CLASSICS OF ROMAN LITERATURE

CLASSICS OF ROMAN LITERATURE

CLASSICS
OF
ROMAN LITERATURE

From the literary beginnings to the end of the Silver Age

Edited by

HARRY E. WEDECK

Lecturer in Classics, Brooklyn College of the City University of N. Y.

Member, Mediaeval Academy of America

Member, The Renaissance Society of America

PHILOSOPHICAL LIBRARY
New York

Copyright, 1963, by

Philosophical Libary, Inc.

15 East 40th Street, New York, N. Y.

All rights reserved

Library of Congress Catalog Number: 63-13350

PA
6163
W4

PREFACE

This treasury is an anthology, in English translation, of the most distinctive literary achievements of the Romans, in the fields of drama, philosophy, history, satire, oratory and analogous categories.

The passages selected are of such a nature as to be complete in themselves or so self-contained as to be readily understandable.

Some of the versions have long been standard renderings; in other instances, the editor has himself contributed a translation. In its totality, this chrestomathy should confirm the enduring impact made by Roman civilization, and furnish evidence of the heritage that they have bequeathed to us.

Springing from a small pastoral colony on the Tiber banks, the Romans became the masters of the universe. They were a more earthy, a more practical and pragmatic and realistic people than the Greeks. They absorbed Greece, and built on the foundations of the conquered nation. What they contributed to the West is primarily the concept of colonial administration. They codified law. They built—aqueducts and forts, bridges and military highways, across Europe, from Hadrian's Wall to the garrison town of Lambaesis in North Africa, from the Danube to the Asiatic frontiers. They subjugated most of the nations of Europe, Egypt, and Asia Minor; and after their military conquests they offered the *Pax Romana*.

In the Sixth Book of the *Aeneid*, Vergil, the national poet, presents a summation of Roman capacities and potentialities in contrast with the skills of the Greeks:

Others will hammer out breathing bronze objects more
delicately (that I quite admit) and will mould living
countenances from marble, and plead cases more effectively
and trace the motions of the heavens with the
measuring rod and name the rising stars. You, Roman,
remember to govern the nations under your rule (these will be
your skills), and to impose the institution of peace, to spare
the subjugated peoples, and to crush the proud.

H. E. W.

v

72514

CONTENTS

POETRY

Catullus	*Attack on Rufus*	2
	Attis	3
	Epithalamium	5
	Smiling Egnatius	12
	Lesbia's Allure	13
	Homage to Lesbia	13
	Eternal Kisses	14
	Lesbia's Sparrow	14
	Lament on Lesbia's Sparrow	15
	Fickle Lesbia	15
	Amorous Frenzy	16
	Ideal Love	16
	Fickle Love	18
	Perplexity of Love	18
	Nuptial Chant	18
	Unfaithful Lesbia	21
	The Poet Travels	22
	Lament for a Brother	23
	Sirmio	23
	Veranius	23
	An Awkward Guest	24
	Dinner Invitation	24
	Varus	25
	Homage to Cicero	26
	Arrius	26
Lucretius	*Book I — An Exposition of the Composition of the Universe*	27
Vergil	*Eclogue I*	50
	Eclogue III	53
	Eclogue IV	56
	Book I — The Aeneid	58
	Book VI	75

Horace	To Virgil	96
	To his Slave	97
	Moderation	97
	The Just Man	98
	The Muses in the Ascendant	101
	Degenerate Man	103
	Fountain of Bandusia	105
	To a Faun	105
	To Lyce	106
Tibullus	Rustic Pleasure	107
	Delia	111
	Unfaithful Delia	112
	Ambarvalia: A Country Festival	115
	Love's Bonds	118
	Contempt of Wealth	120
	Lover	121
	Praise of Sulpicia	122
	The Poet to his Mistress	123
	Poet's Dreams	124
	Birthday Greetings	126
Propertius	Warning to Cynthia	129
	Of Himself	129
	Love's Finery	130
	Fickle Love	131
	Appeal to Bacchus	132
Ovid	Book I — Metamorphoses	
	The World Begins	134
	Heroides: Helen Writes to Paris	148
	Tristia: 111.10: Ovid in Exile	154
Lucan	Book I — Lucan's Pharsalia	157
Statius	Book I — Thebais	174
Martial	Epigrams	198

DRAMA

Plautus	Rudens; The Fisherman's Rope	206
Terence	The Andrian	260

HISTORY and BIOGRAPHY

Livy	*Book XXI — Hannibal Crosses the Alps* ...	307
Tacitus	*Book V — History*	320
Suetonius	*The Historie of Tiberius Nero Caesar*	335

PHILOSOPHY

Cicero	*Book I — On Moral Duties*	348
M. Aurelius	*Book I*	390
	Book II	395
Seneca	*Clemency*	401

ORATORY

Cicero	*The First Oration Against Verres*	413
Tacitus	*A Dialogue Concerning Oratory*	430

THE NOVEL

Petronius	*The Banquet of Trimalchio*	449
Apuleius	*How Apuleius by Roses and Prayer Returned to his Humane Shape*	485

LETTERS

Cicero	*To Atticus — I*	494
	To Atticus — II	495
	To Atticus — III	496
	To P. Lentulus Spinther	496
	To Cn. Pompey, Commander-in-Chief	498
Pliny The Younger	*To Romanus*	499
	To Tacitus	500
	To Cornelius Tacitus	503
	To Caninius	505
	To Sparsus	506
	To Calvisius	506
	To Hispulla	507

ix

	To Minutianus	507
	To Genialis	508
	To The Emperor Trajan	509
	Trajan to Pliny	510
Seneca	Epistle I — Speech as an Index of the Mind	511
	Epistle IV — Correspondence Among Friends. Precepts and Wisdom	513
	Epistle V — Seneca's Studies. Reflections on Human Life	517
	Epistle XIX — An Exposition of True Courage	521
	Epistle XX — Learning. Private and Public Life	523
	Epistle XXI — A Sound Body and a Quiet Mind	525
	Epistle XXV — Protections Against Fate	529

SATIRE

Horace	Book I — Satire I	533
	Book I — Satire IX — The Bore	536
Persius	Satire I	539
Juvenal	Book I — Satire III	544
Selective Bibliography		556

CLASSICS OF ROMAN LITERATURE

CLASSICS OF ROMAN LITERATURE

POETRY

Catullus

Lucretius

Vergil

Horace

Tibullus

Propertius

Ovid

Lucan

Statius

Martial

CATULLUS

GAIUS VALERIUS CATULLUS (c. 84 - c. 54 b c.) was one of the most notable Roman lyric poets. In universal literary history, he ranks, for his passionate amorous exultations, with the greatest erotic poets.

The life of Catullus was brief and tumultuous. He was wealthy, a member of the highest intellectual and social circles of the metropolis, and an aide in colonial administration. But particularly his life was notable for his wild and frenzied infatuation for Lesbia, who was actually Clodia, a woman of the highest social level but also a woman of very indulgent virtues and of many lovers.

Many of Catullus' poems consist of rapturous declarations of eternal love for Lesbia or, in darker interludes, of reproaches and condemnation for her wayward erotic mores.

Some 113 authentic poems of Catullus are extant, dealing, apart from the love motif, with abusive, personal, satiric topics, or with interesting trivia of daily life, sifted through a poet's sensitiveness.

ATTACK ON RUFUS

That no fair woman will, wonder not why,
Clap (Rufus) under thine her tender thigh;
Not a silk gown shall once melt one of them,
Nor the delights of a transparent gemme.
A scurvy story kills thee, which doth tell
That in thine armpits a fierce goat doth dwell.
Him they all fear full of an ugly stinch,
Nor's fit he should lye with a handsome wench;
Wherefore this Nose's cursed plague first crush,
Or cease to wonder why they fly you thus.

Richard Lovelace

ATTIS

(Lament of a priest of Cybele. Such priests, Gallae,
castrated themselves)

Across the roaring ocean, with heart and with eye of flame,
To the Phrygian forest Attis in an eager frenzy came:
And he leapt from his lofty vessel, and he stood in the groves of pine
That circled round with shadows Cybele's mystic shrine:
And there in a frantic fury, as one whose sense has flown,
He robbed himself of his manhood with an edge of sharpened stone.
But as soon as he felt his body bereft of its manly worth,
And saw the red blood trickle on the virgin soil of earth,
With his blanched and womanish fingers a timbrel he gan to smite
(A timbrel, a shawm, Cybele, thine, mother, O thine the rite!),
And he beat the hollow ox-hide with a furious feminine hand,
As he cried in trembling accents to the listening Gallic band:

"Arise, away, ye Gallae! to Cybele's lofty grove!
Together away, ye straylings of our Lady of Dindyma's drove!
Who have sought with me, like exiles, a far and a foreign home:
Who have borne with me the buffets of the sea and the fleeting foam:
Who have followed me, your leader, through the savage storms of night:
Who have robbed your frames of manhood in dainty love's despite.
Make glad the soul of our Lady with the rapid mazy dance.
Away with slothful loitering. Together arise, advance
To Cybele's Phrygian forest, to the Goddess's Phrygian home,
Where ring the clanging cymbals, where echoes the bellowing drum,
Where slow the Phrygian minstrel on his reed drones deep and dread,
Where the Maenad tosses wildly her ivy-encinctured head,
Where the mystic rites of the Goddess with piercing shrieks they greet,
Where our Lady's vagrant votaries together are wont to meet—
Thither must we betake us with triply-twinkling feet."

And thus to his eager comrades the unsexed Attis cries,
In a sudden shriek the chorus with quivering tongue replies:
The hollow timbrel bellows, the tinkling cymbals ring.
Up Ida's slopes the Gallae with feverish footsteps spring.
At their head goes frantic, panting, as one whose senses rove,
With his timbrel, fragile Attis, their guide through the glimmering grove,
Like a heifer that shuns, unbroken, the yoke's unaccustomed weight;
And with hurrying feet impetuous the Gallae follow straight.

3

So, when Cybele's precinct they reached in the inmost wood,
With over-travail wearied they slept without taste of food.
On their eyelids easy Slumber with gliding languor crept,
And their spirit's fanatic ecstasy went from them as they slept.
But when golden-visaged Phoebus with radiant eyes again
Surveyed the fleecy aether, solid land, and roaring main,
And with mettlesome chargers scattered the murky shades of night,
Then Attis swift awakened, and Sleep fled fast from his sight.
(In her bosom divine Pasithea received the trembling sprite.)
So, roused from gentle slumber and of feverish frenzy freed,
As soon as Attis pondered in heart on his passionate deed,
And with mind undimmed bethought him where he stood and how
                                                         unmanned,
Seething in soul he burried back to the seaward strand;
And he gazed on the waste of waters, and the tears brimmed full in his
                                                              eye;
And he thus bespake his fatherland with a plantive, womanish cry:
"O fatherland that bore me! O fatherland my home!
In an evil hour I left thee on the boundless deep to roam.
As a slave who flees his master I fled from thy nursing breast,
To dwell in the desolate forest upon Ida's rugged crest:
To lurk in the snows of Ida, by the wild beast's frozen lair:
To haunt the lonely thickets in the icy upper air.
O where dost thou lie, my fatherland, in the ocean's broad expanse?
For my very eyeball hungers upon thee to turn its glance.
While my soul for a little moment is free from its frenzied trance.
Shall I from my home be hurried to this grove so far away?
So far from my goods and my country, from my kith and my kin shall
                                                              stray?
From the games and the crowded market, from the course and the
                                                    wrestling-plain?
Ah, hapless, hapless Attis, thou must mourn it again and again.
For what form or fashion is there, what sex that I have not known?
I was a child and a stripling, a youth, and a man full grown:
I was the flower of the athletes, the pride of the wrestlers' zone.
My gates were thronged with comrades, my threshold warm with feet;
My home was fair encircled with flowery garlands sweet,
When I rose from my couch at sunrise the smiling day to greet.
Shall I be our Lady's bondmaid? a slave at Cybele's hand?
Shall I be a sexless Maenad, a minion, a thing unmanned?
Shall I dwell on the icy ridges under Ida's chilly blast?
Shall I pass my days in the shadows that the Phrygian summits cast,
With the stag that haunts the forest, with the boar that roams the glade?
Even now my soul repents me: even now is my fury stayed."

4

From the rosy lips of Attis such plaint forth issuing flowed,
And straight the rebellious message rose up to the Gods' abode.
From the brawny neck of her lion Cybele loosed the yoke,
And, goading on his fury, to the savage beast she spoke:
"Up, up!" she cried; "dash onward! Drive back with a panic fear,
Drive back to the lonely wilderness the wretch who lingers here!
Who dares to flee so lightly from the doom that I impose!
Lash, lash thy side in anger with thine own impetuous blows!
Let the din of thy savage bellowing roar loud on the startled plain,
And thick on thy tawny shoulders shake fierce thy shaggy mane!"

So threatening spoke Cybele and loosed from his neck the yoke;
And the brute, himself inciting, with a roar through the thicket broke:
And lashed his side in anger, and he rushed to the hoary main
Till he found the fragile Attis by the shore of the watery plain:
Then he gave one bound. But Attis fled back to the grove aghast.
There all the days of his lifetime as Cybele's thrall he passed.

Goddess! Mighty Goddess! Cybele! who rulest Dindyma's height,
Far from my home, O Lady, let thy maddening wrath alight!
Upon others rain thy frenzy! Upon others wreak thy might!

Grant Allen

EPITHALAMIUM

(Wedding song)

Urania's son, whose home is on
The heights of skyey Helicon,
Who the virgin in her bloom
Bringest to her lusty groom,
Hymen, hear, thou lovers' friend!
Hear, and hither blithely wend!

Flowers around these brows of thine
Of sweet marjoram entwine;
Bring the scarf with hue of flame,
Type and veil of maiden shame;
Come, and on thy snowy feet
Let the saffron sandals meet!

5

In this day, when all rejoice,
Laugh, and, with thy silvery voice
Carolling the nuptial song,
Dance with jocund feet along,
And aloft within thy hand
Wave the blazing pine-tree brand!

Vinia doth with Manlius wed;
Omens blest surround their bed:
Good she is, and fair, and bright
As the Queen of Ida's height,
Venus, when the prize to claim
To the Phrygian judge she came.

As the fragrant myrtle, found
Flourishing on Asian ground,
Thick with blossoms overspread,
By the Hamadryads fed
For their sport with honey-dew,
All so sweet is she to view.

Hither, then, thyself betake,
And a little while forsake
The Aonian grottoes hid
Thespia's rocky wolds amid,
Washed in many a plashy pool
By Aganippe's waters cool.

And call the lady home with soul
Submissive to her lord's control;
Around her heart love's tendrils bind,
Until, like clasping ivy twined
Around a stately tree, they hold
It mazed in meshes manifold.

And you ye stainless virgins, whom
A day awaits of kindred doom,
Combine to give her welcoming,
And here with us in measure sing,
Oh Hymen, Hymenaeus, thou
Attend us with thy blessing now!

That summoned by your voices chaste,
He may to do his office haste,
And hither wend more swift and sure,
The harbinger of blisses pure,
Who doth for evermore delight
True hearts in wedlock to unite.

What god shall worshipped be above
This god, yea this, by all who love?
Or which of the celestials find
More adoration from mankind?
Oh Hymen, Hymenaeus, thou
Attend us with thy blessing now!

Thee doth the parent full of dread
Implore to bless his children's bed;
For thee, for thee, the virgin chaste
Unclasps the girdle from her waist;
The bridegroom lists with throbbing heart,
Till thou within the chamber art.

The maiden all in blushes dressed,
Thou bearest from her mother's breast,
And giv'st into her lover's arms,
That close triumphant on her charms.
Oh Hymen, Hymenaeus, thou
Attend us with thy blessing now;

Without thee love no bliss can reap,
And its good name unsullied keep;
But it is blest, yet pure the while,
If thou upon its raptures smile.
Oh, which of all the gods in bliss
Is worthy to compare with this?

Without thee can no home beget
An honoured progeny, nor yet
The parent in the heir survive —
But with thee all his blossoms thrive.
Oh, which of all the gods in bliss
Is worthy to compare with this?

The lands from which thy rites are barred,
Can ne'er, their frontier-bounds to guard,
Breed chiefs whom all revere; but they,
If thou conferr'st thy blessing, may.
What god of all the gods in bliss
Is worthy to compare with this?

And now, ye gates, your wings unfold!
The virgin draweth nigh. Behold
The torches, how upon the air
They shake abroad their gleaming hair!
Come, bride, come forth! no more delay!
The day is hurrying fast away!

But lost in shame and maiden fears
She stirs not, — weeping, as she hears
The friends that to her tears reply,
Thou must advance, the hour is nigh!
Come, bride, come forth! no more delay!
The day is hurrying fast away!

Dry up thy tears! For well I trow,
No woman lovelier than thou,
Aurunculeia, shall behold
The day all panoplied in gold
And rosy light uplift his head
Above the shimmering ocean's bed!

As in some rich man's garden-plot,
With flowers of every hue inwrought,
Stands peerless forth with drooping brow
The hyacinth, so standest thou!
Come, bride, come forth! no more delay!
The day is hurrying fast away!

Come forth, fair bride! Delay no more!
Come forth and hear the hymn we pour
To Hymen, mighty god, for thee!
Come forth, sweet bride! The torches, see,
Are waving high their golden hair!
Then come in all thy beauty rare!

8

No base adult'ress from his vows
Shall ever wean thy constant spouse,
Nor any lure of pleasures vile
His loyalty from thee beguile;
But, nestling to thy gentle breast,
He'll live in thee supremely blest.

As round its wedded elm the vine
Doth all its clinging tendrils twine,
So in thy loving arms will he
Be twined and circled round by thee.
But day is hurrying fast away;
Come, bride, come forth! no more delay!

And thou white-footed couch, in pride
That wait'st the coming of the bride,
Above all couches blest, do thou
From yonder flowers that deck thee now
A perfume breathe so exquisite,
Shall steep the lovers in delight!

What joys ecstatic soon shall greet
Thy lord, what thrilling raptures sweet,
Beneath the glimpses of the moon,
And in the hush of sultry noon!
But day is hurrying fast away;
Then come, sweet bride, no more delay!

Raise, boys, your torches! raise them high!
I see the scarf of crimson nigh.
On! To her home the bride to bring,
And, as ye move, in measure sing
Hail, Hymen! Hymenaeus, hail!
    Hail, Hymen, Hymenaeus!

*   *   *

Oh happy bride, how richly blest,
Of such a lordly home possessed,
As from thy spouse thou tak'st to-day,
Which to the end shall own thy sway!
Hail, Hymen! Hymenaeus, hail!
    Hail, Hymen, Hymenaeus!

Till hoary age shall steal on thee,
With loitering step, and trembling knee,
And palsied head, that, ever bent,
To all in all things nods assent!
Hail, Hymen! Hymenaeus, hail!
  Hail, Hymen, Hymenaeus!

Thy golden-sandalled feet do thou
Lift lightly o'er the threshold now!
Fair omen this! And pass between
The lintel-post of polished sheen!
Hail, Hymen! Hymenaeus, hail!
  Hail, Hymen, Hymenaeus!

See where, within, thy lord is set
On Tyrian-tinctured coverlet,
His eyes upon the threshold bent,
And all his soul on thee intent!
Hail, Hymen! Hymenaeus, hail!
  Hail, Hymen, Hymenaeus!

Within his inmost heart a fire
Is flaming up of sweet desire,
As warm as that which flames in thine,
Yea, warmer, wilder, more divine!
Hail, Hymen! Hymenaeus, hail!
  Hail, Hymen, Hymenaeus!

Thou purple-vestured youth, untwine
The rounded arm that rests on thine,
And let the maid, by others led,
Advance to climb her husband's bed!
Hail, Hymen! Hymenaeus, hail!
  Hail, Hymen, Hymenaeus!

Ye dames, who have your husband's praise
Well-earned through length of many days,
In bonds of single wedlock tied,
Advance, 'tis yours to place the bride!
Hail, Hymen! Hymenaeus, hail!
  Hail, Hymen, Hymenaeus!

Enter, husband! Now thou mayst!
In the couch thy wife is placed;
And her cheeks with shame aglow
'Neath the veil of saffron show,
Like the pale parthenium through
Poppy-beds of saffron hue.

Thou too, by the gods I vow,
Not less beautiful art thou!
Venus, who endows the fair,
Hath on thee bestowed her care.
Soon the day will disappear;
Tarry not, but enter here.

Tarried hast thou not, indeed.
Now, to recompense thy speed,
Venus aid thy genial task,
Since thou scorn'st thy love to mask;
What thou wishest boldly taking,
Of thy joy no secret making.

Let him first compute the grains
Of the sand on Egypt's plains,
Or the stars that gem the nights,
Who could count the rare delights,
Which thy spousals yet shall bless,
Joys in number numberless!

Now disport, and stint ye not!
Children be anon begot.
'Tis not meet so old a stem
Should be left ungraced by them,
To transmit its fame unshorn
Down through ages yet unborn.

Soon my eyes shall see, mayhap,
Young Torquatus on the lap
Of his mother, as he stands
Stretching out his tiny hands,
And his little lips the while
Half open on his father smile.

11

And oh! may he in all be like
Manlius his sire, and strike
Strangers, when the boy they meet,
As his father's counterfeit,
And his face the index be
Of his mother's chastity!

Him, too, such fair fame adorn,
Son of such a mother born,
That the praise of both entwined
Call Telemachus to mind,
With her who nursed him on her knee,
Unparagoned Penelope!

Now, virgins, let us shut the door!
Enough we've toyed, enough and more!
But fare ye well, ye loving pair,
We leave ye to each other's care;
And blithely let your hours be sped
In joys of youth and lustyhed!

Theodore Martin

SMILING EGNATIUS

Egnatius has teeth that gleam
So shining white, they always seem
To make him smile at any time.
An innocent's accused of crime?
The jury weeps so tearfully?
But he keeps smiling beamingly.
There's mourning at a dead son's bier?
Bereft, a mother sheds a tear?
He's still a-smile. No matter where,
No matter what, his smile's still there.
I think it is a kind of vice
That's neither urbane nor quite nice.
So I must warn you, friend of mine,
—Assume you're Sabine, Tiburtine,
Gaunt Umbrian, or Tuscan plump,
Lanuvian dark and toothy chump,

12

From 'cross the Po, where my kin dwell,
Or anyone who cleans teeth well—
Do stop your everlasting grin.
For what can be a greater sin
Than smiling when there is no reason,
And grinning in and out of season?

H. E. W.

LESBIA'S ALLURE

Lesbia for ever on me rails.
To talk of me she never fails.
Now, hang me, but for all her art,
I find that I have gained her heart.
My proof is this: I plainly see
The case is just the same with me;
I curse her every hour sincerely,
Yet, hang me, but I love her dearly.

Jonathan Swift

HOMAGE TO LESBIA

Him rival to the gods I place,
    Him loftier yet, if loftier be,
Who, Lesbia, sits before thy face,
    Who listens and who looks on thee;

Thee smiling soft. Yet this delight
    Doth all my sense consign to death;
For when thou dawnest on my sight,
    Ah, wretched! flits my labouring breath.

My tongue is palsied. Subtly hid
    Fire creeps me through from limb to limb;
My loud ears tingle all unbid:
    Twin clouds of night mine eyes bedim.

Ease is my plague: ease makes thee void,
    Catullus, with these vacant hours,
And wanton: ease that hath destroyed
    Great kings, and states with all their powers.

W. E. Gladstone

ETERNAL KISSES

Come and let us live, my dear,
Let us love and never fear
What the sourest fathers say:
Brightest Sol that dies to-day
Lives again as blithe to-morrow;
But if we dark sons of sorrow
Set, O then, how long a night
Shuts the eyes of our short sight!
Then let amorous kisses dwell
On our lips, begin and tell
A thousand, and a hundred score,
An hundred and a thousand more,
Till another thousand smother
That, and that wipe off another.
Thus at last when we have numbred
Many a thousand, many a hundred,
We'll confound the reckoning quite,
And lose ourselves in wild delight:
While our joys so multiply
As shall mock the envious eye.

Richard Crashaw

LESBIA'S SPARROW

Sparrow, pet of the lady of my love, who
Will with thee toy, will in her bosom nurse thee,
Her forefinger resign to thy caressings,
And provoke thee to peck at it with fury,
When she is minded, that lady whom I dote on,
Pretty tricks to play, all maddeningly charming,
Finding balm so in this for her emotion,
Else too tense, I believe, for her endurance.
Oh, like her, that I might with thee make pastime,
Ease the pangs so that agitate and rend me!
Dear then wert thou to me, as in the legend
Was to the swift-footed maid the golden apple,
Which ungirdled her zone so long unyielding.

Theodore Martin

14

LAMENT ON LESBIA'S SPARROW

Loves and Graces mourn with me,
Mourn, fair youths, where'er ye be!
Dead my Lesbia's sparrow is,
Sparrow, that was all her bliss,
Than her very eyes more dear;
For he made her dainty cheer,
Knew her well, as any maid
Knows her mother, never strayed
From her bosom, but would go
Hopping round her to and fro,
And to her, and her alone,
Chirrup'd with such pretty tone.
Now he treads that gloomy track,
Whence none ever may come back.
Out upon you, and your power,
Which all fairest things devour,
Orcus' gloomy shades, that e'er
Ye took my bird that was so fair!
Ah, the pity of it! Thou
Poor bird, thy doing 'tis, that now
My loved one's eyes are swoll'n and red,
With weeping for her darling dead.

Theodore Martin

FICKLE LESBIA

My mistress says, there's not a man
    Of all the many that she knows,
She'd rather wed than me, not one,
    Though Jove himself were to propose.

She says so; — but what woman says
    To him who fancies he has caught her,
'Tis only fit it should be writ
    In air or in the running water.

Theodore Martin

15

AMOROUS FRENZY

None could ever say that she,
Lesbia! was so loved by me;
Never, all the world around,
Faith so true as mine was found.
If no longer it endures,
(Would it did!) the fault is yours.
I can never think again
Well of you: I try in vain.
But, be false, do what you will,
Lesbia! I must love you still.

Walter Savage Landor

IDEAL LOVE

Whilst on Septimius' panting Breast
(Meaning nothing less than rest)
Acme lean'd her loving head
Thus the pleas'd Septimius said:

My dearest Acme, if I be
Once alive, and love not thee
With a passion far above
All that e're was called love,
In a Libyan desert may
I become some lion's prey,
Let him, Acme, let him tear
My breast, when Acme is not there.

The God of Love who stood to hear him,
(The God of Love was always near him)
Pleas'd and tickl'd with the sound,
Sneez'd aloud, and all around
The little Loves that waited by,
Bow'd and blest the augury.
Acme, enflam'd with what he said,
Rear'd her gently-bending head,
And her purple mouth with joy
Stretching to the delicious boy

Twice (and twice would scarce suffice)
She kist his drunken, rolling eyes.

My little life, my all (said she)
So may we ever servants be
To this best God, and n'er retain
Our hated liberty again,
So may thy passion last for me,
As I a passion have for thee
Greater and fiercer much than can
Be conceiv'd by thee a man.
Into my marrow it is gone,
Fixt and settled in the bone,
It reigns not only in my heart,
But runs, like life, through ev'ry part.

She spoke; the God of Love aloud,
Sneez'd again and all the crowd
Of little Loves that waited by
Bow'd and blest the augury.

This good omen thus from Heaven
Like a happy signal given,
Their loves and lives (all four) embrace,
And hand in hand run all the race.
To poor Septimius (who did now
Nothing else but Acme grow)
Acme's bosom was alone
The whole world's imperial throne,
And to faithful Acme's mind
Septimius was all human kind.

If the Gods would please to be
But advis'd for once by me,
I'd advise 'em when they spy
Any illustrious piety,
To reward her, if it be she,
To reward him, if it be he;
With such a husband, such a wife,
With Acme's and Septimius' life.

Abraham Cowley

17

FICKLE LOVE

You told me, Lesbia, once, that you
    For your Catullus only cared,
That, though imperial Jove might sue,
    My empire should by none be shared.

I loved you then with love beyond
    The transient flush of passion wild;
Ay, with a tenderness as fond,
    As binds the parent to the child.

I know you now. Alas! and though
    Your fall, your fickleness I spurn,
Yet, can I not forget you, no!
    But with a wilder passion burn.

How this can be so, you inquire.
    'Tis that thy very shamelessness
But fans the fire of base desire,
    Although it makes me love the less.

Theodore Martin

PERPLEXITY OF LOVE

I hate and love — the why I cannot tell,
But by my tortures know the fact too well.

Theodore Martin

NUPTIAL CHANT

YOUTHS:

Lo, Hesper is at hand! Rise, youths! His light
Expected long now harbingers the night.
'Tis time to quit the feast. We must away.
Swell high with me the hymeneal lay.
Anon the virgin comes in blushes by.
Oh Hymen, Hymenaeus, be thou nigh!

18

MAIDENS:

       Mark you the youths? Rise up, rise up, each maid!
       Already hath the evening star displayed
       In the dim welkin his Oetean flame.
       Mark you their nimbleness? Then know their aim!
       Anon they'll sing a lay we must outvie.
       Oh Hymen, Hymenaeus, be thou nigh!

YOUTHS:

       No easy triumph, comrades, shall we gain.
       See how the maids are practising their strain!
       Nor vainly so. With undivided care
       Their task is wrought — what marvel, if 'tis fair?
       Whilst we, who labour with distracted wit,
       Are like to lose the palm, and so 'tis fit,
       Bestowing here our voice, and there our ear.
       Well studied work to victory is dear —
       Pains undivided, toil that will not tire;
       Then kindle to your task with answering fire!
       Anon they will begin; we must reply.
       Oh Hymen, Hymenaeus, be thou nigh!

MAIDENS:

       Say, Hesper, say, what fire of all that shine
       In Heaven's great vault more cruel is than thine?
       Who from the mother's arms her child can tear —
       The child that clasps her mother in despair;
       And to the youth whose blood is all aflame,
       Consigns the virgin sinking in her shame!
       When towns are sacked, what cruelty more drear?
       Oh Hymen, Hymenaeus, Hymen, hear!

YOUTHS:

       Say, Hesper, say, what fire of all that shine
       In Heaven's great vault more jocund is than thine?
       Who with thy flame dost ratify the bond
       Of wedlock-troth first vowed by lovers fond,
       By parents vowed, but consummated ne'er,
       Until thy star hath risen upon the air?
       What choicer hour sends heaven our life to cheer?
       Oh Hymen, Hymenaeus, Hymen, hear!

19

MAIDENS:

Woe, my companions, woe, that Hesper thus
Hath reft the fairest of our mates from us!
Why were we heedless of thy coming—why?
For most it fits to watch, when thou art nigh.
To stolen delights by night the lover hies,
And him wilt thou, oh Hesper, oft surprise,
When thou in other name dost reappear.
Oh Hymen, Hymenaeus, Hymen, hear!

YOUTHS:

Heed not the railing of the virgin choir!
They joy to chide thee with fictitious ire.
How, if within their secret soul they long
For what they so vituperate in song?
Then to their chiding turn a heedless ear.
Oh Hymen, Hymenaeus, draw thou near!

MAIDENS:

As in a garden grows some floweret fair,
Safe from the flocks, safe from the ploughman's share,
Nursed by the sun, by gentle breezes fanned,
Fed by the showers, admired on every hand,
There as it coyly blossoms in the shade,
Desired by many a youth, by many a maid;
But pluck that flower, its witchery is o'er,
And neither youth nor maid desires it more.
So is the virgin prized, endeared as much,
Whilst yet unsullied by a lover's touch;
But if she lose her chaste and virgin flower,
Her beauty's bloom is blighted in an hour:
To youths no more, no more to maidens dear.
Oh Hymen, Hymenaeus, be thou near!

YOUTHS:

As grows a widowed vine in open fields,
It hangs its head, no mellow clusters yields;
So droops the fragile stem, its topmost shoot
With nerveless tendril hangs about its root;
That vine no husbandman nor rustic swain
Hath cared to tend or cultivate or train;
But if by happier chance that self-same vine
Around a husband elm its tendrils twine,

20

Then many a husbandman and rustic swain
Its shoots will tend and cultivate and train.
Even such the virgin, and unprized as much,
That fades, untended by a lover's touch;
But when, in fulness of her maiden pride,
Some fitting mate has won her for his bride,
She's loved as never she was loved before,
And parents bless her, and are stern no more.

YOUTHS and MAIDENS:
Then spurn not, oh ye virgins, such a groom!
Unmeet it is to spurn the man to whom
Thy father gave thee, and thy mother too;
For unto them is thy obedience due.
Not wholly thine is thy virginity;
Thy parents own some part of it in thee.
One third thy father's is by right divine,
One third thy mother's; one alone is thine.
Then war not with these twain, who with thy dower
Have given their son-in-law their rights and power.
Come! to the bridal-chamber hence — away!
Oh Hymen, Hymenaeus, bless our rites to-day!

Theodore Martin

UNFAITHFUL LESBIA

Our Furius and Aurelius! comrades sweet!
    Who to Ind's farthest shore with me would roam,
Where the far-sounding Orient billows beat
    Their fury into foam;

Or to Hyrcania, balm-breathed Araby,
    The Sacian's or the quivered Parthian's land,
Or where seven-mantled Nile's swoll'n waters dye
    The sea with yellow sand;

Or cross the lofty Alpine fells, to view
    Great Caesar's trophied fields, the Gallic Rhine,
The paint-smeared Briton race, grim-visaged crew,
    Placed by earth's limit line;

21

To all prepared with me to brave the way,
  To dare whate'er the eternal gods decree —
These few unwelcome words to her convey
  Who once was all to me.

Still let her revel with her godless train,
  Still clasp her hundred slaves to passion's thrall,
Still truly love not one, but ever drain
  The life-blood of them all.

Nor let her more my once fond passion heed,
  For by her faithlessness 'tis blighted now,
Like flow'ret on the verge of grassy mead
  Crushed by the passing plow.

J. Cranstoun

THE POET TRAVELS

A balmy warmth comes wafted o'er the seas,
  The savage howl of wintry tempests drear
In the sweet whispers of the western breeze
  Has died away; the spring, the spring is here!

Now quit, Catullus, quit the Phrygian plain,
  Where days of sweltering sunshine soon shall crown
Nicaea's fields with wealth of golden grain,
  And fly to Asia's cities of renown!

Already through each nerve a flutter runs
  Of eager hope, that longs to be away,
Already 'neath the light of other suns
  My feet, new-winged for travel, yearn to stray.

And you, ye band of comrades tried and true,
  Who side by side went forth from home, farewell!
How far apart the paths shall carry you
  Back to your native shore, ah, who can tell?

Theodore Martin

22

LAMENT FOR A BROTHER

Brother! o'er many lands and oceans borne,
I reach thy grave, death's last sad rite to pay;
To call thy silent dust in vain, and mourn,
Since ruthless fate has hurried thee away;
Woe's me! yet now upon thy tomb I lay,
All soak'd with tears for thee, thee loved so well,
What gifts our fathers gave the honour'd clay
Of valued friends; take them, my grief they tell:
And now, for ever hail! for ever fare-thee-well!

J. Cranstoun

SIRMIO

Gem of all isthmuses and isles that lie,
    Fresh or salt water's children, in clear lake
Or ampler ocean: with what joy do I
    Approach thee, Sirmio! Oh! am I awake,
Or dream that once again mine eye beholds
Thee, and has looked its last on Thracian wolds?
    Sweetest of sweets to me that pastime seems,
When the mind drops her burden: when — the pain
Of travel past — our own cot we regain,
    And nestle on the pillow of our dreams!
'Tis this one thought that cheers us as we roam.
Hail, O fair Sirmio! Joy, thy lord is here!
Joy too, ye waters of the Golden Mere!
And ring out, all ye laughter-peals of home!

C. S. Calverley

VERANIUS

Dearest of all Veranius! Oh my friend!
    Hast thou come back from thy long pilgrimage,
With brothers twin in soul thy days to spend,
    And by thy hearthfire cheer thy mother's age?

23

And art thou truly come? Oh welcome news!
    And I shall see thee safe, and hear once more
Thy tales of Spain, its tribes, its feats, its views,
    Flow as of old from thy exhaustless store.

And I shall gaze into thine eyes again!
    And I again shall fold thee to my breast!
Oh you, who deem yourselves most blest of men,
    Which of you all like unto me is blest?

Theodore Martin

AN AWKWARD GUEST

Marrucinus Asinius, you ply your left hand
In a fashion that gentlemen don't understand;
Their napkins you steal, when the rest of the guests
Are intent on the flow of the wine and the jests.
You fancy this fun? Why, you goose, don't you know
That this sort of thing is unseemly and low?
You think, I'm no judge? But that you'll scarce say
Of Pollio, your brother, a talent who'd pay,
Yourself of these pilfering habits to free,
For who knows so well, what is true fun, as he?
So I give you your choice. Send my napkin, and soon,
Or expect to be lashed by whole yards of lampoon.
'Tis not for its value I prize it — don't sneer!
But as a memento of friends who are dear.
'Tis one of a set that Fabullus from Spain
And Veranius sent me — a gift from the twain;
So the napkins, of course, are as dear to Catullus
As the givers, Veranius himself and Fabullus.

Theodore Martin

DINNER INVITATION

If the gods will, Fabullus mine,
With me right heartily you'll dine.
Bring but good cheer — that chance is thine

Some days hereafter;
Mind, a fair girl too, wit, and wine,
And merry laughter.

Bring these — you'll feast on kingly fare;
But bring them — for my purse I swear
The spiders have been weaving there;
        But thee I'll favor
With a pure love, or what's more rare,
        More sweet of savor,

An unguent I'll before you lay
The Loves and Graces t'other day
Gave to my girl — smell it — you'll pray
        The gods, Fabullus,
To make you turn all nose straightway.
        Yours aye, Catullus.

J. Cranstoun

VARUS

Suffenus, whom so well you know,
My Varus, as a wit and beau,
Of smart address and smirking smile,
Will write you verses by the mile.
You cannot meet with daintier fare
Than title-page and binding are;
But when you once begin to read
You find it sorry stuff indeed,
And you are ready to cry out
Upon this beau — "O what a lout!"
No man on earth so proud as he
Of his own precious poetry,
Or knows such perfect bliss as when
He takes in hand that nibbled pen.

Have we not all some faults like these?
Are we not all Suffenuses?
In others the defect we find,
But cannot see our sack behind.

W. S. Landor

25

HOMAGE TO CICERO

Tully, most eloquent of all the line
Of Romulus, past, present, or to be,
Catullus sends sincerest thanks to thee,
Poorest of bards — as far the poorest he
As thou art first in eloquence divine.

J. Cranstoun

ARRIUS

Arrius *commodious* aye *chommodious* called,
And for *insidious* out *hinsidious* bawled,
And then he thought his accent wondrous good
When he had mouthed them rough as e'er he could.
His mother, and his uncle Liber, too,
And their good parents thus, methinks, would do.
He went to Syria, — all our ears had then
A sweet repose, — smooth flowed the words again,
Vanished the fears that put us nigh distraught,
When, suddenly, the direful news was brought,
That Arrius, when in Syria, said that he
Just came from crossing the *Hionian* Sea.

J. Cranstoun

LUCRETIUS

TITUS LUCRETIUS CARUS (c. 94 - c. 55 B. C.) was a poet of whose life
little is known. He is the author of *De Rerum Natura*, a didactic poem, in six
books. Herein Lucretius expounds the atomic theory and the physical composition
of the cosmos. His object was to banish superstitious fear of the gods and to
demonstrate the mortality of the soul. The universe, in short, consists of matter
and void.

Book I — *An Exposition of the Composition of the Universe*

Mother of the Aeneadae, darling of men and gods, increase-
giving Venus, who beneath the gliding signs of heaven fillest with thy
presence the ship-carrying sea, the corn-bearing lands, since through
thee every kind of living things is conceived, rises up and beholds the
light of the sun. Before thee, goddess, flee the winds, the clouds of
heaven; before thee and thy advent; for thee earth manifold in works
puts forth sweet-smelling flowers; for thee the levels of the sea do laugh
and heaven propitiated shines with outspread light. For soon as the
vernal aspect of day is disclosed, and the birth-favouring breeze of
favonius unbarred is blowing fresh, first the fowls of the air, o lady,
shew signs of thee and thy entering in, throughly smitten in heart by
thy power. Next the wild herds bound over the glad pastures and
swim the rapid rivers: in such wise each made prisoner by thy charm
follows thee with desire, whither thou goest to lead it on. Yes throughout seas and mountains and sweeping rivers and leafy homes of birds
and grassy plains, striking fond love into the breasts of all thou con-
strainest them each after its kind to continue their races with desire.
Since thou then art sole mistress of the nature of things, and without
thee nothing rises up into the divine borders of light, nothing grows
to be glad or lovely, I would have thee for a helpmate in writing the
verses which I essay to pen on the nature of things for our own son
of the Memmii, whom thou, goddess, hast willed to have no peer, rich
as he ever is in every grace. Wherefore all the more, o lady, lend my
lays an everliving charm. Cause meanwhile the savage works of war

27

to be lulled to rest throughout all seas and lands; for thou alone canst bless mankind with calm peace, seeing that Mavors lord of battle controls the savage works of war, Mavors who often flings himself into thy lap quite vanquished by the never-healing wound of love; and then with upturned face and shapely neck thrown back feeds with love his greedy sight gazing, goddess, open-mouthed on thee; and as backward he reclines, his breath stays hanging on thy lips. While then, lady, he is reposing on thy holy body, shed thyself about him and above, and pour from thy lips sweet discourse, asking, glorious dame, gentle peace for the Romans. For neither can we in our country's day of trouble with untroubled mind think only of our work, nor can the illustrious offset of Memmius in times like these be wanting to the general weal.

For what remains to tell, apply to true reason unbusied ears and a keen mind withdrawn from cares, lest my gifts set out for you with stedfast zeal you abandon with disdain, before they are understood. For I will essay to discourse to you of the most high system of heaven and the gods and will open up the first-beginnings of things, out of which nature gives birth to all things and increase and nourishment, and into which nature likewise dissolves them back after their destruction. These we are accustomed in explaining their reason to call matter and begetting bodies of things and to name seeds of things and also to term first bodies, because from them as first elements all things are.

When human life to view lay foully prostrate upon earth crushed down under the weight of religion, who shewed her head from the quarters of heaven with hideous aspect lowering upon mortals, a man of Greece ventured first to lift up his mortal eyes to her face and first to withstand her to her face. Him neither glory of gods nor thunderbolts nor heaven with threatening roar could quell, but only stirred up the more the eager courage of his soul, filling him with desire to be the first to burst the fast bars of nature's portals. Therefore the living force of his soul gained the day: on he passed far beyond the flaming walls of the world and traversed throughout in mind and spirit the immeasurable universe; whence he returns a conqueror to tell us what can, what cannot come into being; in short on what principle each thing has its powers defined, its deep-set boundary mark. Therefore religion is put under foot and trampled upon in turn; us his victory brings level with heaven.

This is what I fear herein, lest haply you should fancy that you are entering on unholy grounds of reason and treading the path of sin; whereas on the contrary often and often that heinous religion has given birth to sinful and unholy deeds. Thus in Aulis the chosen chieftains

28

of the Danai foremost of men foully polluted with Iphianassa's blood the altar of the Trivian maid. Soon as the fillet encircling her maiden tresses shed itself in equal length adown each cheek, and soon as she saw her father standing sorrowful before the altars and beside him the ministering priests hiding the knife and her countrymen at sight of her shedding tears, speechless in terror she dropped down on her knees and sank to the ground. Nor aught in such a moment could it avail the luckless girl that she had first bestowed the name of father on the king. For lifted up in the hands of the men she was carried shivering to the altars, not after due performance of the customary rites to be escorted by the clear-ringing bridal song, but in the very season of marriage, stainless maid mid the stain of blood, to fall a sad victim by the sacrificing stroke of a father, that thus a happy and prosperous departure might be granted to the fleet. So great the evils to which religion could prompt!

You yourself some time or other overcome by terror-speaking tales of the seers will seek to fall away from us. Ay indeed, for how many dreams may they now imagine for you, enough to upset the calculations of life and trouble all your fortunes with fear! And with good cause; for if men saw that there was a fixed limit to their woes, they would be able in some way to withstand the religious scruples and threatenings of the seers. As it is, there is no way, no means of resisting, since they must fear after death everlasting pains. For they cannot tell what is the nature of the soul, whether it be born or on the contrary find its way into men at their birth, and whether it perish together with us when severed from us by death or visit the gloom of Orcus and wasteful pools or by divine decree find its way into brutes in our stead, as sang our Ennius who first brought down from delightful Helicon a crown of unfading leaf, destined to bright renown throughout Italian clans of men. And yet with all this Ennius sets forth that there are Acherusian quarters, publishing it in immortal verses; though in our passage thither neither our souls nor bodies hold together, but only certain idols pale in wondrous wise. From these places he tells us the ghost of everliving Homer uprose before him and began to shed salt tears and to unfold in words the nature of things. Wherefore we must well grasp the principle of things above, the principle by which the courses of the sun and moon go on, the force by which every thing on earth proceeds, but above all we must find out by keen-sighted reason what the soul and the nature of the mind consist of, and what thing it is which meets us and frightens our minds when we are awake and under the influence of disease and when we are buried in sleep, so that we seem to see and hear speaking to us face to face them who are dead and whose bones earth holds in its embrace.

Nor does my mind fail to perceive how hard it is to make clear in Latin verses the dark discoveries of the Greeks, especially as many points must be dealt with in new terms on account of the poverty of the language and the novelty of the questions. But yet your worth and the looked for pleasure of sweet friendship prompt me to undergo any labour and lead me on to watch the clear nights through, seeking by what words and in what verse I may be able in the end to shed on your mind so clear a light that you can thoroughly scan hidden things.

This terror then and darkness of mind must be dispelled not by the rays of the sun and glittering shafts of day, but by the aspect and the law of nature; the warp of whose design we shall begin with this first principle, nothing is ever gotten out of nothing by divine power. Fear in sooth takes such a hold of all mortals, because they see many operations go on in earth and heaven, the causes of which they can in no way understand, believing them therefore to be done by power divine. For these reasons when we shall have seen that nothing can be produced from nothing, we shall then more correctly ascertain that which we are pursuing, both the elements out of which every thing can be produced and the manner in which all things are done without the hand of the gods.

If things came from nothing, any kind might be born of any thing, nothing would require seed. Men, for instance, might rise out of the sea, the scaly race out of the earth, and birds might burst out of the sky; horned and other herds, every kind of wild-beasts would haunt with changing brood tilth and wilderness alike. Nor would the same fruits keep constant to trees, but would change; any tree might bear any fruit. For if there were not begetting bodies for each, how could things have a fixed unvarying mother? But in fact because things are all produced from fixed seeds, each thing is born and goes forth into the borders of light out of that in which resides its matter and first bodies; and for this reason all things cannot be gotten out of all things because in particular things resides a distinct power. Again why do we see the rose put forth in spring, corn in the season of heat, vines yielding at the call of autumn, if not because, when the fixed seeds of things have streamed together at the proper time, whatever is born discloses itself, while the due seasons are there and the quickened earth brings its weakly products in safety forth into the borders of light? But if they came from nothing, they would rise up suddenly at uncertain periods and unsuitable times of year, inasmuch as there would be no first-beginnings which might be kept from a begetting union by the unpropitious season. No nor would time be required for the growth of things after the meeting of the seed, if they could increase out of

30

nothing. Little babies would at once grow into men and trees in a moment would rise and start out of the ground. But none of these events it is plain ever comes to pass, since all things grow step by step, as is natural, since they all grow from a fixed seed and in growing preserve their kind; so that you may be sure that all things increase in size and are fed out of their own matter. Furthermore without fixed seasons of rain the earth is unable to put forth its gladdening produce, nor again if kept from food could the nature of living things continue its kind and sustain life; so that you might hold with greater truth that many bodies are common to many things, as we see letters common to different words, than that anything could come into being without first-beginnings. Again why could not nature have produced men of such a size and strength as to be able to wade on foot across the sea and rend great mountains with their hands and outlive many generations of living men, if not because an unchanging matter has been assigned for begetting things and what can arise out of this matter is fixed? We must admit therefore that nothing can come from nothing, since things require seed before they can severally be born and be brought out into the buxom fields of air. Lastly since we see that tilled grounds surpass untilled and yield a better produce by the labour of hands, we may infer that there are in the earth first-beginnings of things which we by turning up the fruitful clods with the share and labouring the soil of the earth stimulate to rise. But if there were no such, you would see all things without any labour of ours spontaneously come forth in much greater perfection.

Moreover nature dissolves every thing back into its first bodies and does not annihilate things. For if aught were mortal in all its parts alike, the thing in a moment would be snatched away to destruction from before our eyes; since no force would be needed to produce disruption among its parts and undo their fastenings. Whereas in fact, as all things consist of an imperishable seed, nature suffers the destruction of nothing to be seen, until a force has encountered it sufficient to dash things to pieces by a blow or to pierce through the void places within them and break them up. Again if time, whenever it makes away with things through age, utterly destroys them eating up all their matter, out of what does Venus bring back into the light of life the race of living things each after its kind, or, when they are brought back, out of what does earth manifold in works give them nourishment and increase, furnishing them with food each after its kind? Out of what do its own native fountains and extraneous rivers from far and wide keep full the sea? Out of what does ether feed the stars? For infinite time gone by and lapse of days must have eaten up all things which are of mortal body. Now if in that period of time gone by those

31

things have existed, of which this sum of things is composed and recruited, they are possessed no doubt of an imperishable body, and cannot therefore any of them return to nothing. Again the same force and cause would destroy all things without distinction, unless everlasting matter held them together, matter more or less closely linked in mutual entanglement: a touch in sooth would be sufficient cause of death, inasmuch as any amount of force must of course undo the texture of things in which no parts at all were of an everlasting body. But in fact, because the fastenings of first-beginnings one with the other are unlike and matter is everlasting, things continue with body uninjured, until a force is found to encounter them strong enough to overpower the texture of each. A thing therefore never returns to nothing, but all things after disruption go back into the first bodies of matter. Lastly rains die, when father ether has tumbled them into the lap of mother earth; but then goodly crops spring up and boughs are green with leaves upon the trees, trees themselves grow and are laden with fruit; by them in turn our race and the race of wild beasts are fed, by them we see glad towns teem with children and the leafy forests ring on all sides with the song of new birds; through them cattle wearied with their load of fat lay their bodies down about the glad pastures and the white milky stream pours from the distended udders; through them a new brood with weakly limbs frisks and gambols over the soft grass, their young minds smitten with the love of pure milk. None of the things therefore which seem to be lost is utterly lost, since nature replenishes one thing out of another and does not suffer any thing to be begotten, before she has been recruited by the death of some other.

Now mark me: since I have taught that things cannot be born from nothing, cannot when begotten be brought back to nothing, that you may not haply yet begin in any shape to mistrust my words, because the first-beginnings of things cannot be seen by the eyes, take moreover this list of bodies which you must yourself admit are in the number of things and cannot be seen. First of all the force of the wind when aroused beats on the harbours and whelms huge ships and scatters clouds; sometimes in swift whirling eddy it scours the plains and straws them with large trees and scourges the mountain summits with forest-rending blasts: so fiercely does the wind rave with a shrill howling and rage with threatening roar. Winds therefore sure enough are unseen bodies which sweep the seas, the lands, ay and the clouds of heaven, tormenting them and catching them up in sudden whirls. On they stream and spread destruction abroad in just the same way as the soft liquid nature of water when all at once it is borne along in an overflowing stream, and a great downfall of water from the high hills augments it with copious rains, flinging together fragments of forests and entire trees; nor can the strong bridges sustain the sudden force of coming water: in such wise turbid with much rain the river dashes upon the piers with mighty strength. With a loud noise the water makes havoc and rolls under its eddies huge stones and throws down whatever opposes its waves. In this way then must the blasts of winds as well move on, and when they like a mighty stream have borne down in any direction, they push things before them and throw them down with repeated assaults, sometimes catch them up in curling eddy and carry them away in swift-circling whirl. Wherefore once and again I say winds are unseen bodies, since in their works and ways they are found to rival great rivers which are of a visible body. Then again we perceive the different smells of things, yet never see them coming to our nostrils; nor do we behold heats nor can we observe cold with the eyes nor are we used to see voices. Yet all these things must consist of a bodily nature, since they are able to move the senses; for nothing but body can touch and be touched. Again clothes hung up on a shore which waves break upon become moist, and then get dry if spread out in the sun. Yet it has not been seen in what way the moisture of water has sunk into them nor again in what way this has been dispelled by heat. The moisture therefore is dispersed into small particles which the eyes are quite unable to see. Again after the revolution of many of the sun's years a ring on the finger is thinned on the under side by wearing, the dripping from the eaves hollows a stone, the bent plough-share of iron imperceptibly decreases in the fields, and we behold the stone-paved streets worn down by the feet of the multitude; the brass statues too at the gates shew their right hands to be wasted by the touch of the numerous passers by who greet them. These things then we see are lessened, since they have been thus worn down; but what bodies depart at any given time the nature of vision has jealously shut out our seeing. Lastly the bodies which time and nature add to things by little and little, constraining them to grow in due measure, no exertion of the eyesight can behold; and so too wherever things grow old by age and decay, and when rocks hanging over the sea are eaten away by the fine salt spray, you cannot see what they lose at any given moment. Nature therefore works by unseen bodies.

And yet all things are not on all sides jammed together and kept in by body: there is also void in things. To have learned this will be good for you on many accounts; it will not suffer you to wander in doubt and be to seek in the sum of things and distrustful of our words. If there were not void, things could not move at all; for that which is the property of body, to let and hinder, would be present to all things at all times; nothing therefore could go on, since no other thing would be the first to give way. But in fact throughout seas and lands and the heights of heaven we see before our eyes many things move in many ways for various reasons, which things, if there were no void, I need not say would lack and want restless motion: they never would have been begotten at all, since matter jammed on all sides would have been at rest. Again however solid things are thought to be, you may yet learn from this that they are of rare body: in rocks and caverns the moisture of water oozes through and all things weep with abundant drops; food distributes itself through the whole body of living things; trees grow and yield fruit in season, because food is diffused through the whole from the very roots over the stem and all the boughs. Voices pass through walls and fly through houses shut, stiffening frost pierces to the bones. Now if there are no void parts, by what way can the bodies severally pass? You would see it to be quite impossible. Once more, why do we see one thing surpass another in weight though not larger in size? For if there is just as much body in a ball of wool as there is in a lump of lead, it is natural it should weigh the same, since the property of body is to weigh all things downwards, while on the contrary the nature of void is ever without weight. Therefore when a thing is just as large, yet is found to be lighter, it proves sure enough that it has more of void in it; while on the other hand that which is heavier shews that there is in it more of body and that it contains within it much less of void. Therefore that which we are seeking with keen-sighted reason exists sure enough, mixed up in things; and we call it void.

And herein I am obliged to forestall this point which some raise, lest it draw you away from the truth. The waters they say make way for the scaly creatures as they press on, and open liquid paths, because the fish leave room behind them, into which the yielding waters may stream; thus other things too may move and change place among themselves, although the whole sum be full. This you are to know has been taken up wholly on false grounds. For on what side I ask can the scaly creatures move forwards, unless the waters have first made room? Again on what side can the waters give place, so long as the fish are unable to go on? Therefore you must either strip all bodies of motion or admit that in things void is mixed up from which every thing gets its first start in moving. Lastly if two broad bodies after contact quickly spring asunder, the air must surely fill all the void which is formed between the bodies. Well however rapidly it stream together with swift-circling currents, yet the whole space will not be able to be filled up in one moment; for it must occupy first one spot and then another, until the whole is taken up. But if haply anyone supposes that, when the bodies have started asunder, that result follows because the air condenses, he is mistaken; for a void is then formed which was not before, and a void also is filled which existed before; nor can the air condense in such a way, nor supposing it could, could it methinks without void draw into itself and bring its parts together.

Wherefore however long you hold out by urging many objections, you must needs in the end admit that there is a void in things. And many more arguments I may state to you in order to accumulate proof on my words; but these slight footprints are enough for a keen-searching mind to enable you by yourself to find out all the rest. For as dogs often discover by smell the lair of a mountain-ranging wild beast though covered over with leaves, when once they have got on the sure tracks, thus you in cases like this will be able by yourself alone to see one thing after another and find your way into all dark corners and draw forth the truth. But if you lag or swerve a jot from the reality, this I can promise you, O Memmius, at once without more ado: such plenteous draughts from abundant wellsprings my sweet tongue shall pour from my richly furnished breast, that I fear slow age will steal over our limbs and break open in us the fastnesses of life, ere the whole store of reasons on any one question has by my verses been dropped into your ears.

But now to resume the thread of the design which I am weaving in verse: all nature then, as it exists by itself, has been founded on two things: there are bodies and there is void in which these bodies are placed and through which they move about. For that body exists by itself the general feeling of mankind declares; and unless the first foundation of belief shall be firmly grounded on this, there will be nothing to which we can appeal on hidden things in order to prove anything by reasoning of mind. Then again, if room and space which we call void did not exist, bodies could not be placed anywhere nor move about at all in any direction; as we have demonstrated to you a little before. Moreover there is nothing which you can affirm to be once separate from all body and quite distinct from void, which would so to say count as the discovery of a third nature. For whatever shall exist, this of itself must be something or other. Now if it shall admit of touch in however slight and small a measure, it will, be it with a large or be it with a little addition, provided it do exist, increase the amount of body and join the sum. But if it shall be intangible and unable to hinder any thing from passing through it on any side, this you are to know will be that which we call empty void. Again whatever shall exist by itself, will either do something or will itself suffer by the action of other things, or else in it things will be able to exist and go on. But no thing can do and suffer without body nor aught furnish room except void and vacancy. Therefore beside void and bodies no third nature taken by itself can be left in the number of things, either such as to fall at any time under the ken of our senses or such as any one can grasp by the reason of his mind.

For whatever things are named, you will either find to be properties linked to these two things or you will see to be accidents of these things. That is a property which can in no case be disjoined and separated without destruction accompanying the severance, such as the weight of a stone, the heat of fire, the fluidity of water. Slavery on the other hand, poverty and riches, liberty war concord and all other things which may come and go while the nature of the thing remains unharmed, these we are wont, as it is right we should, to call accidents. Time also exists not by itself, but simply from the things which happen the sense apprehends what has been done in time past, as well as what is present and what is to follow after. And we must admit that no one feels time by itself abstracted from the motion and calm rest of things. So when they say that the daughter of Tyndarus was ravished and the Trojan nations were subdued in war, we must mind that they do not force us to admit that these things are by themselves, since those generations of men, of whom these things were accidents, time now gone by has irrevocably swept away. For whatever shall have been done may be termed an accident in one case of the Teucran people, in another of the countries simply. Yes for if there had been no matter of things and no room and space in which things severally go on, never had the fire, kindled by love of the beauty of Tyndarus' daughter, blazed beneath the Phrygian breast of Alexander and lighted up the famous struggles of cruel war, nor had the timber-horse unknown to the Trojans wrapt Pergama in flames by its night-issuing brood of sons of the Greeks; so that you may clearly perceive that all actions from first to last exist not by themselves and are not by themselves in the way that body is, nor are terms of the same kind as void is, but are rather of such a kind that you may fairly call them accidents of body and of the room in which they severally go on.

Bodies again are partly first-beginnings of things, partly those which are formed of a union of first-beginnings. But those which are first-beginnings of things no force can quench: they are sure to have the better by their solid body. Although it seems difficult to believe that aught can be found among things with a solid body. For the lightning of heaven passes through the walls of houses, as well as noise and voices; iron grows red-hot in the fire and rocks burning with fierce heat burst asunder; the hardness of gold is broken up and dissolved by heat; the ice of brass melts vanquished by the flame; warmth and piercing cold coze through silver, since we have felt both, as we held cups with the hand in due fashion and the water was poured down into them. So universally there is found to be nothing solid in things. But yet because true reason and the nature of things constrains, attend until we make clear in a few verses that there are such things as consist of solid and everlasting body, which we teach are seeds of things and first-beginnings, out of which the whole sum of things which now exists has been produced.

First of all then since there has been found to exist a two-fold and widely dissimilar nature of two things, that is to say of body and of place in which things severally go on, each of the two must exist for and by itself and quite unmixed. For wherever there is empty space which we call void, there body is not; wherever again body maintains itself, there empty void no wise exists. First bodies therefore are solid and without void. Again since there is void in things begotten, solid matter must exist about this void, and no thing can be proved by true reason to conceal in its body and have within it void, unless you choose to allow that that which holds it in is solid. Again that can be nothing but a union of matter which can keep in the void of things. Matter therefore, which consists of a solid body, may be everlasting, though all things else are dissolved. Moreover if there were no empty void, the universe would be solid; unless on the other hand there were certain bodies to fill up whatever places they occupied, the existing universe would be empty and void space. Therefore sure enough body and void are marked off in alternate layers, since the universe is neither of a perfect fulness nor a perfect void. There are therefore certain bodies capable of marking off void spaces from full. These can neither be broken in pieces by the stroke of blows from without nor have their texture undone by aught piercing to their core nor give way before any other kind of assault; as we have proved to you a little before. For without void nothing seems to admit of being crushed in or broken up or split in two by cutting, or of taking in wet or permeating cold or penetrating fire, by which all things are destroyed. And the more anything contains within it of void, the more thoroughly it gives way to the assault of these things. Therefore if first bodies are as I have shewn, solid and without void, they must be everlasting. Again unless matter had been eternal all things before this would have utterly returned to nothing and whatever things we see would have been born anew from nothing. But since I have proved above that nothing can be produced from nothing, and that what is begotten cannot be recalled to nothing, first-beginnings must be of an imperishable body, into which all things can be dissolved at their last hour, that there may be a supply of matter for the reproduction of things. Therefore first-beginnings are of solid singleness, and in no other way can they have been preserved through ages during infinite time past in order to reproduce things.

Again if nature had set no limit to the breaking of things, by this time the bodies of matter would have been so far reduced by the breaking of past ages that nothing could within a fixed time be conceived out of them and reach its utmost growth of being. For we see that anything is more quickly destroyed than again renewed; and therefore that which the long, the infinite duration of all bygone time had broken up demolished and destroyed, could never be reproduced in all remaining time. But now sure enough a fixed limit to their breaking has been set, since we see each thing renewed, and at the same time definite periods fixed for things to reach the flower of their age. Moreover while the bodies of matter are most solid, it may yet be explained in what way all things which are formed soft, as air water earth fires, are so formed and by what force they severally go on, since once for all there is void mixed up in things. But on the other hand if the first-beginnings of things be soft, it cannot be explained out of what enduring basalt and iron can be produced; for their whole nature will utterly lack a first foundation to begin with. First-beginnings therefore are strong in solid singleness, and by a denser combination of these all things can be closely packed and exhibit enduring strength.

Again if no limit has been set to the breaking of bodies, nevertheless the several bodies which go to things must survive from eternity up to the present time, not yet assailed by any danger. But since they are possessed of a frail nature, it is not consistent with this that they could have continued through eternity harassed through ages by countless blows. Again too since a limit of growing and sustaining life has been assigned to things each after its kind, and since by the laws of nature it stands decreed what they can each do and what they cannot do, and since nothing is changed, but all things are so constant that the different birds all in succession exhibit in their body the distinctive marks of their kind, they must sure enough have a body of unchangeable matter also. For if the first-beginnings of things could in any way be vanquished and changed, it would be then uncertain too what could and what could not rise into being, in short on what principles each thing has its powers defined, its deep-set boundary mark; nor could the generations reproduce so often each after its kind the nature habits way of life and motions of the parents.

Then again since there is ever a bounding point to that first body which already is beyond what our senses can perceive, that point sure enough is without parts and consists of a least nature and never has existed apart by itself and will not be able in future so to exist, since it is in itself part of that other; and so a first and single part and then other and other similar parts in succession fill up in close serried mass the nature of the first body; and since these cannot exist by themselves, they must cleave to that from which they cannot in any way be torn. First-beginnings therefore are of solid singleness, massed together and cohering closely by means of least parts, not compounded out of a union of those parts, but, rather, strong in everlasting singleness. From them nature allows nothing to be torn, nothing further to be worn away, reserving them as seeds for things. Again unless there shall be a least, the very smallest bodies will consist of infinite parts, inasmuch as the half of the half will always have a half and nothing will set bounds to the division. Therefore between the sum of things and the least of things what difference will there be? There will be no distinction at all; for how absolutely infinite soever the whole sum is, yet the things which are smallest will equally consist of infinite parts. Now since on this head true reason protests and denies that the mind can believe it, you must yield and admit that there exist such things as are possessed of no parts and are of a least nature. And since these exist, those first bodies also you must admit to be solid and everlasting. Once more, if nature creatress of things had been wont to compel all things to be broken up into least parts, then too she would be unable to reproduce anything out of those parts, because those things which are enriched with no parts cannot have the properties which begetting matter ought to have, I mean the various entanglements weights blows clashings motions by means of which things severally go on.

For which reasons they who have held fire to be the matter of things and the sum to be formed out of fire alone, are seen to have strayed most widely from true reason. At the head of whom enters Heraclitus to do battle, famous for obscurity more among the frivolous than the earnest Greeks who seek the truth. For fools admire and like all things the more which they perceive to be concealed under involved language, and determine things to be true which can prettily tickle the ears and are varnished over with finely sounding phrase.

For I want to know how things can be so various, if they are formed out of fire one and unmixed: it would avail nothing for hot fire to be condensed or rarified, if the parts of fire had always the same nature which the whole fire likewise has. The heat would be more intense by compression of parts, more faint by their severance and dispersion. More than this you cannot think it in the power of such causes to effect, far less could so great a diversity of things come from mere density and rarity of fires. Observe also, if they suppose void to be mixed up in things, fire may then be condensed and left rare; but because they see many things rise up in contradiction to them and

39

shrink from leaving unmixed void in things, fearing the steep, they lose the true road, and do not perceive on the other hand that if void is taken from things, all things are condensed and out of all things is formed one single body, which cannot briskly radiate anything from it, in the way heat-giving fire emits light and warmth, letting you see that it is not of closely compressed parts. But if they haply think that in some other way fires may be quenched in the union and change their body, you are to know that if they shall scruple on no side to do this, all heat sure enough will be utterly brought to nothing, and all things that are produced will be formed out of nothing. For whenever a thing changes and quits its proper limits, at once this change of state is the death of that which was before. Therefore something or other must needs be left to those fires of theirs undestroyed, that you may not have all things absolutely returning to nothing, and the whole store of things born anew and flourishing out of nothing. Since then in fact there are some most unquestionable bodies which always preserve the same nature, on whose going or coming and change of order things change their nature and bodies are transformed, you are to know that these first bodies of things are not of fire. For it would matter nothing that some should withdraw and go away and others should be added on and some should have their order changed, if they yet one and all retained the nature of heat; for whatever they produced would be altogether fire. But thus methinks it is: there are certain bodies whose clashings motions order position shapes produce fires, and which by a change of order change the nature of the things and do not resemble fire nor anything else which has the power of sending bodies to our senses and touching by its contact our sense of touch.

Again to say that all things are fire and that no real thing except fire exists in the number of things, as this same man does, appears to be sheer dotage. For he himself takes his stand on the side of the senses to fight against the senses and shakes their authority, on which rests all our belief, ay from which this fire as he calls it is known to himself; for he believes that the senses can truly perceive fire, he does not believe they can perceive all other things which are not a whit less clear. Now this appears to me to be as false as it is foolish; for to what shall we appeal? what surer test can we have than the senses, whereby to note truth and falsehood? Again why should any one rather abolish all things and choose to leave the single nature of heat, than deny that fires exist, while he allows any thing else to be? it seems to be equal madness to affirm either this or that.

For these reasons they who have held that fire is the matter of things and that the sum can be formed out of fire, and they who have determined air to be the first-beginning in begetting things, and all who have held that water by itself alone forms things, or that earth produces all things and changes into all the different natures of things, appear to have strayed exceedingly wide of the truth; as well as they who make the first-beginnings of things two-fold coupling air with fire and earth with water, and they who believe that all things grow out of four things, fire earth and air and water. Chief of whom is Agrigentine Empedocles: him within the three-cornered shores of its lands that island bore, about which the Ionian sea flows in large cranklings, and splashes up brine from its green waves. Here the sea racing in its straitened firth divides by its waters the shores of Italia's lands from the other's coasts: here is wasteful Charybdis and here the rumblings of Aetna threaten anew to gather up such fury of flames, as again with force to belch forth the fires bursting from its throat and carry up to heaven once more the lightnings of flame. Now though this great country is seen to deserve in many ways the wonder of mankind and is held to be well worth visiting, rich in all good things, guarded by large force of men, yet seems it to have held within it nothing more glorious than this man, nothing more holy marvellous and dear. The verses too of his godlike genius cry with a loud voice and set forth in such wise his glorious discoveries that he hardly seems born of a mortal stock.

Yet he and those whom we have mentioned above immeasurably inferior and far beneath him, although the authors of many excellent and godlike discoveries they have given responses from so to say their heart's holy of holies with more sanctity and on much more unerring grounds than the Pythia who speaks out from the tripod and laurel of Phoebus, have yet gone to ruin in the first-beginnings of things: it is there they have fallen, and great themselves, great and heavy has been that fall; first because they have banished void from things and yet assign to them motions, and allow things soft and rare, air sun fire earth living things corn, and yet mix not up void in their body; next because they suppose that there is no limit to the division of bodies and no stop set to their breaking and that there exists no least at all in things; though we see that that is the bounding-point of any thing which seems to be least in reference to our senses, so that from this you may infer that because the things which you do not see have a bounding-point, there is a least in them. Moreover since they assign soft first-beginnings of things, which we see to have birth and to be of a body altogether mortal, both the sum of things must in that case revert to nothing and the store of things be born anew and flourish out of nothing: now how wide of the truth both of these doctrines are you will already comprehend. In the next place these bodies are in many ways mutually hostile and poisonous; and therefore they will either perish when they have met, or will fly asunder just as we see, when a storm has gathered, lightnings and rains and winds fly asunder.

Again if all things are produced from four things and all again broken up into those things, how can they more be called first-beginnings of things than things be called their first-beginnings, the supposition being reversed? For they are begotten time about and interchange colour and their whole nature without ceasing. But if haply you suppose that the body of fire and of earth and air and the moisture of water meet in such a way that none of them in the union changes its nature, nothing I can tell you will be able to be thus produced out of them, neither living thing nor thing with inanimate body, as a tree; in fact each thing amid the medley of this discordant mass will display its own nature and air will be seen to be mixed up with earth and heat to remain in union with moisture. But first-beginnings ought in begetting things to bring with them a latent and unseen nature in order that no thing stand out, to be in the way and prevent whatever is produced from having its own proper being.

Moreover they go back to heaven and its fires for a beginning, and first suppose that fire changes into air, next that from air water is begotten and earth is produced out of water, and that all in reverse order come back from earth, water first, next air, then heat, and that these cease not to interchange, to pass from heaven to earth, from earth to the stars of ether. All which first-beginnings must on no account do; since something unchangeable must needs remain over, that things may not utterly be brought back to nothing. For whenever a thing changes and quits its proper limits, at once this change of state is the death of that which was before. Wherefore since those things which we have mentioned a little before pass into a state of change, they must be formed out of others which cannot in any case be transformed, that you may not have things returning altogether to nothing. Why not rather hold that there are certain bodies possessed of such a nature, that, if they have haply produced fire, the same may, after a few have been taken away and a few added on and the order and motion changed, produce air; and that all other things may in the same way interchange with one another?

'But plain matter of fact clearly proves' you say 'that all things grow up into the air and are fed out of the earth; and unless the season at the propitious period send such abundant showers that the trees reel beneath the soaking storms of rain, and unless the sun on its part foster them and supply heat, corn trees living things could not grow.' Quite true, and unless solid food and soft water should recruit us, the body would waste away and then the whole life would break up out of all the sinews and bones; for we beyond doubt are recruited and fed by certain things, this and that other thing by certain other things. Because many first-beginnings common to many things in many ways are mixed up in things, therefore sure enough different things are fed by different things. And it often makes a great difference with what things and in what position the same first-beginnings are held in union, and what motions they mutually impart and receive; for the same make up heaven sea lands rivers sun, the same make up corn trees living things; but they are mixed up with different things and in different ways as they move. Now you see throughout even in these verses of ours many words, though you must needs admit that the lines and words differ one from the other both in meaning and in the sound wherewith they sound. So much can elements effect by a mere change of order; but those elements which are the first-beginnings of things can bring with them more combinations out of which different things can severally be produced.

Let us now also examine the homoeomeria of Anaxagoras as the Greeks term it, which the poverty of our native speech does not allow us to name in our own tongue; though it is easy enough to set forth in words the thing itself. First of all then, when he speaks of the homoeomeria of things, you must know he supposes bones to be formed out of very small and minute bones and flesh of very small and minute fleshes and blood by the coming together of many drops of blood, and gold he thinks can be composed of grains of gold and earth be a concretion of small earths and fires can come from fires and water from waters, and everything else he fancies and supposes to be produced on a like principle. And yet at the same time he does not allow that void exists anywhere in things, or that there is a limit to the division of things. Wherefore he appears to me on both these grounds to be as much mistaken as those whom we have already spoken of above. In addition to this the first-beginnings which he supposes are too frail; if first-beginnings they be which are possessed of a nature like to the things themselves and are just as liable to suffering and death, and which nothing reins back from destruction. For which of them will hold out against a strong crushing force, so as to escape death, in the very jaws of destruction? fire or water or air? which of these? blood or bones? Not one methinks, since everything will be just as essentially mortal as those things which we see with the senses perish before our eyes vanquished by some force. But I appeal to facts demonstrated above for proof that things cannot fall away to nothing nor on the other hand grow from nothing. Again since food gives increase and nourishment to the body, you are to know that our veins and blood and bones and the like are formed of things foreign to them in kind; or if they shall say that all foods are of a mixed body and contain in them small bodies of sinews and bones and veins as well and particles

43

of blood, it will follow that all food, solid as well as liquid, must be held to be composed of things foreign to them in kind, of bones that is and sinews and matter and blood mixed up. Again if all the bodies which grow out of the earth, are in the earths, the earth must be composed of things foreign to them in kind which grow out of these earths. Apply again this reasoning to other things, and you may use just the same words. If flame and smoke and ash are latent in woods, woods must necessarily be composed of things foreign to them in kind. Again all those bodies, to which the earth gives food, it increases out of things foreign to them in kind which rise out of the earth: thus too the bodies of flame which issue from the woods, are fed out of things foreign to them in kind which rise out of these woods.

Here some slight opening is left for evasion, which Anaxagoras avails himself of, choosing to suppose that all things though latent are mixed up in things, and that is alone visible of which there are the largest number of bodies in the mixture and these more ready to hand and stationed in the first rank. This however is far banished from true reason. For then it were natural that corn too should often, when crushed by the formidable force of the stone, shew some mark of blood or some other of the things which have their nourishment in our body; and when we rub one stone on another, blood should ooze out. For like reasons it were fitting that grasses too should yield sweet drops of liquid, like in flavour to the udder of milk in sheep; yes and that often, when clods of earth have been crumbled, kinds of grasses and corn and leaves should be found to lurk distributed among the earth in minute quantities; and lastly that ash and smoke and minute fires should be found latent in woods, when they were broken off. Now since plain matter of fact teaches that none of these results follows, you are to know that things are not so mixed up in things; but rather seeds common to many things must in many ways be mixed up and latent in things.

'But it often comes to pass on high mountains' you say 'that contiguous tops of tall trees rub together, the strong southwinds constraining them so to do, until the flower of flame has broken out and they have burst into a blaze.' Quite true and yet fire is not innate in woods; but there are many seeds of heat, and when they by rubbing have streamed together, they produce conflagrations in the forests. But if the flame was stored up ready made in the forests, the fire could not be concealed for any length of time, but would destroy forests, burn up trees indiscriminately. Do you now see, as we said a little before, that it often makes a very great difference with what things and in what position the same first-beginnings are held in union and what motions they mutually impart and receive, and that the same may when a little

44

changed in arrangement produce say fires and a fir? just as the words too consist of elements only a little changed in arrangement, though we denote firs and fires with two quite distinct names. Once again, if you suppose that whatever you perceive among visible things cannot be produced without imagining bodies of matter possessed of a like nature, in this way, you will find, the first-beginnings of things are destroyed: it will come to this that they will be shaken by loud fits of convulsive laughter and will bedew with salt tears face and cheeks.

Now mark and learn what remains to be known and hear it more distinctly. Nor does my mind fail to perceive how dark the things are; but the great hope of praise has smitten my heart with sharp thyrsus, and at the same time has struck into my breast sweet love of the muses, with which now inspired I traverse in blooming thought the pathless haunts of the Pierides never yet trodden by sole of man. I love to approach the untasted springs and to quaff, I love to cull fresh flowers and gather for my head a distinguished crown from spots whence the muses have yet veiled the brows of none; first because I teach of great things and essay to release the mind from the fast bonds of religious scruples, and next because on a dark subject I pen such lucid verses o'erlaying all with the muses' charm. For that too would seem to be not without good grounds; but even as physicians when they purpose to give nauseous wormwood to children, first smear the rim round the bowl with the sweet yellow juice of honey, that the unthinking age of children may be fooled as far as the lips, and meanwhile drink up the bitter draught of wormwood and though beguiled yet not be betrayed, but rather by such means recover health and strength; so I now, since this doctrine seems generally somewhat bitter to those by whom it has not been handled, and the multitude shrinks back from it in dismay, I have resolved to set forth to you our doctrine in sweet-toned Pierian verse and o'erlay it as it were with the pleasant honey of the muses, if haply by such means I might engage your mind on my verses, till such time as you clearly perceive with what shape the whole nature of things has been put together.

But since I have taught that most solid bodies of matter fly about for ever unvanquished through all time, mark now, let us unfold whether there is or is not any limit to their sum; likewise let us clearly see whether that which has been found to be void, or room and space, in which things severally go on, is all of it altogether finite or stretches without limits and to an unfathomable depth.

Well then the existing universe is bounded in none of its dimensions; for then it must have had an outside. Again it is seen that there can be an outside of nothing, unless there be something beyond to bound it, so that that is seen, farther than which this our nature of sense does not follow the thing. Now since we must admit that there is nothing outside the sum, it has no outside, and therefore is without end and limit. And it matters not in which of its regions you take your stand; so invariably, whatever position any one has taken up, he leaves the universe just as infinite as before in all directions. Again if for the moment all existing space be held to be bounded, supposing a man runs forward to its outside borders and stands on the utmost verge and then throws a winged javelin, do you choose that it when hurled with vigorous force shall advance to the point to which it has been sent and fly to a distance, or do you decide that something can get in its way and stop it? for you must admit and adopt one of the two suppositions; either of which shuts you out from all escape and compels you to grant that the universe stretches without end. For whether there is something to get in its way and prevent its coming whither it was sent and placing itself in the point intended, or whether it is carried forward, in either case it has not started from the end. In this way I will go on and, wherever you have placed the outside borders, I will ask what then becomes of the javelin. The result will be that an end can no where be fixed, and that the room given for flight will still prolong the power of flight. Lastly one thing is seen by the eyes to end another thing; air bounds off hills, and mountains air, earth limits sea and sea again all lands; the universe however there is nothing outside to end.

Again if all the space of the whole sum were enclosed within fixed borders and were bounded, in that case the store of matter by its solid weights would have streamed together from all sides to the lowest point nor could anything have gone on under the canopy of heaven, no nor would there have been a heaven nor sunlight at all, inasmuch as all matter, settling down through infinite time past, would lie together in a heap. But as it is, sure enough no rest is given to the bodies of the first-beginnings, because there is no lowest point at all, to which they might stream together as it were, and where they might take up their positions. All things are ever going on in ceaseless motion from all quarters and bodies of matter stirred to action are supplied from beneath out of infinite space. Therefore the nature of room and the space of the unfathomable void is such as bright thunderbolts cannot race through in their course though gliding on through endless tract of time, no nor lessen one jot the journey that remains to go by all their travel; so huge a room is spread out on all sides for things without any bounds in all directions round.

Again nature keeps the sum of things from setting any limit to itself, since she compels body to be ended by void and void in turn by body, so that either she thus renders the universe infinite by this alternation of the two, or else the one of the two, in case the other does not bound it, with its single nature stretches nevertheless immeasurably. But void I have already proved to be infinite; therefore matter must be infinite: for if void were infinite, and matter finite, neither sea nor earth nor the glittering quarters of heaven nor mortal kind nor the holy bodies of the gods could hold their ground one brief passing hour; since forced asunder from its union the store of matter would be dissolved and borne along the mighty void, or rather I should say would never have combined to produce anything, since scattered abroad it could never have been brought together. For verily not by design did the first-beginnings of things station themselves each in its right place guided by keen-sighted intelligence, nor did they bargain sooth to say what motions each should assume, but because many in number and shifting about in many ways throughout the universe they are driven and tormented by blows during infinite time past, after trying motions and unions of every kind at length they fall into arrangements such as those out of which this our sum of things has been formed, and by which too it is preserved through many great years when once it has been thrown into the appropriate motions, and causes the streams to replenish the greedy sea with copious river waters and the earth fostered by the heat of the sun, to renew its produce, and the race of living things to come up and flourish, and the gliding fires of ether to live: all which these several things could in no wise bring to pass, unless a store of matter could rise up from infinite space, out of which store they are wont to make up in due season whatever has been lost. For as the nature of living things when robbed of food loses its body and wastes away, thus all things must be broken up, as soon as matter has ceased to be supplied, diverted in any way from its proper course. Nor can blows from without hold together all the sum which has been brought into union. They can it is true frequently strike upon and stay a part, until others come and the sum can be completed. At times however they are compelled to rebound and in so doing grant to the first-beginnings of things room and time for flight, to enable them to get clear away from the mass in union. Wherefore again and again I repeat many bodies must rise up; nay more that the blows themselves may not fail, there is need of an infinite supply of matter on all sides.

And herein, Memmius, be far from believing this, that all things as they say press to the centre of the sum, and that for this reason the nature of the world stands fast without any strokes from the outside and the uppermost and lowest parts cannot part asunder in any direction, because all things have been always pressing towards the centre (if you can believe that anything can rest upon itself); or that the heavy bodies which are beneath the earth all press upwards and are at rest

47

on the earth, turned topsyturvy, just like the images of things which we see before us in the waters. In the same way too they maintain that living things walk head downwards and cannot tumble out of earth into the parts of heaven lying below them any more than our bodies can spontaneously fly into the quarters of heaven; that when those see the sun, we behold the stars of night; and that they share with us time about the seasons of heaven and pass nights equal in length to our days. But groundless error has devised such dreams for fools, because they have embraced false principles of reason. For there can be no centre where the universe is infinite; no nor, even if there were a centre, could anything take up a position there any more on that account than for some quite different reason be driven away. For all room and space, which we term void, must through centre, through no-centre alike give place to heavy bodies, in whatever directions their motions tend. Nor is there any spot of such a sort that when bodies have reached it, they can lose their force of gravity and stand upon void; and that again which is void must not serve to support anything, but must, as its nature craves, continually give place. Things cannot therefore in such a way be held in union, o'ermastered by love of a centre.

Again since they do not suppose that all bodies press to the centre, but only those of earth and water, and such things as are held together by a body of an earthly nature, the fluid of the sea and great water from the mountains; while on the other hand they teach that the subtle element of air and hot fires at the same time are carried away from the centre and that for this reason the whole ether round bickers with signs and the sun's flame is fed throughout the blue of heaven, because heat flying from the centre all gathers together there, and that the topmost boughs of trees could not put forth leaves at all, unless from time to time nature supplied food from the earth to each, their reasons are not only false, but they contradict each other. Space I have already proved to be infinite; and space being infinite matter as I have said must also be infinite lest after the winged fashion of flames the walls of the world should suddenly break up and fly abroad along the mighty void, and all other things follow for like reasons and the innermost quarters of heaven tumble in from above and the earth in an instant withdraw from beneath our feet and amid the commingled ruins of things in it and of heaven, ruins unloosing the first bodies, should wholly pass away along the unfathomable void, so that in a moment of time not a wrack should be left behind, nothing save untenanted space and viewless first-beginnings. For on whatever side you shall first determine first bodies to be wanting, this side will be the gate of death for things, through this the whole crowd of matter will fling itself abroad.

If you will well learn these things, then carried to the end with slight trouble (you will be able by yourself to understand all the rest). For one thing after another will grow clear and dark night will not rob you of the road, to keep you from surveying the utmost ends of nature: in such wise things will light the torch for other things.

H. A. J. Munro

VERGIL

PUBLIUS VERGILIUS MARO (70-19 B. C.) was one of the most notable
ancient poets. Born near Mantua, he finally reached Rome, where he studied
rhetoric, astronomy, and medicine: but ultimately dedicated himself to poetry.
He became a member of the literary coterie that centred round the Emperor
Augustus, was a friend of Maecenas, patron of the arts, and was particularly
attached to the poet Horace. Vergil made a trip to Greece, but fell ill on his
return, died, and was buried at Naples.

Vergil's poetic reputation has been great and continuous for two thousand
years. His output includes short miscellaneous pieces, a series of pastoral sketches
called *Eclogues* or *Bucolics*: a poem on husbandry, the *Georgics*: and a long
epic poem, in twelve books, entitled the *Aeneid*, in which he glorifies the
Roman Emperor and the Roman race.

The three Eclogues that follow are imitative of the Sicilian idylls
of Theocritus. Eclogue I deals with the cares of shepherds and with
their love affairs. Eclogue III presents a bucolic singing contest.
Eclogue IV is sometimes called the Messianic Eclogue, because it
alludes to a child who will bring back a golden age. The reference,
however, is must probably to the expected child of Octavian, the Emperor Augustus.

ECLOGUE I

MELIBOEUS

TITYRUS

MELIBOEUS: Stretched in the shadow of the broad beech, thou
  Rehearsest, Tityrus, on the slender pipe
  Thy woodland music. We our fatherland
  Are leaving, we must shun the fields we love:
  While, Tityrus, thou, at ease amid the shade,
  Bidd'st answering woods call Amaryllis 'fair.'

50

TITYRUS: O Meliboeus! 'Tis a god that made
    For me this holiday: for god I'll aye
    Account him; many a young lamb from my fold
    Shall stain his altar. Thanks to him, my kine
    Range, as thou seest them; thanks to him, I play
    What songs I list upon my shepherd's pipe.
MELIBOEUS: For me, I grudge thee not; I marvel much:
    So sore a trouble is in all the land.
    Lo! feeble I am driving hence my goats —
    Nay dragging, Tityrus, one, and that with pain.
    For, yeaning here amidst the hazel-stems,
    She left her twin kids — on the naked flint
    She left them; and I lost my promised flock.
    This evil, I remember, oftentimes,
    (Had not my wits been wandering), oaks foretold
    By heaven's hand smitten: oft the wicked crow
    Croaked the same message from the rifted holm.
    —Yet tell me, Tityrus, of this 'God' of thine.
TITYRUS: The city men call Rome my folly deemed
    Was e'en like this of ours, where week by week
    We shepherds journey with our weanling flocks.
    So whelp to dog, so kid (I knew) to dam
    Was likest: and I judged great things by small.
    But o'er all cities this so lifts her head,
    As doth o'er osiers lithe the cypress tree.
MELIBOEUS: What made thee then so keen to look on Rome?
TITYRUS: Freedom: who marked, at last, my helpless state:
    Now that a whiter beard than that of yore
    Fell from my razor: still she marked, and came
    (All late) to help me — now that all my thought
    Is Amaryllis, Galatea gone.
    While Galatea's, I despaired, I own,
    Of freedom, and of thrift. Though from my farm
    Full many a victim stept, though rich the cheese
    Pressed for yon thankless city: still my hand
    Returned not, heavy with brass pieces, home.
MELIBOEUS: I wondered, Amaryllis, whence that woe,
    And those appeals to heav'n: for whom the peach
    Hung undisturbed upon the parent tree.
    Tityrus was gone! Why, Tityrus, pine and rill,
    And all these copses, cried to thee, "Come home!"

TITYRUS: What could I do? I could not step from out
My bonds; nor meet, save there, with Pow'rs so kind.
There, Meliboeus, I beheld that youth
For whom each year twelve days my altars smoke.
Thus answered he my yet unanswered prayer;
"Feed still, my lads, your kine, and yoke your bulls."
MELIBOEUS: Happy old man! Thy lands are yet thine own!
Lands broad enough for thee, although bare stones
And marsh choke every field with reedy mud.
Strange pastures shall not vex thy teeming ewes,
Nor neighbouring flocks shed o'er them rank disease.
Happy old man! Here, by familiar streams
And holy springs, thou'lt catch the leafy cool.
Here, as of old, yon hedge, thy boundary line,
Its willow-buds a feast for Hybla's bees,
Shall with soft whisperings woo thee to thy sleep.
Here, 'neath the tall cliff, shall the vintager
Sings carols to the winds: while all the time
Thy pets, the stockdoves, and the turtles make
Incessantly their moan from aery elms.
TITYRUS: Aye, and for this shall slim stags graze in air,
And ocean cast on shore the shrinking fish;
For this, each realm by either wandered o'er,
Parthians shall Arar drink, or Tigris Gauls;
Ere from this memory shall fade that face!
MELIBOEUS: And we the while must thirst on Libya's sands,
O'er Scythia roam, and where the Cretan stems
The swift Oaxes; or, with Britons, live
Shut out from all the world. Shall I e'er see,
In far-off years, my fatherland? the turf
That roofs my meagre hut? see, wondering, last,
Those few scant cornblades that are realms to me?
What! must rude soldiers hold these fallows trim?
That corn barbarians? See what comes of strife,
Poor people — where we sowed, what hands shall reap!
Now, Meliboeus, pr'ythee graft thy pears,
And range thy vines! Nay on, my she-goats, on,
Once happy flock! For never more must I,
Outstretched in some green hollow, watch you hang
From tufted crags, far up: no carols more
I'll sing: nor, shepherded by me, shall ye
Crop the tart willow and the clover-bloom.

TITYRUS: Yet here, this one night, thou may'st rest with me,
Thy bed green branches. Chestnuts soft have I
And mealy apples, and our fill of cheese.
Already, see, the far-off chimneys smoke,
And deeper grow the shadows of the hills.

C. S. Calverley

ECLOGUE III

MENELCAS

DAMOETAS

PALAEMON

MENELCAS: Whose flock, Damoetas? Meliboeus's?
DAMOETAS: No, Aegon's. Aegon left it in my care.
MENELCAS: Unluckiest of flocks! Your master courts
Neaera, wondering if she like me more:
Meanwhile a stranger milks you twice an hour,
Saps the flock's strength, and robs the sucking lambs.
DAMOETAS: Yet fling more charily such words at men.
You — while the goats looked goatish — we know who,
And in what chapel — (but the kind Nymphs laughed) —
MENELCAS: Then (was it?) when they saw me Micon's shrubs
And young vines hacking with my rascally knife?
DAMOETAS: Or when by this old beech you broke the bow
And shafts of Daphnis: which you cried to see,
You crossgrained lad, first given to the boy;
And harm him somehow you must needs, or die.
MENELCAS: Where will lords stop, when knaves are come to this?
Did not I see you, scoundrel, in a snare
Take Damon's goat, Wolf barking all the while?
And when I shouted, "Where's he off to? Call,
Tityrus, your flock," — you skulked behind the sedge.
DAMOETAS: Beaten in singing, should he have withheld
The goat my pipe had by its music earned?
That goat was mine, you mayn't p'raps know: and he
Owned it himself: but said he could not pay.

53

MENELCAS: He beat by you? You own a decent pipe?
Used you not, dunce, to stand at the crossroads,
Stifling some lean tune in a squeaky straw?
DAMOETAS: Shall we then try in turn what each can do?
I stake yon cow — nay hang not back — she comes
Twice daily to the pail, is suckling twins.
Say what you'll lay.
MENELCAS: I durst not wager aught
Against you from the flock: for I have at home
A father, I have a tyrant stepmother.
Both count the flock twice daily, one the kids.
But what you'll own far handsomer, I'll stake
(Since you will be so mad) two beechen cups,
The carved work of the great Alcimedon.
O'er them the chiseller's skill has traced a vine
That drapes with ivy pale her wide-flung curls.
Two figures in the centre: Conon one,
And — what's that other's name, who'd take a wand
And shew the nations how the year goes round;
When you should reap, when stoop behind the plough?
Ne'er yet my lips came near them, safe hid up.
DAMOETAS: For me two cups the selfsame workman made,
And clasped with lissom briar the handles round.
Orpheus i' the centre, with the woods behind.
Ne'er yet my lips came near them, safe hid up.
— This talk of cups, if on my cow you've fixed
Your eye, is idle.
MENELCAS: Nay you'll not this day
Escape me. Name your spot, and I'll be there.
Our umpire be — Palaemon; here he comes!
I'll teach you how to challenge folks to sing.
DAMOETAS: Come on, if aught is in you. I'm not loth,
I shrink from no man. Only, neighbour, thou
('Tis no small matter) lay this well to heart.
PALAEMON: Say on, since now we sit on softest grass;
And now buds every field and every tree,
And woods are green, and passing fair the year.
Damoetas, lead. Menalcas, follow next.
Sing verse for verse: such songs the Muses love.
DAMOETAS: With Jove we open. Jove fills everything,
He walks the earth, he listens when I sing.
MENELCAS: Me Phoebus loves. I still have offerings meet
For Phoebus; bay, and hyacinth blushing sweet.

54

DAMOETAS: Me Galatea pelts with fruit, and flies
    (Wild girl) to the woods: but first would catch my eyes.
MENELCAS: Unbid Amyntas comes to me, my flame;
    With Delia's self my dogs are not more tame.
DAMOETAS: Gifts have I for my fair: who marked but I
    The place where doves had built their nest sky-high?
MENELCAS: I've sent my poor gift, which the wild wood bore,
    Ten golden apples. Soon I'll send ten more.
DAMOETAS: Oft Galatea tells me — what sweet tales!
    Waft to the god's ears just a part, ye gales.
MENELCAS: At heart Amyntas loves me. Yet what then?
    He mates with hunters, I with servingmen.
DAMOETAS: Send me thy Phillis, good Iolas, now.
    Today's my birthday. When I slay my cow
    To help my harvest — come, and welcome, thou.
MENELCAS: Phillis is my love. When we part, she'll cry;
    And fain would bid Iolas' self goodbye.
DAMOETAS: Wolves kill the flocks, and storms the ripened corn;
    And winds the tree; and me a maiden's scorn.
MENELCAS: Rain is the land's delight, weaned kids' the vine;
    Big ewes' lithe willow; and one fair face mine.
DAMOETAS: Pollio loves well this homely muse of mine.
    For a new votary fat a calf, ye Nine.
MENELCAS: Pollio makes songs. For him a bull demand,
    Who butts, whose hoofs already spurn the sand.
DAMOETAS: Who loves thee, Pollio, go where thou art gone.
    For him flow honey, thorns sprout cinnamon.
MENELCAS: Who loathes not Bavius, let him love thy notes,
    Maevius: — and yoke the fox, and milk he-goats.
DAMOETAS: Flowers and ground-strawberries while your prize ye make,
    Cold in the grass — fly hence, lads — lurks the snake.
MENELCAS: Sheep, banks are treacherous: draw not overnigh:
    See, now the lordly ram his fleece doth dry.
DAMOETAS: Tityrus, yon she-goats from the river bring.
    I in due time will wash them at the spring.
MENELCAS: Call, lads, your sheep. Once more our hands, should heat
    O'ertake the milk, will press in vain the teat.
DAMOETAS: How rich these vetches, yet how lean my ox.
    Love kills alike the herdsman and the flocks.
MENELCAS: My lambs — and here love's not in fault, you'll own —
    Witched by some jealous eye, are skin and bone.
DAMOETAS: Say in what land — and great Apollo be
    To me — heaven's arch extends just cubits three.

MENELCAS: Say in what land with kings' names grav'n are grown
  Flowers — and be Phillis yours and yours alone.
PALAEMON: Not mine such strife to settle. You have earned
  A cow, and you: and whoso else shall e'er
  Shrink from love's sweets or prove his bitterness.
  Close, lads, the springs. The meads have drunk enough.

C. S. Calverley

ECLOGUE IV

Muses of Sicily, a loftier song
Wake we! Some tire of shrubs and myrtles low.
Are woods our theme? Then princely be the woods.

Come are those last days that the Sybil sang:
The ages' mighty march begins anew.
Now comes the virgin, Saturn reigns again:
Now from high heaven descends a wondrous race.
Thou on the newborn babe — who first shall end
That age of iron, bid a golden dawn
Upon the broad world — chaste Lucina, smile:
Now thy Apollo reigns. And, Pollio, thou
Shalt be our Prince, when he that grander age
Opens, and onward roll the mighty moons:
Thou, trampling out what prints our crimes have left,
Shalt free the nations from perpetual fear.
While he to bliss shall waken; with the Blest
See the Brave mingling, and be seen of them,
Ruling that world o'er which his father's arm shed peace. —

On thee, child, everywhere shall earth, untilled,
Show'r, her first baby-offerings, vagrant stems
Of ivy, foxglove, and gay briar, and bean;
Unbid the goats shall come big-uddered home,
Nor monstrous lions scare the herded kine.
Thy cradle shall be full of pretty flowers:
Die must the serpent, treacherous poison-plants
Must die; and Syria's roses spring like weeds.

But, soon as thou canst read of hero-deeds
Such as thy father wrought, and understand
What is true worth: the champaign day by day
Shall grow more yellow with the waving corn;
From the wild bramble purpling then shall hang
The grape; and stubborn oaks drop honeydew.
Yet traces of that guile of elder days
Shall linger; bidding men tempt seas in ships,
Gird towns with walls, cleave furrows in the land.
Then a new Tiphys shall arise, to man
New argosies with heroes: then shall be
New wars; and once more shall be found for Troy,
A mightier Achilles.

                    After this,
When thou hast grown and strengthened into man,
The pilot's self shall range the seas no more;
Nor, each land teeming with the wealth of all,
The floating pines exchange their merchandise.
Vines shall not need the pruning-hook, nor earth
The harrow: ploughmen shall unyoke their steers.
Nor then need wool be taught to counterfeit
This hue and that. At will the meadow ram
Shall change to saffron, or the gorgeous tints
Of Tyre, his fair fleece; and the grazing lamb
At will put crimson on.
             So grand an age
Did those three Sisters bid their spindles spin;
Three, telling with one voice the changeless will of Fate.

Oh draw—the time is all but present—near
To thy great glory, cherished child of heaven,
Jove's mighty progeny! And lo! the world,
The round and ponderous world, bows down to thee;
The earth, the ocean-tracts, the depths of heaven.
Lo! nature revels in the coming age.
Oh! may the evening of my days last on,
May breath be mine, till I have told thy deeds!
Not Orpheus then, not Linus, shall outsing
Me: though each vaunts his mother or his sire,
Calliopea this, Apollo that.
Let Pan strive with me, Arcady his judge;
Pan, Arcady his judge, shall yield the palm.

Learn, tiny babe, to read a mother's smile:
Already ten long months have wearied her.
Learn, tiny babe. Him, who ne'er knew such smiles,
Nor god nor goddess bids to board or bed.

C. S. Calverley

Book I — *The Aeneid*

Aeneas leads his Trojans toward Italy. Shipwrecked, however, on the coast of Libya, by Juno's contrivance, they are received by Queen Dido in Carthage. At a banquet, Aeneas relates his adventures.

Arms and the man I sing, who at the first from Troy's shores the exile of destiny, won his way to Italy and her Latian coast — a man much buffeted on land and on the deep by violence from above, to sate the unforgetting wrath of Juno the cruel — much scourged too in war, as he struggled to build him a city, and find his gods a home in Latium — himself the father of the Latian people, and the chiefs of Alba's houses, and the walls of high towering Rome.

Bring to my mind, O Muse, the causes — for what treason against her godhead, or what pain received, the queen of heaven drove a man of piety so signal to turn the wheel of so many calamities, to bear the brunt of so many hardships? Can heavenly natures hate so fiercely and so long?

Of old there was a city, its people emigrants from Tyre, Carthage, over against Italy and Tiber's mouth, yet far removed — rich and mighty, and formed to all roughness by war's iron trade — a spot where Juno, it was said, loved to dwell more than in all the world beside, Samos holding but the second place. Here was her armor, here her chariot — here to fix by her royal act the empire of the nations, could Fate be brought to assent, was even then her aim, her cherished scheme. But she had heard that the blood of Troy was sowing the seed of a race to overturn one day those Tyrian towers — from that seed of a nation, monarch of broad realms and glorious in war, was to bring ruin on Libya — such the turning of Fate's wheel. With these fears Saturn's daughter, and with a lively memory of that old war which at first she had waged at Troy for her loved Argos' sake — nor indeed had the causes of that feud and the bitter pangs they roused yet vanished from her mind — no, stored up in her soul's depths remains the judgment of Paris, and the wrong done to her slighted beauty, and

58

the race abhorred from the womb, and the state enjoyed by the ravished Ganymede. With this fuel added to the fire, the Trojans, poor remains of Danaan havoc and Achilles' ruthless spear, she was tossing from sea to sea, and keeping far away from Latium; and for many long years they were wandering, with destiny still driving them, the whole ocean round. So vast the effort it cost to build up the Roman nation!

Scarce out of sight of the land of Sicily were they spreading their sails merrily to the deep, and scattering with their brazen prows the briny spray, when Juno, the everlasting wound still rankling in her heart's core, thus communed with herself: "And am I to give up what I have taken in hand, baffled, nor have power to prevent the king of the Teucrians from reaching Italy—because, forsooth, the Fates forbid me? What! was Pallas strong enough to burn up utterly the Grecian fleet, and whelm the crews in the sea, for the offense of a single man, the frenzy of Ajax, Oileus' son? Aye, she with her own hand launched from the clouds Jove's winged fire, dashed the ships apart, and turned up the sea-floor with the wind—him, gasping out the flame which pierced his bosom, she caught in the blast, and impaled on a rock's point—while I, who walk the sky as its queen, Jove's sister and consort both, am battling with a single nation these many years. And are there any found to pray to Juno's deity after this, or lay on her altar a suppliant's gift?"

With such thoughts sweeping through the solitude of her enkindled breast, the goddess comes to the storm-cloud's birthplace, the teeming womb of fierce southern blasts, Aeolia. Here, in a vast cavern, King Aeolus is bowing to his sway struggling winds and howling tempests, and bridling them with bond and prison. They, in their passion, are raving at the closed doors, while the huge rock roars responsive: Aeolus is sitting aloft in his fortress, his sceptre in his hand, soothing their moods and allaying their rage; were he to fail in this, why sea and land, and the deep of heaven, would all be forced along by their blast, and swept through the air. But the almighty sire has buried them in caverns dark and deep, with this fear before his eyes, and placed over them giant bulk and tall mountains, and given them a king who, by the terms of his compact, should know how to tighten or slacken the reins at his patron's will. To him it was that Juno then, in these words, made her humble request:—

"Aeolus—for it is to thee that the sire of gods and king of men has given it with the winds now to calm, now to rouse the billows— there is a race which I love not now sailing the Tyrrhene sea, carrying Ilion into Italy and Ilion's vanquished gods; do thou lash the winds to fury, sink and whelm their ships, or scatter them apart, and strew the ocean with their corpses. Twice seven nymphs are of my train,

59

all of surpassing beauty; of these her whose form is fairest, Deiopea, I will unite to thee in lasting wedlock, and consecrate her thine own, that all her days, for service so great, she may pass with thee, and make thee father of a goodly progeny."

Aeolus returns: "Thine, great Queen, is the task to search out on what thou mayest fix thy heart; for me to do thy bidding is but right. Thou makest this poor realm mine, mine the sceptre and Jove's smile; thou givest me a couch at the banquets of the gods, and makest me lord of the storm-cloud and of the tempest."

So soon as this was said, he turned his spear, and pushed the hollow mountain on its side; and the winds, as though in column formed, rush forth where they see an outlet, and sweep over the earth in hurricane. Heavily they fall on the sea, and from its very bottom crash down the whole expanse — one and all, east and south, and south-west, with his storms thronging at his back, and roll huge billows shoreward. Hark to the shrieks of the crew, and the creaking of the cables! In an instant the clouds snatch sky and daylight from the Teucrians' eyes — night lies on the deep, black and heavy — pole thunders to pole; heaven flashes thick with fires, and all nature brandishes instant death in the seaman's face. At once Aeneas' limbs are unstrung and chilled — he groans aloud, and, stretching his clasped hands to the stars, fetches from his breast words like these: — "O happy, thrice and again, whose lot it was, in their fathers' sight under Troy's high walls to meet death! O thou, the bravest of the Danaan race, Tydeus' son, why was it not mine to lay me low on Ilion's plains, and yield this fated life to thy right hand? Aye, there it is that Hector, stern as in life, lies stretched by the spear of Aeacides — there lies Sarpedon's giant bulk — there it is that Simois seizes and sweeps down her channel those many shields and helms, and bodies of the brave!"

Such words as he flung wildly forth, a blast roaring from the north strikes his sail full in front and lifts the billows to the stars. Shattered are the oars; then the prow turns and presents the ship's side to the waves; down crashes in a heap a craggy mountain of water. Look! these are hanging on the surge's crest — to those the yawning deep is giving a glimpse of land down among the billows; surf and sand are raving together. Three ships the south catches, and flings upon hidden rocks — rocks which, as they stand with the waves all about them, the Italians call Altars, an enormous ridge rising above the sea. Three the east drives from the main on to shallow sand Syrtes, a piteous sight, and dashes them on shoals, and embanks them in mounds of sand. One in which the Lycians were sailing, and true Orontes, a mighty sea strikes from high on the stem before Aeneas' very eyes; down goes the helmsman, washed from his post, and topples

60

on his head, while she is thrice whirled round by the billow in the spot where she lay, and swallowed at once by the greedy gulf. You might see them here and there swimming in that vast abyss—heroes' arms, and planks, and Troy's treasures glimmering through the water. Already Ilioneus' stout ship, already brave Achates', and that in which Abas sailed, and that which carried old Aletes, are worsted by the storm; their side-jointings loosened, one and all give entrance to the watery foe, and part failingly asunder.

Meantime the roaring riot of the ocean and the storm let loose reached the sense of Neptune, and the still waters disgorged from their deep beds, troubling him grievously; and casting a broad glance over the main he raised at once his tranquil brow from the water's surface. There he sees Aeneas' fleet tossed hither and thither over the whole expanse—the Trojans whelmed under the billows, and the crashing ruin of the sky—nor failed the brother to read Juno's craft and hatred there. East and West he calls before him, and bespeaks them thus:—"Are ye then so wholly o'ermastered by the pride of your birth? Have ye come to this, ye Winds, that, without sanction from me, ye dare to confound sea and land, and upheave these mighty mountains? ye! whom I—but it were best to calm the billows ye have troubled. Henceforth ye shall pay me for your crimes in far other coin. Make good speed with your flight, and give your king this message. Not to him did the lot assign the empire of the sea and the terrible trident, but to me. His sway is over those enormous rocks, where you, Eurus, dwell, and such as you; in that court let Aeolus lord it, and rule in the prisonhouse of the winds when its doors are barred."

He speaks, and ere his words are done soothes the swelling waters, and routs the mustered clouds, and brings back the sun in triumph. Cymothoë and Triton combine their efforts to push off the vessels from the sharp-pointed rock. The god himself upheaves them with his own trident, and levels the great quicksands, and allays the sea, and on chariot-wheels of lightest motion glides along the water's top. Even as when in a great crowd tumult is oft stirred up, and the base herd waxes wild and frantic, and brands and stones are flying already, rage suiting the weapon to the hand—at that moment, should their eyes fall on some man of weight, for duty done and public worth, tongues are hushed and ears fixed in attention, while his words sway the spirit and soothe the breast—so fell all the thunders of the ocean, so soon as the great father, with the waves before him in prospect, and the clear sky all about him, guides his steeds at will, and as he flies flings out the reins freely to his obedient car.

Spent with toil, the family of Aeneas labor to gain the shore that may be nearest, and are carried to the coasts of Libya. There is a spot retiring deep into the land, where an island forms a haven by the barrier of its sides, which break every billow from the main and send it shattered into the deep indented hollows. On either side of the bay are huge rocks, and two great crags rising in menace to the sky; under their summits far and wide the water is hushed in shelter, while a theatric background of waving woods, a black forest of stiffening shade, overhangs it from the height. Under the brow that fronts the deep is a cave with pendent crags; within there are fresh springs and seats in the living rock — the home of the nymphs; no need of cable here to confine the weary bark or anchor's crooked fang to grapple her to the shore. Here with seven ships mustered from his whole fleet Aeneas enters; and with intense yearning for dry land the Trojans disembark and take possession of the wished-for shore, and lay their brine-drenched limbs upon the beach. And first Achates from a flint struck out a spark, and received the fire as it dropped in a cradle of leaves, and placed dry wood all about it, and spread the strong blaze among the tinder. Then their corn, soaked and spoiled as it was, and the corn-goddess's armory they bring out, sick of fortune; and make ready to parch the rescued grain at the fire, and crush it with the millstone.

Aeneas meanwhile clambers up a rock, and tries to get a full view far and wide over the sea, if haply he may see aught of Antheus, driven by the gale, and the Phrygian biremes, or Capys, or high on the stern the arms of Caicus. Sail there is none in sight; three stags he sees at distance straying on the shore; these the whole herd follows in the rear, and grazes along the hollows in long array. At once he took his stand, and caught up a bow and fleet arrows, which true Achates chanced to be carrying, and lays low first the leaders themselves, as they bear their heads aloft with tree-like antlers, then the meaner sort, and scatters with his pursuing shafts the whole rout among the leafy woods; nor stays his hand till he stretches on earth victoriously seven huge bodies, and makes the sum of them even with his ships. Then he returns to the haven and gives all his comrades their shares. The wine next, which that good Acestes had stowed in casks on the Trinacrian shore, and given them at parting with his own princely hand, he portions out, and speaks words of comfort to their sorrowing hearts: —

"Comrades! for comrades we are, no strangers to hardships already; hearts that have felt deeper wounds! for these too heaven will find a balm. Why, men, you have even looked on Scylla in her madness, and heard those yells that thrill the rocks; you have even made trial of the crags of the Cyclopes. Come, call your spirits back, and banish these doleful fears — who knows but some day this too will be remembered with pleasure? Through manifold chances, through these many perils of fortune, we are making our way to Latium, where the Fates hold out to us a quiet settlement; there Troy's empire has leave to rise again from its ashes. Bear up, and reserve yourselves for brighter days."

Such were the words his tongue uttered: heart-sick with overwhelming care, he wears the semblance of hope in his face, but has grief deep buried in his heart. They gird themselves to deal with the game, their forthcoming meal; strip the hide from the ribs, and lay bare the flesh — some cut it into pieces and impale it yet quivering on spits, others set up the cauldrons on the beach, and supply them with flame. Then with food they recall their strength, and, stretched along the turf, feast on old wine and fat venison to their hearts' content. Their hunger sated by the meal, and the boards removed, they vent in long talk their anxious yearning for their missing comrades — balanced between hope and fear, whether to think of them as alive, or as suffering the last change, and deaf already to the voice that calls on them. But good Aeneas' grief exceeds the rest; one moment he groans for bold Orontes' fortune, another for Amycus', and in the depth of his spirit laments for the cruel fate of Lycus; for the gallant Gyas and the gallant Cloanthus.

And now at last their mourning had an end, when Jupiter from the height of ether, looking down on the sea with its fluttering sails, on the flat surface of earth, the shores, and the broad tribes of men, paused thus upon heaven's very summit, and fixed his downward gaze on Libya's realms. To him, revolving in his breast such thoughts as these, sad beyond her wont, with tears suffusing her starry eyes, speaks Venus: "O thou, who by thy everlasting laws swayest the two commonwealths of men and gods, and awest them by thy lightning! What can my poor Aeneas have done to merit thy wrath? What can the Trojans? yet they, after the many deaths they have suffered already, still find the whole world barred against them for Italy's sake. From them assuredly it was that the Romans, as years rolled on — from them were to spring those warrior chiefs, aye from Teucer's blood revived, who should rule sea and land with absolute sway — such was thy promise: how has thy purpose, O my father, wrought a change in thee? This, I know, was my constant solace when Troy's star set in grievous ruin, as I sat balancing destiny against destiny. And now here is the same Fortune, pursuing the brave men she has so oft discomfited already. Mighty king, what end of sufferings hast thou to give them? Antenor, indeed, found means to escape through the midst of the Achæans, to thread in safety the windings of the Illyrian coast, and the realms of the Liburians, up at the gulf's head, and to pass the

63

springs of Timavus, whence through nine mouths, 'mid the rocks' responsive roar, the sea comes bursting up, and deluges the fields with its thundering billows. Yet in that spot he built the city of Patavium for his Trojans to dwell in, and gave them a place and a name among the nations, and set up a rest for the arms of Troy: now he reposes, lapped in the calm of peace. Meantime we, of thine own blood, to whom thy nod secures the pinnacle of heaven, our ships, most monstrous, lost, as thou seest, all to sate the malice of one cruel heart, are given up to ruin, and severed far from the Italian shores. Is this the reward of piety? Is this to restore a king to his throne?"

Smiling on her, the planter of gods and men, with that face which calms the fitful moods of the sky, touched with a kiss his daughter's lips, then addressed her thus "Give thy fears a respite, lady of Cythera: the people's destiny abides still unchanged for thee; thine eyes shall see the city of thy heart, the promised walls of Lavinium; thine arms shall bear aloft to the stars of heaven thy hero Aeneas; nor has my purpose wrought a change in me. Thy hero — for I will speak out, in pity for the care that rankles yet, and awaken the secrets of Fate's book from the distant pages where they slumber — thy hero shall wage a mighty war in Italy, crush its haughty tribes, and set up for his warriors a polity and a city, till the third summer shall have passed over the Rutulians' defeat. But the boy Ascanius, who has now the new name of Iulus — Ilus he was, while the royalty of Ilion's state stood firm — shall let thirty of the sun's great courses fulfil their monthly rounds while he is sovereign, then transfer the empire from Lavinium's seat, and build Alba the Long, with power and might. Here for full three hundred years the crown shall be worn by Hector's line, till a royal priestess, teeming by the war-god, Ilia, shall be the mother of twin sons. Then shall there be one, proud to wear the tawny hide of the wolf that nursed him, Romulus, who will take up the sceptre, and build a new city, the city of Mars, and give the people his own name of Roman. To them I assign no limit, no date of empire: my grant to them is dominion without end. Nay, Juno, thy savage foe, who now, in her blind terror, lets neither sea, land, nor heaven rest, shall amend her counsels and vie with me in watching over the Romans, lords of earth, the great nation of the gown. So it is willed. The time shall come, as Rome's years roll on, when the house of Assaracus shall bend to its yoke Phthia and renowned Mycenae, and queen it over vanquished Argos. Then shall be born the child of an illustrious line, one of thine own Trojans, Caesar, born to extend his empire to the ocean, his glory to the stars, — Julius, in name as in blood the heir of great Iulus. Him thou shalt one day welcome in safety to the sky, a warrior laden with Eastern spoils; to him, as to

64

Aeneas, men shall pray and make their vows. In his days war shall cease, and savage times grow mild. Faith with her hoary head, and Vesta, Quirinus, and Remus his brother, shall give law to the world: grim, iron-bound, closely welded, the gates of war shall be closed; the fiend of Discord a prisoner within, seated on a pile of arms deadly as himself, his hands bound behind his back with a hundred brazen chains, shall roar ghastly from his throat of blood."

So saying, he sends down from on high the son of Maia, that Carthage the new, her lands and her towers, may open themselves to welcome in the Teucrians, lest Dido, in her ignorance of Fate, should drive them from her borders. Down flies Mercury through the vast abyss of air, with his wings for oars, and has speedily alighted on the shores of Libya. See! he is doing his bidding already: the Punic nation is resigning the fierceness of its nature at the god's pleasure; above all the rest, the queen is admitting into her bosom thoughts of peace toward the Teucrians, and a heart of kindness.

But Aeneas the good, revolving many things the whole night through, soon as the gracious dawn is vouchsafed, resolves to go out and explore this new region; to inquire what shores be these on which the wind has driven him; who their dwellers, for he sees it is a wilderness, men or beasts; and bring his comrades back the news. His fleet he hides in the wooded cover under a hollow rock, with a wall of trees and stiffening shade on each side. He moves on with Achates, his single companion, wielding in his hands two spear shafts, with heads of broad iron. He had reached the middle of the wood, when his way was crossed by his mother, wearing a maiden's mien and dress, and a maiden's armor, Spartan, or even as Harpalyce of Thrace tires steed after steed, and heads the swift waters of her own Hebrus as she flies along. For she had a shapely bow duly slung from her shoulders in true huntress fashion, and her hair streaming in the wind, her knee bare, and her flowing scarf gathered round her in a knot. Soon as she sees them, "Oh! youths," cries she, "if you have chanced to see one of my sisters wandering in these parts, tell me where to find her — wandering with a quiver, and a spotted lynx hide fastened about her; or, it may be, pressing on the heels of the foaming boar with her hounds in full cry."

Thus Venus spoke, and Venus' son replied: — "No sight or hearing have we had of any sister of thine, O thou — what name shall I give thee? maiden; for thy face is not of earth, nor the tone of thy voice human: some goddess surely thou art. Phœbus' sister belike, or one of the blood of the nymphs? be gracious, whoe'er thou art, and relieve our hardship, and tell us under what sky now, on what realms of earth we are thrown. Utter strangers to the men and the place, we are wan-

65

dering, as thou seest, by the driving of the wind and of the mighty waters. Do this, and many a victim shall fall to thee at the altar by this hand of mine."

Then Venus: — "Nay, I can lay claim to no such honors. Tyrian maidens, like me, are wont to carry the quiver, and tie the purple buskin high up the calf. This that you now see is the Punic realm, the nation Tyrian and the town Agenor's; but on the frontiers are the Libyans, a race ill to handle in war. The queen is Dido, who left her home in Tyre to escape from her brother. Lengthy is her tale of wrong, lengthy the windings of its course; but I will pass rapidly from point to point. Her husband was Sychæus, wealthiest of Phœnician land-owners, and loved by his poor wife with fervid passion; on him her father had bestowed her in her maiden bloom, linking them together by the omens of a first bridal. But the crown of Tyre was on the head of her brother, Pygmalion, in crime monstrous beyond the rest of men. They were two, and fury came between them. Impious that he was, at the very altar of the palace, the love of gold blinding his eyes, he surprises Sychæus with his stealthy steel, and lays him low, without a thought for his sister's passion; he kept the deed long concealed, and with many a base coinage sustained the mockery of false hope in her pining love-lorn heart. But lo! in her sleep there came to her no less than the semblance of her unburied spouse, lifting up a face of strange unearthly pallor; the ruthless altar and his breast gored with the steel, he laid bare the one and the other, and unveiled from first to last the dark domestic crime. Then he urges her to speed her flight, and quit her home for ever, and in aid of her journey unseals a hoard of treasure long hid in the earth, a mass of silver and gold which none else knew. Dido's soul was stirred; she began to make ready her flight, and friends to share it. There they meet, all whose hate of the tyrant was fell or whose fear was bitter; ships, that chanced to lie ready in the harbor, they seize, and freight with gold. Away it floats over the deep, the greedy Pygmalion's wealth; and who heads the enter-prise? a woman! So they came to the spot where you now see yonder those lofty walls, and the rising citadel of Carthage the new; there they bought ground, which got from the transaction the name of Byrsa, as much as they could compass round with a bull's hide. But who are you after all? What coast are you come from, or whither are you hold-ing on your journey?" That question he answers thus, with a heavy sigh, and a voice fetched from the bottom of his heart: — "Fair goddess! should I begin from the first and proceed in order, and hadst thou leisure to listen to the chronicle of our sufferings, eve would first close the Olympian gates and lay the day to sleep. For us, bound from ancient Troy, if the name of Troy has ever chanced to pass through a

66

Tyrian ear, wanderers over divers seas already, we have been driven by a storm's wild will upon your Libyan coasts. I am Aeneas, styled the good, who am bearing with me in my fleet the gods of Troy rescued from the foe; a name blazed by rumor above the stars. I am in quest of Italy, looking there for an ancestral home, and a pedigree drawn from high Jove himself. With twice ten ships I climbed the Phrygian main, with a goddess mother guiding me on my way, and a chart of oracles to follow. Scarce seven remain to me now, shattered by wind and wave. Here am I, a stranger, nay, a beggar, wandering over your Libyan deserts, driven from Europe and Asia alike." Venus could bear the complaint no longer, so she thus struck into the middle of his sorrows: — "Whoever you are, it is not, I trow, under the frown of heavenly powers that you draw the breath of life, thus to have arrived at our Tyrian town. Only go on, and make your way straight hence to the queen's palace. For I give you news that your comrades are returned and your fleet brought back, wafted into shelter by shifting gales, unless my learning of augury was vain, and the parents who taught me cheat. Look at these twelve swans exultant in victorious column which the bird of Jove, swooping from the height of ether, was just now driving in confusion over the wide unsheltered sky; see now how their line stretches, some alighting on the ground, others just looking down on those alighted. As they, thus rallied, ply their whirling wings in sport, spreading their train round the sky, and uttering songs of triumph, even so your vessels and your gallant crews are either safe in the port, or entering the haven with sails full spread. Only go on, and where the way leads you direct your steps."

She said, and as she turned away, flashed on their sight her neck's roseate hue; her ambrosial locks breathed from her head a heavenly fragrance; her robe streamed down to her very feet; and in her walk was revealed the true goddess. Soon as he knew his mother, he pursued her flying steps with words like these: — "Why wilt thou be cruel like the rest, mocking thy son these many times with feigned semblances? Why is it not mine to grasp thy hand in my hand, and hear and return the true language of the heart?" Such are his upbraidings, while he yet bends his way to the town. But Venus fenced them round with a dim cloud as they moved, and wrapped them as a goddess only can in a spreading mantle of mist, that none might be able to see them, none to touch them, or put hindrances in their path, or ask the reason of their coming. She takes her way aloft to Paphos, glad to revisit the abode she loves, where she has a temple and a hundred altars, smoking with Sabæan incense, and fragrant with garlands ever new.

They, meanwhile, have pushed on their way, where the path guides them, and already they are climbing the hill which hangs heavily over the city, and looks from above on the towers that rise to meet it. Aeneas marvels at the mass of building, once a mere village of huts; marvels at the gates, and the civic din, and the paved ways. The Tyrians are alive and on fire — intent, some on carrying the walls aloft and upheaving the citadel, and rolling stones from underneath by force of hand; some on making choice of a site for a dwelling, and enclosing it with a trench. They are ordaining the law and its guardians, and the senate's sacred majesty. Here are some digging out havens; there are others laying deep the foundations of a theatre, and hewing from the rocks enormous columns, the lofty ornaments of a stage that is to be. Such are the toils that keep the commonwealth of bees at work in the sun among the flowery meads when summer is new, what time they lead out the nation's hope, the young now grown, or mass together honey, clear and flowing, and strain the cells to bursting with its nectarous sweets, or relieve those who are coming in of their burdens, or collect a troop and expel from their stalls the drones, that lazy, thriftless herd. The work is all afire, and a scent of thyme breathes from the fragrant honey. "O happy they, whose city is rising already!" cries Aeneas, as he looks upward to roof and dome. In he goes, close fenced by his cloud, miraculous to tell, threads his way through the midst, and mingles with the citizens, unperceived of all.

A grove there was in the heart of the city, most plenteous of shade — the spot where first, fresh from the buffeting of wave and wind, the Punic race dug up the token which queenly Juno had bidden them expect, the head of a fiercy steed — for even thus, said she, the nation should be renowned in war and rich in sustenance for a life of centuries. Here Dido, Sidon's daughter, was building a vast temple to Juno, rich in offerings and in the goddess's especial presence; of brass was the threshold with its rising steps, clamped with brass the doorposts, the hinge creaked on a door of brass. In this grove it was that first a new object appeared, as before, to soothe away fear: here it was that Aeneas first dared to hope that all was safe, and to place a better trust in his shattered fortunes. For while his eyes range over each part under the temple's massy roof, as he waits there for the queen — while he is marvelling at the city's prosperous star, the various artist-hands vying with each other, their tasks and the toil they cost, he beholds, scene after scene, the battles of Ilion, and the war that Fame had already blazed the whole world over — Atreus's sons, and Priam, and the enemy of both, Achilles. He stopped short, and breaking into tears, "What place is there left?" he cries, "Achates, what clime on earth that is not full of our sad story? See the Priam. Here, too, worth finds its due rewards; here, too, there are tears for human fortune, and hearts are touched by mortality. Be free from fear: this

68

renown of ours will bring you some measure of safety." So speaking, he feeds his soul on the empty portraiture, with many a sigh, and lets copious rivers run down his cheeks. For he still saw how, as they battled round Pergamus, here the Greeks were flying, the Trojan youth in hot pursuit; here the Phrygians, at their heels in his car Achilles, with that dreadful crest. Not far from this he recognizes with tears the snowy canvas of Rhesus' tent, which, all surprised in its first sleep, Tydeus' son was devastating with wide carnage, himself bathed in blood — see! he drives off the fiery steeds to his own camp, ere they have had time to taste the pastures of Troy or drink of Xanthus. There in another part is Troilus in flight, his arms fallen from him — unhappy boy, confronted with Achilles in unequal combat — hurried away by his horses, and hanging half out of the empty car, with his head thrown back, but the reins still in his hand; his neck and his hair are being trailed along the ground, and his inverted spear is drawing lines in the dust. Meanwhile to the temple of Pallas, not their friend, were moving the Trojan dames with locks dishevelled, carrying the sacred robe, in suppliant guise of mourning, their breasts bruised with their hands — the goddess was keeping her eyes riveted on the ground, with her face turned away. Thrice had Achilles dragged Hector round the walls of Ilion, and was now selling for gold his body, thus robbed of breath. Then, indeed, heavy was the groan that he gave from the bottom of his heart when he saw the spoils, the car, the very body of his friend and Priam stretching out those helpless hands. Himself, too, he recognizes in the forefront of the Achaean ranks, and the squadrons of the East, and the arms of the swarthy Memnon. There, leading the columns of her Amazons, with their moony shields is Penthesilea in her martial frenzy, blazing out, the centre of thousands, as she loops up her protruded breast with a girdle of gold, the warrior queen, and nerves herself to the shock of combat, a maiden against men.

While these things are meeting the wondering eyes of Aeneas the Dardan — while he is standing bewildered, and continues riveted in one set gaze — the queen has moved towards the temple, Dido, of loveliest presence, with a vast train of youths thronging round her. Like as on Eurotas' banks, or along the ridges of Cynthus, Diana is footing the dance, while attending her, a thousand mountain nymphs are massing themselves on either side; she, her quiver on her shoulder, as she steps, towers over the whole goddess sisterhood, while Latona's bosom thrills silently with delight; such was Dido — such she bore herself triumphant through the midst to speed the work which had empire for its prospect. Then, at the doors of the goddess, under the midmost vaulting of the temple, with a fence of arms round her, supported high on a throne, she took her seat. There she was giving laws and judgments to her citizens and equalizing the burden of their tasks by fair partition, or draughting it by lot, when suddenly Aeneas sees coming among the great crowd Antheus and Sergestus, and brave Cloanthus, and other of the Teucrians, whom the black storm had scattered over the deep and carried far away to other coasts. Astounded was he, overwhelmed, too, was Achates, all for joy and fear; eagerly were they burning to join hands with theirs but the unexplained mystery confounds their minds. They carry on the concealment, and look out from the hollow cloud that wraps them, to learn what fortune their mates have had, on what shore they are leaving their fleet, what is their errand here — for they were on their way, a deputation from all the crews, suing for grace, and were making for the temple with loud cries.

After they had gained an entrance, and had obtained leave to speak in the presence, Ilioneus, the eldest, thus began calm of soul: —

"Gracious queen to whom Jupiter has given to found a new city, and to restrain by force of law the pride of savage nations, we, hapless Trojans, driven by the winds over every sea make our prayer to you — keep off from our ships the horrors of fire, have pity on a pious race, and vouchsafe a nearer view to our affairs. We are not come to carry the havoc of the sword into the homes of Libya — to snatch booty and hurry it to the shore; such violence is not in our nature; such insolence were not for the vanquished. There is a place — the Greeks call it Hesperia — a land old in story, strong in arms and in the fruitfulness of its soil; the Oenotrians were its settlers; now report says that later generations have called the nation Italian, from the name of their leader. Thither were we voyaging, when rising with a sudden swell, Orion lord of the storm carried us into hidden shoals and far away by the stress of reckless gales over the water, the surge mastering us, and over pathless rocks scattered us here and there: a small remnant, we drifted hither on to your shores. What race of men have we here? What country is so barbarous as to sanction a native usage like this? Even the hospitality of the sand is forbidden us — they draw the sword, and will not let us set foot on the land's edge. If you defy the race of men, and the weapons that mortals wield, yet look to have to do with gods, who watch over the right and the wrong. Aeneas was our king, than whom never man breathed more just, more eminent in piety, or in war and martial prowess. If the Fates are keeping our hero alive — if he is feeding on this upper air, and not yet lying down in death's cruel shade — all our fears are over, nor need you be sorry to have made the first advance in the contest of kindly courtesy. The realm of Sicily, too, has cities for us, and store of arms, and a hero-king of Trojan blood, Acestes. Give us leave but to lay up on shore our storm-beaten fleet, to fashion timber in your forests, and strip boughs for our oars, that, if we are allowed to sail for Italy, our comrades and king restored to us, we may make our joyful way to Italy and to Latium; or, if our safety is swallowed up, and thou, best father of the Teucrians, art the prey of the Libyan deep, and a nation's hope lives no longer in Iulus, then, at least, we may make for Sicania's straits, and the houses standing to welcome us, when we came hither, and may find a king in Acestes." Such was the speech of Ilioneus; an accordant clamor burst at once from all the sons of Dardanus.

Then briefly Dido, with downcast look, makes reply: — "Teucrians! unburden your hearts of fear, lay your anxieties aside. It is the stress of danger and the infancy of my kingdom that makes me put this policy in motion and protect my frontiers with a guard all about. The men of Aeneas and the city of Troy — who can be ignorant of them? — the deeds and the doers, and all the blaze of that mighty war? Not so blunt are the wits we Punic folk carry with us, not so wholly does the sun turn his back on our Tyrian town when he harnesses his steeds. Whether you make your choice of Hesperia the great, and the old realm of Saturn, or of the borders of Eryx and their king Acestes, I will send you on your way with an escort to protect you, and will supply you with stores. Or would you like to settle along with me in my kingdom here? Look at the city I am building, it is yours, lay up your ships, Trojan and Tyrian shall be dealt with by me without distinction. Would to heaven your king were here too, driven by the gale that drove you hither — Aeneas himself! For myself, I will send trusty messengers along the coast, with orders to traverse the furthest parts of Libya, in case he should be shipwrecked and wandering anywhere in forest or town."

Excited by her words, brave Achates and father Aeneas, too, were burning long ere this to break out of their cloud. Achates first accosts Aeneas: — "Goddess-born, what purpose now is foremost in your mind? All you see is safe, our fleet and our mates are restored to us. One is missing, whom our own eyes saw in the midst of the surge swallowed up, all the rest is even as your mother told us."

Scarce had he spoken when the cloud that enveloped them suddenly parts asunder and clears into the open sky. Out stood Aeneas, and shone again in the bright sunshine, his face and his bust the image of a god, for his great mother had shed graceful tresses over her son's brow, and the glowing flush of youth, and had breathed the breath of beauty and gladness into his eyes, loveliness such as the artist's touch imparts to ivory, or when silver or Parian marble is enchased with yellow gold. Then he addresses the queen, and speaks suddenly to the astonishment of all: — "Here am I whom you are seeking, before you,

71

—Aeneas, the Trojan, snatched from the jaws of the Libyan wave. O heart that alone of all has found pity for Troy's cruel agonies — that makes us, poor remnants of Danaan fury, utterly spent by all the chances of land and sea, destitute of all, partners of its city, of its very palace! To pay such a debt of gratitude, Dido, is more than we can do — more than can be done by all the survivors of the Dardan nation, now scattered the wide world over. May the gods — if there are powers that regard the pious, if justice and conscious rectitude count for aught anywhere on earth — may they give you the reward you merit! What age had the happiness to bring you forth? what god-like parents gave such nobleness to the world? While the rivers run into the sea, while the shadows sweep along the mountain-sides, while the stars draw life from the sky, your glory and your name and your praise shall endure, whatever the land whose call I must obey." So saying, he stretches out his right hand to his friend Ilioneus, his left to Serestus, and so on to others, gallant Gyas and gallant Cloanthus.

Astounded was Dido, Sidon's daughter, first at the hero's presence, then at his enormous sufferings, and she bespoke him thus: — "What chance is it, goddess-born, that is hunting you through such a wilderness of perils? what violence throws you on our savage coasts? Are you, indeed, the famed Aeneas, whom to Anchises the Dardan, Venus, queen of light and love, bore by the stream of Simois? Aye, I remember Teucer coming to Sidon, driven from the borders of his fatherland, hoping to gain a new kingdom by the aid of Belus. Belus, my sire, was then laying waste the rich fields of Cyprus, and ruling the isle with a conqueror's sway. Ever since that time I knew the fate of the Trojan city, and your name, and the Pelasgian princes. Foe as he was, he would always extol the Teucrians with signal praise, and profess that he himself came of the ancient Teucrian stock. Come then, brave men, and make our dwellings your home. I, too, have had a fortune like yours, which, after the buffeting of countless sufferings, has been pleased that I should find rest in this land at last. Myself no stranger to sorrow, I am learning to succor the unhappy." With these words, at the same moment she ushers Aeneas into her queenly palace, and orders a solemn sacrifice at the temples of the gods. Meantime, as if this were nought, she sends to his comrades at the shore twenty bulls, a hundred huge swine with back all bristling, a hundred fat lambs with their mothers, and the wine-god's jovial bounty.

But the palace within is laid out with all the splendor of regal luxury, and in the centre of the mansion they are making ready for banquet; the coverlets are embroidered, and of princely purple — on the tables is massy silver, and chased on gold the gallant exploits of

Tyrian ancestors, a long, long chain of story, derived through hero after hero ever since the old nation was young.

Aeneas, for his fatherly love would not have his heart at rest, sends on Achates with speed to the ships to tell Ascanius the news and conduct him to the city. On Ascanius all a fond parent's anxieties are centered. Presents, moreover, rescued from the ruins of Ilion, he bids him bring — a pall stiff with figures of gold, and a veil with a border of yellow acanthus, adornments of Argive Helen, which she carried away from Mycenae, when she went to Troy and to her unblessed bridal, her mother Leda's marvellous gift; the sceptre, too, which Ilione had once borne, the eldest of Priam's daughters, and the string of pearls for the neck, and the double coronal of jewels and gold. With this to despatch, Achates was bending his ways to the ships.

But the lady of Cythera is casting new wiles, new devices in her breast, that Cupid, form and feature changed, may arrive in the room of the charmer Ascanius, and by the presence he brings influence the queen to madness, and turn the very marrow of her bones to fire. She fears the two-faced generation, the double-tongued sons of Tyre; Juno's hatred scorches her like a flame, and as night draws on the care comes back to her. So then with these words she addresses her winged Love: — "My son, who art alone my strength and my mighty power, my son, who laughest to scorn our great father's Typhoean thunderbolts, to thee I fly for aid, and make suppliant prayer of thy majesty. How thy brother Aeneas is tossed on the ocean the whole world over by Juno's implacable rancor I need not tell thee — nay, thou hast often mingled thy grief with mine. He is now the guest of Dido, the Phoenician woman, and the spell of a courteous tongue is laid on him, and I fear what may be the end of taking shelter under Juno's wing; she will never be idle at a time on which so much hangs. Thus then I am planning to be first in the field, surprising the queen by stratagem, and encompassing her with fire, that no power may be able to work a change in her, but that a mighty passion for Aeneas may keep her mine. For the way in which thou mayest bring this about, listen to what I have been thinking. The young heir of royalty, at his loved father's summons, is making ready to go to this Sidonian city — my soul's darling that he is — the bearer of presents that have survived the sea and the flames of Troy. Him I will lull in deep sleep and hide him in my hallowed dwelling high on Cythera or Idalia, that by no chance he may know or mar our plot. Do thou then for a single night, or more, artfully counterfeit his form, and put on the boy's usual look, thyself a boy, that when Dido, at the height of her joy, shall take thee into her lap while the princely board is laden and the vine-god's liquor flowing, when she shall be caressing thee and printing her fondest kisses on thy cheek, thou mayest breathe concealed fire into her veins, and steal upon her with poison."

At once Love complies with his fond mother's words, puts off his wings, and walks rejoicing in the gait of Iulus. As for Ascanius, Venus sprinkles his form all over with the dew of gentle slumber, and carries him, as a goddess may, lapped in her bosom, into Idalia's lofty groves, where a soft couch of amaracus enfolds him with its flowers, and the fragrant breath of its sweet shade. Meanwhile, Cupid was on his way, all obedience, bearing the royal presents to the Tyrians, and glad to follow Achates. When he arrives, he finds the queen already settled on the gorgeous tapestry of a golden couch, and occupying the central place. Already father Aeneas, already the chivalry of Troy are flocking in, and stretching themselves here and there on coverlets of purple. There are servants offering them water for their hands, and deftly producing the bread from the baskets, and presenting towels with shorn nap. Within are fifty maidens, whose charge is in course to pile up provisions in lasting store, and light up with fire the gods of the hearth. A hundred others there are, and male attendants of equal number and equal age, to load the table with dishes, and set on the cups. The Tyrians, too, have assembled in crowds through the festive hall, and scatter themselves as invited over the embroidered couches. There is marvelling at Aeneas' presents, marvelling at Iulus, at those glowing features, where the god shines through, and those words which he feigns so well, and at the robe and the veil with the yellow acanthus border. Chief of all, the unhappy victim of coming ruin cannot satisfy herself with gazing, and kindles as she looks, the Phœnician woman, charmed with the boy and the presents alike. He, after he has hung long in Aeneas' arms and round his neck, gratifying the intense fondness of the sire he feigned to be his, finds his way to the queen. She is riveted by him — riveted, eye and heart, and ever and anon fondles him in her lap — poor Dido, unconscious how great a god is sitting heavy on that wretched bosom. But he, with his mind still bent on his Acidalian mother, is beginning to efface the name of Sychæus letter by letter, and endeavoring to surprise by a living passion affections long torpid, and a heart long unused to love.

When the banquet's first lull was come, and the board removed, then they set up the huge bowls and wreathe the wine. A din rings to the roof — the voice rolls through those spacious halls; lamps hang from the gilded ceiling, burning brightly, and flambeau-fires put out the night. Then the queen called for a cup, heavy with jewels and gold, and filled it with unmixed wine; the same which had been used by Belus, and every king from Belus downward. Then silence was commanded through the hall. "Jupiter, for thou hast the name of law-

74

giver for guest and host, grant that this day may be auspicious alike for the Tyrians and the voyagers from Troy, and that its memory may long live among our posterity. Be with us, Bacchus, the giver of jollity, and Juno, the queen of our blessings; and you, the lords of Tyre, may your good will grace this meeting." She said, and poured on the table an offering of the wine, and, the libation made, touched the cup first with her lips, then handed it to Bitias, rallying his slowness. Eagerly he quaffed the foaming goblet, and drenched himself deep with its brimming gold. Then came the other lords in order. Iopas, the long-haired bard, takes his gilded lyre, and fills the hall with music; he, whose teacher was the mighty Atlas. His song is of the wanderings of the moon and the agonies of the sun, whence sprung man's race and the cattle, whence rain-water and fire; of Arcturus and the showery Hyades, and the twin Bears; why the winter suns make such haste to dip in ocean, or what is the retarding cause that bids the nights move slowly. Plaudits redouble from the Tyrians, and the Trojans follow the lead. With varied talk, too, she kept lengthening out the night, unhappy Dido, drinking draughts of love long and deep, as she asked much about Priam, about Hector much; now what were the arms in which Aurora's son had come to battle; now what Dio-mede's steeds were like; now how great was Achilles. "Or rather, gentle guest," cries she, "tell us the story from the very first — all about the stratagems of the Danaans, and the sad fate of your country, and your own wanderings — for this is now the seventh summer that is wafting you a wanderer still over every land and wave."

John Conington

Book VI

Aeneas lands at Cumae, on the western coast of Italy. With the Sibyl's help, he visits the Underworld. There he meets his father Anchises, who prophesies the coming greatness of Rome.

So saying and weeping, he gives rope to his fleet, and in due time is wafted smoothly to Cumae's shores of Euboean fame. They turn their prows seaward: then the anchor with griping fang began to moor vessel after vessel, and crooked keels fringe all the coast. With fiery zeal the crews leap out on the Hesperian shore: some look for the seed of fire where it lies deep down in the veins of flint: some strip the woods, the wild beast's shaggy covert, and point with joy to the streams they find. But good Aeneas repairs to the heights on which Apollo sits exalted, and the privacy of dread Sibyl, stretching far away into a vast cavern — the Sibyl, into whose breast the prophet that speaks at Delos breathes his own mighty mind and soul, and opens the future to her eye. And now they are entering the groves of the Trivian goddess and the golden palace.

Daedalus, so runs the legend, flying from Minos' sceptre, dared to trust himself in air on swift wings of his own workmanship, sailed to the cold north along an unwonted way, and at last stood buoyant on the top of this Eubœan hill. Grateful to the land that first received him, he dedicated to thee, Phoebus, his feathery orage, and raised a mighty temple. On the doors was seen Androgeos' death: there too were the sons of Cecrops, constrained — O cruel woe! — to pay in penalty the yearly tale of seven of their sons' lives: the urn is standing, and the lots drawn out. On the other side, breasting the wave, the Cnossian land frowns responsive. There is Pasiphaë's tragic passion for the bull, and the mingled birth, the Minotaur, half man, half brute, a monument of monstrous love. There is the edifice, that marvel of toiling skill, and its inextricable maze — inextricable, had not Daedalus in pity for the enthralling passion of the royal princess, himself unravelled the craft and mystery of those chambers, guiding the lover's dark steps with a clue of thread. You too, poor Icarus, had borne no mean part in that splendid portraiture, would grief have given art its way. Twice the artist essayed to represent the tragedy in gold: twice the father's hands dropped down palsied. So they would have gone on scanning all in succession, had not Achates returned from his errand, and with him the priestess of Phoebus and Diana, Deiphobe, Glaucus' daughter, who thus bespeaks the king: "Not this the time for shows like these; your present work is to sacrifice seven bullocks untouched by the yoke, seven sheep duly chosen."

This said to Aeneas, whose followers swiftly perform the prescribed rites, she summons the Teucrians into the lofty temple, herself its priestess. One huge side of the Euboean cliff has been hollowed into a cave, approached by a hundred broad avenues, a hundred mouths — from these a hundred voices are poured, the responses of the Sibyl. Just as they were on the threshold, "It is the moment to pray for the oracle," cries the maiden; "the god, the god is here." Thus as she spoke at the gate, her visage, her hue changed suddenly — her hair started from its braid — her bosom heaves and pants, her wild soul swells with frenzy — she grows larger to the view, and her tones are not of earth, as the breath of the divine presence comes on her nearer and nearer. "What! a laggard at vows and prayers? Aeneas of Troy

76

a laggard? for that is the only spell to part asunder the great closed lips of the terror-smitten shrine." She said, and was mute. A cold shudder runs through the Teucrians' iron frames, and their king pours out his very soul in prayer: "Phoebus, ever Troy's pitying friend in her cruel agonies — thou who didst level Paris' Dardan bow and string his Dardan arm against the vast frame of Aeacides — by thy guidance I have penetrated all these unknown seas that swathe mighty continents. The Massylian tribes, thrust away by Nature out of view, and the quicksands that environ their coasts — now at last our hands are on the flying skirts of Italy. Oh let it suffice Troy's fortune to have followed us thus far! Ye too may now justly spare our nation of Pergamus, gods and goddesses all, whose eyes were affronted by Troy and the great glories of Dardan land. And thou, most holy prophetess, that canst read the future as the present, grant me — I am asking for no crown that Fate does not owe me — grant a settlement in Latium to the Teucrians and their wandering gods, even the travel-tost deities of Troy. Then to Phoebus and his Trivian sister I will set up a temple of solid marble, and appoint feast-days in Phoebus' name. For thee too an august shrine is in store in that our future realm. For there I will lodge thy oracles and the secret words of destiny which thou shalt speak to my nation, and consecrate chosen men to thy gracious service. Only commit not thy strains to leaves, lest they float all confusedly the sport of the whirling winds. Utter them with thine own mouth, I implore thee." So his prayer ended.

But the prophetess, not yet Phoebus' willing slave, is storming with giant frenzy in her cavern, as though she hoped to unseat from her bosom the mighty god. All the more sharply he plies her mouth with his bit till its fury lags, tames her savage soul, and moulds her to his will by strong constraint. And now the hundred mighty doors of the chamber have flown open of their own accord, and are wafting through the air the voice of prophecy: "Oh you whose vast perils by sea are over at length! but on land there are heavier yet in store. The sons of Dardanus shall come to the realm of Lavinium — from this care set your mind at rest — but think not that they shall also have joy of their coming. War, savage war, and the Tiber foaming with surges of blood, is the vision I see. No lack for you of Simois, or Xanthus, or a Dorian camp. Another Achilles is reserved for Latium, he too goddess-born — nor will Juno ever be seen to quit her fastened hold on Troy — while you, a needy suppliant — what nation, what city in Italy will not have had you knocking at its gates! Once more will an alien bride bring on the Teucrians all this woe — once more a foreign bed. But you, yield not to affliction, but go forth all the bolder to meet

77

it, so far as your destiny gives you leave. The first glimpse of safety, little as you dream it, shall dawn on you from a Grecian town."

Such are the words with which Cumae's Sibyl from her cell shrills forth awful mysteries and booms again from the cavern, robing her truth in darkness — such the violence with which Apollo shakes the bridle in her frenzied mouth and plies her bosom with his goad. Soon as her frenzy abated and the madness of her lips grew calm, Aeneas the hero began: "No feature, awful maiden, that suffering can show rises on my sight new or unlooked-for — I have foreseen all and scanned all in fancy already. I have but one prayer to make: since here it is that Fame tells of the gate of the infernal monarch, and the murky pool of Acheron's overflow, grant me to pass to the sight, to the presence of my loved father — teach the way, and unlock the sacred doors. Him I bore away through flames and a driving tempest of darts on these my shoulders and rescued him from the midst of the foe: he was the companion of my journey, and encountered with me all the waves of ocean, all the terrors of sea and sky in his own feeble frame, beyond the strength and the day of old age. Nay more — that I would kneel to thee and approach thy dwelling — this was his charge, his oft-repeated prayer. Oh, of thy grace, pity the son and the sire; for thou art all-powerful, nor is it for nought that Hecate has set thee over the groves of Avernus. If Orpheus had the power to fetch back the shade of his wife, by the help of his Thracian lyre and its sounding strings — if Pollux redeemed his brother by dying in turn with him, and went and returned on the path those many times — why talk of Theseus, why of great Alcides? my line, like theirs, is from Jove most high."

Such were his prayers, while his hands clasped the altar, when thus the prophetess began: "Heir of the blood of gods, son of Anchises of Troy, easy is the going down to Avernus — all night and all day the gate of gloomy Pluto stands unbarred; but to retrace your footsteps, and win your way back to the upper air, that is the labor, that the task. There have been a few, favorites of gracious Jove, or exalted to heaven by the blaze of inborn worth, themselves sprung from the gods, who have had the power. The whole intervening space is possessed by woods, and lapped round by the black windings of Cocytus' stream. And now, if your heart's yearning is so great, your passion so strong, twice to stem the Stygian pool, twice to gaze on the night of Tartarus — if it be your joy to give scope to a madman's striving — hear what must first be done. Deep in the shade of a tree lurks a branch, all of gold, foliage alike and limber twig, dedicated to the service of the Juno of the shades; it is shrouded by the whole labyrinth of the forest, closed in by the boskage that darkens the glens. Yet none may pierce the subterranean mystery, till a man have gathered from the tree that leafy sprout of gold, for this it is that fair Proserpine has ordained to be brought her as her own proper tribute. Pluck off one, another is there unfailing, of gold as pure, a twig burgeoning with as fine an ore. Let then your eye be keen to explore it, your hand quick to pluck it when duly found, for it will follow the touch with willingness and ease, if you have a call from Fate; if not, no strength of yours will overcome it, no force of steel tear it away. But, besides this, you have the breathless corpse of a friend lying unburied — alas! you know it not — tainting your whole fleet with the air of death, while you are asking Heaven's will, and lingering on this our threshold. Him first consign to his proper place, and hide him in the grave. Lead black cattle to the altar: be this the expiation to pave your way. Thus at last you shall look on the groves of Styx and the realms untrodden of the living." She said, and closed her lips in silence.

Aeneas, with saddened face and steadfast eye, moves on, leaving the cave behind, and revolves in his mind the secrets of the future. Achates, ever faithful, walks at his side, and plants his foot with no less consciousness of care. Many were the things exchanged in their ranging talk — who could be the dead comrade that the priestess spoke of, what the corpse that needed burial. And lo! Misenus, soon as they came, there on the dry beach they see him, snatched by death that should have spared him — Misenus, son of Aeolus, than whom none was mightier to stir men's hearts with his clarion, and kindle with music the war-god's flame. Hector the great had been his chief: in Hector's service he performed a warrior's part famous alike with the trumpet and the spear. But after the conquering arm of Achilles robbed his master of life, valiant hero, he made himself the comrade of the Dardan Aeneas, nor found the standard he followed meaner than of old. But in those days, as he was making his hollow shell ring over the waters, infatuate mortal, challenging the gods to compete, Triton, roused to jealousy, seized him, if the story be true, and plunged him in a moment in the billow that laps among the rocks. So they all stood round, uttering loud shrieks; louder than the rest Aeneas the good. And then without delay they set about the Sibyl's bidding, weeping sore, and in mournful rivalry heap up the funeral pyre with trees, and carry it into the sky.

Away they go to an ancient wood, the wild beast's tall covert — down go the pitch-trees; the holm-oak rings with the axe's blows, and so do the ashen beams; the wedge cleaves through the fissile oak; they roll down from the heights huge mountain ashes. There is Aeneas, in this, as in other labors, the first to cheer on his comrades, and wielding a weapon like theirs; and thus he ponders in the sad silence of his own breast, looking at the immeasurable wood, and thus gives utterance to his prayer: "Oh that at this moment that golden branch on the tree would reveal itself to our sight in all this depth of forest! for I see that in all things the prophetess has told us of you, Misenus, alas! too truly!" Scarce had he spoken, when, as by chance, a pair of doves come flying along the sky, under the hero's very eyes and settle on the turf at his feet. At once the mighty chief recognizes his mother's birds and gladly breathes a second prayer: "Oh guide us on our way wherever it be, and as ye fly direct our steps into the grove where the precious branch casts its shade on the rich ground! Thou too forsake not our perplexity, O goddess mother!" Thus much he said, and checked his advancing foot, watching to see what prognostics they bring, whither they aim their onward course. They, as they graze, go ever forward on the wing, as far as the eyes of the travellers can keep them in view. Then when they come to Avernus' noisome jaws, swiftly they soar aloft, and gliding through the clear sky, settle twain on the same tree, their chosen seat, whence there flashed through the branches the contrasted gleam of gold. Even as in the woods, in the cold of mid-winter, the mistletoe is wont to put forth new leaves a vegetable growth, but of no parent tree, and with its yellow produce to surround the tapering boles, so looked the leafy gold among the holm-oak's dark shade — so in the light breeze tinkled the foil. Aeneas snatches it at once, plucks it off with eagerness overpowering its delay, and carries it to the home of the prophetic Sibyl.

Meantime, with not less zeal, the Teucrians on the shore were mourning for Misenus, and paying the last honor to the thankless ashes. First they raised a pile, unctuous with pinewood, and high-heaped with planks of oak: they wreath its sides with gloomy foliage, and set up before it funeral cypresses, and adorn it with a covering of refulgent armor. Some make ready heated water and cauldrons bubbling over the fire, and wash and anoint the cold corpse. Loud rings the wail: then, the dirge over, they place the limbs on the couch that claims them, and fling over them purple garments, the dead man's usual covering. Some put their shoulders to the heavy bier in melancholy service, and after ancestral fashion, with averted eyes, apply the torch from under. The rich heap is ablaze — offerings of incense, sacrificial viands, oil streaming from the bowl. After that the ashes were fallen in and the blaze was lulled, they drenched with wine the relics and the thirsty embers on the pyre, and Corynaeus gathered up the bones, and stored them in a brazen urn. He, too, carried round pure water, and sprinkled thrice the comrades of the dead, scattering the thin drops with a branch of fruitful olive — so he expiated the company, and spoke the last solemn words. But good Aeneas raises over the dead the arms, the oar and the trumpet, in a huge pile under a skyey mountain, which is now from him called Misenus, and retains from age to age the everlasting name.

This done, he hastens to execute the Sibyl's bidding. A deep cave there was, yawning wide with giant throat, rough and shingly, shadowed by the black pool and the gloom of the forest — a cave, over whose mouth no winged thing could fly unharmed, so poisonous the breath that exhaling from its pitchy jaws steamed up to the sky — whence Greece has given the spot the name *Aornos*. Here first the priestess places in sacrificial station four black-skinned bullocks, and empties wine over their brows, and plucking from between their horns the hairs of the crown, throws them into the hallowed flame, as the first fruits of worship, with loud cries on Hecate, queen in heaven and Erebus both. Others put the knife to the throat, and catch in chargers the steaming blood. With his own sword Aeneas strikes down a lamb of sable fleece, for the Furies' mother and her mighty sisters, and a barren heifer for thee, dread Proserpine. Then to the Stygian monarch he rears altars, blazing through the darkness, and piles on the flame the bulls' carcasses entire, pouring fat oil on the entrails all aglow. When, hark! as the sun began to glimmer and dawn, the ground is bellowing under their feet, and the wood-crowned heights are nodding, and the baying of dogs sounds through the gloom, for the goddess is at hand. "Hence, hence with your unhallowed feet!" clamors the prophetess, "and rid the whole grove of your presence. And you — strike into the road, and pluck your sword from its scabbard — now is the hour for courage, Aeneas, now for a stout heart." No more she said, but flung herself wildly into the cavern's mouth; and he, with no faltering step, keeps pace with his guide.

Ye gods, whose empire is the shades — spirits of silence, Chaos and Phlegethon, stretching wide in the stillness of night, suffer me to tell what has reached my ears; grant me your aid to reveal things buried underground, deep and dark.

On they went, darkling in solitary night, far into the gloom, through Pluto's void halls and ghostly realms — like a journey in woods under the niggard beams of a doubtful moon, when Jupiter has shrouded heaven in shadow, and black Night has stolen the color from Nature's face. There before the threshold, in the very mouth of Hell, Agony and the fiends of Remorse have made their lair; there dwell wan Diseases, and woeful Age, and Terror, and Hunger that prompts to Sin, and loathly Want — shapes of hideous view — and Death, and Suffering; then comes Sleep, Death's blood-brother, and the soul's guilty joys, and deadly War couched in the gate, and the Furies' iron chambers, and frantic Strife, with bloody fillets wreathed in her snaky hair.

In the midst there stands, with boughs and aged arms outspread, a massive elm, of broad shade, the chosen seat, so Rumor tells, of bodiless dreams, which cling close to its every leaf. There, too, are a hundred monstrous shapes of wild beasts of divers kinds, Centaurs stalled in the entrance and two-formed Scyllas, and Briareus, the hundred-handed, and the portent of Lerna, hissing fearfully, and Chimaera in her panoply of flames, Gorgons, and Harpies, and the semblance of the three-bodied spectre. At once Aeneas grasps his sword, in the haste of sudden alarm, and meets their advance with its drawn blade; and did not his companion warn him, of her own knowledge, that they are but thin unbodied spirits flitting in a hollow mask of substance, he would be rushing among them, and slashing shadows asunder with the steel's unavailing blows.

Hence runs the road that leads to the waters of Tartarean Acheron, whose gulfy stream, churning mud in its monstrous depths, is all aglow, and disgorges into Cocytus the whole of its sand. These waters are guarded by a grisly ferryman, frightful and foul—Charon; his chin an uncleared forest of hoary hair; his eyes a mass of flames; while his uncleanly garb hangs from his shoulders, gathered into a knot. With his own hand he pushes on the craft with a pole, and trims the sails, and moves the dead heavily along in his boat of iron-gray, himself already in years; but a god's old age is green and vigorous. Towards him the whole crowd was pouring to the bank: matrons and warriors, and bodies of mighty heroes discharged of life, boys and unwedded maidens, and youths laid on the pile of death in their parents' eyes— many as are the leaves that drop and fall in the woods in autumn's early cold, or many as are the birds that flock massed together from the deep to the land, when the wintry year drives them over sea to tenant a sunnier clime. There they stood, each praying that he might be the first to cross, with hands yearningly outstretched towards the further shore; but the grim boatman takes on board now these, now those, while others he drives away, and bars them from the river's brink. Aeneas cries as a man perplexed and startled by the tumult: "Tell me, dread maiden, what means this concourse to the stream? Of what are the spirits in quest? What choice decides that these shall retire from the shore, while those are rowing through that leaden pool?" To him in brief returned the aged priestess: "Son of Anchises, Heaven's undoubted offspring, before you are Cocytus' depths and the marshy flood of Styx, that power by whose name the gods fear to swear in vain. The whole multitude you see here is helpless and tombless; Charon is the ferryman; those who ride the wave are the buried. He may not ferry them from the dreadful banks across that noisy current till their bones have found a place of rest. A hundred years they wander hovering about these shores; then at last they embark, and see again the flood of their longing." Anchises' son stood and paused, musing deeply, and pitying at his heart a lot so unkind. Yes, there he sees, sadly wandering without death's last tribute, Leucaspis and Orontes, the captain of Lycia's fleet: both had sailed with him from Troy over the stormy water, and the south wind whelmed them both, engulfing the vessel and its crew.

Lo! he sees his pilot, Palinurus, moving along — Palinurus, who but now, while voyaging from Libya, his eyes bent on the stars, had fallen from the stern, flung out into the wide waste of waters. So when he had at last taken knowledge of his features, now saddened, in the deep gloom, he thus accosts him first: "Who was it, Palinurus, of all the gods, that tore you from us, and whelmed you in the wide sea? Tell me who. Till now I never found him false; but in this one response Apollo has proved a cheat, foretelling that you would be unharmed on the deep, and win your way to the Ausonian frontier, and thus it is that he keeps his word!" "Nay," returned he, "my chief, Anchises' son, Phoebus' tripod has told you no lie, nor did any god whelm me in the sea. No, I chanced to fall, tearing away by main force the rudder, to which I was clinging like sentry to his post, as I guided your course, and dragging it with me in my headlong whirl. Witness those cruel waters, I felt no fear for my own life like that which seized me for your ship, lest, disarmed and disabled, shaken loose from her ruler's hand, she should give way under the great sea that was rising then. Three long nights of storm the south wind swept me over the vast wilderness of convulsed ocean. Hardly at last, at the fourth dawn, I looked out aloft upon Italy from the crest of the wave. Stroke by stroke I was swimming to shore; and now I was just laying hold on safety, had not the savage natives come on me, sword in hand, clogged as I was with my dripping clothes, and clutching with talon fingers the steep mountain-top, and deemed blindly they had found a prize. Now the wave is my home, and the winds keep tossing me on the beach. Oh, by heaven's pleasant sunshine and bright sky; by your father, I adjure you; by the promise growing up with your Iulus, rescue me with that unconquered arm from this cruel fate: be yourself, and either spread earth upon me, for that you can surely do, and put back to Velia's haven; or, if any way there be, any that your goddess mother can reveal — for well I ween it is not without Heaven's leave that you purpose to stem these fearful tides and the reluctant pool of Styx — stretch your hand to your poor friend, and take me with you over the water, that at least I may find in death a place of rest and peace." So had he spoken, when thus the priestess began: "What demon, Palinurus, has set on you so monstrous a desire? You, unburied, look on the

83

Stygian water, and the dread river of the furies? You set foot on the bank unbidden? Cease to dream that Heaven's destiny can be swayed by prayer. Yet hear and retain a word which may console your hard lot. For know that the dwellers in that fatal border, goaded far and wide through their cities by prodigies from heaven, shall propitiate your dust: they shall erect a tomb, and through that tomb send down your funeral dues, and the spot shall bear for ever the name of Palinurus." These words allayed his cares, and banished for awhile grief from that sad bosom: his heart leaps to the land that is called by his name.

They accordingly continue their journey, and approach the river. Soon as the boatman saw them, at the moment, from the wave of Styx, moving through the stilly forest, and turning their steps to the bank, he first bespeaks them thus, and assails them unaccosted: "You, whoever you are, that are making for these waters of ours in warlike trim, speak your errand from the spot where you are, and come no nearer. This is the place for the shadows, for Sleep and slumberous Night. The bodies of the living may not be ferried in my Stygian barque. Nay, it was not to my joy that I gave Alcides a passage over the lake, nor Theseus and Pirithous, born of gods though they were, and of strength unsubdued. The one laid a jailer's hand on the warder of Tartarus, even at the foot of the king's own throne, and dragged him trembling along: the others essayed to carry off the queen from Pluto's bridal chamber." To which the Amphrysian priestess replied in brief: "Here there are no stratagems like those; be not discomposed; these weapons are not borne for violence; the monstrous guardian of your gate is free to terrify the bloodless spectres from his den with his unending bark; Proserpine is free to keep her uncle's home as faithful wife should. This is Aeneas of Troy, renowned for piety and arms alike: it is to see his father that he is going down to Erebus' lowest depth of gloom. If thou art moved in nought by the spectacle of piety so signal, yet let this branch" — and she uncovered the branch which was concealed in her robe — "claim recognition." At once the angry swell subsides, and the breast is calm. No further parley. Gazing in wonder at the sacred offering of the fated bough, last seen so long ago, he turns to them the sea-green boat, and draws near the bank. Then he dislodges other ghostly passengers who were sitting along the benches, and clears the gangways, while he takes into the vessel's hollow the mighty Aeneas. The sutures of the boat cracked beneath the weight, as through its rents it drew in large draughts of marsh-water. At length priestess and prince are safe across the flood, set down amid featureless mud and blue-green rushes.

Cerberus, the monster, makes the whole realm ring with his three barking throats, as he lies in giant length fronting them in his den's mouth. The priestess, seeing the snakes already bristling on his neck, throws him a morsel steeped in the slumber of honey and medicated meal. He, in the frenzy of hunger, opens his triple jaws to catch it as it comes, and stretches his enormous back at length on the ground, till his huge bulk covers the den. Aeneas masters the approach while the warder sleeps, and swiftly passes from the bank of the river without return.

At once there breaks on his ear a voice of mighty wailing, infant spirits sobbing and crying on the threshold, babes that, portionless of the sweets of life, were snatched from the breast by the black death-day's tyranny, and whelmed in untimely night. Next to them are those who were done to death by false accusation. Yet let none think that the lot of award or the judge's sentence are wanting here. There sits Minos, the president, urn in hand: he summons an assembly of the speechless, and takes cognizance of earthly lives and earthly sins.

Next to them comes the dwelling-place of the sons of sorrow, who, though guiltless, procured their own death by violence, and, for mere hatred of the sunshine flung their lives away. Oh, how gladly would they now, in the air above, bear to the end the load of poverty and the full extremity of toil! But Fate bars the way: the unlovely pool swathes them round in her doleful waters, and Styx, with her ninefold windings, keeps them fast.

Not far hence the traveller's eye sees stretching on every side the Mourning Fields: such the name they bear. Here dwell those whom cruel Love's consuming tooth has eaten to the heart, in the privacy of hidden walks and enshrouding myrtle wood; their tender sorrows quit them not even in death. In this region he sees Phaedra and Procris, and sad Eriphyle, pointing to the wounds of her ruthless son, and Evadne, and Pasiphaë: along with them moves Laodamia, and Caeneus, once a man, now a woman, brought back by the turn of fate, to her former self. Among these was Phoenicia's daughter, Dido, fresh from her death-wound, wandering in that mighty wood: soon as the Trojan hero stood at her side, and knew her, looming dimly through the dusk — as a man sees or thinks he sees through the clouds, when the month is young, the rising moon — his tears broke forth, and he addressed her tenderly and lovingly. "Unhappy Dido! and was it then a true mes-senger that reached me with the tale that you were dead: that the sword had done its worst? Was it, alas, to the grave that I brought you? By the stars of heaven I swear, by the powers above, by all that is most sacred here underground, against my will, fair queen, I quitted your coast. No; it was the command of the gods; the same stern force which compels me now to pass through this realm of shade, this wilder-ness of squalor and abysmal night; it was that which drove me by its uttered will: nor could I have thought that my departure would bring on you such violence of grief. Stay your step, and withdraw not from the look I bend on you. Whom would you shun? the last word which fate suffers me to address you is this." With words like these, Aeneas kept soothing the soul that blazed forth through those scowling eyes, and moving himself to tears. She stood with averted head and eyes on the ground, her features as little moved by the speech he essayed as if she held the station of a stubborn flint, or a crag of Marpessa. At length she flung herself away, and, unforgiving still, fled into the shadow of the wood, where her former lord, Sychaeus, answers her sorrows with his, and gives her full measure for her love. Yet, none the less, Aeneas, thrilled through and through by her cruel fate, follows far on her track with tears, and sends his pity along with her.

Then he turns, to encounter the appointed way. And now they were already in the furthest region, the separate place tenanted by the great heroes of war. Here there meets him Tydeus, here Parthenopaeus, illustrious in arms, and the spectre of pale Adrastus. Here are chiefs of Dardan line, wailed long and loudly in the upper air as they lay low in fight. As he saw them all in long array, he groaned heavily: Glaucus and Medon, and Thersilochus, the three sons of Antenor, and Poly-phoetes, Ceres' priest, and Idaeus, with his hand still on the car, still on the armor. They surround him, right and left, the ghostly crowd; one look is not sufficient: they would fain linger on and on, and step side by side with him, and learn the cause of his coming. But the nobles of the Danaans, and the flower of Agamemnon's bands, when they saw the hero and his armor gleaming through the shade, were smitten with strange alarm: some turn their back in flight, as erst they fled to the ships: others raise a feeble war-shout. The cry they essay mocks their straining throats.

Here it is that he sees Priam's son, mangled all over, Deiphobus, his face cruelly marred — face and both hands — his temples despoiled of his ears, and his nose lopped by unseemly carnage. Scarce, in truth, he recognized him, trembling as he was and trying to hide the terrible vengeance wreaked on him: unaccosted he addresses him in the tones he knew of old: "Deiphobus, mighty warrior, scion of Teucer's illus-trious stock, who has had the ambition to avenge himself so cruelly? who has had his will of you thus? For me, Rumor told me on that fatal night that you had sunk down, tired with the work of slaughtering the Greeks, on a heap of undistinguished carnage. Then with my own hand, I set up an empty tomb on the Rhoetean shore, and thrice with a loud voice invoked your spirit. There are your name and your arms to keep the spot in memory: your self, dear friend, I could not see, so as to give you repose in the fatherland I was leaving." To whom the son of Priam: "Dear friend, you have failed in naught: all that Deiphobus could claim has been paid by you to him and to his shade. No; it was my own destiny and the deadly wickedness of the Spartan woman that plunged me thus deep in ill: these tokens are of her leaving. How we spent that fatal night in treacherous joyance you knew well: too good cause is there to bear it in mind. When the fateful horse at one bound surmounted the height of Pergamus, and brought a mail-clad infantry in its laden womb, she feigned a solemn dance, and led round the city Phrygian dames in Bacchic ecstasy; herself in their midst raising a mighty torch aloft, and calling to the Danaans from the top of the citadel. That hour I, spent with care and overborne with sleep, was in the hold of our ill-starred bridal chamber, weighed down as I lay, by slumber sweet and sound, the very image of the deep calm of death. Meantime, my peerless helpmate removes from the house arms of every sort: yes, my trusty sword she had withdrawn from my pillow, and now she calls Menelaus to come in, and throws wide the door, hoping, I doubt not, that the greatness of the boon would soften her lover's heart, and that the memory of her crime of old could thus be wiped from men's minds. Why make the story long? They burst into the chamber, along with them that child of Aeolus, then as ever the counselor of evil. Recompense, ye gods, the Greeks in kind, if these lips, that ask for retribution, are pure and loyal. But you; what chance has brought you here in your lifetime, let me ask in turn? Are you come under the spell of ocean-wandering, or by the command of heaven? or what tyranny of fortune constrains you to visit these sad, sunless dwellings, the abode of confusion?"

In this interchange of talk, the Dawn-goddess in her flushing car, careering through the sky, had well passed the summit of the arch; and perchance they had spent all their allotted time in converse like this, had not the Sibyl warned her companion with brief address: "Night is hastening, Aeneas; and we, as we weep, are making hours pass. This is the spot where the road parts in twain. The right, which goes under the palace-wall of mighty Dis — there lies our way to Elysium; the left puts in motion the tortures of the wicked, and sends them to Tartarus, the home of crime." Deiphobus replied: "Frown not, dread priestess: I depart, to make the ghostly number complete, and plunge again in darkness. Go on your way, our nation's glory, go: may your experience of fate be more blest." He said, and, while yet speaking, turned away.

Suddenly, Aeneas looks back, and, under a rock on the left, sees a broad stronghold, girt by a triple wall; a fierce stream surrounds it with surges of fire, Tartarean Phlegethon, and tosses craggy fragments in thunder. Full in front is a vast gate, its pillars of solid adamant. No force of man, not even the embattled powers of heaven, could break it down. Rising in air is a turret of iron, and Tisiphone, with a gory robe girt round her, sits at the vestibule with sleepless vigilance night and day. Hence sounds of wailing meet the ear, and the crack of remorseless whips; the clank of steel follows, and the trailing of the chain. Aeneas stood still, riveted by the terror of the noise. "What shapes is guilt wearing now? tell me, dread maiden. What are the torments that lie on it so hard? what mean these loud upsoaring shrieks?" The priestess returned: "Noble leader of the Teucrians, no innocent foot may tread that guilty threshold; but the day when Hecate set me over the groves of Avernus, she taught me from her own lips the punishments of Heaven, and led me through from end to end. Here rules Gnossian Rhadamanthus, a reign of iron — avenger, at once, and judge of cowering guilt, he compels a confession of what crimes soever men in upper air, blindly rejoicing in the cheat, have kept secret till the hour of death, to be expiated then. In a moment, Tisiphone the torturer, with uplifted scourge, lashes from side to side the spurned and guilty soul: and brandishing in her left hand knots of serpents, summons her unpitying sisterhood. Then at last, grating on their dread-sounding hinge, the awful gates are opened. See you what manner of sentry is seated at the entrance? what a presence is guarding the threshold? Know that a Hydra fiercer yet with fifty monstrous throats, each a yawning pit, holds her seat within. Then there is the abyss of Tartarus in sheer descent, extending under the shades, twice as far as man's skyward gaze from earth to the heaven of Olympus. Here are earth's ancient progeny, the Titan brood, hurled down by the thunderbolt to wallow in the depths of the gulf. Here too I saw the twin sons of Aloeus, frames of giant bulk, who essayed by force of hand to pluck down the mighty heavens, and dislodge Jove from his realm in the sky. I saw too Salmoneus, smitten with cruel vengeance, while mimicking the fires of Jove and the rumblings of Olympus. Borne in a four-horse car, a flaring torch in hand, he was making his triumphal progress through the tribes of Greece, and the midst of Elis' city, and bidding men accord him a god's homage. Madman! to counterfeit the storm-cloud and the unrivalled thunderbolt with the rattle of brass and the beat of horses' horny hoofs. But the almighty sire from the depth of his cloudy dwelling hurled his weapon — no futile firebrand his, no pinewood's smoky glare — and dashed him headlong down with that tremendous blast. Tityos, too, the foster-child of Earth's common breast, it was mine to see: his body lies extended over nine whole acres, and there is a monstrous vulture with hooked beak shearing away his imperishable liver, and reaping a harvest of suffering from his vitals, as it digs deep for its meal, and burrows in the cavern of his breast, nor gives the new-growing filaments rest or respite. What need to tell of the Lapithae, of Ixion and Pirithoüs — men who live under a black crag, ever falling, and just in act to drop? The lofty couch is spread for the banquet, and the pillar of gold gleams underneath: the feast is before them, served in kingly luxury; but the eldest of the Furies is couched at their side: she will not let them stretch a hand to the board: she starts up with torch uplifted and thunder in her tones. Here are they who lived in hatred with their brethren while life yet was; who smote a parent or wove for a client the web of fraud; who gained a treasure and brooded over it alone, and never shared it with their kin — a mighty number these — adulterers, who were slain for their crime; citizens who followed the standard of treason; slaves who shrunk not from breaking their troth to their lords: all in prison awaiting their doom. Ask not what doom is theirs, what phase, what fate has whelmed them so deep. Others roll the huge stone up the hill, or hang dispread from the spokes of the wheel: there sits, as he will sit for evermore, unhappy Theseus: and Phlegyas, from the depth of his agony, keeps warning all, and proclaiming with a voice of terror through the shades: 'Learn hereby to be righteous, and not to scorn the gods.' This sold his country for gold, and saddled her with a tyrant; for gain he made and unmade laws: this assailed his daughter's bed, and essayed a forbidden union: all dared some monstrous crime, and enjoyed their daring. No; had I even a hundred tongues, and a hundred mouths, and lungs of iron, not then could I embrace all the types of crime, or rehearse the whole muster-roll of vengeance."

So spoke Apollo's aged priestess; and then resuming: "But come," she cries, "speed on your way, and fulfil the duty you have essayed: quicken we our pace. I see the walls which the Cyclopian forge raised in air, and the arched gates confronting us, where sacred rule bids us set down our offering." As she spoke, they step side by side through the dusky ways, dispatch the interval of distance, and draw near the gate. Aeneas masters the approach, sprinkles his body with pure spring water, and fixes the branch on the portal's front.

And now these things done at length, and the offering to the goddess accomplished, they have reached the regions of bliss, green pleasaunces of happy groves, and the abodes of the blest. Here ether clothes the plains with an ampler plenitude and a dazzling lustre; and the eye beholds a sun and stars of its own. There are some, plying their limbs on the grassy wrestling-ground, conflicting in sport, and grappling each other on the yellow sand: some are beating their feet in the dance, and chanting songs. There, too, is the Thracian priest in his flowing robe, singing the seven notes in unison with the dancer's measure, and striking them now with his fingers, now with the quill of ivory. Here are the old race of Teucer, a goodly family, heroes of lofty soul, born in earth's better days, Ilus and Assaracus, and Dardanus, founder of Troy. From afar he gazes wonderingly on their warrior arms and their ghostly chariots. Their spears stand rooted in the ground, and their unyoked steeds graze dispersedly over the meadow. All the delight they knew when alive in chariots and armor, all their pride in grooming and feeding their horses, goes with them underground, and animates them there. See, too, his eyes rests on others regaling on either hand upon the grass, and singing in chorus a joyous paean, all in a fragrant grove of bay, the source whence, welling forth into the upper world, Eridanus flows in broad current between his wooded banks. Here is a noble company who braved wounds in fight for fatherland; all the priests who kept their purity while life was; all the poets whose hearts were clean, and their songs worthy of Phoebus' ear; all who by cunning inventions gave a grace to life, and whose worthy deeds made their fellows think of them with love; each has his brow cinctured with a snow-white fillet. Looking on the multitude as it streamed around, the Sibyl bespoke them thus — Musaeus before all; for he stands the centre of that vast crowd, which looks up to him, as with rising shoulders he towers above them: "Tell us, happy spirits, and you, best of bards, which is Anchises' haunt? which his home? for it is to see him that we have come hither, and won our way over the mighty river of Erebus." Instant the hero replied in brief: "Here there are no fixed abodes; our dwellings are in shadowy groves; our settlements on the velvet slope of banks and meadows fresh with running streams. But come, if you will, climb this hill with me, and I will set your feet at once on a road that will lead you." So saying, he moves on before, and from the top of the ridge points to broad fields of light, while they descend from the summit.

But father Anchises, down in the depth of the green dell, was surveying with fond observance the spirits now confined there, but hereafter to pass into the light of day, and scanning, as chance would have it, the whole multitude of his people, even his loved posterity, their destinies, their warrior deeds, their ways, and their works. Soon as he saw Aeneas advancing through the grass to meet him, he stretched out both his hands with eager movement, tears gushed over his cheeks, and words escaped his lips: "And are you come at last? has love fulfilled a father's hopes and surmounted the perils of the way? is it mine to look on your face, my son, and listen and reply as we talked of old? Yes; I was even thinking so in my own mind. I was reckoning that it would be, counting over the days. Nor has my longing played me false. Oh, the lands and the mighty seas from which you have come to my presence! the dangers, my son, that have tossed and smitten you! Oh, how I have feared lest you should come to harm in that realm of Libya!" The son replied: "Your shade it was, father, your melancholy

90

shade, that, coming to me oft and oft, constrained me to knock at these doors: here, in the Tyrrhene deep my ships are riding at anchor. Let us grasp hand in hand: let us, my father! Oh, withdraw not from my embrace!" As he spoke, the streaming tears rolled down his face. Thrice, as he stood, he essayed to fling his arms round that dear neck: thrice the phantom escaped the hands that caught at it in vain, impalpable as the wind, fleeting as the wings of sleep.

Meanwhile Aeneas sees in the retired vale a secluded grove with brakes and rustling woods, and the river of Lethe, which floats along by those abodes of peace. Round it were flying races and tribes untold: even as in the meadows when bees in calm summer-tide settle on flower after flower, and stream over the milk-white lilies, the humming fills the plain. Startled at the sudden sight, Aeneas wonderingly inquires what it means, what are those waters in the distance, or who the men that are thronging the banks in crowds so vast. To him his father Anchises: "They are spirits to whom Destiny has promised new bodies, there at the side of Lethe's water, drinking the wave of carelessness, and the long draught of oblivion. In truth I have long wished to tell you of them and show them before you, to recount the long line of my kindred, that you may rejoice with me now that Italy is found." "Oh, my father! and must we think that there are souls that fly hence aloft into the upper air, and thus return to the sluggish fellowship of the body? can their longing for light be so mad as this?" "I will tell you, my son, nor hold you longer in doubt." So replies Anchises, and unfolds the story in order.

"Know, first, that heaven and earth, and the watery plains, and the Moon's lucid ball, and Titan's starry fires are kept alive by a spirit within; a mind pervading each limb stirs the whole frame and mingles with the mighty mass. Hence spring the races of men and beasts, and living things with wings, and the strange forms that Ocean carries beneath his marble surface. These particles have a fiery glow, a heavenly nature, struggling against the clogs of corrupting flesh, the dullness of limbs of clay and bodies ready to die. Hence come their fears and lusts, their joys and griefs: nor can they discern the heavenly light, prisoned as they are in night and blind dungeon walls. Nay, when life's last ray has faded from them, not even then, poor wretches, are they wholly freed from ill, freed from every plague of the flesh: those many taints must needs be ingrained strangely in the being, so long as they have grown with it. So they are schooled with punishment, and pay in suffering for ancient ill: some are hung up and dispread to the piercing winds: others have the stain of wickedness washed out under the whelming gulf, or burnt out with fire: each is chastized in his own spirit: then we are sped through the breadth of Elysium, while some few remain to inhabit these happy plains, till the lapse of ages, when time's cycle is complete, has cleansed the ingrained blot and left a pure residue of heavenly intelligence, the flame of essential ether. All of these, when they have rounded the circle of a thousand years, Heaven summons to the stream of Lethe, a mighty concourse, to the end that with memory effaced they may return to the vault of the sky, and learn to wish for a new union with the body."

Anchises ended: he draws his son and the Sibyl with him into the midst of the assemblage, the heart of that buzzing crowd, and mounts an eminence, whence he might see face to face the whole of the long procession, and learn each comer's looks.

"Now then, for the glories of the Dardan race from this time onward, the posterity reserved for you in the Italian line, noble spirits, the ordained heirs of our proud name: of these I will tell you, and inform you of your destiny. He whom you see there, the youth leaning on the pointless spear, his lot is to fill the next place in light: he will be first to rise to upper day, born from the admixture of Italian blood, Silvius, that great Alban name, your latest offspring, whom in your old age at set of life your spouse Lavinia will bear you in the woods, himself a king and the father of kings to be: from him it is that our race shall rule over Alba the Long. Next comes mighty Procas, the pride of the people of Troy, and Capys, and Numitor, and a second bearer of your name, Silvius Aeneas, himself renowned alike for piety and for valor, if ever he should come to the throne of Alba. What glorious youths! look what strength they carry in their port, while their brows are shaded by the civic oak! These shall uprear for you, high on the mountains, Nomentum, and Gabii, and Fidenae's town, and the towers of Collatia, Pometii and Inuus' camp, and Bola, and Cora; names which shall one day be named: now they are mere nameless lands. Romulus, too, the child of Mars, shall come along with his grandsire. Romulus, whom a mother, bearing Ilium's name, shall produce from the blood of Assaracus. See you the two plumes standing on his crest, how his sire marks him even now for the upper world by his own token of honor? Yes, my son, it is by his auspices that our glorious Rome shall extend her empire to earth's end, her ambition to the skies, and embrace seven hills with the wall of a single city, blest parent of a warrior brood: even as the mighty Berecyntian mother rides tower-crowned through the towns of Phrygia, proud of the gods that have sprung from her, a hundred grandchildren at her knee, all dwellers in heaven, all lords of the lofty sky. Hither now turn your two rays of vision: look at this family, at Romans of your own. Here is Caesar: here the whole progeny of Iulus, as it will pass one day under heaven's mighty cope. This, this is he, the man promised to you so

92

often, Augustus Caesar, true child of a god, who shall establish again for Latium a golden age in that very region where Saturn once reigned, while he stretches his sway alike beyond Garamantian and Indian. See, the land is lying outside the stars, outside the sun's yearly path, where heaven-carrier Atlas turns round on his shoulder the pole, studded with burning constellations. In view of his approach, a shiver runs already by oracular warning through Caspian realms and Maeotian land, and there is stir and confusion at the mouths of sevenfold Nile. Nay, even Alcides traversed no such length of earth, though he stalked the brazen-footed deer, or tamed Erymanthus' savage wilds, and appalled Lerna with his arrows: no, nor he who guides his triumphal car with reins of ivy-leaf, Bacchus, driving his tigers down from Nysa's lofty top. And do we still hesitate to let prowess give scope to power, or does fear prevent our setting foot on Ausonian soil? But who is he in the distance, conspicuous with a wreath of olive, with sacred vessels in his hand? Ah! I know the hoary hair and beard of the king of Rome, who shall give the infant city the support of law, sent from his homely Cures and a land of poverty into a mighty empire. Next shall come one doomed to break his country's peace, Tullus, and stir up warriors rusting in ease and squadrons that have forgotten their triumphs. Ancus follows, a greater boaster, even now too ready to catch the breath of a popular cheer. Would you look too at the kings of Tarquin's house, at the haughty spirit of Brutus the avenger, and the fasces retrieved? He shall be the first to take the consul's power and the axes of doom: the father will bring his rebel sons to death, all for fair freedom's sake. Unhappy man! let after ages speak of that deed as they will, strong over all will be patriot passion and unmeasured thirst of praise. Look, there are the Drusi and Decii, and Torquatus with his unpitying axe, and Camillus the restorer of the standards. But those whom you see there, dressed alike in gleaming armor — spirits at harmony now and so long as they are confined in darkness — alas! how vast a war will they wage, each with each, if they shall attain the light of day, what arraying of hosts, what carnage will there be! Father-in-law and son-in-law, the one coming down from Alpine ramparts and the stronghold of Monoecus: the other drawn up against him with the forces of the east. Do not, do not, my children, make wars like these familiar to your spirits: turn not your country's valor against your country's vitals: and you, restrain yourself the first: you, whose lineage is from heaven, drop the steel from your grasp, heir of Anchises' blood. See here, a conqueror who shall drive to the lofty Capitol the car of triumph over Corinth, glorious from Achaean slaughter: here one who shall lay Argus in dust, and Agamemnon's own Mycenae, ay, and the heir of Aeacus, with Achilles' martial blood

93

in his veins: a Roman's vengeance for his Trojan grandsires, and for Pallas' insulted fame. What tongue would leave you unpraised, great Cato, or Cossus, you? or the race of the Gracchi, or those twin thunderbolts of war, the Scipios, Libya's ruin, or Fabricius, princely in his poverty, or you, Serranus, sowing your own plowed fields? When, ye Fabii, will panting praise overtake you? You are in truth our greatest, the single savior of our state by delay. Others, I doubt not, will plead better at the bar, will trace with the rod the courses of heaven, and foretell the risings of the stars. Yours, Roman, be the lesson to govern the nations as their lord: this is your destined culture, to impose the settled rule of peace, to spare the humbled, and to crush the proud."

Father Anchises paused; and, as they wondered, went on to say: "See how Marcellus advances in the glory of the general's spoils, towering with conqueror's majesty over all the warriors near! When the state of Rome reels under the invader's shock, he shall stay it; his horse's hoofs shall trample the Carthaginian and the revolted Gaul; and he shall dedicate the third suit of armor to Quirinus the sire." Hereupon Aeneas, for he saw walking at Marcellus' side a youth of goodly presence and in gleaming armor, but with little joy on his brow and downcast eyes: "Who, my father, is he that thus attends the warriors' march? his son, or one of the glorious line of his posterity? What a hum runs through the attendant train! how lofty his own mien! but the shadow of gloomy night hovers saddening round his head." Father Anchises began, tears gushing forth the while: "Alas, my son! ask not of the heavy grief that those of your blood must bear. Of him the fates shall give but a glimpse to earth, nor suffer him to continue longer. Yes, powers of the sky! Rome's race would have been in your eyes too strong, had a boon like this been its own forever. What groanings of the brave shall be wafted from Mars' broad field to Mars' mighty town! What a funeral, father Tiber, shall thine eyes behold, as thou flowest past that new-built sepulchre! No child of the stock of Ilion shall raise his Latin ancestors to such heights of hope: never while time lasts shall the land of Romulus take such pride in any that she has reared. Woe for the piety, for the ancient faith, for the arm unconquered in battle! Never would foeman have met that armed presence unscathed, marched he on foot into the field or tore with bloody spur the flank of his foaming steed. Child of a nation's sorrow! were there hope of the breaking the tyranny of fate, thou shalt be Marcellus. Bring me handfuls of lilies, that I may strew the grave with their dazzling hues, and crown, if only with these gifts, my young descendant's shade, and perform the vain service of sorrow." Thus they wander here and there through the whole expanse in the broad fields of shadow and take note of all. Soon as Anchises had taken his son from end to end, and fired his mind with the prospect of that glorious history, he then tells the warrior of the battles that he must fight at once, and informs him of the Laurentian tribes and Latinus' town, and how to shun or stand the shock of every peril.

There are two gates of Sleep: the one, as story tells, of horn, supplying a ready exit for true spirits: the other gleaming with the polish of dazzling ivory, but through it the powers below send false dreams to the world above. Thither Anchises, talking thus, conducts his son and the Sibyl, and dismisses them by the gate of ivory. Aeneas traces his way to the fleet and returns to his comrades; then sails along the shore for Caieta's haven. The anchor is cast from the prow: the keels are ranged on the beach.

John Conington

HORACE

QUINTUS HORATIUS FLACCUS (65-8 B. C.) was the most famous Roman lyric poet. Born at Venusia, he later settled in Rome, becoming intimate, like Vergil, with the imperial court. His greatest friend was Vergil himself, whom he calls *half of my life*.

A kind of poet laureate, Horace glorified the state and its Emperor. As a hedonist, he chanted the pleasures of wine, women, and song. He also produced a body of satires. Indulgently but shrewdly he presents a picture of contemporary Roman life, its foibles and weaknesses.

Horace's works include four books of Odes, Carmina: seventeen Epodes: an *Ars Poetica*, a discussion of poetry: and the *Satires*.

TO VIRGIL

Unshamed, unchecked, for one so dear
   We sorrow. Lead the mournful choir,
   Melpomene, to whom thy sire
Gave harp, and song-notes liquid-clear!

Sleeps He the sleep that knows no morn?
   Oh Honour, oh twin-born with Right
   Pure Faith, and Truth that loves the light,
When shall again his like be born?

Many a kind heart for Him makes moan;
   Thine, Virgil, first. But ah! in vain
   Thy love bids heaven restore again
That which it took not as a loan:

Were sweeter lute than Orpheus given
   To thee, did trees thy voice obey;
   The blood revisits not the clay
Which He, with lifted wand, hath driven

Into his dark assemblage, who
   Unlocks not fate to mortal's prayer.
   Hard lot! Yet light their griefs who BEAR
The ills, which they may not undo.

                      C. S. Calverley

TO HIS SLAVE

Persian grandeur I abhor;
　　Linden-wreathed crowns, avaunt:
Boy, I bid thee not explore
　　Woods which latest roses haunt:

Try on naught thy busy craft
　　Save plain myrtle; so arrayed
Thou shalt fetch, I drain, the draught
　　Fitliest 'neath the scant vine-shade.

C. S. Calverley

MODERATION

I scorn and shun the rabble's noise.
　　Abstain from idle talk. A thing
　　That ear hath not yet heard, I sing,
The Muses' priest, to maid and boys.

To Jove the flocks which great kings sway,
　　To Jove great kings allegiance owe.
　　Praise him: he laid the giants low:
All things that are, his nod obey.

This man may plant in broader lines
　　His fruit-trees: that, the pride of race
　　Enlists a candidate for place:
In worth, in fame, a third outshines

His mates; or, thronged with clients, claims
　　Precedence. Even-handed Fate
　　Hath but one law for small and great:
That ample urn holds all men's names.

He o'er whose doomed neck hangs the sword
　　Unsheathed, the dainties of the South
　　Shall lack their sweetness in his mouth:
No note of bird or harpsichord

97

Shall bring him Sleep. Yet Sleep is kind,
  Nor scorns the huts of labouring men;
  The bank where shadows play, the glen
Of Tempe dancing in the wind.

He, who but asks 'Enough,' defies
  Wild waves to rob him of his ease;
  He fears no rude shocks, when he sees
Arcturus set or Haedus rise:

When hailstones lash his vines, or fails
  His farm its promise, now of rains
  And now of stars that parch the plains
Complaining, or unkindly gales.

—In straitened seas the fish are pent;
  For dams are sunk into the deep:
  Pile upon pile the builders heap,
And he, whom earth could not content,

The Master. Yet shall Fear and Hate
  Climb where the Master climbs: nor e'er
  From the armed trireme parts black Care;
He sits behind, the horseman's mate.

And if red marble shall not ease
  The heartache; nor the shell that shines
  Star-bright; nor all Falernum's vines,
All scents that charmed Achaemenes:

Why should I rear me halls of rare
  Design, on proud shafts mounting high?
  Why bid my Sabine vale goodbye
For doubled wealth and doubled care?

                                    C. S. Calverley

THE JUST MAN

The just man's single-purposed mind
  Not furious mobs that prompt to ill
  May move, nor kings' frowns shake his will
Which is as rock; not warrior winds

That keep the seas in wild unrest;
    Nor bolt by Jove's own finger hurled:
    The fragments of a shivered world
Would crash round him still self-possest.

Jove's wandering son reached, thus endowed,
    The fiery bastions of the skies;
    Thus Pollux; with them Caesar lies
Beside his nectar, radiant-browed.

Honoured for this, by tigers drawn
    Rode Bacchus, reining necks before
    Untamed; for this War's horses bore
Quirinus up from Acheron.

To the pleased gods had Juno said
    In conclave: "Troy is in the dust;
    Troy, by a judge accursed, unjust,
And that strange woman prostrated.

"The day Laomedon ignored
    His god-pledged word, resigned to me
    And Pallas ever pure, was she,
Her people, and their traitor lord.

"Now the Greek woman's guilty guest
    Dazzles no more: Priam's perjured sons
    Find not against the mighty ones
Of Greece a shield in Hector's breast:

"And, long drawn out by private jars,
    The war sleeps. Lo! my wrath is o'er:
    And him the Trojan vestal bore
(Sprung of that hated line) to Mars,

"To Mars restore I. His be rest
    In halls of light: by him be drained
    The nectar-bowl, his place obtained
In the calm companies of the blest.

"While betwixt Rome and Ilion raves
    A length of ocean, where they will
    Rise empires for the exiles still:
While Paris's and Priam's graves

"Are trod by kine, and she-wolves breed
    Securely there, unharmed shall stand
    Rome's lustrous Capitol, her hand
Curb with proud laws the trampled Mede.

"Wide-feared, to far-off climes be borne
    Her story; where the central main
    Europe and Libya parts in twain,
Where full Nile laves a land of corn:

"The buried secret of the mine,
    (Best left there) let her dare to spurn,
    Nor unto man's base uses turn
Profane hands laying on things divine.

"Earth's utmost end, where'er it be,
    Let her hosts reach; careering proud
    O'er lands where watery rain and cloud,
Or where wild suns hold revelry.

"But, to the warriors of Rome,
    Tied by this law, such fates are willed;
    That they seek never to rebuild,
Too fond, too bold, their grandsires' home.

"With darkest omens, deadliest strife,
    Shall Troy, raised up again, repeat
    Her history; I the victor-fleet
Shall lead, Jove's sister and his wife.

"Thrice let Apollo rear the wall
    Of brass; and thrice my Greeks shall hew
    The fabric down; thrice matrons rue
In chains their sons,' their husbands' fall."

Ill my light lyre such notes beseem.
    Stay, Muse; nor, wayward still, rehearse
    Sayings of Gods in meagre verse
That may but mar a mighty theme.

C. S. Calverley

100

Come, Music's Queen, from yonder sphere:
    Bid thy harp speak: sing high and higher —
    Or take Apollo's lute and lyre,
And play, and cease not. Did ye hear?

Or is some sweet Delusion mine?
    I seem to hear, to stray aside
    Groves that are holy; whither glide
Fair brooks, where breezes are benign.

Me, on Mount Vultur once — a lad,
    O'ercome with sleepiness and play —
    (I had left Apulia miles away,
That nursed me) doves from Fayland clad

With leaflets. Marvelled all whose nest
    Is Acherontia's cliff; who fell
    The Bantine forest trees, or dwell
On rich Ferentium's lowly breast;

How I could sleep, unharmed by bear
    Or dusky serpent. There I lay,
    In myrtle hid and holy bay,
A lusty babe, the Great ones' care.

Yours, Sisters, yours, the Sabine hills
    I climb: at cool Praeneste yours,
    Yours by flat Tibur, or the shores
Of Baiae. I have loved your rills,

Your choirs: for this Philippi's slaughter,
    When fled our captains, harmed not me;
    I died not 'neath the cursed tree,
Nor sank in Palinurus' water: —

Be with me still: and, fears at rest,
    I'll launch on raving Bosphorus, stand
    Upon Assyria's sultry sand,
With Britons mate, who slay the guest,

Sit down with Spaniard, wild to sate
    Their thirst with horses' blood: or roam
    Far o'er quivered Scythian's home
By Tanais' banks, inviolate.

—High Caesar ye (his warn-torn braves
    Safe housed at last in thorpe and town)
    Asking to lay his labours down,
Make welcome in Pierian caves.

—Kind ones! Ye give sweet counsel, love
    Its givers. We know how He slew
    The Titans, and their hideous crew,
Hurling his thunder from above,

Who the dull earth, the windy sea,
    The cities, and the realms of woe,
    And gods above, and men below,
Rules, and none other, righteously.

In truth Jove's terrors had been great;
    So bold a front those warriors shewed
    These brethren, on his dark abode
Striving to pile all Pelion's weight.

But Mimas and Typhoeus were
    As naught, and huge Porphyrion too,
    And Rhoecus, and the arm that threw,
Undaunted, tree-trunks through the air;

With ringing shield when Pallas met
    Their rush. Hot Vulcan too stood there,
    And Juno sage, and he, who ne'er
Eased from the bow his shoulder yet;

Who bathes in pure Castalian dew
    His locks; in Lycian bowers adored,
    And his own woods, — Apollo, lord
Of Delos and of Patara too.

—Brute force its own bulk foils. But force
    By reason led, the gods make great

102

And greater; while the strong they hate,
Whose brain revolves each evil course.

This Gyas, hundred-armed, could tell;
    And that Orion, who with wild
    Violence assailed the Undefiled,
And by Diana's arrows fell.

— Earth, grieved, her monster brood entombed:
    Mourns them, by Jove's bolts hurled to hell.
    Still living fires 'neath Aetna dwell,
Yet Aetna still is unconsumed:

O'er wanton Tityus' heart the bird,
    That miscreant's gaoler, still doth hover;
    And still Pirithous, lawless lover,
Do thrice a hundred fetters gird.

C. S. Calverley

DEGENERATE MAN

Thou'lt rue thy fathers' sins, not thine,
    Till built the temples be, replaced
    The statues, foul and smoke-defaced, —
Roman, — and reared each tottering shrine.

Thou rul'st but under heaven's hand.
    Thence all beginnings come, all ends.
    Neglected, mark what woes it sends
On this our miserable land.

Twice Pacorus and Monaeses foiled
    Our luckless onset: huge their glee,
    When to their necklaces they see
Hanging the wealth of Rome despoiled.

Dacian and Aethiop nigh laid low
    Our state, with civil feuds o'errun;
    One with his fleet dismayed her, one
Smote her with arrows from his bow.

103

A guilty age polluted first
    Our beds, hearths, families: from that source
    Derived, the foul stream, gathering force,
O'er the broad land, a torrent, burst.

Pleased, now, the maiden learns to move
    To soft Greek airs: already knows —
    Fresh from the nursery — how to pose
Her graceful limbs; and dreams of love:

Next, while her lord drinks deep, invited
    Her gallants in: nor singles one,
    Into whose guilty arms to run,
Stealthy and swift, when dim the lights:

No! in her lord's sight up springs she:
    Alike at some small tradesman's beck,
    As his who walks a Spanish deck
And barters wealth for infamy.

— Were those lads of such parents bred
    Who dyed the seas with Punic blood?
    Pyrrhus, Antiochus withstood,
And Hannibal, the nation's dread?

Rude soldiers' sons, a rugged kind,
    They brake the soil with Sabine spade:
    Or shouldered stakes their axe had made
To a right rigorous mother's mind.

What time the shadows of the rocks
    Change, as the sun's departing car
    Sends on the hours that sweetest are,
And men unyoke the wearied ox.

Time mars not — what? A spoiler he.
    Our sires were not so brave a breed
    As their sires: we, a worse, succeed;
To raise up sons more base than we.

C. S. Calverley

FOUNTAIN OF BANDUSIA

Bandusia, stainless mirror of the sky!
Thine is the flower-crown'd bowl, for thee shall die,
    When dawns yon sun, the kid;
    Whose horns, half-seen, half-hid,

Challenge to dalliance or to strife — in vain!
Soon must the firstling of the wild herd be slain,
    And those cold springs of thine
    With blood incarnadine.

Fierce glows the Dogstar, but his fiery beam
Toucheth not thee: still grateful thy cool stream
    To labour-wearied ox,
    Or wanderer from the flocks:

And henceforth thou shalt be a royal fountain:
My harp shall tell how from yon cavernous mountain,
    Where the brown oak grows tallest,
    All babblingly thou fallest.

C. S. Calverley

TO A FAUN

Wooer of young Nymphs who fly thee,
    Lightly o'er my sunlit lawn,
Trip, and go, nor injured by thee
    Be my weanling herds, O Faun:

If the kid his doomed head bows, and
    Brims with wine the loving cup,
When the year is full; and thousand
    Scents from altars hoar go up.

Each flock in the rich grass gambols
    When the month comes which is thine;
And the happy village rambles
    Fieldward with the idle kine:

Lambs play on, the wolf their neighbour:
    Wild woods deck thee with their spoil;
And with glee the sons of labour
    Stamp upon their foe soil.

C. S. Calverley

TO LYCE

Lyce, the gods have listened to my prayer:
The gods have listened, Lyce. Thou art grey,
    And still would'st thou seem fair;
    Still unshamed drink, and play,

And, wine-flushed, woo slow-answering Love with weak
Shrill pipings. With young Chia He doth dwell,
    Queen of the harp; her cheek
    Is his sweet citadel: —

He marked the withered oak, and on he flew
Intolerant; shrank from Lyce grim and wrinkled,
    Whose teeth are ghastly-blue,
    Whose temples snow-besprinkled: —

Not purple, not the brightest gem that glows,
Brings back to her the years which, fleeting fast,
    Time hath once shut in those
    Dark annals of the Past.

Oh, where is all thy loveliness? soft hue
And motions soft? Oh, what of Her doth rest,
    Her, who breathed love, who drew
    My heart out of my breast?

Fair, and far-famed, and subtly sweet, thy face
Ranked next to Cinara's. But to Cinara fate
    Gave but a few years' grace;
    And lets live, all too late,

Lyce, the rival of the beldam crow:
That fiery youth may see with scornful brow
    The torch that long ago
    Beamed bright, a cinder now.

C. S. Calverley

106

TIBULLUS

ALBUS TIBULLUS (C. 48-19 B.C.) was a poet who preferred the pastoral tranquillity of rusticity to the appeals of social life, public affairs, and political intrigues. His wealth enabled him to live alternately in Rome and at his country estate. Poet laureate of the literary coterie of his contemporaries, he had a brief experience in the East, in the entourage of Messala.

His poetic corpus consists of four books of Elegies. Like Catullus, Tibullus had an infatuation for a faithless woman of a low social level: called, in his poems, Delia. Although his amours with Delia and others form the theme of most of Tibullus' elegiac pieces, there are glimpses of rural rites, seasonal ceremonials, and the attractions of country life.

RUSTIC PLEASURE

The glittering ore let others vainly heap,
    O'er fertile vales extend th'enclosing mound;
With dread of neighb'ring foes forsake their sleep,
    And start aghast at every trumpet's sound.

Me humbler scenes delight, and calmer days;
    A tranquil life fair poverty secure!
Then boast, my hearth, a small but cheerful blaze,
    And, riches grasp who will, let me be poor.

Nor yet be hope a stranger to my door,
    But o'er my roof, bright goddess, still preside!
With many a bounteous autumn heap my floor,
    And swell my vats with must, a purple tide.

My tender vines I'll plant with early care,
    And choicest apples with a skilful hand;
Nor blush, a rustic, oft to guide the share,
    Or goad the tardy ox along the land.

Let me, a simple swain, with honest pride,
    If chance a lambkin from its dam should roam,
Or sportful kid, the little wanderer chide,
    And in my bosom bear exulting home.

Here Pales I bedew with milky showers,
    Lustrations yearly for my shepherd pay,
Revere each antique stone bedeck'd with flowers
    That bounds the field, or points the doubtful way.

My grateful fruits, the earliest of the year,
    Before the rural god shall duly wait.
From Ceres' gifts I'll cull each browner ear,
    And hang a wheaten wreath before her gate.

The ruddy god shall save my fruit from stealth,
    And far away each little plunderer scare:
And you, the guardians once of ampler wealth,
    My household gods, shall still my off'rings share.

My num'rous herds that wanton'd o'er the mead
    The choicest fatling then could richly yield;
Now scarce I spare a little lamb to bleed
    A mighty victim for my scanty field.

And yet a lamb shall bleed, while, ranged around,
    The village youths shall stand in order meet,
With rustic hymns, ye gods, your praise resound,
    And future crops and future wines entreat.

Then come, ye power, nor scorn my frugal board,
    Nor yet the gifts clean earthen bowls convey;
With these the first of men the gods adored,
    And form'd their simple shape of ductile clay.

My little flock, ye wolves, ye robbers, spare,
    Too mean a plunder to deserve your toil;
Or wealthier herds the nightly theft prepare;
    There seek a nobler prey, and richer spoil.

For treasured wealth, nor stores of golden wheat,
    The horde of frugal sires, I vainly call;
A little farm be mine, a cottage neat,
    And wonted couch where balmy sleep may fall.

"What joy to hear the tempest howl in vain,
    And clasp a fearful mistress to my breast;

108

Or lull'd to slumber by the beating rain,
    Secure and happy sink at last to rest."

These joys be mine! — O grant me only these,
    And give to others bags of shining gold,
Whose steely heart can brave the boist'rous seas,
    The storm wide-wasting, or the stiff'ning cold.

Content with little, I would rather stay
    Than spend long months amid the wat'ry waste;
In cooling shades elude the scorching ray,
    Beside some fountain's gliding waters placed.

Oh perish rather all that's rich and rare,
    The diamond quarry, and the golden vein,
Than that my absence cost one precious tear,
    Or give some gentle maid a moment's pain.

With glittering spoils, Messala, gild thy dome,
    Be thine the noble task to lead the brave;
A lovely foe me captive holds at home,
    Chain'd to her scornful gate, a watchful slave.

Inglorious post! — and yet I heed not fame:
    Th'applause of crowds for Delia I'd resign:
To live with thee I'd bear the coward's name,
    Nor 'midst the scorn of nations once repine.

With thee to live I'd mock the ploughman's toil.
    Or on some lonely mountain tend my sheep;
At night I'd lay me on the flinty soil,
    And happy 'midst thy dear embraces sleep.

What drooping lover heeds the Tyrian bed,
    While the long night is pass'd with many a sigh;
Nor softest down with richest carpets spread,
    Nor whisp'ring rills can close the weeping eye.

Of threefold iron were his rugged frame,
    Who, when he might thy yielding heart obtain,
Could yet attend the calls of empty fame,
    Or follow arms in quest of sordid gain.

Unenvied let him drive the vanquish'd host,
    Through captive lands his conquering armies lead;
Unenvied wear the robe with gold emboss'd,
    And guide with solemn state his foaming steed.

Oh may I view thee with life's parting ray,
    And thy dear hand with dying ardour press:
Sure thou wilt weep — and on thy lover's clay,
    With breaking heart, print many a tender kiss!

Sure thou wilt weep — and woes unutter'd feel,
    When on the pile thou seest thy lover laid!
For well I know, nor flint, nor ruthless steel,
    Can arm the breast of such a gentle maid.

From the sad pomp, what youth, what pitying fair,
    Returning slow, can tender tears refrain?
O Delia, spare thy cheeks, thy tresses spare,
    Nor give my ling'ring shade a world of pain.

But now while smiling hours the Fates bestow,
    Let love, dear maid, our gentle hearts unite!
Soon death will come and strike the fatal blow;
    Unseen his head, and veil'd in shades of night.

Soon creeping age will bow the lover's frame,
    And tear the myrtle chaplet from his brow:
With hoary locks ill suits the youthful flame,
    The soft persuasion, or the ardent vow.

Now the fair queen of gay desire is ours,
    And lends our follies an indulgent smile:
'Tis lavish youth's t'enjoy the frolic hours,
    The wanton revel and the midnight broil.

Your chief, my friends and fellow-soldiers, I
    To these light wars will lead you boldly on:
Far hence, ye trumpets, sounds, and banners fly;
    To those who covet wounds and fame begone.

And bear them fame and wounds; and riches bear;
    There are that fame and wounds and riches prize.
For me, while I possess one plenteous year,
    I'll wealth and meagre want alike despise.

James Grainger

With wine, more wine, my recent pains deceive,
Till creeping slumber send a soft reprieve:
Asleep, take heed no whisper stirs the air,
For waked, my boy, I wake to heart-felt care.
Now is my Delia watch'd by ruthless spies,
And the gate, bolted, all access denies.
Relentless gate! may storms of wind and rain
With mingled violence avenge my pain!
May forky thunders, hurl'd by Jove's red hand,
Burst every bolt, and shatter every band!
Ah no! rage turns my brain; the curse recall;
On me, devoted, let the thunder fall!
Then recollect my many wreaths of yore,
How oft you've seen me weep, insensate door!
No longer then our interview delay,
And as you open let no noise betray.

In vain I plead! — dare then my Delia rise!
Love aids the dauntless, and will blind your spies!
Those who the godhead's soft behests obey,
Steal from their pillows unobserv'd away;
On tip-toe traverse unobserv'd the floor;
The key turn noiseless, and unfold the door:
In vain the jealous each precaution take,
Their speaking fingers assignations make.
Nor will the god impart to all his aid:
Love hates the fearful, hates the lazy maid:

But through sly windings and unpractis'd ways
His bold knight-errants to their wish conveys:
For those whom he with expectation fires
No ambush frightens, and no labour tires;
Sacred the dangers of the dark they dare,
No robbers stop them, and no bravoes scare.
Though wintry tempests howl, by love secure,
The howling tempest I with ease endure:
No watching hurts me, if my Delia smile,
Soft turn the gate, and beckon me the while.

She's mine. Be blind, ye ramblers of the night,
Lest angry Venus snatch your guilty sight:

The goddess bids her votaries' joys to be
From every casual interruption free:
With prying steps alarm us not, retire,
Nor glare your torches, nor our names inquire:
Or if ye know, deny, by heaven above,
Nor dare divulge the privacies of love.
From blood and seas vindictive Venus sprung,
And sure destruction waits the babbling tongue!
Nay, should they prate, you, Delia, need not fear;
Your lord (a sorceress swore) should give no ear!
By potent spells she cleaves the sacred ground,
And shuddering spectres wildly roam around!
I've seen her tear the planets from the sky!
Seen lightning backward at her bidding fly!
She calls? from blazing pyres the corse descends,
And, re-enliven'd, clasps his wondering friends!
The friends she gathers with a magic yell,
Then with aspersions frights them back to hell!
She wills, — glad summer gilds the frozen pole!
She wills, — in summer wintry tempests roll!
She knows ('tis true) Medea's awful spell!
She knows to vanquish the fierce guards of hell!
To me she gave a charm for lovers meet,
("Spit thrice, my fair, and thrice the charm repeat.")
Us in soft dalliance should your lord surprise,
By this imposed on he'd renounce his eyes!
But bless no rival, or th'affair is known;
This incantation me befriends alone.
Nor stopp'd she here; but swore, if I'd agree,
By charms or herbs to set thy lover free.
With dire lustrations she began the rite!
(Serenely shone the planet of the night,)
The magic gods she call'd with hellish sound,
A sable sacrifice distain'd the ground —
I stopp'd the spell: I must not, cannot part:
I begg'd her aid to gain a mutual heart.

James Grainger

UNFAITHFUL DELIA

Love still invites me with a smiling eye!
Beneath his smiles what pains and anguish lie!

Yet since the gods, dread power, must yield to thee,
What laurels canst thou gain from conquering me?
Me Delia loved; but by thy subtle wiles,
The fair, in secret, on another smiles:
That my suspicion's false, 'tis true, she swears;
And backs her imprecations with her tears!
False fair, your oaths and Syren tears refrain;
Your Syren tears and oaths no credit gain;
For when your lord suspected me of yore,
As much you wept, as many oaths you swore.

Yet wherefore blame I love? the blame is mine;
I, wretched I, first taught her to design!
I first instructed her her spies to foil;
Back on myself my wanton arts recoil:
Herbs of rare energy my skill supplied,
All marks of too-fond gallantry to hide!
More artful now, alone the wanton lies;
And new pretexts her cozening brains devise.

Uncautious lord of a too cunning spouse!
Admittance grant me, she shall keep her vows!
Be warn'd, my friend, observe her when her tongue
Commends in wanton phrase the gay-dress'd young;
Oh let her not her heaving bosom bare,
Exposed to every fop's immodest stare.
When leaning on the board, with flowing wine,
She seems to draw some inconsiderate line;
Take heed, take heed, (I know the warning true,)
These random lines assign an interview.
Nor let your wife to fanes so frequent roam,
A modest wife's best temple is at home:
But if your prohibitions all are vain,
Give me the hint, I'll dodge her to the fane;
What though the goddess snatch my curious sight,
I'll bring her wanton privacies to light.

Some gem she wore, I'd oft pretend to view
But squeez'd her fingers unperceiv'd of you:
Oft with full racy bowls I seal'd your eyes,
Water my bev'rage, and obtain'd the prize.
Yet since I tell, forgive the pranks I play'd,
Love prompted all, and Love must be obey'd!

113

Nay, 'twas at me (be now the truth avow'd)
Your watchful mastiff used to bark so loud;
But now some other, with insidious wait,
Intent observes each creaking of your gate,
At which, whoever of the house appears,
Passing, the mien of quick despatch he wears;
But comes again the minute they remove,
And coughs, sure signal of impatient love!

What boots, though marriage gave a wife so fair,
If careless you, or she eludes your care?
While men are artful, and your wife can feign,
Vain are your brazen bolts, your mastiffs vain.

Cold to the raptures of the genial bed,
She lays the fault upon an aching head:
'Tis false; the wanton for some other sighs;
From this her coolness, this her aches arise.

Then, then be warn'd, intrust her to my care;
Whips, chains I laugh at, if you grant my prayer.
"Hence, from my ward, ye sparkish essenced beaus;
Illegal love oft springs from essenced clothes."
Where'er she walks, not distant I'll attend,
And guard your honour from the casual friend!
"Off, gallants, off: for so the gods ordain,
So the dread priestess in unerring strain!"
(When holy fury fires the frantic dame,
She mocks all torture, and exults in flame;
Her snow-white arms and heaving breast she tears;
And with the gushing gore Bellona smears;
Deep in her side she plants the glittering sword;
And the dread goddess prompts each fateful word.)
"Ye youths, beware, nor touch whom Cupid guards,
Unpunish'd none attempt his gentle wards:
As my blood flows, and as these ashes fly,
Their wealth shall perish, and their manhood die."

She menaced, then the fair with dreadful pain:
E'en were you guilty, may her threats be vain:
Not on your own account; your mother's age,
Your worthy mother deprecates my rage:
When Love and Fortune smiled, her gentle aid

114

Oft me conducted to the blooming maid;
My footsteps, wakeful, from afar she knew,
Unbarr'd the gate, nor fear'd the nightly dew:
Half of my life's long thread I'd pleas'd resign,
My sweet conductress, could I lengthen thine!
Still, still, though much abus'd, I Delia prize:
She's still thy daughter, and enchants my eyes.

Yet though no coy cimarr invest the fair,
Nor vestal fillet bind her auburn hair;
Teach her what decent modesty requires,
To crown my fire, alone, with equal fires.
Me too confine; and if, in wanton praise
Of other maids, my tongue luxuriant strays,
Let thy suspicion then no limits know,
Insult me, spurn me, as thy greatest foe!
But if your jealousies are built in air,
And patient love your usage cannot bear;
What wrath may perpetrate, my soul alarms,
Nor yet be chaste from mean unamorous fear;
Be still most modest when I am not near.

For those, whom neither wit nor worth secure,
Grow old, unpitied; palsied, worthless, poor;
Yet with each servile drudgery they strive,
To keep their being's wretchedness alive!
The gay regard their woe with laughing eyes;
Swear they deserve it, and absolve the skies!
Nor Venus less exults! "May such a fate,
(From heaven she prays) upon th'inconstant wait."

The same my wish! but oh may we two prove,
In age, a pattern of unalter'd love!

James Grainger

AMBARVALIA: A COUNTRY FESTIVAL

Attend! and favour! as our sires ordain,
The fields we lustrate, and the rising grain:
Come, Bacchus, and thy horns with grapes surround;
Come, Ceres, with thy wheaten garland crown'd;

This hallow'd day suspend each swain his toil,
Rest let the plough, and rest th'uncultured soil:
Unyoke the steer, his racks heap high with hay,
And deck with wreaths his honest front to-day.
Be all your thoughts to this grand work applied!
And lay, ye thrifty fair, your wool aside!
Hence I command you mortals from the rite,
Who spent in amorous blandishment the night,
The vernal powers in chastity delight.
But come, ye pure, in spotless garbs array'd!
For you the solemn festival is made;
Come! follow thrice the victim round the lands!
In running water purify your hands!
See! to the flames the willing victim come.
Ye swains with olive crown'd, be dumb! be dumb!
"From ills, O sylvan gods, our limits shield,
To-day we purge the farmer and the field;
Oh let no weeds destroy the rising grain;
By no fell prowler be the lambkin slain;
So shall the swain dread penury no more,
But gaily smiling o'er his plenteous store,
With liberal hand shall larger billets bring,
Heap the broad hearth, and hail the genial spring.
His numerous bond-slaves all in goodly rows,
With wicker huts your altars shall enclose.
That done, they'll cheerly laugh, and dance, and play,
And praise your goodness in their uncouth lay."

The gods assent! see! see! those entrails show
That heaven approves of what is done below!
Now quaff Falernian, let my Chian wine,
Pour'd from the cask, in massy goblets shine!
Drink deep, my friends; all, all, be madly gay,
'Twere irreligion not to reel to-day!
Health to Messala, every peasant toast,
And not a letter of his name be lost!

O come, my friend, whom Gallic triumphs grace,
Thou noblest splendour of an ancient race;
Thou whom the arts all emulously crown,
Sword of the state, and honour of the gown;
My theme is gratitude, inspire my lays!
Oh be my Genius! while I strive to praise

The rural deities, the rural plain,
The use of foodful corn they taught the swain.
They taught man first the social hut to raise,
And thatch it o'er with turf, or leafy sprays:
They first to tame the furious bull essay'd,
And on rude wheels the rolling carriage laid,
Man left his savage ways; the garden glow'd,
Fruits not their own admiring trees bestow'd,
While through the thirsty ground meandering runnels flow'd.
There bees of sweets despoil the breathing spring,
And to their cells the dulcet plunder bring.
The ploughman first to soothe the toilsome day,
Chanted in measur'd feet his sylvan lay:
And, seed-time o'er, he first in blithesome vein,
Piped to his household gods the hymning strain.
Then first the press with purple wine o'erran,
And cooling water made it fit for man.
The village lad first made a wreath of flowers
To deck in spring the tutelary powers:
Blest be the country, yearly there the plain
Yields, when the dog-star burns, the golden grain;

Thence too thy chorus, Bacchus, first began,
The painted clown first laid the tragic plan.
A goat, the leader of the shaggy throng,
The village sent it, recompensed the song.
There too the sheep his woolly treasure wears;
There too the swain his woolly treasure shears;
This to the thirsty dame long work supplies;
The distaff hence, and basket took their rise.
Hence too the various labours of the loom,
Thy praise, Minerva, and Arachne's doom!
Mid mountain herds Love first drew vital air,
Unknown to man, and man had nought to fear;
'Gainst herds, his bow th'unskilful archer drew;
Ah my pierced heart, an archer now too true!
Now herds may roam untouch'd, 'tis Cupid's joy,
The brave to vanquish, and to fix the coy.
The youth whose heart the soft emotion feels,
Nor sighs for wealth, nor waits at grandeur's heels;
Age fired by Love is touch'd by shame no more,
But blabs its follies at the fair one's door!
Led by soft Love, the tender, trembling fair

Steals to her swain, and cheats suspicion's care,
With outstretched arms she wins her darkling way,
And tiptoe listens that no noise betray!

Ah wretched those on whom dread Cupid frowns!
How happy they whose mutual choice he crowns!
Will Love partake the banquet of the day?
O come — but throw thy burning shafts away.

Ye swains, begin to mighty Love the song,
Your songs, ye swains, to mighty Love belong.
Breathe out aloud your wishes for my fold,
Your own soft vows in whispers may be told.
But hark! loud mirth and music fire the crowd —
Ye now may venture to request aloud!

Pursue your sports; night mounts her curtain'd wain;
The dancing stars compose her filial train;
Black muffled sleep steals on with silent pace,
And dreams flit past, imaginations race.

James Grainger

LOVE'S BONDS

I see my slavery, and a mistress near;
    Oh, freedom of my fathers! fare thee well!
A slavery wretched, and a chain severe,
    Nor Love remits the bonds that o'er me fell.

How have I then deserved consuming pain?
    Or for what sin am I of flames the prey?
I burn, ah me! I burn in every vein!
    Take, cruel girl, oh take thy torch away!

Oh! how to'scape this agonizing heat,
    Might I a stone on icy mountains lie!
Stand a bleak rock by wreaking billows beat,
    And swept by madding whirlwinds of the sky!

Bitter the day, and ah! the nightly shade;
    And all my hours in venom'd stream have roll'd;

118

No elegies, no lays of Phoebus, aid;
    With hollow palm she craves the tinkling gold.

Away, ye Muses! if ye serve not Love:
    I, not to sing of battles, woo your strain;
How walks the bright-hair'd sun the heavens above,
    Or turns the full-orb'd moon her steeds again.

By verse I seek soft access to my fair;
    Away, ye Muses! with the useless lore;
Through blood and pillage I must gifts prepare;
    Or weep, thrown prostrate at her bolted door.

Suspended spoils I'll snatch from pompous fanes;
    But Venus first shall violated be;
She prompts the sacrilege, who forged the chains;
    And gave that nymph insatiable to me.

Perish the wretch! who culls the emerald green,
    Or paints the snowy fleece with Tyrian red!
Through filmy Coan robes her limbs are seen,
    And India's pearls gleam lucid from her head.

'Tis pamper'd avarice thus corrupts the fair;
    The key is turn'd; the mastiff guards the door.
The guard's disarm'd, if large the bribe you bear;
    The dog is hush'd; the key withstands no more.

Alas! that e'er a heavenly form should grace
    The nymph that pants with covetous desires!
Hence tears and clamorous brawls, and sore disgrace
    E'en to the name of love, that bliss inspires.

For thee, that shutt'st the lover from thy door,
    Foil'd by a price, the gilded hire of shame,
May tempests scatter this thy ill-got ore,
    Strewn on the winds, or melted in the flame.

May climbing fires thy mansion's roof devour,
    And youths gaze glad, nor throw the quenching wave;
May none bemoan thee at thy dying hour,
    None pay the mournful tribute to thy grave.

119

But she, unbribed, unbought, yet melting kind,
    May she a hundred years, unfading, bloom;
Be wept, while on the flaming pile reclined,
    And yearly garlands twine her pillar'd tomb.

Some ancient lover, with his locks of grey,
    Honouring the raptures that his youth had blest,
Shall hang the wreath, and slow-departing say,
    "Sleep! — and may earth lie light upon thy breast!"

Truth prompts my tongue; but what can truth avail?
    The love her laws prescribe must now be mine;
My ancestor's loved groves I set to sale —
    My household gods, your title I resign!

Nay — Circe's juice, Medea's drugs, each plant
    Oh Thessaly, whence dews of poison fall; —
Let but my Nemesis's soft smile enchant,
    Then let her mix the cup — I'll drink them all.

C. A. Elton

CONTEMPT OF WEALTH

Why should my vows, Neaera! fill the sky,
    And the sweet incense blend with many a prayer?
Not forth to issue on the gazing eye
    From marble vestibule of mansion fair.

Not that unnumber'd steers may turn my field,
    And the kind earth its copious harvests lend:
But that with thee the joys of life may yield
    Their full satiety, till life has end.

And, when my days have measured out their light,
    And, naked, I must Lethe's bark survey;
I on thy breast may close my fading sight,
    And feel my dying age fall soft away.

For what avails the pile of massive gold:
    What the rich glebe by thousand oxen plough'd?
Roofs, that the Phrygian pillars vast uphold,
    Taenarian shafts, Carystian columns proud?

Mansions, whose groves might seem some temple's wood;
   The gilded cornice, or the marble floor?
Pearls glean'd from sands of Persia's ruddy flood,
   Sidon's red fleece, and all the crowd adore?

For envy clings to these: the crowd still gaze,
   Charm'd with false shows, and love with little skill:
Not wealth the cares of human souls allays,
   Since fortune shifts their happiness at will.

With thee, O sweet Neaera! want were bliss;
   Without thee I the gifts of kings disdain:
Oh clear the light! blest day, that brings me this;
   Thrice blest, that yields thee to my arms again.

If to my vows for this thy sweet return,
   Love's god, kind, listen, nor avert his ear;
Then Lydia's river, rolling gold, I'll spurn:
   Kingdoms and wealth of worlds shall poor appear.

Seek these who may: a frugal fare be mine:
   With my dear consort let me safely dwell:
Come, Juno! to my timid prayers incline.
   Come, Venus! wafted on thy scallop'd shell.

But, if the Sister Fates refuse my boon,
   Who draw the future day with swift-spun thread,
Hell to its gulfy rivers call me soon,
   To sluggish lurid lakes, where haunt the dead.

C. A. Elton

LOVER

Ah me! how hard, the mask of joy to wear
And feign the jest, with thoughts of brooding care!
Ill suits the smile with looks that joy belie,
Or wine's gay wit with mental misery.
Fond wretch! what boots complaint? vile cares, away!
Know, father Bacchus hates the mournful lay.
So thou, O Cretan maid! didst once deplore

121

A perjured tongue, left lonely on the shore,
As skill'd Catullus tells, who paints in song
The ingrate Theseus, Ariadne's wrong.
Take warning, youths! oh blest! whoe'er shall know
The art to profit by another's woe.
Let not the hanging nymph's embrace deceive,
Nor protestations of base tongues believe:
Not though the traitress by her eyes may swear
Her Juno, Venus; for no faith is there.
Jove laughs at lovers' perjuries; the gales
Of heaven disperse these light protesting tales.
Why, then, so oft the treacherous nymph arraign?
Begone sad words! begone the pensive strain!
How would I rest whole nights within thy bower!
And share whole days thy every waking hour!
Faithless! with undeserved disdain severe!
Faithless! yet faithless as thou art, most dear.
Bacchus the Naiad loves: quick — loitering slave!
Temper the mellow wine with Martian wave:
No — if the giddy nymph my board has fled,
And fickle sought some unknown lover's bed:
I will not through the night in sighings pine:
Boy! mix it pure: come — dash it strong with wine:
Nay — long ago the Syrian nard should breathe
Round my moist brow, and flowers my hair inwreath.

                                    C. A. Elton

PRAISE OF SULPICIA

Mars! on thy calends, fair Sulpicia see,
Deck'd in her gay habiliments for thee.
Come — Venus will forgive: descend, if wise:
To view her beauties leave thyself the skies.
But oh beware! lest, gazing on her charms,
Fierce as thou art, thou drop thy shameful arms.
For from her eyes, when gods are Cupid's aim,
He lights two lamps, that burn with keenest flame.
In every act, and step, and motion seen,
Grace stealthy glides, and forms her easy mien:
Graceful her locks in loose disorder spread;

Graceful the smoother braid that binds her head:
She charms, when Tyrian purple folds her limbs;
She charms, when white her snowy drapery swims:
Thus blithe Vertumnus in th'Olympian hall
Shifts all his thousand shapes, and charms in all.
She only of her sex deserves the grain
Of wool twice dipp'd in Tyrus' crimson stain:
Hers to possess whate'er the Arab reaps
Of harvest shrubs, whence liquid fragrance weeps:
Whatever pearls the sable Indian's hand
Culls on his eastern ocean's ruddy sand.
Her on these calends, O ye Muses! sing:
Let thy shell'd harp, exulting Phoebus! ring:
The festal rite let future years prolong:
No nymph more worthy of your choral song.

C. A. Elton

THE POET TO HIS MISTRESS

"Never shall woman's smile have power
    To win me from those gentle charms!"
Thus swore I in that happy hour
    When Love first gave them to my arms.

And still alone thou charm'st my sight—
    Still, though our city proudly shine
With forms and faces fair and bright,
    I see none fair or bright but thine.

Would thou wert fair for only me,
    And couldst no heart but mine allure!
To all men else unpleasing be,
    So shall I feel my prize secure.

Oh, love like mine ne'er wants the zest
    Of others' envy, others' praise;
But in its silence safely blest,
    Broods o'er a bliss it ne'er betrays.

123

Charm of my life! by whose sweet power
    All cares are hush'd, all ills subdued —
My light in ev'n the darkest hour,
    My crowd in deepest solitude.

No; not though heaven itself sent down
    Some maid of more than heavenly charms,
With bliss undreamt thy bard to crown,
    Would I for her forsake those arms.

T. Moore

POET'S DREAMS

Now heaven forfend! — nor bring those dreams to light
That haunted the pale close of yesternight!
Away! far hence, ye false, vain shadows, fly!
Hope not to win my fond credulity:
From gods alone unerring warnings come,
When seers in entrails read the future doom.
Dreams, like the cheating shades of night, we find,
Play with false fears upon the timid mind.
Such midnight omens superstition sees,
Which crackling salt and holy meal appease.
But whether truth to others shadow'd seem
In the seer's warning, or the lying dream;
At least may Luna chase these fears in air,
Which my poor heart has ill deserved to bear:
If pure my conscience from crime's deepening dye,
Nor e'er my tongue blasphemed the powers on high.

Night now had measured heaven's caerulean steep
With sable steeds; her laved wheels touch'd the deep
But sleep, that soothes the wretched, soothed not me;
Still from an anxious chamber prompt to flee:
Till, when the sun peep'd faint from eastern skies,
Late slumber settled on my languid eyes.
When lo! a youth was seen my floor to tread,
Chaste laurels nodding round his wreathed head.
No form so fair adorn'd the age of gold:
No form so fair could spring from human mould:
Loose o'er his tapering neck the ringlets flew,

That breathing myrtle dropp'd with Tyrian dew:
White as the moon did his complexion show,
And tinting crimson flush'd his skin of snow.
As virgin cheeks with tender blushes dyed,
When to the youth consents the yielded bride:
As girls with purple amranth lilies spread;
As apples pale catch autumn's streaky red.
A sweeping robe around his ankles trail'd;
His dazzling limbs the gorgeous vesture veil'd:
On his left side a harp suspended hung,
Of precious shell, with gold resplendent strung:
Soft, at his first approach, the chord he smote
With ivory quill, with sweet-breathed vocal note:
His fingers and his voice preluded clear,
Then sweet, but sad, his accents thrill'd my ear.
"Hail, care of heaven! the bard of spotless love
Apollo, Bacchus, and the Nine approve:
But ah! not Bacchus, not the Nine, have power
To read the shadows of the future hour:
To me the father gave the laws of doom,
The mystic volume of events to come.
What I, unerring prophet, tell, receive:
The god's true lips shall speak; do thou believe.
She whom thou dear hast held, and loved to prize,
Dear as a daughter in her mother's eyes;
Dear as the virgin when, with blushing charms,
She sinks within her panting bridegroom's arms;
For whom thy voice has wearied heaven with prayer;
For whom thy feverish days are cross'd with care;
And who, when sleep its umber'd mantle throws,
With nightly phantoms haunts thy vain repose:
She — fair Neaera — in thy verse divine,
Inconstant sighs for other arms than thine;
Far other wishes heave her sinful breast,
Nor in her chaster home is Neaera blest.
Ah, cruel sex! ah woman! faithless name!
Be every man-deceiver's portion, shame!
Yet may she bend; for mutable the race:
Do thou, still patient, stretch thy true embrace.
Fell Love has taught the hardest toils to dare:
Fell Love has taught e'en cruel stripes to bear:
I once Admetus' snowy heifers fed;
Not vain the tale in sportful fictions read:

No more my hand the harp sonorous play'd;
No more my voice responsive cadence made;
But on a flimsy oat I whisper'd love:
E'en I, Latona's son, the son of Jove.
Ah! youth! thou know'st not love! unless thou bear
A thorny pillow, an unfeeling fair.
Yet doubt not, nor despair: but soft complain:
Hard hearts at soft complaint have turn'd again.
If true my temple's oracles, now go:
This in my name let false Neaera know:
'Phoebus himself insures this marriage tie:
Here blest, no longer for another sigh'."

He said: the idle slumber took its flight:
Ah! from such ills I turn my loathing sight:
I dare not think thy vows are vow'd from me;
That sins can harbour'd in thy bosom be:
For not from ocean's depths thy being came,
Nor fierce Chimaera breathed thee forth in flame:
Not hell's grim dog with viperous brood o'erhung,
Monster of triple head and triple tongue;
Not Scylla, twi-form'd maid, thy nature gave,
Around whose waist the dogs engendering rave;
No lioness produced thee in the wild,
Nor Syrt, nor Scythia, rear'd thee as its child.
But thine a polish'd and humane abode,
Where never cruelty its features show'd:
In thy mild mother all her sex we view,
Thine, amiablest of men, a father too.
Now, pray the gods! these dreams befall me fair!
Light may they vanish on the tepid air!

C. A. Elton

BIRTHDAY GREETINGS

"This day" (the Fates foretold in sacred song,
And singing drew the vital twine along)
"He comes, nor shall the gods the doom recall,
He comes, whose sword shall quell the rebel Gaul.
With all her laurels him shall Conquest crown,
And nations shudder at his awful frown;

126

Smooth Atur, now that flows through peaceful lands,
Shall fly affrighted at his hostile band."
'Tis done! this prophecy Rome joys to see,
Far-famed Messala, now fulfill'd in thee:
Long triumphs ravish the spectators' eyes,
And fetter'd chieftains of enormous size:
An ivory car, with steeds as white as snow,
Sustains thy grandeur through the pompous show.

Some little share in those exploits I bore;
Witness Taebella, and the Santoigne shore;
Witness the land where steals the silent Saone,
Where rush the Garonne, and th'impetuous Rhone;
Where Loire, enamour'd of Carnutian bounds,
Leads his blue water through the yellow grounds.

Or shall his other acts adorn my theme? —
Fair Cydnus, winding with a silver stream?
Taurus, that in the clouds his forehead hides,
And rich Cilicia from the world divides;
Taurus, from which unnumber'd rivers spring,
The savage seat of tempests, shall I sing?
Why should I tell, how sacred through the skies
Of Syrian cities, the white pigeon flies?
Why sing of Tyrian towers, which Neptune laves;
Whence the first vessel, venturous, stemm'd the waves?
How shall the bard the secret source explore,
Whence, father Nile, thou draw'st thy watery store?
Thy fields ne'er importune for rain the sky,
Thou dost benignly all their wants supply:
As Egypt, Apis mourns in mystic lays,
She joins thy praises to Osiris' praise.

Osiris first contrived the crooked plough,
And pull'd ripe apples from the novice bough;
He taught the swains the savage mould to wound,
And scatter'd seed-corn in th'unpractised ground.
He first with poles sustain'd the reptile vine,
And show'd its infant tendrils how to twine;
Its wanton shoots instructed man to shear,
Subdue their wildness, and mature the year:
Then too the ripen'd cluster first was trod;
Then in gay streams its cordial soul bestow'd;

127

This as swains quaff'd, spontaneous numbers came,
They praised the festal cask, and hymn'd thy name;
All ecstasy, to certain time they bound,
And beat in measured awkwardness the ground.
Gay bowls serene the wrinkled front of care;
Gay bowls the toil-oppressed swain repair!
And let the slave the laughing goblet drain;
He blithesome sings, though manacles enchain.

Thee sorrow flies, Osiris, god of wine:
But songs, enchanting Love, and dance are thine:
But flowers and ivy thy fair head surround,
And a loose saffron mantle sweeps the ground.
With purple robes invested, now you glow;
The shrine is shown, and flutes melodious blow:
Come then, my god, but come bedew'd with wine!
Attend the rites, and in the dance combine.
The rites and dances are to Genius due.
Benign Osiris, stand confess'd to view.
Rich unguents drop already from his hair,
His head and neck soft flowery garlands share.
O come, so shall my grateful incense rise,
And cakes of honey meet thy laughing eyes.

On thee, Messala, ('tis my fervent prayer,)
May heaven bestow a wise, a warlike heir:
In whom, increased, paternal worth may shine,
Whose acts may add a lustre to thy line,
And transports give thee in thy life's decline.
But should the gods my fervent prayer deny,
Thy fame, my glorious friend, shall never die.
Long as (thy bounteous work) the well-made way
Shall its broad pavement to the sun display,
The bards of Alba shall in lofty rhyme
Transmit thy glory down the tide of time:
They sing from gratitude: nor less the clown
Whom love or business have detained in town
Till late, as home he safely plods along,
Thee chants, Messala, in his village song.

Blest morn, which still my grateful Muse shall sing,
Oft rise, and with you greater blessings bring.

James Grainger

128

PROPERTIUS

SEXTUS PROPERTIUS (c. 48 b. c. - 16 b. c.), the supreme Roman elegiac poet, was intimate with the prominent contemporaries of the capital. The erotic poet Ovid was his particular friend, while Maecenas, the confidant of the Emperor Augustus, was his patron.

Propertius' poems, constituting four books of Elegies, deal with early myths and Roman cults, with his friends, his poetic art, and largely, in so far as his poetic reputation is concerned, with his love for Cynthia, the poetic pseudonym of a pliant lady named Hostia. As in the case of Catullus, the path of love was marked by infatuation and quarrels, by Cynthia's faithlessness, by the poet's continuous protestations of his passion, and finally by his renunciations.

WARNING TO CYNTHIA

Your charms let other poets tell:
Or time oblivion on you bring.
If praises of your gifts outpour,
It's wasted effort, nothing more.
For, mark this now, your graces death
Will carry off in one fell breath.
The wayfarer in dudgeon high
Will scorn your tomb and pass it by.
And no one shall in tribute say:
Underneath these ashes laid,
Stranger, is a learned maid.

H. E. W.

OF HIMSELF

In the name of our longstanding friendship, Tullus,
You ask me what stock I'm of, my birthplace, my household gods.
If you know Perusia, grave of the men of our country
Who died in the grim days of Italy,

When Roman conflict pursued its own citizens:
Hence, Tuscan dust, my especial sorrow:
For on you lie scattered the bones of my kinsman:
On your soil they lie, unburied —
The neighboring region of Umbria,
Close to the plain beneath, a fertile spot,
Is my birthplace.

H. E. W.

LOVE'S FINERY

Why wear, my Life, when thou abroad dost stir,
   A head trimmed up to fashion's latest laws?
   A Coan vestment of transparent gauze,
And hair perfumed with Orontean myrrh.

Why set thyself on gems and costly dress?
   Why mar with trinkets Nature's form divine,
   And not allow thy beauties forth to shine
In all their own, their matchless loveliness?

To thee such aids can add no charms: ah no!
   True love will aye disdain the artist's care.
   See! the fair fields a thousand colours wear
And ivy-sprays far best spontaneous grow.

Fairer in lone rock-clefts green arbutes rise,
   Fairer the streamlet wends its wandering way,
   Lovelier bright pebbles gem their native bay,
Sweetlier song-birds trill artless melodies.

Not so did Phoebe merit Castor's hand,
   Nor Hilaïra win her Pollux' love;
   Not so, when Idas erst with Phoebus strove,
Appeared Marpesa by Evenus' strand.

With no false glare Hippodamia drew
   Her Phrygian lord, to reign a foreign queen;
   Her face no gems adorned, though fair, I ween,
As e'er Apelles on the canvas threw.

130

No fear for lack of lovers tortured these —
    Their wealth of beauty was their modesty;
    I, too, repose unwavering faith in thee:
She's rich in charms who can one lover please.

And richer thou: for Phoebus gives thee song,
    And fond Calliope the Aonian lyre;
    Yea, thy sweet speech my eager soul shall fire
With love for thee, my Cynthia, all life long.

Thine Beauty's charms and Wisdom's priceless prize,
    The brightest jewels that adorn a wife;
    With these thou'lt shed a lustre round my life,
If thou wilt wretched luxuries despise.

J. Cranstoun

FICKLE LOVE

Why charge me still with inactivity,
    As if from conscious Rome I would not go?
Lo! Cynthia sleeps as far from where I lie
    As Hypanis from the Venetian Po.

No more she holds me clasped in fond embrace,
    Nor with sweet accents glads my listening ear,
I once was dear: nor bosoms e'er bore trace
    Of happier loves than ours or more sincere.

Does heaven with envy sting, our hearts estrange?
    Does Promethean herb our union rend?
I'm altered: distance too doth maidens change;
    How soon doth love to sore disfavour tend.

Now first I'm forced long nights' lone hours to bear;
    My very sighs are painful to my ears;
Blest he who still may weep before his fair —
    For love rejoices in a lover's tears.

Blest he who still may weep before his fair —
For love transferred may find felicity:
None else I'll love — I cannot, cannot change:
Cynthia — my first — my latest love shall be.

J. Cranstoun

APPEAL TO BACCHUS

Humbly to thine altars now I hasten,
  Fill my sails, and waft me o'er the brine;
Bacchus! thou canst haughty Venus chasten,
  And dispel the cares of love with wine.

By thy power are lovers joined and parted;
  Soothe my troubled soul, for thou as I —
Witness Ariadne — must have smarted —
  Ere thy lynxes bore her to the sky.

In my bones the old flames ever-burning
  Death or wine shall doom to disappear;
Sober nights keep lonely lovers turning
  On their couch, distraught by hope and fear.

But if thou this fever fierce dispellest,
  Wooing o'er my weary soul to sleep,
I thy vines will plant, train trimly-trellised,
  And secure from prowling wild beast keep —

Foam my vats with purple must, and tender
  Grapes ne'er fail my treading feet to stain!
And to thee, O horned god! I'll render
  Homage all my days that yet remain.

I, thy poet styled, shall sing thy valour —
  Sing thy birth when bolts Aetnean flew —
Tell how Indian armed hosts in pallor
  Fled before thy dread Nysaean crew —

132

Sing Lycurgus' fury, unavailing,
    At the planting of thy gladsome tree —
Sing of impious Pentheus — theme ne'er failing
    To delight thee — slain by Maenads three —

Tyrrhene pirates, changed to dolphins, leaping
    From the ship where sprang the sprouting vine;
And thy sweet-breath'd streams through Naxos sweeping,
    Whence the men of Naxos quaff thy wine —

Neck with clustered ivy-berries glowing —
    Streaming locks with Tyrian turban bound —
Ivory shoulders with sweet unguents flowing —
    Trailing robe thy snow-white feet around —

Here, Dircaean nymphs soft tabors dashing,
    Horn-hoofed Fauns with gaping reeds in hand —
There, hoarse cymbals great Cybele clashing,
    Turret-crowned, 'mid Ida's roving band —

Golden bowl to pay the meet oblation, —
    Ministering priest before thy shrine,
Crowning all the rites with due libation,
    From the cup a-brim with purple wine —

In no humble strain these themes I'll thunder
    Like a peal from deep-mouthed Pindar's breast, —
Only burst this cruel bond asunder —
    Lull, oh lull my aching head to rest!

                                        J. Cranstoun

133

OVID

The reputation of Publius Ovidius Naso (43 B. C. - C. 17 A. D.) rests largely on his erotic writings. He is the archpoet of love, its technique and its manifestations. For centuries after his death Ovid was considered the supreme guide in the amatory field.

Born at Sulmo, Ovid was educated in Rome and studied also at Athens. He was intimate with many of the younger poets of his day, notably Tibullus. Endowed with a sufficiency of wealth, he dedicated himself to poetry and the social life. Banished by the Emperor Augustus on grounds that are still obscure, he spent his remaining years in the Euxine Sea, at Tomis.

His works include fifteen books of *Metamorphoses*, dealing with mythological transformations: *Fasti,* a poetic calendar: *Heroides,* fictitious love-letters: *Amores,* love poems: *Ars Amatoria,* an amatory manual: *Remedia Amoris,* a kind of counterfoil to the *Ars Amatoria.*

Book I — *Metamorphoses*

THE WORLD BEGINS

Before the seas, and this terrestrial ball,
And Heav'ns high canopy, that covers all,
One was the face of Nature, if a face;
Rather a rude and indigested mass:
A lifeless lump, unfashion'd, and unfram'd;
Of jarring seeds; and justly chaos nam'd.
No sun was lighted up the world to view;
No moon did yet her blunted horns renew:
Nor yet was Earth suspended in the sky;
Nor, pois'd, did on her own foundations lie:
Nor seas about the shores their arms had thrown;
But earth and air and water were in one.
Thus air was void of light, and earth unstable,
And water's dark abyss unnavigable.
No certain form on any was imprest;
All were confus'd, and each disturb'd the rest.
For hot and cold were in one body fixt.

And soft with hard, and light with heavy mixt.
    But God, or nature, while they thus contend,
To these intestine discords put an end.
Then earth from air, and seas from earth were driv'n,
And grosser air sunk from ethereal heav'n.
Thus disembroil'd, they take their proper place;
The next of kin contiguously embrace;
And foes are sunder'd by a larger space.
The force of fire ascended first on high,
And took its dwelling in the vaulted sky:
Then air succeeds, in lightness next to fire:
Whose atoms from unactive earth retire.
Earth sinks beneath, and draws a numerous throng
Of pondrous, thick, unwieldy seeds along.
About her coasts, unruly waters roar,
And, rising on a ridge, insult the shore.
Thus when the God, what ever God was he,
Had form'd the whole, and made the parts agree,
That no unequal portions might be found,
He moulded earth into a spacious round:
Then with a breath, he gave the winds to blow;
And bad the congregated waters flow.
He adds the running springs, and standing lakes;
And bounding banks for winding rivers makes.
Some part, in earth are swallow'd up, the most
In ample oceans, disimbogu'd, are lost.
He shades the woods, the vallies he restrains
With rocky mountains, and extends the plains.
And as five zones th'ethereal regions bind,
Five correspondent, are to earth assign'd:
The sun, with rays directly darting down,
Fires all beneath, and fries the middle zone:
The two beneath the distant poles complain
Of endless winter, and perpetual rain.
Betwixt th'extremes, two happier climates hold
The temper that partakes of hot and cold.
The fields of liquid air, inclosing all,
Surround the compass of this earthly ball:
The lighter parts lie next the fires above;
The grosser near the watry surface move:
Thick clouds are spread, and storms engender there,
And thunder's voice, which wretched mortals fear,
And winds that on their wings cold winter bear.

135

Nor were those blustring brethren left at large,
On seas and shores their fury to discharge:
Bound as they are, and circumscrib'd in place,
They rend the world, resistless, where they pass;
And mighty marks of mischief leave behind;
Such is the rage of their tempestuous kind.
First Eurus to the rising morn is sent,
(The regions of the balmy continent;)
And Eastern realms, where early Persians run,
To greet the blest appearance of the sun.
Westward, the wanton Zephyr wings his flight;
Pleas'd with the remnants of departing light:
Fierce Boreas with his offspring issues forth,
T'invade the frozen waggon of the North.
While frowning Auster seeks the southern sphere,
And rots with endless rain, th'unwholesome year.

  High o'er the clouds, and empty realms of wind,
The God a clearer space for heav'n design'd;
Where fields of light, and liquid ether flow,
Purg'd from the pondrous dregs of earth below.
Scarce had the pow'r distinguish'd these, when straight
The stars, no longer overlaid with weight,
Exert their heads from underneath the mass,
And upward shoot, and kindle as they pass
And with diffusive light, adorn their heav'nly place.
Then, every void of nature to supply,
With forms of gods he fills the vacant sky:
New herds of beasts he sends the plains to share;
New colonies of birds, to people air;
And to their oozy beds the finny fish repair.
A creature of a more exalted kind
Was wanting yet, and then was man design'd:
Conscious of thought, of more capacious breast,
For empire form'd, and fit to rule the rest:
Whether with particles of heav'nly fire
The god of nature did his soul inspire;
Or earth, but new divided from the sky,
And, pliant, still, retain'd th'ethereal energy:
Which wise Prometheus temper'd into paste,
And mixt with living streams, the godlike image cast.
Thus, while the mute creation downward bend
Their sight, and to their earthy mother tend,
Man looks aloft; and with erected eyes

Beholds his own hereditary skies.
From such rude principles our form began,
And earth was metamorphos'd into man.
     The Golden Age was first; when men yet new,
No rule but uncorrupted reason knew;
And, with a native bent, did good pursue.
Un-forc'd by punishment, un-aw'd by fear,
His words were simple, and his soul sincere:
Needless was written law, where none opprest:
The law of man was written in his breast:
No suppliant crowds before the judge appear'd:
No court erected yet, nor cause was hear'd;
But all was safe, for conscience was their guard.
The mountain trees in distant prospect please,
E're yet the pine descended to the seas;
E're sails were spread, new oceans to explore;
And happy mortals, unconcern'd for more,
Confin'd their wishes to their native shore.
No walls were yet; nor fence, nor moat nor mound;
Nor drum was heard, nor trumpets' angry sound:
Nor swords were forg'd; but, void of care and crime,
The soft creation slept away their time.
The teeming earth, yet guiltless of the plough,
And unprovok'd, did fruitful stores allow:
Content with food, which Nature freely bred,
On wildings, and on strawberries they fed;
Cornels and bramble-berries gave the rest,
And falling acorns furnisht out a feast.
The flow'rs unsown, in fields and meadows reign'd,
And western winds immortal spring maintain'd.
In following years, the bearded corn ensu'd
From earth unask'd, nor was that earth renew'd.
From veins of vallies, milk and nectar broke;
And honey sweating through the pores of oak.
     But when good Saturn, banish'd from above,
Was driv'n to Hell, the world was under Jove.
Succeeding times a Silver Age behold,
Excelling brass, but more excell'd by gold.
Then summer, autumn, winter did appear;
And spring was but a season of the year.
The sun his annual course obliquely made,
Good days contracted, and enlarg'd the bad.
Then air with sultry heats began to glow,

The wings of winds were clogg'd with ice and snow;
And shivering mortals, into houses driven,
Sought shelter from th'inclemency of Heav'n.
Those houses, then, were caves, or homely sheds,
With twining oziers fenc'd; and moss their beds.
Then ploughs, for seed, the fruitful furrows broke,
And oxen labour'd first beneath the yoke.

To this next came in course the Brazen Age:
A warlike offspring prompt to bloody rage,
Not impious yet —
—— Hard Steel succeeded then;
And stubborn as the metal, were the men.
Truth, Modesty, and Shame, the world forsook:
Fraud, Avarice, and Force, their places took.
Then sails were spread, to every wind that blew;
Raw were the sailors, and the depths were new:
Trees rudely hollow'd, did the waves sustain;
E're ships in triumph plough'd the watry plain.

Then land-marks limited to each his right:
For all before was common, as the light.
Nor was the ground alone requir'd to bear
Her annual income to the crooked share;
But greedy mortals, rummaging her store,
Digg'd from her entrails first the precious ore;
Which next to Hell the prudent Gods had laid;
Thus cursed steel, and more accursed gold,
Gave mischief birth, and made that mischief bold:
And double death did wretched man invade,
By steel assaulted, and by gold betray'd.
Now, (brandish'd weapons glitt'ring in their hands)
Mankind is broken loose from moral bands;
No rights of hospitality remain:
The guest by him who harbour'd him, is slain:
The son-in-law pursues the father's life;
The wife her husband murders, he the wife.
The step-dame poison for the son prepares;
The son inquires into his father's years.
Faith flies, and Piety in exile mourns;
And Justice, here opprest, to Heav'n returns.

Nor were the Gods themselves more safe above;
Against beleagur'd heav'n, the giants move.
Hills piled on hills, on mountains, mountains lie,
To make their mad approaches to the sky.

Till Jove, no longer patient, took his time
T'avenge with thunder their audacious crime:
Red light'ning play'd along the firmament,
And their demolish't works to pieces rent.
Sing'd with the flames, and with the bolts transfixt,
With native earth their blood the monsters mixt;
The blood, indu'd with animating heat,
Did in th'impregnant earth, new sons beget:
They, like the seed from which they sprung, accurst,
Against the Gods immortal hatred nurst:
An impious, arrogant, and cruel brood;
Expressing their original from blood.
Which when the King of Gods beheld from high
(Withal revolving in his memory,
What he himself had found on earth of late,
Lycaon's guilt, and his inhuman treat)
He sigh'd; nor longer with his pity strove;
But kindled to a wrath becoming Jove;
Then, call'd a general council of the Gods;
Who summon'd, issue from their blest abodes,
And fill th'assembly, with a shining train.
A way there is, in Heaven's expanded plain,
Which when the skies are clear, is seen below,
And mortals, by the name of Milky, know.
The ground-work is of stars; through which the road
Lies open to the thunderer's abode.
The Gods of greater nations dwell around,
And on the right and left the palace bound;
The commons where they can, the nobler sort,
With winding-doors wide open, front the court.
This place, as far as earth with heav'n may vie,
I dare to call the Loovre of the sky.
When all were plac'd, in seats distinctly known,
And he, their father, had assum'd the throne,
Upon his iv'ry sceptre first he leant,
Then shook his head, that shook the firmament:
Air, earth, and seas, obey'd th'almighty nod;
And with a gen'ral fear, confess'd the God.
At length, with indignation, thus he broke
His awful silence, and the pow'rs bespoke.
"I was not more concern'd in that debate
Of empire, when our universal state
Was put to hazard, and the giant race

139

Our captive skies were ready to imbrace;
For tho' the foe was fierce, the seeds of all
Rebellion, sprung from one original;
Now wheresoever ambient waters glide,
All are corrupt, and all must be destroy'd.
Let me this holy protestation make,
By Hell, and Hell's inviolable lake,
I try'd whatever in the god-head lay;
But gangreen'd members must be lopt away,
Before the nobler parts are tainted to decay.
There dwells below, a race of demi-gods,
Of nymphs in waters, and of fawns in woods;
Who, tho' not worthy yet, in heav'n to live,
Let 'em, at least, enjoy that earth we give.
Can these be thought securely lodg'd below,
When I my self, who no superior know,
I, who have heav'n and earth at my command,
Have been attempted by Lycaon's hand?"
     At this a murmur thro' the synod went,
And with one voice they vote his punishment.
Thus, when conspiring traitors dar'd to doom
The fall of Caesar, and in him of Rome,
The nations trembled, with a pious fear;
All anxious for their earthly thunderer:
Nor was their care, O Caesar! less esteem'd
By thee, than that of Heav'n for Jove was deem'd;
Who with his hand and voice, did first restrain
Their murmurs, then resum'd his speech again.
The Gods to silence were compos'd and sate
With reverence, due to his superior state.
"Cancel your pious cares; already he
Has paid his debt to Justice, and to me.
Yet what his crimes, and what my judgments were,
Remains for me thus briefly to declare.
The clamours of this vile degenerate age,
The cries of orphans, and th'oppressor's rage,
Had reach'd the stars; I will descend, said I,
In hope to prove this loud complaint a lie.
Disguis'd in human shape, I travell'd round
The world, and more than what I hear'd I found.
O'er Maenalus I took my steepy way,
By caverns infamous for beasts of prey.
Then cross'd Cyllenè, and the piny shade,

More infamous by curst Lycaon made.
Dark night had cover'd Heaven and Earth, before
I enter'd his unhospitable door.
Just at my entrance, I display'd the sign
That somewhat was approaching of divine.
The prostrate people pray: the tyrant grins,
And, adding Profanation to his sins,
'T'll try,' said he, 'and if a God appear,
To prove his deity, shall cost him dear.'
'Twas late; the graceless wretch my death prepares,
When I shou'd soundly sleep, opprest with cares:
This dire experiment he chose, to prove
If I were mortal, or undoubted Jove;
But first he had resolv'd to taste my pow'r:
Not long before, but in a luckless hour
Some legates sent from the Molossian state,
Were on a peaceful errand come to treat:
Of these he murders one, he boils the flesh,
And lays the mangl'd morsels in a dish:
Some part he roasts; then serves it up, so drest,
And bids me welcome to this human feast.
Mov'd with disdain, the table I o'er-turn'd;
And with avenging flames, the palace burn'd.
The tyrant in a fright, for shelter, gains
The neighb'ring fields, and scours along the plains.
Howling he fled, and fain he would have spoke,
But human voice his brutal tongue forsook.
About his lips, the gather'd foam he churns,
And breathing slaughters, still with rage he burns,
But on the bleating flock his fury turns.
His mantle, now his hide, with rugged hairs
Cleaves to his back; a famish'd face he bears;
His arms descend, his shoulders sink away,
To multiply his legs for chase of prey.
He grows a wolf, his hoariness remains,
And the same rage in other members reigns.
His eyes still sparkle in a narr'wer space,
His jaws retain the grin, and violence of his face.
        This was a single ruin, but not one
Deserves so just a punishment alone.
Mankind's a monster, and th'ungodly times,
Confed'rate into guilt, are sworn to crimes.
All are alike involv'd in ill, and all

Must by the same relentless fury fall."
    Thus ended he; the greater Gods assent,
By clamours urging his severe intent;
The less fill up the cry for punishment.
Yet still with pity they remember man;
And mourn as much as heav'nly spirits can.
They ask, when those were lost of human birth,
What he wou'd do with all this waste of earth:
If his dispeopl'd world he would resign
To beasts, a mute, and more ignoble line;
Neglected altars must no longer smoke,
If none were left to worship and invoke.
To whom the Father of the Gods reply'd:
"Lay that unnecessary fear aside:
Mine be the care, new people to provide.
I will from wondrous principles ordain
A race unlike the first, and try my skill again."
    Already had he toss'd the flaming brand,
And roll'd the thunder in his spacious hand;
Preparing to discharge on seas and land:
But stopp'd, for fear thus violently driv'n,
The sparks should catch his axle-tree of Heav'n.
Rememb'ring, in the Fates, a time when fire
Shou'd to the battlements of Heav'n aspire,
And all his blazing worlds above shou'd burn,
And all th'inferior globe to cinders turn.
His dire Artill'ry thus dismist, he bent
His thoughts to some securer punishment:
Concludes to pour a watry deluge down;
And what he durst not burn, resolves to drown.
    The Northern breath, that freezes floods, he binds;
With all the race of cloud-dispelling winds
The South he loos'd, who night and horror brings;
And fogs are shaken from his flaggy wings.
From his divided beard, two streams he pours;
His head and rhumy eyes distil in showers.
With rain his robe and heavy mantle flow:
And lazy mists are lowring on his brow.
Still as he swept along, with his clench't fist,
He squeez'd the clouds; th'imprison'd clouds resist:
The skies, from pole to pole, with peals resound:
And show'rs inlarg'd come pouring on the ground.
Then, clad in colours of a various dye,

142

Junonian Iris breeds a new supply
To feed the clouds: impetuous rain descends;
The bearded corn beneath the burden bends:
Defrauded clowns deplore their perish'd grain;
And the long labours of the year are vain.

Nor from his patrimonial heav'n alone
Is Jove content to pour his vengeance down:
And from his brother of the seas he craves,
To help him with auxiliary waves.
The watry tyrant calls his brooks and floods,
Who roll from mossy caves (their moist abodes;)
And with perpetual urns his palace fill:
To whom in brief, he thus imparts his will.

Small exhortation needs; your pow'rs employ:
And this bad world, so Jove requires, destroy,
Let loose the reins to all your watry store:
Bear down the dams, and open every door.

The floods, by nature enemies to land,
And proudly swelling with their new command,
Remove the living stones, that stop their way,
And gushing from their source, augment the sea.
Then, with his mace, their monarch struck the ground:
With inward trembling, Earth receiv'd the wound;
And rising streams a ready passage found.
Th'expanded waters gather on the plain,
They flote the fields, and over-top the grain;
Then rushing onwards, with a sweepy sway,
Bear flocks, and folds, and lab'ring hinds away.
Nor safe their dwellings were; for, sapp'd by floods,
Their houses fell upon their household gods.
The solid piles, too strongly built to fall,
High o'er their heads, behold a watry wall:
Now seas and earth were in confusion lost;
A world of waters, and without a coast.

One climbs a cliff; one in his boat is born,
And ploughs above, where late he sow'd his corn.
Others o'er chimney tops and turrets row,
And drop their anchors on the meads below:
Or downward driv'n, they bruise the tender vine,
Or tost aloft, are knock't against a pine.
And where of late the kids had cropt the grass,
The monsters of the deep now take their place.
Insulting Nereids on the cities ride,

143

And wondring dolphins o'er the palace glide.
On leaves and masts of mighty oaks they browse.
And their broad fins entangle in the boughs.
The frighted wolf now swims amongst the sheep;
The yellow lion wanders in the deep:
His rapid force no longer helps the boar:
The stag swims faster, than he ran before.
The fowls, long beating on their wings in vain,
Despair of land, and drop into the main.
Now hills and vales no more distinction know,
And levell'd nature lies oppress'd below.
The most of mortals perish in the flood:
The small remainder dies for want of food.
A mountain of stupendous height there stands
Betwixt th'Athenian and Boeotian lands,
The bound of fruitful fields, while fields they were,
But then a field of waters did appear:
Parnassus is its name; whose forky rise
Mounts through the clouds, and mates the lofty skies.
High on the summit of this dubious cliff,
Deucalion wafting, moor'd his little skiff.
He with his wife were only left behind
Of perish'd man; they two were human kind.
The mountain nymphs and Themis they adore,
And from her oracles relief implore.
The most upright of mortal men was he;
The most sincere and holy woman, she.
         When Jupiter, surveying Earth from high,
Beheld it in a lake of water lie,
That, where so many millions lately liv'd,
But two, the best of either sex, surviv'd,
He loos'd the northern wind; fierce Boreas flies
To puff away the clouds, and purge the skies:
Serenely, while he blows, the vapours, driven,
Discover Heav'n to Earth, and Earth to Heaven.
The billows fall, while Neptune lays his mace
On the rough sea, and smooths its furrow'd face,
Already Triton, at his call appears
Above the waves; a Tyrian robe he wears;
And in his hand a crooked trumpet bears.
The sovereign bids him peaceful sounds inspire,
And give the waves the signal to retire.
His writhen shell he takes; whose narrow vent

144

Grows by degrees into a large extent;
Then gives it breath; the blast with doubling sound,
Runs the wide circuit of the world around.
The sun first heard it, in his early East,
And met the rattling echo's in the West.
The waters, listning to the trumpets' roar,
Obey the summons, and forsake the shore.
    A thin circumference of land appears;
And earth, but not at once, her visage rears,
And peeps upon the seas from upper grounds:
The streams, but just contain'd within their bounds,
By slow degrees into their channels crawl
And earth increases as the waters fall.
In longer time the tops of trees appear,
Which mud on their dishonour'd branches bear.
    At length, the world was all restor'd to view,
But desolate, and of a sickly hue:
Nature beheld herself, and stood aghast,
A dismal desert and silent waste.
    Which when Deucalion, with a piteous look,
Beheld, he wept, and thus to Pyrrha spoke:
"Oh wife, oh sister, oh oh all thy kind
The best and only creature left behind,
By kindred, love, and now by dangers join'd;
Of multitudes, who breath'd the common air,
We two remain; a species in a pair;
The rest the seas have swallow'd; nor have we
Ev'n of this wretched life a certainty.
The clouds are still above; and, while I speak,
A second deluge o'er our heads may break.
Shou'd I be snatch'd from hence, and thou remain,
Without relief, or partner of thy pain,
How cou'd'st thou such a wretched life sustain?
Shou'd I be left, and thou be lost, the sea,
That bury'd her I lov'd, shou'd bury me.
Oh cou'd our father his old arts inspire,
And make me heir of his informing fire,
That so I might abolisht man retrieve,
And perisht people in new souls might live.
But Heav'n is pleas'd, nor ought we to complain,
That we, th'examples of mankind remain."
He said: the careful couple join their tears,
And then invoke the Gods, with pious prayers.
Thus, in devotion having eas'd their grief,

From sacred oracles they seek relief:
And to Cephysus' brook their way pursue:
The stream was troubl'd, but the foord they knew.
With living waters in the fountain bred,
They sprinkle first, their garments, and their head,
Then took the way which to the temple led.
The roofs were all defil'd with moss and mire,
The desert altars void of solemn fire.
Before the gradual, prostrate they ador'd,
The pavement kiss'd, and thus the saint implor'd.
"O righteous Themis, if the pow'rs above
By pray'rs are bent to pity and to love;
If human miseries can move their mind;
If yet they can forgive, and yet be kind;
Tell how we may restore, by second birth,
Mankind, and people desolated earth."
Then thus the gracious Goddess, nodding, said;
"Depart, and with your vestments veil your head;
And stooping lowly down, with loosn'd zones,
Throw each behind your back, your mighty mother's bones."
Amaz'd the pair; and mute with wonder, stand,
Till Pyrrha first refus'd the dire command.
"Forbid it heav'n," said she, "that I shou'd tear
Those holy reliques from the sepulchre."
They ponder'd the mysterious words again,
For some new sense; and long they sought in vain.
At length Deucalion clear'd his cloudy brow,
And said; "The dark enigma will allow
A meaning, which, if well I understand,
From sacrilege will free the God's command:
This earth our mighty mother is, the stones
In her capacious body, are her bones.
These we must cast behind." With hope and fear,
The woman did the new solution hear:
The man diffides in his own augury,
And doubts the Gods; yet both resolve to try.
Descending from the mount, they first unbind
Their vests, and veil'd, they cast the stones behind:
The stones (a miracle to mortal view,
But long tradition makes it pass for true)
Did first the rigour of their kind expell,
And suppl'd into softness as they fell;
Then swell'd, and swelling, by degrees grew warm;
And took the rudiments of human form;

146

Imperfect shapes: in marble such are seen,
When the rude chisel does the man begin;
While yet the roughness of the stone remains,
Without the rising muscles, and the veins.
The sappy parts, and next resembling juice,
Were turn'd to moisture, for the bodies' use:
Supplying humours, blood, and nourishment:
The rest, (too solid to receive a bent;)
Converts to bones; and what was once a vein,
Its former name and nature did retain.
By help of pow'r divine, in little space,
What the man threw, assum'd a manly face;
And what the wife, renew'd the female race.
Hence we derive our nature, born to bear
Laborious life; and harden'd into care.

    The rest of animals, from teeming earth
Produc'd, in various forms receiv'd their birth.
The native moisture, in its close retreat,
Digested by the sun's ethereal heat,
As in a kindly womb, began to breed:
Then swell'd and quicken'd by the vital seed.
And some in less, and some in longer space,
Were ripen'd into form, and took a several face.
Thus when the Nile from Pharian fields is fled,
And seeks, with ebbing tides, his ancient bed,
The fat manure with heav'nly fire is warm'd:
And crusted creatures, as in wombs are form'd:
These, when they turn the glebe, the peasants find:
Some rude, and yet unfinish'd in their kind:
Short of their limbs, a lame imperfect birth;
One half alive; and one of lifeless earth.

    For heat and moisture, when in bodies join'd,
The temper that results from either kind,
Conception makes; and fighting, till they mix,
Their mingl'd atoms in each other fix.
Thus Nature's hand the genial bed prepares
With friendly discord, and with fruitful wars.

    From hence the surface of the ground with mud
And slime besmear'd (the faeces of the flood),
Receiv'd the rays of Heav'n; and sucking in
The seeds of heat, new creatures did begin:
Some were of sev'ral sorts produc'd before;
But of new monsters, earth created more.

John Dryden

When loose epistles violate chaste eyes,
She half consents, who silently denies:
How dares a stranger with designs so vain,
Marriage and hospitable rights profane?
Was it for this, your fleet did shelter find
From swelling seas, and ev'ry faithless wind?
(For tho' a distant country brought you forth,
Your usage here was equal to your worth.)
Does this deserve to be rewarded so?
Did you come here a stranger or a foe?
Your partial judgment may perhaps complain,
And think me barbarous for my just disdain;
Ill-bred then let me be, but not unchaste
Nor my clear fame with any spot defac'd.
Tho' in my face there's no affected frown,
Nor in my carriage a feign'd niceness shown,
I keep my honor still without a stain,
Nor has my love made any coxcomb vain.
Your boldness I with admiration see;
What hope had you to gain a queen like me?
Because a hero forc'd me once away
Am I thought fit to be a second prey?
Had I been won, I had deserv'd your blame,
But sure my part was nothing but the shame.
Yet the base theft to him no fruit did bear,
I 'scap'd unhurt by any thing but fear.
Rude force might some unwilling kisses gain,
But that was all he ever could obtain.
You on such terms would ne'er have let me go;
Were he like you, we had not parted so.
Untouch'd the youth restor'd me to my friends,
And modest usage made me some amends.
'Tis virtue to repent a vicious deed,
Did he repent, that Paris might succeed?
Sure 'tis some fate that sets me above wrongs,
Yet still exposes me to busy tongues.
I'll not complain; for who's displeas'd with love,
If it sincere, discreet, and constant prove?
But that I fear; not that I think you base,
Or doubt the blooming beauties of my face;
But all your sex is subject to deceive,

And ours, alas, too willing to believe.
Yet others yield; and love o'ercomes the best:
But why should I not shine above the rest?
Fair Leda's story seems at first to be
A fit example ready found for me.
But she was cozen'd by a borrow'd shape,
And under harmless feathers felt a rape:
If I should yield, what reason could I use?
By what mistake the loving crime excuse?
Her fault was in her pow'rfull lover lost;
But of what Jupiter have I to boast?
Tho' you to heroes and to kings succeed,
Our famous race does no addition need;
And great alliances but useless prove
To one that comes herself from mighty Jove.
Go then, and boast in some less haughty place
Your Phrygian blood, and Priam's ancient race;
Which I wou'd shew I valu'd, if I durst;
You are the fifth from Jove, but I the first.
The crown of Troy is pow'rful I confess;
But I have reason to think ours no less.
Your letter fill'd with promises of all,
That men can good, and women pleasant call,
Gives expectation such an ample field,
As wou'd move goddesses themselves to yield.
But if I e'er offend great Juno's laws,
Yourself shall be the dear, the only cause:
Either my honour I'll to death maintain,
Or follow you, without mean thoughts of gain.
Not that so fair a present I despise;
We like the gift, when we the giver prize.
But 'tis your love moves me, which made you take
Such pains, and run such hazards for my sake;
I have perceiv'd (though I dissembled too)
A thousand things that love has made you do.
Your eager eyes would almost dazzle mine,
In which (wild man) your wanton thoughts wou'd shine.
Sometimes you'd sigh, sometimes disorder'd stand,
And with unusual ardor, press my hand;
Contrive just after me to take the glass,
Nor wou'd you let the least occasion pass:
Which oft I fear'd, I did not mind alone,
And blushing sate for things which you have done:

149

Then murmur'd to myself, he'll for my sake
Do any thing; I hope 'twas no mistake.
Oft have I read within this pleasing grove,
Under my name, those charming words, I Love.
I frowning seem'd not to believe your flame,
But now, alas, am come to write the same.
If I were capable to do amiss,
I could not but be sensible of this.
For oh! your face has such peculiar charms,
That who can hold from flying to your arms!
But what I ne'er can have without offence,
Pleasure may tempt but virtue more should move;
O learn of me to want the thing you love.
What you desire is sought by all mankind:
As you have eyes, so others are not blind.
Like you they see, like you my charms adore:
They wish not less, but you dare venture more.
Oh! had you then upon our coasts been brought,
My virgin love when thousand rivals sought,
You had I seen, you should have had my voice;
Nor could my husband justly blame my choice.
For both our hopes, alas you come too late!
Another now is master of my fate.
More to my wish I cou'd have liv'd with you,
And yet my present lot can undergo.
Cease to solicit a weak woman's will,
And urge not her you love, to so much ill.
But let me live contented as I may,
And make not my unspotted fame your prey.
Some right you claim, since naked to your eyes
Three Goddesses disputed beauty's prize:
One offer'd valour, t'other crowns; but she
Obtain'd her cause, who smiling promis'd me.
But first I am not of belief so light,
To think such nymphs woud shew you such a sight:
Yet granting this, the other part is feign'd;
A bribe so mean your sentence had not gain'd.
With partial eyes I shou'd my self regard,
To think that Venus made me her reward:
I humbly am content with human praise;
A Goddess's applause would envy raise:
But be it as you say: for, 'tis confest,
The men, who flatter highest, please us best.

150

That I suspect it, ought not to displease;
For miracles are not believ'd with ease.
One joy I have, that I had Venus' voice;
A greater yet, that you confirm'd her choice;
That proffer'd laurels, promis'd sov'reignty,
Juno and Pallas, you contemn'd for me.
Am I your empire then, and your renown?
What heart of rock, but must by this be won?
And yet bear witness, O you pow'rs above,
How rude I am in all the arts of love!
My hand is yet untaught to write to men:
This is th'essay of my unpractis'd pen:
Happy those nymphs whom use has perfect made;
I think all crime, and tremble at a shade.
Ev'n while I write, my fearful conscious eyes
Look often back, misdoubting a surprize.
For now the rumour spreads among the crowd,
At court in whispers, but in town aloud.
Dissemble you, what e'er you hear 'em say:
To leave off loving were your better way;
Yet if you will dissemble it, you may.
Love secretly: the absence of my lord
More freedom gives, but does not all afford:
Long is his journey, long will be his stay;
Call'd by affairs of consequence away.
To go or not when unresolv'd he stood,
I bid him make what swift return he cou'd:
Then kissing me, he said, 'I recommend
All to thy care, but most my Trojan friend.'
I smil'd at what he innocently said,
And only answer'd, you shall be obey'd.
Propitious winds have borne him far from hence,
But let not this secure your confidence.
Absent he is, yet absent he commands:
You know the proverb, Princes have long hands.
My fame's my burden: for the more I'm prais'd,
A juster ground of jealousy is rais'd.
Were I less fair, I might have been more blest:
Great beauty through great danger is possest,
To leave me here his venture was not hard,
Because he thought my virtue was my guard.
He fear'd my face, but trusted to my life,
The beauty doubted, but believ'd the wife.

151

You bid me use th'occasion while I can,
Put in our hands by the good easy man.
I wou'd, and yet I doubt, 'twixt love and fear;
One draws me from you, and one brings me near.
Our flames are mutual; and my husband's gone:
The nights are long; I fear to lie alone.
One house contains us, and weak walls divide,
And you're too pressing to be long denied:
Let me not live, but every thing conspires
To join our loves, and yet my fear retires.
You court with words, when you should force imploy:
A rape is requisite to shamefac'd joy.
Indulgent to the wrongs which we receive,
Our sex can suffer what we dare not give.
What have I said! for both of us 'twere best,
Our kindling fires if each of us supprest.
The faith of strangers is too prone to change,
And, like themselves, their wandering passions range.
Hipsypyle, and the fond Minoian maid,
Were both by trusting of their guests betray'd.
How can I doubt that other men deceive,
When you yourself did fair Oenone leave?
But lest I shou'd upbraid your treachery,
You make a merit of that crime to me.
Yet grant you were to faithful love inclin'd,
Your weary Trojans wait but for a wind.
Should you prevail; while I assign the night,
Your sails are hoisted, and you take your flight:
Some bawling mariner our love destroys,
And breaks asunder our unfinish'd joys.
But I with you may leave the Spartan port,
To view the Trojan wealth, and Priam's court:
Shown while I see, I shall expose my fame,
And fill a foreign country with my shame.
In Asia what reception shall I find?
And what dishonour leave in Greece behind?
What will your brothers, Priam, Hecuba,
And what will all your modest matrons say?
Ev'n you, when on this action you reflect,
My future conduct justly may suspect;
And what e're stranger lands upon your coast,
Conclude me, by your own example, lost.

152

I from your rage a strumpet's name shall hear,
While you forget what part in it you bear.
You, my crime's author, will my crime upbraid:
Deep under ground, Oh let me first be laid!
You boast the pomp and plenty of your land,
And promise all shall be at my command:
Your Trojan wealth, believe me, I despise;
My own poor native land has dearer ties.
Shou'd I be injur'd on your Phrygian shore,
What help of kindred cou'd I there implore?
Medea was by Jason's flatt'ry won:
I may, like her, believe, and be undone.
Plain honest hearts, like mine, suspect no cheat,
And love contributes to its own deceit.
The ships, about whose sides loud tempests roar,
With gentle winds were wafted from the shore.
Your teeming mother dreamt a flaming brand,
Sprung from her womb, consum'd the Trojan land.
To second this, old prophecies conspire,
That Ilium shall be burnt with Grecian fire.
Both give me fear; nor is it much allay'd,
That Venus is oblig'd our loves to aid.
For they who lost their cause, revenge will take;
And for one friend two enemies you make.
Nor can I doubt, but shou'd I follow you,
The sword wou'd soon our fatal crime pursue:
A wrong so great my husband's rage wou'd rouse,
And my relations wou'd his cause espouse.
You boast your strength and courage; but alas!
Your words receive small credit from your face.
Let heroes in the dusty field delight,
Those limbs were fashion'd for another fight.
Bid Hector sally from the walls of Troy;
A sweeter quarrel shou'd your arms employ.
Yet fears like these, shou'd not my mind perplex,
Were I as wise as many of my sex.
But time and you may bolder thoughts inspire;
And I perhaps may yield to your desire.
You last demand a private conference,
These are your words, but I can guess your sense.
Your unripe hopes their harvest must attend:
Be rul'd by me, and time may be your friend.

153

This is enough to let you understand;
For now my pen has tir'd my tender hand:
My woman knows the secret of my heart,
And may hereafter better news impart.

John Dryden

TRISTIA: 111.10: OVID IN EXILE

Should any one there in Rome remember Ovid the exile,
    And without me, my name still in the city survive;
Tell him that under stars which never set in the ocean
    I am existing still, here in a barbarous land.
Fierce Sarmatians encompass me round, and the Bessi and Getae;
    Names how unworthy to be sung by a genius like mine!
Yet when the air is warm, intervening Ister defends us:
    He, as he flows, repels inroads of war with his waves.
But when the dismal winter reveals its hideous aspect,
    When all earth becomes white with a marble-like frost;
And when Boreas is loosed, and the snow hurled under Arcturus,
    Then these nations, in sooth, shudder and shiver with cold.
Deep lies the snow, and neither the sun nor the rain can dissolve it;
    Boreas hardens it still, makes it forever remain.
Hence, ere the first has melted away, another succeeds it.
    And two years it is wont, in many places, to lie.
And so great is the power of the North-wind awakened, it levels
    Lofty towers with the ground, roofs uplifted bears off.
Wrapped in skins, and with trousers sewed, they contend with the
    And their faces alone of the whole body are seen.   [weather,
Often their tresses, when shaken, with pendent icicles tinkle,
    And their whitened beards shine with the gathering frost.
Wines consolidate stand, preserving the form of the vessels;
    No more draughts of wine, — pieces presented they drink.
Why should I tell you how all the rivers are frozen and solid,
    And from out of the lake frangible water is dug?
Ister, — no narrower stream than the river that bears the papyrus, —
    Which through its many mouths mingles its waves with the deep;
Ister, with hardening winds, congeals its cerulean waters,

154

Under a roof of ice winding its way to the sea.
There where ships have sailed, men go on foot, and the billows,
Solid made by the frost, hoof-beats of horses indent.
Over unwonted bridges, with water gliding beneath them,
The Sarmatian steers drag their barbarian carts.
Scarcely shall I be believed; yet when naught is gained by a falsehood,
Absolute credence then should to a witness be given.
I have beheld the vast Black Sea of ice all compacted,
And a slippery crust pressing its motionless tides.
'Tis not enough to have seen, I have trodden this indurate ocean;
Dry shod passed my foot over its uppermost wave.
If thou hadst had of old such a sea as this is, Leander!
Then thy death had not been charged as a crime to the Strait.
Nor can the curved dolphins uplift themselves from the water;
All their struggles to rise merciless winter prevents;
And though Boreas sound with roar of wings in commotion,
In the blockaded gulf never a wave will there be;
And the ships will stand hemmed in by the frost, as in marble,
Nor will the oar have power through the stiff waters to cleave.
Fast-bound in the ice have I seen the fishes adhering,
Yet notwithstanding this some of them still were alive.
Hence. if the savage strength of omnipotent Boreas freezes
Whether the salt-sea wave, whether the refluent stream, —
Straightway, — the Ister made level by arid blasts of the North-wind, —
Comes the barbaric foe borne on his swift-footed steed;
Foe. that powerful made by his steed and his far-flying arrows,
All the neighboring land void of inhabitants makes.
Some take flight, and none being left to defend their possessions,
Unprotected their goods pillage and plunder become;
Cattle and creaking carts, the little wealth of the country,
And what riches beside indigent peasants possess,
Some as captives are driven along, their hands bound behind them,
Looking backward in vain toward their Lares and lands.
Others, transfixed with barbed arrows, in agony perish.
For the swift arrow-heads all have in poison been dipped.
What they cannot carry or lead away they demolish,
And the hostile flames burn up the innocent cots.
Even when there is peace, the fear of war is impending;
None, with the ploughshare pressed, furrows the soil any more.
Either this region sees, or fears a foe that it sees not,
And the sluggish land slumbers in utter neglect.
No sweet grape lies hidden here in the shade of its vine-leaves,

155

No fermenting must fills and o'erflows the deep vats.
Apples the region denies; nor would Acontius have found here
   Ought upon which to write words for his mistress to read.
Naked and barren plains without leaves or trees we behold here, —
   Places, alas! unto which no happy man would repair.
Since then this mighty orb lies open so wide upon all sides,
   Has this region been found only my prison to be?

H. W. Longfellow

L U C A N

MARCUS ANNAEUS LUCANUS (39 - 65 A.D.) was born at Cordoba in Spain
and brought to Rome as a child. Here he distinguished himself in the schools
of rhetoric, studied in Athens, and held official positions under the Emperor
Nero. Implicated in the conspiracy of Piso against the Emperor, Lucan was
forced to end his life.
His chief work is the epic poem *Pharsalia* or *Bellum Civile,* in ten books.
The subject is the conflict between Caesar and Pompey.

Book I — *Lucan's Pharsalia*

Wars more than civil upon Emathian plains, and license con-
ceded to lawlessness, I sing; and a powerful people turning with victorious right-hand against its own vitals, and kindred armies *engaged*;
and, the compact of rule rent asunder, a contest waged with all the
might of the shaken earth for the universal woe, and standards meeting
with hostile standards, the eagles alike, and darts threatening darts.

What madness, this, O citizens! what lawlessness so great of the
sword, while nations are your hate, for you to shed the Latian blood?
And, while proud Babylon was to be spoiled of the Ausonian trophies,
and the shade of Crassus was wandering unavenged, has it pleased you
that wars, doomed to produce no triumphs, should be waged? Alas!
how much of land and of sea might have been won with that self-same
blood which the right-hands of fellow-citizens have shed. Whence Titan
makes his approach, and where the night conceals the stars, and where
the mid-day intensely burns with its scorching moments; where too, the
winter, frozen and unused to be relaxed by the spring, binds fast the
icy ocean with Scythian cold! By this beneath the yoke should the Seres,
by this the barbarian Araxes, have come, and the race, if any there be,
that lies situate contiguous to the rising Nile.

Then, Rome, if so great thy love for an accursed warfare, when
thou hast subjected the whole earth to Latian laws, turn thy hands
against thyself; not as yet has a foe been wanting to thee. But now that
the walls are tottering with the dwellings half overthrown throughout
the cities of Italy, and, the fortifications falling away, vast stones are
lying *there,* and the houses are occupied by no protector, and but few
inhabitants are wandering amid the ancient cities, that Hesperia has

157

remained unsightly with brambles and unploughed for many a year, and that hands are wanting for the fields requiring them — not thou, fierce Pyrrhus, nor yet the Carthaginian, will prove the cause of ruin so great; to no sword has it been allowed to penetrate the vitals; deep-seated are the wounds of the fellow-citizen's right hand.

But if the Fates have decreed no other way for Nero to succeed, and at a costly price eternal realms are provided for the Gods, and heaven could only obey its own Thunderer after the wars of the raging Giants; then in no degree, O Gods above, do we complain; crimes themselves, and lawlessness, on these conditions, are approved; let Pharsalia fill her ruthless plains, and let the shades of the Carthaginians be sated with blood; let the hosts meet for the last time at tearful Munda. To these destined *wars*, Caesar, let the famine of Perusia and the struggles of Mutina be added, the fleets, too, which rugged Leucadia overwhelmed, and the servile wars beneath the burning Aetna; still, much does Rome owe to the arms of her citizens, since for thy sake these events have come to pass.

When, thy allotted duties fulfilled, thou shalt late repair to the stars, the palace of heaven, preferred *by thee*, shall receive thee, the skies rejoicing; whether it please thee to wield the sceptre, or whether to ascend the flaming chariot of Phoebus, and with thy wandering fire to survey the earth, in no way alarmed at the change of the sun; by every Divinity will it be yielded unto thee, and to thy free choice will nature leave it what God thou shalt wish to be, where to establish the sovereignty of the world. But do thou neither choose thy abode in the Arctic circle, nor where the sultry sky of the south behind us declines; whence with thy star obliquely thou mayst look upon Rome. If thou shouldst press upon one side of the boundless aether, the sky will be sensible of the burden. Keep thy weight in the mid sphere of the balanced heavens; may all that part of the aether with sky serene be free *from mist*, and may no clouds interpose before Caesar.

Then, arms laid aside, may the human race consult its own good, and may all nations love one another; may Peace, sent throughout the world, keep close the iron thresholds of the warlike Janus. But to myself already *art thou* a Divinity; and, if I, a bard, receive thee in my breast, I could not wish to invoke the God who moves the mystic shrines of Cirrha, and to withdraw Bacchus from Nysa. Sufficient art thou to supply inspiration for Roman song.

My design leads me to recount the causes of events so great, and a boundless task is commenced upon; what it was that impelled a frantic people to arms — what that drove away Peace from the world. The envious course of the Fates, and the denial to what is supreme to be of long duration; the heavy fall, too, beneath a weight too great;

and Rome that could not support herself. So when, its structure dissolved, the last hour shall have closed so many ages of the universe, all things shall return once more to former chaos; constellations shall rush on against mingled constellations; fiery stars shall fall into the deep; earth shall refuse to extend her shores, and shall cast away the ocean; Phoebe shall come into collision with her brother, and, disdaining to guide her two-horsed chariot in its sidelong course, will demand the day for herself; and the whole mechanism, discordant, will confuse the ties of the universe rent asunder.

Mighty things fall of themselves; this limit to increase have the Deities assigned to a prosperous state. Nor yet to the advantage of any *other* nations does Fortune turn her hate against a people all-powerful by land and by sea. Thou, Rome, *wast* the cause of *thy own* woes, becoming the common property of three masters; the fatal compact, too, for sway never *successfully* entrusted to a number. O ye, disastrously concordant, and blinded by desires too great, why does it please you to unite your strength and to share the world in common? While the earth shall support the sea, and the air the earth, and his long courses shall whirl on Titan *in his career*, and night shall succeed the day through signs as many, no faith is there in partners in rule, and all power will be impatient of a sharer.

And believe not any nations, nor let the examples of *this* fatality be sought from afar; the rising walls *of Rome* were steeped with a brother's blood. Nor was the earth and the ocean then the reward of frenzy so great; an humble retreat brought into collision its lords.

The discordant concord lasted for a short time; and peace there was, through no inclination of the chieftains. For Crassus, interposing, was the sole impediment to the destined war. Just as the narrow Isthmus which cleaves and barely divides the two seas, nor yet allows them to meet together; if the earth were to withdraw, the Ionian would dash itself against the Aegean main; so, when Crassus, who kept asunder the ruthless arms of the chieftains, by a fate much to be deplored stained Assyrian Carrhae with Latian blood, the Parthian misfortunes let loose the frenzy of Rome. More, ye descendants of Arsaces, was effected by you in that battle than you suppose; civil warfare you conferred upon the conquered.

The sway is cut asunder by the sword; and the fortunes of a powerful people, which embrace the sea, the land, the whole earth, brook not two *leaders*. For Julia, cut off by the ruthless hand of the Destinies, bore away to the shades below the ties of allied blood, and the marriage torches, with direful omen, portentous of woe. But if the Fates had allowed thee a longer sojourn in life, thou alone hadst been able to restrain on the one side the husband and on the other the parent, and, the sword dashed down, to join the armed hands, just as the Sabine women, interposing, united the sons-in-law with the fathers-in-law. By thy death is friendship rent asunder, and license granted to the chieftains to commence the warfare. The ambition of rivalry adds its spur.

Thou, Magnus, art afraid lest recent exploits should eclipse former triumphs, and the laurels gained from the pirates should be eclipsed by the conquest of the Gauls: thee, *Caesar*, does the continuance of thy labours and thy experience *gained by them* now elevate, and Fortune that cannot brook a second place. Neither can Caesar now endure any one his superior, nor Pompey *Anyone his equal*. Who with the more justice took up arms it is not permitted us to know; each one defends himself with a mighty abettor; the conquering cause was pleasing to the Gods, but the conquered one to Cato.

Nor did they meet on equal terms; the one, with his years tending downward to old age, and grown tranquil amid a long practice of the arts of peace, had now in tranquillity forgotten the general; and, an aspirant for fame, *had been wont to confer* upon the public many a largess; solely to be wafted on by the popular gales, and to exult in the applause of a theatre his own; not to recruit his strength afresh, and principally to rely upon his former successes. *There* stood the shadow of a glorious name: just as the lofty oak, in a fertile field, which bears the spoils of an ancient people and the consecrated gifts of chieftains, now no longer standing fast by its firm roots, is fixed by its own weight: and sending forth its bared branches into the air, with its trunk, and not its leaves, forms a shade; and although it threatens to fall at the first eastern blast, *and trees* so many around it lift themselves with firmly-rooted strength, still it alone is venerated.

But in Caesar not only was there a name as great, and the fame of the general: but a valour that knew not how to rest in *one* place, and a shame only *felt* at not conquering in war. Fierce and unrestrained; *ready* to lead his troops whither hope and whither vengeance should summon, and never to spare fleshing his sword: to press on his own advantages, to rely on the favour of the Deity; bearing down whatever opposed himself as he sought the summit, and rejoicing amid ruin to have made his way.

Just as the lightning forced by the winds through the clouds flashes forth with the echoes of the riven aether and with a crash throughout the universe, and overwhelms the light of day, and terrifies the alarmed nations, dazzling the eyes with its sidelong flame. It rages against temples its own; and, no matter impeding its going forth, both falling, it sends vast, and returning, vast devastation far and wide, and collects again its scattered fires.

These were the motives secretly existing with the chieftains; but *there were* public grounds for the warfare, which have ever overwhelmed mighty nations. For when, the world subdued, Fortune introduced wealth too great, and the manners gave way before prosperity, and booty and the spoils of the enemy induced luxurious habits; no moderation *was there* in gold or in houses; hunger, too, distained the tables of former times; dresses hardly suitable for the matrons to wear, the males seized hold upon; poverty fruitful in men was shunned; and that was fetched from the entire earth by means of which each nation falls. Then did they join the lengthened boundaries of the fields, and the extended lands once turned up by the hard ploughshare of Camillus, and which had submitted to the ancient mattocks of the Curii, lay far and wide beneath the charge of husbandmen unknown *to their employers.*

This was not the people whom tranquil peace might avail, whom its own liberty might satisfy with arms unmoved. Thence *arose* ready broils, and the contemptible wickedness which poverty could prompt; and the great honor, and one worthy to be sought with the sword, to have been able to do more than one's own country; might, too, was the measure of right; hence laws and decrees of the people constrained, and Tribunes confounding their rights with Consuls. Hence the Fasces snatched up at a price, and the populace itself the vendor of its own applause, and canvassing fatal to the city, bringing round the annual contests on the venal Plain *of Mars*; hence devouring usury, and interest greedy for each moment, and credit shaken, and warfare profitable to the many.

Now had Caesar in his course passed the icy Alps, and revolved in his mind the vast commotions and the future war. When he had arrived at the waves of the little Rubicon, the mighty image of his trembling country distinctly appeared to the chieftain in the darkness of the night, bearing marks of extreme sadness on her features, letting loose the white hair from her tower-bearing head, with her long locks dishevelled, standing with her arms *all* bare, and uttering *these words,* mingled with sighs:

"Whither beyond this do you proceed? Whither, ye men, do you bear my standards? If rightfully you come, if as citizens, thus far you may." Then did horror smite the limbs of the chieftain, his hair stood on end, and a languor that checked his course withheld his steps on the verge of the bank. Soon he exclaims, "O Thunderer, who dost look down upon the walls of the mighty city from the Tarpeian rock, and ye Phrygian Penates of the Julian race, ye secret mysteries, too, of Quirinus borne away, and Jove of Latium, who dost reside in lofty Alba, and ye Vestal hearths, and thou, O Rome, equal to a supreme

161

Deity, favour my designs! With no fatal arms am I pursuing thee; lo! here am I, Caesar, the conqueror by land and by sea, everywhere (if only it is permitted me) thine own soldier even still. He will it be, he the guilty one, who shall make me thy foe!"

Then did he end the respite from the warfare, and swiftly bore the standards through the swollen stream. Just as when in the parched plains of sultry Libya a lion, his enemy perceived at hand, crouches undecided until he collects all his fury; soon as he has aroused himself by the lashings of his infuriate tail, and has raised his mane erect, and from his vast throat the loud roar re-echoes; then, if the light lance of the Moor, hurled, pierces him, or the hunting spears enter his broad chest, amid the weapons, careless of wounds so great, he rushes on.

From a small spring rises the ruddy Rubicon, and, when fervid summer glows, is impelled with humble waves, and through the lowly vales it creeps along, and, a fixed boundary, separates from the Ausonian husbandmen the Gallic fields. At that time winter gave it strength, and now the showery Cynthia with her blunted horn for the third time had swollen the waves, and the Alps were thawed by the watery blasts of the eastern breeze. First of all the charger is opposed obliquely to the stream, to bear the brunt of the floods; then the rest of the throng bursts through the pliant waves of the river, now broken *in its course*, across the easy ford. When Caesar, the stream surmounted, reached the opposite banks, and stood upon the forbidden fields of Hesperia; "Here," said he, "here do I leave peace, and the violated laws behind; thee, Fortune, do I follow; henceforth, far hence be treaties! The Destinies have we trusted; War as our umpire we must adopt."

Thus having said, the active leader in the shades of night hurries on his troops, and swifter than the hurled charge of the Balearic sling, and the arrow shot behind the back of the Parthian; and threatening he surprises Ariminum. Lucifer left behind, the stars fled from the fires of the sun, and now arose the day doomed to behold the first outbreak of the war. Whether by the will of the Gods, or whether the murky south wind impelled them, clouds obscured the saddened light. When in the captured Forum the soldier halted, commanded to pitch his standard, the clash of clarions and the clang of trumpets sounded the ill-omened signals together with the hoarse-sounding horn. The rest of the people was broken, and, aroused from their beds, the youth snatched down the arms fixed up near the hallowed Penates, which a prolonged peace *still* afforded; they laid hold of shields decaying with the frames now bare, and darts with blunted points, and swords rough with the cankering of swarthy rust.

When the well-known eagles glittered, and the Roman standards, and Caesar mounted aloft was beheld in the midst of the ranks, they grew chilled with alarm, icy dread bound fast their limbs, and they resolved *these* silent complaints within their speechless breasts: — "O walls ill founded, these with the Gauls for their neighbours! O *walls* condemned to a hapless site! Profound peace and tranquil repose is there throughout all nations; we are the prey and the first encampment for *these thus* frenzied. Far better, Fortune, wouldst, thou have afforded an abode in an eastern clime, and under the icy north, and wandering abodes, rather than to have to protect the threshold of Latium. We were the first to behold the commotions of the Senones, the Cimbrian, too, rushing on, and the hosts of Libya, and the career of the Teutonic rage. As oft as Fortune aims a blow at Rome, this is the passage for the warfare."

Thus with a secret sigh *spoke each*, not venturing to express his alarm aloud; no voice was entrusted to anguish; but in the same degree in which, when the winter keeps in the birds, the fields are silent, and the mid ocean without a murmur is still, thus profound was the silence. Light has *now* dispelled the cold shades of night; lo! the Fates supply to his wavering mind the torches of war and inducements provoking to battle, and rend asunder all the pauses of moderation; Fortune struggles that the movements of the chieftain shall be justified, and discovers pretexts for his arms.

The threatening Senate, the law violated, expelled from the divided city the differing Tribunes, the Gracchi being thrown in their teeth. These now repairing to the standards of the chieftain moving *onward* and in their vicinity, the daring Curio, with his venal tongue, accompanies; a voice that once was the people's, and that had dared to defend liberty, and to place armed potentates on a level with the lower classes.

And when he beheld the chieftain revolving his various cares in his breast, he said, "While, Caesar, thy party could be aided by my voice, although against the will of the Senate, then did we prolong thy rule, so long as I had the liberty to occupy the Rostra, and to bring over to thee the wavering Quirites. But after the laws, coerced by warfare, were dumb, we were driven from our paternal homes, and of our own accord we endured exile; 'tis thy victory will make us citizens *again*. While, strengthened with no support, the factions are *still* in doubt, away with delay! it always injures *men* prepared to procrastinate. Equal labours and anxieties are being sought for a greater reward. Gaul has kept thee engaged in war for twice five years, a portion of the earth how trifling! If with a happy result thou hast fought a few battles, Rome for thee will subdue the world!

"Now neither does the procession of the lengthened triumph receive thee returning, nor does the Capitol demand the consecrated

163

laurels. Cankering envy denies thee everything; and hardly wilt thou escape with impunity having subdued the foe: it is the determination of the son-in-law to deprive the father-in-law of the sway. Thou canst not share the earth; alone thou mayst possess it."

After he had thus spoken, and had aroused in him, though eager already for the war, much anger *still*, and had inflamed the chieftain, in the same degree as the Elean courser is urged on by the shouts, although, the starting place now closed, he struggles against the door, and headlong loosens the bolts. Forthwith he summons the armed maniples to the standards, and when, the multitudes collecting, he has well calmed their hurrying tumultuousness, with his countenance and his right hand he enjoins silence:

"O companions in war!" he exclaims, "who together with me have experienced the thousand hazards of battle, now in the tenth year that you have conquered, has your blood, shed in the regions of the north, deserved this, and wounds and death, and winters passed at the foot of the Alps? Not otherwise is Rome convulsed by the vast tumultuous preparations for war, than if the Punic Hannibal were descending from the Alps. With stout recruits the cohorts are being filled; for the fleet every forest is falling; and both by sea and by land is Caesar ordered to be expelled. What, if my standards had lain prostrate in adverse warfare, and if the fierce nations of the Gauls had been rushing close on our backs? Now, when Fortune acts with me in prospering circumstances, and the Gods *are* summoning us to the mastery, we are challenged. Let him come to the war, the chieftain, enfeebled by prolonged peace, with his soldiery *so* hastily levied, his toga-clad partisans, too, and the loquacious Marcellus, the Catos as well, *mere* idle names. Will, forsooth, men from afar and purchased dependants still associate Pompey with the sway for years so many? Is he to be guiding the *triumphal* chariot, his years not yet permitting it? Is he never to resign the honors which he has once usurped? Why need I now complain of the fields placed under restraint throughout the whole earth, and how that starvation at his command has become his slave? Who does not know how the camp has been intermingled with the trembling Forum? When the swords ominously threatening surrounded the terrified judgment seat with an unwonted array, and, the soldiery presuming to burst in upon the midst of the legal proceedings, the standards of Pompey closed around the accused Milo. Now, too, lest an old age spent in privacy should await him in his feebleness, he is preparing for contests accursed, accustomed to civil warfare, and, trained by crimes, to surpass his master Sulla. And as the fierce tigers never lay aside their fury, which, in the Hyrcanian forest, while they haunted the lairs of their dams, the blood deep-drawn of the slain herds has nurtured; so too, Magnus, does thy thirst survive to thee accustomed to lick the sword of Sulla. Once received within the lips, no blood allows the polluted jaws to become satiated. Still, what end will power meet with, thus prolonged? What limit is there to crimes? At least, dishonorable man, let this Sulla of thine teach thee now to dismount from this supreme sway. Shall then, after the wandering Cilicians, and the Pontic battles of the exhausted monarch, with difficulty ended through barbarian poison, Caesar be granted to Pompey as a last province, because, commanded to lay down my conquering eagles, I did not obey? If from myself the reward of my labours is torn away, to these, at least, let the rewards of their prolonged service be granted, *though* not with their general; under some leader, whoever he is, let these troops enjoy their triumph. Whither, after the wars, shall pallid old age betake itself? What settlement is there to be for those who have served their time? What lands shall be granted for our veterans to plough? What walls for the invalided? Or, Magnus, shall pirates, in preference, become the settlers? Victorious already, raise, raise your standards: the might we must employ, which we have acquired; to him who wields arms does he surrender everything who refuses what is his due. The Deities, too, will not forsake us; for neither is plunder nor sovereignty sought by my arms; we are tearing away its tyrants from a City ready to be enslaved."

Thus he speaks; but the hesitating ranks mutter among themselves words of indecision in whispers far from distinct; duty and their paternal Penates check their feelings although rendered fierce with carnage, and their swelling spirits; but through ruthless love of the sword and dread of their general, they are brought back. Then Laelius, who held the rank of first centurion, and wore the insignia of the decoration won in service, the oak that bespoke the reward for saving a citizen, exclaimed:

"If it is lawful, O greatest guardian of the Roman fame, and if it is allowed to utter the accents of truth — that a patience so long enduring has withheld thy might, do we complain. Was it that confidence in us was wanting to thee? So long as the warm blood imparts motion to these breathing bodies, and so long as stalwart arms have might to hurl the javelin, wilt thou be submitting to the degenerate arts of peace, and the sovereign sway of the Senate? Is it so very dreadful to prove the conqueror in civil war? Come, lead us amid the tribes of Scythia, amid the inhospitable shores of Syrtis, amid the sultry sands of thirsting Libya. This army, when it left the conquered world behind its back, stilled the swelling waves of Ocean with its oars, and subdued the foaming Rhine at its northern mouth. To me, in following thy commands, it is as much a matter of course to do, as *it is* to will. And

165

no fellow-citizen of mine, Caesar, is he against whom I shall hear thy trumpet-signal. By the prospering standards of thy ten campaigns I swear, and by thy triumphs *gained* over every foe; if thou shouldst bid me bury my sword in the breast of my brother, in the throat too of my parent, and in the entrails of my wife teeming with her burden, still, though with unwilling right hand, I will do all this; if to despoil the Gods, and to set fire to the Temples, the flames of thy camp shall envelope the Divinity of *Juno* Moneta; if to pitch the camp above the waves of Etrurian Tiber, a bold marker-out of the encampment will I enter upon the Hesperian fields. Whatever walls thou shalt desire to level with the plain, impelled by these arms the battering-ram shall scatter the stones far and wide; even though that city which thou shouldst order to be utterly razed should be Rome *herself*."

To these words the cohorts at once shout assent, and pledge themselves with hands lifted on high, for whatever wars he shall summon them to. An uproar ascends to the skies as vast, as, when the Thracian Boreas beats against the crags of pine-bearing Ossa, the trunks bending of the woods bowed down, or returning again *upright* into the air, the roar *of the forests* arises.

Caesar, when he perceives that the war is embraced by the soldiers thus heartily, and that the Fates are favouring, that by no indecision he may impede his fortune, summons forth the cohorts scattered throughout the Gallic fields, and with standard moved from every direction marches upon Rome. They deserted the tents pitched by the cavity of Lemannus, and the camp which soaring aloft above the curving rock of Vogesus used to overawe the pugnacious Lingones with their painted arms. Those left the shallows of Isara, which running with its own flood through such an extent, falling into a stream of greater name, bears not *its own* name down to the ocean waves. The yellow-haired Ruteni are relieved from the prolonged garrison; the placid Atax rejoices at no longer bearing the Latian keels; the Varus, too, the limit of Hesperia, her boundaries *now* extended; where, too, beneath the divine authority of Hercules, the consecrated harbour adjoins the sea with its hollowed rocks; no Corus holds sway over it, nor yet the Zephyr; alone does Circius disturb the shores his own, and withholds *the ships* from the safe harbour of Monoecus. Where, too, the doubtful coast extends, which land and sea claim at alternate periods, when the vast ocean is poured forth *upon it*, or when with ebbing waves it retreats. *Whether it is that* the wind thus rolls on the sea from distant climes, and bearing it on *there* leaves it; or whether the waves of wandering Tethys, influenced by the second of the heavenly bodies, flow at the lunar hours; or whether the flaming Titan, that he may quaff the refreshing waves, uplifts the ocean, and raises the billows to the

166

stars — do you enquire, whom the economy of the universe engages; but to me, thou Cause, whatever thou art, that dost govern movements thus regular, as the Gods of heaven have willed it *so*, for ever lie concealed!

Then does he, who occupies the field of Nemetis and the banks of the Aturus, where on the curving shore, flowing by Tarbela, it encloses the sea gently flowing in, move his standards, and the Santonian exults, the enemy removed; the Biturigian, too, and the active Suessones with their long arms; the Leucan and the Rheman, most adroit in extending the arm *with the poised javelin*; the Sequanian race most adroit with the reins guided in the circle; the Belgian, too, the skilful guide of the scythed chariot; the Arverni, likewise, who have presumed to pretend themselves of Latian brotherhood, descended from the race of the people of Ilium; the Nervian, also, too fatally rebellious, and defiled by the *broken* treaty with the slaughtered Cotta; the Vangiones, too, who imitate thee, Sarmatian, with the looselyflowing trowsers; the fierce Batavians, too, whom the harsh-sounding trumpets of crooked brass inflame *to war*; where Cinga flows around with its tide; where the Rhone bears to the sea the Arar, swept along with its impetuous waves; where the race dwells upon the heights on the mountain summits, the Gebennae precipitous with their snowwhite crags. (The Pictones, left at liberty, cultivate their fields; and no more does the camp pitched around keep in check the fickle Turones. The Andian disdaining, Meduana, to pine amid thy fogs, is now refreshed by the placid stream of Liger; from the squadrons of Caesar renowned Genabos is set free.)

Thou, too, Trevirian, overjoyed that the course of warfare is turned back; and *thou*, Ligurian, now shorn, in former times with thy locks hanging adown thy graceful neck, preferred to the whole of long-haired Gaul; *those*, too, by whom the relentless Teutates is appeased by direful bloodshed, and Hesus, dreadful with his merciless altars; and the shrine of Taranis, not more humane than *that* of Scythian Diana. You, too, *ye* Bards, who, *as* poets, hand down in your praises to remote ages spirits valiant, and cut off in war, freed from alarm, did *then* pour forth full many a strain; and you, Druids, after arms were laid aside, sought once again your barbarous ceremonials and the ruthless usages of your sacred rites. To you alone has it been granted to know the Gods and the Divinities of heaven, or alone to know that they do not exist. In remote forests do you inhabit the deep glades. On your authority the shades seek not the silent abodes of Erebus, and the pallid realms of Pluto in the depths below; the same spirit controls other limbs in another world; death is the mid space in a prolonged existence, if you sing what is ascertained *as truth*. Assuredly

167

the nations whom the Northern Bear looks down upon *are* happy in their error, whom this, the very greatest of terrors, does not move, the fear of death. Thence have the people spirits *ever* ready to rush to arms, and souls that welcome death; and *they deem* it cowardice to be sparing of a life destined to return. You, too, stationed to prevent the Cauci, with their curling locks, from warfare, repair to Rome, and desert the savage banks of the Rhine, and the world *now* laid open to the nations.

Caesar, when his immense resources, with their collected strength, had created confidence for daring still greater things, spread throughout all Italy, and filled the neighbouring fortified towns. Idle rumours, too, were added to well-founded fears, and burst upon the feelings of the public, and presented to them the destined slaughter, and, a swift forerunner of the hastening warfare, let loose tongues innumerable to false alarms. Some there are who, where Mevania displays itself in the plains that rear the bulls, aver that the audacious squadrons are pushing onward to the combat, and that, where Nar flows on to the stream of Tiber, the barbarian troops of the ruthless Caesar are spreading far and wide; that he himself, leading all his eagles and his collected standards, is advancing with no single column, and with a camp densely thronged. And not such as they remember him do they *now* behold him; both more terrible and relentless does he seem to their imaginations, and more inhuman than the conquered foe. That after him the nations lying between the Rhine and the Alps, torn from the Arctic regions and from their paternal homes, are following close, and that the City has been ordered, a Roman looking on, to be sacked by barbarous tribes.

Thus, by his fears, does each one give strength to rumour; and no one the author of their woes, what they have invented they dread. And not alone is the lower class alarmed, smitten by a groundless terror; but the Senate house, and the Fathers themselves rush forth from their seats, and the Senate taking to flight gives its hateful decrees for the warfare into the charge of the Consuls. Then uncertain what to seek as safe, and what to leave as worthy to be feared, whither the anxiety for flight directs each one, it urges the populace headlong, and the throng, connected in *one* long line, bursts forth.

You would suppose either that accursed torches had set fire to the abodes, or that now, the ruins shaking, the nodding houses were tottering to their fall; thus does the panic-stricken multitude at random rush throughout the City with precipitate steps, as though there had been but one hope in their ruined fortunes, to desert their paternal walls. Just as, when the stormy south wind has repulsed from the Libyan Syrtes the boundless ocean, and the broken mass of the sail-bearing mast has sent forth its crash, and the pilot, the ship deserted, leaps into the waves, the seaman, too, and *thus*, the structure of the vessel not yet torn asunder, each one makes a shipwreck for himself; so the City forsaken, do they fly unto the warfare. The parent, now weakened with old age, was able to call no one back; nor yet the wife her husband with her tears; nor did the household Lares detain them, while they were breathing prayers for their safety *thus* doubtful; nor did any one pause at the threshold, and then, filled with perhaps his last glimpse of the beloved City, take his departure; not to be called back, the crowd rushes on.

O Deities, ready to grant supreme prosperity, and loth to preserve the same! The cowardly throngs left the City a prey on Caesar's approach, filled with the people and with conquered nations, and able to hold the human race, if the multitude were collected together. When, in foreign regions, the Roman soldier, pressed by the foe, is hemmed in, he escapes the dangers of the night by a simple trench; and the rampart suddenly formed with the protection of some clods torn up affords secure slumbers within the tents. Thou Rome, on the name only of war being heard art being deserted; a single night has not been trusted to thy walls.

Still, pardon must be granted, *yes*, must be granted for alarms thus great. Pompey flying, they were in dread. Besides, that even no hope in the future might cheer their failing spirits, there was added the disclosed assurance of a still worse future, and the threatening Gods of heaven filled with prodigies the earth, the seas, the skies. The gloomy nights beheld stars unknown, and the sky burning with flames, and torches flying obliquely through the expanse along the heavens, and the train of a fear-inspiring meteor, and a comet threatening sky, and the fire described various forms in the dense atmosphere; now a javelin, with a prolonged *flame*, and now a torch, with a scattered light, flashed in the heavens. Lightning in silence without any clouds, and bringing its fires from the Arctic regions, smote the Capital of Latium; the lesser stars, too, that were wont to speed onwards in the still hours of the night, came in the middle of the day; and, her horns closed, when Phoebe was now reflecting her brother on her whole orb, struck by the sudden shadow of the earth she turned pale. Titan himself, when he was raising his head in mid Olympus, concealed his glowing chariot in dense darkness, and enwrapped the earth in shade, and forced the nations to despair of day; just as, the Sun retreating by the east, Mycenae of Thyestes brought on the night.

Grim Mulciber opened the mouths of Sicilian Etna; nor did it raise its flames to the heavens, but with its crest bending low the flame fell downwards on the Hesperian side. The black Charybdis stirred up from her depths sea of the colour of blood; the savage dogs barked in dismal tones. The fire was torn from the Vestal altars; and the flame that showed that the Latin rites were completed was divided into *two* parts, and rose with a twofold point, resembling the funeral piles of Thebes. Then did the Earth withdraw from her axis, and, their ridges quaking, the Alps shook off their ancient snows. With billows more mighty Tethys did overwhelm Hesperian Calpe and the heights of Atlas. We have heard how that the native Deities wept, and how with sweat the Lares attested the woes of the City, how, too, that the presented gifts fell down in their Temples, and birds of ill omen polluted the day; and how that the wild beasts, emboldened, the woods at nightfall deserted, made their lairs in the midst of Rome. Then were the tongues of cattle adapted to human accents; monstrous births, too, *there were* of human beings, both as to the number and the formation of the limbs, and her own infant struck the mother with horror; the fatal lines, too, of the Prophetess of Cumae were repeated among the populace. Then did those, whom with their hacked arms the savage Bellona inspires, sing of the Gods enraged; and tossing their blood-stained hair, the Galli howled forth sad accents to the throng. Urns filled with bones laid at rest sent forth groans.

Then arose the crash of arms, and loud voices were heard amid the remote parts of the groves, and ghosts came nigh to *men*. Those, too, who till the fields adjacent to the extremities of the walls, fled in all directions; the mighty Erinys was encompassing the City about, shaking her pitch-tree torch down-turned with flaming top, and her hissing locks; such as when the Fury impelled the Theban Agave, or whirled *in air* the weapons of the savage Lycurgus; or such as, when, by the command of the unjust Juno, Pluto now visited, Alcides shuddered at Megaera. Trumpets resounded, and black night, amid the silent shades, sent forth an uproar as loud as that with which the cohorts are mingled *in combat*. The shade of Sulla, too, seeming to arise in the middle of the Plain *of Mars*, uttered ill-boding prophecies; and the husbandmen fled from Marius raising his head at the cold waves of Anio, his sepulchre burst asunder.

By reason of these things it seemed good that, according to the ancient usage, the Etrurian prophets should be summoned. Of whom, Aruns, the one most stricken in years, inhabited the walls of deserted Luca, well-skilled in the movements of the lightnings, and the throbbing veins of the entrails, and the warnings of the wing hovering in the air. In the first place he orders the monsters, which revolting nature has produced from no seed, to be seized, and *then bids them* burn the accursed progeny of the barren womb in ill-omened flames. Then next he orders the whole City to be perambulated by the trembling citizens,

170

and the priests, who purify the walls at the festive lustrum, to whom is granted the power to perform the rite, to go round about the lengthened spaces without the walls, at the extreme boundaries. The inferior throng follows, tightly girt in the Gabinian fashion, and the filleted priestess leads the Vestal choir, to whom alone it is permitted to behold the Trojan Minerva. Next, those who have charge of the decrees of the Gods and the mystic prophecies, and who reconduct Cybele, when bathed, from the little Almo: the Augur, too, skilled in observing the birds on the left hand; and the Septemvir, joyous at the festivals, and the fellowship of the Titii, — the Salian, likewise, carrying the ancilia on his exulting neck; and the Flamen, who wears the tuft upon his noble head.

And while in prolonged circuit they go round about the emptied City, Aruns collects the dispersed *objects struck by* flames of lightning, and with a lamenting murmur buries them in the earth, and bestows a name upon the consecrated spots. Then does he urge onward to the altar a male, with selected neck. Now had he begun to pour the wine, and to place on it the salted corn, with knife pointed downwards; and long was the victim impatient of the rites not grateful to him; when the aproned attendants pressed upon the threatening horns, sinking on his knees he presented his subdued neck. And no blood as usual spurted forth; but from the gaping wound there was black venom poured forth instead of ruddy gore. Astounded at the ill-omened rites Aruns turned pale, and sought the wrath of the Gods of heaven in the torn-out entrails. The very colour alarmed the prophet; for a pervading lividness streaked with spots of blood the pallid vitals, tinted with foul spots and gorged with congealed blood. He perceives the liver reeking with corruption, and beholds the veins threatening on the enemy's side. The fibres of the panting lungs lie concealed, and a narrow line separates the vital parts. The heart lies still; and through gaping clefts the vitals emit corrupt matter; the cauls, too, disclose their retreats; and, shocking sign! that which has appeared with impunity in no entrails, lo! he sees growing upon the head of the entrails the mass of another head — a part hangs weak and flabby, a part throbs and with a rapid pulsation incessantly moves the veins.

When, by these means, he understood the fated allotment of vast woes, he exclaimed, "Hardly is it righteous, Gods of heaven, for me to disclose to the people what you warn me of! nor indeed, supreme Jupiter, have I propitiously offered unto thee this sacrifice; and into the breast of the slaughtered bull have the infernal Deities entered! Things not to be uttered too we dread; but things still greater than our apprehensions will come to pass. May the Gods grant a prosperous result to what has been seen, and may there be no truth in the entrails;

but *rather* may Tages, the founder of the art, have *fondly* invented *all* these things!" Thus did the Etrurian, obscuring the omens and concealing them in much perplexing doubt, utter his prophecies.

But Figulus, to whom it was a care to know the Gods and the secrets of the heavens, whom not Egyptian Memphis could equal in the science of the stars and in the principles which regulate the heavenly bodies, exclaimed: — "Either this world wanders without any laws throughout all ages, and the Constellations run to and fro with uncertain movements; or else, if the Fates hold sway, a speedy destruction is preparing for the City and the human race. Will the earth yawn, and cities be swallowed up? Or will the glowing atmosphere deprive us of all moderate temperature? Will the faithless earth refuse her crops of corn? Will all the water be mingled with poison infused *therein*? What kind of ruin, O Gods of heaven, with what plagues do you furnish your vengeance? At the same instant the closing days of many have met. If the cold star of Saturn, with its evil influence in the lofty heaven, had lighted up its dusky fires, Aquarius would have poured forth showers worthy of Deucalion, and the whole earth would have been concealed in the ocean spread over it. If, Phoebus, thou wast now urging the fierce Nemean lion with thy rays, flames would be making their way over the whole world, and, set on fire by thy chariot, the sky would be in a blaze. Those fires pause; thou, Gradivus, who dost inflame the threatening Scorpion with his burning tail, and dost thou make preparations thus mighty? For with his remote setting propitious Jupiter is going down, and the healthful star of Venus is dim, and the Cyllenian *Deity*, rapid in his movements, is retarded, and Mars occupies the heavens alone.

"Why have the Constellations forsaken their courses, and *why* in obscurity are they borne along throughout the universe? Why *thus* intensely shines the side of the sword-girt Orion? The frenzy of arms is threatening; and the might of the sword shall confound all right by force; and for many a year shall this madness prevail. And what avails it to ask an end from the Gods of heaven? That peace comes with a tyrant *alone*. Prolong, Rome, the continuous series of thy woes; protract for a length of time thy calamities, only now free during civil war."

These presages greatly alarm the trembling multitude, but greater ones confound them. For just as on the heights of Pindus the Edonian female, filled with the Ogygian Lyaeus, hurries along, so likewise is a matron, borne along through the astounded City, disclosing by these words how Phoebus is exciting her breast: "Whither, O Paean, am I being borne? In what land art thou placing me, hurried along amid the skies? I see Pangaeum, white with its snowy ridges, and extended Philippi beneath the crags of Haemus. What frenzy this is, O Phoebus, tell *me*; why do Roman armies mingle their weapons and their bands? Without an enemy is there war? Torn away, whither am I being borne? Thou art conducting me to the distant east, where the sea is changed by the stream of the Nile of Lagus. Him who is lying a hideous trunk on the river's sand, do I recognize. Over the seas am I borne to the shifting Syrtes and the parched Libya, whither the direful Erinys has transferred the ranks of Emathia. Now above the heights of the cloud-capt Alps and the aërial Pyrenees am I torn away. To the abodes of my native City I return, and in the midst of the Senate impious warfare is being waged. Factions again arise, and once more throughout all the earth do I proceed. Permit me to behold fresh shores of the sea, and fresh lands; now, Phoebus, have I beheld Philippi!"

Thus she said; and exhausted by her wearied frenzy she laid her down.

H. T. Riley

STATIUS

PUBLIUS PAPINIUS STATIUS (c. 45 - 96 A.D.) was born in Naples. He settled in Rome, acquired great popularity as a poet, and was attached to the court of the Emperor Domitian.

In addition to a series of occasional poems entitled *Silvae*, in five books, Statius composed two epics: *Thebais*, in twelve books, and *Achilleis*, in two books unfinished.

Book I — *Thebais*

THE ARGUMENT

Eteocles and Polynices having dethroned their father, Oedipus, king of Thebes, agree to reign alternately. Oedipus invokes the fury Tisiphone to punish them; she sows dissension between them. Eteocles is chosen by lot to reign the first year. An universal discontent prevails among the Thebans. Jupiter calls a council of the Gods, and declares his intention of punishing Thebes and Argos. He sends Mercury to call up the ghost of Laius from the shades. On Eteocles's refusing to give up the sceptre at the expiration of his year, Polynices goes to Argos to solicit the aid of Adrastus against him. He is overtaken by a heavy storm, and being very much fatigued, lies down at Adrastus's gate. Tydeus arrives at the same place by chance. They quarrel and fight. Adrastus, alarmed at the noise, comes out, reconciles, and entertains them very hospitably. He relates the origin of a sacrifice which was then celebrating, and addresses a prayer to Apollo, which concludes the book.

Of guilty Thebes, to foreign arms a prey,
Fraternal rage, and impious lust of sway,
My daring Muse would sing, so Phoebus deign
To prompt the bard, and harmonize the strain.
Say, goddess, whence shall I my subject trace,
From Cadmus, author of the vicious race?
Shall I describe him on the raging sea,
Obsequious to the monarch's stern decree?

Then tell, from whence th' aspiring nation rose,
And to what source proud Thebes its grandeur owes,
How soften'd rocks (so will'd resistless fate)
Danc'd into form, to grace a future state?
What fatal causes could so far incense
The queen of Heav'n, and what the dire offence,
When Athamas, by wrath divine pursu'd,
His trembling hands in filial blood imbrued,
And his pale spouse, to shun his angry bow,
Sprung from the beach, and sought the depths below?
Waive then, whate'er to Cadmus may belong,
O Muse, and date the subject of thy song
From wretched Oedipus; — nor yet aspire
In Caesar's praise to string thy feeble lyre,
Or tell, how twice he bade the Rhine obey,
How twice the Danube roll'd beneath his sway:
(While Dacia, daring impious war to wage,
Fell the just object of the victor's rage:)
Or how, in youthful armour clad, he strove
To vindicate the sacred rites of Jove.
Nor thou, commission'd in the rolls of fate,
To swell the glories of the Latian state,
By wild ambition led away, resign
The Roman helm to feebler hands than thine.
What tho' the stars contract their liquid space,
Well pleas'd to yield thee a serener place;
Tho' Phoebus, conscious of superior blaze,
Would intermix with thine his friendly rays;
And Jove his wide-extended empire share,
Content to rule an equal tract of air;
Yet may thy people's wishes thee detain,
And Jove enjoy an undivided reign.
The time will come, when a diviner flame
Shall prompt me to resound thy ripen'd flame,
Meanwhile permit my Muse to seek renown
In Theban wars, a prelude to thy own.
She sings of souls discordant e'en in death,
And hate, that fled not with the vital breath;
A throne, for which the vengeful fates decreed,
Two rival kings by mutual arms should bleed,
And scepter'd chiefs; who long unbury'd lay,
To birds and beasts an undistinguish'd prey;
When Dirce's source was stain'd with kindred gore,

175

And Thetis from the blood-impurpled shore
Beheld Ismenos roll a mingled heap
Of arms and warriors to the frighted deep.
What first, O Clio, shall adorn thy page,
Th' expiring prophet, or Aetolian's rage?
Say, wilt thou sing, how grim with hostile blood,
Hippomedon repell'd the rushing flood;
Lament th' Arcadian youth's untimely fate,
Or Jove, oppos'd by Capaneus, relate?
    Now Oedipus, inur'd to deepest night,
No more in sighs bewails the loss of sight;
And tho' the rays of Phoebus ne'er invade
His dark abode, or pierce th' eternal shade,
Yet conscience haunts him with reflecting glass,
Thro' which his sins, too well distinguish'd, pass.
Their torches o'er his head the furies rear,
And threats and harsh reproaches grate his ear,
Now to th' unpitying ruler of the skies
He lifts the gloomy sockets of his eyes,
Then strikes the gaping void with impious hands,
And thus aloud infernal aid demands.
"Ye gods, who sway in Tartarus maintain,
Where guilty spirits howl with endless pain;
Thou Styx, whose gloomy banks, and shady lake
A sad impression on my senses make;
Tisiphone, on whose repeated name
I've dwelt; if Oedipus attention claim,
Oh! lend an ear, and from the realms below
Accord my wishes, and assist my vow.
If from my sire misdeem'd I took my way
To Cyrrha's fane on that important day,
When Laius bled beneath these impious hands,
Where the three paths divide the Phocian lands:
If seconded by thee, I durst chastise
Th' insidious Sphinx, and gain'd the glitt'ring prize;
Or, by thy fav'ring torch conducted, strove
To meet with equal fires Jocasta's love:
If studious of thy cause, I now prepare
Two sons, whose rising merits claim thy care;
And, too impatient of the vital light,
Forc'd from these streaming orbs the balls of sight:
Attend, and aid the vengeance I request;
If worthy thee, and what thou would'st suggest,

176

My sons (if sons they are) their sire disown,
Spoil'd of his eyes, and driven from his throne;
And, while a guideless, helpless wretch I roam,
Deride my groans in pamp'ring ease at home.
Such is their pity, such their filial love,
And yet inactive sleep the bolts of Jove.
Then be the place of Jove by thee supply'd,
To check their insults, and reward their pride;
Let them some lasting stroke of vengeance mourn,
Which may extend to ages yet unborn:
Give them the crown, which steep'd in recent gore,
From the cleft temples of my sire I tore.
Go then, dissolve the sacred bonds of peace,
Bid discord rise, and love fraternal cease:
Urge them to dare, what may to latest times
Transmit their guilt, some yet unacted crimes.
Soon thou'lt experience (do but lead the way)
Their headstrong wills, impatient of delay;
And in the outlines of their tempers find
The truest portrait of their father's mind."
The list'ning fury now prepares to rise,
And tow'rds the suppliant wretch directs her eyes.
On sad Cocytos' banks she sate reclin'd,
And to the breeze her flowing locks resign'd.
Her snakes, unbound, along the margin glide,
Sport on the waves, or lash the sulph'ry tide.
From thence she springs; not swifter lightnings fly,
Or falling stars, that cleave the mid-way sky.
The phantoms ken her, as she soars in air,
And to the distant shades in haste repair.
Thro' dreary realms, and Pluto's wide domains
She roams, and soon th' infernal mansion gains.
The day beheld her dire approach, and shrouds
Her sick'ning glories in encircling clouds,
E'ven Atlas labour'd with unwonted fears,
And shook beneath the burden of the spheres.
From Malea's humble vale she rose in flight,
And sped to Thebes, the monster's chief delight.
Not Hell itself, nor the Tartarean coast
An equal share of her esteem can boast.
A hundred serpents on her visage glare
With horrid scales, and mingle with her hair:
Her eyes, intrench'd within her bristling head,

By fits, a livid, fainty splendour shed.
Thus Cynthia blushes thro' the midnight shade,
When magic charms her lab'ring beams invade.
Her bloated skin with gather'd venom teems,
And her foul mouth exhales sulphureous steams.
Disease and death's annihilating force
From hence, as she commissions, bend their course.
Some stiffen'd rags were o'er her shoulders thrown,
And the dire monster by her dress was known.
A crested serpent arm'd her better hand,
And in the left she toss'd a flaming brand.
When now she stood where craggy cliffs arise,
And proud Cithaeron threats the neighb'ring skies,
Rang'd on her head, the scaly monsters glare,
And hiss, entwin'd in her envenom'd hair.
A signal to the Earth the shores resound,
And Greece from far returns the deaf'ning sound.
The distant summons fam'd Parnassus took,
And old Eurotas from its summit shook:
Huge Oeta nods, half sunk with all her pines,
And Isthmos scarce the parted waves disjoins;
While starting at the shock, Leucothoe press'd
The young Palaemon closer to her breast.
The fury to the palace now had come,
And shaded with her wings the splendid dome,
When here and there each furious brother flies,
And rage the place of mutual love supplies:
While jealousy and hate-ingend'ring fears
Flame in their breasts, and haunt their cred'lous ears.
Their restless minds then wild ambition fires
To break the league, and deadly wrath inspires.
Their haughty souls superior pow'r disown,
And scorn th' alternate splendours of a crown.
Such discord rises from divided sway,
When each will rule, and neither will obey.
As two young steers, when first compell'd to bow
Their stubborn necks, and trail the galling plow,
Frisk here and there, impatient of the toil,
And spread disorder o'er the furrowy soil;
Thus Discord arms the brothers in her cause,
And urges them to cancel nature's laws.
First they decreed, that each in turn should wear
The diadem in his successive year.

Unhappy youths, no longer doom'd to prove
The joys of friendship, and fraternal love!
While that in exile mourns his present state,
This dreads, alas! the same impending fate.
Nor long this league withheld their impious hands,
From executing Discord's dire commands:
But ere one year was clos'd, they both gave away
To fierce contention, and desire of sway.
Yet then no gates of iv'ry did unfold
The palace, beaming with barbaric gold;
No polish'd arches, fram'd of Parian stone,
Beneath th' incumbent dome in order shone;
No guards, reclining on erected spears,
Essay'd to chase the sleepless tyrant's fears;
Nor curious gems, inlaid with art divine,
Flam'd on the brim, and sparkled in the wine.
Mere lust of pow'r the rival brothers arms,
And fills a narrow realm with war's alarms.
But while their claims yet undetermin'd stand,
And none enjoys in peace supreme command;
Law gives a sanction to injurious might,
And pow'r is hallow'd with the name of right.
Say, rivals, why ye rush to mutual death,
And why so lavish of your vital breath?
Not all th' united realms, which Sol surveys,
Adorn'd with orient, or declining rays,
When to the south he bends his rapid course,
Or the bleak north enjoys his temp'rate force;
Not all the wealth that fertile Tyre can boast,
Nor all that glitters on the Phrygian coast;
Could claim such deeds, or merit such regard,
Were all those realms the conqueror's reward.
Meanwhile the lots for the first year were thrown,
And proud Eteocles ascends the throne.
How grateful then, O tyrant, was the day,
When all around were subject to thy sway!
How pleas'd, without contention to devour
The wish'd-for sweets of undivided pow'r!

And now the disaffected Thebans vent
In whisper'd tales their growing discontent.
To th' absent prince in secret they adhere,
And curse the slow progression of the year.
Then one, by nature ready to complain,

Alike dissatisfy'd with every reign,
Well taught to feel rebellious faction's flame,
And brand with calumny the royal name,
Exclaim'd aloud: "Shall then the Theban state
Feel each vicissitude of cruel fate?
Still must our slavish necks with patience bear
Th' alternate yoke of each tyrannic heir;
Who now reverse our fates, divide the land,
And hold inferior fortune at command?
For e'er shall Thebes her sad condition mourn,
And dread each exil'd tyrant's quick return?
Is this thy fixt decree, almighty Jove,
Is this a proof of thy paternal love?
Was this a curse entail'd upon our race?
Say, from what time the omen we may trace;
When Cadmus sought his sister on the main,
Sow'd with the serpent's teeth the fertile plain,
And, forc'd on fair Boeotia's soil by fate,
Laid the foundation of the Theban state?
See, how elate with pride our king appears,
Free from competitors, and void of fears!
What threat'ning looks he wears, as if again
He scorn'd to yield his temporary reign.
Yet none before was easier of access,
More affable, or prone to give redress.
Nor wonder we: he was not then alone,
Nor without dread of a divided throne.
While we stand here, a patient servile band,
Prepar'd to act whate'er our lords command.
As when two winds contend with adverse force,
And influence by turns the vessel's course,
On this side now, obsequious to the blast,
Now there she nods, and still obeys the last:
Thus fares our state, between the doubtful sway
Of either prince, unknowing which t'obey.
Distracted, tortur'd with suspense she stands,
While this repeats his threats, and that commands."
    Meanwhile the king of Heav'n, imperial Jove,
Convenes a synod of the pow'rs above;
Full in the midst, enthron'd, the thund'rer sate,
Sublime in all the pomp of regal state.
Beneath his piercing eye, in full survey,
The spacious earth, and seas contracted lay.

His brow was void of frowns, serene his look,
Yet at his nod the whole creation shook.
Their heav'nly king the rising senate greet,
And at his word resume their starry seat.
Inferior gods from ev'ry quarter come,
By rank distinguish'd in the starry dome.
None absent were of all whose force can bind,
Or on the deep discharge, the furious wind;
No rosy dryad of the shady wood,
Nor azure sister of the crystal flood.
But here, obedient to their sov'reign's will,
The winds are silent, and the waves lie still.
Thro' Heav'n's expanse a gath'ring horrour rolls,
And huge Olympus trembles to the poles.
With rays serene the wreathed pillars glare,
And a new lustre gilds the fields of air.
Its tremours now the globe began to cease,
And nature lay resign'd to downy peace;
When thus the thund'rer spoke: assenting fate
On ev'ry accent stamp'd resistless weight.
"Say, must I still of human crimes complain,
And must the thund'rer's bolts be hurl'd in vain?
Why seek they thus my tardy wrath to prove,
And scorn my proffer'd clemency and love;
While yet the Cyclops ply their arms no more,
And Aetna weeps for her exhausted store?
For this I suffer'd headstrong Phaeton
To mount the car of the reluctant Sun;
And Neptune bade th' imprison'd water flow,
And hills and vales no more distinction know:
But all in vain; our vengeance they defy,
And triumph o'er the ruler of the sky.
To punish these, I leave the realms above,
A race descended from imperial Jove:
With Perseus Argo's sons alliance claim,
From Cadmus Thebes derives immortal fame.
Who has not heard of wretched Cadmus' fate,
And the long labours of the Theban state;
When from the silent regions of the night,
The furies sprang, and rush'd to mortal fight?
Why should I publish the fierce mother's shame,
And deeds, the pow'rs of Heav'n would blush to name?
Before I cou'd recount their num'rous crimes

From Cadmus' days unto the present times,
Phoebus wou'd seek the chambers of the main,
And rise to gild the courts of Heav'n again.
Say, without horrour can the tale be read
Of Laius slain, and his dishonour'd bed?
Dire monster! first to cause his father's death,
Then stain the womb, from whence he drew his breath.
Yet th' angry pow'rs he satisfies with groans,
And gloom eternal for his sins atones.
No more he breathes at large our upper air,
But feeds the worms of conscience with despair.
Yet say, what fury cou'd his sons inspire
Thus to torment their old, unhappy sire;
To trample on his eyes with impious feet,
And hurl him headlong from the regal seat?
Then let us pity him; nor let in vain
The wretched king of filial rage complain;
Hence shall it be my bus'ness to redress
His wrongs, and crown his wishes with success.
The day shall come, when discord from afar
Shall give whole nations to the waste of war;
When the whole guilty race in fight shall fall,
And one incircling ruin swallow all.
Adrastus shall in dire alliance join
With Heaven, and so complete the Fates' design.
Nor let proud Argos triumph: 'tis decreed,
That she amid the gen'ral carnage bleed:
The craft of Tantalus, and impious feast,
Yet wake my vengeance, and inflame my breast."
        Then Juno, impotent of passion, broke
Her sullen silence, and with fury spoke.
"Why urge me thus to deeds of martial rage?
Shall Juno still in mortal strife engage?
Thou know'st, no mortals merit more my grace,
Than Argos, and the fam'd Inachian race,
By me for e'er enrich'd, and taught to wield
Tho' there thy wiles, and providential care
O'ercame the keeper of the Pharian fair,
And the fam'd Argive was debauch'd of old,
Too fond, alas! of all-bewitching gold.
Yet these obscurer crimes I could forgive,
Did not proud Thebes my stifled ire revive;
Where Jove in all his dazzling glory shone,

And hurl'd the bolts to Juno due alone.
Let punish'd Thebes absolve th' injurious deed,
Nor both beneath divided vengeance bleed.
But if, tenacious of thy right divine,
Thou'lt thwart my will, and frustrate my design,
Descend from Heav'n, fulfil thy stern desire,
Raze Samos, wrap Mycenae's walls in fire,
The guiltless Spartan race at once confound,
And their fair structures level with the ground.
With incense why should Juno's altars blaze,
And joyful paeans swell the note of praise?
Transfer to more deserving Isis' fane
The fatten'd victim, destin'd to be slain.
For her in Egypt bid the timbrel sound,
And Nile from ev'ry mouth her praise rebound.
But if thou wilt chastise the present age,
And sacrifice whole nations to thy rage,
If thou wilt trace obliterated crimes
From the dark annals of preceding times,
Say, from what period then it is decreed,
And to what times the guilty world shall bleed.
Begin, from whence in many a winding maze
To the Sicilian stream Alphaeus strays:
There dire Arcadia's swains presum'd to found
Thy sacred temple on polluted ground;
Where stern Oenomaus' car was wont to stand,
And mould'ring skulls lie scatter'd on the sand.
Since such oblations please, since patient Jove
Yet courts the shades of Ida's guilty grove,
And favours Crete, whose impious sons presume
To show the king of Heav'n's fictitious tomb;
In Argos let thy spouse unenvy'd reign,
And share the mystic honours of the fane:
Nor waste in fight a race deriv'd from Jove,
A race, whose merits claim paternal love.
Let more detested realms in wars engage,
And feel the sad effects of filial rage."
Thus strove in vain th' indignant queen of air,
And blended in her speech reproach and prayer;
Unmov'd remains the ruler of the skies,
And thus with calmness from his throne replies.
" 'Twas thus I deem'd the queen of Heav'n would plead,
Whene'er the fate of Argos was decreed:

Nor less might Bacchus thwart the fate,
Bacchus, the guardian of the Theban state,
But he not dares the lifted bolt to stay,
Reveres our pow'r and gives the vengeance way.
For by thy waves, tremendous Styx! that flow
Thro' the drear realms of gliding ghosts below,
Not all the gods, who reign in Heav'n above,
Shall change this fixt decree, or influence Jove.
Thus have I sworn, and what I swear shall stand,
That none but Jove shall exercise command.
Haste then, my son, our orders to perform,
Mount the fleet wind, and ride the rapid storm,
To Pluto's realms with willing haste repair,
And summon Laius to the fields of air,
Whose shiv'ring ghost with lifted hands implores
A speedy passage to the farther shores.
Let his proud grandson, taught by him, disown
The mutual compact, nor resign the crown
To banish'd Polynices, who relies
On Tydeus, and his Argive sire's supplies.
From hence shall spring the seeds of mutual hate,
The rest shall follow in the course of fate."
Swift as the word, the sprightly son of May
Prepares th' Almighty's orders to obey;
The glitt'ring sandals to his feet applies,
And to his heels the well-trim'd pinion ties.
His hat's wide-spread circumference confines
The starry radiance, that around him shines.
He grasps the wand, which draws from hollow graves,
Or drives the trembling shades to Stygian waves;
With magic power seals up the watchful eye
In slumbers soft, or causes sleep to fly.
From the vast height with swift descent he springs;
(A slender gale supports his steady wings)
Then thro' th' etherial void conspicuous flew,
And a long trail of light behind him drew.
Meanwhile from Thebes the banish'd hero roves
Thro' barren tracts, and wide Aonian groves;
And while the flatt'ring hopes of distant sway
Chear the bleak horrours of the tedious way,
The partial signs enlarge their heav'nly space,
And the Sun seems to run a double race:
His cares arise with each revolving ray,

And night renews the labours of the day.
In prospect he prevents his future joy,
And snatches at the visionary toy,
Surveys the glitt'ring tow'rs of Thebes his own,
Or deals out justice from a fancied throne.
Would fate permit, he'd give an age away,
And lavish all on one luxurious day:
Despair renews, now hope dispels his gloom,
And fruitless wishes all his joys consume.
The prince at length resolves to seek for aid,
Where Danaus once th' Inachian sceptre sway'd,
From whence th' indignant Sun withdrew his light,
And hid the tyrant's crimes in sudden night:
And now, impell'd by furies, chance or fate,
He rush'd impetuous from the well-known gate,
And quits the caves, where howling matrons toil,
And slaughter'd Pentheus fertiliz'd the soil;
Then views from whence Cithaeron's less'ning steep
Receives its limits from th' adjoining deep,
Or trembling hangs on Scyron's noted rock,
And from afar surveys the wat'ry shock.
To Megara the warrior next repairs,
Fam'd for the rape of Nisus' purple hairs,
From thence the straits of Corinth passes o'er,
And hears the billows break on either shore.
Now Phoebus, conscious of exhausted light,
Resigns his empire to succeeding night,
And rising Cynthia thro' the realms above
Her dew-bespangled car in silence drove.
All things were hush'd: sleep quits the fields of air,
And steals upon the watchful miser's care:
No future toils alarm his peaceful breast,
Steep'd in oblivion, and consign'd to rest.
Yet no red cloud, edg'd with a golden ray,
Foretold the glad approach of hast'ning day,
No faint reflection of the Sun invades
The night, or glimmers on the less'ning shades:
From Earth ascending, thicker vapours roll,
From one black mist, and darken either pole.
The winds arise, and with tumultuous rage
The gath'ring horrours of the storm presage;
And whilst in Heav'n superior sway they claim,
Earth labours, and resounds the starry frame.

185

But Auster chiefly checks the breaking light,
In clouds encircled, and renews the night;
Then opes the sluices of the pregnant sky,
And bids the tempest from each quarter fly,
Which the fierce north, ere finish'd was its course,
Congeals to show'rs of hail with wond'rous force.
The thunder rolls, with lightning ether glows,
And bursting clouds unweary'd fires disclose.
Now Nemea, now Arcadia's cloud-capt hills
Pour on the subject vales their murm'ring rills.
His waves in troops old Inachus sends forth,
And Erasinus, rising to the north.
Where late was dust, unnumber'd billows roar,
And Lerna spews around its liquid store:
Nor art, nor nature can the war sustain;
Mounds fail, and damms are interpos'd in vain
Beneath its force the tallest oaks give way,
And gaping groves admit a sudden day;
Roots, leaves and boughs are hurry'd o'er the wood,
Float on the waves, and swell the loaded flood.
Meantime the Theban views with wond'ring eyes
The rocky ruin, that around him flies:
Now rural cots, and sheep-folds borne away
By the mad whirlwind's unresisted sway,
Then show'r-fed rivers from the mountain's height
Strike his quick ear, and fill his soul with fright.
Yet not more slow, unknowing where he strays,
The madding youth thro' dark and trackless ways
Pursues his course: Fear follows close behind,
And his stern brother's image haunts his mind.
As fares a mariner, when storms arise,
And clouded Phoebe quits th' unwilling skies,
Nor shines the Northern Wain: amid the strife
Of Heav'n and ocean, thoughtful for his life,
And doubtful, whether to expect his death
From storms above, or dangers underneath,
Starts at the thunder, which around him rolls,
Or dreads destruction from the neighb'ring shoals.
Not less perplex'd, the Theban warrior roves
Thro' shadowy thickets, and surrounding groves.
In vain the brambles his huge shield oppose,
His courage to his toils superior rose;
Till now he views, where from Larissa's brow
The shelving walls with light reflected glow;

186

Thither he posts, and from Prosymna's plain
Surveys the sacred grove, and Juno's fane;
And on the right fam'd Lerna's lake beheld,
Where fierce Alcides the fierce hydra quell'd.
At length he pass'd the gates, which open lay,
And to the royal dome pursu'd his way;
O'er the cold marble then his limbs he threw,
And sought in sleep his vigour to renew.
Adrastus o'er fair Argos sway maintain'd,
And long in peace the hoary prince had reign'd;
He drew his birth on both sides from above,
And claim'd alliance with almighty Jove.
Fate would not with a manly offspring crown
His nuptial bed. Two daughters heir'd his throne.
To him Apollo, monstrous to relate!
Disclos'd the secrets of unerring fate,
And said: "Expect thy sons on Argos' shore,
A tawny lion, and a bristling boar."
Long this revolv'd within his tender breast,
Engross'd his thoughts, and broke his nightly rest;
Long sage Amphiaraus essay'd in vain
This seeming menace of the gods t' explain,
At length perceiv'd the pow'rs' superior will,
And fate oppos'd to his predicting skill.
Here Tydeus, by resistless fortune led,
From Caledon's suspected vengeance fled,
And strove, too conscious of his brother slain,
His people's love by absence to regain.
Long sought the toiling chief a safe retreat
From the rough storm, till chance directs his feet
To the same place, where, stretch'd upon the ground,
The Theban warrior a like shelter found.
But Discord, ever fond of human blood,
Forbids the chiefs to plan each other's good;
Nor suffers them beneath one roof to share
A common shelter from th' inclement air.
Awhile harsh words, and mingled threats delay
Th' alternate labours of the bloody fray:
Then, of their garments strip'd, they both engage,
And mutual blows succeed to mutual rage.
With youth and stature flush'd, the Theban glows,
And on his lowly rival deals his blows;
But valiant Tydeus, though his dwarfish size

Could promise little to the partial eyes,
With greater confidence arose to fight,
And courage that disown'd superior might.
With swift repeated strokes their hands fly round
Their heads and cheeks; their cracking jaws resound:
Thick as in war an iron tempest flies,
Or hail, that quits in rattling show'rs the skies.
Thus, when the trumpet's clanging sound proclaims
The wish'd renewal of th' Olympic games,
When clouds of dust from ev'ry part ascend,
And equal chance suspends th' impatient friend,
The different clamours of the pit engage
The list'ning rivals, and provoke their rage,
While from afar each partial mother eyes
The contest, and foredooms her son the prize.
Thus hatred, not desire of praise provokes
The sprightly chiefs, and arms their heavy strokes.
Their eyes start inward from beneath each blow,
And from their faces bloody currents flow.
Now had each vig'rous candidate for fame
With flaming sword renew'd his double claim,
And the proud Theban, stretch'd beneath the hand
Of Tydeus, dy'd with gore a foreign strand;
But old Adrastus, who with cares oppress'd,
Sigh'd for the distant joys of balmy rest,
With wonder heard th' unwonted clamours rise,
And deep-fetch'd groans, that echo'd through the skies.
But when, Aurora bringing back the day,
Through the wide op'ning gates he took his way,
And saw their manly features rough with blood,
And their gash'd cheeks emit a crimson flood,
He thus exclaims. —— " Say, what provokes your rage,
O foreign youths, and why you thus engage?
(For sure my subjects would not dare to stain
My courts with blood, and Cynthia's rule profane.
Say, is the day too scanty, or the night
Once sacred to repose, reserv'd for fight?
But come, your country, birth, and names relate,
Say, whither bound, and whence this mutual hate?
For such high spirit, and resentment shows
A breast, that with no common ardour glows,
And in that stream of honour we may trace
A gen'rous birth, and more than vulgar race."

Scarce had he spoke, when in a mingled din
The chiefs abash'd with mutual shame, begin:
"Useless are words, O king, when wounds display
The bloody labours of this casual fray."
In vain they strive, while mutual scoffs confound
Their diff'rent accents, and perplex the sound,
Till glowing with the prospect of relief,
Intrepid Tydeus thus imparts his grief.
"From fam'd Aetolia's monster-bearing plains
I stray'd an exile, till in your domains
The night my progress check'd: and shall he dare
Deny me shelter from th' inclement air,
Because he first obtain'd a safe retreat
Beneath this roof, and hospitable seat?
Shall man alone, by boasted reason led,
Refuse to share with man the social bed,
When fiercer Cyclops live in mutual peace,
And fights between the stabled Centaurs cease?
E'en rav'ning brutes defend the common cause,
Nor deviate thus from Nature's sacred laws.
But why this flow of words? this fatal morn
Shall see my bloody spoils in triumph borne,
Or should my breast with equal vigour glow,
Nor my brisk blood forget, as erst, to flow,
This arm shall soon display my lineal fire,
And prove me worthy my celestial sire."
"Nor shall the want to martial heat disgrace,"
The Theban prince replies, "my godlike race,"
For conscious pride forbad him yet to own
His wretched sire, and claim the Theban crown.
To them the king. — "This causeless strife surceas'd,
Advance, and with us share the solemn feast.
But first resign your threats, and rage of blood
To mutual love, and cares of mutual good;
And let your hands, in sacred union join'd,
Attest the fixt intentions of the mind.
For some mysterious cause was this decreed,
Nor are the gods unconscious of the deed.
Perhaps, when length of time has seal'd the vow,
And your firm hearts with holy friendship glow,
With joy you may review the bloody fray,
Nor blush to trace this e'er-auspicious day."
Thus Jove's decree, unconscious he foreshows;

The sequel far transcends his warmest vows:
For Pylades was not more known to fame,
Nor Theseus, burning with an equal flame,
Tho' to redeem his bold companion lost,
He brav'd the dangers of the Stygian coast.
At length, the chiefs to reason yield the sway,
And the sage dictates of the king obey:
An air of mutual friendship they assume,
And enter, hand in hand, the spacious room.
Thus when the ruler of the stormy main
Is pleas'd the tempest's fury to restrain,
The winds, abating, smooth the vessel's course,
And on the slack'ning sails exhaust their force.
Here first the monarch, fix'd in deep amaze,
The dress and arms of either guest surveys,
A lion's tawny hide the Theban wore
(Such grac'd the godlike Hercules of yore,
Ere Nemea's boast resign'd his shaggy spoils,
To deck his shoulders, and reward his toils):
Th' Aetolian monster's pride young Tydeus bears,
Horrid with tusks, and rough with bristling hairs.
The hoary chief, astonish'd to behold
Th' events, by Phoebus' oracles foretold,
Acknowledges with joy the voice of Heav'n,
And answers, from the vocal cavern giv'n.
Then to the skies he lifts his grateful hands,
And thus the future aid of night demands,
(While thro' each vein mysterious transports roll,
And awful pleasure thrills thro' all his soul.)
"O gloomy queen of shades, whose ebon throne
The sparkling gems of Heav'n in order crown,
Beneath whose reign indulgent sleep repairs
The busy world, and buries mortal cares,
Till rising Sol warms India's fragrant soil,
And with his rays renews our daily toil;
Whose aid alone could free the doubtful way,
And the dark fates disclose to sudden day;
O speed my cause, nor let me still complain
Of lying oracles and omens vain:
So shall our sons renew these rites divine
For ages hence at this thy honour'd shrine,
And while the priests thy sacred name invoke,
Black sheep cull'd out shall fall beneath their stroke,

In curling spires the sable smoke shall rise,
And waft its grateful odours to the skies.
Hail, ancient tripods, and ye dark abodes!
Exult we, fortune, for th' acknowledg'd gods,
Whose tutelary pow'r with joy I own,
And you, O long desired to heir my throne!"
He spoke, and with the princes bent his way
To th' inner court, impatient of delay,
Where yet thin fumes a fainty odour yield,
And mould'ring embers dying sparks conceal'd.
He then enjoins his servants to repair
The fire, and make the genial feast their care.
Swift at the word they run: the court replies
To ev'ry voice, and echoes back their cries.
With Tyrian carpets this adorns the ground,
That smooths the beds with gold and purple crown'd;
While some the tables range, count ev'ry guest,
And artfully adjust the future feast;
Others with salted entrails heap the fire,
And bid the flames from ev'ry part aspire.
From gilded roofs depending, lamps display
Nocturnal beams, and emulate the day:
The canisters are pil'd with Ceres' spoils,
And the king views with joy their rival toils.
On tapestry reclin'd, Adrastus shone
Afar conspicuous, from his iv'ry throne;
A broider'd couch supports the foreign guests,
Nor love of discord longer fires their breasts.
The monarch bids Acestes then appear,
And whispers his injunctions in her ear,
Whose bright example had to virtue train'd
His daughters, and preserv'd their fame unstain'd.
The nymphs the summons of their sire attend,
And to the hall their steps obsequious bend:
Minerva's features, and Diana's grace,
Conspir'd to stamp perfection on their face.
But as in prospect they perus'd the feast,
And met the glances of each unknown guest,
In blushes they reveal'd the first surprise,
And to their sire recall'd their wand'ring eyes.
While gath'ring shame their conscious face o'er spread,
Varying their cheeks by turns with white and red.
But when the rage of hunger was repress'd,

191

The meat remov'd, and satiate ev'ry guest,
A goblet in the midst Adrastus plac'd,
With sculptur'd gold, and glitt'ring figures grac'd,
In which his ancestors were wont to pour
Libations, and indulge the genial hour.
Here fraught with Gorgon's spoils, the winged horse
O'er Heav'n's expanse was seen to stretch his course
While she her eyes in dying motions roll'd,
Her paleness imag'd in th' impassion'd gold.
There the commission'd eagle seems to bear
The Phrygian youth through tracts of yielding air;
Proud Ida's summit lessens to his sight,
And Troy rolls back beneath his rising flight;
While his sad comrades on the crowded coast
View both in clouds of ambient ether lost,
And each lov'd hound, in deeper notes of woe,
Demands his master of th' unheeding foe.
This old Adrastus fills with sacred wine,
And then in pray'r invokes the pow'rs divine:
But Phoebus, first of the celestial train,
Receives the mystic off'rings of the fane;
Him with united shouts the crowd demands,
And waves the flow'ring branches in their hands;
For him this annual sacrifice prepares,
While with incessant flames each altar glares.
Then thus the king. — "Perhaps these youths would know,
What claims this strict observance of our vow;
And why the pious sons of Argos pay
Such special honours to the god of day.
No superstitious zeal our sires impell'd
To constitute these rites, which you've beheld:
But when and whence these solemn customs rose,
(So ye but lend attention,) I'll disclose.
When now the Python had by Phoebus bled,
And with his bulk the Delphic plain o'erspread,
(As hanging o'er the fair Castalian flood
He fills his turgid maw with noxious food)
To th' Argive court repair'd the victor-god,
And with his presence honour'd our abode.
The king Crotopus (as the fates decreed)
Was blest with no male issue to succeed:
A nymph, unmatch'd in manners as in face,
Was the sole product of his first embrace:

Thrice happy maid! had Phoebus fail'd to move
Her tender breast, nor kindled mutual love;
For by th' enamour'd god compress'd, she bore
A godlike son on Nemea's winding shore,
Ere the tenth moon had with her borrow'd light
Supply'd the want of day, and rul'd the night.
For this constrain'd to quit her native place,
And shun approaching vengeance and disgrace,
Among the rustic swains she seeks a friend,
To whom she might her precious charge commend.
The wretched babe, beneath an homely shed,
With bleating lambkins shares a common bed;
While with the pipe his foster-father tries
To soothe his plaints, and close his infant eyes.
Hard was his lot. Yet still relentless fate
Forbad him to enjoy his poor retreat:
For while abandon'd to blind Fortune's care,
Beneath the shade he breathes the morning air,
The furious dogs his tender carcase tore,
And fed luxurious on the recent gore.
But when the tidings reach'd the mother's ears,
Unmindful of her former shame and fears,
She raves, the palace fills with piercing cries,
Nor shuns her father's once-avoided eyes:
Then hears, impatient of her vital breath,
The fatal sentence, and demands her death.
But Phoebus, mindful of his stol'n embrace,
Prepares t' avenge her suff'rings and disgrace,
And bids ascend, to plague the guilty Earth,
A horrid monster of infernal birth:
Her face and breast a female form disclose,
But from her head a crested serpent rose,
Whose hideous length disparts her livid brows,
And from afar with dreadful splendour glows.
When fav'ring night the busy world o'erspreads,
She roams the streets, or haunts the children's beds,
Consigns to Pluto, and a sudden night,
Those new-born babes, who scarce had seen the light,
And, unresisted by the heartless foe,
Thrives, and collects fresh strength from public woe,
With grief Choroebus ey'd the wasteful pest,
And gen'rous rage inflam'd his patriot breast;
To some few chosen youths, who life disclaim,

And think it oversold to purchase fame,
He pleads his country's cause, and undismay'd
Extorts a promise of united aid.
These soon descry'd her, fir'd with vengeful hate,
Where the broad path, divided, fronts the gate:
Two infants, borne from some unguarded home,
Hang at her side, unconscious what's to come,
Till her sharp claws explore their inner parts,
And seek the nearest passage to their hearts.
So sad a sight Choroebus could not bear,
But buried in her breast his rushing spear.
The springs of life emit their crimson store,
And thro' the gap, discharg'd in issuing gore,
Her soul revisits the Tartarian coast,
And native Styx, — a lonely dreaded ghost.
Eager they press to view the monster's eyes
Livid in death, her womb's enormous size,
And breasts more filthy with the clotted blood
Of Grecian babes. The youths of Argos stood
In wonder lost; and to their recent tears
Great joys succeed, but joys appall'd with fears.
Their sole vexation now remains to find
Their rage exhausted, their revenge confin'd.
Some seem'd displeas'd, they can no longer kill,
And wish their pow'r was equal to their will:
Whilst others mangling her detested corse
With furious zeal her limbs asunder force.
To distant roosts the birds of night repair,
And shriek, impatient of the scented air:
E'en hungry dogs, and monsters of the wood,
Start from the sight, and loathe the direful food.
This but increas'd Apollo's former hate,
And urg'd him to revenge the monster's fate.
From cleft Parnassus' heights he bent his bow.
And hurl'd his vengeance on the realms below.
Around the god unnumber'd mischiefs wait,
And ev'ry shaft contains resistless fate.
White o'er the horizon gath'ring clouds arise,
Fraught with destruction, and infect the skies.
Death cuts the fatal sisters' threads in haste,
And the dispeopled city soon lays waste.
But Phoebus ask'd, from what mysterious source
Sirius deriv'd such unresisted force,

194

Demands those youths, whose hands in dust had laid
The monster's pride, to glut her vengeful shade.
Thrice happy warrior! may thy worth be crown'd
With fame, nor length of time thy glory bound;
Who, nobly lavish of thy vital breath,
Disdain'st to shun inevitable death:
And, rushing to the temple, durst provoke
The raging god, and thus demand the stroke.
'Think not desire of life, or public force
Hath to thy fane, O Phoebus, urg'd my course:
With conscious virtue arm'd, thy will I wait,
To save my country, and avert its fate.
Behold the man, who durst in fight engage
His country's pest, and bound its wasteful rage:
Whom to revenge, the Sun withheld its light,
And wrapt the skies in pestilential night.
But if such horrid scenes thy thoughts employ,
And death and slaughter are thy savage joy;
If man no more must thy protection claim,
Since the fiend's death has fann'd thy vengeful flame;
Yet why should Argos for my crimes atone,
And share the vengeance due to me alone?
Let me be deem'd the hateful cause of all,
And suffer, rather than my country fall;
Unless you view with joy our desert town,
And fun'ral flames, unrivall'd by your own.
But why do I the fatal dart arrest,
And torture with suspense each matron's breast?
Then fit the arrow to the well-strung bow,
And send me glorying to the shades below.
But, ere the fates suppress my vital breath,
Grant me to see (some solace in my death)
The plague in unoffending Argos cease,
And exil'd health restor'd again to Greece.'
Fortune consigns the coward to the grave,
But for his country's sake preserves the brave.
Relenting Phoebus quits his angry bow,
And blushing longer to remain a foe,
With rev'rence bids th' unwilling patriot live,
And health and peace in sorrowing Greece revive.
From that auspicious day with rites divine,
We worship at Apollo's honour'd shrine:
Such annual feasts his temp'rate rays require,

And thus we shun the god's returning ire.
But say, illustrious youth, from whence you came,
From whence derive your birth, and what's your claim?
Since the brave son of Oeneus stands confest,
A welcome neighbour, and more welcome guest,
And the full bowl, and silent hours invite
With various converse to contract the night."
A rising blush o'erspreads the Theban chief,
Yet glowing with the prospect of relief,
Prone to the earth he fix'd his gloomy eyes,
And with a previous sigh at length replies.
"Before these altars how shall I reveal
What conscious shame enjoins me to conceal?
Too happy! was my fortune not more known
To fame than you, or known to you alone.
But since you take such int'rest in my woe,
And the disast'rous tale desire to know,
Learn, that from Cadmus by descent I come,
Jocasta's son, and Thebes my native home."
Adrastus, touch'd with his unhappy fate,
Replies. — "Forbear the sequel to relate:
Nor think us strangers to the Theban name,
Or deaf to the divulging voice of fame.
Ev'n those who freeze beneath the northern pole,
Or view the swelling waves of Ganges roll,
Who live where ocean bounds th' Hesperian lands,
Or dread the depth of Lybia's burning sands,
All these have known the furies' vengeful ire,
And the rash actions of your wretched sire.
But if the son re-acts the father's crimes,
And shares the lineal guilt of former times,
How curst am I, on whose unhappy race
The feast of Tantalus entail'd disgrace!
Be this thy study then, with inbred worth
T' efface the stains coeval with thy birth.
But see, pale Cynthia quits th' etherial plains,
And of night's empire but a third remains;
With wine then let the sprinkled altars blaze,
And joyful Paeans swell the note of praise.
O Phoebus, author of the rising day,
Whether the Lycian mountains court thy stay,
Or fair Castalia's current claims thy care,
Where oft thou joy'st to bathe thy golden hair:

Whether proud Troy detains thee on her strands,
Rear'd by the labour of celestial hands:
Or, pleas'd to seek thy native isle no more,
Thy genial presence gilds the Cynthian shore;
Whose graceful hand supports the fatal bow,
And darts destruction on the furious foe:
In vain old age assaults thy beardless face,
Crown'd with fresh beauty, and perennial grace.
'Tis thine to warn us with unerring skill
Of Heav'n's decrees, and Jove's resistless will;
To teach, from whence the torch of discord springs,
The change of sceptres, and the fate of kings.
Thy shafts allay'd fierce Tityos' lawless lust,
And humbled haughty Marsyas to the dust,
(Who durst aspire to match thy sacred lays)
And from the Python reap'd immortal praise:
Thy pow'r transform'd proud Niobe to stone,
And to Latona's charms adjudg'd the crown:
Megaera, fiercest fiend, at thy command
For e'er incumbent, shakes her vengeful brand
O'er the devoted head of the rash sire,
Who wrapt the Delphic fane in impious fire:
He views the proffer'd food, yet dares not taste,
And dreads the cavern'd rock above him plac'd.
Let then our fields thy constant influence share,
And Argos, sacred to the queen of air;
Whether the name of Titan please thee most,
A name rever'd on th'Achaemenian coast,
Or great Osiris, whom the Pharian swain
Decks with the first-fruits of the ripen'd grain:
Or Mitra more, to whose prolific rays
The grateful Persian adoration pays,
Who grasps the horns of the reluctant steer,
While on his head encircling lights appear."

W. L. Lewis

MARTIAL

MARCUS VALERIUS MARTIALIS (c. 40 A.D. - c. 104 A.D.) was born in Spain and settled at Rome. His poems kept him in meagre poverty, but in later years he became intimate with the major writers and poets of his day.

His works include a series of poems on contests in the Flavian Amphitheatre: mottoes in elegiac couplets: and twelve books of *Epigrams*. In these epigrams he describes contemporary Rome, bitingly, revealingly, and often obscenely. His fame rests on the epigram, which in his hands acquired its modern witty, condensed expression.

EPIGRAMS

Look around: you see a little supper room;
But from my window, lo! great Caesar's tomb!
And the great dead themselves, with jovial breath
Bid you be merry and remember death.

Robert Louis Stevenson

You ask me, dear friend, what lass I'd enjoy:
I would have one, that's neither too coming nor coy,
A medium is best, that gives us no pain,
By too much indulgence, or too much disdain.

William Hay

Still pants for gold the millionaire,
    He's never done;
To many Fortune gives too large a share,
    Enough to none.

James Cranstoun

198

Tomorrow you will live, you always cry:
In what fair country does this morrow lye,
That 'tis so mighty long ere it arrive?
Beyond the Indies does this morrow live?
'Tis so far fetch'd, this morrow, that I fear
'Twill be both very old and very dear.
Tomorrow I will live, the fool does say;
Today itself's too late, the wise lived yesterday.

William Cowley

To boast, Charmenion, is your practice
That you're from Corinth — now, the fact is
Disputed not by one or other —
But why, for heaven's sake, call me Brother —
Me, born in Celteberia's land,
A citizen from Tagus' strand?
Say, is't that everybody traces
A wondrous likeness in our faces?
You walk with sleek and flowing hair,
While my rough Spanish crop I wear;
Your polished skin of pumice speaks,
While I have hairy limbs and cheeks;
You lisp — your tongue's so plaguy weak,
My infant child could louder speak:
Are doves like eagles, prithee tell,
Or like strong lion lithe gazelle?
From saying Brother then desist, or,
Charmenion, I may call you Sister.

James Cranstoun

Honest and poor, faithful in word and thought,
What hath thee, Fabian, to the city brought?
Thou neither the buffoon nor bawd can'st play;
Nor with false whispers th'innocent betray:
Nor corrupt wives; nor from rich beldams get
A living by thy industry and sweat;
Nor with vain promises and projects cheat;
Nor bribe nor flatter any of the great.

199

But you're a man of learning, prudent, just;
A man of courage, firm, and fit for trust.
Why, you may stay, and live unenvied here.
But (faith) go back, and keep you where you were.

William Cowley

———

Dear, pleasant Martial, listen if you please;
The secrets of a happy life are these:
Wealth, not by labour earned, but from thy sire;
A fertile field; an ever-blazing fire;
No wrangling; clothes to keep your body warm;
A mind at ease, and moderate strength of arm;
A healthful body; wise simplicity;
Friends like thyself, and pleasant company;
A board well furnished aye with homely fare;
Thy nights not riotous, but free from care;
Nowise morose, yet modest be thy bed;
Light be thy slumber, soon night's shadows sped:
Pleased with thy lot, for nothing further pray;
Nor dread, nor wish to see, life's final day.

James Cranstoun

———

Would you be free? 'tis your chief wish, you say;
Come on: I'll shew thee, friend, the certain way:
If to no feasts abroad thou lov'st to go,
Whilst bounteous God does bread at home bestow:
If thou, goodness of thy cloaths do'st prize
By thine own use, and not by other's eyes;
If (only safe from weathers) thou can'st dwell
In a small house, but a convenient shell;
If thou without a sigh, or golden wish,
Canst look upon thy beechen bowl and dish:
If in thy mind such power and greatness be;
The Persian king's a slave compar'd with thee.

William Cowley

Leaves his game the schoolboy sadly,
    At his master's call dismayed,
And the drunken gambler, badly
    By the luring dice betrayed,
Dragged from den where all-unheeding
    He caroused an hour before,
At the Aedile's' bar is pleading
    With a heavy heart and sore.

All the Saturnalia over!
    And no little gift — ah no!
Such as Galla sent her lover —
    Sent her Martial years ago.
So roll past, my dull December,
    And, when you your nuts will crack
On the first of March, remember,
    Galla, I shall pay you back.

James Cranstoun

The spice, cloaths, plate, and jewels, which each day
By you are sold, the buyer bears away.
But your wife's merchandise yields greater gain,
Which you so often sell, yet still retain.

William Hay

Sweet Alcimus, cut off in youth's bright bloom,
Light lies Labici's earth upon thy clay:
No marble pile I rear to crown thy tomb,
The toil were vain — 'twould crumble and decay;
But the frail box, the palm with shady leaf,
The green turf watered with affection's tears,
These are the plain memorials of my grief —
An honour that will live through endless years.
When Fate shall snap my thread, life's journey o'er,
So may my dust repose — I ask no more.

James Cranstoun

201

Sweet as perfume of an apple bit by tooth of tender maiden,
  Or as zephyr from Corycian saffron-glade —
Sweet as branches of the vine with snow-white virgin blossoms laden,
  Or as plains when sheep have newly cropped the blade —

Sweet as myrtle, or as Arab that has come from reaping spices,
  Or as amber warmed by friction's heating power —
Sweet as from Assyrian incense is the pale-blue flame that rises,
  Or as delved soil bedewed by summer shower —

Sweet as breathes the circling garland round the nard-anointed tresses,
  Is thy kiss, cold Diadumenus! to me:
Oh, I would that thou wouldst freely shower on me thy fond caresses,
  All those sweets and more than all I'd find in thee!

James Cranstoun

A little farm you purchase near the town,
With a poor timber house, just dropping down.
And business quit, a better farm by far;
I mean the certain profits of the bar.
Of wheat, oats, beans, and barley, large supplies
The lawyer got; which now the farmer buys.

William Hay

So mayst thou lying on a bank of flowers —
Its rim bedewed around with diamond showers
From rippling rill whose dancing pebbles play, —
All thoughts of trouble banished far away —
In thy dark wine-cup mingle summer snows,
And wreathe thy temples with the blushing rose:

And laughing loves be thine — a gamesome train —
Thine be a maiden chaste, yet fond and fain,
But, Flaccus (and now mark my wish and prayer),
Oh! shun the hot and noxious Cyprus air,
When threshing-floors receive the crackling grain,
And fiercely bristles Leo's tawny mane.

202

Dear Paphian goddess! I implore of thee,
Send back the generous youth unharmed to me,
And so shall March's Kalends aye be thine;
And incense, victims, bowls of rosy wine,
And many a sacred slice — oblations due —
Upon thy shining altars thou shalt view.

James Cranstoun

I drink a pint; a gallon you: for shame!
Can you complain, the wine is not the same?

William Hay

That I your invitation should decline,
Why do you wonder? Why do you repine?
When hundreds you invite to me unknown;
I do not choose, dear friend, to dine alone.

William Hay

A Quack, who stole his patient's cup, did cry,
Caught in the fact, 'What? would you drink, and die?'

William Hay

As oft, Sir Tradewell, as we meet,
You're sure to ask me in the street,
When you shall send your boy to me,
To fetch my book of poetry,
And promise you'll but read it o'er,
And faithfully the loan restore;
But let me tell you as a friend,
You need not take the pains to send;
'Tis a long way to where I dwell

203

At farther end of Clerkenwell;
There in a garret near the sky,
Above five pair of stairs I lie.
But if you'd have what you pretend,
You may procure it nearer hand:
In Cornhill, where you often go,
Hard by th'Exchange, there is, you know,
A shop of rhime, where you may see
The posts all clad in poetry:
There H — lives of high renown,
The noted'st Tory in the town:
Where, if you please, enquire for me,
And he, or's prentice, presently
From the next shelf will reach you down
The piece well bound for half a crown;
The price is much too dear, you cry,
To give for both the book and me;
Yes doubtless for such vanities;
We know, Sir, you are too wise.

John Oldham

When I am half seas o'er, and cannot read,
My lawyer brings me a long parchment deed:
Tells me, I promised when the term began,
To seal a lease to Tim, my father's man.
It will be better by to-morrow's light:
I'll touch no wax but that on corks tonight.

William Hay

DRAMA

Plautus

Terence

205

PLAUTUS

TITUS MACCIUS PLAUTUS (c. 251 - c. 184 B. C.), one of the great writers in the comic tradition, produced twenty-one comedies, imitative of Greek New Comedy. They are lively, occasionally obscene, and packed with humorous types and situations. Throughout the plays there runs a pervasive zestful verbal expressiveness. In respect of their ludicrous situations, of characterization, and of wit and boisterous humor, they remain timeless in their universal appeal.

RUDENS; THE FISHERMAN'S ROPE

DRAMATIS PERSONAE

ARCTURUS, who speaks the Prologue.
DAEMONES, an aged Athenian, now living at Cyrene.
PLESIDIPPUS, a young Athenian, in love with Palæstra.
SCEPARNIO,
GRIPUS,
TURBALIO,
SPARAX,
   Servants of Daemones
TRACHALIO, the servant of Plesidippus.
LABRAX, a Procurer.
CHARMIDES, a Sicilian, his guest.
FISHERMEN of Cyrene.
PTOLEMOCRATIA, Priestess of Venus.
PALAESTRA,
AMPELISCA,   } Young women in the possession of Labrax.
SCENE: Near Cyrene, in Africa; not far from the seashore, and before the cottage of DAEMONES and the Temple of Venus, which has, probably, a small court before it, surrounded with a low wall.

THE SUBJECT

DAEMONES, an aged Athenian, having lost his property, goes to live in retirement near the sea-shore of Cyrene, in the vicinity of the Temple of Venus. It so happens that Labrax, a Procurer, makes purchase of two damsels, Palæstra and Ampelisca, and comes to reside at Cyrene. Plesidippus, a young Athenian, sees Palæstra there, and falls in love

206

with her; and making an arrangement with the Procurer, gives him a sum in part payment for her, on which occasion, Labrax invites him to a sacrifice in the Temple of Venus. A Sicilian guest of his, however, named Charmides, persuades him to carry the young women over to Sicily, where he is sure to make a greater profit by them. On this, the Procurer, accompanied by his guest, sets sail with them. A tempest arises, and they are shipwrecked. The young women escape in a boat, and arriving ashore, are hospitably received by the Priestess of Venus. Labrax and Charmides also escape, and on discovering where the women are, the former attempts to drag them by force from the Temple. On this they are protected by Dæmones and Plesidippus, who, through Trachalio, finds out where they are. In the wreck a wallet has been lost, which belongs to Labrax, and in which is a casket enclosing some trinkets belonging to Palæstra. Gripus, a servant of Dæmones, draws this up with the rope attached to his net; and by means of these trinkets it is discovered that Palæstra is the daughter of Dæmones, whom he had lost in her infancy; on which she is given in marriage to Plesidippus by her father, who becomes reconciled to Labrax.

RUDENS; THE FISHERMAN'S ROPE

THE ACROSTIC ARGUMENT

(Supposed to have been written by Priscian the Grammarian.)

A FISHERMAN draws a wallet out of the sea in his net *(Reti)*, in which *(Ubi)* are the trinkets of his master's daughter, who, having been stolen, had come into the possession of a Procurer as her owner *(Dominum)*. She *(Ea)*, having suffered shipwreck *(Naufragio)*, without knowing it comes under the protection of her own father; she is recognized, and is married to her *(Suo)* lover Plesidippus.

THE PROLOGUE

Spoken by the God Arcturus.

With him who sways all nations, seas, and lands, I am a fellow-citizen in the realms of the Gods. I am, as you see, a bright *and* shining star, a Constellation that ever in its season rises here *on earth* and in the heavens. Arcturus is my name. By night, I am glittering in the heavens and amid the Gods, passing among mortals in the day. Other Constellations, too, descend from the heavens upon the earth; Jove, who is the ruler of Gods and men — he disperses us here in various directions among the nations, to observe the actions, manners, piety, and faith of men, just as the means of each avail him. Those who commence villainous suits at law upon false testimony, and those who, in court, upon false oath deny a debt, their names written down, do we return to Jove. Each day does he learn who here is calling for vengeance. Whatever wicked men seek here to gain their cause through perjury, who succeed before the judge in their unjust demands, the same case adjudged does he judge over again, *and* he fines them in a penalty much greater than the *results of* the judgment they have gained. The good men written down on other tables does he keep. And *still* these wicked persons entertain a notion of theirs, that they are able to appease Jupiter with gifts, with sacrifice; both their labour and their cost they lose. This, for this reason, is so, because no petition of the perjured is acceptable to Him. If any person that is supplicating the Deities is pious, he will more easily procure pardon for himself than he that is wicked. Therefore I do advise you this, you who are good and who pass your lives in piety and in virtue — still persevere, that one day you may rejoice that so you did. Now, the reason for which I've come hither, I will disclose to you. First, then, Diphilus has willed the name of this city to be Cyrene. There *(pointing to the cottage)* dwells Dæmones, in the country and in a cottage very close adjoining to the sea, an old gentleman who has come hither in exile from Athens, no unworthy man. And still, not for his bad deserts has he left his country, but while he was aiding others, meanwhile himself he embarrassed: a property honorably acquired he lost by his kindly ways. Long since, his daughter, *then* a little child, was lost; a most villainous fellow bought her of the thief, *and* this Procurer brought the maiden hither to Cyrene. A certain Athenian youth, a citizen of this city, beheld her as she was going home from the music-school. He begins to love her; to the Procurer he comes; he purchases the damsel for himself at the price of thirty minae, and gives him earnest, and binds *the Procurer* with an oath. This Procurer, just as befitted him, did not value at one straw his word, or what, on oath, he had said to the young man. He had a guest, a fit match for himself, an old man of Sicily, a rascal from Agrigentum, a traitor to his *native* city; this fellow began to extol the beauty of that maiden, and of the other damsels, too, that were belonging to him. *On this* he began to persuade the Procurer to go together with himself to Sicily; he said that there the men were given to pleasure; that there he might be enabled to become a wealthy man; that there was the greatest profit from courtesans. He prevails. A ship is hired by stealth. Whatever he has, by night the Procurer carries it on board ship from his house; the young man who purchased the damsel of him he has told he is desirous of performing a vow to Venus. This is the Temple of Venus, here *(pointing at it)*, and here, for that reason, has he invited the youth hither to a breakfast. From there at once did he embark on board ship, *and* he carried off the courtesans. Some other persons informed the young man what things were going on, *how* that the Procurer had departed. When the young man came to the harbour, their ship had got a great way out to sea. When I beheld too that the maiden was being carried off, I brought at the same instant both relief to her and destruction to the Procurer; the storm I rebuked, and the waves of the sea I aroused. For the most violent Constellation of them all am I, Arcturus; turbulent I am when rising, when I set, more turbulent *still*. Now, cast ashore there, both the Procurer and his guest are sitting upon a rock; their ship is dashed to pieces. But this maiden, and another as well, her attendant, affrighted, have leaped from the ship into a boat. At this moment the waves are bringing them from the rocks to land, to the cottage of this old man, who is living here in exile, whose roof and tiles the storm has stript off. And this is his servant who is coming out of doors. The youth will be here just now, and you shall see him, who purchased the maiden of the Procurer. *Now,* fare ye well, *and* may your foes distrust themselves. *(Exit.)*

Act I — Scene I

Enter Sceparnio, *with a spade on his shoulder.*

SCEPARNIO *(to himself)*: O ye immortal Gods, what a *dreadful* tempest has Neptune sent us this last night! The storm has unroofed the cottage. What need of words is there? It was no storm, but *what* Alcmena *met with* in Euripides; it has so knocked all the tiles from off the roof; more light has it given us, and has added to our windows.

SCENE *II* — *Enter* Plesidippus, *at a distance, talking with three* Citizens.

PLESIDIPPUS: I have both withdrawn you from your avocations, and that has not succeeded on account of which I've brought you; I could not catch the Procurer *down* at the harbour. But I have been un-willing to abandon *all* hope by reason of my remissness; on that account, my friends, have I the longer detained you. Now hither to the Temple of Venus am I come to see, where he was saying that he was about to perform a sacrifice.

SCEPARNIO *(aloud to himself, at a distance)*: If I am wise, I shall be getting ready this clay that is awaiting me. *(Falls to work digging.)*

PLESIDIPPUS *(looking round)*: Some one, I know not who, is speaking near to me.

209

DAEMONES: Hallo! Sceparnio!

SCEPARNIO: Who's calling me by name?

DAEMONES: He who paid his money for you.

SCEPARNIO *(turning round)*: As though you would say, Dæmones, that I am your slave.

DAEMONES: *There's* occasion for plenty of clay, *therefore* dig up plenty of earth, I find that the whole of my cottage must be covered; for now it's shining through it, more full of holes than a sieve.

PLESIDIPPUS *(advancing)*: Health to you, good father, and to both of you, indeed.

DAEMONES: Health to you.

SCEPARNIO *(to* Plesidippus, *who is muffled up in a coat)*: But whether are you male or female, who are calling him father?

PLESIDIPPUS: Why really, I'm a man.

DAEMONES: *Then,* man, go seek a father elsewhere. I once had an only daughter, that only one I lost. Of the male sex I never had a child.

PLESIDIPPUS: But the Gods will give ——

SCEPARNIO *(going on digging)*: A heavy mischance to you indeed, i' faith, whoever you are, who are occupying us, *already* occupied, with your prating.

PLESIDIPPUS *(pointing to the cottage)*: *Pray* are you dwelling there?

SCEPARNIO: Why do you ask that? Are you reconnoitring the place for you to come and rob there?

PLESIDIPPUS: It befits a slave to be right rich in his savings, whom, in the presence of his master, the conversation cannot escape, or who is to speak rudely to a free man.

SCEPARNIO: And it befits a man to be shameless and impudent, for him to whom there's nothing owing, of his own accord to come to the house of another person annoying *people.*

DAEMONES: Sceparnio, hold your tongue. *(To* Plesidippus.) What do you want, young man?

PLESIDIPPUS: A mishap to that fellow, who is in a hurry to be the first to speak when his master's present. But, unless it's troublesome, I wish to make enquiry of you in a few words.

DAEMONES: My attention shall be given *you,* even though in the midst of business.

SCEPARNIO *(to* Plesidippus): Rather, be off with you to the marsh, and cut down some reeds, with which we may cover the cottage, while it is fine weather.

DAEMONES: Hold your tongue. Do you tell me *(to* Plesidippus) if you have need of anything.

PLESIDIPPUS: Inform me on what I ask you; whether you have seen here any frizzle-headed fellow, with grey hair, a worthless, perjured, fawning knave.

DAEMONES: Full many a one; for by reason of fellows of that stamp am I living in misery.

PLESIDIPPUS: Him, I mean, who brought with him to the Temple of Venus *here* two young women, and who was to make preparations for himself to perform a sacrifice either to-day or yesterday.

DAEMONES: By my faith, young man, for these very many days past I haven't seen any one sacrificing there; and yet it can't be unknown to me if any one does sacrifice *there*. They are always asking here for water, or for fire, or for vessels, or for a knife, or for a spit, or for a pot for cooking, or something or other. What need is there of words? I procured my vessels and my well, for *the use of* Venus, *and* not my own. There has now been a cessation *of it* for these many days past.

PLESIDIPPUS: According to the words you utter, you tell me I'm undone.

DAEMONES: Really, so far as I'm concerned, i' faith, you may be safe and sound.

SCEPARNIO *(stopping in his digging)*: Hark you, you that are roaming about Temples for the sake of your stomach, 'twere better for you to order a breakfast to be got ready at home. Perhaps you've been invited here to breakfast. He that invited you, hasn't he come at all?

PLESIDIPPUS: 'Tis the fact.

SCEPARNIO: There's no risk *then* in your betaking yourself hence home without your breakfast. It's better for you to be a waiter upon Ceres than upon Venus; the latter attends to love, Ceres attends to wheat.

PLESIDIPPUS *(to Dæmones)*: This fellow has been making sport of me in a digraceful manner.

DAEMONES *(looking out at the side)*: O ye immortal Gods, Sceparnio, what means those people near the sea-shore?

SCEPARNIO: According to my notion, they've been invited to a parting breakfast.

DAEMONES: How so?

SCEPARNIO: Why, because, after dinner, I fancy, they yesterday washed themselves clean; their ship has gone to pieces out at sea.

DAEMONES *(looking steadfastly)*: Such is the fact.

SCEPARNIO: But, i' faith, on dry land our cottage and tiles *have done the same.*

DAEMONES: Oh dear! what unfortunate creatures you are; *(to* Sceparnio*)* how the shipwrecked people are swimming.

PLESIDIPPUS: Prithee, where are these people?

211

DAEMONES *(pointing to the distance)*: This way, to the right; don't you see them near the shore?

PLESIDIPPUS *(looking the same way)*: I see them; *(to his* Friends*)* follow me. I only wish it may be he that I'm seeking *that* most accursed fellow. *(To* Dæmones *and* Sceparnio.*)* Fare you well.

SCEPARNIO: If you hadn't put us in mind, we should have thought of *that* ourselves. *(Exeunt* Plesidippus *and* Friends.*)*

SCENE IV — SCEPARNIO *and* DAEMONES.

SCEPARNIO *(looking out towards the sea)*: But, O Palæmon, hallowed associate of Neptune, who art said to be the partner of Hercules, what shocking thing do I see?

DAEMONES: What do you see?

SCEPARNIO: I see two young women sitting in a boat alone. How the poor things are being tossed about! That's good, that's good, well done. The surge is driving the boat away from the rock towards the shore. Not a pilot could have ever done it better. I don't think that I ever saw billows more huge. They are saved, if they can escape those waves. Now, now's the danger; it has sent one overboard! See you that one whom the waves have thrown out of the boat? Still, she's in a shallow place; she'll easily wade through it now, she's now on shore. O capital! now she's safe. But that other one has *now* sprung towards the land from the boat — from her alarm she has fallen into the waves upon her knees. She has got up again; if she takes this direction, the matter's safe; *(a pause)* but she has taken to the right, to utter destruction. Ah, she will be wandering all the day ——

DAEMONES: What signifies that to you?

SCEPARNIO: If she should fall down from that rock towards which she is wending her way, she'll be putting a period to her wandering.

DAEMONES: If you are about to dine this evening at their expense, I think you may *then* be concerned for them, Sceparnio; if you are going to eat at my house, I wish your services to be devoted to myself.

SCEPARNIO: You ask what's good and proper.

DAEMONES: Then follow me this way.

SCEPARNIO: I follow. *(Exeunt.)*

SCENE V — *Enter* Palæstra, *at a distance, with her clothes torn and drenched.*

PALAESTRA *(to herself)*: By heavens, the mishaps of mortals are spoken of as much less bitter *than* the sharp *pangs* that are inflicted

212

in the experience of them. Has this *then* pleased the Deity, that I, clad in this guise, should, in my terror, be cast upon a spot unknown? Shall I *then* declare that I have been born to this wretched lot? Do I receive this meed in return for my exemplary piety? For to me it would not prove a hardship to endure this laborious lot, if I had conducted myself undutifully towards my parents or the Gods; but if studiously I have exerted myself to beware *of that*, then, unduly, *and* unjustly Deities, you send upon me this. For what henceforth shall the glaringly impious receive, if after this fashion you pay honor to the guiltless? But if I knew that I or my parents had done anything wicked, now should I have grieved the less. But the wickedness of *this* master *of mine* is pressing hard upon me, his impiety is causing my woes; everything has he lost in the sea; these are the remains *(looking at her dress)* of his property. Even she, who was carried together with me in the boat, was washed out by the violence of the waves; I am now alone. If she at least had been saved for me, through her aid my affliction here would have been lighter to me. Now, what hope or aid or what counsel shall I receive, a spot so lonesome here have I lighted upon alone? Here are the rocks, here roars the sea, and not one individual comes across my path. This *dress* that I am clothed in forms all my riches quite entirely; nor know I with what food or roof I am to be provided. What hope have I through which to desire to live? Neither am I acquainted with the place, nor was I ever here before. At least I could have wished for some one who would point out to me either a road or a path from these spots; so much am I now at a loss for advice whether to go this way or that; neither, indeed, do I see anywhere near here a cultivated spot. Cold, distraction, *and* alarm, have taken possession of all my limbs. My parents, you know not of this, that I am now thus wretched; I that was born a woman entirely free, was so to no purpose. Am I at all the less in servitude now, than if I had been born a slave? And never in any way has it been a profit to those who for their own sakes reared me up. *(She advances forward, and rests on one side against the cliff.)*

SCENE *VI — Enter* Ampelisca, *at a distance, on the other side of the stage, in a similar condition.*

AMPELISCA *(to herself)*: What is there better for me, what more to my advantage, than to shut out life from my body? So wretched am I in my existence, and so many deadening cares are there in my breast; so despicable is my lot; I care not for my life; I have

213

lost the hope with which I used to comfort myself. All places have I now rambled about, and through each covert spot have I crawled along, to seek my fellow-slave with voice, eyes, ears, that I might trace her out. And *still* I find her nowhere, nor have I *yet* determined whither to go, nor where to seek her, nor, in the meantime, do I find any person here to give me an answer, of whom I might make enquiry. No place, too, is there on earth more solitary than are these spots and this locality. And yet, if she lives, never while I exist will I cease before I discover her alive.

PALAESTRA *(aloud)*: Whose voice is it that sounds close by me here?

AMPELISCA *(starting)*: I am alarmed. Who's speaking near me?

PALAESTRA: Prithee, kind Hope, do come to my aid.

AMPELISCA: It's a woman: a woman's voice reaches my ears. Will you not rescue wretched me from this alarm?

PALAESTRA: Surely a woman's voice reached my ears. Prithee, is it Ampelisca?

AMPELISCA: Is it you, Palæstra, that I hear?

PALAESTRA: But why don't I call her by her own name, that she may hear me? *(With a loud voice.)* Ampelisca!

AMPELISCA: Ha! who's that?

PALAESTRA: 'Tis I.

AMPELISCA: Is it Palæstra?

PALAESTRA: It is.

AMPELISCA: Tell me where you are.

PALAESTRA: Troth, I'm in the midst of a multitude of woes.

AMPELISCA: I am your partner; and no less is my own share than yours. But I long to see you.

PALAESTRA: *In that wish* you are my rival.

AMPELISCA: Let's follow our voices with our steps; where are you?

PALAESTRA: See, here am I. Step onward towards me, and come straight on to meet me.

AMPELISCA: I'm doing so with care. *(They meet in front of the stage.)*

PALAESTRA: Give me your hand.

AMPELISCA: Take it.

PALAESTRA: Are you still alive? Prithee, tell me.

AMPELISCA: You, indeed, make me now wish to live, since I'm empowered to touch you. How hardly can I persuade myself of this, that I am holding you. Prithee, do embrace me *(they embrace)*, my *only* hope; how you are now easing me of all my woes.

PALAESTRA: You are beforehand with me in using expressions which belong to me. Now it befits us to be going hence.

AMPELISCA: Prithee, whither shall we go?

PALAESTRA: Let's keep along this sea-shore. *(Pointing to the shore.)*

AMPELISCA: Wherever you please, I'll follow.

214

PALAESTRA: Shall we go along thus with our wet clothing?

AMPELISCA: That which exists, the same must of necessity be borne. *(Looking up at the Temple.)* But, pray, what's this?

PALAESTRA: What is it?

AMPELISCA: Prithee, don't you see this Temple? *(Pointing towards it.)*

PALAESTRA: Where is it?

AMPELISCA: On the right hand.

PALAESTRA: I seem to be looking at a place becoming the Divinities.

AMPELISCA: There must be people not far hence; it is so delightful a spot. Whoever the God is, I pray him to relieve us from these troubles, and to succour us females, wretched, helpless, and in distress. *(They advance towards the Temple, and kneel down before it.)*

SCENE *VII — Enter* Ptolemocratia, *the Priestess, from the Temple of Venus.*

PTOLEMOCRATIA: Who are these, that in their prayers are soliciting aid from my Patroness? For the voice of suppliants has brought me hither out of doors. They pay suit to a kind and compliant Goddess and a Patroness that makes no difficulties, and one *who is* very benevolent.

PALAESTRA: Mother, we bid you hail.

PTOLEMOCRATIA: Maidens, hail to you. But, prithee, whence am I to say that you are hither come with your wet garments, thus wofully arrayed?

PALAESTRA: Just now, we came from a place there *(pointing towards the shore)*, not a great way from this spot; but it is a great way off from here, whence we have been brought hither.

PTOLEMOCRATIA: Have you been borne, do you mean, by a *ship*, the wooden steed, over the azure paths?

PALAESTRA: Even so.

PTOLEMOCRATIA: Then it were more fitting that you should have come arrayed in white and provided with victims; it isn't the practice for people to come to this Temple in that fashion. *(Pointing at their dresses.)*

PALAESTRA: Prithee, whence would you have us, who have been both cast away at sea, to be bringing victims hither? Now, in want of assistance, do we embrace your knees, we who are of hopes undefined in places unknown, that you may receive us under your roof and shelter us, and that you will pity the miseries of us both, who have neither any place *of refuge* nor hope at hand, nor have anything whatever of our own beyond that which you see.

215

PTOLEMOCRATIA: Give me your hands, arise, both of you, from off your knees; no one among women is more compassionate than I *(They arise from the ground.)* But, maidens, my circumstances are poor *and* limited; with difficulty I support my own existence; Venus I serve for my maintenance.

AMPELISCA: Prithee, is this a Temple of Venus?

PTOLEMOCRATIA: I will admit it; I am styled the Priestess of this Temple. But whatever it is, it shall be done by me with a hearty welcome, so far as my means shall suffice. Come with me this way.

PALAESTRA: Kindly and attentively, mother, do you show your attention to us.

PTOLEMOCRATIA: *So* I ought to do. *(They go into the Temple.)*

ACT II — SCENE I

Enter some Fishermen, *with lines and nets.*

A FISHERMAN: Persons who are poor live wretchedly in every way, especially those who have no calling and have learned no art. Of necessity must that be deemed enough, whatever they have at home. From our garb, then, you pretty well understand how wealthy we are. These hooks and these rods here are as good to us as a calling and as our clothing. Each day from the city do we come out hither to the sea to seek for forage. Instead of exertion in the wrestling-school and the place for exercise, we have this: sea-urchins, rockmussels, oysters, limpets, cockles, sea-nettles, sea-mussels, *and* spotted crabs, we catch. After that, we commence our fishing with the hook and among the rocks, *and thus* we take our food from out of the sea. If success does not befall us, and not any fish is taken, soaked in salt water and thoroughly drenched, we quietly betake ourselves home, *and* without dinner go to sleep. And since the sea is now in waves so boisterous, no hopes have we; unless we take some cockles, without a doubt we've had our dinners. Now let's adore good Venus here, that she may kindly befriend us to-day. *(They advance towards the doors of the Temple.)*

SCENE II — *Enter* Trachalio, *at a distance, in haste.*

TRACHALIO *(to himself)*: I've carefully given *all* attention that I mightn't pass my master anywhere; for when some time since he went out

216

of the house, he said that he was going to the harbour, *and* he ordered me to come here to meet him at the Temple of Venus. But see, opportunely do I espy some people standing here of whom I may enquire; I'll accost them. *(Goes up to the* Fishermen.*)* Save you, thieves of the sea, shellfish-gatherers and hook-fishers, hungry race of men, how fare ye? How perish apace?

FISHERMEN: Just as befits a fisherman with hunger, thirst, and expectation.

TRACHALIO: Have you seen to-day, while you've been standing here, any young man, of courageous aspect, ruddy, stout, of genteel appearance, come by this way, who was taking with him three men in scarfs, with swords?

FISHERMEN: We know of no one coming this way of that appearance which you mention.

TRACHALIO: *Have you seen* any old fellow, bald on the forehead and snub-nosed, of big stature, pot-bellied, with eyebrows awry, a narrow forehead, a knave, the scorn of Gods and men, a scoundrel, one full of vile dishonesty and of iniquity, who had along with him two very pretty-looking young women?

FISHERMEN: One who has been born with qualities and endowments of that sort, 'twere really fitter for him to resort to the executioner than to the Temple of Venus.

TRACHALIO: But tell me if you have seen him.

FISHERMEN: Really, no one has passed this way. Fare you well.

TRACHALIO: Fare ye well. *(Exeunt* Fishermen.*)*

SCENE III — Trachalio, *alone.*

TRACHALIO *(to himself)*: I thought *so*; it has come to pass as I suspected; my master has been deceived; the cursed Procurer has taken himself off to distant lands. He has embarked on board ship, *and* carried the women away; I'm a wizard. He invited my master here to breakfast, as well, *this very* spawn of wickedness. Now what is better for me than to wait here in this spot until my master comes? At the same time, if this Priestess of Venus knows anything more, if I see her, I'll make enquiries; she'll give me the information.

SCENE IV — *Enter* Ampelisca, *from the Temple.*

AMPELISCA *(to the* Priestess, *within)*: I understand; *here* at this cottage *(pointing to it),* which is close by the Temple of Venus, you've requested me to knock and ask for water.

TRACHALIO: Whose voice is it that has flown to my ears?

AMPELISCA: Prithee, who's speaking here? Who is it that I see?

217

TRACHALIO: Isn't this Ampelisca that's coming out from the Temple?

AMPELISCA: Isn't this Trachalio that I see, the servant of Plesidippus?

TRACHALIO: It is she.

AMPELISCA: It is he; Trachalio, health to you.

TRACHALIO: Health, Ampelisca, to you; how fare you?

AMPELISCA: In misery *I pass* a life not far advanced.

TRACHALIO: Do give some better omen.

AMPELISCA: Still it behoves all prudent persons to confer and talk together. But, prithee, where's your master, Plesidippus?

TRACHALIO: Marry, well said, indeed; as if he wasn't within *there.* *(Pointing to the Temple.)*

AMPELISCA: By my troth, he isn't, nor, in fact, has he come here at all.

TRACHALIO: He hasn't come?

AMPELISCA: You say the truth.

TRACHALIO: That's not my way, Ampelisca. But how nearly is the breakfast got ready?

AMPELISCA: What breakfast, I beg of you?

TRACHALIO: The sacrifice, I mean, that you are performing here.

AMPELISCA: Prithee, what is it you are dreaming about?

TRACHALIO: For certain, Labrax invited Plesidippus hither to a breakfast, your master, my master.

AMPELISCA: By my troth, you're telling of no wondrous facts: if he has deceived Gods and men, he has *only* acted after the fashion of Procurers.

TRACHALIO: *Then* neither yourselves nor my master are here performing a sacrifice.

AMPELISCA: You are a wizard.

TRACHALIO: What are you doing then?

AMPELISCA: The Priestess of Venus has received here into her abode both myself and Palæstra, after many mishaps and dreadful alarm, and from being in danger of our lives, destitute of aid and of resources.

TRACHALIO: Prithee, is Palæstra here, the beloved my master?

AMPELISCA: Assuredly.

TRACHALIO: Great joyousness is there in your news, my *dear* Ampelisca. But I greatly long to know what was this danger of yours.

AMPELISCA: Last night our ship was wrecked, my *dear* Trachalio.

TRACHALIO: How, ship? What story's this?

AMPELISCA: Prithee, have you not heard in what way the Procurer intended secretly to carry us away hence to Sicily, and *how,* whatever there was at home, he placed on board ship? That has all gone to the bottom now.

TRACHALIO: O clever Neptune, hail to thee! Surely, no dicer is more skilful than thyself. Decidedly a right pleasant throw hast thou made; thou didst break a — villain. But where now is the Procurer Labrax?

AMPELISCA: Perished through drinking, I suppose; Neptune last night invited him to deep potations.

TRACHALIO: By my troth, I fancy it was given him to drink by way of cup of necessity. How much I do love you, my *dear* Ampelisca; how pleasing you are; what honied words you do utter. But you and Palæstra, in what way were you saved?

AMPELISCA: I'll let you know. Both in affright, we leapt from the ship into a boat, because we saw that the ship was being borne upon a rock; in haste, I unloosed the rope, while they were in dismay. The storm separated us from them with the boat in a direction to the right. And so, tossed about by winds and waves, in a multitude of ways, we wretched *creatures,* during the livelong night drifted half dead; the wind this day has scarce borne us to the shore.

TRACHALIO: I understand; thus is Neptune wont *to do*; he is a very dainty Aedile; if any wares are bad, *over* he throws them all.

AMPELISCA: Woe to your head and life!

TRACHALIO: To your own, my *dear* Ampelisca. I was sure that the Procurer would do that which he has done; I often said *so*. It were better I should let my hair grow, and set up for a soothsayer.

AMPELISCA: Did you not take care then, you and your master, that he shouldn't go away, when you knew *this*?

TRACHALIO: What could he do?

AMPELISCA: If he was in love, do you ask what he could do? Both night and day he should have kept watch; he should have been always on his guard. But, by my troth, he has done like many *others*; thus finely has Plesidippus taken care of her.

TRACHALIO: For what reason do you say that?

AMPELISCA: The thing is evident.

TRACHALIO: Don't you know *this*? Even he who goes to the bath to bathe, while there he carefully keeps an eye upon his garments, still they are stolen; inasmuch as some one of those that he is watching is a rogue; the thief easily marks him for whom he's upon the watch; the keeper knows not which one is the thief. But bring me to her; where is she?

AMPELISCA: Well then, go here into the Temple of Venus; you'll find her sitting *there*, and in tears.

TRACHALIO: How disagreeable is that to me already. But why is she weeping?

AMPELISCA: I'll tell you; she's afflicting herself in mind for this; because the Procurer took away a casket from her which she had, and

219

in which she kept that by which she might be enabled to recognize her parents; she fears that this has been lost.

TRACHALIO: Where was that little casket, pray?

AMPELISCA: There, on board the ship; he himself locked it up in his wallet, that there mightn't be the means by which she might recognize her parents.

TRACHALIO: O scandalous deed! to require her to be a slave, who ought to be a free woman.

AMPELISCA: Therefore *she* now *laments* that it has gone to the bottom along with the ship. There, too, was all the gold and silver of the Procurer.

TRACHALIO: Some one, I trust, has dived and brought it up.

AMPELISCA: For this reason is she sad and disconsolate, that she has met with the loss of them.

TRACHALIO: Then have I the greater occasion to do this, to go in and console her, that she mayn't thus distress herself in mind. For I know that many a lucky thing has happened to many a one beyond their hopes.

AMPELISCA: But I *know* too that hope has deceived many who have hoped.

TRACHALIO: Therefore a patient mind is the best remedy for affliction. I'll go in, unless you wish for anything. *(Goes into the Temple.)*

AMPELISCA: Go. *(To herself.)*: I'll do that which the Priestess requested me, and I'll ask for some water here at the neighbour's; for she said if I asked for it in her name, they would give it directly. And I do think that I never saw a more worthy old lady, one to whom I should think that it is more befitting for Gods and men to show kindness. How courteously, how heartily, how kindly, how, without the least difficulty, she received us into her home, trembling in want, drenched, shipwrecked, half dead; not otherwise, *in fact,* than if we had been her own offspring. How *kindly* did she herself, just now, tucking up her garments, make the water warm for us to bathe. Now, that I mayn't keep her waiting, I'll fetch some water from the place where she requested me. *(Knocking at the door of* Dæmones.*)* Hallo, there, is there any one in the cottage? Is any one going to open this *door*? Will any one come out?

SCENE V — *Enter* Sceparnio, *from the cottage of* Dæmones.

SCEPARNIO: Who is it so furiously making an attack upon our door?

AMPELISCA: It's I.

SCEPARNIO: Well now, what good *news* is there? *(Aside.)* Dear me, a lass of comely appearance, i' troth.

220

AMPELISCA: Greeting to you, young man.

SCEPARNIO: And many greetings to you, young woman.

AMPELISCA: I'm come to you——

SCEPARNIO: I'll receive you with a welcome, if you come in the evening, by-and-by, just such as I could like; for just now I've no means to receive you, a damsel, thus early in the morning. But what have you to say, my smiling pretty one. *(Chucks her under the chin.)*

AMPELISCA: Oh, you're handling me too familiarly. *(Moves away.)*

SCEPARNIO: O ye immortal Gods! she's the very image of Venus. What joyousness there is in her eyes, and, only do see what a skin; 'tis of the vulture's tint, — rather, the eagle's, indeed. I meant to say. Her breasts, too, how beautiful; and then what expression on her lips! *(Takes hold of her.)*

AMPELISCA *(struggling)*: I'm no common commodity for the whole township; can't you keep your hands off me?

SCEPARNIO *(patting her)*: Won't you let me touch you, gentle one, in this manner, gently *and* lovingly?

AMPELISCA: When I have leisure, then I'll be giving my attention to toying and dalliance to please you; for the present, prithee, do either say me "Yes" or "No" to the matter for which I was sent hither.

SCEPARNIO: What now is it that you wish?

AMPELISCA *(pointing to her pitcher)*: To a shrewd person, my equipment would give indications of what it is I want.

SCEPARNIO: To a shrewd woman, this equipment, too, of mine would give indication of what it is I want.

AMPELISCA *(pointing to the Temple)*: The Priestess there of Venus, requested me to fetch some water from your house here.

SCEPARNIO: But I'm a lordly sort of person; unless you entreat me, you shan't have a drop. We dug this well with danger to ourselves, and with tools of iron. Not a drop can be got out of me except by means of plenty of blandishments.

AMPELISCA: Prithee, why do you make so much fuss about the water — *a thing* that *even* enemy affords to enemy?

SCEPARNIO: Why do you make so much fuss about granting a favour to me, that citizen grants to citizen?

AMPELISCA: On the contrary, my sweet one, I'll even do everything for you that you wish.

SCEPARNIO: O charming! I am favoured; she's now calling me her sweet one. The water shall be given you, so that you mayn't be coaxing me in vain. Give me the pitcher.

AMPELISCA: Take it *(gives it to him)*: make haste and bring it out, there's a dear.

SCEPARNIO: Stay a *moment*; I'll be here this instant, my sweet one. *(Goes into the cottage.)*

SCENE VI — Ampelisca, *alone.*

AMPELISCA: What shall I say to the Priestess for having delayed here so long a time? How, even still, in my wretchedness do I tremble, when with my eyes I look upon the sea. *(She looks towards the shore.)* But what, to my sorrow, do I see afar upon the shore? My master, the Procurer, and his Sicilian guest, both of whom wretched I supposed to have perished in the deep. Still does thus much more of evil survive for us than we had imagined. But why do I delay to run off into the Temple, and to tell Palæstra this, that we may take refuge at the altar before this scoundrel of a Procurer can come hither and seize us here? I'll betake myself away from this spot; for the necessity suddenly arises *for me to do so. (Runs into the Temple.)*

SCENE VII — *Enter* Sceparnio, *from the cottage.*

SCEPARNIO *(to himself)*: O ye immortal Gods, I never did imagine that there was so great delight in water; how heartily I did draw this. The well seemed much less deep than formerly. How entirely without exertion did I draw this up. With all deference to myself, am I not a very silly fellow, in having only to-day made a commencement of being in love? *(Turning slowly round, he holds out the pitcher.)* Here's the water for you, my pretty one; here now, I would have you carry it with as much pleasure as I carry it, that you may please me. *(Stares around him.)* But where are you? *(Again looks about.)* I'troth, she's in love with me, as I fancy; the roguish one's playing bo-peep. Where are you? Are you going now to take this pitcher? Where are you, *I say*? You've carried the joke far enough. Really, *do be* serious at last. Once more, are you going to take this pitcher? Where in the world are you? *(Looks about.)* I' troth, I don't see her anywhere, for my part; she's making fun of me. I' faith, I shall now set down this pitcher in the middle of the road. But yet, suppose any person should carry away from here this sacred pitcher of Venus, he would be causing me some trouble. I' faith, I'm afraid that this woman's laying a trap for me, that I may be caught with the sacred pitcher of Venus. In such case, with very good reason,

222

the magistrate will be letting me die in prison, if any one shall see me holding this. For it's marked with the name; itself tells its own tale, whose property it is. Troth now, I'll call that Priestess here out of doors, that she may take this pitcher. I'll go there to the door. *(He knocks.)* Hallo there! Ptolemocratia. *(Calling aloud.)* Take this pitcher of yours, please; some young woman, I don't know who, brought it here to me. *(A pause.)* It must *then* be carried in-doors *by me.* I've found *myself* a job, if, in fact, of my own accord, water is to be carried by me for these people as well. *(Goes into the Temple with the pitcher.)*

Scene VIII — *Enter* Labrax, *dripping wet, followed by* Charmides, *at a distance, in the same plight.*

LABRAX *(grumbling to himself)*: The person that chooses himself to be wretched and a beggar, let him trust himself and his life to Neptune. For if any one has any dealings at all with him, he sends him back home equipped in this guise. *(Surveying himself.)* By my troth, Liberty, you were a clever one, who were never willing to put *even* a foot, i' faith, on board ship with me. But *(looking round)* where's this guest of mine that has proved my ruin? Oh, see, here he comes.

CHARMIDES: Where the plague are you hurrying to, Labrax? For really I cannot follow you so fast.

LABRAX: I only wish that you had perished by direful torments in Sicily before I had looked upon with my eyes, *you* on whose account this misfortune has befallen me.

CHARMIDES: I only wish that on the day on which you admitted me into your house, I had laid me down in a prison sooner. I pray the immortal Gods, that so long as you live, you may have all your guests just like your own self.

LABRAX: In your person I admitted misfortune into my house. What business had I to listen to a rogue *like* you, or what to depart hence? Or why to go on board ship, where I have lost even more wealth than I was possessor of?

CHARMIDES: Troth, I'm far from being surprised if your ship has been wrecked, which was carrying yourself, a villain, and your property villainously acquired.

LABRAX: You've utterly ruined me with your wheedling speeches.

CHARMIDES: A more accursed dinner of yours have I been dining upon than the ones that were set before Thyestes and Tereus.

LABRAX: I'm dying; I'm sick at heart. Prithee, do hold up my head.

CHARMIDES: By my troth, I could very much wish that you would vomit up your lungs.

223

LABRAX: Alas! Palæstra and Ampelisca, where are you now?

CHARMIDES: Supplying food for the fishes at the bottom, I suppose.

LABRAX: You have brought beggary upon me by your means, while I was listening to your bragging lies.

CHARMIDES: You have reason deservedly to give me many hearty thanks, who from an insipid *morsel* by my agency have made you salt.

LABRAX: Nay, but do you get out from me to extreme and utter perdition.

CHARMIDES: You be off; I was going to do that very thing.

LABRAX: Alas! what mortal being is there living more wretched than I?

CHARMIDES: I am by very far much more wretched, Labrax, than yourself.

LABRAX: How so?

CHARMIDES: Because I am not deserving of it, whereas you are deserving.

LABRAX: O bulrush, bulrush, I do praise your lot, who always maintain your credit for dryness.

CHARMIDES *(his teeth chattering)*: For my part, I'm exercising myself for a skirmishing fight, for, from my shivering, I utter all my words in piecemeal flashes.

LABRAX: By my troth, Neptune, you are a purveyor of chilly baths; since I got away from you with my clothes, I've been freezing. No hot liquor-shop at all for sure does he provide; so salt and cold the potions that he prepares.

CHARMIDES: How lucky are the blacksmiths, who are always sitting among hot coals; they are always warm.

LABRAX: I only wish that I were now enjoying the lot of the duck, so as, although I had *just* come from out of the water, still to be dry.

CHARMIDES: What if I some way or other let myself out at the games for a hobgoblin?

LABRAX: For what reason?

CHARMIDES: Because, i' faith, I'm chattering aloud with my teeth. But I'm of opinion that, with very good reason, I've had this ducking.

LABRAX: How so?

CHARMIDES: Why, haven't I ventured to go on board ship with yourself, who have been stirring up the ocean for me from the *very* bottom?

LABRAX: I listened to you *when* you were *advising me*; you assured me that there *in Sicily* was very great profit from courtesans; there, you used to say, I should be able to amass wealth.

CHARMIDES: Did you expect, then, you unclean beast, that you were going to gobble up the whole island of Sicily?

LABRAX: What whale, I wonder, has gobbled up my wallet, where all my gold and silver was packed up?

CHARMIDES: That same one, I suppose, that *has swallowed* my purse, which was full of silver in my travelling-bag.

LABRAX: Alas! I'm reduced even to this one poor tunic *(stretching it out)* and to this poor shabby cloak; I'm done for to all intents.

224

CHARMIDES: Then you may even go into partnership with me; we have got equal shares.

LABRAX: If at least my damsels had been saved, there would have been some hope. Now, if the young man Plesidippus should be seeing me, from whom I received the earnest for Palæstra, he'll then be causing me some trouble *in consequence. (He begins to cry.)*

CHARMIDES: Why cry, you fool? Really, by my troth, so long as your tongue shall exist, you have abundance with which to make payment to everybody.

SCENE IX— *Enter* Sceparnio, *from the Temple.*

SCEPARNIO *(to himself, aloud)*: What to-do is this, I'd like to know, that two young women here in the Temple, in tears, are holding in their embrace the statue of Venus, dreading I know not what in their wretchedness? But they say that this last night they have been tossed about, and to-day cast on shore from the waves.

LABRAX *(overhearing)*: Troth now, young man, prithee, where are these young women that you are talking of?

SCEPARNIO: Here *(pointing)* in the Temple of Venus.

LABRAX: How many are there?

SCEPARNIO: Just as many as you and I make.

LABRAX: Surely, they are mine.

SCEPARNIO: Surely, I know nothing about that.

LABRAX: Of what appearance are they?

SCEPARNIO: Good-looking; I could even fall in love with either of them, if I were well liquored.

LABRAX: Surely, they are the damsels.

SCEPARNIO: Surely, you are a nuisance; be off, go in and see, if you like.

LABRAX: These must be my wenches in here, my *dear* Charmides.

CHARMIDES: Jupiter confound you, both if they are and still if they are not.

LABRAX: I'll straightway burst into this Temple of Venus here.

CHARMIDES: Into the bottomless pit, I would rather. (Labrax *rushes into the Temple, and shuts the doors.)*

SCENE X— Charmides *and* Sceparnio.

CHARMIDES: Prithee, stranger, show me some spot where I may go to sleep there, wherever you please *(points to the ground)*; no one hinders, it's free to the public. *(Pointing to his clothes)*: But do you see me, in what wet clothes I'm dressed? Do take me under

225

shelter; lend me some dry clothes, while my own are drying; on some occasion I'll return you the favour.

SCEPARNIO: See, Here's my outer coat, which alone is dry; that, if you like, I'll lend you. *(Takes it off and holds it out to him.)* In that same I'm wont to be clothed, by that same protected, when it rains. Do you give me those *clothes of yours*; I'll *soon* have them dried.

CHARMIDES: How now, are you afraid that, as I've been washed bare last night at sea, I mayn't be made bare again here upon shore?

SCEPARNIO: Wash you bare, or anoint you well, I don't care one fig. I shall never entrust anything to you unless upon a pledge being taken. Do you either sweat away or perish with cold, be you either sick or well. I'll put up with no stranger-guest in my house; I've had disagreements enough. *(Puts on his coat, and goes into the house of* Dæmones.*)*

SCENE XI — Charmides, *alone.*

CHARMIDES: What, are you off? *(A pause.)* He's a trafficker in slaves for money; whoever he is, he has no bowels of compassion. But why in my wretchedness am I standing here, soaking? Why don't I rather go away from here into the Temple of Venus, that I may sleep off this debauch which I got with drinking last night against the bent of my inclination? Neptune has been drenching us with salt water as though we were Greek wines, and so he hoped that our stomachs might be vomited up with his salt draughts. What need of words? If he had persisted in inviting us a little longer, we should have gone fast asleep there; as it is, hardly alive has he sent us off home. Now I'll go see the Procurer, my boon companion, what he's doing within. *(Goes into the Temple.)*

ACT III — SCENE I

Enter Dæmones, *from his house.*

DAEMONES *(to himself)*: In wondrous ways do the Gods make sport of men, in wondrous fashions do they send dreams in sleep. Not the sleeping, even, do they allow to rest. As, for example, I, this last night which has gone by, dreamed a wonderful and a curious dream. A she-ape seemed to be endeavouring to climb up to a swallow's nest; and she was not able thence to take them out.

226

After that, the ape seemed to come to me to beg me to lend a ladder to her. I in these terms gave answer to the ape, that swallows are the descendants of Philomela and of Progne. I expostulated with her, that she might not hurt those of my country. But she began to be much more violent, *and* seemed gratuitously to be threatening me with vengeance. She summoned me to a court of justice. Then, in my anger, I seemed to seize hold of the ape by the middle, in what fashion I know not; and I fastened up with chains *this* most worthless beast. Now to what purpose I shall say that this dream tends, never have I this day been able to come to *any* conclusion. *(A loud noise is heard in the Temple.)* But what's this noise that arises in this Temple of Venus, my neighbour? My mind's in wonder *about it.*

SCENE *II — Enter* Trachalio, *in haste, from the Temple.*

TRACHALIO *(aloud)*: O citizens of Cyrene, I implore your aid, countrymen, you who are near neighbours to these spots, bring aid to helplessness, and utterly crush a most vile attempt. Inflict vengeance, that the power of the wicked, who wish themselves to be distinguished by crimes, may not be stronger than of the guiltless. Make an example for the shameless man, give its reward to modest virtue; cause that one may be allowed to live here rather under the control of the laws than of *brute* force. Hasten hither into the Temple of Venus; again do I implore your aid, you who are here at hand and who hear my cries. Bring assistance to those who, after the recognized usage, have entrusted their lives to Venus and to the priestess of Venus, under their protection. Wring ye the neck of iniquity before it reaches yourselves.

DAEMONES: What's *all* this to-do?

TRACHALIO *(embracing his knees)*: By these knees of yours, I do entreat you, old gentleman, whoever you are ——

DAEMONES: Nay, but do you let go my knees, then, and tell me why it is that you are making a noise?

TRACHALIO: I do beg and entreat you, that if you hope this year that you will have abundance of laserwort and silphium, and that that export will arrive at Capua safe and sound, and that you may ever enjoy freedom from diseased eyes ——

DAEMONES: Are you in your senses?

TRACHALIO: —— Or whether you trust that you will have plenty of juice of silphium, that you will not hesitate to give me the aid which I shall entreat of you, aged sir.

DAEMONES: And I, by your legs, and ankles, and back, do entreat you that, if you hope that you will have a crop of elm-twigs,

227

and that a fruitful harvest of beatings will this year be your lot, you will tell me what's the matter here, by reason of which you are making this uproar.

TRACHALIO: Why do you choose to speak me ill? For my part, I wished you everything that's good.

DAEMONES: *And* for my part, I'm speaking you well, in praying that things which you deserve may befall you.

TRACHALIO: Prithee, do prevent this.

DAEMONES: What's the matter, then?

TRACHALIO *(pointing to the Temple)*: Two innocent women are inside here, in need of your aid, on whom, against law and justice, an injury has been, is being, glaringly committed here in the Temple of Venus. Besides, the Priestess of Venus is being disgracefully insulted.

DAEMONES: What person is there of effrontery so great as to dare to injure the Priestess? But these women, who are they? Or what injury is being done to them?

TRACHALIO: If you give me your attention, I'll tell you. They have clung to the statue of Venus; a most audacious fellow is now trying to tear them away. They ought, *by rights*, both of them to be free.

DAEMONES: What fellow is it that so lightly holds the Gods? In a few words tell me.

TRACHALIO: One most full of fraud, villainy, parricide, *and* perjury; a lawbreaker, an immodest, unclean, most shameless fellow; to sum up all in one word, he is a Procurer; why need I say more about him?

DAEMONES: Troth now, you tell of a man that ought to be handed over to retribution.

TRACHALIO: A villain, to seize the Priestess by the throat.

DAEMONES: By my troth, but he had done it at his own great peril. *(Calls aloud at his door.)* Come you out of doors here, Turbalio *and* Sparax; where are you?

TRACHALIO: Prithee, do go in, and hasten to their rescue.

DAEMONES *(impatiently)*: And am I to call for them once more? Follow me this way.

    Enter Turbalio *and* Sparax, *from the cottage.*

TRACHALIO: Come on now this instant, bid them tear his eyes out, Just in the way that cooks do cuttle-fish.

DAEMONES: Drag the fellow out here by his legs, just like a slaughtered pig. (Dæmones *and his* Servants *go into the Temple.*)

TRACHALIO *(listening at the door)*: I hear a scuffling; the Procurer, I guess, is being belaboured with their fists; I'd very much like them to knock the teeth out of the jaws of the most villainous fellow. But see, here are the women themselves coming out of the Temple in consternation.

SCENE III — *Enter* Palæstra *and* Ampelisca, *in haste, from the Temple, with dishevelled locks.*

PALAESTRA: Now is that *time* arrived when destitution of all resources and aid, succour *and* defence, overtakes us. Neither hope nor means is there to bring us aid, nor know we in what direction we should commence to proceed. In exceeding terror now are we both, in this our wretchedness. Such cruelty and such outrage have been committed towards us just now in-doors by our master, who, in his villainy, pushed down the old lady, the Priestess, headlong, and struck her in a very disgraceful manner, and with his violence tore us away from the inner side of the statue. But as our lot and fortunes are now showing themselves, 'twere best to die, nor in our miseries is there anything better than death.

TRACHALIO *(behind)*: What's this? Whose words are those? *Why* do I delay to console them? *(Aloud.)* Harkye, Palæstra, Ampelisca, harkye!

PALAESTRA: Prithee, who is it that calls *us*?

AMPELISCA: Who is it that calls me by name?

TRACHALIO: If you turn round and look, you'll know.

PALAESTRA *(turning round)*: O hope of my safety!

TRACHALIO: Be silent and of good courage; trust me.

PALAESTRA: If only it can be so, let not violence overwhelm us.

TRACHALIO: What violence?

PALAESTRA: That same which is driving me to commit violence on myself.

TRACHALIO: Oh, do leave off; you are very silly.

PALAESTRA: Then do you leave off at once your consoling me in my misery with words.

AMPELISCA: Unless you afford us protection in reality, Trachalio, it's all over with us.

PALAESTRA: I'm resolved to die sooner than suffer this Procurer to get me in his power. But still I am of woman's heart; when, in my misery, death comes into my mind, fear takes possession of my limbs.

TRACHALIO: By my troth, although this is a bitter *affliction*, do have a good heart.

PALAESTRA: Why where, pray, is a good heart to be found for me?

TRACHALIO: Don't you fear, I tell you; sit you down here by the altar. *(Points to it.)*

AMPELISCA: What can this altar possibly avail us more than the statue here within the Temple of Venus, from which just now, embracing it, in our wretchedness, we were torn by force?

TRACHALIO: Only you be seated here; then I'll protect you in this spot. This altar you possess as though your bulwarks; these your fortifications; from this spot will I defend you. With the aid of Venus, I'll march against the wickedness of the Procurer.

PALAESTRA: We follow your instructions (they advance to the altar and kneel); and genial Venus, we both of us, in tears, implore thee, embracing this thy altar, bending upon our knees, that thou wilt receive us into thy guardianship, and be our protector; that thou wilt punish those wretches who have set at nought thy Temple, and that thou wilt suffer us to occupy this altar with thy permission, we who last night were by the might of Neptune cast away; hold us not in scorn, and do not for that reason impute it to us a fault, if there is anything that thou shouldst think is not so well attended to by us as it ought to have been.

TRACHALIO: I think they ask what's just; it ought, Venus, by thee to be granted. Thou oughtst to pardon them; 'tis terror forces them to do this. They say that thou wast born from a shell; take thou care that thou dost not despise the shells of these. But see, most opportunely the old gentleman is coming out, both my protector and your own. (He goes to the altar.)

SCENE IV — Enter Dæmones, from the Temple, with his two Servants dragging out Labrax.

DAEMONES: Come out of the Temple, you most sacrilegious of men, as many as have ever been born. Do you go (calling to the Women) and sit by the altar. (Not seeing them near the door.) But where are they?

TRACHALIO: Look round here.

DAEMONES (looking round): Very good; I wanted that. Now bid him come this way. (To Labrax.) Are you attempting here among us to commit a violation of the laws against the Deities? (To the Servants, who obey with alacrity.) Punch his face with your fists.

LABRAX: I'm suffering these indignities at your own cost.

DAEMONES: Why, the insolent fellow's threatening even.

LABRAX: I've been robbed of my rights; you are robbing me of my female slaves against my will.

TRACHALIO: Do you then find some wealthy man of the Senate of Cyrene as judge, whether these women ought to be yours, or whether they oughtn't to be free, or whether it isn't right that

230

you should be clapped into prison, and there spend your life, until you have worn the whole gaol out *with your feet.*

LABRAX: I wasn't prepared to prophesy for this day that I should be talking with a hang-gallows *like yourself.* (*Turning to* Daemones.) You do I summon to *judgment.*

DAEMONES (*pointing to* Trachalio): In the first place, try it with him who knows you.

LABRAX (*to* Dæmones): My suit is with yourself.

TRACHALIO: But it must be with myself. (*Pointing to the* Women.) Are these your female slaves?

LABRAX: They are.

TRACHALIO: Just come then, touch either of them with your little finger only.

LABRAX: What if I do touch them?

TRACHALIO: That very instant, upon my faith, I'll make a handball of you, and while you're in the air I'll belabour you with my fists, you most perjured villain.

LABRAX: Am I not to be allowed to take away my female slaves from the altar of Venus?

DAEMONES: You may not; such is the law with us.

LABRAX: I've no concern with your laws; for my part, I shall at once carry them both away from here. If you are in love with them, old gentleman (*holding out his hand*), you must down here with the ready cash.

DAEMONES: But these women have proved pleasing to Venus.

LABRAX: She may have them, if she pays the money.

DAEMONES: A Goddess, *pay* you money? Now then, that you may understand my determination, only do you commence in mere joke to offer them the very slightest violence; I'll send you away from here with such a dressing, that you won't know your own self. You, therefore (*turning to his* Servants), when I give you the signal, if you don't beat his eyes out of his head, I'll trim you round about with rods just like beds of myrtle with bulrushes.

LABRAX: You are treating me with violence.

TRACHALIO: What, do you even upbraid us with violence, you flagrant specimen of flagitiousness?

LABRAX: *You*, you thrice-dotted villain, do you dare to speak abusively to me?

TRACHALIO: I am a thrice-dotted villain; I confess it; you are a strictly honorable man; ought these women a bit the less to be free?

LABRAX: What — free?

TRACHALIO: Aye, and your mistresses, too, i' faith, and from genuine Greece; for one of them was born at Athens of free-born parents.

DAEMONES: What is it I hear from you?

231

TRACHALIO: That she *(pointing to* Palæstra*)* was born at Athens, a free-born woman.

DAEMONES *(to* Trachalio*)*: Prithee, is she a countrywoman of mine?

TRACHALIO: Are you not a Cyrenian?

DAEMONES: No; born at Athens in Attica, bred and educated there.

TRACHALIO: Prithee, aged sir, do protect your countrywomen.

DAEMONES *(aside)*: O daughter, when I look on her, separated from me you remind me of my miseries: *(aloud)* she who was lost by me when three years old; now, if she is living, she's just about as tall, I'm sure, *as she. (Pointing to* Palæstra.*)*

LABRAX: I paid the money down for these two, to their owners, of whatever country they were. What matters it to me whether they were born at Athens or at Thebes, so long as they are rightfully in servitude as my slaves?

TRACHALIO: Is it so, you impudent fellow? What, are you, a cat prowling after maidens, to be keeping children here kidnapped from their parents and destroying them in your disgraceful calling? But as for this other one, I really don't know what her country is; I only know that she's more deserving than yourself, you most abominable rascal.

LABRAX: Are these women your property?

TRACHALIO: Come to the trial, then, which of the two according to his back is the more truthful; if you don't bear more compliments upon your back than any ship of war has nails, then I'm the greatest of liars. Afterwards, do you examine mine, when I've examined yours; if it shall not prove to be so untouched, that any leather flask maker will say that it is a hide most capital and most sound for the purposes of his business, what reason is there why I shouldn't mangle you with stripes, even till you have your belly full? Why do you stare at them? If you touch them I'll tear your eyes out.

LABRAX: Yet notwithstanding, although you forbid me *to do so,* I'll at once carry them off both together with me.

DAEMONES: What will you do?

LABRAX: I'll bring Vulcan; he is an enemy to Venus. *(Goes towards* Dæmones' *cottage.)*

TRACHALIO: Whither is he going?

LABRAX *(calling at the door)*: Hallo! Is there anybody here? Hallo! *I say.*

DAEMONES: If you touch the door, that very instant, upon my faith, you shall get a harvest upon your face with fists for your pitchforks.

SERVANT: We keep no fire, we live upon dried figs.

DAEMONES: I'll find the fire, if only I have the opportunity of kindling it upon your head.

LABRAX: Faith, I'll go somewhere to look for some fire.

DAEMONES: What, when you've found it?

LABRAX: I'll be making a great fire here.

DAEMONES: What, to be burning a mortuary sacrifice for yourself?

LABRAX: No, but I'll burn both of these alive here upon the altar.

DAEMONES: I'd like that. For, by my troth, I'll forthwith seize you by the head and throw you into the fire, and, half-roasted, I'll throw you out as food for the great birds. *(Aside.)* When I come to a consideration of it with myself, this is that ape, that wanted to take away those swallows from the nest against my will, as I was dreaming in my sleep.

TRACHALIO: Aged sir, do you know what I request of you? That you will protect these females *and* defend them from violence, until I fetch my master.

DAEMONES: Go look for your master, and fetch him here.

TRACHALIO: But don't let him ——

DAEMONES: At his own extreme peril, if he touches them, or if he attempts *to do so.*

TRACHALIO: Take care.

DAEMONES: Due care is taken; do you be off.

TRACHALIO: And watch him too, that he doesn't go away anywhere. For we have promised either to give the executioner a great talent, or else to produce this fellow this very day.

DAEMONES: Do you only be off. I'll not let him get away while you are absent.

TRACHALIO: I'll be back here *soon. (Exit* Trachalio.*)*

SCENE V — Dæmones, Labrax, Palæstra, Ampelisca, *and* Servants.

DAEMONES *(to* Labrax, *who is struggling with the* Servants*)*: Which, you Procurer, had you rather do, be quiet with a thrashing, or e'en as it is, without the thrashing, if you had the choice?

LABRAX: Old fellow, I don't care a straw for what you say. My own women, in fact, I shall drag away this instant from the altar by the hair, in spite of yourself, and Venus, and supreme Jove.

DAEMONES: Just touch them.

LABRAX *(going towards them)*: I' troth, I surely will touch them.

DAEMONES: Just come then; only approach this way.

LABRAX: Only bid both those fellows, then, to move away from there.

DAEMONES: On the contrary, they shall move towards you.

LABRAX: I' faith, for my own part, I don't think so.

DAEMONES: If they do move nearer to you, what will you do?

LABRAX: I'll retire. But, old fellow, if ever I catch you in the city, never *again,* upon my faith, shall any one call me a Procurer, if I don't give you some most disagreeable sport.

233

DAEMONES: Do what you threaten. But now, in the meantime, if you do touch them, a heavy punishment shall be inflicted on you.

LABRAX: How heavy, in fact?

DAEMONES: Just as much as is sufficient for a Procurer.

LABRAX: These threats of yours I don't value one straw; I certainly shall seize them both this instant without your leave.

DAEMONES: Just touch them.

LABRAX: By my troth, I surely will touch them.

DAEMONES: You will touch them, but do you know with what result? Go then, Turbalio, with all haste, *and* bring hither from out of the house two cudgels.

LABRAX: Cudgels?

DAEMONES: Aye, good ones; make haste speedily. (Turbalio *goes in.*) I'll let you have a reception this day in proper style, as you are deserving of.

LABRAX *(aside)*: Alas! cursedly unfortunate. I lost my headpiece in the ship; it would now have been handy for me, if it had been saved. *(To* Dæmones.) May I at least address these women?

DAEMONES: You may not (Turbalio *enters, bringing two cudgels.*) Well now, by my faith, look, the cudgel-man is coming very opportunely here.

LABRAX *(aside)*: By my troth, this surely is a tingling for my ears.

DAEMONES: Come, Sparax, do you take this other cudgel. *(Giving him one.)* Come, take your stand, one on one side, the other on the other. Take your stations both of you. *(They stand with lifted cudgels on each side of the altar.)* Just so. Now then attend to me: if, i' faith, that *fellow* there should this day touch these women with his finger against their inclination, if you don't give him a reception with these *cudgels* even to that degree that he shan't know which way he is to get home, you are undone, both of you. If he shall call for any one, do you make answer to this fellow in their stead. But if he himself shall attempt to get away from here, that instant, as hard as you can, lay on to his legs with *your* sticks.

LABRAX: Are they not even to allow me to go away from here?

DAEMONES: I've said sufficient. And when that servant comes here with his master, he that has gone to fetch his master, do you at once go home. Attend to this with great diligence, will you. (Dæmones *goes into his house.*)

SCENE VI — Palæstra, Ampelisca, Labrax, *and the* Servants.

LABRAX: O rare, by my troth, the Temple here is surely changed all of a sudden; this is now the Temple of Hercules which was that

234

of Venus before; in such fashion has the old fellow planted two statues here with clubs. I' faith, I don't know now whither in the world I shall fly from here; so greatly are they both raging now against me, both on land and sea. Palæstra!

SERVANT: What do you want?

LABRAX: Away with you, there is a misunderstanding *between us*; that, indeed, is not my Palæstra that answers. Harkye, Ampelisca.

SERVANT: Beware of a mishap, will you.

LABRAX *(aside)*: So far as they can, the worthless fellows advise me rightly enough. *(Aloud.)* But, harkye, I ask you, whether it is any harm to you for me to come nearer to these women?

SERVANT: Why none at all to ourselves.

LABRAX: Will there be any harm to myself?

SERVANT: None at all, if you *only* take care.

LABRAX: What is it that I'm to take care against?

SERVANT: Why, look you, against a heavy mishap.

LABRAX: Troth now, prithee, do let me approach them.

SERVANT: Approach them, if you like.

LABRAX: I' faith, obligingly done; I return you thanks, I'll go nearer to them. *(Approaches them.)*

SERVANT: Do you stand there on the spot, *where you are. (Drags him to his place, with the cudgel over his head.)*

LABRAX *(aside)*: By my faith, I've come scurvily off in many ways. *Still,* I'm resolved to get the better of them this day by constantly besieging them.

SCENE VII—*Enter* Plesidippus *and* Trachalio, *at a distance, on the other side of the stage.*

PLESIDIPPUS: And did the Procurer attempt by force *and* violence to drag my mistress away from the altar of Venus?

TRACHALIO: Even so.

PLESIDIPPUS: Why didn't you kill him on the instant?

TRACHALIO: I hadn't a sword.

PLESIDIPPUS: You should have taken either a stick or a stone.

TRACHALIO: What! ought I to have pelted *this* most villainous fellow with stones like a dog?

LABRAX *(aside, on seeing them)*: By my troth, but I'm undone now; see, here's Plesidippus; he'll be sweeping me away altogether this moment with the dust.

PLESIDIPPUS: Were the damsels sitting on the altar even then when you set out to come to me?

TRACHALIO: *Yes, and* now they are sitting in the same place.

PLESIDIPPUS: Who is now protecting them there?

235

TRACHALIO: Some old gentleman, I don't know who, a neighbour of the Temple of Venus — he gave very kind assistance; he is now protecting them with his servants — I committed them to *his* charge.

PLESIDIPPUS: Lead me straight to the Procurer. Where is this fellow? *(They go towards* Labrax.*)*

LABRAX: Health to you.

PLESIDIPPUS: I want none of your healths. Make your choice quickly, whether you had rather be seized by your throat wrenched, or be dragged along; choose whichever you please, while you may.

LABRAX: I wish for neither.

PLESIDIPPUS: Be off then, Trachalio, with all speed to the sea-shore; bid those persons that I brought with me to hand over this *rascal* to the executioner, to come from the harbour to the city to meet me; afterwards return hither and keep guard here. I'll now drag this scoundrelly outcast to justice. *(Exit* Trachalio.*)*

SCENE VIII — Plesidippus, Labrax, Palæstra, *and* Servants.

PLESIDIPPUS *(to* Labrax*)*: Come, proceed to a court of justice.

LABRAX: In what have I offended?

PLESIDIPPUS: Do you ask? Didn't you receive an earnest of me for *this* woman *(pointing to* Palæstra*)*, and carry her off from here?

LABRAX: I didn't carry her off.

PLESIDIPPUS: Why do you deny it?

LABRAX: Troth now, because I put her on board ship; carry her off, unfortunately, I couldn't. For my part, I told you that this day I would make my appearance at the Temple of Venus; have I swerved at all *from that*? Am I not there?

PLESIDIPPUS: Plead your cause in the court of justice; here a word is enough. Follow *me. (They lay hold of him.)*

LABRAX *(calling aloud)*: I entreat you, my *dear* Charmides, do come to my rescue; I am being seized with my throat wrenched.

SCENE IX — *Enter* Charmides, *from the Temple.*

CHARMIDES *(looking about)*: Who calls my name?

LABRAX: Do you see me how I'm being seized?

CHARMIDES: I see, and view it with pleasure.

LABRAX: Don't you venture to assist me?

CHARMIDES: What person is seizing you?

LABRAX: Young Plesidippus.

CHARMIDES: What you've got, put up with; 'twere better for you, with a cheerful spirit, to slink to gaol; that has befallen you which many greatly wish for for themselves.

LABRAX: What's that?

CHARMIDES: To find for themselves that which they are seeking.

LABRAX: I entreat you, do follow me.

CHARMIDES: You try to persuade me just like what you are: you are being taken off to gaol, for that reason is it you entreat me to follow you?

PLESIDIPPUS *(to* Labrax*)*: Do you still resist?

LABRAX: I'm undone.

PLESIDIPPUS: I trust that may prove the truth. You, my *dear* Palæstra and Ampelisca, do you remain here in the meanwhile, until I return hither.

SERVANT: I would advise them rather to go to our house, until you return.

PLESIDIPPUS: I'm quite agreeable; you act obligingly. *(The Servants open the door of the cottage, and* Palæstra *and* Ampelisca *go in.)*

LABRAX: You are thieves to me.

SERVANT: How, thieves?

PLESIDIPPUS: Lead him along. *(The* Servants *seize him.)*

LABRAX *(calling out)*: I pray *and* entreat you. Palæstra.

PLESIDIPPUS: Follow, you hand-dog.

LABRAX: Guest, *Charmides*!

CHARMIDES: I am no guest *of yours*; I repudiate your hospitality.

LABRAX: What, do you slight me in this fashion?

CHARMIDES: I do so; I've been drinking *with you* once already.

LABRAX: May the Deities confound you.

CHARMIDES: To that person *of yours*, say that. (Plesidippus *leads* Labrax *off, followed by the* Servants.)

SCENE X — Charmides, *alone*

CHARMIDES: I do believe that men are transformed, each into a different beast. That Procurer, I guess, is transformed into a stock-dove; for, before long, his neck will be in the stocks. He'll to-day be building his nest in the gaol. Still, however, I'll go, that I may be his advocate, — if by my aid he may possibly be sentenced any the sooner.

ACT IV — SCENE I

Enter Dæmones, *from his cottage.*

DAEMONES *(to himself)*: 'Twas rightly done, and it is a pleasure this day for me to have given aid to these young women; I have now found some dependants, and both of them of comely looks and

237

youthful age. But my plaguy wife is watching me in all ways, lest I should be giving any hint to the young women. But I wonder what in the world my servant Gripus is about, who went last night to the sea to fish. Troth, he had done wiser if he had slept at home; for now he throws away both his pains and his nets, seeing what a storm there now is and was last night. I'll thoroughly cook upon my fingers what he has caught to-day; so violently do I see the ocean heaving. *(A bell rings.)* But my wife's calling me to breakfast; I'll return home. She'll now be filling my ears with her silly prating. *(Goes into the cottage.)*

SCENE II — *Enter* Gripus, *dragging a net enclosing a wallet, by a rope.*

GRIPUS *(to himself)*: These thanks do I return to Neptune, my patron, who dwells in the salt retreats, the abode of fishes, inasmuch as he has despatched me finely laden on my return from his retreats, and from his Temples, laden with most abundant booty, with safety to my boat, which in the stormy sea made me master of a singular and rich haul. In a wondrous and incredible manner has this haul turned out prosperously for me, nor yet have I this day taken a single ounce weight of fish, but only that which I am here bringing with me in my net. For when I arose in the middle of the night, and without sloth, I preferred profit to sleep and rest; in the raging tempest, I determined to try how I might lighten the poverty of my master and my own servitude, not sparing of my own exertions. Most worthless is the man that is slothful, and most detestably do I hate that kind of men. It behoves him to be vigilant who wishes to do his duty in good time; for it befits him not to be waiting until his master arouses him to his duties. For those who sleep on for the love of it, rest without profit *to themselves* and to their own cost. But now I, who have not been slothful, have found that for myself through which to be slothful if I should choose. *(Points to the wallet.)* This have I found in the sea to-day; whatever's in it, it's something heavy that's in it; I think it's gold that's in it. And not a single person is there my confidant *in the matter.* Now, Gripus, this opportunity has befallen you, that the Prætor might make you a free man from among the multitude. Now, thus shall I do, this is my determination; I'll come to my master cleverly *and* cunningly, little by little I'll promise money for my freedom, that I may be free. Now, when I shall be free, then, in fine, I'll provide me land and houses *and* slaves: I'll carry on merchandize with large ships: among the grandees I shall be considered a

238

grandee. Afterwards for the sake of pleasing myself, I'll build me a ship and I'll imitate Stratonicus, and I'll be carried about from town to town. When my greatness is far-spread, I shall fortify some great city: to that city I shall give the name of "Gripus," a memorial of my fame and exploits, and there I'll establish a mighty kingdom. I am resolving here in my mind to prepare for mighty matters. At present I'll hide this booty. But this grandee *(pointing to himself)* is about to breakfast upon vinegar and salt, without *any* good *substantial* meat. *(Gathers up the net, and drags it after him.)*

SCENE III — *Enter* Trachalio, *in haste.*

TRACHALIO: Hallo there! stop.

GRIPUS: Why should I stop?

TRACHALIO: While I coil up this rope for you that you are dragging.

GRIPUS: Now let it alone.

TRACHALIO: Troth, but I'll assist you. What's kindly done to worthy men, isn't thrown away.

GRIPUS: There was a boisterous tempest yesterday; no fish have I, young man; don't you be supposing I have. Don't you see that I'm carrying my dripping net without the scaly race?

TRACHALIO: I' faith, I'm not wishing for fish so much as I am in need of your conversation.

GRIPUS: Then, whoever you are, you are worrying me to death with your annoyance.

TRACHALIO *(takes hold of him)*: I'll not allow you to go away from here; stop.

GRIPUS: Take you care of a mishap, if you please; but why the plague are you dragging me back?

TRACHALIO: Listen.

GRIPUS: I won't listen.

TRACHALIO: But, upon my faith, you shall listen.

GRIPUS: Nay but, another time, tell me what you want.

TRACHALIO: Come now, it's worth your while at once to hear what I want to tell you.

GRIPUS: Say on, whatever it is.

TRACHALIO: See whether any person is following near us. *(Looks back.)*

GRIPUS: Why, what reason is there that it should matter to me?

TRACHALIO: So it is; but can you give me some good advice?

GRIPUS: What's the business? Only tell me.

TRACHALIO: I'll tell you; keep silence; if only you'll give me your word that you won't prove treacherous to me.

GRIPUS: I do give you my word; I'll be true *to you,* whoever you are.

239

TRACHALIO: Listen. I saw a person commit a theft; I knew the owner to whom that same *property* belonged. Afterwards I came myself to the thief, and I made him a proposal in these terms: "I know *the person* on whom that theft was committed; now if you are ready to give me half, I'll not make a discovery to the owner." He didn't even give me an answer. What is it fair should be given me out of it? Half, I trust you will say.

GRIPUS: Aye, even more; but unless he gives it you, I think it ought to be told to the owner.

TRACHALIO: I'll act on your advice. Now give me your attention; for it is to yourself all this relates.

GRIPUS: What has been done *by me*?

TRACHALIO *(pointing at the wallet)*: I've known the person for a long time to whom that wallet belongs.

GRIPUS: What do you mean?

TRACHALIO: And in what manner it was lost.

GRIPUS: But I know in what manner it was found; and I know the person who found it, and who is now the owner. That, i' faith, is not a bit the more your matter than it is my own. I know the person to whom it now belongs; you, the person to whom it formerly belonged. This shall no individual get away from me; don't you be expecting *to get it* in a hurry.

TRACHALIO: If the owner comes, shan't he get it away?

GRIPUS: That you mayn't be mistaken, no born person is there that's owner of this but my own self — who took this in my own fishing.

TRACHALIO: Was it really so?

GRIPUS: Which fish in the sea will you say "is my own?" When I catch them, if indeed I do catch them, they are my own; as my own I keep them. They are not claimed as having a right to freedom, nor does any person demand a share in them. In the market I sell them all openly as my own wares. Indeed, the sea is, surely, common to all persons.

TRACHALIO: I agree to that; prithee, *then*, why any the less is it proper that this wallet should be common to me? It was found in the sea.

GRIPUS: Assuredly you are an outrageously impudent fellow; for if this is justice which you are saying, *then* fishermen would be ruined. Inasmuch as, the moment that the fish were exposed upon the stalls, no one would buy them; every person would be demanding his own share of the fish for himself; he would be saying that they were caught in the sea that was common *to all*.

TRACHALIO: What do you say, you impudent *fellow*? Do you dare to compare a wallet with fish? Pray, does it appear to be the same thing?

240

GRIPUS: *The matter* doesn't lie in my power; when I've cast my hook and net *into the sea,* whatever has adhered I draw out. Whatever my net and hooks have got, that in especial is my own.

TRACHALIO: Nay but, i' faith, it is not; if indeed, you've fished up any article that's made.

GRIPUS: Philosopher, *you.*

TRACHALIO: But look now, you conjurer, did you ever see a fisherman who caught a wallet-fish, or exposed one for sale in the market? But, indeed, you shan't here be taking possession of all the profits that you choose; you expect, you dirty fellow, to be both a maker of wallets and a fisherman. Either you must show me a fish that is a wallet, or else you shall carry nothing off that wasn't produced in the sea and has no scales.

GRIPUS: What, did you never hear before to-day that a wallet was a fish?

TRACHALIO: Villain, there is no *such fish.*

GRIPUS: Yes, there certainly is; I, who am a fisherman, know it. But it is seldom caught; no fish more rarely comes near the land.

TRACHALIO: It's to no purpose; you hope that you can be cheating me, you rogue. Of what colour is it?

GRIPUS *(looking at the wallet)*: Of this colour very few are caught: some of a purple skin; there are great and black ones also.

TRACHALIO: I understand; by my troth, you'll be turning into a wallet-fish I fancy, if you don't take care; your skin will be purple, and then afterwards black.

GRIPUS *(aside)*: What a villain this that I have met with to-day!

TRACHALIO: We are wasting words; the day wears apace. Consider, please, by whose arbitration do you wish us to proceed?

GRIPUS: By the arbitration of the wallet.

TRACHALIO: Really so, indeed? You are a fool.

GRIPUS: My respects to you, *Mister* Thales. *(Going.)*

TRACHALIO *(holding him)*: You shan't carry that off this day, unless you find a place of safe keeping *for it,* or an umpire, by whose arbitration this matter may be settled.

GRIPUS: Prithee, are you in your senses?

TRACHALIO: I'm mad, in need of hellebore.

GRIPUS: But I'm troubled with sprites; still I shan't let this go. *(Hugs the wallet.)*

TRACHALIO: Only add a single word more, that instant I'll drive my fists smash into your brains. This instant on this spot, just as a new napkin is wont to be wrung, I'll wring out of you whatever moisture there is, if you don't let this go. *(Seizes the wallet.)*

GRIPUS: Touch me; I'll dash you down on the ground just in such fashion as I'm in the habit of doing with a polypus fish. Would you like to fight? *(Assumes a boxing attitude.)*

TRACHALIO: What need is there? Nay, in preference, divide the booty.

GRIPUS: You can't get anything from here but harm *to yourself*, so don't expect it. I'm taking myself off.

TRACHALIO: But I'll turn aside your ship from that direction, that you mayn't be off anywhere — stop. *(Stands in front of him, and holds the rope.)*

GRIPUS: If you are the helmsman of this ship, I'll be the pilot. Let go of the rope now, you villain.

TRACHALIO: I will let go; do you let go of the wallet.

GRIPUS: I' faith, you shall never this day become a scrap the more wealthy from this.

TRACHALIO: You cannot convince me by repeatedly denying, unless either a part is given me, or it is referred to arbitration, or it is placed in safe keeping.

GRIPUS: What, that which I got out of the sea——?

TRACHALIO: But I spied it out from the shore.

GRIPUS: — With my own pains and labour, and net and boat.

TRACHALIO: If *now* the owner, whose property it is, were to come, how am I, who espied from afar that you had taken this, a bit the less the thief than yourself?

GRIPUS: None whatever. *(Going.)*

TRACHALIO *(seizing the net)*: Stop, you whip-knave; just let me learn of you by what reasoning I am not the sharer, and *yet* the thief.

GRIPUS: I don't know; neither do I know these city laws of yours, only that I affirm that this is mine. *(Looks at the wallet.)*

TRACHALIO: And I, too, say it is mine.

GRIPUS: Stay now; I've discovered by what method you may be neither thief nor sharer.

TRACHALIO: By what method?

GRIPUS: Let me go away from here; you quietly go your own way, and don't you inform against me to any one, and I won't give anything to you. You hold your tongue; I'll be mum. This is the best and the fairest *plan*.

TRACHALIO: Well, what proposition do you venture to make?

GRIPUS: I've made it already; for you to go away, to let go of the rope, *and* not to be a nuisance to me.

TRACHALIO: Stop while I propose terms.

GRIPUS: I' faith, do, prithee, dispose of yourself forthwith.

TRACHALIO: Do you know any one in these parts?

GRIPUS: My own neighbours I must *know*.

TRACHALIO: Where do you live here?

GRIPUS *(pointing)*: At a distance out away yonder, as far off as the farthest fields.

TRACHALIO *(pointing to the cottage of* Dæmones*)*: The person that lives in that cottage, should you like it to be decided by his arbitration?

GRIPUS: Let go of the rope for a moment while I step aside and consider.

TRACHALIO: Be it so. *(Lets go the rope.)*

GRIPUS *(aside)*: Capital, the thing's all right; the whole of this booty is my own. He's inviting me here inside of my own abode to my own master as umpire. By my troth, he never this day will award three obols away from his own servant. Assuredly, this fellow doesn't know what proposal he has been making. *(To* Trachalio.*)* I'll go to the arbitrator *with you.*

TRACHALIO: What then?

GRIPUS: Although I know for sure that this is my own lawful right, let that be done rather than I should now be fighting with you.

TRACHALIO: Now you satisfy me.

GRIPUS: Although you are driving me before an arbitrator whom I don't know, if he shall administer justice, although he is unknown, he is *as good as* known *to me*; if he doesn't, though known, he is *the same as though* entirely unknown.

SCENE IV — *Enter* Dæmones, *from his cottage, with* Palæstra *and* Ampelisca, *and* Servants.

DAEMONES *(to the* Women*)*: Seriously, upon my faith, *young* women, although I wish what you desire, I'm afraid that on your account my wife will be turning me out of doors, who'll be saying that I've brought harlots here before her *very* eyes. Do you take refuge at the altar rather than I.

THE WOMEN: We, wretched creatures, are undone. *(They weep.)*

DAEMONES: I'll place you in safety; don't you fear. But why *(turning to the* Servants*)* are you following me out of doors? Since I'm here, no one shall do them harm. Now then, be off, I say, indoors, both of you, you guards from off guard. *(They go in.)*

GRIPUS: O master, save you.

DAEMONES: Save you. How goes it?

TRACHALIO *(pointing to* Gripus*)*: Is he your servant?

GRIPUS: I'm not ashamed *to say yes.*

TRACHALIO: I've nothing to do with you.

GRIPUS: Then get you gone hence, will you.

TRACHALIO: Prithee, do answer me, aged sir; is he your servant?

DAEMONES: He is mine.

TRACHALIO: Oh then, that is very good, since he is yours. Again I salute you.

DAEMONES: And I you. Are you he who, not long since, went away

243

from here to fetch his master?

TRACHALIO: I am he.

DAEMONES: What now is it that you want?

TRACHALIO *(pointing to* Gripus*)*: This is your servant, you say?

DAEMONES: He is mine.

TRACHALIO: That is very good, since he is yours.

DAEMONES: What's the matter?

TRACHALIO *(pointing to* Gripus*)*: That's a rascally fellow there.

DAEMONES: What has the rascally fellow done to you?

TRACHALIO: I wish the ankles of that fellow were smashed.

DAEMONES: What's the thing about which you are now disputing between yourselves?

TRACHALIO: I'll tell you.

GRIPUS: No, I'll tell you.

TRACHALIO: I fancy I'm to move the matter first.

GRIPUS: If indeed you were a decent person, you would be moving yourself off from here.

DAEMONES: Gripus, give attention, and hold your tongue.

GRIPUS: In order that that fellow may speak first?

DAEMONES: Attend, *I tell you. (To* Trachalio.*)* Do you say on.

GRIPUS: Will you give the right of speaking to a stranger sooner than to your own *servant*?

TRACHALIO: O dear! how impossible it is for him to be kept quiet. As I was beginning to say, that Procurer, whom some little time since you turned out of the Temple of Venus — see *(pointing at the wallet)*, he has got his wallet.

GRIPUS: I haven't got it.

TRACHALIO: Do you deny that which I see with my own eyes?

GRIPUS: But I *only* wish you couldn't see. I have got it, *and* I haven't got it; why do you trouble yourself about me, what things I do?

TRACHALIO: In what way you got it does matter, whether rightfully or wrongfully.

GRIPUS: If I didn't take it *in the sea*, there's not a reason why you shouldn't deliver me up to the cross. If I took it in the sea with my net, how is it yours rather than my own?

TRACHALIO *(to* Dæmones*)*: He is deceiving you; the matter happened in this way, as I am telling you.

GRIPUS: What do you say?

TRACHALIO: So long as the person that has the first right to speak is speaking do *(to* Dæmones*)* put a check on him, please, if he belongs to you.

GRIPUS: What, do you wish the same thing to be done to myself, that your master has been accustomed *to do* to yourself? If he is in the habit of putting a check upon you, this *master* of ours isn't in the habit *of doing so* with us.

DAEMONES *(to* Trachalio*)*: In that remark only has he got the better of you. What do you want now? Tell me.

TRACHALIO: For my part, I neither ask for a share of that wallet there, nor have I ever said this day that it is my own; but in it there is a little casket that belongs to this female *(pointing to* Palæstra*)*, whom a short time since I averred to be free born.

DAEMONES: You are speaking of her, I suppose, who a short time since you said was my countrywoman?

TRACHALIO: Just so; and those trinkets which formerly, when little, she used to wear, are there in that casket, which is in that wallet. This thing is of no service to him, and will be of utility to her, poor creature, if he gives it up, by means of which to seek for her parents.

DAEMONES: I'll make him give it up; hold your tongue.

GRIPUS: I' faith, I'm going to give nothing to that fellow.

TRACHALIO: I ask for nothing but the casket and the trinkets.

GRIPUS: What if they are made of gold?

TRACHALIO: What's that to you? Gold shall be paid for gold, silver shall have its weight in silver in return.

GRIPUS: Please let me see the gold; after that I'll let you see the casket.

DAEMONES *(to* Gripus*)*: Do you beware of punishment, and hold your tongue. *(To* Trachalio.*)* As you commenced to speak do you go on.

TRACHALIO: *This* one thing I entreat of you, that you will have compassion on this female, if, indeed, this wallet is that Procurer's, which I suspect it is. In this matter, I'm saying nothing of certainty to you, but only on conjecture.

GRIPUS: Do you see how the rascal's wheedling him?

TRACHALIO: Allow me to say on as I commenced. If this is the wallet that belongs to that villain whose I say it is, these women here will be able to recognize it; order him to show it to them.

GRIPUS: Say you so? To show it to them?

DAEMONES: He doesn't say unreasonably, Gripus, that the wallet should be shown.

GRIPUS: Yes, i' faith, confoundedly unreasonably.

DAEMONES: How so?

GRIPUS: Because, if I do show it, at once they'll say, of course, that they recognize it.

TRACHALIO: Source of villainy, do you suppose that all other people are just like yourself, you author of perjury?

GRIPUS: All this I easily put up with, so long as he *(pointing to* Dæmones*)* is of my way of thinking.

245

TRACHALIO: But now he is against you; from this *(pointing to the wallet)* will he obtain true testimony.

DAEMONES: Gripus, do you pay attention. *(To* Trachalio.*)* You explain in a few words what it is you want.

TRACHALIO: For my part, I have stated it; but if you haven't understood me, I'll state it over again. Both of these women *(pointing to them)*, as I said a short time since, ought to be free; *(pointing to* Palæstra*)* she was stolen at Athens when a little girl.

GRIPUS: Tell me what that has got to do with the wallet, whether they are slaves or whether free women?

TRACHALIO: You wish it all to be told over again, you rascal, so that the day may fail us.

DAEMONES: Leave off your abuse, and explain to me what I've been asking.

TRACHALIO: There ought to be a casket of wicker-work in that wallet, in which are tokens by means of which she may be enabled to recognize her parents, by whom, when little, she was lost at Athens, as I said before.

GRIPUS: May Jupiter and the Gods confound you. What do you say, you sorcerer of a fellow? What, are these women dumb, that they are not able to speak for themselves?

TRACHALIO: They are silent for this reason, because a silent woman is always better than a talking one.

GRIPUS: Then, i' faith, by your way of speaking, you are neither a man nor a woman to my notion.

TRACHALIO: How so?

GRIPUS: Why, because neither talking nor silent are you ever good *for anything.* Prithee *(to* Dæmones*)* shall I ever be allowed to-day to speak?

DAEMONES: If you utter a single word more this day, I'll break your head for you.

TRACHALIO: As I had commenced to say it, old gentleman, I beg you to order him to give up that casket to these *young women;* if for it he asks any reward for himself, it shall be paid; whatever else is there besides, let him keep for himself.

GRIPUS: Now at last you say that, because you are aware it is my right; just now you were asking to go halves.

TRACHALIO: Aye, and even still I ask it.

GRIPUS: I've seen a kite making a swoop, even when he got nothing at all however.

DAEMONES *(to* Gripus*)*: Can't I shut your *mouth* without a drubbing?

GRIPUS *(pointing to* Trachalio*)*: If that fellow is silent, I'll be silent; if he talks, allow me to talk in my own behalf.

246

DAEMONES: Please now give me this wallet, Gripus.

GRIPUS: I'll trust it to you; but for you to return it me, if there are none of those things in it.

DAEMONES: It shall be returned.

GRIPUS: Take it. *(Gives him the wallet.)*

DAEMONES: Now then listen, Palæstra and Ampelisca, to this which I say. Is this the wallet, in which this *Procurer* said that your casket was?

PALAESTRA: It is the same.

GRIPUS *(aside)*: Troth, to my sorrow, I'm undone; how on the instant, before she well saw it, she said that it was it.

PALAESTRA: I'll make this matter plain to you, instead of difficult. There ought to be a casket of wicker-work there in that wallet; whatever is in there I'll state by name; don't you show me anything. If I say wrong, I shall *then* have said *this* to no purpose; then you shall keep these things, whatever is in there for yourselves. But if the truth, then I entreat you that what is my own may be restored to me.

DAEMONES: I agree; you ask for bare justice *only*, in my way of thinking, at least.

GRIPUS: But, i' faith, in mine, for extreme injustice; what if she is a witch or a sorceress, and shall mention exactly everything that's in it? Is a sorceress to have it?

DAEMONES: She shan't get it, unless she tells the truth; in vain will she be conjuring. Unloose the wallet, then *(giving it to* Gripus*)*, that as soon as possible I may know what is the truth.

GRIPUS *(first unfastens the straps of the wallet, and then hands it to his* Master*)*: Take it, it's unfastened. (Dæmones *takes out the casket.*) Alas, I'm undone; I see the casket.

DAEMONES *(holding it up, and addressing* Palæstra*)*: Is this it?

PALAESTRA: That is it. O my parents, here do I keep you locked up; here have I enclosed both my wealth and my hopes of recognizing you.

GRIPUS *(aside)*: Then, by my faith, the Gods must be enraged with you, whoever you are, who fasten up your parents in so narrow a compass.

DAEMONES: Gripus, come hither, your cause is being tried. *(To* Palæstra.*)* Do you, young woman, away at a distance there say what's in it, and of what appearance; mention them all. By my troth, if you make ever so slight a mistake, even if afterwards you wish, madam, to correct yourself, you'll be making a great mistake.

GRIPUS: You demand what's real justice.

TRACHALIO: By my troth, then, he doesn't demand yourself; for you are the opposite of justice.

DAEMONES: Now then, say on, young woman. Gripus, give attention and hold your tongue.

PALAESTRA: There are some trinkets.

DAEMONES *(looking in the casket)*: See, here they are, I espy them.

GRIPUS *(aside)*: In the first onset I am worsted; *(takes hold of the arm of* Dæmones*)* hold, don't be showing.

DAEMONES: Of what description are they? Answer in their order.

PALAESTRA: In the first place, there's a little sword of gold, with an inscription.

DAEMONES: Just tell me, what the characters are upon that little sword.

PALAESTRA: The name of my father. Next, on the other side, there's a little two-edged axe, of gold likewise, with an inscription: there on the axe is the name of my mother.

DAEMONES: Stay; tell me, what's the name of your father upon the little sword?

PALAESTRA: Dæmones.

DAEMONES: Immortal Gods! where in the world are my hopes?

GRIPUS: Aye, by my troth, *and where are* mine?

DAEMONES: Do proceed forthwith, I entreat you.

GRIPUS: Cautiously, or else *(aside)* away to utter perdition.

DAEMONES: Say, what's the name of you mother, here upon the little axe?

PALAESTRA: Dædalis.

DAEMONES: The Gods will that I should be preserved.

GRIPUS: But that I should be ruined.

DAEMONES: This must be my own daughter, Gripus.

GRIPUS: She may be for me, indeed. *(To* Trachalio.*)* May all the Gods confound you who this day saw me with your eyes, and myself as well for a blockhead, who didn't look about a hundred times first *to see* that no one was watching me, before I drew the net out of the water.

PALAESTRA: Next, *there's* a little knife of silver, and two little hands linked together, and *then* a little sow.

GRIPUS *(aside)*: Nay, then, go and be hanged, you with your little sow and your little pigs.

PALAESTRA: There's also a golden drop, which my father presented to me upon my birthday.

DAEMONES: Undoubtedly there is; *but* I cannot restrain myself any longer from embracing you. My daughter, blessings on you; I am that father who begot you; I am Dæmones, and see, your mother Dædalis is in the house here *(pointing to his cottage)*.

AMPELISCA *(embracing him)*: Blessing on you, my unlooked-for father.

DAEMONES: Blessings on you; how joyously do I embrace you.

248

TRACHALIO: 'Tis a pleasure *to me*, inasmuch as this falls to your lot from your feelings of affection.

DAEMONES: Come then, Trachalio, if you can, bring that wallet into the house.

TRACHALIO *(taking the wallet)*: See the villainy of Gripus; inasmuch, Gripus, as this matter has turned out unfortunately for you, I congratulate you.

DAEMONES: Come, *then*, let's go, my daughter, to your mother, who will be better able to enquire of you into this matter from proofs; who had you more in her hands, and is more thoroughly acquainted with your tokens.

TRACHALIO: Let's all go hence in-doors, since we are giving our common aid.

PALAESTRA: Follow me, Ampelisca.

AMPELISCA: That the Gods favour you, it is a pleasure to me. *(They all go into the cottage of* Dæmones, *except* Gripus.*)*

SCENE V — Gripus, *alone.*

GRIPUS *(to himself)*: Am I not a blockhead of a fellow, to have this day fished up that wallet? Or, when I had fished it up, not to have hidden it somewhere in a secret spot? By my troth, I guessed that it would be a troublesome booty for me, because it fell to me in such troublous weather. I' faith, I guess that there's plenty of gold and silver there. What is there better for me than to be off hence in-doors and secretly hang myself — at least for a little time, until this vexation passes away from me? *(Goes into the cottage.)*

SCENE VI — *Enter* Dæmones, *from his cottage.*

DAEMONES *(to himself)*: O ye immortal Gods, what person is there more fortunate than I, who unexpectedly have discovered my daughter? Isn't it the fact, that if the Gods will a blessing to befall any person, that longed-for *pleasure* by some means or other, falls to the lot of the virtuous? I this day, a thing that I never hoped for nor yet believed, have unexpectedly discovered my daughter, and I shall bestow her upon a respectable young man of noble family, an Athenian, and my kinsman. For that reason I wish him to be fetched hither to me as soon as possible, and I've requested my servant to come out here, that he may go to the Forum. Still, I'm surprised at it that he isn't yet come out. I think I'll go to the door. *(Opens the door, and looks in.)*

249

What do I behold? Embracing her, my wife is clasping my daughter around her neck. Her caressing is *really* almost too foolish and sickening. *(Goes to the door again, and calls out.)* 'Twere better, wife, for an end to be made at last of your kissing; and make all ready that I may perform a sacrifice, when I come in-doors, in honor of the household Gods, inasmuch as they have increased our family. At home I have lambs and swine for sacred use. But why, ladies, are you detaining that Trachalio? Oh, I see he's coming out of doors, very seasonably.

SCENE VII — *Enter* Trachalio, *from the cottage.*

TRACHALIO *(speaking to those within)*: Wheresoever he shall be, I'll seek Plesidippus out at once, and bring him together with me to you.

DAEMONES: Tell him how this matter has fallen out about my daughter. Request him to leave other occupations and to come here.

TRACHALIO: Very well.

DAEMONES: Tell him that I'll give him my daughter for a wife.

TRACHALIO: Very well.

DAEMONES: And that I knew his father, and that he is a relation of my own.

TRACHALIO: Very well.

DAEMONES: But do make haste.

TRACHALIO: Very well.

DAEMONES: Take care and let a dinner be prepared here at once.

TRACHALIO: Very well.

DAEMONES: What, all very well?

TRACHALIO: Very well. But do you know what it is I want of you? That you'll remember what you promised, that this day I'm to be free.

DAEMONES: Very well.

TRACHALIO: Take care and entreat Plesidippus to give me my freedom.

DAEMONES: Very well.

TRACHALIO: And let your daughter request it; she'll easily prevail.

DAEMONES: Very well.

TRACHALIO: And that Ampelisca may marry me, when I'm a free man.

DAEMONES: Very well.

TRACHALIO: And that I may experience a pleasing return to myself in kindness for my actions.

DAEMONES: Very well.

TRACHALIO: What, all very well?

DAEMONES: Very well. Again I return you thanks. But do you make haste to proceed to the city forthwith, and betake yourself hither again.

TRACHALIO: Very well. I'll be here directly. In the meanwhile, do you make the other preparations that are necessary. *(Exit* Trachalio.*)*

DAEMONES: Very well — may Hercules ill befriend him with his "very-welling;" he has so stuffed my ears *with it.* Whatever it was I said, "very well" *was the answer.*

SCENE VIII — *Enter* Gripus, *from the cottage.*

GRIPUS: How soon may I have a word with you, Dæmones?

DAEMONES: What's your business, Gripus?

GRIPUS: Touching that wallet, if you are wise, be wise; keep what goods the Gods provide you.

DAEMONES: Does it seem right to you, that, what belongs to another I should assert to be my own?

GRIPUS: *What*, not a thing that I found in the sea?

DAEMONES: So much the better does it happen for him who lost it; none the more is it necessary that it should be your wallet.

GRIPUS: For this reason are you poor, because you are too scrupulously righteous.

DAEMONES: O Gripus, Gripus, in the life of man very many traps there are, in what they are deceived by guile. And, by my troth, full often is a bait placed in them, which bait if any greedy person greedily snaps at, through his own greediness he is caught in the trap. He who prudently, skilfully, and warily takes precaution, full long he may enjoy that which is honestly acquired. This booty seems *to me* to be about to be made a booty of *by me,* that it may go hence with a greater blessing than it *first* came. What, ought I to conceal what I know was brought to me as belonging to another? By no means will my friend Dæmones do that. 'Tis ever most becoming for prudent men to be on their guard against this, that they be not themselves confederates with their servants in evil-doing. Except only when I'm gaming, I don't care for any gain.

GRIPUS: At times, I've seen the Comedians, when acting, in this fashion repeat saying in a wise manner, and be applauded for them, when they pointed out this prudent conduct to the public. But when each person went thence his own way home, there wasn't one after the fashion which they had recommended.

DAEMONES: Go in-doors, don't be troublesome, moderate your tongue. I'm going to give you nothing, don't you deceive yourself.

251

GRIPUS *(apart)*: Then I pray the Gods that whatever's in that wallet, whether it's gold, or whether silver, it may all become ashes. *(Goes into the cottage.)*

SCENE IX — Dæmones, *alone.*

DAEMONES: This is the reason why we have bad servants. For this *master*, if he had combined with any servant, would have made both himself and the other guilty of a theft. While he was thinking that he himself had made a capture, in the meantime he himself would have been made a capture: capture would have led to capture. Now will I go in-doors from here and sacrifice; after that, I'll at once order the dinner to be cooked for us. *(Goes into the cottage.)*

ACT V — SCENE I

Enter Plesidippus *and* Trachalio, *at the further end of the stage.*

PLESIDIPPUS: Tell me all these things over again my life, my Trachalio, my free-man, my patron, aye rather, my father; has Palæstra found her father and mother?
TRACHALIO: She has found them.
PLESIDIPPUS: And is she my countrywoman?
TRACHALIO: So I think.
PLESIDIPPUS: And is she to marry me?
TRACHALIO: So I suspect.
PLESIDIPPUS: Prithee, do you reckon that he will betroth her to me?
TRACHALIO: So I reckon.
PLESIDIPPUS: Well, shall I congratulate her father too upon his finding her?
TRACHALIO: So I reckon.
PLESIDIPPUS: Well, her mother *too*?
TRACHALIO: So I reckon.
PLESIDIPPUS: What then do you reckon?
TRACHALIO: What you ask me, I reckon.
PLESIDIPPUS: Tell me then how much do you reckon it at?
TRACHALIO: What I, I reckon ——
PLESIDIPPUS: Then really, do carry over. Don't be always making a reckoning.
TRACHALIO: So I reckon.
PLESIDIPPUS: What, did I run? *(Pretends to run.)*
TRACHALIO: So I reckon.

PLESIDIPPUS: Or rather gently, this way? *(He walks slowly.)*
TRACHALIO: So I reckon.
PLESIDIPPUS: Ought I to salute her as well when I arrive?
TRACHALIO: So I reckon.
PLESIDIPPUS: Her father too?
TRACHALIO: So I reckon.
PLESIDIPPUS: After that, her mother?
TRACHALIO: So I reckon.
PLESIDIPPUS: And what after that? When I arrive, should I also embrace
her father?
TRACHALIO: So I don't reckon.
PLESIDIPPUS: Well, her mother?
TRACHALIO: So I don't reckon.
PLESIDIPPUS: Well, her own self?
TRACHALIO: So I don't reckon.
PLESIDIPPUS: Confusion, he has closed his reckoning; now when I wish
him, he doesn't reckon.
TRACHALIO: You are not in your senses; follow me.
PLESIDIPPUS: Conduct me, my patron, where you please. *(They go into
the cottage of* Dæmones.*)*

SCENE II — *Enter* Labrax, *at a distance.*

LABRAX *(to himself)*: What other mortal being is there living this day
more wretched than myself, whom before the commissioned judges
Plesidippus has just now cast? Palæstra has just been taken from
me. I'm ruined outright. But I do believe that Procurers
were procreated for *mere* sport; so much do all persons make
sport if any misfortune befalls a Procurer. Now I'll go look here,
in the Temple of Venus, for that other female, that her at least
I may take away, the *only* portion of my property that remains.
(He retires a little distance.)

SCENE III — *Enter* Gripus, *from the cottage of* Dæmones,
with a spit in his hand.

GRIPUS *(calling to the* People *within)*: By the powers, you shall never
this day at nightfall behold Gripus alive, unless the wallet is
restored to me.
LABRAX *(behind)*: I'm ready to die; when I hear mention made anywhere
of a wallet, I'm thumped, as it were with a stake, upon the breast.
GRIPUS *(at the door, continuing)*: That scoundrel is free; I, the person
that held the net in the sea, and drew up the wallet, to him you
refuse to give anything.

LABRAX *(behind)*: O ye immortal Gods! by his talk this person has made me prick up my ears.

GRIPUS *(continuing)*: By my troth, in letters a cubit long, I'll immediately post it up in every quarter, "If any person has lost a wallet with plenty of gold and silver, let him come to Gripus." You shan't keep it as you are wishing.

LABRAX *(behind)*: I' faith, this person knows, as I think, who has got the wallet. This person must be accosted by me; ye Gods, aid me, I do entreat you.

(Some one calls Gripus, *from within.)*

GRIPUS: Why are you calling me back in-doors? *(He rubs away at the spit.)* I want to clean this here before the door. But surely this, i' faith, has been made of rust, *and* not of iron; so that the more I rub it, it becomes *quite* red and more slender. Why surely this spit has been drugged; it does waste away so in my hands.

LABRAX *(accosting him)*: Save you, young man.

GRIPUS: May the Gods prosper you with your shorn pate.

LABRAX: What's going on?

GRIPUS: A spit being cleaned.

LABRAX: How do you do?

GRIPUS: What are you? Prithee, are you a medicant?

LABRAX: No, i' faith, I am more than a medicant by one letter.

GRIPUS: Then you are a "mendicant."

LABRAX: You've hit it to a nicety.

GRIPUS: Your appearance seems suitable to it. But what's the matter with you?

LABRAX: Troth, this last night I was shipwrecked at sea; the vessel was cast away, *and* to my misfortune I lost there everything that I had.

GRIPUS: What did you lose?

LABRAX: A wallet with plenty of gold and silver.

GRIPUS: Do you at all remember what there was in the wallet which was lost?

LABRAX: What matters for us now to be talking of it, if, in spite of it, it's lost?

GRIPUS: What if I know who has found it? I wish to learn from you the tokens.

LABRAX: Eight hundred golden pieces were there in a purse, besides a hundred Philippean minæ in a wash-leather bag apart.

GRIPUS *(aside)*: Troth, it is a noble prize; I shall be getting a handsome

254

reward. The Gods show respect to mortals; therefore I shall come off bounteously rewarded. No doubt, it is this man's wallet. *(To* Labrax*)* Do you proceed to relate the rest.

LABRAX: A large talent of silver of full weight was in a purse, besides a bowl, a goblet, a beaker, a boat, *and* a cup.

GRIPUS: Astonishing! you really did have some splendid riches.

LABRAX: A shocking expression is that, and a most abominable one. "You did have, and *now* have not."

GRIPUS: What would you be ready to give to one who should find these out for you, and give you information? Say, speedily *and* at once.

LABRAX: Three hundred didrachms.

GRIPUS: Rubbish.

LABRAX: Four hundred.

GRIPUS: Old Thrums.

LABRAX: Five hundred.

GRIPUS: A rotten nut.

LABRAX: Six hundred.

GRIPUS: You are prating about mere tiny weevils.

LABRAX: I'll give seven hundred.

GRIPUS: Your mouth is hot, you are cooling it just now.

LABRAX: I'll give a thousand didrachms.

GRIPUS: You are dreaming.

LABRAX: I add no more; be off with you.

GRIPUS: Hear me then; if, i' faith, I should be off from here, I shan't be here.

LABRAX: Would you like a hundred as well as the thousand?

GRIPUS: You are asleep.

LABRAX: Say how much you ask.

GRIPUS: That you mayn't be adding anything against your inclination, a great talent; it's not possible for three obols to be bated thence; then do you say either "yes" or "no" at once.

LABRAX *(aside)*: What's *to be done* here? It's a matter of necessity, I see: *(to* Gripus*)* the talent shall be paid.

GRIPUS *(going towards the altar)*: Just step this way; I wish Venus here to put the question to you.

LABRAX: Whatever you please, that command me.

GRIPUS: Touch this altar of Venus.

LABRAX *(touching it)*: I am touching it.

GRIPUS: By Venus here must you swear *to me.*

LABRAX: What must I swear?

GRIPUS: What I shall bid you.

LABRAX: Dictate in words just as you like. *(Aside.)* What I've got at home, I shall never beg of any one else.

255

GRIPUS: Take hold of this altar.

LABRAX *(taking hold of it)*: I am taking hold of it.

GRIPUS: Swear that you will pay me the money on that same day on which you shall gain possession of the wallet.

LABRAX: Be it so.

GRIPUS *(speaking, while* Labrax *repeats after him)*: Venus of Cyrene, I invoke thee as my witness, if I shall find that wallet which I lost in the ship, safe with the gold and silver, and it shall come into my possession ——

GRIPUS: "Then to this Gripus *do I promise;*" say so and place your hand upon me.

LABRAX: Then to this Gripus do I promise, Venus, do thou hear me ——

GRIPUS *(followed by* Labrax*)*: "That I will forthwith give him a great talent of silver."

LABRAX: That I will forthwith give him a great talent of silver.

GRIPUS: If you defraud me, say, may Venus utterly destroy your body, and your existence in our calling *(aside.)* As it is, do you have this for yourself, when you've *once* taken the oath.

LABRAX: If, Venus, I shall do anything amiss against this *oath,* I supplicate thee that all Procurers may *henceforth* be wretched.

GRIPUS *(aside)*: As it is, it shall be so, even if you do keep your oath. Do you wait here; *(going towards the cottage)* —I'll at once make the old gentleman come out; do you forthwith demand of him that wallet. *(Goes in.)*

LABRAX *(to himself)*: If ever so much he shall restore to me this wallet, I'm not this day indebted to him three obols even. It's according to my own intention what my tongue swears. *(The door opens.)* But I'll hold my peace; see, here he's coming out, and bringing the old man.

SCENE IV — *Enter Gripus, followed by* Dæmones, *with the wallet.*

GRIPUS: Follow this way. Where is this Procurer? Hark you *(to* Labrax*)*, see now; this person *(pointing at* Dæmones*)* has got your wallet.

DAEMONES: I have got it, and I confess that it is in my possession; and if it's yours, you may have it. Everything, just as each particular was in it, shall in like manner be given safe to you. *(Holding it out.)* Take it, if it's yours.

LABRAX: Immortal Gods, it is mine. *(Takes it.)* Welcome *dear* wallet.

DAEMONES: Is it yours?

LABRAX: Do you ask the question? If indeed, i' faith, it were in Jove's possession, still it is my own.

DAEMONES: Everything in it is safe; there has only been one casket taken out of it with some trinkets, by means of which this day I have found my daughter.

256

LABRAX: What person?

DAEMONES: Palæstra, who was your property, she has been discovered to be my own daughter.

LABRAX: By my troth, it has happily turned out so; since this matter has happened so fortunately for you according to your wishes, I'm rejoiced.

DAEMONES: In that I don't readily believe you.

LABRAX: Aye, by my faith, that you may be sure that I'm rejoiced, you shan't give me three obols for her; I excuse you.

DAEMONES: I' faith, you are acting kindly.

LABRAX: No, troth; it's really yourself, indeed, *that's doing so. (Going off with the wallet.)*

GRIPUS: Hark you, you've got the wallet now.

LABRAX: I have got it.

GRIPUS: Make haste.

LABRAX: Make haste about what?

GRIPUS: To pay me the money.

LABRAX: By my troth, I'll neither give you anything nor do I owe you anything.

GRIPUS: What mode of proceeding is this? Don't you owe it me?

LABRAX: Troth, not I indeed.

GRIPUS: Didn't you promise it me upon your oath?

LABRAX: I did take an oath, and now I'll take an oath, if it is in any way my own pleasure; oaths were invented for preserving property, not for losing it.

GRIPUS: Give me, will you, a great talent of silver, you most perjured fellow.

DAEMONES: Gripus, what talent is it you are asking him for?

GRIPUS: He promised it me on oath.

LABRAX: I chose to swear; *(turning to* Dæmones*)* are you the priest as to my perjury?

DAEMONES *(to* Gripus*)*: For what reason did he promise you the money?

GRIPUS: If I restored this wallet into his hands, he swore that he would give me a great talent of silver.

LABRAX: Find me a person with whom I may go to the judge, *to decide* whether you did not make the bargain with wicked fraudulence, and whether I am yet five-and-twenty years old.

GRIPUS *(pointing to* Dæmones*)*: Go *to the judge* with him.

LABRAX: No; I must have some other person.

DAEMONES *(to* Labrax*)*: Then I shan't allow you to take it away from him, unless I shall have found him guilty. Did you promise him the money?

LABRAX: I confess it.

257

DAEMONES: What you promised my slave must needs be my own. Don't you be supposing, Procurer, that you are to be using your pimping honesty here. That can't be.

GRIPUS (to Labrax): Did you fancy now that you had got hold of a person whom you might cheat? It must be paid down here (holding his hand), good silver coin; I shall, at once, pay it to him (pointing to Dæmones), so that he may give me my liberty.

DAEMONES: Inasmuch, therefore, as I have acted courteously towards you, and by my means these things (pointing to the wallet) have been saved for you——

GRIPUS: I' faith, by my means, rather; don't say by yours.

DAEMONES (to Gripus): If you are prudent you'll hold your tongue. (To Labrax.) Then it befits you in a like courteous manner kindly to return the obligation to myself, who so well merit the same.

LABRAX: You are pleading, of course, for my right?

DAEMONES (ironically): It would be a wonder if I didn't, at a loss to myself, ask you to forego your right.

GRIPUS (aside): I'm all right; the Procurer's giving way; my freedom is at hand.

DAEMONES (pointing to Gripus): He found this wallet; he is my slave. I therefore have preserved this for you, together with a large sum of money.

LABRAX: I return you thanks, and with regard to the talent that I promised on oath to him, there's no reason that you shouldn't receive it.

GRIPUS: Hark you, give it me then, if you are wise.

DAEMONES (to Gripus): Will you hold your tongue, or not?

GRIPUS: You pretend to be acting on my side: I tell you, by my troth, you shan't do me out of that, if I did lose the other booty.

DAEMONES: You shall have a beating if you add a single word.

GRIPUS: Troth now, do you kill me even; I'll never be silent on any terms, unless my mouth is shut with the talent.

LABRAX: For yourself, in fact, is he using his exertions; do hold your tongue.

DAEMONES: Step this way, Procurer.

LABRAX: Very well. (They walk on one side.)

GRIPUS: Proceed openly; I don't want any whisperings or mumblings to be going on.

DAEMONES: Tell me, at what price did you buy that other young woman, Ampelisca?

LABRAX: I paid down a thousand didrachms.

DAEMONES: Should you like me to make you a handsome offer?

LABRAX: I should like it much.

DAEMONES: I'll divide the talent.

LABRAX: You act fairly.

DAEMONES: For that other woman *Ampelisca*, that she may be free, take you one half, *and* give the other half to him.

LABRAX: By all means.

DAEMONES: For that half I'll give his freedom to Gripus, by means of whom you found your wallet, and I my daughter.

LABRAX: You act fairly; I return you many thanks. *(They return to Gripus.)*

GRIPUS: How soon then is the money to be returned to me?

DAEMONES: The money's paid, Gripus; I've got it.

GRIPUS: You, faith; but I had rather it were myself.

DAEMONES: I' faith, there's nothing for you here, *so* don't you be expecting it. I wish you to release him from his oath.

GRIPUS *(aside)*: Troth, I'm undone; if I don't hang myself, I'm utterly done for. *(Aloud.)* I' faith, after this day you certainly shall never be cheating me again.

DAEMONES: Dine here to-day, Procurer.

LABRAX: Be it so; the proposal is to my taste.

DAEMONES: Do you *both* follow me in-doors. *(He comes forward and addresses the Audience.)* Spectators, I would invite you to dinner as well, were it not that I'm going to give nothing, and that there is no good cheer at all at home; and if, too, I didn't believe that you are invited to dinner elsewhere. But if you shall be willing to give hearty applause to this Play, do you all come to make merry at my house *some* sixteen years hence. Do you *(to* Labrax *and* Gripus*)* both dine here *with me* to-day.

GRIPUS: Be it so.

AN ACTOR *(To the* Audience.*)*: Now give us your applause.

H. T. Riley

259

TERENCE

PUBLIUS TERENTIUS AFER (c. 195-159 b. c.) was reputedly born in Carthage and brought to Rome as a slave. Here his talents gave him entrance into Roman cultured circles. Terence fulfilled the promise of his gifts by composing six comedies, all of which are extant.

THE ANDRIAN

PROLOGUE

The Bard, when first he gave his mind to write,
Thought it his only business, that his plays
Should please the people: but it now falls out,
He finds, much otherwise, and wastes, perforce,
His time in writing Prologues; not to tell
The argument, but to refute the slanders
Broach'd by the malice of an older Bard.
　　　And mark what vices he is charg'd withal!
Menander wrote the 'Andrian' and 'Perinthian':
Know one, and you know both; in argument
Less diff'rent than in sentiment and style.
What suited with the 'Andrian' he confesses
From the 'Perinthian' he transferr'd, and us'd
For his: and this it is these sland'rers blame,
Proving by deep and learned disputation,
That Fables should not be confounded thus.
Troth! all their knowledge is, they nothing know:
Who, blaming him, blame Naevius, Plautus, Ennius,
Whose great example is his precedent;
Whose negligence he'd wish to emulate
Rather than *their dark diligence*. Henceforth,
Let them, I give them warning, be at peace,
And cease to rail, lest they be made to know
Their own misdeeds. Be favourable! Sit
With equal mind, and hear our play; that hence
Ye may conclude, what hope to entertain,
Whether the plays he may hereafter write,
Shall merit approbation or contempt.

PROLOGUE.
SIMO, Father of Pamphilus.
CHREMES, Father of Glycerium and Philomena.
PAMPHILUS, Son of Simo.
CHARINUS, A young Man.
CRITO, A native of Andros.
SOSIA, Freedman of Simo.
DAVUS, Servant to Simo.
BYRRHIA, Servant to Charinus.
DROMO.
SERVANTS, &c.
GLYCERIUM, Daughter of Chremes.
MYSIS, Maidservant to Glycerium.
LESBIA, A midwife attendant on Glycerium.
ARCHYLLIS.

SCENE — ATHENS.

THE ANDRIAN

ACT I — SCENE I

Simo, Sosia, *and* Servants *with provisions*

SIMO: Carry those things in: go! *(Ex. servants.)*
    Sosia, come here:
    A word with you!
SOSIA: I understand: — that these
    Be ta'en due care of.
SIMO: Quite another thing.
SOSIA: What can my art do more for you?
SIMO: This business
    Needs not that art; but those good qualities,
    Which I have ever known abide in you,
    Fidelity and secrecy.
SOSIA: I wait
    Your pleasure.
SIMO: Since I bought you, from a boy,
    How just and mild a servitude you've pass'd
    With me, you're conscious: from a purchas'd slave

I made you free, because you serv'd me freely:
The greatest recompence I could bestow.
SOSIA: I do remember.
SIMO: Nor do I repent.
SOSIA: If I have ever done, or now do aught
That's pleasing to you, Simo, I am glad,
And thankful that you hold my service good.
And yet this troubles me: for this detail,
Forcing your kindness on my memory,
Seems to reproach me of ingratitude.
Oh, tell me then at once, what would you, sir?
SIMO: I will; and this I must advise you first:
The nuptial you suppose preparing now,
Is all unreal.
SOSIA: Why pretend it then?
SIMO: You shall hear all from first to last: and thus
The conduct of my son, my own intent,
And what part you're to act, you'll know at once.
For my son, Sosia, now to manhood grown,
Had freer scope of living: for before
How might you know, or how indeed divine
His disposition, good or ill, while youth,
Fear, and a master, all constrain'd him?
SOSIA: True.
SIMO: Though most, as is the bent of youth, apply
Their mind to some one object, horses, hounds,
Or to the study of philosophy;
Yet none of these, beyond the rest, did he
Pursue; and yet, in moderation, all.
I was o'erjoy'd.
SOSIA: And not without good cause.
For this I hold to be the Golden Rule
Of life: Too much of one thing's good for nothing.
SIMO: So did he shape his life to bear himself
With ease and frank good-humour unto all:
Mixt in what company soe'er, to them
He wholly did resign himself; complied
With all their humours, checking nobody,
Nor e'er assuming to himself: and thus
With ease, and free from envy, may you gain
Praise, and conciliate friends.
SOSIA: He rul'd his life
By prudent maxims: for, as times go now,
Compliance raises friends, and truth breeds hate.

SIMO: Meanwhile, ('tis now about three years ago,)
       A certain woman from the isle of Andros,
       Came o'er to settle in this neighbourhood,
       By poverty and cruel kindred driv'n;
       Handsome and young.

SOSIA: Ah! I begin to fear
       Some mischief from this Andrian.

SIMO: At first,
       Modest and thriftily, tho' poor, she liv'd,
       With her own hands a homely livelihood
       Scarce earning from the distaff and the loom.
       But when a lover came, with promis'd gold,
       Another, and another; as the mind
       Falls easily from labour to delight,
       She took their offers, and set up the trade.
       They, who were then her chief gallants, by chance
       Drew thither, as oft happens with young men,
       My son to join their company. "So so!
       (Said I within myself,) he's smit! he has it!"
       And in the morning as I saw their servants
       Run to and fro, I'd often call, "Here, boy!
       Prithee now, who had Chrysis yesterday?"
       The name of this same Andrian.

SOSIA: I take you.

SIMO: Phaedrus, they said, Clinia, or Niceratus;
       For all these three then follow'd her — "Well, well,
       But what of Pamphilus?" — "Of Pamphilus!
       He supt, and paid his reck'ning." — I was glad.
       Another day I made the like enquiry,
       But still found nothing touching Pamphilus.
       Thus I believ'd his virtue prov'd, and hence
       Thought him a miracle of continence:
       For he who struggles with such spirits, yet
       Holds in that commerce an unshaken mind,
       May well be trusted with the governance
       Of his own conduct. Nor was I alone
       Delighted with his life, but all the world
       With one accord said all good things, and prais'd
       My happy fortunes, who possess'd a son
       So good, so lib'rally disposed. — In short,
       Chremes, seduc'd by this fine character,
       Came of his own accord, to offer me
       His only daughter with a handsome portion
       In marriage with my son. I lik'd the match;

	Betroth'd my son; and this was pitch'd upon,
	By joint agreement, for the wedding-day.
SOSIA:	And what prevents its being so?
SIMO:	I'll tell you.
	In a few days, the treaty still on foot,
	This neighbour Chrysis dies.
SOSIA:	In happy hour:
	Happy for you! I was afraid of Chrysis.
SIMO:	My son, on this event, was often there
	With those who were the late gallants of Chrysis;

SOSIA: And what prevents its being so?

SIMO: I'll tell you.
In a few days, the treaty still on foot,
This neighbour Chrysis dies.

SOSIA: In happy hour:
Happy for you! I was afraid of Chrysis.

SIMO: My son, on this event, was often there
With those who were the late gallants of Chrysis;
Assisted to prepare the funeral,
Ever condol'd, and sometimes wept with them.
This pleas'd me then; for in myself I thought,
"Since merely for a small acquaintance-sake
He takes this woman's death so nearly, what
If he himself had lov'd? What would he feel
For me, his father?" All these things, I thought,
Were but the tokens and the offices
Of a humane and tender disposition.
In short, on his account, e'en I myself
Attend the funeral, suspecting yet
No harm.

SOSIA: And what —

SIMO: You shall hear all. The corpse
Borne forth, we follow: when among the women
Attending there, I chanc'd to cast my eyes
Upon one girl, in form ——

SOSIA: Not bad, perhaps ——

SIMO: And look, so modest, and so beauteous, Sosia!
That nothing cou'd exceed it. As she seem'd
To grieve beyond the rest; and as her air
Appear'd more liberal and ingenuous,
I went and ask'd her women, who she was.
Sister, they said, to Chrysis: when at once
It struck my mind; "So! so! the secret's out;
Hence were those tears, and hence all that compassion!"

SOSIA: Alas! I fear how this affair will end.

SIMO: Meanwhile the funeral proceeds: we follow;
Come to the sepulchre: the body's plac'd
Upon the pile, lamented: whereupon
This sister I was speaking of, all wild,
Ran to the flames with peril of her life.
Then! there! the frighted Pamphilus betrays
His well-dissembled and long-hidden love;

Runs up, and takes her round the waist, and cries,
"Oh my Glycerium! what is it you do?
Why, why endeavour to destroy yourself?"
Then she, in such a manner, that you thence
Might easily perceive their long, long love,
Threw herself back into his arms, and wept,
Oh, how familiarly!

SOSIA: How say you!

SIMO: I
Return in anger thence, and hurt at heart,
Yet had not cause sufficient for reproof.
"What have I done? (he'd say;) or how deserv'd
"Reproach? or how offended, father? — Her,
"Who meant to cast herself into the flames,
"I stopt." A fair excuse!

SOSIA: You're in the right;
For him, who sav'd a life, if you reprove,
What will you do to him that offers wrong?

SIMO: Chremes next day came open-mouth'd to me:
Oh monstrous! he had found that Pamphilus
Was married to this stranger woman. I
Deny the fact most steadily, and he
As steadily insists. In short, we part
On such bad terms, as let me understand
He would refuse his daughter.

SOSIA: Did not you
Then take your son to task?

SIMO: Not even this
Appear'd sufficient for reproof.

SOSIA: How so?

SIMO: "Father, (he might have said,) you have, you know,
"Prescrib'd a term to all these things yourself.
"The time is near at hand, when I must live
"According to the humour of another.
"Meanwhile, permit me now to please my own!"

SOSIA: What cause remains to chide him then?

SIMO: If he
Refuses, on account of this amour,
To take a wife, such obstinate denial
Must be considered as his first offence.
Wherefore I now, from this mock-nuptial,
Endeavour to draw real cause to chide:
And that same rascal Davus, (if he's plotting,)

265

That he may let his counsel run to waste,
Now, when his knaveries can do no harm:
Who, I believe, with all his might and main,
Will strive to cross my purposes; and that
More to plague me, than to oblige my son.

SOSIA: Why so?

SIMO: Why so! Bad mind, bad heart: But if
I catch him at his tricks! — But what need words?
— If, as I wish it may, it should appear
That Pamphilus objects not to the match,
Chremes remains to be prevail'd upon,
And will, I hope, consent. 'Tis now your place
To counterfeit these nuptials cunningly;
To frighten Davus; and observe my son,
What he's about, what plots they hatch together.

SOSIA: Enough; I'll take due care. Let's now go in.

SIMO: Go first: I'll follow you. *(Exit Sosia.)*
Beyond all doubt
My son's averse to take a wife: I saw
How frighten'd Davus was but even now,
When he was told a nuptial was preparing. —
But here he comes.

SCENE II. — *Enter* Davus.

DAVUS *(to himself)*: I thought 'twere wonderful
If this affair went off so easily;
And dreaded where my master's great good-humour
Would end at last: who, after he perceiv'd
The lady was refus'd, ne'er said a word
To any of us, nor e'er took it ill.

SIMO *(behind)*: But now he will; to your cost too, I warrant you!

DAVUS: This was his scheme; to lead us by the nose
In a false dream of joy; then all agape
With hope, even then that we were most secure,
To have o'erwhelm'd us, nor allow'd us time
To cast about which way to break the match.
Cunning old gentleman!

SIMO: What says the rogue?

DAVUS: My master, and I did not see him!

SIMO: Davus!

DAVUS: Well! what now? *(pretending not to see him)*.

SIMO: Here! this way!

DAVUS: What can he want? *(to himself.)*

266

SIMO (overhearing): What say you?

DAVUS: Upon what, sir?

SIMO: Upon what!
The world reports that my son keeps a mistress.

DAVUS: Oh, to be sure, the world cares much for that.

SIMO: D'ye mind what I say, sirrah?

DAVUS: Nothing more, sir.

SIMO: But for me now to dive into these matters
May seem perhaps like too severe a father:
For all his youthful pranks concern not me.
While 'twas in season, he had my free leave
To take his swing of pleasure. But to-day
Brings on another stage of life, and asks
For other manners: wherefore I desire,
Or, if you please, I do beseech you, Davus,
To set him right again. (ironically).

DAVUS: What means all this?

SIMO: All, who are fond of mistresses, dislike
The thoughts of matrimony.

DAVUS: So they say.

SIMO: And then, if such a person entertains
An evil counsellor in those affairs,
He tampers with the mind, and makes bad worse.

DAVUS: Troth, I don't comprehend one word of this.

SIMO: No?

DAVUS: No. I'm Davus, and not Oedipus.

SIMO: Then for the rest I have to say to you,
You choose I should speak plainly?

DAVUS: By all means.

SIMO: If I discover then, that in this match
You get to your dog's tricks to break it off,
Or try to shew how shrewd a rogue you are,
I'll have you beat to mummy, and then thrown
In prison, sirrah! upon this condition,
That when I take you out again, I swear
To grind there in your stead. D'ye take me *now*?
Or don't you understand *this* neither?

DAVUS: Clearly.
You have spoke out at last: the very thing!
Quite plain and home; and nothing round about.

SIMO: I could excuse your tricks in any thing,
Rather than this. (angrily).

DAVUS: Good words! I beg of you.

267

SIMO: You laugh at me: well, well! — I give you warning,
    That you do nothing rashly, nor pretend
    You were not advertis'd of this — Take heed! *(Exit.)*

SCENE III — Davus.

DAVUS: Troth, Davus, 'tis high time to look about you;
    No room for sloth, as far as I can sound
    The sentiments of our old gentleman
    About this marriage; which if not fought off,
    And cunningly, spoils me, or my poor master.
    I know not what to do; nor can resolve
    To help the son, or to obey the father.
    If I desert poor Pamphilus, alas!
    I tremble for his life; if I assist him,
    I dread his father's threats: a shrewd old Cuff,
    Not easily deceiv'd. For, first of all,
    He knows of this amour; and watches me
    With jealous eyes, lest I devise some trick
    To break the match. If he discovers it,
    Woe to poor Davus! nay, if he's inclin'd
    To punish me, he'll seize on some pretence
    To throw me into prison, right or wrong.
    Another mischief too, to make bad worse;
    This Andrian, wife or mistress, is with child
    By Pamphilus. And do but mark the height
    Of their assurance! for 'tis certainly
    The dotage of mad people, not of lovers.
    Whate'er she shall bring forth, they have resolv'd
    To educate: and have among themselves
    Devis'd the strangest story! that Glycerium
    Is an Athenian citizen. "There was
    "Once on a time a certain merchant, shipwreckt
    "Upon the isle of Andros; there he died:
    "And Chrysis' father took this orphan-wreck,
    "Then but an infant, under his protection."
    Ridiculous! 'tis all romance to me:
    And yet the story pleases them. But see!
    Mysis comes forth. But I must to the Forum,
    To look for Pamphilus, for fear his father
    Should find him first, and take him unawares. *(Exit.)*

Mysis: I hear, Archyllis; I hear what you say:
    You beg me to bring Lesbia. By my troth
    That Lesbia is a drunken wretch, hot-headed,
    Nor worthy to be trusted with a woman
    In her first labour. — Well, well! she shall come. —
    Observe how earnest the old gossip is, *(coming forward)*.
    Because this Lesbia is her pot-companion.
    — Oh grant my mistress, Heav'n, a safe delivery,
    And let the midwife trespass any where
    Rather than here! — But what is it I see?
    Pamphilus all disorder'd: How I fear
    The cause! I'll wait awhile, that I may know
    If this commotion means us any ill.

Scene V — Pamphilus, Mysis, *behind.*

Pamphilus: Is this well done? or like a man? — Is this
    The action of a father?
Mysis: What's the matter?
Pamphilus: Oh all ye pow'rs of heav'n and earth! what's wrong,
    If this is not so? — If he was determin'd
    That I to-day should marry, should I not
    Have had some previous notice? — ought not he
    To have inform'd me of it long ago?
Mysis: Alas! what's this I hear?
Pamphilus: And Chremes too,
    Who had refus'd to trust me with his daughter,
    Changes his mind, because I change not mine.
    Can he then be so obstinately bent
    To tear me from Glycerium? To lose her
    Is losing life — Was ever man so crost,
    So curst as I? — Oh pow'rs of heav'n and earth!
    Can I by no means fly from this alliance,
    With Chremes' family? — so oft contemn'd
    And held in scorn! — all done, concluded all! —
    Rejected, then recall'd: — and why? — unless,
    For so I must suspect, they breed some monster,
    Whom as they can obtrude on no one else,
    They bring to me.
Mysis: Alas, alas! this speech
    Has struck me almost dead with fear.

PAMPHILUS: And then
My father! — what to say of him? — Oh shame!
A thing of so much consequence to treat
So negligently! — For but even now
Passing me in the Forum, "Pamphilus!
"To day's your wedding-day, (said he): prepare;
"Go, get you home!" — This sounded in my ears
As if he said, "Go, hang yourself!" — I stood
Confounded. Think you I could speak one word?
Or offer an excuse, how weak soe'er?
No, I was dumb: — and had I been aware,
Should any ask what I'd have done, I would,
Rather than this, do any thing. — But now
What to resolve upon? — So many cares
Entangle me at once, and rend my mind,
Pulling it diff'rent ways. My love, compassion,
This urgent match, my rev'rence for my father,
Who yet has ever been so gentle to me,
And held so slack a rein upon my pleasures.
— And I oppose him? — Racking thought! — Ah me!
I know not what to do.
MYSIS: Alas, I fear
Where this uncertainty will end. 'Twere best
He should confer with her; or I at least
Speak touching her to him. For while the mind
Hangs in suspense, a trifle turns the scale.
PAMPHILUS: Who's there? what, Mysis! Save you!
MYSIS: Save you, sir! (coming forward).
PAMPHILUS: How does she?
MYSIS: How! opprest with wretchedness.
To-day supremely wretched, as to-day
Was formerly appointed for your wedding:
And then she fears lest you desert her.
PAMPHILUS: I!
Desert her? Can I think on't? or deceive
A wretched maid, who trusted to my care
Her life and honour! Her whom I have held
Near to my heart, and cherish'd as my wife?
Or leave her modest and well nurtur'd mind
Through want to be corrupted? Never, never.
MYSIS: No doubt, did it depend on you alone;
But if constrain'd——
PAMPHILUS: D'ye think me then so vile?
Or so ungrateful, so inhuman, savage,

270

Neither long intercourse, nor love, nor shame,
Can move my soul, or make me keep my faith?
MYSIS: I only know, my mistress well deserves
You should remember her.
PAMPHILUS: I should remember her? Oh, Mysis, Mysis!
The words of Chrysis touching my Glycerium
Are written in my heart. On her death-bed
She call'd me. I approach'd her. You retir'd.
We were alone; and Chrysis thus began:
"My Pamphilus, you see the youth and beauty
"Of this unhappy maid: and well you know,
"These are but feeble guardians to preserve
"Her fortune or her fame. By this right hand
"I do beseech you, by your better angel,
"By your tried faith, by her forlorn condition,
"I do conjure you, put her not away,
"Nor leave her to distress. If I have ever,
"As my own brother, lov'd you; or if she
"Has ever held you dear 'bove all the world,
"And ever shewn obedience to your will ——
"I do bequeath you to her as a husband,
"Friend, guardian, father: all our little wealth
"To you I leave, and trust it to your care." ——
She join'd our hands, and died. —— I did receive her,
And once receiv'd will keep her.
MYSIS: So we trust.
PAMPHILUS: What make you from her?
MYSIS: Going for a midwife.
PAMPHILUS: Haste then! and hark, be sure take special heed,
You mention not a word about the marriage,
Lest this too give her pain.
MYSIS: I understand.

ACT II — SCENE I

Charinus, Byrrhia.

CHARINUS: How, Byrrhia? Is she to be married, say you,
To Pamphilus to-day?
BYRRHIA: 'Tis even so.
CHARINUS: How do you know?
BYRRHIA: I had it even now
From Davus at the Forum.

271

CHARINUS: Woe is me!
    Then I'm a wretch indeed: till now my mind
    Floated 'twixt hope and fear: now, hope remov'd,
    Stunn'd and o'erwhelm'd, it sinks beneath its cares.
BYRRHIA: Nay, prithee, master, since the thing you wish
    Cannot be had, e'en wish for that which may!
CHARINUS: I wish for nothing but Philomena.
BYRRHIA: Ah, how much wiser were it, that you strove
    To quench this passion, than, with words like these,
    To fan the fire, and blow it to a flame?
CHARINUS: How readily do men at ease prescribe
    To those who're sick at heart! Distrest like me,
    You would not talk thus.
BYRRHIA: Well, well, as you please.
CHARINUS: Ha! I see Pamphilus. I can resolve
    On any thing, ere give up all for lost.
BYRRHIA: What now?
CHARINUS: I will entreat him, beg, beseech him,
    Tell him our course of love, and thus perhaps,
    At least prevail upon him to defer
    His marriage some few days: meanwhile, I hope,
    Something may happen.
BYRRHIA: Ay, that something's nothing.
CHARINUS: Byrrhia, what think you? Shall I speak to him?
BYRRHIA: Why not? For tho' you don't obtain your suit,
    He will at least imagine you're prepar'd
    To cuckold him, in case he marries her.
CHARINUS: Away, you hang-dog, with your base suspicions!

SCENE II — *Enter* Pamphilus.

PAMPHILUS: Charinus, save you!
CHARINUS: Save you, Pamphilus!
    Imploring comfort, safety, help, and counsel,
    You see me now before you.
PAMPHILUS: Help and counsel!
    I can afford you neither — But what mean you?
CHARINUS: Is this your wedding-day?
PAMPHILUS: Ay, so they say.
CHARINUS: Ah, Pamphilus, if it be so, this day
    You see the last of me.
PAMPHILUS: How so?
CHARINUS: Ah me!
    I dare not speak it: prithee tell him, Byrrhia.

272

BYRRHIA: Ay, that I will.
PAMPHILUS: What is't?
BYRRHIA: He is in love
    With your bride, sir
PAMPHILUS: I'faith so am not I.
    Tell me, Charinus, has aught further past
    'Twixt you and her?
CHARINUS: Ah, no, no.
PAMPHILUS: Would there had!
CHARINUS: Now by our friendship, by my love, I beg
    You would not marry her. ————
PAMPHILUS: I will endeavour.
CHARINUS: If that's impossible, or if this match
    Be grateful to your heart ————
PAMPHILUS: My heart!
CHARINUS: At least
    Defer it some few days; while I depart,
    That I may not behold it.
PAMPHILUS: Hear, Charinus;
    It is, I think, scarce honesty in him
    To look for thanks, who means no favour. I
    Abhor this marriage, more than you desire it.
CHARINUS: You have reviv'd me.
PAMPHILUS: Now if you, or he,
    Your Byrrhia here, can do or think of aught;
    Act, plot, devise, invent, strive all you can
    To make her yours; and I'll do all I can
    That she may not be mine.
CHARINUS: Enough.
PAMPHILUS: I see
    Davus, and in good time: for he'll advise
    What's best to do.
CHARINUS: But you, you sorry rogue, *(to Byrrhia)*.
    Can give me no advice, nor tell me aught,
    But what it is impertinent to know.
    Hence, sirrah, get you gone!
BYRRHIA: With all my heart. *(Exit.)*

SCENE III—*Enter* Davus *hastily.*

DAVUS: Good heav'ns, what news I bring! what joyful news!
    But where shall I find Pamphilus, to drive
    His fears away, and make him full of joy?

273

CHARINUS: There's something pleases him.

PAMPHILUS: No matter what.

       He has not heard of our ill fortune yet.

DAVUS: And he, I warrant, if he has been told
       Of his intended wedding———

CHARINUS: Do you hear?

DAVUS: Poor soul, is running all about the town
       In quest of me. But whither shall I go?
       Or which way run?

CHARINUS: Why don't you speak to him?

DAVUS: I'll go.

PAMPHILUS: Ho! Davus! Stop, come here!

DAVUS: Who calls?
       O, Pamphilus! the very man. — Heyday!
       Charinus too! — Both gentlemen, well met!
       I've news for both.

PAMPHILUS: I'm ruin'd, Davus.

DAVUS: Hear me!

PAMPHILUS: Undone!

DAVUS: I know your fears.

CHARINUS: My life's at stake.

DAVUS: Your's I know also.

PAMPHILUS: Matrimony mine.

DAVUS: I know it.

PAMPHILUS: But to-day.

DAVUS: You stun me; plague!
       I tell you I know ev'ry thing: you fear *(to Charinus)*.
       You should *not* marry her — you fear you *should. (To Pamphilus.)*

CHARINUS: The very thing.

PAMPHILUS: The same.

DAVUS: And yet the *same*
       Is nothing. Mark!

PAMPHILUS: Nay, rid me of my fear.

DAVUS: I will then. Chremes don't intend his daughter
       Shall marry you to-day.

PAMPHILUS: No! How d'ye know?

DAVUS: I'm sure of it. Your father but just now
       Takes me aside, and tells me 'twas his will,
       That you should wed to-day; with much beside,
       Which now I have not leisure to repeat.
       I, on the instant, hastening to find you,
       Run to the Forum to inform you of it:
       There, failing, climb an eminence; look round;
       No Pamphilus: I light by chance on Byrrhia;

Enquire; he hadn't seen you. Vext at heart,
What's to be done? thought I. Returning thence,
A doubt arose within me. Ha! bad cheer,
The old man melancholy, and a wedding
Clapt up so suddenly! This don't agree.
PAMPHILUS: Well, what then?
DAVUS: I betook me instantly
To Chremes' house; but thither when I came,
Before the door all hush. This tickled me.
PAMPHILUS: You're in the right. Proceed.
DAVUS: I watch'd awhile:
Meantime no soul went in, no soul came out;
No matron; in the house no ornament;
No note of preparation. I approach'd,
Look'd in ———
PAMPHILUS: I understand: a potent sign!
DAVUS: Does this seem like a nuptial?
PAMPHILUS: I think not.
DAVUS: Think not, d'ye say? Away! you don't conceive:
The thing is evident. I met beside,
As I departed thence, with Chremes' boy,
Bearing some pot-herbs, and a pennyworth
Of little fishes for the old man's dinner.
CHARINUS: I am deliver'd, Davus, by your means,
From all my apprehensions of to-day.
DAVUS: And yet you are undone.
CHARINUS: How so? since Chremes
Will not consent to give Philomena
To Pamphilus.
DAVUS: Ridiculous! As if,
Because the daughter is denied to him,
She must of course wed you. Look to it well;
Court the old gentleman thro' friends, apply,
Or else ———
CHARINUS: You're right: I will about it straight,
Altho' that hope has often fail'd. Farewell.

SCENE IV — Pamphilus, Davus.

PAMPHILUS: What means my father then? why counterfeit?
DAVUS: That I'll explain. If he were angry now,
Merely that Chremes has refus'd his daughter,
He'd think himself in fault; and justly too,

275

Before the bias of your mind is known.
But granting you refuse her for a wife,
Then all the blame devolves on you; and then
Comes all the storm.

PAMPHILUS: What course then shall I take?
Shall I submit———

DAVUS: He is your father, sir,
Whom to oppose were difficult; and then,
Glycerium's a lone woman; and he'll find
Some course, no matter what, to drive her hence.

PAMPHILUS: To drive her hence?

DAVUS: Directly.

PAMPHILUS: Tell me then,
Oh tell me, Davus, what were best to do?

DAVUS: Say that you'll marry.

PAMPHILUS: How!

DAVUS: And where's the harm?

PAMPHILUS: Say that I'll marry!

DAVUS: Why not?

PAMPHILUS: Never, never.

DAVUS: Do not refuse!

PAMPHILUS: Persuade not!

DAVUS: Do but mark
The consequence.

PAMPHILUS: Divorcement from Glycerium,
And marriage with the other.

DAVUS: No such thing.
Your father, I suppose, accosts you thus:
I'd have you wed to-day;—I will, quoth you:
What reason has he to reproach you then?
Thus shall you baffle all his settled schemes,
And put him to confusion; all the while
Secure yourself: for 'tis beyond a doubt
That Chremes will refuse his daughter to you;
So obstinately too, you need not pause,
Or change these measures, lest he change his mind:
Say to your father then, that you will wed,
That, with the will, he may want cause to chide.
But if, deluded by fond hopes, you cry,
"No one will wed their daughter to a rake,
"A libertine."—Alas! you're much deceiv'd.
For know, your father will redeem some wretch
From rags and beggary to be your wife,
Rather than see your ruin with Glycerium.

276

But if he thinks you bear an easy mind,
He too will grow indiff'rent, and seek out
Another match at leisure: i'the mean while
Affairs may take a lucky turn.

PAMPHILUS: D'ye think so?

DAVUS: Beyond all doubt.

PAMPHILUS: See, what you lead me to.

DAVUS: Nay, peace!

PAMPHILUS: I'll say so then. But have a care
He knows not of the child, which I've agreed
To educate.

DAVUS: Oh confidence!

PAMPHILUS: She drew
This promise from me, as a firm assurance
That I would not forsake her.

DAVUS: We'll take care.
But here's your father: let him not perceive
You're melancholy.

SCENE V — *Enter* Simo *at a distance.*

SIMO: I return to see
What they're about, or what they meditate.

DAVUS: Now is he sure that you'll refuse to wed.
From some dark corner brooding o'er black thoughts
He comes, and fancies he has fram'd a speech
To disconcert you. See, you keep your ground!

PAMPHILUS: If I can, Davus.

DAVUS: Trust me, Pamphilus,
Your father will not change a single word
In anger with you, do but say you'll wed.

SCENE VI — *Enter* Byrrhia *behind.*

BYRRHIA: To-day my master bade me leave all else
For Pamphilus, and watch how he proceeds,
About his marriage; where for I have now
Followed the old man hither: yonder too
Stands Pamphilus himself, and with him Davus.
To business then!

277

SIMO: I see them both together.

DAVUS: Now mind. *(Apart to* Pamphilus.*)*

SIMO: Here, Pamphilus!

DAVUS: Now turn about,
>   As taken unawares. *(Apart.)*

PAMPHILUS: Who calls? my father!

DAVUS: Well said! *(Apart.)*

SIMO: It is my pleasure, that to-day,
>   As I have told you once before, you marry.

BYRRHIA: Now on our part, I fear what he'll reply. *(Aside.)*

PAMPHILUS: In that, and all the rest of your commands,
>   I shall be ready to obey you, sir.

BYRRHIA: How's that! *(overhearing).*

DAVUS: Struck dumb. *(Aside.)*

BYRRHIA: What said he? *(Listening.)*

SIMO: You perform
>   Your duty, when you cheerfully comply
>   With my desires.

DAVUS: There! said I not the truth *(Apart to* Pamphilus.*)*

BYRRHIA: My master then, so far as I can find,
>   May whistle for a wife.

SIMO: Now then go in,
>   That when you're wanted you be found.

PAMPHILUS: I go. *(Exit.)*

BYRRHIA: Is there no faith in the affairs of men?
>   Tis an old saying and a true one too;
>   "Of all mankind, each loves himself the best."
>   I've seen the lady; know her beautiful;
>   And therefore sooner pardon Pamphilus,
>   If he had rather win her to his arms,
>   Than yield her to th' embraces of my master.
>   I will go bear these tidings, and receive
>   Much evil treatment for my evil news. *(Exit.)*

SCENE VII—*Manent* Simo *and* Davus.

DAVUS: Now he supposes I've some trick in hand,
>   And loiter here to practice it upon him!

SIMO: Well, what now, Davus?

DAVUS: Nothing.

SIMO: Nothing, say you?

DAVUS: Nothing at all.

278

SIMO: And yet I look'd for something.

DAVUS: So, I perceive, you did. — This nettles him. *(Aside.)*

SIMO: Can you speak truth?

DAVUS: Most easily.

SIMO: Say then,
    Is not this wedding irksome to my son.
    From his adventure with the Andrian?

DAVUS: No, faith; or if at all, 'twill only be
    Two or three days' anxiety, you know;
    Then 'twill be over: for he sees the thing
    In its true light.

SIMO: I praise him for't.

DAVUS: While you
    Restrain'd him not, and while his youth allow'd,
    'Tis true he lov'd; but even then by stealth,
    As wise men ought, and careful of his fame.
    Now his age calls for matrimony, now
    To matrimony he inclines his mind.

SIMO: Yet, in my eyes, he seem'd a little sad.

DAVUS: Not upon that account. He has, he thinks,
    Another reason to complain of you.

SIMO: For what?

DAVUS: A trifle.

SIMO: Well, what is't?

DAVUS: Nay, nothing.

SIMO: Tell me, what is't?

DAVUS: You are then, he complains,
    Somewhat too sparing of expense.

SIMO: I?

DAVUS: You.
    A feast of scarce ten drachms! Does this, says he,
    Look like a wedding-supper for his son?
    What friends can I invite? especially
    At such a time as this? — And, truly, sir,
    You have been very frugal; much too sparing.
    I can't commend you for it.

SIMO: Hold your peace.

DAVUS: I've ruffled him. *(Aside.)*

SIMO: I'll look to that. Away! *(Exit Davus.)*
    What now? What means the varlet? Precious rogue!
    For if there's any knavery on foot,
    He, I am sure, is the contriver on't. *(Exit.)*

Simo, Davus, *coming out of* Simo's *house.* — Mysis,
Lesbia, *going towards the house of* Glycerium.

MYSIS: Ay, marry, 'tis as you say, Lesbia:
Women scarce ever find a constant man.
SIMO: The Andrian's maid-servant? Is't not?
DAVUS: Ay.
MYSIS: But Pamphilus——
SIMO: What says she? *(Overhearing.)*
MYSIS: — Has been true.
SIMO: How's that? *(overhearing.)*
DAVUS: Wou'd he were deaf, or she were dumb! *(Aside.)*
MYSIS: — For the child, boy, or girl, he has resolv'd
To educate.
SIMO: O Jupiter! what's this
I hear? If this be true, I'm lost indeed!
LESBIA: A good young gentleman!
MYSIS: Oh, very good.
But in, in, lest you make her wait.
LESBIA: I follow. *(Exeunt* Mysis *and* Lesbia.*)*

SCENE II — *Manent* Simo, Davus.

DAVUS: Unfortunate! What remedy! *(Aside.)*
SIMO: How's this? *(To himself.)*
And can he be so mad? What! educate
A harlot's child! — Ah, now I know their drift:
Fool that I was, scarce smelt it out at last!
DAVUS *(listening)*: What's this he says he has smelt out?
SIMO: Imprimis, *(to himself).*
'Tis this rogue's trick upon me. All sham:
A counterfeit deliv'ry and mock-labour,
Devis'd to frighten Chremes from the match.
GLYCERIUM *(within)*: Juno Lucina, save me! help, I pray thee.
SIMO: Hey-day! Already? Oh ridiculous!
Soon as she heard that I was at the door,
She hastens to cry out: Your incidents
Are ill-tim'd, Davus.
DAVUS: Mine, sir?
SIMO: Are your players
Unmindful of their cues, and want a prompter?
DAVUS: I do not comprehend you.

SIMO *(apart)*: If this knave
Had in the real nuptial of my son,
Come thus upon me unprepar'd, what sport,
What scorn he'd have expos'd me to? But now
At his own peril be it. I'm secure.

SCENE III — *Re-enter* Lesbia. — Archyllis *appears at the door.*

LESBIA *(to* Archyllis *within)*: As yet, Archyllis, all the symptoms seem
As good as might be wish'd in her condition:
First, let her make ablution; after that,
Drink what I've order'd her, and just so much:
And presently I will be here again. *(Coming forward.)*
Now, by this good day, master Pamphilus
Has got a chopping boy: Heav'n grant it live!
For he's a worthy gentleman, and scorn'd
To do a wrong to this young innocent. *(Exit.)*

SCENE IV — *Manent* Simo, Davus.

SIMO: This too, where's he that knows you would not swear
Was your contrivance?
DAVUS: My contrivance! What, sir?
SIMO: While in the house, forsooth, the midwife gave
No orders for the lady in the straw:
But having issued forth into the street,
Bawls out most lustily to those within.
— Oh Davus, am I then so much your scorn?
Seem I so proper to be play'd upon,
With such a shallow, barefac'd imposition?
You might at least, in reverence, have us'd
Some spice of art, were't only to pretend
You fear'd my anger, should I find you out.
DAVUS: I' faith, now he deceives himself, not I. *(Aside.)*
SIMO: Did not I give you warning? threaten too,
In case you play'd me false? But all in vain:
For what car'd you? — What! think you I believe
This story of a child by Pamphilus?
DAVUS: I see his error: Now I know my game. *(Aside.)*
SIMO: Why don't you answer?
DAVUS: What! you don't believe it!
As if you had not been inform'd of this? *(Archly).*
SIMO: Inform'd?
DAVUS: What then you found it out yourself? *(Archly).*

SIMO: D'ye laugh at me?

DAVUS: You must have been inform'd;
  Or whence this shrewd suspicion?

SIMO: Whence! from you:
  Because I know you.

DAVUS: Meaning, this was done
  By my advice?

SIMO: Beyond all doubt; I know it.

DAVUS: You do not know me, Simo. ———

SIMO: I not know you?

DAVUS: For if I do but speak, immediately
  You think yourself impos'd on. ———

SIMO: Falsely, hey?

DAVUS: So that I dare not ope my lips before you.

SIMO: All that I know is this; that nobody
  Has been deliver'd here.

DAVUS: You've found it out?
  Yet by-and-by they'll bring the bantling here,
  And lay it at our door. Remember, sir,
  I give you warning that will be the case;
  That you may stand prepar'd, nor after say,
  'Twas done by Davus's advice, his tricks!
  I would fain cure your ill opinion of me.

SIMO: But how d'ye know?

DAVUS: I've heard so, and believe so.
  Besides, a thousand different things concur to lead
  To this conjecture. First, Glycerium
  Profess'd herself with child by Pamphilus:
  That proves a falsehood. Now, as she perceives
  A nuptial preparation at our house,
  A maid's dispatch'd immediately to bring
  A midwife to her, and withal a child.
  You too, they will contrive, shall see the child,
  Or else the wedding must proceed.

SIMO: How's this?
  Having discover'd such a plot on foot,
  Why did not you directly tell my son?

DAVUS: Who then has drawn him from her but myself?
  For me all know how much he doated on her:
  But now he wishes for a wife. In fine,
  Leave that affair to me; and you mean while
  Pursue as you've began, the nuptials; which
  The gods, I hope, will prosper!

282

SIMO: Get you in.
    Wait for me there, and see that you prepare
    What's requisite. *(Exit* Davus.*)*
    He has not wrought upon me
    To yield implicit credit to his tale,
    Nor do I know if all he said be true.
    But, true or false, it matters not: to me
    My son's own promise is the main concern.
    Now to meet Chremes, and to beg his daughter
    In marriage with my son. If I succeed,
    What can I rather wish, than to behold
    Their marriage-rites to-day? For since my son
    Has given me his word, I've not a doubt,
    Should he refuse, but I may force him to it:
    And to my wishes, see where Chremes comes.

SCENE V — *Enters* Chremes.

SIMO: Chremes, good day!
CHREMES: The very man I look'd for.
SIMO: And I for you.
CHREMES: Well met. — Some persons came
    To tell me you inform'd them, that my daughter
    Was to be married to your son to-day:
    And therefore came I here, and fain would know
    Whether 'tis you or they have lost their wits.
SIMO: A moment's hearing; you shall be inform'd
    What I request, and what you wish to know.
CHREMES: I hear: what would you? speak.
SIMO: Now by the gods;
    Now by our friendship, Chremes, which, begun
    In infancy, has still increas'd with age;
    Now by your only daughter, and my son,
    Whose preservation wholly rests on you;
    Let me entreat this boon: and let the match
    Which should have been, still be.
CHREMES: Why, why entreat?
    Knowing you ought not to beseech this of me.
    Think you, that I am other than I was,
    When first I gave my promise? If the match
    Be good for both, e'en call them forth to wed.
    But if their union promises more harm
    Than good to both; you also, I beseech you,

283

Consult our common interest, as if
You were her father, Pamphilus my son.
SIMO: E'en in that spirit, I desire it, Chremes,
Entreat it may be done; nor would entreat,
But that occasion urges.
CHREMES: What occasion?
SIMO: A difference 'twixt Glycerium and my son.
CHREMES: I hear. *(Ironically.)*
SIMO: A breach so wide as gives me hopes
To separate them for ever.
CHREMES: Idle tales!
SIMO: Indeed 'tis thus.
CHREMES: Ay marry, thus it is.
Quarrels of lovers but renew their love.
SIMO: Prevent we then, I pray, this mischief now;
While time permits, while yet his passion's sore
From contumelies; ere these women's wiles,
Their wicked arts, and tears made up of fraud,
Shake his weak mind, and melt it to compassion.
Give him a wife: By intercourse with her,
Knit by the bonds of wedlock, soon, I hope,
He'll rise above the guilt that sinks him now.
CHREMES: So you believe: for me, I cannot think
That he'll be constant, or that I can bear it.
SIMO: How can you know, unless you make the trial?
CHREMES: Ay, but to make that trial on a daughter
Is hard indeed.
SIMO: The mischief, should he fail,
Is only this: divorce, which heav'n forbid!
But mark what benefits, if he amend!
First, to your friend you will restore a son;
Gain to yourself a son-in-law; and match
Your daughter to an honest husband.
CHREMES: Well!
Since you're so throughly convinc'd 'tis right,
I can deny you nought that lies in me.
SIMO: I see I ever lov'd you justly, Chremes.
CHREMES: But then —
SIMO: But what?
CHREMES: From whence are you appris'd
That there's a difference between them?
SIMO: Davus,
Davus (in all their secrets) told me so;
Advis'd me, too, to hasten on the match

284

As fast as possible. Wou'd he, d'ye think,
Do that, unless he were full well assur'd
My son desir'd it too? — Hear what he says.
Ho there! call Davus forth. — But here he comes.

SCENE VI — *Enter* Davus.

DAVUS: I was about to seek you.
SIMO: What's the matter?
DAVUS: Why is not the bride sent for? it grows late.
SIMO: D'ye hear him? — Davus, I for some time past
　　　Was fearful of you; lest, like other slaves,
　　　As slaves go now, you should put tricks upon me,
　　　And baffle me, to favour my son's love.
DAVUS: I, sir?
SIMO: I thought so: and in fear of that,
　　　Conceal'd a secret which I'll now disclose.
DAVUS: What secret, sir?
SIMO: I'll tell you: for I now
　　　Almost begin to think you may be trusted.
DAVUS: You've found what sort of man I am at last.
SIMO: No marriage was intended.
DAVUS: How! none!
SIMO: None.
　　　All counterfeit, to sound my son and you.
DAVUS: How say you?
SIMO: Even so.
DAVUS: Alack, alack!
　　　I never could have thought it. Ah, what art! *(Archly.)*
SIMO: Hear me. No sooner had I sent you in,
　　　But opportunely I encounter'd Chremes.
DAVUS: How! are we ruin'd then? *(Aside.)*
SIMO: I told him all,
　　　That you had just told me. ——
DAVUS: Confusion! how? *(Aside.)*
SIMO: Begg'd him to grant his daughter, and at length
　　　With much ado prevail'd.
DAVUS: Undone! *(Aside.)*
SIMO: How's that? *(Overhearing.)*
DAVUS: Well done! I said.
SIMO: My good friend Chremes, then,
　　　Is now no obstacle.
CHREMES: I'll home awhile,
　　　Order due preparations, and return. *(Exit.)*

SIMO: Prithee, now, Davus, seeing you alone
  Have brought about this match——
DAVUS: Yes, I alone.
SIMO: —Endeavour further to amend my son.
DAVUS: Most diligently.
SIMO: It were easy now,
  While his mind's irritated.
DAVUS: Be at peace.
SIMO: Do then: where is he?
DAVUS: Probably, at home.
SIMO: I'll in, and tell him, what I've now told you. *(Exit.)*

SCENE VII — Davus *alone.*

DAVUS: Lost and undone! To prison with me straight!
  No prayer, no plea: for I have ruin'd all!
  Deceiv'd the old man, hamper'd Pamphilus
  With marriage; marriage, brought about to-day
  By my sole means; beyond the hopes of one;
  Against the other's will.——Oh cunning fool!
  Had I been quiet, all had yet been well.
  But see, he's coming. Would my neck were broken! *(Retires.)*

SCENE VIII — *Enter* Pamphilus; Davus *behind.*

PAMPHILUS: Where is this villain that has ruin'd me?
DAVUS: I'm a lost man.
PAMPHILUS: And yet I must confess,
  That I deserv'd this, being such a dolt,
  A very idiot, to commit my fortunes
  To a vile slave. I suffer for my folly,
  But will at least take vengeance upon him.
DAVUS: Let me but once escape the present danger,
  I'll answer for hereafter.
PAMPHILUS: To my father
  What shall I say? — And can I then refuse,
  Who have but now consented? With what face?
  I know not what to do.
DAVUS: I'faith, nor I;
  And yet it takes up all my thoughts. I'll tell him
  I've hit on something to delay the match.
PAMPHILUS: Oh! *(Seeing* Davus.*)*
DAVUS: I am seen.

286

PAMPHILUS: So, good sir! What say you?
　　　　See, how I'm hamper'd with your fine advice.
DAVUS *(coming forward)*: But I'll deliver you.
PAMPHILUS: Deliver me?
DAVUS: Certainly, sir.
PAMPHILUS: What, as you did just now?
DAVUS: Better, I hope.
PAMPHILUS: And can you then believe
　　　　That I would trust you, rascal? You amend
　　　　My broken fortunes, or redeem them lost?
　　　　You, who to-day, from the most happy state,
　　　　Have thrown me upon marriage! — Did not I
　　　　Foretell it would be thus?
DAVUS: You did indeed.
PAMPHILUS: And what do you deserve for this?
DAVUS: The gallows.
　　　　—Yet suffer me to take a little breath,
　　　　I'll devise something presently.
PAMPHILUS: Alas!
　　　　I have not leisure for your punishment;
　　　　The time demands attention to myself,
　　　　Nor will be wasted in revenge on you.

ACT IV — SCENE I

Charinus *alone.*

CHARINUS: Is this to be believ'd, or to be told?
　　　　Can then such inbred malice live in man,
　　　　To joy in ill, and from another's woes
　　　　To draw his own delight? — Ah, is't then so?
　　　　—Yes, such there are, the meanest of mankind,
　　　　Who, from a sneaking bashfulness, at first
　　　　Dare not refuse; but when the time comes on
　　　　To make their promise good, then force perforce
　　　　Open themselves and fear: yet must deny.
　　　　Then too, oh shameless impudence! they cry,
　　　　"Who then are you? and what are you to me?
　　　　"Why should I render up my love to you?
　　　　"Troth, neighbour, charity begins at home."
　　　　— Speak of their broken faith, they blush not, they,
　　　　Now throwing off that shame they ought to wear,
　　　　Which they before assum'd without a cause.

—What shall I do? accost him? tell my wrongs?
Expostulate, and throw reproaches on him?
What will that profit, say you? — Very much:
I shall at least embitter his delight,
And gratify my anger.

SCENE II — *To him* Pamphilus *and* Davus.

PAMPHILUS: Oh, Charinus,
By my imprudence, unless Heav'n forefend,
I've ruin'd both myself and you.
CHARINUS: Imprudence!
Paltry evasion! You have broke your faith.
PAMPHILUS: What now?
CHARINUS: And do you think that words like these
Can baffle me again?
PAMPHILUS: What means all this?
CHARINUS: Soon as I told you of my passion for her,
Then she had charms for you. —— Ah, senseless fool,
To judge your disposition by my own!
PAMPHILUS: You are mistaken.
CHARINUS: Was your joy no joy,
Without abusing a fond lover's mind,
Fool'd on with idle hopes? — Well, take her.
PAMPHILUS: Take her?
Alas! you know not what a wretch I am;
How many cares this slave has brought upon me,
My rascal here!
CHARINUS: No wonder, if he takes
Example from his master.
PAMPHILUS: Ah, you know not
Me, or my love, or else you would not talk thus.
CHARINUS: Oh yes, I know it all. You had but now
A dreadful altercation with your father:
And therefore he's enrag'd, nor could prevail
On you, forsooth, to wed. *(Ironically.)*
PAMPHILUS: To shew you then,
How little you conceive of my distress,
These nuptials were mere semblance, mock'ry all,
Nor was a wife intended me.
CHARINUS: I know it:
You are constrain'd, poor man, by inclination.
PAMPHILUS: Nay, but have patience! you don't know —

288

CHARINUS: I know
    That you're to marry her.
PAMPHILUS: Why rack me thus?
        Nay hear! He never ceas'd to importune
        That I would tell my father, I would wed ;
        So prest, and urg'd, that he at length prevail'd.
CHARINUS: Who did this?
PAMPHILUS: Davus.
CHARINUS: Davus!
PAMPHILUS: Davus all.
CHARINUS: Wherefore?
PAMPHILUS: I know not: but I know the gods
        Meant in their anger I should listen to him.
CHARINUS: Is it so, Davus?
DAVUS: Even so.
CHARINUS: How, villain?
        The gods confound you for it! — Tell me, wretch,
        Had all his most inveterate foes desir'd
        To throw him on this marriage, what advice
        Could they have given else?
DAVUS: I am deceiv'd,
        But not dishearten'd.
CHARINUS: True. *(Ironically.)*
DAVUS: This way has fail'd;
        We'll try another way: unless you think,
        Because the business has gone ill at first,
        We cannot graft advantage on misfortune.
PAMPHILUS: Oh ay, I warrant you, if you look to't,
        Out of one wedding you can work me two.
DAVUS: Pamphilus, 'tis my duty, as your slave,
        To strive with might and main, by day and night,
        With hazard of my life, to do you service:
        Tis your's, if I am crost, to pardon me.
        My undertakings fail indeed, but then
        I spare no pains. Do better, if you can,
        And send me packing.
PAMPHILUS: Ay, with all my heart:
        Place me but where you found me first.
DAVUS: I will.
PAMPHILUS: But do it instantly
DAVUS: Hist! hold awhile:
        I hear the creaking of Glycerium's door.
PAMPHILUS: Nothing to you.
DAVUS: I'm thinking.

289

PAMPHILUS: What, at last?

DAVUS: Your business shall be done, and presently.

SCENE III—*Enter* Mysis.

MYSIS *(To* Glycerium, *within)*: Be where he will, I'll find your **Pamphilus**,
 And bring him with me. Meanwhile, you, my soul,
 Forbear to vex yourself.

PAMPHILUS: Mysis!

MYSIS: Who's there?
 Oh Pamphilus, well met, sir!

PAMPHILUS: What's the matter?

MYSIS: My mistress, by the love you bear her, begs
 Your presence instantly. She longs to see you.

PAMPHILUS: Ah, I'm undone: This sore breaks out afresh.
 Unhappy that we are, thro' your curst means,
 To be tormented thus. *(To* Davus.*)* — She has been told
 A nuptial is prepar'd, and therefore sends.

CHARINUS: From which how safe you were, had he been quiet. *(Pointing*

DAVUS: Ay, if he raves not of himself enough,   [*to* **Davus.***)*
 Do, irritate him. *(To* Charinus.*)*

MYSIS: Truly that's the cause;
 And therefore 'tis, poor soul, she sorrows thus.

PAMPHILUS: Mysis, I swear to thee by all the gods,
 I never will desert her: tho' assur'd
 That I for her make all mankind my foes.
 I sought her, carried her: our hearts are one,
 And farewell they that wish us put asunder!
 Death, only death shall part us.

MYSIS: I revive.

PAMPHILUS: Apollo's oracles are not more true.
 If that my father may be wrought upon,
 To think I hinder'd not the match, tis well:
 But if that cannot be, come what come may,
 Why let him know, 'twas I—What think you now? *(To* Charinus.*)*

CHARINUS: That we are wretches both.

DAVUS: My brain's at work.

CHARINUS: Oh brave!

PAMPHILUS: I know what you'd attempt.

DAVUS: Well, well!
 I will effect it for you.

PAMPHILUS: Ay, but now.

DAVUS: E'en now.

CHARINUS: What is't?

290

DAVUS: For him, sir, not for you.
    Be not mistaken.
CHARINUS: I am satisfied.
PAMPHILUS: Well, what do you propose?
DAVUS: This day, I fear,
    Is scarce sufficient for the execution,
    So think not I have leisure to relate.
    Hence then! You hinder me: hence, hence! I say.
PAMPHILUS: I'll to Glycerium. *(Exit.)*
DAVUS: Well, and what mean you?
    Whither will you, sir?
CHARINUS: Shall I speak the truth?
DAVUS: Oh, to be sure: now for a tedious tale!
CHARINUS: What will become of me?
DAVUS: How! not content!
    It is not then sufficient, if I give you
    The respite of a day, a little day,
    By putting off this wedding?
CHARINUS: Ay, but, Davus, ——
DAVUS: But what?
CHARINUS: That I may wed ——
DAVUS: Ridiculous!
CHARINUS: If you succeed, come to me.
DAVUS: Wherefore come?
    I can't assist you.
CHARINUS: Should it so fall out. —
DAVUS: Well, well, I'll come.
CHARINUS: If aught, I am at home. *(Exit.)*

SCENE IV — *Manent* Davus, Mysis.

DAVUS: Mysis, wait here till I come forth.
MYSIS: For what?
DAVUS: It must be so.
MYSIS: Make haste then.
DAVUS: In a moment. *(Exit to* Glycerium's.*)*

SCENE V — Mysis *alone.*

MYSIS: Can we securely then count nothing our's?
    Oh all ye gods! I thought this Pamphilus
    The greatest good my mistress could obtain,
    Friend, lover, husband, ev'ry way a blessing:
    And yet what woe, poor wretch, endures she not

On his account? Alas! more ill than good.
But here comes Davus.

SCENE VI. — *Re-enter* Davus, *with the child.*

MYSIS: Prithee, man, what now?
    Where are you carrying the child?
DAVUS: Oh, Mysis,
    Now have I need of all your ready wit,
    And all your cunning.
MYSIS: What are you about?
DAVUS: Quick, take the boy, and lay him at our door.
MYSIS: What, on the bare ground?
DAVUS: From the altar then
    Take herbs and strew them underneath.
MYSIS: And why
    Can't you do that yourself?
DAVUS: Because, supposing
    There should be need to swear to my old master
    I did not lay the bantling there myself,
    I may with a safe conscience. *(Gives her the child.)*
MYSIS: I conceive.
    But pray how came this sudden qualm upon you?
DAVUS: Nay, but be quick, that you may comprehend
    What I propose. — (Mysis *lays the child at* Simo's *door.)* Oh
MYSIS: What now?   [Jupiter! *(Looking out.)*
DAVUS: Here comes the father of the bride! ——I change
    My first intended purpose.
MYSIS: What you mean
    I can't imagine.
DAVUS: This way, from the right
    I'll counterfeit to come: — And be't your care
    To throw in aptly now and then a word,
    To help out the discourse as need requires.
MYSIS: Still what you're at, I cannot comprehend.
    But if I can assist, as you know best,
    Not to obstruct your purposes, I'll stay. (Davus *retires.)*

SCENE VII — *Enter* Chremes, *going towards* Simo's.

CHREMES: Having provided all things necessary,
    I now return to bid them call the bride.
    What's here? *(seeing the child.)* By Hercules, a child! Ha, woman,
    Was't you that laid it here?

MYSIS: Where is he gone? *(Looking after* Davus.*)*
CHREMES: What, won't you answer me?
MYSIS *(looking about)*: Not here: Ah me!
  The fellow's gone, and left me in the lurch.
  (Davus, *coming forward, and pretending not to see them.*)
DAVUS: Good heavens, what confusion at the Forum!
  The people all disputing with each other!
  The market-price is so confounded high! *(Loud.)*
  What to say else I know not. *(Aside.)*
MYSIS *(to* Davus*)*: What d'ye mean
  (Chremes *retires, and listens to their conversation.*)
  By leaving me alone?
DAVUS: What farce is this?
  Ha, Mysis, whence this child? Who brought it here?
MYSIS: Have you your wits, to ask me such a question?
DAVUS: Whom should I ask, when no one else is here?
CHREMES *(behind)*: I wonder whence it comes. *(To himself.)*
DAVUS: Wilt answer me? *(Loud.)*
MYSIS: Ah! *(Confused.)*
DAVUS: This way, to the right! *(Apart to* Mysis.*)*
MYSIS: You're raving mad.
  Was't not yourself?
DAVUS: I charge you not a word,
  But what I ask you. *(Apart to* Mysis.*)*
MYSIS: Do you threaten me?
DAVUS: Whence comes this child? *(Loud.)*
MYSIS: From our house.
DAVUS: Ha! ha! ha!
  No wonder, that a harlot has assurance.
CHREMES: This is the Andrian's servant-maid, I take it.
DAVUS: Do we then seem to you such proper folks
  To play these tricks upon? *(Loud to* Mysis.*)*
CHREMES: I came in time. *(To himself.)*
DAVUS: Make haste, and take your bantling from our door *(loud)*.
  Hold! do not stir from where you are, be sure. *(Softly.)*
MYSIS: A plague upon you: you so terrify me!
DAVUS: Wench, did I speak to you or no? *(Loud.)*
MYSIS: What would you?
DAVUS: What would I? Say, whose child have you laid here?
  Tell me. *(Loud.)*
MYSIS: You don't know?
DAVUS: Plague of what I know:
  Tell what I ask. *(Softly.)*
MYSIS: Yours.

293

DAVUS: Ours! Whose? *(Loud.)*

MYSIS: Pamphilus's.

DAVUS: How say you? Pamphilus's? *(Loud.)*

MYSIS: To be sure.

CHREMES: I had good cause to be against this match. *(To himself.)*

DAVUS: O monstrous impudence! *(Bawling.)*

MYSIS: Why all this noise?

DAVUS: Did not I see this child convey'd by stealth
    Into your house last night?

MYSIS: Oh rogue!

DAVUS: 'Tis true.
    I saw old Canthara stuff'd out.

MYSIS: Thank heav'n,
    Some free-women were present at her labour.

DAVUS: Troth, she don't know the gentleman, for whom
    She plays this game. She thinks, should Chremes see
    The child laid here, he would not grant his daughter.
    Faith, he would grant her the more willingly.

CHREMES: Not he indeed. *(To himself.)*

DAVUS: But now, one word for all,
    Take up the child; or I shall trundle him
    Into the middle of the street and roll
    You, madam, in the mire.

MYSIS: The fellow's drunk.

DAVUS: One piece of knavery begets another:
    Now, I am told, 'tis whisper'd all about,
    That she's a citizen of Athens — *(loud)*.

CHREMES: How!

DAVUS: And that by law he will be forc'd to wed her.

MYSIS: Why prithee is she not a citizen?

CHREMES: What a fine scrape was I within a hair
    Of being into! *(To himself)*

DAVUS: What voice is that?
    Oh Chremes! you are come in time. Attend!

CHREMES: I have heard all already.

DAVUS: You've heard all?

CHREMES: Yes, all, I say, from first to last.

DAVUS: Indeed?
    Good lack, what knaveries! This lying jade
    Should be dragg'd hence to torture. — This is he! *(To Mysis.)*
    Think not 'twas Davus you impos'd upon.

MYSIS: Ah me! — Good sir, I spoke the truth indeed.

CHREMES: I know the whole. — Is Simo in the house?

DAVUS: Yes, sir. *(Exit Chremes.)*

294

SCENE VIII — *Manent* Davus, Mysis. Davus *runs up to her.*

MYSIS: Don't offer to touch me, you villain!
 If I don't tell my mistress every word —
DAVUS: Why, you don't know, you fool, what good we've done.
MYSIS: How should I?
DAVUS: This is father to the bride:
 Nor could it otherwise have been contriv'd
 That he should know what we would have him.
MYSIS: Well,
 You should have giv'n me notice.
DAVUS: Is there then
 No diff'rence, think you, whether all you say
 Falls naturally from the heart, or comes
 From dull premeditation?

SCENE IX — *Enter Crito.*

CRITO: In this street
 They say that Chrysis liv'd: who rather chose
 To heap up riches here by wanton ways,
 Than to live poor and honestly at home:
 She dead, her fortune comes by law to me.
 But I see persons to enquire of. *(Goes up.)* Save you!
MYSIS: Good now, who's that I see? is it not Crito,
 Chrysis' kinsman? Ay, the very same.
CRITO: O Mysis, save you!
MYSIS: Save you, Crito!
CRITO: Chrysis
 Is then —— ah?
MYSIS: Ay, she has left us, poor soul!
CRITO: And ye; how go you on here? — pretty well?
MYSIS: We? — as we *can*, as the old saying goes,
 When, as we *would*, we cannot.
CRITO: And Glycerium,
 Has she found out her parents?
MYSIS: Wou'd she had!
CRITO: Not yet! An ill wind blew me hither then.
 For truly, had I been appris'd of that,
 I'd ne'er have set foot here: For this Glycerium
 Was always call'd and thought to be her sister.
 What Chrysis left, she takes possession of:
 And now for me, a stranger, to commence
 A law-suit here, how good and wise it were,

295

Other examples teach me. She, I warrant,
Has got her some gallant too, some defender:
For she was growing up a jolly girl
When first she journied hither. They will cry
That I'm a pettifogger, fortune-hunter,
A beggar. — And besides it were not well
To leave her in distress.

MYSIS: Good soul! Troth, Crito,
You have the good old-fashion'd honesty.

CRITO: Well, since I am arriv'd here, bring me to her,
That I may see her.

MYSIS: Ay, with all my heart.

DAVUS: I will in with them: for I would not chuse
That our old gentleman should see me now. *(Exeunt.)*

ACT V — SCENE I

Chremes, Simo.

CHREMES: Enough already, Simo, and enough
I've shewn my friendship for you; hazarded
Enough of peril: Urge me then no more!
Wishing to please you, I had near destroy'd
My daughter's peace and happiness for ever.

SIMO: Ah, Chremes, I must now entreat the more,
More urge you to confirm the promis'd boon.

CHREMES: Mark, how unjust you are thro' wilfulness!
So you obtain what you demand, you set
No bounds to my compliance, nor consider
What you request; for if you *did* consider,
You'd cease to load me with these injuries.

SIMO: What injuries?

CHREMES: Is that a question now?
Have you not driven me to plight my child
To one possest with other love, averse
To marriage; to expose her to divorce,
And crazy nuptial; by her woe and bane
To work a cure for your distemper'd son?
You had prevail'd: I travell'd in the match,
While circumstances would admit; but now
The case is chang'd, content you: — It is said,
That she's a citizen; a child is born:
Prithee excuse us!

SIMO: Now, for heaven's sake,
    Believe not them, whose interest it is
    To make him vile and abject as themselves.
    These stories are all feign'd, concerted all,
    To break the match: When the occasion's past,
    That urges them to this, they will desist.

CHREMES: Oh, you mistake: E'en now I saw the maid
    Wrangling with Davus.

SIMO: Artifice! mere trick.

CHREMES: Ay, but in earnest; and when neither knew
    That I was there.

SIMO: It may be so: and Davus
    Told me before-hand they'd attempt all this;
    Though I, know now, forgot to tell you.

SCENE II — *Enter* Davus *from* Glycerium's.

DAVUS *(to himself)*: He may be easy now, I warrant him —

CHREMES: See, yonder's Davus.

SIMO: Ha! whence comes the rogue?

DAVUS: By my assistance, and this stranger's safe. *(To himself.)*

SIMO: What mischief's this? *(Listening.)*

DAVUS: A more commodious man,
    Arriving just in season, at a time
    So critical, I never knew. *(To himself.)*

SIMO: A knave!
    Who's that he praises? *(Listening.)*

DAVUS: All is now secure. *(To himself.)*

SIMO: Why don't I speak to him?

DAVUS: My master here! *(Turning about.)*
    What shall I do? *(To himself.)*

SIMO: Good sir, your humble servant! *(Sneering.)*

DAVUS: Oh, Simo! and our Chremes! — All is now
    Prepar'd within.

SIMO: You've taken special care. *(Ironically.)*

DAVUS: E'en call them when you please.

SIMO: Oh, mighty fine!
    That to be sure is all that's wanting now.
    — But tell me, sir! what business had you there? *(Pointing to*

DAVUS: I? *(Confused.)*   [Glycerium's.)*

SIMO: You.

DAVUS: I —— ? *(Stammering.)*

SIMO: You, sir.

DAVUS: I went in but now. *(Disordered.)*

297

SIMO: As if I ask'd, how long it was ago!
DAVUS: With Pamphilus.
SIMO: Is Pamphilus within?
— Oh torture! — Did not you assure me, sirrah,
    They were at variance?
DAVUS: So they are.
SIMO: Why then
    Is Pamphilus within?
CHREMES: Oh, *why* d'ye think?
    He's gone to quarrel with her. *(Sneering.)*
DAVUS: Nay but, Chremes,
    There's more in this, and you shall hear strange news.
    There's an old countryman, I know not who,
    Is just arriv'd here; confident and shrewd;
    His look bespeaks him of some consequence.
    A grave severity is in his face,
    And credit in his words.
SIMO: What story now?
DAVUS: Nay, nothing, sir, but what I hear him say.
SIMO: And what says he, then?
DAVUS: That he's well assur'd
    Glycerium's an Athenian citizen.
SIMO: Ho, Dromo! Dromo! *(Calling.)*
DAVUS: What now?
SIMO: Dromo!
DAVUS: Hear me,
SIMO: Speak but a word more — Dromo!
DAVUS: Pray, sir, hear!

SCENE III — *Enter* Dromo.

DROMO: Your pleasure, sir?
SIMO: Here drag him headlong in,
    And truss the rascal up immediately.
DROMO: Whom?
SIMO: Davus.
DAVUS: Why?
SIMO: Because I'll have it so.
    Take him, I say.
DAVUS: For what offence?
SIMO: Off with him.
DAVUS: If it appear that I've said aught but truth,
    Put me to death.
SIMO: I will not hear. I'll trounce you!

298

DAVUS: But tho' it should prove true, sir!
SIMO: True or false.
      See that you keep him bound: and, do you hear?
      Bind the slave hand and foot. Away! *(Exeunt* Dromo *and* Davus.*)*

SCENE IV—*Manent* Simo, Chremes.

SIMO: By heav'n,
      As I do live, I'll make you know this day
      What peril lies in trifling with a master,
      And make *him* know what 'tis to plague a father.
CHREMES: Ah, be not in such rage.
SIMO: Oh Chremes, Chremes!
      Filial unkindness! — Don't you pity me?
      To feel all this for such a thankless son! —
      Here, Pamphilus, come forth! ho, Pamphilus!
      Have you no shame? *(Calling at* Glycerium's *door.)*

SCENE V — *Enter* Pamphilus.

PAMPHILUS: Who calls — Undone! my father!
SIMO: What say you? Most ———
CHREMES: Ah, rather speak at once
      Your purpose, Simo, and forbear reproach.
SIMO: As if 'twere possible to utter aught
      Severer than he merits! Tell me then; *(to* Pamphilus*)*
      Glycerium is a citizen?
PAMPHILUS: They say so.
SIMO: They say so! — Oh amazing impudence! —
      Does he consider what he says? does he
      Repeat the deed? or does his colour take
      The 'hue of shame? — To be so weak of soul,
      Against the custom of our citizens,
      Against the law, against his father's will,
      To wed himself to shame and this vile woman.
PAMPHILUS: Wretch that I am!
SIMO: Ah, Pamphilus! d'ye feel
      Your wretchedness at last? Then, then, when first
      You wrought upon your mind at any rate
      To gratify your passion; from that hour
      Well might you feel your state of wretchedness.
      But why give in to this? Why torture thus,
      Why vex my spirit? Why afflict my age
      For his distemp'rature? Why rue his sins?

299

— No; let him have her, joy in her, live with her.

PAMPHILUS: My father! ——

SIMO: How, *my father!* — Can I think
    You want this father? You that for yourself
    A home, a wife, and children have acquir'd
    Against your father's will? and witnesses
    Suborn'd, to prove that she's a citizen?
    — You've gain'd your point.

PAMPHILUS: My father, but one word!

SIMO: What would you say?

CHREMES: Nay, hear him, Simo.

SIMO: Hear him?
    What must I hear then, Chremes?

CHREMES: Let him speak.

SIMO: Well, let him speak: I hear him.

PAMPHILUS: I confess,
    I love Glycerium: if it be a fault,
    That too I do confess. To you, my father,
    I yield myself: dispose me as you please!
    Command me! Say, that I shall take a wife;
    Leave; — I will endure it, as I may. —
    This only I beseech you, think not I
    Suborn'd this old man hither. — Suffer me
    To clear myself, and bring him here before you.

SIMO: Bring him here!

PAMPHILUS: Let me, father!

CHREMES: 'Tis but just:
    Permit him!

PAMPHILUS: Grant me this!

SIMO: Well, be it so. *(Exit* Pamphilus.*)*
    I could bear all this bravely, Chremes; more,
    Much more, to know that he deceiv'd me not.

CHREMES: For a great fault a little punishment
    Suffices to a father.

SCENE VI — *Re-enter* Pamphilus *with* Crito.

CRITO: Say no more!
    Any of these inducements would prevail:
    Or your entreaty, or that it is truth,
    Or that I wish it for Glycerium's sake.

CHREMES: Whom do I see? Crito, the Andrian?
    Nay certainly 'tis Crito.

CRITO: Save you, Chremes!

CHREMES: What has brought you to Athens?
CRITO: Accident.
     But is this Simo?
CHREMES: Ay.
SIMO: Asks he for me?
     So, sir, you say that this Glycerium
     Is an Athenian citizen?
CRITO: Do you
     Deny it?
SIMO: What then, are you come prepar'd?
CRITO: Prepar'd! for what?
SIMO: And dare you ask for what?
     Shall you proceed thus with impunity?
     Lay snares for inexperienc'd, lib'ral youth,
     With fraud, temptation, and fair promises
     Soothing their minds? ——
CRITO: Have you your wits?
SIMO: — And then
     With marriage solder up their harlot loves?
PAMPHILUS: Alas! I fear the stranger will not bear this. *(Aside.)*
CHREMES: Knew you this person, Simo, you'd not think thus:
     He's a good man.
SIMO: A good man he? — To come,
     Altho' at Athens never seen till now,
     So opportunely on the wedding-day! —
     Is such a fellow to be trusted, Chremes?
PAMPHILUS: But that I fear my father, I could make
     That matter clear to him. *(Aside.)*
SIMO: A sharper!
CRITO: How?
CHREMES: It is his humour, Crito: do not heed him.
CRITO: Let him look to't. If he persists in saying
     Whate'er he pleases, I shall make him hear
     Something that may displease him. — Do I stir
     In these affairs, or make them my concern?
     Bear your misfortunes patiently! For me,
     If I speak true or false, shall now be known.
     — "A man of Athens once upon a time
     "Was shipwreck'd on the coast of Andros: with him
     "This very woman, then an infant. He
     "In this distress applied, it so fell out,
     "For help to Chrysis' father ——"
SIMO: All romance.
CHREMES: Let him alone.

301

CRITO: And will he interrupt me?

CHREMES: Go on.

CRITO: "Now Chrysis' father, who receiv'd him,
"Was my relation. There I've often heard
"The man himself declare, he was of Athens.
"There too he died."

CHREMES: His name?

CRITO: His name, so quickly? —
Phania.

CHREMES: Amazement!

CRITO: Troth, I think 'twas Phania;
But this I'm sure, he said he was of Rhamnus.

CHREMES: Oh Jupiter!

CRITO: These circumstances, Chremes,
Were known to many others, then in Andros.

CHREMES: Heav'n grant it may be as I wish! Inform me,
Whose daughter, said he, was the child? his own?

CRITO: No, not his own.

CHREMES: Whose then?

CRITO: His brother's daughter.

CHREMES: Mine, mine, undoubtedly!

CRITO: What say you?

SIMO: How!

PAMPHILUS: Hark, Pamphilus!

SIMO: But why believe you this?

CHREMES: That Phania was my brother.

SIMO: True. I knew him.

CHREMES: He, to avoid the war, departed hence:
And fearing 'twere unsafe to leave the child,
Embark'd with her in quest of me for Asia:
Since when I've heard no news of him till now.

PAMPHILUS: I'm scarce myself, my mind is so enrapt
With fear, hope, joy, and wonder of so great,
So sudden happiness.

SIMO: Indeed, my Chremes,
I heartily rejoice she's found your daughter.

PAMPHILUS: I do believe you, father.

CHREMES: But one doubt
There still remains, which gives me pain.

PAMPHILUS: Away
With all your doubts! You puzzle a plain cause. (Aside.)

CRITO: What is that doubt?

CHREMES: That name does not agree.

302

CRITO: She had another, when a child.
CHREMES: What, Crito?
    Can you remember?
CRITO: I am hunting for it.
PAMPHILUS: Shall then his memory oppose my bliss,
    When I can minister the cure myself?
    No, I will not permit it. — Hark you, Chremes,
    The name is Pasibula.
CRITO: True.
CHREMES: The same.
PAMPHILUS: I've heard it from herself a thousand times.
SIMO: Chremes, I trust you will believe, we all
    Rejoice at this.
CHREMES: 'Fore heaven I believe so.
PAMPHILUS: And now, my father——
SIMO: Peace, son! the event
    Has reconcil'd me.
PAMPHILUS: O thou best of fathers!
    Does Chremes too confirm Glycerium mine?
CHREMES: And with good cause, if Simo hinder not.
PAMPHILUS: Sir! *(To* Simo.*)*
SIMO: Be it so.
CHREMES: My daughter's portion is
    Ten talents, Pamphilus.
PAMPHILUS: I am content.
CHREMES: I'll to her instantly: and prithee, Crito,
    Along with me! for sure she knows me not *(Exeunt* Chremes
SIMO: Why do you not give orders instantly   [*and* Crito.*)*
    To bring her to our house?
PAMPHILUS: Th' advice is good.
    I'll give that charge to Davus.
SIMO: It can't be.
PAMPHILUS: Why?
SIMO: He has other business of his own,
    Of nearer import to himself.
PAMPHILUS: What business?
SIMO: He's bound.
PAMPHILUS: Bound! how, sir!
SIMO: How, sir? — Neck and heels.
PAMPHILUS: Ah, let him be enlarg'd!
SIMO: It shall be done.
PAMPHILUS: But instantly.
SIMO: I'll in, and order it. *(Exit.)*
PAMPHILUS: Oh what a happy, happy, day is this!

303

SCENE VII — *Enter* Charinus *behind.*

CHARINUS: I come to see what Pamphilus is doing:
    And there he is!
PAMPHILUS: And is this true? — Yes, yes,
    I know 'tis true, because I wish it so.
        Therefore I think the life of gods eternal,
    For that their joys are permanent: and now,
        My soul hath her content so absolute,
    That I too am immortal, if no ill
    Step in betwixt me and this happiness.
    Oh, for a bosom-friend now to pour out
    My ecstasies before him!
CHARINUS: What's this rapture? *(Listening.)*
PAMPHILUS: Oh, yonder's Davus: nobody more welcome:
    For he, I know, will join in transport with me.

SCENE THE LAST — *Enter* Davus.

DAVUS *(entering)*: Where's Pamphilus?
PAMPHILUS: Oh, Davus!
DAVUS: Who's there?
PAMPHILUS: I.
DAVUS: Oh, Pamphilus!
PAMPHILUS: You know not my good fortune.
DAVUS: Do you know my ill fortune?
PAMPHILUS: To a tittle.
DAVUS: 'Tis after the old fashion, that my ills
    Should reach your ears, before your joys reach mine.
PAMPHILUS: Glycerium has discover'd her relations.
DAVUS: Oh excellent!
CHARINUS: How's that? *(Listening.)*
PAMPHILUS: Her father is
    Our most near friend.
DAVUS: Who?
PAMPHILUS: Chremes.
DAVUS: Charming news!
PAMPHILUS: And I'm to marry her immediately.
CHARINUS: Is this man talking in his sleep, and dreams
    On what he wishes waking? *(Listening.)*
PAMPHILUS: And moreover,
    For the child, Davus ——
DAVUS: Ah, sir, say no more.
    You're th' only favourite of the gods.

304

CHARINUS: I'm made,
If this be true. I'll speak to them. *(Comes forward.)*
PAMPHILUS: Who's there?
Charinus! oh, well met.
CHARINUS: I give you joy.
PAMPHILUS: You've heard then —
CHARINUS: Ev'ry word: and prithee now,
In your good fortune, think upon your friend,
Chremes is now your own; and will perform
Whatever you shall ask.
PAMPHILUS: I shall remember.
'Twere tedious to expect his coming forth:
Along with me then to Glycerium!
Davus, do you go home, and hasten them
To fetch her hence. Away, away!
DAVUS: I go. *(Exeunt* Pamphilus *and* Charinus.*)*
(Davus addressing the Audience.)
DAVUS: Wait not till they come forth: Within
She'll be betroth'd; within, if aught remains
Undone, 'twill be concluded. — Clap your hands!

George Colman

305

HISTORY and BIOGRAPHY

Livy

Tacitus

Suetonius

LIVY

TITUS LIVIUS (59 B.C. - 17 A.D.) was a Roman historian who presented Roman history as a sequence of scenes and people, memorable events and heroic deeds that enhanced Roman prestige and stimulated patriotic feelings.

Born at Patavium, Livy settled in Rome and devoted himself to writing. His literary activities brought him into intimate contacts with the circle of the Imperial court. His *History of Rome, Ab Urbe Condita Libri,* consisted originally of 142 books, of which 35 are extant.

Book XXI — Hannibal Crosses the Alps

The three Punic Wars constituted a long conflict between Rome and Carthage, at the end of which Rome became the dominant power in the Mediterranean area. The first Punic War ran from 264-241 B.C. In the second Punic War (218-201 B. C.) Hannibal the Carthaginian commander invaded Italy. The third Punic War (149-146 B. C.) ended with the Carthaginian surrender.

Then, lest delay and ease might unsettle their minds, he crosses the Pyrenees with the rest of his forces and pitches his camp at the town Illiberis. The Gauls, though they had heard that the war was directed against Italy, yet because there was a report that the Spaniards on the other side of the Pyrenees had been reduced by force, and that strong forces had been imposed on them, being roused to arms through the fear of slavery, assembled certain tribes at Ruscino. When this was announced to Hannibal, he, having more fear of the delay than of the war, sent envoys to say to their princes, "that he wished to confer with them; and that they should either come nearer to Illiberis, or that he would proceed to Ruscino, that their meeting might be facilitated by vicinity: for that he would either be happy to receive them into his camp, or would himself without hesitation come to them: since he had entered Gaul as a friend, and not as an enemy, and would not draw the sword, if the Gauls did not force him, before he came to Italy." These proposals, indeed, were made by his messengers. But when the princes of the Gauls, having immediately moved their camp to Illiberis, came without reluctance to the Carthaginians, being won by his presents, they suffered his army to pass through their territories, by the town of Ruscino, without any molestation.

In the mean time no further intelligence had been brought into Italy to Rome by the ambassadors of Marseilles, than that Hannibal had passed the Iberus; when the Boii, as if he had already passed the Alps, revolted after instigating the Insubrians; not so much through their ancient resentment towards the Roman people, as on account of their having felt aggrieved that the colonies of Placentia and Cremona had been lately planted in the Gallic territory about the Po. Having, therefore, suddenly taken up arms, and made an attack on that very territory, they created so much of terror and tumult, that not only the rustic population, but even the Roman triumvirs, Caius Lutatius, Caius Servilius, and Titus Annius, who had come to assign the lands, distrusting the walls of Placentia, fled to Mutina. About the name of Lutatius there is no doubt: in place of Caius Servilius and Titus Annius, some annals have Quintus Acilius and Caius Herennius; others, Publius Cornelius Asina and Caius Papirius Maso. This point is also uncertain, whether the ambassadors sent to expostulate to the Boii suffered violence, or whether an attack was made on the triumvirs while measuring out the lands. While they were shut up in Mutina, and a people unskilled in the arts of besieging towns, and, at the same time, most sluggish at military operations, lay inactive before the walls, which they had not touched, pretended proposals for a peace were set on foot; and the ambassadors, being invited out to a conference by the chiefs of the Gauls, are seized, not only contrary to the law of nations, but in violation of the faith which was pledged on that very occasion; the Gauls denying that they would set them free unless their hostages were restored to them. When this intelligence respecting the ambassadors was announced, and that Mutina and its garrison were in danger, Lucius Manlius, the praetor, inflamed with rage, led his army in haste to Mutina. There were then woods on both sides of the road, most of the country being uncultivated. There, having advanced without previously exploring his route, he fell suddenly into an ambuscade; and after much slaughter of his men, with difficulty made his way into the open plains. Here a camp was fortified, and because confidence was wanting to the Gauls to attack it, the spirit of the soldiers revived, although it was sufficiently evident that their strength was much clipped. The journey was then commenced anew; nor while the army was led in march through the open tracts did the enemy appear: but, when the woods were again entered, then attacking the rear, amid great confusion and alarm of all, they slew eight hundred soldiers, and took six standards. There was an end to the Gauls of creating, and to the Romans of experiencing terror, when they escaped from the pathless and entangled thicket; then easily defending their march through the open ground, the Romans directed their course to Tanetum, a village near the Po; where, by a temporary fortification, and the supplies conveyed by the river, and also by the aid of the Brixian Gauls, they defended themselves against the daily increasing multitude of their enemies.

When the account of this sudden disturbance was brought to Rome, and the senators heard that the Punic had also been increased by a Gallic war, they order Caius Atilius, the praetor, to carry assistance to Manlius with one Roman legion and five thousand of the allies, enrolled in the late levy by the consul: who, without any contest, for the enemy had retired through fear, arrived at Tanetum. At the same time Publius Cornelius, a new legion having been levied in the room of that which was sent with the praetor, setting out from the city with sixty ships of war, by the coast of Etruria and Liguria, and then the mountains of the Salyes, arrived at Marseilles, and pitched his camp at the nearest mouth of the Rhone, (for the stream flows down to the sea divided into several channels,) scarcely as yet well believing that Hannibal had crossed the Pyrenean mountains; whom when he ascertained to be also meditating the passage of the Rhone, uncertain in what place he might meet him, his soldiers not yet being sufficiently recovered from the tossing of the sea, he sends forward, in the mean time, three hundred chosen horses, with Massilian guides and Gallic auxiliaries, to explore all the country, and observe the enemy from a safe distance. Hannibal, the other states being pacified by fear or bribes, had now come into the territory of the Volcae, a powerful nation. They, indeed, dwell on both sides of the Rhone: but doubting that the Carthaginian could be driven from the hither bank, in order that they might have the river as a defence, having transported almost all their effects across the Rhone, occupied in arms the farther bank of the river. Hannibal, by means of presents, persuades the other inhabitants of the river-side, and some even of the Volcae themselves, whom their homes had detained, to collect from every quarter and build ships; and they at the same time themselves desired that the army should be transported, and their country relieved, as soon as possible, from the vast multitude of men that burthened it. A great number, therefore, of ships and boats rudely formed for the neighbouring passages, were collected together; and the Gauls, first beginning the plan, hollowed out some new ones from single trees; and then the soldiers themselves, at once induced by the plenty of materials and the easiness of the work, hastily formed shapeless hulks, in which they could transport themselves and their baggage, caring about nothing else, provided they could float and contain their burthen.

And now, when all things were sufficiently prepared for crossing, the enemy over against them occupying the whole bank, horse and foot, deterred them. In order to dislodge them, Hannibal orders Hanno, the son of Bomilcar, at the first watch of the night, to proceed with a part of the forces, principally Spanish, one day's journey up the river; and having crossed it where he might first be able, as secretly as possible, to lead round his forces, that when the occasion required he might attack the enemy in the rear. The Gauls, given him as guides for the purpose, inform him that about twenty-five miles from thence, the river spreading round a small island, broader where it was divided, and therefore with a shallower channel, presented a passage. At this place timber was quickly cut down and rafts formed, on which men, horses, and other burthens might be conveyed over. The Spaniards, without making any difficulty, having put their clothes in bags of leather, and themselves leaning on their bucklers placed beneath them, swam across the river. And the rest of the army, after passing on the rafts joined together, and pitching their camp near the river, being fatigued by the journey of the night and the labour of the work, are refreshed by the rest of one day, their leader being anxious to execute his design at a proper season. Setting out next day from this place, they signify by raising a smoke that they had crossed, and were not far distant; which when Hannibal understood, that he might not be wanting on the opportunity, he gives the signal for passing. The infantry already had the boats prepared and fitted; a line of ships higher up transporting the horsemen for the most part near their horses swimming beside them, in order to break the force of the current, rendered the water smooth to the boats crossing below. A great part of the horses were led across swimming, held by bridles from the stern, except those which they put on board saddled and bridled, in order that they might be ready to be used by the rider the moment he disembarked on the strand.

The Gauls run down to the bank to meet them with various whoopings and songs according to their custom, shaking their shields above their heads, and brandishing their weapons in their right hands, although such a multitude of ships in front of them alarmed them, together with the loud roaring of the river, and the mingled clamours of the sailors and soldiers, both those who were striving to break through the force of the current, and those who from the other bank were encouraging their comrades on their passage. While sufficiently dismayed by this tumult in front, more terrifying shouts from behind assailed them, their camp having been taken by Hanno; presently he himself came up, and a twofold terror encompassed them, both such a multitude of armed men landing from the ships, and this unexpected army pressing on their rear. When the Gauls, having made a prompt and bold effort to force the enemy, were themselves repulsed, they break through where a way seemed most open, and fly in consternation to their villages around. Hannibal, now despising these tumultuary onsets of the Gauls, having

310

transported the rest of his forces at leisure, pitches his camp. I believe that there were various plans for transporting the elephants; at least there are various accounts of the way in which it was done. Some relate, that after the elephants were assembled together on the bank, the fiercest of them being provoked by his keeper, pursued him as he swam across the water, to which he had run for refuge, and drew after him the rest of the herd; the mere force of the stream hurrying them to the other bank, when the bottom had failed each, fearful of the depth. But there is more reason to believe that they were conveyed across on rafts; which plan, as it must have appeared safer before execution, is after it the more entitled to credit. They extended from the bank into the river one raft two hundred feet long and fifty broad, which, fastened higher up by several strong cables to the bank, that it might not be carried down by the stream they covered, like a bridge, with earth thrown upon it, so that the beasts might tread upon it without fear, as over solid ground. Another raft equally broad and a hundred feet long, fit for crossing the river, was joined to this first; and when the elephants, driven along the stationary raft as along a road, had passed, the females leading the way, on to the smaller raft which was joined to it, the lashings, by which it was slightly fastened, being immediately let go, it was drawn by some light boats to the opposite side. The first having been thus landed, the rest were then returned for and carried across. They gave no signs of alarm whatever while they were driven along as it were on a continuous bridge. The first fear was, when, the raft being loosed from the rest, they were hurried into the deep. Then pressing together, as those at the edges drew back from the water, they produced some disorder, till mere terror, when they saw water all around, produced quiet. Some, indeed, becoming infuriated, fell into the river; but, steadied by their own weight, having thrown off their riders, and seeking step by step the shallows, they escaped to the shore.

Whilst the elephants were conveyed over, Hannibal, in the mean time, had sent five hundred Numidian horsemen towards the camp of the Romans, to observe where and how numerous their forces were, and what they were designing. The three hundred Roman horsemen sent, as was before said, from the mouth of the Rhone, meet this band of cavalry; and a more furious engagement than could be expected from the number of the combatants takes place. For, besides many wounds, the loss on both sides was also nearly equal: and the flight and dismay of the Numidians gave victory to the Romans, now exceedingly fatigued. There fell of the conquerors one hundred and sixty, not all Romans, but partly Gauls: of the vanquished more than two hundred. This commencement, and at the same time omen of the war, as it portended to the Romans a prosperous issue of the whole, so did it also the success of a doubtful and by no means bloodless contest. When, after the action had thus occurred, his own men returned to each general, Scipio could adopt no fixed plan of proceeding, except that he should form his measures from the plans and undertakings of the enemy: and Hannibal, uncertain whether he should pursue the march he had commenced into Italy, or fight with the Roman army which had first presented itself, the arrival of ambassadors from the Boii, and of a petty prince called Magalus, diverted from an immediate engagement; who, declaring that they would be the guides of his journey and the companions of his dangers, gave it as their opinion, that Italy ought to be attacked with the entire force of the war, his strength having been nowhere previously impaired. The troops indeed feared the enemy, the remembrance of the former war not being yet obliterated; but much more did they dread the immense journey and the Alps, a thing formidable by report, particularly to the inexperienced.

Hannibal, therefore, when his own resolution was fixed to proceed in his course and advance on Italy, having summoned an assembly, works upon the minds of the soldiers in various ways, by reproof and exhortation. He said, that "he wondered what sudden fear had seized breasts ever before undismayed: that through so many years they had made their campaigns with conquest; nor had departed from Spain before all the nations and countries which two opposite seas embrace, were subjected to the Carthaginians. That then, indignant that the Romans demanded those, whosoever had besieged Saguntum, to be delivered up to them, as on account of a crime, they had passed the Iberus to blot out the name of the Romans, and to emancipate the world. That then the way seemed long to no one, though they were pursuing it from the setting to the rising of the sun. That now, when they saw by far the greater part of their journey accomplished, the passes of the Pyrenees surmounted, amid the most ferocious nations, the Rhone, that mighty river, crossed, in spite of the opposition of so many thousand Gauls, the fury of the river itself having been overcome, when they had the Alps in sight, the other side of which was Italy, should they halt through weariness at the very gates of the enemy, imagining the Alps to be — what else than lofty mountains? That supposing them to be higher than the summits of the Pyrenees, assuredly no part of the earth reached the sky, nor was insurmountable by mankind. The Alps in fact were inhabited and cultivated; — produced and supported living beings. Were they passable by a few men and impassable to armies? That those very ambassadors whom they saw before them had not crossed the Alps borne aloft through the air on wings; neither were their ancestors indeed natives of the soil, but settling in Italy from foreign countries, had often as emigrants safely crossed these very Alps in immense bodies, with their wives and children. To the armed soldier, carrying nothing with him but the instruments of war, what in

312

reality was impervious or insurmountable? That Saguntum might be taken, what dangers, what toils were for eight months undergone? Now, when their aim was Rome, the capital of the world, could any thing appear so dangerous or difficult as to delay their undertaking? That the Gauls had formerly gained possession of that very country which the Carthaginian despairs of being able to approach. That they must, therefore, either yield spirit and valour to that nation which they had so often during those times overcome; or look forward, as the end of their journey, to the plain which spreads between the Tiber and the walls of Rome."

He orders them, roused by these exhortations, to refresh themselves and prepare for the journey. Next day, proceeding upward along the bank of the Rhone, he makes for the inland part of Gaul: not because it was the more direct route to the Alps, but believing that the farther he retired from the sea, the Romans would be less in his way; with whom, before he arrived in Italy, he had no intention of engaging. After four days' march he came to the Island; there the streams of the Arar and the Rhone, flowing down from different branches of the Alps, after embracing a pretty large tract of country, flow into one. The name of the Island is given to the plains that lie between them. The Allobroges dwell near, a nation even in those days inferior to none in Gaul in power and fame. They were at that time at variance. Two brothers were contending for the sovereignty. The elder, named Brancus, who had before been king, was driven out by his younger brother and a party of the younger men, who, inferior in right, had more of power. When the decision of this quarrel was most opportunely referred to Hannibal, being arbitrator of the kingdom, he restored the sovereignty to the elder, because such had been the opinion of the senate and the chief men. In return for this service, he was assisted with a supply of provisions, and plenty of all necessaries, particularly clothing, which the Alps, notorious for extreme cold, rendered necessary to be prepared. After composing the dissensions of the Allobroges, when he now was proceeding to the Alps, he directed his course thither, not by the straight road, but turned to the left into the country of the Tricastini, thence by the extreme boundary of the territory of the Vocontii he proceeded to the Tricorii; his way not being any where obstructed, till he came to the river Druentia. This stream, also arising amid the Alps, is by far the most difficult to pass of all the rivers in Gaul; for though it rolls down an immense body of water, yet it does not admit of ships; because, being restrained by no banks, and flowing in several and not always the same channels, and continually forming new shallows and new whirlpools, (on which account the passage is also uncertain to a person on foot,) and rolling down besides gravelly stones, it affords no firm or safe passage to those who enter it; and having been at that time swollen by showers, it created great disorder among the soldiers as they crossed, when, in addition to other difficulties, they were of themselves confused by their own hurry and uncertain shouts.

Publius Cornelius the consul, about three days after Hannibal moved from the bank of the Rhone, had come to the camp of the enemy, with his army drawn up in square, intending to make no delay in fighting: but when he saw the fortifications deserted, and that he could not easily come up with them so far in advance before him, he returned to the sea and his fleet, in order more easily and safely to encounter Hannibal when descending from the Alps. But that Spain, the province which he had obtained by lot, might not be destitute of Roman auxiliaries, he sent his brother Cneius Scipio with the principal part of his forces against Hasdrubal, not only to defend the old allies and conciliate new, but also to drive Hasdrubal out of Spain. He himself, with a very small force, returned to Genoa, intending to defend Italy with the army which was around the Po. From the Druentia, by a road that lay principally through plains, Hannibal arrived at the Alps without molestation from the Gauls that inhabit those regions. Then, though the scene had been previously anticipated from report, (by which uncertainties are wont to be exaggerated,) yet the height of the mountains when viewed so near, and the snows almost mingling with the sky, the shapeless huts situated on the clffs, the cattle and beasts of burden withered by the cold, the men unshorn and wildly dressed, all things animate and inanimate, stiffened with frost, and other objects more terrible to be seen than described, renewed their alarm. To them, marching up the first acclivities, the mountaineers appeared occupying the heights overhead; who, if they had occupied the more concealed valleys, might, by rushing out suddenly to the attack, have occasioned great flight and havoc. Hannibal orders them to halt, and having sent forward Gauls to view the ground, when he found there was no passage that way, he pitches his camp in the widest valley he could find, among places all rugged and precipitous. Then having learned from the same Gauls, when they had mixed in conversation with the mountaineers, from whom they differed little in language and manners, that the pass was only beset during the day, and that at night each withdrew to his own dwelling, he advanced at the dawn to the heights, as if designing openly and by day to force his way through the defile. The day then being passed in feigning a different attempt from that which was in preparation, when they had fortified the camp in the same place where they had halted, as soon as he perceived that the mountaineers had descended from the heights, and that the guards were withdrawn, having lighted for show a greater number of fires than was proportioned to the number that remained, and having left the baggage in the camp, with the cavalry and the principal part of the infantry, he himself with a party of light-armed, consisting of all the most courageous of his troops, rapidly cleared the defile, and took post on those very heights which the enemy had occupied.

At dawn of light the next day the camp broke up, and the rest of the army began to move forward. The mountaineers, on a signal being given, were now assembling from their forts to their usual station, when they suddenly behold part of the enemy over-hanging them from above, in possession of their former position, and the others passing along the road. Both these objects, presented at the same time to the eye and the mind, made them stand motionless for a little while; but when they afterwards saw the confusion in the pass, and that the marching body was thrown into disorder by the tumult which itself created, principally from the horses being terrified, thinking that whatever terror they added would suffice for the destruction of the enemy, they scramble along the dangerous rocks, as being accustomed alike to pathless and circuitous ways. Then indeed the Carthaginians were opposed at once by the enemy and by the difficulties of the ground; and each striving to escape first from the danger, there was more fighting among themselves than with their opponents. The horses in particular created danger in the lines, which, being terrified by the discordant clamours which the groves and re-echoing valleys augmented, fell into confusion; and if by chance struck or wounded, they were so dismayed that they occasioned a great loss both of men and baggage of every description: and as the pass on both sides was broken and precipitous, this tumult threw many down to an immense depth, some even of the armed men; but the beasts of burden, with their loads, were rolled down like the fall of some vast fabric. Though these disasters were shocking to view, Hannibal however kept his place for a little, and kept his men together, lest he might augment the tumult and disorder; but afterwards, when he saw the line broken, and that there was danger that he should bring over his army, preserved to no purpose if deprived of their baggage, he hastened down from the higher ground; and though he had routed the army by the first onset alone, he at the same time increased the disorder in his own army: but that tumult was composed in a moment, after the roads were cleared by the flight of the mountaineers; and presently the whole army was conducted through, not only without being disturbed, but almost in silence. He then took a fortified place, which was the capital of that district, and the little villages that lay around it, and fed his army for three days with the corn and cattle he had taken; and during these three days, as the soldiers were neither obstructed by the mountaineers, who had been daunted by the first engagement, nor yet much by the ground, he made considerable way.

315

He then came to another state, abounding, for a mountainous country, with inhabitants; where he was nearly overcome, not by open war, but by his own arts of treachery and ambuscade. Some old men, governors of forts, came as deputies to the Carthaginians, professing "that having been warned by the useful example of the calamities of others, they wished rather to experience the friendship than the hostilities of the Carthaginians: they would, therefore, obediently execute his commands, and begged that he would accept of a supply of provisions, guides of his march, and hostages for the sincerity of their promises." Hannibal, when he had answered them in a friendly manner, thinking that they should neither be rashly trusted nor yet rejected, lest if repulsed they might openly become enemies, having received the hostages whom they proffered, and made uses of the provisions which they of their own accord brought down to the road, follows their guides, by no means as among a people with whom he was at peace, but with his line of march in close order. The elephants and cavalry formed the van of the marching body; he himself, examining everything around, and intent on every circumstance, followed with the choicest of the infantry. When they came into a narrower pass, lying on one side beneath an overhanging eminence, the barbarians, rising at once on all sides from their ambush, assail them in front and rear, both at close quarters, and from a distance, and roll down huge stones on the army. The most numerous body of men pressed on the rear; against whom the infantry, facing about and directing their attack, made it very obvious, that had not the rear of the army been well supported, a great loss must have been sustained in that pass. Even as it was they came to the extremity of danger, and almost to destruction: for while Hannibal hesitates to lead down his division into the defile, because, though he himself was a protection to the cavalry, he had not in the same way left any aid to the infantry in the rear; the mountaineers, charging obliquely, and on having broken through the middle of the army, took possession of the road; and one night was spent by Hannibal without his cavalry and baggage.

Next day, the barbarians running in to the attack between the two divisions less vigorously, the forces were re-united, and the defile passed, not without loss, but yet with a greater destruction of beasts of burden than of men. From that time the mountaineers fell upon them in smaller parties, more like an attack of robbers than war, sometimes on the van, sometimes on the rear, according as the ground afforded them advantage, or stragglers advancing or loitering gave them an opportunity. Though the elephants were driven through steep and narrow roads with great loss of time, yet wherever they went they rendered the army safe from the enemy, because men unacquainted with such animals were afraid of approaching too nearly. On the ninth day they came to a summit of the Alps, chiefly through places trackless; and after many mistakes of their way, which were caused either by the treachery of the guides, or when they were not trusted, by entering valleys at random, on their own conjectures of the route. For two days they remained encamped on the summit; and rest was given to the soldiers, exhausted with toil and fighting: and several beasts of burden, which had fallen down among the rocks, by following the track of the army arrived at the camp. A fall of snow, it being now the season of the setting of the constellation of the Pleiades, caused great fear to the soldiers, already worn out with weariness of so many hardships. On the standards being moved forward at day-break, when the army proceeded slowly over all places entirely blocked up with snow, and languor and despair strongly appeared in the countenances of all, Hannibal, having advanced before the standards, and ordered the soldiers to halt on a certain eminence, whence there was a prospect far and wide, points out to them Italy and the plains of the Po, extending themselves beneath the Alpine mountains; and said "that they were now surmounting not only ramparts of Italy, but also of the city of Rome; that the rest of the journey would be smooth and down-hill; that after one, or, at most, a second battle, they would have the citadel and capital of Italy in their power and possession." The army then began to advance, the enemy now making no attempts beyond petty thefts, as opportunity offered. But the journey proved much more difficult than it had been in the ascent, as the declivity of the Alps being generally shorter on the side of Italy is consequently steeper; for nearly all the road was precipitous, narrow, and slippery, so that neither those who made the least stumble could prevent themselves from falling, nor, when fallen, remain in the same place, but rolled, both men and beasts of burden, one upon another.

They then came to a rock much more narrow, and formed of such perpendicular ledges, that a light-armed soldier, carefully making the attempt, and clinging with his hands to the bushes and roots around, could with difficulty lower himself down. The ground, even before very steep by nature, had been broken by a recent falling away of the earth into a precipice of nearly a thousand feet in depth. Here when the cavalry had halted, as if at the end of their journey, it is announced to Hannibal, wondering what obstructed the march, that the rock was impassable. Having then gone himself to view the place, it seemed clear to him that he must lead his army round it, by however great a circuit, through the pathless and untrodden regions around. But this route also proved impracticable; for while the new snow of a moderate depth remained on the old, which had not been removed, their footsteps were planted with ease as they walked upon the new snow, which was soft and not too deep; but when it was dissolved by the trampling of so many men and beasts of burden, they then walked on the bare ice below, and through the dirty fluid formed by the melting snow. Here there was a wretched struggle, both on account of the slippery ice not affording any hold to the step, and giving way beneath the foot more readily by reason of the slope; and whether they assisted themselves in rising by their hands or their knees, their supports themselves giving way, they would tumble again; nor were there any stumps or roots near, by pressing against which, one might with hand or foot support himself; so that they only floundered on the smooth ice and amid the melted snow. The beasts of burden sometimes also cut into this lower ice by merely treading upon it, at others they broke it completely through, by the violence with which they struck in their hoofs in their struggling, so that most of them, as if taken in a trap, stuck in the hardened and deeply frozen ice.

At length, after the men and beasts of burden had been fatigued to no purpose, the camp was pitched on the summit, the ground being cleared for that purpose with great difficulty, so much snow was there to be dug out and carried away. The soldiers being then set to make a way down the cliff, by which alone a passage could be effected, and it being necessary that they should cut through the rocks, having felled and lopped a number of large trees which grew around, they make a huge pile of timber; and as soon as a strong wind fit for exciting the flames arose, they set fire to it, and, pouring vinegar on the heated stones, they render them soft and crumbling. They then open a way with iron instruments through the rock thus heated by the fire, and soften its declivities by gentle windings, so that not only the beasts of burden, but also the elephants could be led down it. Four days were spent about this rock, the beasts nearly perishing through hunger: for the summits of the mountains are for the most part bare, and if there is any pasture the snows bury it. The lower parts contain valleys, and some sunny hills, and rivulets flowing beside woods, and scenes more worthy of the abode of man. There the beasts of burden were sent out to pasture, and rest given for three days to the men, fatigued with forming the passage; they then descended into the plains, the country and the dispositions of the inhabitants being now less rugged.

In this manner chiefly they came to Italy in the fifth month (as some authors relate) after leaving New Carthage, having crossed the Alps in fifteen days. What number of forces Hannibal had when he had passed into Italy is by no means agreed upon by authors. Those who state them at the highest, make mention of a hundred thousand foot and twenty thousand horse; those who state them at the lowest, of twenty thousand foot and six thousand horse. Lucius Cincius Alimentus, who relates that he was made prisoner by Hannibal, would influence me most as an authority, did he not confound the number by adding the Gauls and Ligurians. Including these, (who, it is more probable, flocked to him afterwards, and so many authors assert,) he says, that eighty thousand foot and ten thousand horse were brought into Italy; and that he had heard from Hannibal himself, that after crossing the Rhone he had lost thirty-six thousand men, and an immense number of horses, and other beasts of burden, among the Taurini, the next nation to the Gauls, as he descended into Italy. As this circumstance is agreed on by all, I am the more surprised that it should commonly be believed that he passed over the Pennine mountain, and that thence the name was given to that ridge of the Alps. Coelius says, that he passed over the top of Mount Cremo; both which passes would have brought him, not to the Taurini, but through the Salassian mountaineers to the Libuan Gauls. Neither is it probable that these roads into Gaul were then open, especially since those which lead to the Pennine mountain would have been blocked up by nations half German; nor by Hercules (if this argument has weight with any one) do the Veragri, the inhabitants of the ridge, know of the name being given to these mountains from the passage of the Carthaginians, but from the divinity, whom the mountaineers style Penninus, worshipped on the highest summit.

D. Spillan and *C. Edmonds*

TACITUS

CORNELIUS TACITUS (c. 55 - c. 117 A.D.) was the greatest Roman historian. Of distinguished family, he was trained in the schools of rhetoric, pursued an official career, and ultimately became proconsul of Asia.

His works include a dialogue on oratory, a biography of his father-in-law Agricola, an account of Germany, and, chiefly, his *Annales* and *Historiae,* historical surveys written dramatically and with a remarkable analytical understanding.

Book V — History

Titus in Judaea. Conflict between Civilis and Cerealis. Battle on the Banks of the Rhine.

In the beginning of the same year, Titus, who was appointed by his father to complete the subjugation of Judaea, and who, when both were no higher than subjects, had gained a reputation for military talents, now exercised a more extended influence, and shone with augmented lustre; the provinces and armies emulating each other in their zeal and attachment to him. Titus, on his part, that he might be thought deserving of still higher distinctions, appeared in all the splendor of external embellishments, and showed himself a prompt and resolute soldier, challenging respect by courtesy and affability; mixing with the common soldiers when engaged in the works and on their march, without impairing the dignity of the general. He succeeded to the command of three legions in Judaea, the fifth, the tenth, and the fifteenth; who had long served under Vespasian. To these he added the twelfth, from Syria, and the third and twenty-second, withdrawn from Alexandria. He was attended, besides, by twenty cohorts of the allies, and eight squadrons of horse, with the two kings Agrippa and Sohemus, and auxiliaries from Antiochus. He had also a band of Arabs, formidable in themselves, and harboring toward the Jews the bitter animosity usually subsisting between neighboring nations. Many persons had come from Rome and Italy, each impelled by the hopes he had of preoccupying the favor of a prince who had not yet chosen his friends. With this force Titus, advancing into the enemy's country in order of battle, by his scouts diligently exploring the motions of the enemy, and prepared for action, formed a camp a short distance from Jerusalem.

Being now about to relate the catastrophe of that celebrated city, it seems fitting that I should unfold the particulars of its origin. The Jews, we are told, escaping from the island of Crete, at the time when Saturn was driven from his throne by the violence of Jupiter, settled in the extreme parts of Libya. Their name is adduced as a proof. Ida, it is alleged, is a well-known mountain in Crete: the neighboring Idaeans, by an addition to the name to adapt it to the language of barbarians, are ordinarily called Judaeans. Some say that the population, overflowing throughout Egypt, in the reign of Isis, was relieved by emigration into the neighboring countries, under the conduct of Hierosolymus and Juda. Many state that they are the progeny of the Aethiopians, who were impelled by fear and detestation to change their abode in the reign of King Cepheus. There are those who report that they are a heterogeneous band from Assyria, a people who, being destitute of a country, made themselves masters of a portion of Egypt, and subsequently settled in cities of their own in the Hebrew territories, and the parts bordering on Syria. Others, ascribing to the Jews an illustrious origin, say that the Solymi, a nation celebrated in the poetry of Homer, called the city which they built Hierosolyma, from their own name.

Very many authors agree in recording that pestilential disease, which disfigured the body in a loathsome manner, spreading over Egypt, Bocchoris, at that time king, repairing to the oracle of Jupiter Hammon, in quest of a remedy, was directed to purify his kingdom, and exterminate that race of men as being detested by the gods: that a mass of people thus searched out and collected together were in a wild and barren desert abandoned to their misery, when, all the rest being bathed in tears and torpid with despair, Moses, one of the exiles, admonished them not to look for any aid from gods or men, being deserted of both, but to trust themselves to him as a heaven-commissioned guide, by whose aid already they had warded off the miseries that beset them. They assented, and commenced a venturous journey, not knowing whither they went. But nothing distressed them so much as want of water; and now they lay stretched through all the plains, ready to expire, when a herd of wild asses, returning from pasture, went up a rock shaded with a grove. Moses followed them, and forming his conjecture by the herbage that grew upon the ground, opened copious springs of water. This was a relief; and pursuing their journey for six days without intermission, on the seventh, having expelled the natives, they took possession of a country where they built their city, and dedicated their temple.

In order to bind the people to him for the time to come, Moses prescribed to them a new form of worship, and opposed to those of all the world beside. Whatever is held sacred by the Romans, with the Jews is profane: and what in other nations is unlawful and impure, with them is permitted. The figure of the animal through whose guidance they slaked their thirst, and were enabled to terminate their wanderings, is consecrated in the sanctuary of their temple; while in contempt of Jupiter Hammon, they sacrifice a ram. The ox, worshiped in Egypt for the god Apis, is slain as a victim by the Jews. They abstain from the flesh of swine, from the recollection of the loathsome affliction which they had formerly suffered from leprosy, to which that animal is subject. The famine, with which they were for a long time distressed, is still commemorated by frequent fastings; and the Jewish bread, made without leaven, is a standing evidence of their seizure of corn. They say that they instituted a rest on the seventh day because that brought them rest from their toils; but afterward, charmed with the pleasures of idleness, the seventh year also was devoted to sloth. Others allege that this is an honor rendered to Saturn, either because their religious institutes were handed down by the Idaeans, who, we are informed, were expelled from their country with Saturn, and were the founders of the nation; or else because, of the seven stars by which men are governed, the star of Saturn moves in the highest orbit, and exercises the greatest influence; and most of the heavenly bodies complete their effects and course by the number seven.

These rites and ceremonies, howsoever introduced, have the support of antiquity. Their other institutions, which have been extensively adopted, are tainted with execrable knavery; for the scum and refuse of other nations, renouncing the religion of their country, were in the habit of bringing gifts and offerings to Jerusalem, — hence the wealth and grandeur of the state; and also because faith is inviolably observed, and compassion is cheerfully shown toward each other, while the bitterest animosity is harbored against all others. They eat and lodge with one another only; and though a people of unbridled lust, they admit no intercourse with women from other nations. Among themselves no restraints are imposed. That they may be known by a distinctive mark, they have established the practice of circumcision. All who embrace their faith submit to the same operation. The first thing instilled into their proselytes is to despise the gods, to abjure their country, to set at naught parents, children, brothers. They show concern, however, for the increase of their population, for it is forbidden to put any of their brethren to death; and the souls of such as die in battle, or by the hand of the executioner, are thought to be immortal. Hence their desire of procreation, and contempt of death. The bodies of the deceased they choose rather to bury than burn, following in this the Egyptian custom; with whom they also agree in their attention to the dead, and their persuasion as to the regions below, but are opposed to them in their notions about celestial things. The Egyptians worship various animals and images, the work of men's hands; the Jews acknowledge one God only, and conceive of him by the mind alone, condemning, as impious, all who, with perishable materials, wrought into the human shape, form representations of the Deity. That Being, they say, is above all, and everlasting, neither susceptible of likeness nor subject to decay. In consequence, they allow no resemblance of him in their city, much less in their temples. In this they do not flatter their kings, nor show their respect for the Caesars. But because their priests performed in concert with the pipe and timbrels, were crowned with ivy, and a golden vine was found in the temple, some have supposed that Bacchus, the conqueror of the East, was the object of their adoration; but the Jewish institutions have no conformity whatever to the rites of Bacchus. For Bacchus has ordained festive and jocund rites, while the usages of the Jews are dull and repulsive.

Their land is bounded and their borders are formed on the east by Arabia; on the southern confine lies Egypt; on the west Phoenicia and the sea: they command an extended range northward on the side of Syria. The natives are robust, and patient of labor. Rain is seldom seen, and the soil is rich and fertile. The productions of the earth are such as are usually found with us, and besides them palms and the balm-tree flourish in great luxuriance. The palm groves are beautiful and lofty; the balm is of moderate size. As the branches successively swell, if you apply the force of iron the veins shrink, but they may be made to discharge by the fragment of a stone or by a shell; the fluid is employed as a medicine. The principal mountain which this country rears aloft is Libanus, which, astonishing to be related, in a climate intensely hot, is kept cool by its shady groves, and affords a secure retreat for snows. From this mountain the river Jordan springs and receives its supply of waters. The stream does not discharge itself into the sea; it runs into two different lakes, without mixing with them, and is absorbed into a third. The last of these lakes is of immense circuit, resembling a sea, but more nauseous in taste, and by the offensiveness of its odor, pestiferous to the neighborhood. The wind does not stir its surface, nor can fish or water-fowl endure it. The equivocal waters sustain things thrown upon them as if they were thrown upon a solid material; those who are able to swim and those who are not are equally upborne. At a stated season of the year, the lake throws up bitumen. Experience, the mother of all useful arts, has taught men the method of gathering it. It is liquid substance, naturally of a black hue, and by sprinkling vinegar upon it, it floats on the surface in a condensed mass, which those whose business it is lay hold of with the hand, and draw to the upper parts of the vessel; thence it continues to flow in and load the vessel, till you cut it off. Nor could you cut it off with brass or iron. It shrinks from the touch of blood, or a garment stained with menstrual evacuations. Such is the account transmitted to us by ancient authors; but persons acquainted with the country record that waving masses of bitumen are driven toward the shore, or drawn by the hand; and when by the vapor from the land, or the heat of the sun, they have dried, they are cut asunder, like wood or stone, by wedges, or the stroke of the hatchet.

At a small distance from the lake are plains, which tradition says were formerly a fruitful country, and occupied by populous cities, but had been destroyed by thunder-bolts. Traces still remain, we are told, and that the soil, in appearance parched with fire, has lost the power of bringing forth fruits. For all things, whether spontaneously produced or planted by the hand of man, whether they grow to the extent of the blade only and the flower, or their ordinary form, blackened and unsubstantial, crumble into ashes. For my part, as I would admit that cities once famous have been destroyed by fire from heaven, so am I of opinion that the earth is tainted by the exhalation from the lake, the superincumbent air contaminated, and that, therefore, the young plants of corn, and the fruits of autumn, wither away, the soil and air alike being infected. There is also a river named Belus, which glides into the Judaean sea; sands are found in the neighborhood of its mouth, which, mixed with nitre, are fused into glass. The shore is of moderate extent, and affords an exhaustless supply to those who dig it out.

A great portion of Judaea consists of scattered villages. They have likewise towns. Jerusalem is the capital of the nation: there stands a temple of immense wealth; the city is inclosed by the first fortifications you meet with; the royal palace by the second; the temple by the inmost. A Jew is not admitted beyond the portal; all, except the priests, are excluded from the threshold. While the Assyrians, and after them the Medes and Persians, were masters of the East, the Jews, of all the nations then held in subjection, were deemed the vilest. After the Macedonian monarchy was established, King Antiochus having formed a plan to abolish their superstition, and introduce the manners and institutions of Greece, was prevented by a war with the Parthians (for Arsaces had then revolted) from reforming this execrable nation. In process of time, when the Macedonians were by degrees enfeebled, when the Parthian state was in its infancy, and the Romans were at a distance, the Jews seized the opportunity to erect a monarchy of their own. Their kings were soon deposed by the caprice and levity of the people; but having recovered the throne by force of arms, and having dared to drive citizens into exile, demolish cities, put to death brothers, wives, and parents, and all the cruelties usual with despotic kings, they encouraged the superstition, because they took to themselves the dignity of the priesthood as a support of their power.

Pompey was the first Roman that subdued the Jews, and by right of conquest entered their temple. Thenceforward it became generally known that the habitation was empty, and the sanctuary unoccupied, no representation of the Deity being found within it. The walls of the city were leveled to the ground, the Temple remained. In the civil wars that afterward shook the empire, when the eastern provinces fell to the lot of Mark Antony, Pacorus, the Parthian king, made himself master of Judaea; but was, in a short time after, put to death by Ventidius, and his forces retired beyond the Euphrates. Caius Socius once more reduced the Jews to obedience. Herod was placed on the throne by Mark Antony, and Augustus enlarged his privileges. On the death of Herod, a man of the name of Simon, without waiting for the authority of the emperor, seized the sovereignty. He, however, was punished for his ambition by Quinctilius Varus, the governor of Syria; and the nation, reduced to submission, was divided in three portions between the sons of Herod. During the reign of Tiberius things remained in a state of tranquillity. Afterward, being ordered by Caligula to place his statue in the Temple, the Jews, rather than submit, had recourse to arms. This commotion the death of Caligula extinguished. Claudius, the Jewish kings being either dead or their dominion reduced to narrow limits, committed the province of Judaea to Roman knights, or his freedmen. One of these, Antonius Felix, exercised the prerogatives of a king with the spirit of a slave, rioting in cruelty and licentiousness. He married Drusilla, the granddaughter of Antony and Cleopatra, that he might be grandson-in-law of Mark Antony, who was the grandfather of Claudius.

The patience, however, of the Jews held out to the time of Cassius Florus, the procurator. Under him a war broke out. Cestius Gallus, the governor of Syria, endeavored to crush the revolt. He fought some obstinate battles, most of them unsuccessfully. After his death, which happened either by destiny or from disappointment and vexation, Vespasian, who was sent by Nero, succeeded to the command. By his character, the good fortune that attended his arms, and with the advantage of excellent officers, in two summer campaigns he overran the whole country, and made himself master of all the cities except Jerusalem. The following year, which was devoted to civil war, passed in tranquillity so far as concerned the Jews. The peace of Italy restored, the care of foreign affairs returned. It inflamed his resentment that the Jews were the only nation that had not submitted. At the same time it was deemed politic for Titus to remain at the head of the armies, with a view to any events or casualties that might arise under the new reign. Accordingly, the prince, as already mentioned, encamped under the walls of Jerusalem, and displayed his legions in the face of the enemy.

The Jews formed in order of battle under the very walls, determined, if successful, to push forward; and, if obliged to give ground, secure of a retreat. The cavalry, with the light-armed cohorts, sent against them, fought with doubtful success. Soon the enemy gave way, and on the following days engaged in frequent skirmishes before the gates, till at length, after a series of losses, they were forced to retire within the walls. The Romans resolved now to carry the place by storm. To linger before it till famine compelled a surrender, appeared indeed unworthy of them, and the soldiers demanded the post of danger, some from courage, many from hardihood and the hope of gaining rewards. Rome, her splendors and her pleasures, kept flitting before the eyes of Titus himself; and if Jerusalem did not fall at once, he looked upon it as obstructing his enjoyments. But Jerusalem, standing upon an eminence, naturally difficult of approach, was rendered still more impregnable by redoubts and bulwarks by which even places on a level plain would have been competently fortified. Two hills that rose to a prodigious height were inclosed by walls constructed so as in some places to project in angles, in others to curve inward. In consequence, the flanks of the besiegers were exposed to the enemy's weapons. The extremities of the rock were abrupt and craggy; and the towers were built, upon the mountain, sixty feet high; in the low ground, a hundred and twenty feet. These works presented a spectacle altogether astonishing. To the distant eye they seemed to be of equal elevation. Within the city there were other fortifications inclosing the palace of the kings, and the tower of Antonia, with its conspicuous pinnacles, so-called by Herod, in honor of Mark Antony.

The Temple itself was in the nature of a citadel, inclosed in walls of its own, and more elaborate and massy than the rest. The very porticoes that surrounded it were a capital defense. A perennial spring supplied the place with water. Subterraneous caverns were scooped out in the mountains, and there were basins and tanks as reservoirs of rain-water. It was foreseen by the founders of the city that the manners and institutions of the nation, so repugnant to the rest of mankind, would be productive of frequent wars; hence every kind of provision against a siege, howsoever protracted; and exposed as they had been to the successful assault of Pompey, their fears and experience had taught them many expedients. On the other hand, having purchased the privilege of raising fortifications through the venality of the Claudian times, they constructed such walls in a period of peace as showed they had an eye to war, while their numbers were augmented by a conflux of people from every quarter, and from the overthrow of other cities; for all the most indomitable spirits took refuge with them, and, by consequence, they lived in a state of greater dissension. They had three armies, and as many generals. The outward walls, which were of the widest extent, were defended by Simon: John, otherwise called Bargioras, guarded the middle precinct; and Eleazar the Temple. The two former were strong in the number of men, the latter in situation. But battles, plots, and burnings occurred among themselves, and a large quantity of grain was consumed by fire. After a short time, John, sending a band of assassins under color of performing a sacrifice, to cut off Eleazar and his party, gained possession of the Temple. From that time the citizens separated into two factions; and in this state they continued till, the Romans approaching, an enemy without produced unanimity within.

Prodigies had occurred which that race, enslaved to superstition, but opposed to religion, held it unlawful, either by vows or victims, to expiate. Embattled armies were seen rushing to the encounter, with burnished arms, and the whole Temple appeared to blaze with fire that flashed from the clouds. Suddenly the portals of the sanctuary were flung wide open, and a voice, in more than mortal accents, was heard to announce that the gods were going forth; at the same time, a prodigious bustle, as of persons taking their departure; occurrences which few interpreted as indicative of impending woe: the majority were deeply impressed with a persuasion that it was contained in the ancient writings of the priests, that it would come to pass at that very time, that the east would renew its strength, and they that should go forth from Judaea should be rulers of the world. Mysterious words, which foreshowed Vespasian and Titus: but the people, according to the usual course of human fondness, interpreting this consummation of destiny as referring to themselves, were not induced to abandon their error even by affliction. We learn that the number of the besieged of every age, male and female, was six hundred thousand; all that were capable bore arms, and more than could be expected out of that number had the fortitude to do so. The devotion of the women was equal to that of the men; and if they must needs move their seat, and quit the habitation of their fathers, they dreaded to live more than to die. Such was the city, such the nation, against which Titus Caesar determined to act by means of mounds and mantelets, since the nature of the locality was adverse to assault and sudden attacks. The legions had each of their several duties assigned them, and there was a cessation of fighting until all the engines and appliances for reducing cities, invented by ancient or modern genius, were prepared.

As for Civilis, after the check he had received in the country of the Treverians, having recruited his army by supplies in Germany, he fixed his station in the Old Camp, depending on the strength of the place, and that the recollection of the exploits already performed there might increase the confidence of the barbarians. Cerealis followed him thither, with an army doubled by the junction of the second, sixth, and fourteenth legions; and the cohorts and cavalry, which had some time before received orders to come up to his assistance, had quickened their motions after the victory. Neither of the commanders was an advocate for slow operations; but the extent of the plains, naturally marshy, kept them apart; and Cerealis had increased their moisture by erecting a mole athwart the Rhine, by which obstruction the water was thrown back and spread over the adjacent regions. Such was the nature of the place, deceptive from the unknown variations in the depth, and unfavorable to us, inasmuch as the Roman soldiers wore heavy armor, and were fearful of getting out of their depth; the Germans, on the contrary, accustomed to rivers, were enabled to keep their heads above water, from the lightness of their arms and the height of their persons.

The Batavians therefore endeavoring to provoke a battle, the most forward of our men commenced an engagement. A scene of confusion followed, when arms and horses as well disappeared in the deeper parts of the marshes. The Germans, who knew the shallow places, skipped about with ease and safety, for the most part declining an attack in front, but wheeling round upon our flank and rear. Nor was the contest carried on at close quarters as in a regular engagement upon land, but as if it were a naval combat the men shifted about amidst the waters, or if any firm footing presented itself, there grappling with their whole bodies at liberty, the wounded with the unwounded, those who could swim with those who could not, were inextricably engaged in mutual destruction. The carnage, however, was not proportioned to the confusion, because the Romans, not venturing to quit the marsh, returned to their camp. The issue of this encounter stimulated both the generals, but with opposite motives, to expedite a decisive engagement; Civilis to follow up his good fortune, Cerealis to efface the stain of failure. The Germans were flushed with their success, the Romans were goaded on by a sense of shame. The night was spent by the barbarians in songs and shouting; by our men in rage and menaces.

Next day Cerealis formed his entire front with his cavalry and auxiliary cohorts; the legions were posted behind them. He reserved for himself a chosen band, to act as occasion might require. Civilis formed not in an extended line, but in platoon. On the right stood the Batavians and Gugernians; the left was occupied by the Germans, with the Rhine on their flank. No general harangue was made to either army, the commanders on both sides exhorting their men as they came up to them. Cerealis called to mind the established renown of the Roman name, and their victories of ancient as well as modern date. "In order to extirpate forever a faithless, dastard, vanquished enemy, it was necessary to go and inflict the punishment due to his guilt, rather than to fight with him. In the late engagement they were inferior in number, and yet the Germans, the bravest of the enemy's troops, fled before them. There remained some still who in their minds bore the memory of their flight, and on their backs the marks of wounds." He next applied to the legions the incitements peculiarly suited to each. The fourteenth he called the conquerors of Britain; the example of the sixth, he said, raised Galba to the imperial dignity. The soldiers of the second, in that battle for the first time were to consecrate their new banners and their new eagle. From the legions he passed to the German army, and, with hands outstretched, called upon them to redeem by the blood of the enemy their own bank of the Rhine, their own camp. The acclamations were the heartier of all those, who either after a long peace were eager for war, or from weariness of war longed for peace, and who anticipated rewards and tranquillity for the future.

Nor did Civilis, when he had formed his troops, omit to address them, appealing to the ground whereon they stood as the witness of their valor. "The Batavians and the Germans," he said, "were standing on the monuments of their own fame, treading on the ashes and bones of legions. The Romans, whichever way they turned their eyes, had nothing before them but memorials of captivity and defeat. They ought not to be discouraged at the unfavorable turn of the battle in the Treverian territory; their own victory on that occasion stood in the way of the Germans, while, neglecting to use their weapons, they encumbered their hands with plunder. From that moment they met with nothing but success, while the Romans had had to struggle with every difficulty. Whatever provision ought to be made by the skill of a general, had been made —the fields were inundated, while they themselves were aware of their nature, and swamps formed which would prove fatal to their enemies. The Rhine and the gods of Germany were before their eyes, under whose protection he bade them apply themselves to the battle, mindful of their wives, their parents, and their country. That day would either rank them among the most renowned of their ancestors, or hand them down to posterity with infamy." When his words had been applauded by the clangor of arms and dancing (such is their custom), they commenced the battle by a discharge of stone balls and other missiles; but our men did not enter the fens, though the Germans annoyed them for the purpose of drawing them forward.

Their store of darts exhausted, and the battle kindling, the enemy charged with greater determination. With their long spears and towering persons, they were able at a distance to pierce the Romans, who were tossed to and fro, and could not keep their footing. A solid mass of the Bructerians, in the form of a wedge, swam across from the mole which, as I have stated, had been extended into the Rhine. In that quarter the Romans were thrown into disorder, and the auxiliary cohorts began to give way, when the legions advanced to sustain the fight, and checking the impetuous career of the enemy, the battle was restored to an equal footing. In that moment a Batavian deserter came up to Cerealis, and assured him that the enemy might be attacked in the rear, if some cavalry were sent round the extremity of the fen. The ground, he said, was in that part firm, and the Gugernians who guarded that quarter were not on the alert. Two squadrons of horse, sent with the deserter, surrounded the unsuspecting enemy; and the event being announced by a shout, the legions at the same time bore down in front. The barbarians gave way, and fled toward the Rhine. Had the fleet been diligent in pursuing them, that day would have closed the war. The approach of night and a sudden storm of rain, hindered even the cavalry from following them up.

Next day, the fourteenth legion was sent into the upper province to Annius Gallus; Cerealis made up the deficiency thus occasioned in his army by the tenth from Spain. Civilis was reinforced by the Chaucians; but without attempting to take active measures in defense of the Batavian cities. After carrying off whatever was portable, he set fire to the rest, and retired to the island; aware that the Romans could not follow him without constructing a bridge, and for that purpose they had no boats in readiness; nay, he even demolished the mole formed by Drusus Germanicus, and by dissipating the obstruction caused the river to pursue its rapid course toward Gaul. The river being thus as it were swept away, its diminished stream made the space between the island and Germany assume the form of an uninterrupted continent. Tutor also and Classicus passed over the Rhine, with a hundred and thirteen Treverian senators. Alpinus Montanus, the deputy sent, as above mentioned, from Cremona by Antonius Primus to the states of Gaul, was one of the number. He was accompanied by his brother Decimus Alpinus. At the same time, the rest of his adherents exerted themselves in collecting troops among those nations that delighted in dangerous enterprises, by exciting compassion, and by gifts.

And so great were the means of prosecuting the war still left, that Civilis, dividing his army into four parts, attacked on the same day the Roman cohorts, the cavalry, and the legions; the tenth legions at Arenacum; the second at Batavodurum; and the auxiliaries in their intrenchments at Grinnes and Vada. In this enterprise, Civilis headed one of the divisions Verax, his sister's son, led the second; Classicus and Tutor had their separate commands: nor in all their attempts did they act in confidence of success; but where much was hazarded, the issue in some quarter might be prosperous. They knew that Cerealis was not an officer of the strictest caution; and therefore hoped that, while he was distracted by different tidings, hastening from one post to another, he might be intercepted on his march. The party destined to storm the quarters of the tenth legion, judging it an enterprise of too much danger, were content with surprising such of the soldiers as had gone out of the camp, and were occupied in hewing wood. In this attack, the praefect of the camp, five principal centurions, and a few soldiers, were cut to pieces. The rest took shelter within the intrenchments. Meanwhile at Batavodurum they exerted themselves to destroy a bridge which the Romans had in part constructed over the river; the troops engaged, but night parted them before the victory was decided.

The affairs at Grinnes and Vada were of a more critical character. Civilis led the assault on Grinnes, Classicus that on Vada; nor could they be checked, the bravest of the troops having fallen in the attempt, and among them Briganticus, at the head of a squadron of horse; a man, as already stated, distinguished by his fidelity to Rome, and his hostility to Civilis, his uncle. But when Cerealis, with a select body of cavalry, came up to their relief, the fortune of the day was changed, and the Germans were sent flying into the river. Civilis, while attempting to stop their flight, was recognized, and assailed with a shower of darts; but he quitted his horse and swam across the river. Verax escaped in the same way: Tutor and Classicus were conveyed away in boats that were brought to the shore for the purpose. The Roman fleet, notwithstanding positive orders, failed again to co-operate with the land forces; but they were restrained by fear, and the circumstance of the rowers being dispersed on various other duties. It must be admitted that Cerealis did not allow due time for the execution of his orders; hasty in taking his measures, but eminently successful in their issue. Where his conduct was liable to censure, fortune aided him; and, by consequence, discipline fell into neglect with himself and army. Only a few days after, though he had the luck to escape being made a prisoner, he fell under merited censure.

Going to Bonna and Novesium occasionally to inspect the camps erecting at those places for the winter-quarters of the legions, he was in the habit of returning with his fleet, his forces proceeding in a disorderly manner, and no attention being paid to the watches. The Germans observed their negligence, and concerted a plan of surprising them. They chose a night overcast with clouds, and, shooting down the river, entered the intrenchments without opposition. They began the carnage with a stratagem; they cut the cords of the tents, and butchered the men as they lay enveloped in their own dwellings. Another party, in the mean time, surprised the fleet, threw grappling instruments on the vessels, and hauled them away. And as they approached in silence to escape discovery, so, when the slaughter was begun, they raised a deafening shout to add to the alarm. Roused by the wounds inflicted on them, the Romans seek their arms, hurry through the avenues of the camp; a few of them properly armed, most of them with their vestments wrapped round their arms, and with their swords drawn. The general, half asleep and almost naked, was saved by a blunder of the enemy; for they carried off the praetorian ship, in which a flag was hoisted, under an impression that the general was aboard.

331

Cerealis had been passing the night elsewhere, as was generally believed, on account of an illicit amour with Claudia Sacrata, a Ubian woman. The sentinels made an excuse for their guilt that did no honor to the general; alleging that their orders were to observe silence, that they might not disturb his rest, and, by consequence, making no signal, and using no watch-word, they themselves were overpowered with sleep. It was broad daylight when the Germans sailed back, towing with them the captured vessels, and among them the praetorian galley, which they hauled up the River Luppia, as an offering to Veleda.

Civilis conceived a vehement desire of exhibiting a naval armament: he manned all the vessels with two ranks of oars, and even those which were impelled by one rank. To these he added a prodigious number of small craft, among which were thirty or forty fitted out like the Roman Liburnian galleys. The barks lately taken from the Romans were supplied, in lieu of sails, with mantles of various colors, which made no unbecoming appearance. The spot chosen for this naval exhibition was a space resembling a sea, where the Rhine discharges itself through the mouth of the Mosa into the ocean. The motives for fitting out this fleet, in addition to the inherent vanity of the Batavians, was to prevent the supplies on their way from Gaul, by the terror it would inspire. Cerealis, from the strangeness of the thing rather than apprehension, drew out against it a fleet inferior in number, but in the skill of the mariners, the experience of the pilots, and the size of the vessels, superior. The Romans sailed with the current; the enemy had the wind in their favor. Thus, brushing by each other, they parted after a faint discharge of light darts. Civilis, without attempting any thing further, retired beyond the Rhine; Cerealis laid waste the isle of Batavia with determined hostility, leaving, however, the lands and houses of Civilis untouched, according to the known policy of military commanders. But during these proceedings, as it was now the latter end of autumn, and the rainy season had set in, the river, swelling above its banks, so completely inundated the naturally low and swampy island, that it presented the appearance of a lake. No ships were at hand; no means of getting provisions; and the tents, which stood on a flat, were carried away by the force of the waters.

Civilis pleaded it as a merit on his part that the Roman army, in this juncture, might have been cut off, and that the Germans wished it, but were by his artifices diverted from the enterprise. The surrender by that chief, which followed soon after, made this account not improbable. For Cerealis, by secret agents, offered terms of peace to the Batavians, and a promise of pardon to Civilis; and at the same time suggested to Veleda and her family to change the fortune of the war, hitherto pregnant with disasters of them, by conferring a well-timed favor upon the Romans. "The Treverians were cut to pieces, the Ubians reduced, and the Batavians shorn of their country; nor did aught result from the friendship of Civilis, but wounds, banishment, and mourning. Civilis was now an exile and outcast from his country, a burden to those who harbored him. Enough of error had they committed in so often crossing the Rhine. If they carried their machination further, iniquity and guilt would be on one side; on the other, a just retribution and the gods."

Menaces were mingled with his promises. The attachment of the nations beyond the Rhine giving way, the Batavians also began to express dissatisfaction. "It was unwise," they said, "to persist in a desperate cause; nor was it possible that a single nation could deliver the world from bondage. By the slaughter of the legions, and the firing of the Roman camps, what end had been answered, except that of bringing into the field a greater number of legions and more efficient? If the war was waged for Vespasian, Vespasian was master to a trial of strength, what proportion did the Batavians bear to the whole human race? Let them turn their eyes to Rhaetia, to Noricum, and the burdens borne by the other allies of Rome. From the Batavians Rome exacted no tribute: men and valor were all she enjoined. This was all but freedom; and if they were to choose who should rule over them, it was more honorable to submit to the emperor of Rome, than the female rulers of the Germans." Such was the reasoning of the common people. The nobles complained that, "exasperated themselves, they were hurried into the war by the mere violent frenzy of Civilis; that he had sought to avert the calamities of his house by the ruin of his country. Then it was that the gods were offended at the Batavians, when the legions were being besieged, commanders murdered, and a war undertaken which held out the only hope to one man, but was fatal to themselves. They were now on the brink of destruction, unless they set about retracing their steps, and demonstrating their contrition, by punishing the originator of their guilt."

Civilis perceived this turn in the sentiments of his countrymen, and resolved to be beforehand with them; not only because he was weary of the calamities of war, but from the hope of saving his life, a feeling which often subdues noble minds. He desired a conference. The bridge over the Nabalia was broken through in the middle; the two chiefs advanced to the extremities of the chasm, when Civilis thus began: "Were I pleading my cause before a commander of Vitellius, I should neither deserve pardon for what I have done, nor credit for what I state. Vitellius and I were mortal foes; we acted with avowed hostility. The quarrel was begun by him; it was inflamed by me. Toward Vespasian I have long behaved with respect. While he was yet a private man, we were reputed friends. This was well understood by Antonius

Primus, by whose letters I was urged to kindle the flame of war, lest the German legions and the youth of Gaul should pass over the Alps. The instructions Antonius communicated by letters, Hordeonius Flaccus gave in person. I stirred up a war in Germany in the same manner as Mucianus did in Syria, Aponianus in Moesia, and Flavianus in Pannonia."

Anonymous
19th century

SUETONIUS

C. SUETONIUS TRANQUILLUS (C. 69 - C. 140 A.D.) was a prolific biographer. He served as an officer in the Roman army and became a kind of secretary under the Emperor Hadrian. Dismissed from office, he devoted his remaining years to literature.

Among his works are *De Viris Illustribus*, biographies of literary men: and *De Vita Caesarum*, biographies of the Roman Emperors. Suetonius' value and appeal lie in the personal glimpses he affords of his subjects, in his anecdotes, and miscellaneous and intimate revelations.

The Historie of Tiberius Nero Caesar

The following sixteen sections on the life of the Emperor Tiberius Nero Caesar indicate the character of the context, the style, and the general attitude of the biographer.

I

The Patritian familie Claudia (for, there was likewise another Plebeian of that name, neither in power nor dignity inferiour) had the first beginning out of Regillum a Towne of the Sabines. From thence they came with a great retinue of vassals to Rome newly founded, there to dwell: induced thereto by the counsel of T. Tatius, fellow in government of the kingdom with Romulus; or (which is the more received opinion) through the persuasion of Atta Claudius, a principal person of that house, about the 6 years after the kings were expelled: and so, by the Senatours of Rome, raunged they were among the Patritii. Upon this, soon after, they received by vertue of a graunt from the whole City, for their Clients and vassals, lands to occupy beyond the river Anio: and for themselves a place of sepulture under the Capitol: and so forth, in process of time obtained 28 Consulates, five Dictatures, Censures seven, Triumphs six, and two Ovations. This family being distinguished by sundry fore-names and surnames both, in a general consent rejected the fore-name of Lucius, after that two of their linage bearing that name were convict, the one of robberie, the other of murder. Among surnames it assumed the addition of Nero, which in the Sabine tongue signified Strong or stout.

335

II

Many of these Claudii, as they deserved many ways passing well of the Common-wealth: so, in as many sorts they faulted and did amisse. But to relate the principal examples only in both kinds; Appius surnamed Caecus was he, who disswaded the entering into league and society with King Pyrrhus, as prejudicial unto the State: Claudius Caudex was the first man that passed over the narrow Seas with a fleete, and drave the Carthaginians out of Sicilie: Claudius Nero surprised and defaited Asdrubal comming out of Spain with a very great and puissant armie before he could joyn with his brother Annibal. Contrariwise, Claudius Appius Regillanus being Decemver chosen to frame and pen the Romaine Lawes, went about by violence (for the satisfaction of his fleshly lust) to enthrall a virgine Freeborne: and thereby gave occasion to the Commons for to fall away and forsake the Nobles a second time. Claudius Drusus having his own statue erected with a Diademe in a Town called Forum Appii, attempted with the help of his favorites and dependants to hold all Italy in his own hands. Claudius Pulcher, when as in taking of his Auspicia before Sicile, the sacred pullets would not feed, caused them, in contempt of Religion, to be plunged into the Sea, That they might drink seeing they would not eat: and thereupon strucke a battaile at Sea: in which, beeing vanquished, and commaunded by the Senate to nominate a Dictator, scorning, as it were, and making but a jest at the publique danger and calamity of the State, named a (base) Sergeant of his own called Glycia. There stand likewise upon record, the examples of women, and those as divers and contrary. For, two Claudiae there were of the same house: both she that drew forth the ship with the sacred images of the Idaean mother of the Gods sticking fast and grounded within the shelves of Tiberis, having before made her praier openly, That as she was a true and pure virgin, so the ship might follow her, and not otherwise: as also another, who after a strange and new manner, being a woman, was araigned before the people of high treason, for that when her Coach wherein she rode could hardly pass forward by reason of a thick throng and preasse of people, she had openly wished, That her brother Pulcher were alive again, and might lose a fleet the second time, to the end and there might be by that meanes a less multitude at Rome. Moreover, very well known it is, that all the Claudii, excepting only that P. Clodius who for expelling Cicero out of Rome, suffered himself to be adopted by a Commoner and one younger also than himself, were always Optimates, the only maintainers or patrons of the dignity and power of the Patritians: yea, and in opposition of the Commons so violent, stubborn and self-willed that not one of them, although he stood upon his trial

336

for life and death before the people, could find in his hart so much as to change his weed, or to crave any favour at their hands. Nay, some of them there were, who in a brawl and altercation, stuck not to beat the very Tribune of the Commons. Furthermore, a virgin vestal there was of that name, who when a brother of hers triumphed without a warrant from the people, mounted up with him into the chariot, and accompanied him even into the Capitol: to this end, that none of the Tribunes might lawfully oppose themselves and forbid the Triumph.

III

From this race and linage Tiberius Caesar deriveth his Genealogy, and that verily in the whole bloud and of both sides: by his Father, from Tiberius Nero: by his mother from Appius Pulcher, who were both of them the sons of Appius Caecus. Incorporate he was besides into the familie of the Livii, by reason that his Grandfather by the mothers side was adopted thereinto: which family (Commoners though they were) flourished notwithstanding and was highly reputed; as being honoured and graced with eight Consulships, two Censureships, and three triumphs: with a Dictatourship also and Maistership of the Horsemen: renowned likewise and ennobled for brave and notable men, Salinator especially and the Drusi: as for Salinator, in his Censureship he noted and taxed all the Tribes every one and whole body of the people, for unconstant levitie, for that having uppon his former consulship condemned him and set a fine uppon his head, yeat afterwards they made him Consul a second time and Censour besides. Drusus, upon the killing of one Drausus the General of his enemies in close combat and single fight, purchased unto himself and his posterity after him that surname. It is reported also, that this Drusus beeing propretour, recovered and fetched again out of his province Gaule, that gold which in times past had been given unto the Senones when they besieged the Capitol: and that it was not Camillus (as the voice goes) that wrested the same perforce out of their hands. His son in the 4 degree of descent, called for his singular imployment against the Gracchi, Patron of the Senate, left behind him a son: whom in the like variance and debate, as he was busy in devising and putting in practise sundrie plots, the adverse faction treacherously slew.

IV

But, the Father of this Tiberius Caesar, being Treasurer unto C. Caesar, and Admiral of a fleet in the Alexandrine warre performed very good service for the achieving of victory, whereupon he was both substituted Pontifex in steed of Scipio, and also sent with commission

337

to plant Colonies in Gaule, among which were Narbona and Arelate. Howbeit, after that Caesar was slaine, when as all men for fear of troubles and uprores decreed a final abolition and oblivion of that fact and all other quarrels thereupon depending, he proceeded farther and opined, That they should consult about the rewards of such Tyrant-killers. After this, having borne his Pretourship (in the end of which year there arose some discord between the Triumvirs) he retaining by him still the ensignes and ornaments of that office after the time fully expired, and following L. Antonius the Consul and the Triumvirs brothers, as far as to Perusia, when the rest yeelded themselves, continued along fast, and stuck to the faction (that sided against Octavious) and first escaped to Preneste, then to Naples: where when he had proclaimed (but in vain) freedom for all bondslaves, he fled into Sicilie. But taking it to the heart, that he was not immediatly admitted to the presence of Sextus Pompeius, but debarred the use of his Knitches of rods to be borne afore him, he crossed the Seas into Achaia, and went to M. Antonius. With whom, by occasion that shortly after, an attonement and peace was made between all parties, he returned to Rome; and at the request of Augustus, yeelded unto him his own wife Livia Drusilla, who both at that time was great with child, and also had already before brought him a son named Tiberius, in his own house. Not long after, he departed this life, and left his children surviving him, namely Tiberius Nero and Drusus Nero.

V

Some have thought that this Tiberius (Caesar) was born at Fundae, grounding uppon a light conjecture, because his mothers Grandame was a Fundane born; and for that soon after the image of Felicitie, by vertue of an Act of the Senate was there publiquely set up. But, as the most Authors and those of better credite do write, born he was at Rome in the Mount Palatium, the sixteenth day before the Calendes of December, when M. Aemilius Lepidus was Consul the second time together with Munatius Plancus, even after the war at Philippi: for so it stands upon record and in the publique Registers. Yet there want not some who write otherwise: partly that he was born a year before in the Consulship of Hirtius and Pansa, and partly the year next following, wherein Servilius Isauricus and Antonius were Consuls.

VI

His infancy and childhood both were exceeding forward and the same full of toilesome travaile and daunger, by occasion that every where, he accompanied his Parents still, in their flights and escapes. And verily, twice he had like to have descried them with his wrawling at Naples, what time as a little before the forcible and suddaine entry of the enemy, they made shift secretly to get into a ship: namely once, when he was taken hastily from his Nources breast: and a second time out of his Mothers lap and armes, by those who as the necessity of the time required, did their best to ease the poor women of their burden and loade. He was caried away with them likewise through Sicilie and Achaia; yea, and beeing recommended to the Lacedae-monians (who were under the protection of the Claudii their Patrons) for to take the charge of him in publique, as he departed from thence by night, he was in danger of his life by reason of a light flaming fire, which suddainly from all parts arose out of a wood: and compassed all the company in his traine so, as that some part of Liviaes apparel and the hair of her head was scorched and sienged therewith. The giftes bestowed upon him in Sicilie by Pompeia the sister of Sextus Pompeius, to wit, a little Cloake with a button or clasp to it: likewise studds and bosses of gold, continue and are yet shewed to be seen at Baie. After his return into the City of Rome, beeing adopted by M. Gallius a Senatour in his last will and testament, he accepted of the inheritance and entred upon it: but within a while forbare the name, because Gallius had sided with the adverse faction and taken part against Augustus. Being 9 years old he praised his father deceased openly from the *Rostra*. Afterwards, as he grewe to be a springal, he accompanied in the Actiacke tryumph the Chariot of Augustus, ryding upon the steede drawing without the yoke on the left hand, when as Marcellus the son of Octavia rode upon the other on the right hand. He was president also at the Actiack Games and plaies, yea and the Troian Turnament in the Circean solemnities, where he led the troupe of the bigger boyes.

VII

After he had put on his virile robe, his whole youth and all the time besides of the age next ensuing, even unto the beginning of his Empire, he passed for the most part in these affaires following. He exhibited one sword fight performed by fencers to the outrance, in memorial of his father: likewise another in the honourable remembrance of his Grandfather Drusus: and those at sundry times and in diverse places: the former in the Forum of Rome: the second in the Amphi-theatre: having brought again into the Lists, even those that were free before time and discharged from that profession: whom he now hired and bound to fight, with the summe of one hundred thowsand sesterces. He did set foorth stage playes also, but whiles himself was absent: all with great magnificence, and also at the charges of his mother and father in Law. Agrippina the daughter also of M. Agrippa, and neice to Pomponius Atticus a Gentleman of Rome, him I mean, unto whom Cicero wrote his Epistles, he tooke to wife. And when he had begotten of her a son named Drusus, albeit she fitted him well enough and was besides with Childe again, enforced he was to put her away; and foorthwith to wed Julia the daughter of Augustus: not without much grief and heart break: considering that he both desired still the company of Agrippina and also misliked the conditions and demeanour of Julia, as whom he perceived to have had a mind and fancy unto him while she was the wife of a former husband. Which verily was thought also abroad. But as he grieved, that after the divorce he had driven away Agrippina, so when he chanced but once (as she met him) to see her, he followed her still with his eyes so bent, so swelling, and staring, that streight order was given, and a watch set, she should never after come in his way nor within his sight. With Julia he lived at the first in great concord and mutual love: but afterwards he began to estrange himself, and (that which was the more grief) he proceeded to part bedds and to lie from her continually, namely, after that the pledge of love, their son begotten between them, was untimely taken away: who beeing born at Aquileia died a very infant. His own brother Drusus he lost in Germanie, whose body he conveyed throughout to Rome going before it all the way on foot.

VIII

In his first rudiments and beginnings of civil offices, he pleaded at the barre in defence of Archelaus; of the Trallians and Thessalians: all of them in sundry causes while Augustus sat in judgment to heere their tryall: in the behalf also of the Laodicenes, Thyaterenes and Chians, who had suffered great losse by Earthquake, and humbly sought for relief, he intreated the Senate. As for Fannius Caepio, who together with Varro Muraena had conspired against Augustus, he arraigned of high treason before the judges, and caused him to be condemned: and amid these affairs, he executed a duple charge and function: to witte, the purveyance of Corne and Victualles, whereof there happened to be scarcity: and the skouringe or riddance of the worke-house prisons: the Lordes and Maisters whereof were become odious, as if they had caught up and held to work not only waifaring persons, but those also who for fear of taking a military oath and to be enrolled, were driven to shrowd themselves in such corners and starting holes.

IX

His first service in the war was in the expedition of Cantabria, what time he had the place of a Tribune Military. Afterwards, having the conduct of an army into the East parts, he restored the kingdom of Armenia unto Tigranes, and from the Tribunal seat did put the Diademe upon his head. He recovered also those military ensignes which the Parthians had taken from M. Crassus. After this he governed as Regent that part of Gaule beyond the Alpes, called Comata: which was full of troubles, partly by the incursions of barbarous nations, and in part through the intestine discorde of Princess and Nobles of the Country. Then, warred he upon the Rhetians and Vindelici, and so forward upon the Pannonians and Germaines whom he vanquished all. In the Rhaetian and Vindelicke war, he subdued the Nations inhabiting the Alpes: in the Pannonian, he conquered the Breuci and Dalmatians. In the Germaine war he brought over into Gaule 40000 that yeelded unto him, and placed them near unto the Rhene bank, where they had there habitations assigned. For which Acts, he entred the City of Rome both *Ovant* (ryding on horseback) and also Triumphant mounted upon a Chariot: being the first (as some think) that was honoured with Triumphant ornaments, a new kind of honour and never granted to any man before: to bear Magistracy he both began betimes, and also ran through them all in manner joyntly and without intermission, namely his Quaesture, Praeture and Consulate. After some space between he became Consul a second time, yea and also received the Tribunitian Authority for five years together.

X

In this confluence of so many prosperous successes, in the strength also of his years and perfect health, he had a full purpose, sodainely to retire himself and remove out of the way as far as he could. Whether it were for the weariness hee had of his wife, whom neither he durst plainely charge or put away, nor was able to endure any longer, or to the end that by avoyding contempt incident to daily and continual residence, hee might maintaine and increase his authority by absenting himself, if at any time the State stood in need of him, it is uncertain. Some are of opinion, that considering Augustus his children were now well grown, he of his own accorde yeelded up unto them the place and possession, as it were, of the second degree, which himself had usurped and held a long time; following herein the example of M. Agrippa, who having preferred M. Marcellus, to be imployed in public affairs, departed unto Mitylenae; least by his presence he might seem to hinder them or deprave their proceedings. Which cause even

341

himself, but afterwards, alleadged: mary, for the present, pretending the satiety that he had of honorable places, and rest from his travailes, he made suite for licence to depart: neither gave he any care to his own mother humbly beseeching him to stay; nor to his father in law, who complained also that he should be forsaken thereby and left desolate in the Senate. Moreover, when they were instant still to hold him back, he abstained from all kind of meat four days together. At length having obtained leave to be gone, he left his wife and son behind him at Rome, and forthwith went down to Ostia: giving not so much as one word again to any that accompanied him thither, and kissing very few of them at the parting.

XI

As he sayled from Ostia along the coast of Campanie, upon news that he heard of Augustus weakeness, he stayed a while and went not forward: but when a rumor began to be spred of him, (as if he lingred there, waiting some opportunity of greater hopes,) he made no more adoe, but even against wind and wether sayled through and passed over to Rhodes: having taken a delight to the pleasant and healthfull situation of that Iland, ever since he arrived there in his returne from Armenia. Contenting himself here, with a mean and small habitation, with a ferme house likewise by the City side not much larger nor of greater receite, he purposed to lead a very civil and private life: walking otherwhile in the Gymnase without lictor or other officer, performing acts and duties in maner one for another with the Greeks conversing there. It happened upon a time, when he disposed of the business which he would dispatch one day, that he gave it out before hand, He was desirous to visite all the sick in the City. These words of his were mistaken by those next about him. Whereupon all the lazars and diseased persons were by commandement brought into a public porch or gallerie and placed there in order according to the sundrie sorts of their maladies. At which unexpected sight, being much troubled and perplexed, he wist not for a good while what to do: howbeit he went round about from one to another, excusing himself for this that was done even to the meanest, poorest and basest of them all. This only thing and nothing else beside was noted, wherein he seemed to exercise the power of his Tribunes authority. Being daily and continually conversant about the Schools and Auditories of professors, by occasion that there arose a great braule among the Sophisters opposite in arguing cases and declaiming one against other, there chanced to be one who perceiving him comming between and inclining to favorize one part above the other, rayled bitterly at him. With drawing himself therefore by little and little, and retyring home to his house, he came forth sodainely again and appeared with his Lictours: where he cited by the voice of his cryer to appeare judicially before his Tribunal, that foule mouthed rayling fellow, and so commanded him to be had away to prison. After this, he had certain intelligence given him that Julia his wife was convict and condemned for her incontinency and adulteries; also that in his name (by a warrant directed from Augustus) she had a bill of divorse sent unto her. And albeit, he was glad of these tidings, yet he thought it his part, as much as lay in him, by many letters to reconcile the father unto his daughter: yea and how ever she had deserved badly at his hands, yet to suffer her for to have whatsoever he had at any time given unto her in free gift. Now, after he had passed through the time of his Tribunes authority, and confessed at last, that by this retyring of his out of the way he sought to avoide nought else but the suspition of Jelousie and emulation with Caius and Lucius: he made suite, That seeing he was now secured in this behalf, and they strengthened enough and able with ease to manage and maintain the second place in government, he might be permitted to returne and see his friends and acquaintance again, whose presence he missed and longed after. But he could not obtain so much: nay, admonished he was and warned before hand, to lay a side all regard of his friends and kinsfolk, whom he was so willing to leave and abandon before.

XII

He abode therefore still at Rhodes, even against his will: and hardly by the means and intercession of his own mother wrought thus much, that for to cover his ignominy and shame, he might be absent under this pretence, as if he were Augustus his Lieutenant. And then verily, lived he not only private to himself, but also exposed to danger, and in great fear of some hard measure: lying close and hidden in the uplandish and inward parts of the Iland; and avoyding the offices of them that made saile by those coasts, who had frequented him continually: for as much as no man went into any province that way, as Lord General or Magistrate, but he struck a side and turned to Rhodes. Besides, other causes there were of greater fear and trouble presented unto him. For when as he crossed the seas to Samos for to visit Caius, his wives son, president of the East parts, he perceived him to be more estranged than before time through the slaunders and criminous imputations which M. Lollius companion and governor to the said Caius had put into his head. He was drawen also into suspition by certaine Centurions, whom his favour had advanced, and who at the day limited in their pasport were returned to the camp, That he had delivered unto many (of them) Mandates of an ambiguous and duple construction, such as might seem to sound the minds of every one and

343

sollicite them to rebellion. Of which suspition being certified by Augustus, he never rested to call for, and require to have some one of any degree and order what soever, to observe all his deeds and words.

XIII

He neglected also his wonted exercises of horse and armour: yea, and having laid by the habit of his native Country, he betook himself to a clok and slippers. In such a state and condition as this, continued he almost two years throughout, more dispised and hatefull every day then other: insomuch as the Meniansians overthrew his Images and statues: and upon a time, at a certain feast, where familiar friends were met together (by occasion that mention was made of him,) there was one stood up who promised Caius, That in case he did but command and say the word, he would immediatly sayle to Rhodes and fetch unto him the head of that exiled person: for so was he commonly called. And chiefly upon this which was now no bare fear, but plain peril, enforced he was by most earnest prayers not only of his own but also of his mother, to require and seek for to returne: which he obtained at length with the help somewhat of good fortune. Augustus had fully set down with himself to resolve upon nothing as touching that point, but with the will and good liking of his elder son: now was he, as it happened at that time much offended and displeased with M. Lollius, but to his father in law (Tiberius) well affected, and easy to be by him intreated. By the permission therefore and good leave of Caius called home he was; but with this condition, That he should not meddle one Jote in the affairs of State.

XIV

Thus in the 8 yeare after his departure, returned he full of great hopes and nothing doubtfull of future fortunes, which he had conceived as well by strang sights, as also by predictions and prophesies even from his very birth. For Livia while she went with child of him, among many and sundrie experiments which she made, and signes that she observed (and all to know whether she should bring forth a man child or no?) took closely an egge from under an hen that was sitting, and kept it warm sometime in her own, otherwhiles in her women hands by turns one after another, so long, untill there was hatched a cock-chicken with a notable combe upon the head. And when he was but a very babe, Scribonius the Astrologer gave out and warranted great matters of him, and namely, That he should one day raign as Monarch, but yet without the royall Ensignes. For as yet, ye must note, the soveraigne power of the Caesars was unknown. Also, as he entred into

344

his first expedition, and led an army into Syria, through Macedonie: it chanced that the consecrated Altars of the victorious Legions in time past at Philippi shone out sodainely of themselves all on a light fire. And soon after, when in his journey toward Illyricum he went to the Oracle of Geryon near unto Padua, and drew forth his lotte, whereby he was advised that for counsel and resolution in such particulars as he required after, he should throw golden dies into the fountaine Aponus, it fell out so that the dies thus cast by him shewed the greatest number: and even at this very day these dies are seen under the water. Some few days likewise before he was sent for home, an Aegle, (never seen afor time at Rhodes) perched upon the very top and ridge of his house: and the very day before he had intelligence given him of his return, as he was changing his apparel, his shirt was seen on fire. Thrasyllus also the Astrologer, whom for his great profession of wisedom and cunning he had taken into his house to bear him company, he made then most trial of; namely, when upon kenning a ship a far of, he affirmed, That joyfull news was comming, whereas at the very same instant as they walked together Tiberius was fully purposed to have turned him headlong down into the sea, as being a false prophet, (for that things fell out untowardly and contrarie to his former predictions) and one besides who chanced for the most part to be privy unto him of all his secrets.

XV

Being returned to Rome, and having brought his son Drusus solemnly into the Forum, he removed immediatly out at Carina and the house of Pompeius unto Esquilia, and the Hort-yards of Maecenas: where he gave himself wholly to quietness performing private duties only and not medling at all in public offices. After that Caius and Lucius were dead within the compasse of 3 years, he together with their brother M. Agrippa was adopted by Augustus, but compelled first himself to adopt Germanicus his brothers son. Neither did he ought afterwards as an housholder, nor retained one jote of that right which he had forgon by his adoption. For, he gave no donations, he manumised no person: nor yet made benefit of any inheritance or legacies otherwise then in the nature of *Peculium*: and so he did put them down in his book of receits. But from that time forward was there nothing pretermitted for the augmentation of his state and Majesty: and much more after that Agrippa once was in disfavour and sent away: whereby the world took knowledge for certain, that the hope of succession rested only in him.

345

XVI

Now was the Tribunitian Authority conferred a second time upon him, and that for the term of 5 years; the honorable charge and commission likewise, for to pacific the State of Germanie was assigned unto him: and the Parthian Embassadours, after they had declared their message at Rome unto Augustus, were commanded to repair unto him also into his province. But upon the news that Illyricum revolted, he removed from thence to the charge of a new warre, which, being of all foraine warres the most dangerous since those with the Carthaginians, he menaged with the power of 15 Legions, and equal forces of Auxiliaries, for the space of 3 years in great extremity of all things, but especially in exceeding scarcety of Corne. And notwithstanding that he was oftentimes revoked from this service yet persisted he unto the end, fearing least the enemy so near a neighbour and so puissant with all, should make head and come upon them, if they first did quit the place and retire. And verily, passing well paied and rewarded was he for this perseverance of his, as having thereby fully subdued and brought under his subjection all Illirycum as far as reacheth and spreadeth between Italy, the kingdom of Noricum, Thracia, and Macedonie: between the river Danubius also and the gulf of the Adriaticke sea.

Philemon Holland

PHILOSOPHY

Cicero

M. Aurelius

Seneca

CICERO

For biographical note, see under Oratory.

Book I — *On Moral Duties*

Classification of duties: the four cardinal virtues: riches and avarice: conditions of human society: wisdom and justice.

Although, after twelve months spent in the school of Cratippus, and that at Athens too, you cannot, my son Marcus, but be abundantly instructed in the precepts and institutions of philosophy, by reason of the great authority of the master as well as of the place, the one for erudition, the other for example; I am yet of opinion that you shall do well, nevertheless, to take the same course in your studies that I have done in mine, and to mingle your Latin with your Greek, as a method which I have ever found very much conducing to the business both of an orator and of a philosopher, besides that it will give you the command, indifferently, of both languages. In this particular I am persuaded that I have done my countrymen no small service, and that not only those who have no skill at all in Greek, but even the learned themselves, will acknowledge that I have in some sort contributed to the advantage both of their eloquence and judgment. Wherefore, as you have the greatest philosopher of this age for your master, you shall also learn of him as long as you please; and so long, certainly, you ought to desire to learn, as you find yourself the better for it. Upon the reading of my writings you will see a great deal in them of the peripatetic, for I am a follower of Socrates and of Plato both. As to the matter itself, you are at liberty to use your own judgment, but yet the acquainting of yourself with my style will undoubtedly be of some use towards the improvement of our Latin tongue. And let me not in this be thought arrogant neither, for, allowing myself the meanest of many philosophers, I have yet some right methinks, after an age spent upon this study, to value myself upon all the parts of an orator, as propriety, perspicuity, and the flowers and ornaments of well-speaking. Wherefore I must earnestly recommend unto you the perusal, not only of

348

my Orations, but likewise of my Philosophical Discourses, which are now swelled almost to the bulk of the other; and that you will read them with intention and care, for though there may be in the other a greater force and dignity, yet this smooth and temperate mixture is not to be neglected. Among the Greeks I have not found any man that has successfully applied himself to the language of the Bar and to this gentle way of argumentation both at once, unless I should reckon Demetrius Phalereus for one, who was indeed a subtle disputant, no very powerful orator, but then such a vein of sweetness with him, that a body might imagine Theophrastus had been his tutor. For my own part, I have laboured in both these kinds, and with what effect let the world judge. Plato, I believe, would have made a ready and a weighty pleader if he had bent his mind to't; and Demosthenes, a quaint and a polite philosopher, if he would have treated of and stuck to what he had from Plato. And this was the case also of Aristotle and Isocrates, they were both of them fond of their own way and slighted one another.

But being resolved to write somewhat to you at present, and more hereafter, I have made it my choice to begin upon that subject which I look upon to be most accommodate to your age and best becoming the authority of a parent. There are many profitable and important points in philosophy which have been accurately and copiously handled by divers learned men, but that which I take to be of the greatest latitude falls under the head of offices or duties betwixt man and man, whereof we have many precepts and traditions transmitted to us from our forefathers. For there is no condition of life, either public or private, from courts of justice to particular families, either solitary or in society, but there is still a place for human duty; and it is the well or ill discharging of this office that makes our character in the world either glorious or shameful. And this is the common theme, too, of all philosophers; for who shall dare to usurp that sacred name that never prescribed rules for the government of life? But there are some sects yet that, upon a mistake concerning the measures of good and evil, render these offices wholly vain and useless; for whosoever thinks of separating the supreme good from virtue, consulting his own ease in the case, that man can never be either a friend or a just or a generous person upon that bottom — that is to say, so long as he agrees with himself, and without hearkening sometime to the direction of a better nature. Can any man be brave that makes pain the worst of evils? or temperate that makes pleasure the sovereign good? This is so clear that it is not worth a dispute, besides that I have expressly discoursed upon it in another place. The patrons of these opinions cannot pretend in any sort to intermeddle in this matter without contradicting themselves; for there can be no sound, stable, and natural principle of duty erected upon any other foundation than this that virtue is only, or at least chiefly, desirable for its proper self. Wherefore the Stoics, Academics, and Peripatetics were much in the right in this particular, as the whimsies of Aristo, Pyrrho, and Erillus are long since out of doors; not but that they had as much right as other people to a freedom of debate, if they had but left us in a state or capacity of election without cutting off the very means of any communication with human duties. Therefore at this time, and in this question, I shall follow the Stoics, not as an expositor, but, after my usual custom, I shall draw as much water at their well as I think fit, and then make use of it according to my own discretion.

Being in this book to treat of the offices or duties of mankind, it will be proper, in the first place, to define what is intended by the word office — a thing omitted by Panaetius, which I wonder at, for all reasonable propositions ought to be introduced by a definition, for the better understanding of the point in debate.

Of duties, or offices, there are two kinds: the one respects the ends of good men, the other consists in certain rules and precepts to be applied to the use and conduct of human life. Under the former are these questions: Whether all offices be perfect or not? Whether one office be greater or less than another? and, what offices are found to be of the same sort and degree? But those offices which are delivered to us by precept, though they have a regard also to the life of good men, yet it does not so much appear, because they seem to be rather a provision for the ordering of life in society. These are offices which we shall discourse of in this book. There is also another division of offices; some are called middle and imperfect, others perfect. We may call the latter a right (according to the Greek word *Katorthema*) and the other a common office *(kathekon)*, defining that to be perfect which they call right, and that to be a middle office when a man may give a reasonable accompt for the doing of it.

It is natural to deliberate before we resolve: and Panaetius reduces the subject matter of deliberation into three general heads. The first question is, Whether the thing deliberated upon be good or evil? wherein several men are many times of several opinions. The second inquiry or consult refers to the ease, pleasure, or convenience of life, as estate for the purpose, wealth, or power by which we are enabled to be helpful both to ourselves and our friends: Whether the matter in debate be convenient or not? And this question is carried by the appearance of profit. The third point of deliberation lies in a case where the honest and the profitable come in competition, for when utility drives one way, and virtue invites us another, there follows a distraction of mind and a dubious anxiety of thought. It is a great failing to leave out anything in a division, and yet there are two things omitted in this. For the question is not only whether a thing be honest or not, but, where there are two things honest before us, which is the honester? and of two profitables, whether one is the more profitable? So that his three branches must be extended to five: first, the concurrence of two good things; secondly, that of two profitables; and lastly, both of them in comparison. Of which in order.

All living creatures are originally moved by a natural instinct towards the means of self-preservation: as the defence of their lives and bodies; the avoidance of things hurtful to them; the search and provision of all necessaries for life, as food, shelter, and the like. It is likewise common to them all the appetite of propagating and continuing their kind, with a certain care and tenderness for their issue. Now, betwixt a man and a brute there is eminently this difference: the one is carried on by sense, and to that only which is present, with little or no regard to what is either past or to come; whereas the other, by the benefit of reason, sees the consequences of things, their rise and their progress, and couples together causes and effects, compares resemblances of times, actions, and events, tacks the present to the future, and so, taking in his whole life at a view, he prepares all things for the use and comfort of it.

It is by force of the same reason that Nature makes one man a friend to another, that she moves us to the love of communication and society, that she implants in us a particular affection to our children, and dictates to us the necessity of communities and councils. This is it that puts us upon providing for food and clothing, and not for ourselves alone, but for our wives, our children, our friends, and for all those that are under our protection. This impression raises great thoughts in us, and fits us for action; but there is nothing so appropriate and peculiar to mankind as the love and faculty of tracing out the truth, insomuch that we are no sooner at liberty from common cares and business but our heads are presently at work upon something to be either seen, or heard, or understood, accompting upon the knowledge of things wonderful and hidden as a necessary ingredient into a happy and a virtuous life. From whence may be drawn this conclusion, that whatsoever is true, simple, and sincere, is most congruous to the nature of man. This love of truth is accompanied with a desire of rule, so that a generous and well-qualified mind will never be brought into subjection unless either for learning or instruction sake, or in submission to a just and lawful governor for the common good. This elevation begets a contempt of fortune and dignity of spirit. And it is no small matter neither, the power of reasonable nature even in this respect, that man alone understands order, the bounds of decency in words and actions, and the terms of moderation; that only man is affected with the beauty, the gracefulness, and the symmetry of visible objects. Now, if Nature and reason take such care to convey the images, even

351

of sensible things, from the eye to the mind, how much a greater value must she set upon the grace and constancy of our manners, and the keeping such a guard upon all our words and deeds, that no unmanly thing, not a loose syllable or thought, escape us. This is the composition of that honesty we look for, which is nevertheless venerable for being little esteemed; for without any approbation from abroad, the whole earth cannot yet hinder it from being praiseworthy in its own nature. Oh! my son Marcus, we may fashion to ourselves some faint idea of virtue or wisdom, but if it could be presented to our eyes in its genuine lustre, how should we be transported (says Plato) with the love of it!

There is not any virtue whatsoever but arises from one or other of these four heads, and consists either, first, in the search and perception of the truth; or secondly, in the conservation of human society, giving every man his due, and keeping faith in all promises and contracts; or thirdly, in the greatness and force of a brave and invincible courage; or fourthly, in the order and measure of all our words and actions, according to the rules of modesty and temperance.

Now though these four virtues may be complicate and linkt together, there are yet certain distinct duties that issue severally from each of them; as the scrutiny and bolting out of a truth, from prudence, which is a faculty particularly appertaining to that virtue. For he that makes the best judgment of the truth of things, he that most readily finds the way to't, and gives the best account of the reason of it, we conclude him, without all dispute, to be the wisest man. So that effectually the proper subject of this virtue is truth. But the business of the other three virtues is to procure and maintain necessaries for the commodity of life, the upholding of communities and society, and to show the dignity of the mind, as well in the communicating of our fortunes as in the acquiring of them, and more yet (if there shall be occasion) in the despising of them. But order, constancy, moderation, and the like require something of action in concurrence with the operations of the mind; and he that would acquit himself in the course of his life with reputation and a good grace, must observe order and measure.

Of these four parts, into which we have divided the nature and the power of virtue, that which concerns the disquisition of truth holds most affinity with the soul of man. We are all of us both drawn and led to a desire of knowledge, and every man values himself upon being wiser than his neighbour; but on the other side, to fail, to wander, to be ignorant, and to be deceived, we look upon as a wretched and a reproachful thing.

In the pursuit of this most natural virtue, we must take heed of two mistakes: first, the taking up of things upon trust, and flattering ourselves that we know more than effectually we do. He that would keep clear of this rock (as every man should endeavour it) must diligently attend his business, and allow himself time to consider of it. The other in the bestowing of more pains and study upon things that are obscure, hard, and superfluous than the matter is worth, whereas, by avoiding these errors, and employing the same application upon profitable knowledge and the study of virtue, a man gains to himself deserved commendation. We have heard of Caius Sulpicius for his astrology, of Sextus Pompeius for his geometry, and of other persons eminent for logic and civil law, which sciences are all of them exercised in the investigation of truth; and yet for a man to divert himself by these studies from common offices and business, is against the nature of human duty. For the excellency of virtue lies in action, but yet not without intervals, for we must work and rest by turns. Not that the mind is ever idle, but still in a constant agitation of thought, even when the body is most at repose. And all the motions of it applied either to the deliberating and advising upon things honest and tending to a good and happy life, or upon the acquiring of wisdom and knowledge. And so much for prudence, which is the first fountain of virtue.

Of the other three virtues, we find that to be of the largest extent, which directs the ordering of men in society, and in a kind of community of life. Of this there are two parts: justice, which is the more glorious virtue, and entitles us to the very name and character of good men; and beneficence, which we may otherwise call liberality or bounty. The first duty of justice is this, that we hurt no man, unless provoked to it by an injury and in our own defence. We are then to distinguish betwixt things common and particular, and to use them accordingly. Not that anything is private in its own nature, but as it becomes so, either by ancient possession, as appropriated by the first occupant, or by conquest, upon the right of arms, or else by law, agreement, condition, or lot. From hence comes the field Arpinus to be called of the Arpinates, and Tusculanus to be called the field of the Tusculanes, and in like manner is it of private possessions. Now, since custom and usage have rendered many things private which Nature made common, let every man quietly enjoy his lot, and be reputed an enemy to the public if he attempt anything beyond it. But because (as Plato says singularly well) we are not born for ourselves alone, but for our country, our parents, and our friends: and with the Stoics, that the earth, and all the productions of it, were created for the use of man, and man only for man's sake begotten, that one might be helpful to another: what can we do better than to follow, where Nature is our guide? To lay common benefits in common, and by an intercourse of good offices, as giving and receiving, by arts, industry, and all our faculties, to incorporate mankind into one society.

The foundation of justice is faith, that is to say, a firmness and truth in our words, promises, and contracts. The Stoics that are great etymologists will have *fides* to be as much as *fiat*, and that is therefore called faith, *quia fit quod dictum est*, because that which is said is done. This may seem to be far-fetch'd, but however, we have taken the freedom to apply it.

There are two sorts of injustice: one is the immediate doing of an injury, and the other is the not protecting or defending the injured person for so much as in us lies. For he that injuriously offers violence to any man, either in his rage or any other passion whatsoever, may be taken to be in some degree constructively a murderer; and he that does not his best to save his neighbour from harm and to keep off the blow, is as well to blame (though not so much) as the deserter of his parents, his friends, his country, or his companions. Now there are many injuries done us, upon set purpose to hurt us, which arise yet from fear, as when he that watches to do another man mischief does it upon prevention for fear the other should hurt him. But the greater part of injuries are done with a design to compass something we have a mind to, wherein avarice has a very great share. As to the matter of riches, they are desired partly for our necessities and partly for our pleasures. The desire of money in great minds is to make an interest by it, and to get into our power the means of obliging. It was the saying of Crassus that he that would be uppermost in a commonwealth, could never have money enough till he was able to maintain an army at his own charge. There is a pleasure also in a splendid and magnificent appearance, rich furniture; and men take delight to live in reputation, glory, and plenty, which begets an insatiable thirst of money to maintain it. And yet we are not forbidden to advance or increase our fortunes, provided it be done without wrong to another, and by fair means. But men are apt to forget the rules and measures of justice when they come once to be transported with the desire of empire, high places, and titles. It goes a great way that saying of Ennius: "There is no faith or fellowship in empire." 'Tis a hard matter to preserve friendship and agreement in a case where there are many competitors and but one succeed, which manifestly appeared in that tempest which C. Caesar lately brought upon the government, who confounded heaven and earth, and overturned all laws divine and human for the compassing of that power which he vainly propounded to get wholly to himself. And great pity it is that this inordinate desire of honour, dominion, power, and glory does for the most famous wits and the largest minds, so that an error in this case is the more to be avoided.

Now in all injuries there is a great difference betwixt that which is done upon the sudden and in hot blood (which is commonly but short and transient) and that which is done upon forethought and counsel, for those in a heat are much lighter than those upon preparation; and this shall suffice of injuries offered or done.

Now why do we not protect and defend the oppressed, but abandon our duties, there may be several reasons. We are not willing to be at the charge or trouble; we are loth to make enemies; or, it may be, we are negligent, lazy, sluggish, taken up with particular studies, or hindered by business; and this makes us leave those exposed to ruin whom it is our duty to preserve. Wherefore we must take heed not to rest upon that which Plato observes of the philosophers, as if the studying and endeavouring to find out the truth, the vilifying and despising of the things that most men vehemently desire and quarrel about, entitled them presently to the character of honest men, not considering that while they are so just on the one side as to wrong nobody themselves, they are yet so unjust on the other as to leave other people to do it; and so, rather than quit their studies, they forsake their duties and their friends whom they ought to defend. And therefore, says he, they would have nothing to do with the community itself if they were not compelled by force, a thing which ought rather to be done by goodwill and by choice; for it is not the quality of the act, let it be never so right, but the intention of it, that makes the virtue. There are some that, either for saving of their own sake or out of an averseness even to dealing with mankind, cry, "Let every man look to his own business; I meddle with nobody." And all this to get the reputation of harmless people. These men, while they shun one injustice, they fall into another; for he that contributes neither study, labour, nor fortune to the public, is a deserter of the community. Now these two sorts of injuries being laid down, together with the causes of them, and having stated beforehand the bounds of justice, it will be no hard matter to assign unto every person and occasion its proper duty, if we be not over partial to ourselves; but in another body's case it is quite another matter, although Terence's *Chremes* will have every individual to be concerned in the common interest of mankind. But yet being more sensible and quicker-sighted in our own concerns than for the good or evil that befalls others (which we look upon as more remote), we pass upon the one and the other (though in the very same case) a quite different judgment. It is good advice, therefore, to forbear coming to a resolution where we doubt whether the thing be good or bad, for the right is as clear as the sun, but a wavering implies the deliberation of an injustice.

But it often falls out that the same thing which at one time would become a man of honour and justice would at another time not only vary, but prove the clear contrary: as the delivering up of a trust to a madman, or keeping promise with him. Nay, in matters of faith and truth, it is just in some cases to deny, and in others not to keep touch; for all must refer to those fundamentals of justice already propounded. At first, to wrong no man, and secondly, in all cases to consult the common good. So that the duty is not always the same, but changes with the occasion. Suppose such a promise or contract passed, as if it were performed would manifestly tend to the damage either of the party promising or of the person to whom the promise was passed to have it performed. If Neptune (as it is in the fable) had not made good his promise to Theseus, his son Hippolytus had been saved. The story goes, that of three wishes the last was in his passion the destruction of Hippolytus. And the grant of that request cast him into inconsolable sorrows; so that neither are we to keep those promises that are unprofitable to the promised, or more hurtful to the promiser than advantageous to the other. Of two evils we are to choose the less; as if I promise to plead any man's cause, and in the interim my son falls dangerously ill, it is no breach of faith or duty in me not to appear, but rather the contrary, and it were yet worse in him to whom the promise was made to complain of such disappointment. And now in matters where a man is under violence, or overawed by fear, or outwitted and over-reached by fraud, everybody knows that those promises are not binding, many of them being discharged in form by the Praetor's Court, and some by the very law itself.

There are several injuries that are merely matter of cavil, and only advantages taken by a crafty and malicious interpretation of the law. From whence comes that saying, "Extreme right is extreme wrong." The proverb is now worn threadbare. Of this sort there have been many practices, even upon a public score. One agreed upon a truce with the enemy for thirty days, and afterward made incursions upon him, and destroyed his country by night, because the cessation was for days, not nights. Neither can I justify our countryman if it be true. Q. Fabius Labeo (or somebody else, for I have it only upon hearsay) was by the Senate constituted arbitrator of the boundaries of Nola and Naples. When he came to the place he took the Commissioners apart and advised them in private not to do anything greedily, or to press too much, but rather to abate of their pretensions than to demand more, and prevailed so far upon them that there was a good space of ground left betwixt them, so that when they had marked out their bounds according to agreement, that which was left in the middle was adjudged to the Romans. This was rather a cheat than a judgment, and this indirect and crafty way of imposing should be avoided in all cases. There are certain duties to be observed also, even to those that do us the greatest wrong, for there must be a meaning in the very punishment and revenge; and I do not know whether it may be sufficient for the aggressor barely to repent of his injury without some penalty over and above, both for his own amendment and the terror and example of others.

The laws of war among all nations should be strictly and punctually observed. For since there are but two ways of contending — the one by dispute, the other by force; the one humane and the other brutal — we must of necessity have recourse to the latter where the former will not take place. Wherefore the end of war is to secure ourselves from violence in a state of peace, and in case of victory we should preserve those that behaved themselves with honour and generosity in the action of the war. As our ancestors received into the very privileges of the city the Tusculans, the Aequi, the Volsci, the Sabines, the Hernici; but Carthage and Numantia they wholly rased. I could wish they had spared Corinth, but they had a respect I suppose to the strength and situation of the place, and so destroyed it, that for the future it might not, some time or other, prove an encouragement to a revolt. In my opinion, peace should be always consulted where it may be had without treachery, and if my advice had been hearkened to in this matter we might yet at this day have had some sort of a republic, though not the best, whereas now we have just none at all. We should provide, likewise, not only for those that are overcome in the field, but for those also that threw down their arms and cast themselves upon the faith of the general. Nay, I would have an enemy received even after the battery is begun and the breach made. In which point we have been so scrupulously just that, according to the custom of our predecessors, those that took cities or nations conquered in war into the Roman allegiance were made patrons and protectors of what they took. And the rights of war are set forth with exact solemnity in the provisions of the Fetial Law, wherein we are given to understand that no war can be just and warrantable unless it be grounded upon some matter of claim, or denounced beforehand by proclamation. Popilius the General held a province, and a son of Cato's listed himself a soldier under his command. Popilius, finding it convenient to discharge one legion, Cato's son serving in that legion was also dismissed, but he continuing still in the army out of a love of action, his father wrote a letter to Popilius requesting him that if his son continued with him in arms he would give him the military oath over again, because his former sacrament being dissolved he could not otherwise justify his putting himself into the quarrel. Such was the reverence they bare even to the conscience of making war! There is extant an epistle of Marcus Cato the elder to his son Marcus, when he was a soldier in Macedonia in the Persian war. Wherein he tells his son that he heard the Consul had dismist him, and charges him not to engage in any combat, as a thing unlawful for him that was no longer a soldier to fight an enemy. It is remarkable the changing of the word Perduellis (a public enemy) into Hostis, to sweeten the foulness of the thing by the softness of the term. For *Hostis* (with our forefathers) was as much as *Peregrinus* (a stranger), as appears by the Twelve Tables: *Aut status dies cum Hoste.* And then, *Adversus hostem, aeterna auctoritas.* What can be gentler than to treat an enemy

357

in this easy language? Although custom, I must confess, has made it harsher by transferring the signification of it from that of a stranger to the proper denomination of one that bears arms against us. Nay, in the case of a war for honour or dominion, there must yet be the same causes and grounds before-mentioned to make it just, but still all contests of this kind must give fairer quarter, for (as in ordinary differences) we distinguish betwixt an enemy and a rival; our title and dignity lies at stake in the one case, but our life and reputation in the other. The war we had with the Celtiberi and the Cimbri (the Spaniards and Danes) was a war of enmity, and the question was not who should govern, but who should live. With the Latins, the Sabines, the Samnites, the Carthaginians, and with Pyrrhus the quarrel was empire. The Carthaginians were perfidious; Hannibal was cruel, but the rest more honourable. It was a glorious declaration that of Pyrrhus about the discharge of some prisoners, as we find it in Ennius —

> Let mercenaries truck and treat for gold;
> Honour's a thing not to be bought or sold.
> Courage and steel must end this glorious strife;
> And in the case of victory or life,
> Fortune's the judge. We'll take the chance of war.
> And what brave man soever she shall spare
> With life, depend upon't, I'll set him free,
> Let him but own the gift to the great gods and me.

This was a royal speech and resolution, and well becoming the blood of Aeacus.

But even in the case of a private promise, and upon what pinch or necessity soever, faith is yet to be kept, even with an enemy. When Regulus was taken prisoner in the first Punic war, and sent to Rome to solicit the exchange of some prisoners, upon his oath to return so soon as ever he came there, he advised the Senate against himself, and that they should not agree to the exchange. His friends and relations pressed him extremely against going back again, but he chose rather to return to the torture than to stay and break his faith to an enemy. In the second Punic war, after the battle of Cannae, Hannibal sent ten prisoners to Rome under an oath of returning, unless they could obtain the liberty of such and such prisoners in exchange. They were no sooner out of the camp, by Hannibal's permission, but one of them found out a shift to evade the oath, and presently went back under colour of something left behind him, and then returning, went his way as if the obligation of the oath had been discharged. And so it was in words, but not in effect; for in all promises the intention is to be considered, not the letter. The censor set a fine during life upon all their heads that were forsworn, and upon his among the rest that invented this shift. But the more generous instance of justice to an enemy was that of our ancestors in the case of Pyrrhus. There was a fugitive that made a proposal to the Senate for the poisoning and despatching of Pyrrhus, but the Senate and Fabricius delivered up the traitor to his master. Such was the detestation they had for treachery that they would not make use of it, though to the destruction of a powerful and an invading enemy. And so much for military duties.

We must not forget neither that toward the meanest of men also there is a justice to be observed, even in the condition and fortune of slaves; and it is good counsel to advise the using of them as hirelings, and for their work to allow them their reward. Now there are two ways of doing a man an injury; the one is by force, the other by fraud. The one is the quality of the fox, the other of the lion. They are neither of them proper for a man, but yet fraud is the more odious of the two; and of all injustices, that is the most abominable and capital which imposes upon us under the colour of kindness and good meaning. And this shall suffice for justice.

To pursue my purpose, I shall now handle the point of liberality, or bounty, than which there is nothing more accommodate to the nature of man; but it falls under many limitations. It should be our first care to see that what we give may not be to the disadvantage of the person we would oblige, or of any other body, and that it be not above our proportion. Secondly, that it be suited to the dignity of the receiver; for this is the foundation of justice, to which all the circumstances of it are to be referred. He that pretends to gratify any man with that which is rather to his damage than to his benefit, is so far from deserving the reputation of being liberal or bountiful, that he is to be accounted as the most pernicious of flatterers. And those also that rob one man to give to another are guilty of the same injustice with them that take money out of their neighbours' pockets to put into their own. There are many people that look big and set up for men of honour that yet have this humour of taking from one and giving to another, and reckon upon it as a high piece of bounty if they can but advance the fortunes of a friend upon what terms soever; but this is so far from a good office that it is the clear contrary. Let us, therefore, so govern our favours that we may oblige those we love, and yet hurt nobody. Shall we call it liberality in L. Sulla and C. Caesar, the translation of so many estates from the right owners into the possession of strangers? There can be no liberality in a case of injustice. The second caution is the keeping of our bounty within compass, and not to give beyond our ability; for they that extend their kindnesses beyond this measure, wrong their relations by transferring those bounties to strangers which they should rather have communicated or left to their friends. This humour of liberality is commonly accompanied with a certain greediness that makes no scruple of getting anything, though by rapine or injury, so they may but have wherewithal to supply a mistaken bounty. Nay, there are many that give largely merely to be thought bountiful, and this only upon a score of vanity, without any frankness of heart, which is rather a flash of ostentation than an act of generosity and virtue. The third caution is the making choice of a worthy person; wherein we should consider the morals of the man that we would oblige, his particular disposition towards us, our intercourse with him in a community and society of life, and the good offices he hath already done us. It would be well if we could find a concurrence of all these; but if not, the more inducements we have, and the greater they are, the more is their weight.

Howbeit, since we do not live with men absolutely perfect, either for virtue or wisdom, but with those that acquit themselves very well, if they can but arrive at some faint resemblances of virtue, let this be also taken into consideration, that no man whatsoever is to be neglected in whom there appears the least sign or glimmering of goodness. But still we are to set the greatest value upon him that we find best endowed with the soft and gentle virtues of modesty, temperance, and that justice of which we have already spoken at large. For a bold and manly courage in a man that is neither good nor wise is commonly more forward and eager, perhaps, than is convenient. The other are more properly the virtues of a good man. And so much for our manners.

Touching the goodwill that any man bears us, it is first our duty to do much good where we are much beloved; but then we are not to express that affection in a childish ardour and fondness of passion, but in a constancy and firmness of mind.

In the case of an antecedent merit, where we are not now to enter into an obligation but to acknowledge and require it, there must be a more than ordinary care taken; for gratitude is the most indispensable of all duties. If Hesiod bids us restore what we borrow, if we can, in a larger measure, what ought we to do in the case of a prior obligation? Are we not to imitate fruitful lands, that still return more than they received? We are ready enough to oblige those that we hope to be the better for hereafter; how should we behave ourselves, then, toward such as we are the better for already? Since so it is that there are two sorts of liberality (the one of bestowing a benefit, and the other of returning it) it is at our choice whether we will give or no; but an honest man is not at liberty in the point of returning it, provided that it may be done without injury. And yet we are to distinguish also betwixt benefits received, and the greater the benefit the greater is the obligation. Now the obligation is to be valued according to the mind, the intention, and goodwill of the giver; for many people do many things rashly, without either judgment or measure. They squander away their donatives indifferently upon all, carried on by sudden and impetuous passions, as if they were driven by the wind. Now these benefits are not so much to be esteemed as those that are conferred with steadiness and consideration. As to the placing of our bounties and returning of acknowledgments (supposing other things to be equal), it is our duty to help him first that is most in want, though most people do the contrary; for they are there most officious to offer their service where they hope for most again, though in cases where their help was not at all needful.

For the preservation of society and good correspondence among men, we should do well to proportion our bounties to our relations, and to give most to those that are our nearest friends. But for those principles of Nature, which regard communities and human society, they must be fetched higher, as the first thing that we take notice of in the fellowship of mankind. Reason and speech are the bond of it which, by teaching, learning communicating, disputing, and judging, accommodate one man to another, and cement the whole body into a kind of natural community. Nor is there anything wherein we are further removed from beasts than in this advantage of society. It is usual for us to speak of courage and boldness in lions and horses, but we hear nothing of either justice, equity, or goodness in them; and the business is that they have neither speech nor reason. This society of one man with another, and of all with all — this society, I say, general and particular, is of a large extent; and herein there must be a community preserved of all those things which Nature hath brought forth for the common use of men, provided always that such things as are limited by laws and civil ordinances may be observed according to the constitution. As to the rest, they may be reduced to the Greek proverb, "Friends have all things in common." Now all those things that men hold in community are such as, Ennius having laid down in one instance, may be applied to many.

> To put a wand'ring traveller in's way
> Is but to light one candle with another:
> I've ne'er the less for what I give.

From this one case we may learn, that whatsoever we may part with to another without any damage to ourselves, it is our duty to give or to lend freely, though to a stranger. Of this sort we reckon many things to be in common, as water from a river, fire from fire, good counsel to a man that is in doubt or distress. All these things are profitable to the receiver, without any loss or burthen to the giver. So that we may both use these things ourselves, and yet be still contributing of somewhat to the common good. But in regard that particular persons

361

have not much to give, and the number of those that want is almost infinite, common liberality must have a respect to that end of Ennius. We must keep wherewithal to give light to ourselves, that we may have the means of being bountiful to our own.

To descend now from human society, in the latitude of which there are many degrees, there is a nearer bond yet betwixt people of the same province, the same nation, and the same language; and it is yet stricter betwixt men of the same city, for among citizens there are many things in common, as courts of justice, temples, walks, ways, lanes, customs, judgments, suffrages, beside frequent meetings and familiarities, common business, commerce, and contract. And there is yet a nearer tie, and that is the society of kindred, which is contracted into a narrow place, apart from the vast society of mankind. It is by nature common to all living creatures, the appetite of producing the kind: and the first society is in wedlock, the next in children; it comes then to a family and a community of all things. And this is the original of a city, and, as it were, the seminary of a commonwealth. The relation of brothers comes next, and after that of brothers' and sisters' children, who, when they are too many for one house, are transplanted into others, as into colonies. And then follow matches and alliances, with increase of kindred, and their off-spring is the beginning of a commonwealth. There is no doubt but relation of blood, and the kindness that arises from it, must necessarily endear men to one another. For it is a great matter to have the same pedigree, to exercise the same religion, and to deposit their ashes in common sepulchres; but of all associations there is none so firm, none so noble, as when virtuous men are linked together by a correspondency of manners and a freedom of conversation. For such is the charm of that honesty which we have often spoken of, that the very encounter of it moves us, though in a stranger, and makes us friends to the possessor of it, wherever we find it. Now, though all virtue whatsoever is of itself amiable and attractive, insomuch that we cannot but have an esteem for those that we find possessed of it, yet justice and liberality gain upon us in a higher degree. But there is nothing more lovely or more engaging than a conformity and agreement of good manners. For where there are the same inclinations, the same desires, and the same will, the one cannot choose but be delighted with the other, as with its proper self; and it effects that which Pythagoras requires in friendship, the making one of many. And it is a great obligation that is created by the reciprocation of benefits that pass forward and backward in exchange, which, being mutual and grateful, must needs, upon the intercourse, produce firm and extraordinary friendship. But when ye shall have looked over all the ties in nature, as far as your mind and your reason can carry you, you will find nothing dearer, no obligation of greater importance, than that by which we are every one of us tied to the commonwealth. Our parents, children, kindred, acquaintance, are all dear to us; but our single country is more than all the rest, and every honest man is ready to lay down his life for the advantage of that sacred interest. How execrable then is the barbarous impiety of those people that have torn their country to pieces by all sorts of villainy, and who not only have been, but are at this instant, conspiring the destruction of it by a final desolation? But if there should be any dispute or comparison where to pay our duty, in the first place, our country and our parents are the principals, to whose benefits we are the most obliged. Our children and our families are next, as depending upon us alone, without any other retreat. After these our friends and relations, which are commonly of our own rank and condition. Wherefore we owe the necessary helps of life to these before-mentioned; but for conversation, table-society, counsels, exhortations, consolation, and (upon occasion) reproofs, these things are found most amongst friends; and let me tell you over again, the pleasantest friendship is that which is contracted by a similitude of manners.

Now in the exercise of all these duties we should observe what every man has most need of, and what with our help he may, and what without our help he cannot, attain; and in some cases there is a respect to be had to times and occasions even before relations. There are some offices that we should rather pay to one than to another: as I would sooner help a neighbour in with his harvest than either a brother or familiar acquaintance, but in a suit of law I'll defend my kinsman or my friend before my neighbour. Wherefore these circumstances, and the like, should be duly considered in all offices. By custom and exercise we shall become good accomptants, for it is by adding and subtracting that we come to know what remains, and consequently, in all cases, the bounds and limits of our duty; but as neither physicians, nor commanders, nor orators, though never so well instructed in the rules of their profession, shall ever be able without use and practice to make themselves eminently famous, to the same end are the precepts of human duties delivered us that we should put them in exercise; but yet the difficulty and condition of the thing does over and above require it. Now in what manner that virtue is derived, and whence that duty arises, which falls under the consideration of sociable rights and common justice, we have almost said enough already.

In the propounding of four general heads from whence all virtues and duties flow, that which is done with a noble and exalted mind — a mind advanced to the contempt of fortune and worldly things — that virtue, I say, ought to be reputed the most glorious, and therefore that reproach of Ennius's is always at hand upon occasion —

Young men in show, but wenches in your hearts,
While Claelia plays the brave and acts your parts.
You're for exploits that cost no sweat, nor blood.

And, on the other side, with what transport and rapture do we extol the humour of brave and generous actions? From hence comes that field of the rhetoricians upon Marathon, Salamis, Plataea, Thermopylae, Leuctra; and from hence it is that our Cocles, the Decii, the two Scipios, Marcellus, and a world of others, especially the Romans themselves, are grown so famous for the greatness of their minds; and their ambition of military honour may appear in this, that almost all the statues they have left us are dressed up in armour.

And yet that elevation of courage which is seen in hazards and adventures, unless accompanied with justice, and contending rather for the public than for itself, that courage, I say, is so far from being a virtue, that it is a fault, and a brutal ferity inconsistent with the tenderness of human nature. Wherefore the Stoics have well defined it, in calling courage a virtue, contending for equity. Nor did any man ever gain the reputation of true valour by treachery or malice. Nothing can be honest but what is just, and therefore it was notably said of Plato. As that knowledge, says he, which is divided from justice, is rather craft than wisdom, so that courage which is bold and adventurous is rather temerity and foolhardiness than valour, if it be carried on by passion or interest rather than for a common good. Wherefore all men of valour and great undertakings should be likewise men of goodness, simplicity, candour, and friends of truth, which are all inseparable from justice. But the mischief is, that this tumour and elation of mind breaks out many times into a pertinacy and an ambitious desire of rule. For as Plato has it, the Lacedaemonians were naturally inflamed with an ardent desire of overcoming; so that whosoever has the greatest soul is the most addicted to aspiring thoughts, and to set himself above all, or, in truth, rather to stand alone. It is a very hard matter for a man to observe the tenor of true equity (which peculiarly belongs to justice) in the inordinate appetite of superiority and dominion. From whence it comes to pass that such men will not be governed either by reason or any public and lawful constitution. This humour starts factions in a commonwealth, that work by bribery and corruption to advance their power and their fortunes, whose business it is rather to make themselves greater by violence than to keep themselves in a station of equality by justice. But the harder anything is, the fairer it is; nor is there any time or season that can dispense a man from justice. Wherefore those are truly brave and magnanimous that keep off an injury, not those that offer it. He that is truly wise and stout places that virtue which is most consonant to nature in action and not in glory, and in making himself

364

more considerable than other men rather than appearing so. No man can be said to be truly heroic, that depends for his reputation upon the opinion of the multitude. But every man, the higher his stomach is, and the greater his thirst of honour, the more easily is he transported to do unjust things. He stands upon a slippery place; for where is the man who, after all his hazards and travels, does not desire and expect glory as a reward of his adventures?

You shall know a man of generosity and courage chiefly by these two marks. First, he despises outward things upon an opinion that a man should not admire, wish for, or desire anything but what is becoming and honest, nor subject himself to any person, passion or fortune. The other is a disposition of mind (as is said before) that spurs a man to attempt things great and profitable; but difficult, laborious, and dangerous, as well in the matter of life itself as in other conveniences that belong to it. All the splendour and reputation (and let me say, the profit also) of these two things rests in the latter, but the cause and the motive is in the former; for there is the rise and spring of great resolves that carry men above the consideration of anything that is below. The thing itself is seen in two particulars: first, in judging that only to be good which is honest; and, secondly, in a freedom of the mind from all perturbations. For it must be confessed to be the part of a brave and generous mind to look upon those as little things which many account to be great and glorious, and to contemn them upon the foundation of a firm and settled judgment. It is likewise the part of a constant and invincible mind so to bear all sorts of calamity and affliction, as neither to depart from the order of Nature nor to descend below the dignities of a wise man. How incongruous is it for a man that stands the shock of danger to be broken with lust, or to endure the fatigue of labour and then to be overcome with pleasure! This must therefore be avoided, and so must the greedy desire of money. There is not a greater argument of a narrow and wretched mind than to dote upon pelf; nothing more humane and honourable than to despise it if we have it not, and to employ it generously and do good with it if we have it. And so for the affectation of glory. We must beware of it (as is said already), for it bars a man of his liberty, which a brave man will rather die than part with. We should not be solicitous neither for power, which in some cases we should not receive, and in others we should lay down. We must deliver ourselves from all disorders of mind, either by fear or appetite; and likewise from all sourness and transport, either of delight or of wrath, that we may be calm and secure; in which state we shall find both steadiness and credit. There are at this day, and there have been many, that to gain this repose have wholly withdrawn themselves from public business. Among these, the noblest and most eminent of philosophers, and men truly of great severity and weight, who could neither endure the people nor government; and so retired into deserts and retreats to live privately with themselves. And these men, in this recess, had the same design with princes (whose privilege is to live as they list) that they might want nothing, but enjoy their freedom without control. Wherefore, since both those that affect power, and the other idle people that I speak of, aim at the same thing and have this in common betwixt them; the one thinks they may gain their end if they had but ample fortunes, and the other, theirs, if they can but be content with their own, and with a little. They may be both (for ought I know) in some measure in the right. But it must yet be allowed that a private and retired life is both easier and safer, and less importune and troublesome to others. But the life of those that apply themselves to public business is more profitable to mankind, and more conducing to the acquisition of honour and reputation in the world. Wherefore, there is something to be said for those excellent wits that dedicate themselves to letters without meddling in public affairs, and also for such other, as either for want of health, or perhaps some more powerful impediment, have quitted their public stations, being well satisfied that others should enjoy the power and the credit of the employment. But for those that have none of this pretence to talk of despising Government and Offices which most people have in great estimation, I do not only not approve of them but take them to be much to blame. Not that I disallow of their judgment in the little consideration they seem to have for glory, but because they are manifestly afraid of the labours, troubles, repulses and displeasures that they are to encounter. For there are many that behave themselves unequally in contrary cases; severe contemners of pleasure, but they sink under pain; regardless of fame, but dejected with scandal. Nor are they steady, even in these very cases. But for those that are by nature fitted and qualified for civil business, I should advise these people to apply themselves to it without delay, and to take some commission in the government. For this is necessary, both as to public administration and to show the greatness of the mind. And public officers, as much perhaps as philosophers themselves (if not more), should be affected with a general disdain of external things (as I have often said), and stated in an immovable tranquility and security of mind which will deliver them from all anxiety for things to come, and establish them in a life of constancy and honour. Now this point is by so much easier for a philosopher to gain, by how much his life is less exposed to the stroke of fortune; for there are not many things that he stands in need of; beside, that in case of any disaster his fall is not so dangerous. It is but reasonable therefore to conclude that men in great and public places are exposed to greater perturbations of thought than those that live in privacy and repose. So that a greater stock of courage is there necessary, and a mind at liberty from trouble and care. But for him that puts himself into business, let him first consider the honesty of the employment, and then his own abilities to go through with it. Wherein let him neither rashly despair out of heartlessness and sloth, nor be over confident neither in the opinion of himself. But in all matters of business a man should diligently prepare himself before he goes about it.

But since most men take military charges to be of a greater consideration than civil, this opinion should be a little qualified. For it is a very common thing for men to apply themselves to that course of life, out of an itch of glory, and this happens most frequently in men of large souls and abilities; especially where the genius lies that way, and the disposition carries them to the profession of arms. But if we would deal impartially, there have been greater and more glorious things done in the Senate than in the field; for although Themistocles be worthy of all honour, and his name and memory more illustrious than that of Solon, Salamis being still mentioned as a memorial of his noble victory over Xerxes, which is still preferred before the counsel of Solon for the institution of the Areopagites: this must not at all give way to that, for the one did once deliver, preserve, and help the city, but the other will ever do it. This council preserves the laws of Athens, and constitutions of their ancestors. Themistocles cannot say that ever he helped Areopagus, but the other may truly boast of serving Themistocles; for Solon was the founder of that Senate which managed the war. And so for Pausanias and Lysander: It is true that their actions and conduct enlarged the territories of the Lacedaemonians, and yet the laws of Lycurgus are incomparably to be preferred. Nay, and upon that very consideration, their armies were both readier and bolder. It was my opinion, even when I was a boy, that Marcus Scaurus was not inferior to Caius Marius; and when I came afterwards into public business I looked upon Q. Catulus not one jot below Cnaeus Pompeius. For what signifies armies abroad without counsel at home? Neither did Africanus (though an excellent man, as well as a great captain) do the commonwealth a nobler service in the rasing of Numantia than Pub. Nasica (a private man) did at the same time in cutting off Tiberius Gracchus. Now this instance is not purely civil, but in some respect military, because it was done by a violent hand; but still it was done by a civil council, and without an army. It was a memorable saying of mine, that is so often cast in my teeth by a sort of malicious and envious people —

> Let swordsmen to the gown give place,
> And crown the orator with bays.

To pass over other instances; did not the sword give place to the gown when the commonwealth was under my administration? Never was there a more malicious conspiracy, and yet by the influence of our diligence and counsel how quickly was it crushed; insomuch that the very arms themselves fell out of the hands of the most audacious of the mutineers. When was there ever any action done in the field or any triumph comparable to it? This boast to you, my son, that are to inherit the honour of my actions, and to whom I would recommend the imitation of them. This boast to you, I say, may be allowed me. Nor is it any more than Cn. Pompey (a man laden with military honours) ascribed to me in a full audience. My third triumph, says he, would have been to little purpose if Cicero, by preserving the commonwealth, had not left me a place wherein to triumph; so that domestic and civil resolution is not inferior to military; and it requires more pains and study to be employed upon it. That virtue without dispute, which we look for from a high and illustrious mind, is acquired by the force of the soul, not of the body; and yet the body is still to be kept in exercise, and so affected as to obey the dictates of counsel and reason in the despatch of business, and in the bearing of toil. But the honesty here in question is wholly placed in the care and consideration of the mind, wherein the men of the robe in civil administration bring no less advantage to the public than those that bear arms. For war is many times either not begun or otherwise finished by their advice, nay, and some brought on too, as the third Punic War of M. Cato was, where his authority prevailed even when he was dead. Wherefore the faculty of determining is more desirable than that of contending; always provided that we steer not our course rather by an aversion to war than a consideration to benefit. In the undertaking of a war there should be such a prospect as if the only end of it were peace. It is the part of a valiant and a resolute man not to be discomposed in disasters, or to make a bustle, and be put beside himself, but to maintain a presence of mind and judgment without departing from reason. As this is the mark and effect of a great courage, so is the other of an excellent understanding, to forecast in our thoughts the events of things to come, and to weigh beforehand the good and the bad, and what's to be done when it happens without being put to the foolish exclamation of, Who would have thought it? These are the works of an elevated soul that supports itself upon prudence and judgment; but he that rashly thrusts himself into dangers without fear or wit, and engages an enemy hand over head, this is only brutality and outrage; but yet when the time comes, and necessity requires it, let a man fight with his sword in his hand, and rather lose his life than his honour and freedom.

In the case of rasing or demolishing of cities, there should be great care taken that nothing be done either headily or cruelly. It is the part of a great man in public broils to punish the guilty, but still to spare the multitude; and in all conditions to adhere to that which is right and honest.

There are some that esteem feats of arms above civil administrations (as is aforesaid), and there are others that think it more estimable to deal in dangerous and crafty, than in quiet and considerate counsels. We must never in such manner avoid dangers as to appear weak and faint-hearted; and we must likewise have a care, on the other side, not to thrust ourselves into unnecessary hazards, which is one of the greatest follies in the world. Wherefore in difficult cases we should do like physicians, that apply gentle remedies to gentle diseases; but in cases of extremity, a desperate disease must have desperate cure. None but a madman will wish for a storm in fair weather; but it is yet the part of a wise man to weather it the best he can if he falls into a tempest. And the honour is so much the more if the advantage of the success be greater than the miscarriage.

Actions are dangerous, partly to the undertakers and in part to the commonwealth. Some run the hazard of their lives, some of their good names, and others of the love of the people. Now we should more frankly venture ourselves than the public, and more cheerfully expose ourselves for honour and reputation than for other commodities. Some there are that make no scruple of hazarding their lives and fortunes in the defence of their country, and yet are so nice and scrupulous in the matter of reputation, that rather than run any risk of their honour they will leave their very country in danger. As Callicratidas, the Lacedaemonian general in the Peloponnesian War, after many glorious exploits ruined all at last by not removing the navy from the Arginusae, and making his retreat without giving the Athenians battle, as he was advised to do; to which he made this answer, that if the Lacedaemonians lost one fleet, they might set out another, but that if he quitted his ground his honour was lost for ever. But the Lacedaemonians, however, might have borne this loss, whereas the other blow was mortal; when Cleombrotus, for fear of an ill report, unadvisedly engaged with Epaminondas, where the whole power of the Lacedaemonians was cut off at a blow. How much better now was the conduct of Q. Fabius Maximus, of whom Ennius —

Fabius was slow, but sure, and his delay
Restored the tottering State. Now it was his way
To mind his business, not what people said:
He lived a great man, but he's greater dead.

This is an error of a quality to be avoided also in civil matters. For there are many that dare not speak their opinions, though for the best reason, for fear of falling under evil tongues.

There are two precepts of Plato to be observed by all men of authority in the government. The one is in some sort to assert and defend the public interest, that all their actions should refer to that, without any regard to their own advantage. The other is, to attend the service of the whole in such sort, that while they are serving one part they do not abandon another. It is in the administration of a government as in the case of a ward: the commission has a regard to the benefit of those that are delivered up in charge, and not those to whom such a charge or care is committed. But they that provide for one part of the people and neglect another, bring into a city the most pernicious thing in the world — that is to say, discord and sedition; and when they are split into parties, some side with the people, others with the nobility, but none mind the whole. This wrought great mischiefs among the Athenians; and in our republic not only sedition, but the most pestilent civil wars. A course not to be endured by a sober and valiant patriot, or any man that deserves a place in the government; for such a man will apply himself wholly to the care of the public, without designing either upon wealth or power to himself, and in such manner defend the whole that he also provide for every part of it. Neither will he bring any man into envy or hatred by calumny or subornation, but resolutely adhere to justice and honesty; maintaining his post in spite of all opposition, and rather die than desert the aforesaid duties.

Ambition or the thirst of honour is a wretched thing, of which Plato says very well, they that strive who shall be uppermost in the republic do as if mariners should contend which should be at the helm. And he tells us further, that we are to account those for enemies that take up arms against the commonwealth and not such as with honesty and judgment labour to defend it. This was the controversy betwixt P. Africanus and Q. Metellus, without any sort of bitterness.

Give no ear to those that take it to be the part of a brave and resolute man to be violently angry with an enemy, for there is nothing more commendable or better becoming a generous person than clemency and good nature. Nay, towards a free people, where all are liable to the law, we should join a facility with that which we call height of courage, least if we should accustom ourselves to transports upon unseasonable addresses or shameful importunities, we should fall into a humour of morose and unprofitable sourness; provided that with these soft and gentle ways we use severity also where the public requires it, for without that a city can never be kept in order.

All reproof and correction let it be without contumely, as being directed only to the profit of the commonwealth, without regard to the gratifying of his passion or interest that gives either the words or the blows. And the punishment likewise should be proportioned to the fault, for it is unjust that one man should have blows, and another not so much as a check for the same transgression. But above all things, correction is not to be given in anger, for a man in passion will never observe the due mean betwixt the two extremes of too much and too little; wherein the peripatetics are much in the right, if they would not also approve of anger given us by Nature for our advantage. But I am for the avoiding of it in all cases; and I could wish that magistrates, like the laws themselves, would never proceed to punish in wrath, but only in equity.

Let us also in prosperity, and when we have the world at will, as much as possible avoid pride, disgust of everything, and arrogance; for it is the same levity to be transported either with good fortune or with bad. And it is an excellent thing to observe an equal tenor of life, and to have still the same humour and the same countenance, as we find it recorded of Socrates and C. Laelius. Philip of Macedon was outstript by his son in glorious achievements and military execution, but in gentleness and humanity of manners Alexander came short of him; so that the one of them was always great, and the other was many times intemperate and brutal. 'Tis good advice that bids us the higher we are to be the more humble. Panaetius tells us of Africanus (his disciple and familiar friend) how he was wont to say, that as we put out horses of service to riders for the training them and making them fitter for use, when they are grown fierce and unmanageable by being chafed and heated by the action of the battle; so should we commit men that are transported with prosperity, and over-confident in themselves, to some guide that should keep them, as it were, in the ring, or within the bounds of reason and good government, to make them understand the uncertainty of human affairs and the changes of fortune. It is in the height of our prosperity that we should chiefly consult our friends, and allow them more authority over us than at other times; but we must have a care of entertaining flatterers, and of being imposed upon by fair words, wherein we are too easy to be mistaken. For such is the conceit we commonly have of ourselves that we think no commendation more than we deserve. From this weakness there arise innumerable errors; for when we come once to be blown up with praises and high opinions of ourselves we do but serve to make sport for others, and labour under grievous mistakes. And so much for this point.

Their business that governs commonwealths must of necessity be of the greatest moment and require the largest souls, because it has the largest prospect and concerns most people. This is to be given for granted; and yet it must not be denied neither, on the other side, that

371

great generosity of mind has been many times shown in a private life, either in the search or attempt of great matters, and the people yet keeping themselves within their own bounds, or else mingling with philosophers and men in public business, contenting themselves in their private condition; neither scraping together estates by all manner of ways, nor debarring their friends from the use of what they had, but rather dividing with them and with the Republic where there was occasion. Now for this estate let it be, first, well gotten, and neither by shameful nor by odious ways; let a man next do good with it to as many as he can (so they be worthy); let him increase it with prudence, diligence, and good husbandry; and let him rather indulge liberality and bounty than luxury and lust. He that observes these rules may live soberly, splendidly, and generously, and no less candidly, faithfully, and amicably with all men.

We are now to speak of the remaining part of duty, wherein bash-fulness and a certain gracefulness of life, temperance, modesty, the composure of all perturbations of the mind, and moderation are to be considered. Here it is that we find that same decorum, or, as the Greeks, *prepon,* which is of so excellent a nature that it is inseparable from virtue; for whatsoever is decent is likewise honest, and whatsoever is honest is becoming. But still there is a difference betwixt this same honesty and decorum which may be better understood than explained; for that which becomes us does only then appear when honesty is gone before.

Now this decorum does not only appear in the virtue now in question, but also in the three former. For the right and prudent use of reason and speech, the doing of everything considerately, the finding out of truth and the defending of it, looks well in any man; as, on the other side, to be deceived, to mistake, to slip, to be imposed upon, is as misbecoming as if a man were in a fit of dotage or out of his wits. And so whatsoever is just is also graceful; and whatsoever is unjust or dishonest is likewise misbeseeming. And the same rule holds in fortitude, for whatsoever is done generously, and like a man of courage, cannot but be graceful too, and well-becoming a man, and the contrary as reproachful and misbecoming. Wherefore the decorum I here speak of appears likewise in all other virtues, and does in such manner appertain to them, that it lies open, and there needs no mystery to the finding of it out. There is in all virtue somewhat that is graceful, and only separable from virtue by imagination. As the gracefulness and beauty of the body cannot well be separated from health; and so it is with the gracefulness here in question. It is a decorum that is in a manner so confused with virtue, that it is incorporated with it, but in the mind and conception it may be distinguished. And there are of it two sorts. The one is a certain general decorum, that shines in all virtues, and there is another that is subject to this, or dependent upon it, which respects every virtue in particular. The former is commonly defined to be a decorum congruous to the excellency of man, in that which differences man from other living creatures. But the special decorum, as dependent upon the general, they define to be a quality so congruous to Nature, that moderation and temperance appear in it, with the very image of a generous soul. This we may judge to be the decorum which the poets observe, whereof we have spoken more in another place. But we are then said to observe the strict decorum of the poets, when every word and action is fitted to the dignity and condition of the person. As what could be more improper and unseemly than to bring in these just judges, Aeacus and Minos, with these words in their mouths, Let them hate, so they fear; or, The father is the grave of his own children. And yet when Atreus says it, what acclamations are there, because the expression suits with the person! But Nature herself, as to us, has given every man his part with great excellency and advantage over other living creatures. So that the poets will see to the accommodating of all parts to the variety of persons, even the observing of decorum towards the worst of men as well as the best. But since Nature has assigned us our parts of constancy, moderation, temperance, modesty; and the same nature teaches us not to be wholly careless how we demean ourselves toward one another; it is clear to us how far that decorum extends that belongs to every virtue, and every kind of honesty. For as the beauty of the body, with an apt disposition of the parts, proves the eye and delights us in the very correspondence, symmetry, and apt disposition of the parts, so this decorum, that illustrates life, gains upon all those we conserve with, by the order, steadiness, and moderation of all our words and deeds. Wherefore there should a certain reverence be used toward all men, both high and low, for 'tis the humour of an arrogant and dissolute man not to care what the world says of him. But there's a great difference betwixt justice and modesty, upon all accounts. It belongs to justice not to wrong men, and to modesty not to offend them; wherein the power and virtue of a decorum does most eminently appear. This is enough said, I suppose, to make it understood what is intended by that which we call a decorum.

The duty that proceeds from it is chiefly to preserve ourselves in a conformity to Nature, a guide that will never mislead us, but conduct those that follow her to all acuteness and perspicacity of understanding, to the best means of uniting men in society to that which is strong and manly. But the mighty power of gracefulness is in that part which we are now upon; for not only the motions of the body, according to Nature, are to be allowed, but the motions of the mind likewise much more.

The force and nature of the mind is twofold. One part is placed in the appetite — the Greeks call it *hormé* — that carries a man hither and thither; the other in reason, that teaches us and explains to us what to do and what to avoid, by which means our appetite shall be kept obedient to our reason. In all cases we should have a care of rashness and negligence, and do nothing but what we can give a fair account of. This is in some degree the image and description of duty; but then we must so order it that the appetite follow the dictate of reason, so as neither rashly to outrun it, nor out of heaviness and sloth to desert it, but keep it quiet and calm, and free from all perturbation. This will make us eminent for constancy and moderation; for those appetites that wander from the rule, and skip from one thing to another, either by coveting or avoiding — those appetites, I say, for want of being governed by reason, will without all question pass bounds and measure, for they relinquish and cast off their allegiance to reason, which they ought to obey by the law of Nature, and their ill effects are imprinted not only upon our minds but also visibly upon our bodies. As in the transports of wrath, lust, fear, pleasure, what an alteration is there of countenance, voice, motion, gesture; from whence we may collect how necessary it is to moderate and govern our passions, and so to keep ourselves upon a guard that we do nothing heedlessly, or as it were by chance, without care or consideration. For man was never made for levity and pleasure, but rather for the severity of grave and weighty studies. Not that we are to be debarred the freedom of frolics and divertissements, provided that we use them only as sleep, and such other ways of repose, after the discharge of our serious and more important duties. And our very liberties in discourse must not be profuse neither, nor immodest, but only candid and facetious; for as we do not allow our children all sorts of games, but only such sports as hold some proportion with honest actions, so in raillery itself there must be a mixture of candour as well as understanding.

There are two sorts of raillery or mirth: the one is coarse, petulant, criminal, and foul; the other cleanly, gracious, ingenuous, and facetious. In which kind not only Plautus and the Greek comedians, but the followers of Socrates, have written much, and stuffed their books with a great many of their saying and conceits, as Cato's collection of apothegms, &c. Now 'tis an easy matter to distinguish betwixt a coarse and a cleanly way of jesting. The one is a word in season, only for recreation, and worthy of a man of honour; the other not fit for an honest man, especially where filthy things are delivered in as unclean words.

Nay, in our very recreations we should keep within compass, and have a care that we do not lash out into excesses and pass the limits of modesty in the transports of our pleasures. The chase of wild beasts, and the military and manly exercises that are practised in our field, or *Campus*

374

Martius, these I reckon to be honourable pleasures, and we need never want these ways of diversion.

But whatever we do, it should be always in our thought the excellency of human nature above that of brutes, which are only pushed on by violent appetites to sensual pleasures; whereas the entertainment of a man's mind is learning and meditation, which is never idle, but still employed either upon inquiry or action, and charmed with a delight that arises from what we hear or see. Nay, the very man himself that is most addicted to his pleasures (if he has but the soul of a man in him, and not only the name without the effect, for such there are), though he may be overcome by his lusts, he yet stands so right as to be ashamed of, to conceal, and to disguise his love of those pleasures even for modesty sake, which shows that the pleasures of the body are not worthy of the dignity of the soul, but rather contemptible and to be rejected. But if any man shall be found to have a great regard for pleasures, let him be sure to use them with moderation. In our very clothes and diet we should still keep an eye rather to matter of health and strength than to the humouring of the fancy or palate; and if we shall but duly weigh and examine the dignity and excellency of Nature, we shall quickly find how shameful a thing it is to dissolve in a luxurious softness and delicacy, and how becoming, on the other side, to live frugally, temperately, gravely, and soberly.

Every man must be understood to be invested with two capacities, the one common to mankind, as endued with reason, and in a preference to beasts, from whence we do not only derive the knowledge of decency and virtue, but the very means of finding out our several duties; the other is a propriety that has a respect particularly to individuals. There is a great difference in bodies: one man is better for a course, another for a scuffle: and so in beauties; one beauty is imperious and majestical, another charming. Now there are at least as great diversities and varieties in our minds. L. Crassus and L. Philippus were both of them of a nature wonderfully gentle and gracious; and both these qualities were yet more eminent and more laboured, too, in C. Caesar, the son of Lucius. There was a strange austerity of humour in M. Scaurus and M. Drusus; and in the same time, and as yet in their youth too. C. Laelius was gay and pleasant; his friend Scipio more ambitious and reserved. It is reported that Socrates, among the Greeks, was a gentle and a pleasant companion; a wit that lay much upon innocent raillery, and had an excellent faculty of speaking his mind under an agreeable disguise. Pythagoras, on the other side, and Pericles, advanced themselves without any gaiety of humour at all. Among the Carthaginians, Hannibal, and among our own commanders, Q. Maximus, have the name of men extremely close and secret, silent, dissembling; notably good at stratagems, or setting spies upon an enemy, and disappointing their counsels. Those that the Greeks have the greatest esteem of are Themistocles the Athenian, and Jason the Pheraean.

But above all they magnify that profound and politic fetch of Solon, who, for the advantage of the commonwealth and for his own security, counterfeited himself mad. There are others now so far from this artifice that they are simple and open: to the degree of not enduring anything but what's done above-board; they will not suffer anything that looks like treachery. These men are the servants of truth and the enemies of fraud. There are others again that will bear anything, and crouch to any man for their own ends, as Sulla and M. Brassus; the Lacedaemonian Lysander is said to have been a great master of his art in this kind, and yet Callicratidas, that succeeded him in the command of the navy, is reported to have been quite of another humour. And we find diversity as well in the style and fashion of speaking as in the difference of manners. As you shall see men of great authority and parts that yet wont themselves to the phrase and language of the common people, as the two Catulus's, father and son, and the like Q. Mucius Mancinus, which I myself am a witness of. Nay, I have heard old men say that P. Scipio Nasica had that way with him; but his father the clean contrary, and no grace of speech in the world. I speak of him that revenged the commonwealth upon the seditious attempts of Tiberius Gracchus. And no more had Xenocrates, the severest of philosophers; and yet famous and eminent for that very sourness. There are a world of other dissimilitudes both of nature and manners which are not yet to be despised, so that every man should do well to stick to that inclination that Nature has given him in particular, provided it be not vicious; and by so doing he shall more easily discover and attain the decorum which we look for in this place.

But yet we are so to behave ourselves, that without opposing common Nature we follow the dictates every man of his own genius; and though other things may perhaps be weightier and better, we are yet to take our measures according to the bent of our own particular. For 'tis in vain to struggle with Nature, or to pursue anything which we cannot attain. From hence it is that we must gather the knowledge of what becomes us. For nothing can be graceful that lays a force upon Nature. In short, there is nothing more becoming in human life than an equability and congruity of our actions, which if ever we depart from and pass to the affectation of another man's nature, we lose our own; for as we use our own native language without forcing foreign words into it (as some people do, and make themselves only ridiculous for their pains), so should we in our lives and actions make ourselves all of a piece.

Nay, so sensible is this difference of natures, that one man shall be honoured for destroying of himself, and another condemned for it; all in the same case, as it was with Marcus Cato that killed himself, and the rest that rendered themselves up to Caesar in Africa. This might perhaps have turned to their reproach if they had laid violent hands upon themselves; for an action so heroical would have borne no proportion with the softness and facility of their ways and manners, but rather have introduced an incongruity betwixt their lives and deaths. But for Cato, that was a man naturally grave and severe, even to a miracle, and hardened to it by a long habit of constancy; a man unalterably firm to his purpose and resolution; it made for the dignity of his humour and character rather to support death itself than the frown and dominion of a tyrant. How many miseries did Ulysses suffer in that tedious ramble of his, enslaving himself to women (if a body may give Circe and Calypso that name), and a complaisance upon all occasions to all sorts of people. Nay, at his own house how patiently did he put the contempts and flouts of the meanest of his servants there? Whereas Ajax, according to the report we have of him, would have borne a thousand deaths rather than those contumelies. This contemplation should make every man look into himself, to see what he has of his own and to make his best of that, without disguising himself to act the part of another. That which every man has peculiar to himself is the thing which best becomes him. Wherefore every man should take a true estimate of what he is, and impartially examine his abilities and defects; what he can do and what he cannot. That we may be, at least, as wise in our lives as comedians are upon the stage; who make choice not so much of the best parts or plays, as of the fittest for their disposition. He that has the strongest voice chooses the tragedy of Epigoni or Medus; the best actor prefers Melanippa or Clytaemnestra. Rutilius (whom I remember) always acted Antiopa, and sometimes Aesopus played Ajax. Shall a stage-player now take more care of himself in a comedy than a wise man in his life? Let every man see, in the first place, which way his talent lies; and, in the next, let him endeavour to improve it. But if we should be forced at any time, by necessity, to play a part that we were never made for, let it be our care, study, and thought so to behave ourselves, that at least we may not lose our credit where we cannot get any. So that the best of this case will be to avoid shame, without pretending to get a reputation by the forcing of our nature.

Now to those two parts already spoken of, that is to say of common nature and particular inclination, there is a third that is cast upon us either by time or chance; and yet a fourth which we accommodate according to our judgment. For kingdoms, empires, dignities, honours, riches, with their contraries, are all of them in the hand of fortune and governed by the revolution of times. Now it is wholly at our own choice what part we will sustain. Wherefore one man takes to philosophy, another to the civil law, a third to rhetoric, and a fourth affects an excellency rather in one virtue than in another. But for those whose ancestors were any of them very famous, they commonly study to get reputation by treading in their steps, as Q. Mucius followed his father Publius in the civil law; and Scipio Africanus emulated his father

377

in feats of arms. Some again are not content with the honour they derive from their predecessors unless they add somewhat to it of their own. As Africanus did yet augment and illustrate the honour of his military knowledge by his particular eloquence. And so did Timotheus, the son of Conon, who being a captain not inferior to his father, made himself yet greater by the addition of letters and understanding. But it happens sometimes that the son declines the imitation of the father, and betakes himself rather to some course or design of his own; which is a thing often found in men of large minds that are descended from obscure parents. All these circumstances must be taken into consideration in the question of this decorum.

The first point in deliberation is this: what it is that we design either to be or to do, and what course of life to take to. In this deliberation there is great hazard and difficulty. For it is in our youth that we are to resolve and pitch upon the condition we propound, at which time we are least able to judge of it. So that we are commonly engaged in some certain purpose of life before we are able to distinguish betwixt a better and a worse. For although (according to the report of Prodicus out of Xenophon) so soon as ever Hercules came out of his minority (the time for every man to choose what course of life he will steer) he retired into a solitude, and upon the sight of two ways, the one of virtue and the other of pleasure, he sat a long time considering with himself which of the two ways he should take. Yet this might do well enough for Hercules that was the son of Jupiter, but not for us I fear that commonly follow those men still that we like best, and take up an affection for their ways and studies. And yet for those that are trained up under the institution of their parents, they do commonly and insensibly contract an affection for the methods and customs of their education. Others are carried away by the stream of popular practice, esteeming that still to be the best that pleases the most. And yet some there are that lead the course of life they ought to do, induced thereunto either by Providence, a certain felicity or goodness of nature, a virtuous inclination, or some particular advantage of their institution. But it is a very rare thing to find a concurrence of eminent wit and learning, or to find either of them with so much time for deliberation as is needful for the election of a profitable course of life. In this deliberation a regard must be had to that which is most proper and natural to every particular; for, as is already said, since in whatever we do, we must inquire into every man's particular genius before we can say what becomes him, so we must be more careful yet in the establishment of our own lives to see that we maintain an equality in the main, and that we never differ from ourselves or falter in our duty.

But since Nature has the greatest power in this case and fortune the next, we must consult them both what course of life to fix upon;

but Nature in the first place, for she is much firmer and more constant, and it is not for fortune, that is frail and mortal, to contend with immortal nature. Whoever, therefore, shall conform in the ordering of his life to the inclinations of an uncorrupted nature, must keep constantly to that tenor which is the decorum of life, unless he find himself mistaken in his choice. And in that case (for it is a case to be put) there must be a change admitted of purposes and manners. And that change will be more easily and commodiously wrought under the favour of times and occasions. But where the season is not favourable it must be introduced by little and little; as wise men say of inconvenient and illgrounded friendships, 'tis better to unstitch than to tear them all to pieces on a sudden. But when we have once altered our course we must be infinitely careful to make it appear that we have done it upon good and weighty reasons. Now whereas I have (in what is aforesaid) propounded the imitation of our predecessors, let me not be thought to advise an imitation of them in their vices; beside that there are many things wherein Nature is not to be imitated. As the son of Africanus the elder (he that adopted the son of Paulus Aemilius). It was not possible for him, by reason of the craziness of his body, to be so like his father as the other was like his. Wherefore, if a man be not in condition to plead at the bar, to harangue the people in public assemblies, or to lead armies, there are some duties yet in his power which he is obliged to perform; as the offices of Justice, Faith, Liberality, Modesty, Temperance, which benefits will fairly supply the want of the other. The best of patrimonies is the reputation of great and virtuous actions and ancestors, and the son that does not uphold the renown of his father is a shame and a scandal to it.

Now in regard that there are several duties properly belonging to several ages, and many things that becoming a young man would be ridiculous in an old, we shall say something also under that distinction.

It is the duty of a young man to reverence his elders, and to make his choice of the best and most approved among them for his directors and governors, for the ignorance and folly of youth should be ordered and instructed by the prudence and experience of the aged; but, above all things, he should be restrained from loose and wanton pleasures, and trained up rather in laborious exercises, and in the fatigue and toils both of body and mind. For it makes men vigorous and industrious, as well in war as in peace; and even in the intervals of liberty and refreshment young men should have a care of intemperance, and not to pass the bounds of modesty, which will be the more easily attained if they be often in the eyes of their seniors and tutors.

When we come to be in years the labour of the body must be abated, and we should increase those of the mind, but striving still by all means to be serviceable to our friends and to our juniors by our advice and wisdom, but principally to the commonwealth. But, above all things, have a care of a drowsy, a languishing, and a lazy old age, and so likewise of a luxurious, which, as it is reproachful and dishonourable, in this case it is most of all. But if the intemperance of lust be added to it, the mischief is double; first the infamy which it reflects upon age itself, and then the ill example in authorising young men to be more shameless and wicked.

It would not be impertinent here to speak something of the duties of magistrates, private citizens, and strangers. The magistrate's part is to consider himself as the representative of the city, and to uphold the honour and dignity of it; to observe the laws and customs; to do justice; and to remember that all these things are committed to his charge. It is the part of a private man to live with his fellow-citizens under one common bond of legal duty, neither falling so low as to make himself despicable, nor too much exalting himself; and never to entertain any thought but to the glory and peace of the commonwealth. This is the man that we esteem, and pronounce to be a worthy citizen. As to the duty of a stranger, let him mind his own business and not intermeddle with other people's, but keep himself within his compass. By these means it will be understood, when it shall come to be diligently examined, what is most becoming us under the several circumstances of persons, times, and ages; but there is nothing so graceful as to behave ourselves equally and steadily in all our actions and counsels.

But this gracefulness shows itself in all our words and deeds, nay, in the very motions and postures of the body, and consists principally in beauty, order, and a kind of air or agreement suitable to everything we do. 'Tis a hard matter to express this, but it shall suffice, that it may be easily understood. In the observance of these three points we render ourselves acceptable in our conversation with all people. And so much for this too.

Nature has undoubtedly taken great care in the forming of man's body, exposing only those parts to sight that are beautiful, comely, and agreeable to the eye, and keeping those parts concealed and covered which would give offence if they were laid open to view, and serve us only for unclean and common necessities. There is no question but the modesty of the mind conforms itself in this particular to the exquisite fabric of the body, for whatsoever Nature has concealed all men in their right wits do naturally keep out of sight, and as private as possible, in compliance with their very necessities. Now for those parts of the body which are of most necessary use to man we neither call the part nor the use of it by the proper name, and that which may be honestly done (if secretly) we cannot so much as honestly name, insomuch that those things cannot be done openly without impudence, nor so much as mentioned without obscenity. Therefore there's no hearkening to the Cynics, or to the old Stoics (which are almost Cynics), and blame and laugh at us for reckoning those things to be foul in words which are not so in truth. And yet those things which we all agree to be foul we can yet call by their own names; as theft, cozenage, adultery, are all dishonest in the deed, and yet we use the words without scruple. To beget children is an honest action, but it wears a coarse name; and we feel a great deal more to this purpose against modesty in their disputations. But we are to follow Nature, and so fly whatsoever may offend either the eye or the ear of a modest man. Nay, in our very postures and gestures, as walking, standing, sitting, lying, in the very countenance, the eye, the motion of the hands, there must a regard be had still to that which is becoming. In all this there are two things we should beware of. The one, not to do anything that is loose, nice, and effeminate; the other, to avoid things that look harsh, rough, and uncivil. For why should that which becomes an orator, or a comedian, misbeseem us? The discipline of the theatre has a long time had such a regard to modesty that no man enters upon the stage without drawers, lest some part of the body should come to be discovered by chance that ought to be concealed. The Roman customs will not allow sons, when they are men grown, so much as to bathe with their fathers, or sons-in-law with their wives' parent. In these points of virtuous modesty nature is both our mistress and our guide.

Of beauty or agreeableness there are two kinds; the one is matter of gracefulness, the other of dignity, and we may call them male and female. It is not for a man to be trickt out with fooleries, or to have anything that is fantastical or effeminate, no, not so much as in his very motion or gesture. How are we disgusted many times at the conceited actions of stage-players, and the more odious and affected motions of wrestlers? And yet we commend that which is natural and simple both in the one and in the other. The dignity of the countenance is maintained by a good colour, and that colour by the exercise of the body; and to all this we should keep ourselves neat and cleanly, not to the degree of niceness and affectation, but only so as not to incur the censure of rudeness, sluttery, and neglect. And the same rule we should observe in our garments, in which particular, as well as in other things, a mediocrity does best. In our walking we must neither march so slow, as if we were officiating at a solemnity, nor yet make such post-haste as to run ourselves out of breath, and put the mouth or the countenance into disorder, which is the sign of a light and unsteady humour. But we must take more pains yet to keep the mind in a temper of conformity to nature, which we may easily compass if we can but preserve ourselves from falling into transports and perturbations, and diligently attend to a conservation of the decorum here prescribed.

The motions of the mind are twofold. Some are of thought and others of appetite. Those of thought are chiefly employed in the finding out of the truth. Those of appetite push a man forward to the doing of something. We must be careful, therefore, first to apply our thoughts to that which is most worthy of them; and, secondly, to keep the appetite in subjection to reason.

As to the matter of speech, the power of it is great, and it is also twofold. The one is a speech of contention, the other of common discourse. The former is for the bar, for public assemblies, and for the Senate; the other is for ordinary conversation, casual disputes, private meetings of company or friends at the table. The masters of rhetoric have given precepts for the former, but we have none for the latter, altho' perhaps that might be done too. But there's nobody that addicts himself that way. For if men would but apply themselves to the study of it they would never want masters to teach it. And yet we are all of us mad upon rhetoric, although for what concerns words and periods the same rules would serve both. It is by the help of the voice that we discourse, and the two great advantages of it are to be clear and sweet. We must stand indebted to nature for them both; and yet exercise and practice will help us in the one, and the imitation of smooth and gentle speakers may be of use to us in the other. What was it but this that gave the Catuli so fair a reputation, both for judgment and language? They were learned men, 'tis true, and so were others, but these yet were lookt upon as the great masters of the Latin tongue. They had a wonderful sweetness of voice, and their pronunciation neither too loud and open, nor yet muffled betwixt the teeth; so that it was both audible and agreeable and without any affectation, the tone without any force, and neither too faint not too shrill. L. Crassus, 'tis true, was a word-flowing speaker, and no less ingenious, but for well-speaking the Catuli were no less esteemed. Now for sharpness and pleasure of wit Caesar, the brother of the elder Catulus, went beyond them all, insomuch that in his ordinary discourses he surpassed the best pleaders of his time. All these things severally must be diligently heeded to make us understand what it is that may best become us in everything.

In familiar speech the followers of Socrates are most worthy of imitation. It should be gentle, without being too pressing or tedious; and I would have it pleasant and entertaining in all cases. Nor would I have any man take possession of a common right in such sort as to talk all himself, to the exclusion of others; but in discourse, as in other things, every man to take his turn. The first thing to be heeded is the subject-matter of the discourse. If serious, it must be seriously handled; if matter of mirth, a freedom of raillery and lightness does well enough with it. But above all things we must be careful in the government of our speech not to discover any vice or defect in our manners, wherein a man is most liable to betray himself when he talks spitefully of the absent, and either in jest or in earnest maliciously exposes them to contumely and reproach. The ordinary matter of familiar discourse is either about domestic affairs, the republic, or matter of studies and learning. If at any time we pass these bounds, we must as soon as may be take up again. But be it as it will, it must be thought upon how far our discourse may be grateful to the company, for we are not equally pleased with the same things at all times. And then, as we begin a discourse upon reason, we must not continue it beyond measure. But as it is laid down upon very good grounds, and as a general rule, that we should keep ourselves clear from perturbations or violent motions of the mind, that rebel against reason, so should we in our speech keep a guard upon ourselves against those intemperate motions, and that we do not lay open our distempers of anger, appetite, laziness, heartlessness, or the like. We should be very careful also in our conversation to possess the company with an opinion of the reverence and goodwill we have for them. There are many occasions wherein we cannot avoid chiding, and we may be allowed some time a more than ordinary contention of voice and a sharper severity of words; but yet this is not to be done neither as if we were angry, but we are to proceed to this kind or reproof as we do to blaming and scarifying, rarely and unwillingly, nor ever at all but upon necessity, and for want of some other way of remedy; but not in anger still upon any terms, for it never does anything either well or wisely: and yet it may do well enough to use a temperate and a mild way of rebuke, but still accompanied with gravity, that the reprehension may be applied without reproach. It must be also signified that the only thing intended by the reproof was the amendment of him that suffers it. Nay, it will become us in our differences even with our greatest enemies, in despite of all indignities, yet to preserve a gravity, to keep ourselves free from passion; for whatsoever we do in distemper can neither be well done in itself nor approved by those that are witnesses to the doing it. It is a lewd thing likewise for a man to talk much of himself, especially, with Thraso, to brag of things that are false, and to make sport for the company.

Being now to go through all the points of decency and duty (as that is my design), I shall say something what kind of house I should think fit for a person of honour or a prince so as to have it accommodate for use, for that is the intent of building it; and there must yet be had a regard to the state and dignity of the person that inhabits it. I have been told of Cn. Octavius (the first consul of that family) that he was highly reverenced for a magnificent pile that he built upon the Palatine Hill, and that the reputation he got by so many people coming to see it, opened his way (being but a new man) to the Consulship. Scaurus afterwards caused that to be demolished for the enlargement of his own. The former brought the Consulship first into his family, and the latter (though the son of an eminent and famous person, and the house enlarged) brought into it not only a repulse, but misery and shame. It does well to have the dignity of the master yet further adorned by house; but not that dignity to be fetched altogether from it. The house should be graced by the master, and not the master by the house; and it is in a house as it is in other cases, a man must have a respect not only to himself, but also to others. In the house of a person of eminent condition, where many guests are to be received and men of all sorts to be admitted, there must great care be taken that it be large enough. But a large house without people disparages the master of it, and especially if it has been more frequented under a former possessor; for 'tis an odious thing to have passengers reflect upon it and say (as in these times there's too much occasion): Here's the old house, but where's the old master? I would have him that sets upon building take special care not to lash out into magnificence and expense as a thing of ill consequence, even in the example, for there are too many imitators in this kind of the doings of princes. How many have we that emulate the splendour of Lucullus's villas, but where is the man that emulates his virtue? There must be a mean observed in these things, and that moderation must be transferred in all cases to the use, ornament, and convenience of life. But enough of this.

In all undertakings there are three things to be observed. First, that we govern our appetites by reason, which is a sure way to keep us to our duties. Secondly, that we take a right estimate of our enterprises, and allow time and pains neither more nor less than the matter requires. Thirdly, that we keep a measure even in those things that are matter of dignity and reputation. We cannot do better than to observe the decorum already spoken of without moving one step beyond it. But the first point is the most excellent of the three.

We come now to the order of things and the opportunity of seasons. Under this science is comprehended that which the Greeks call *eutaxia,* by which we understand the harmony of order, and not that modesty that regards temperament and measure. Now to take it as modesty, the Stoical definition of it is this: it is the skill of disposing all our words and actions in their proper place. So that the ordering of things and the placing of them are much one and the same, for they define order to be only the laying together of things in their due and fitting places. But they tell us that the place of action respects the opportunity of time. Now that seasonable time of action the Greeks call *eukairia,* the Latins *occasio.* So that this modesty, taken in the sense aforesaid, is the knowledge of the opportunities of times fit for action; which is a definition that may as well agree with the prudence which we have treated of in the beginning. But in this place we are discoursing of moderation, temperance, and virtues of that quality. Wherefore having lodged these matters which particularly belong to prudence in their right places, we come now to those virtues that refer to modesty and the gaining of a good opinion and esteem in the world; of which we have spoken largely already.

It should be in the order of life as in that of an artificial and well-governed discourse. All the parts of it should be equal and correspondent one to another. Many things do well enough over a glass of wine that would be most ridiculous and shameful upon a debate. There should be no fooling in serious matters. It was well said of Pericles, at a council of war, to his colleague Sophocles, that was joined with him in the command of the army. As they were upon a consultation, there happened to pass by a very fine youth. What a delicate child is there, says Sophocles, in the middle of the debate. Brother, says Pericles, a general's eyes should be as temperate as his fingers. But if the same thing had been spoken at a public spectacle, nothing could have been said against it, so powerful is the consideration of time and place. If a man were upon a journey, and going to plead a cause, nobody would blame him for thinking of his business and conning of his lesson by the way. But that pensive musing humour, at a jolly entertainment, would be looked upon to be either want of wit or breeding, in the not distinguishing of times. Now for things which are very gross, as for a man to fall a-singing in a court of justice, or to do anything that is notoriously preposterous or improper, these are absurdities so well understood by all people that there needs no precept or caution in the case. But there are certain niceties of conversation which are indeed so minute, that some make slight of them, and others do not so much as perceive them. And yet these are the points that require our most diligent consideration. For as it is in musical instruments, let them be never so little out of tune, a skilful ear presently takes check at it, and that's the case in the least disconsonancy of life. Only the offence is so much the greater here, by how much the agreement of our actions and manners is of greater value and effect than a consent of sounds. Wherefore, as there is no jar or discord in music so small as to escape the animadversion of a critical ear, no less quick and accurate ought we to be in censuring and detecting the venial errors of life; being led to the knowledge of the greatest matters even by the smallest. From the motion of the eye, from a smooth or a contracted brow, from sadness, mirth, laughter, speech, silence — nay, from the very tone of soft or loud speaking, and a thousand such common circumstances, we gather the understanding of human duties, and of what naturally becomes us, and what the contrary.

385

Now toward the erecting of a true judgment upon things in this kind, it were not amiss for us to begin our observations abroad; and then to avoid or correct that in ourselves which we find misbecoming in others. For so it is (I cannot tell how it comes about) that we are much better at spying out our neighbour's faults than our own, and therefore it is a good and a profitable method the teaching of children to do better, by showing them in imitation how ill it becomes them to do amiss. In cases doubtful and hard to be resolved upon, it will behove us to consult men of learning and experience for direction. Now it is very natural for men to follow the bias of their proper inclinations, so that we are not only to attend to what anybody says, but likewise to what he thinks, and even to the very motive that leads him to that thought. For, as it is with painters, statuaries, nay, and with right poets too, they love to have their works exposed, and, as the world find faults, to mend them. They take advice upon what's amiss both with themselves and friends, and are induced to the doing or not doing, to the changing or correcting of many things, by the opinion of others. But for what concerns customs and civil institutions, there can be no place there for the prescribing where the matter itself is a precept. Neither let a man so much deceive himself as to imagine that the example of Socrates for the purpose, or Aristippus in the saying or doing of any ill thing against rules of government must presently authorise him to the same license, for this liberty in those great and divine men we are to look upon as a privilege purchased by their virtues. Now for the Cynics (those enemies of shame, and consequently of honesty and virtue), there's no enduring of them. To magistrates and persons in authority we are to pay all honour and reverence, and so likewise to all those worthy patriots that have spent their lives in great and honest actions, and in the service of their country. We owe a respect also to grey hairs, and even to those that are but designed to any administration in the government. We must distinguish betwixt a citizen and a stranger, and, even in a stranger, betwixt a private person and a public. But to sum up all in a word, it is our duty to cherish, maintain, and preserve unity, peace, and good agreement in human society.

We come now to the matter of trade and profit, which we find to be divided into liberal (or, in vulgar English, creditable) and sordid. There are some painful employments that carry along with them a general odium, as that of a tax-gatherer or an usurer. These, in the first place, I do not like; and I do also look upon all mercenary dealings, where we pay for the work and nor for the art, to be mean and ignoble. The very price of the commodity is a kind of covenanting for slavery. It is also a coarse business that of a retailer, that only buys in a lump to sell again in parcels; for they get their very bread commonly by lying, which is a most unmanly submission. And so for all mechanics, they are men of low and vulgar business, and we are not to expect anything that is clear and generous from the shop. I am likewise with Terence no friend to those trades that minister to luxury, as fishermen, butchers, cooks, pudding-makers, fishmongers; nor to the voluptuous arts, as perfumers, dancing-masters, and the whole mystery of gaming. But for those professions that require a greater measure of prudence, and minister advantage in proportion, as physic, architecture, the furnishing of good instructions, these are commendable employments, where they suit with the condition of him that uses them. And then for merchandising: the driving of a petty trade that way is little better than peddling; but when it comes to be large and general, and to be managed back and forward with candour and credit, it is no contemptible application. Nay, on the contrary, this way of commerce is highly to be esteemed when he that has made his fortune by it sits down, not satiated, but contented, and retires as well from his port to the country, as he has done many a time from the sea to the port, and there quietly enjoys himself and his possessions. Of all beneficial industry certainly there is not anything more agreeable or more worthy of a man of honour and reason than the culture and improvement of the earth, which being a subject handled at large in our *Cato Major,* we shall refer you thither for your satisfaction.

Here is enough said already upon the several parts of virtue and our duties arising from thence. It remains now to consider in a case of two duties before us which to choose (a thing that often happens); and of two honest propositions, which is the honester is the question (a point omitted by Panaetius). For since there is no virtue but what issues from one of these four fountains, and has a respect either to knowledge, society, courage, or moderation, it must necessarily be that upon a complication of these virtues there must likewise ensue a competition of duties. Now it is my opinion that mankind is naturally more concerned in offices that relate to the community than in matters that only affect the understanding, which may be thus made out: take a wise man that has the world at will, both for fortune and leisure, let him consider with himself and contemplate all things whatsoever that are worth the knowing, he would be yet sick of his life for all this if he were to spend his time wholly in solitude and without a companion.

The principal virtue is, as I have said, that which the Greeks call *sophia,* and we wisdom. But their *sophrosyne* (or prudence) is quite another thing, being the skill of judging what we are to do and what not, or of distinguishing betwixt good and evil; whereas wisdom (which we call the principal) is the knowledge of things divine and human, wherein is comprehended a certain correspondence betwixt the gods and men, and a society among themselves. Now if this be the most eminent virtue, as certainly it is, so must that likewise be the most eminent duty which refers to community. For the speculation and perception of things is but lame and imperfect if it be not followed with action, which action is best seen in providing for the common benefits of mankind, and must therefore be reduced to the subject of human society in preference to the naked understanding of things. And this does every good man find to be true upon his own practice and observation. For where's the man that is so transported with a thirst of knowledge or a desire of piercing into the nature of things, that if he should be called upon the sudden to the relief of his country, his father, or his friend that were in danger: where is the man, I say, that in the heat and rapture of his most divine contemplations would not quit all to attend this duty, even supposing him to be in his thoughts already numbering the stars and taking measure of the universe? This gives us to understand that the offices of justice conducing to the common utility of mankind (than which nothing ought to be dearer to us) are of so much greater importance than these of study and science; and never was any man so taken up in his life and application with the search of knowledge as not yet to have an eye to his duty to the public, and to consult the well-being of sociable nature, as we see in the instance of Lysis the Pythagorean to the Theban Epaminondas; and in that of Plato to Dion of Syracuse; and divers others that trained up their disciples to the love, knowledge, and exercise of civil duties. And for the service (if any at all) which I myself have rendered to the republic, I must ascribe it to my masters and to my books that instructed and fitted me for my function. For great men do not only teach the lovers of learning during their lives, but in their very graves too, transmitting their precepts down to after times for the use of posterity. Now to show how much their leisures contributed to our business, these eminent men have not slipt so much as any one point appertaining to the laws, manners, and discipline of the commonwealth, but have still, with all their faculties, applied the fruits of their labours and studies to the well-being of the public. So that a copious eloquence, pointed with prudence, is much more profitable than the most refined subtilty of thought, without speaking. For meditation does only circulate within itself; whereas eloquence works upon others, and insinuates itself into the affections of all that hear it. We must not imagine that bees gather into swarms upon a design to make their cells, but it is in their nature to congregate, and then they work their combs. And so it is with men, who are much more sociable by nature; when they are gotten together they consult their common business. Now for that virtue (of justice) which provides for the defence and conservation of men in society, if it be not accompanied with the understanding of things it is but solitary and fruitless. And what is courage, without the softness of human courtesy and candour, but a savage and outrageous brutality?

From hence we may infer the excellency of a practical justice in the ordering of mankind above the force and effect of a speculative notion. There are some people that fancy all leagues and associations amongst men to arise from the need that one man has for another toward the supplying of our natural and common necessities; because, say they, if Providence had delivered us from this care of looking after food and clothing by appointing some extraordinary way for the furnishing of it, no man of either brains or virtue would ever trouble his head about business, but wholly deliver himself up to the attaining of wisdom. But this is a mistake, for even in that condition a man would fly solitude, and wish for a companion in his very studies; he would be willing to teach and to learn, to hear and to speak. So that beyond question the duties that defend and support men in society are more to be esteemed than those that barely relate to learning and knowledge.

It may be another question whether this community which is so consonant to nature be in all cases to be preferred to modesty and moderation. Now I think not. For there are some things, partly so foul and in part so flagitious, that a wise man (even if it were to save his country) would not be guilty of them. Posidonius has made a large collection of such cases, but so filthy, so obscene, that a man cannot honestly repeat them. Now why should any man do that for the saving of his country which his country itself would rather perish than any member of it should do? But, however, this is the best on't; that it can never be for the interest of the public to have a wise man do any such thing. Let it be therefore concluded that of all duties we are to prefer those that tend toward the maintaining of society; for a considerate action presumes an antecedent cognition and wisdom. So that it is more to do considerately than to think wisely. But let this suffice, for the matter is made so plain that there will be no difficulty to resolve upon two duties in question which to choose. But then in the community itself there are several degrees of duties in subordination one to another. The first is what we owe to the immortal gods, the second to our country, the third to our parents; and so in order, suc- cessively, to others. Upon a brief disquisition of this matter it will appear that the point in debate is not only which is honest and which the contrary, but of two honest propositions which is the honester; and then, which is the honestest of all. This, as I have said, was slipt by Panaetius; but let us now proceed.

Roger L'Estrange

M. AURELIUS

MARCUS AURELIUS (C. 121-180 A.D.) was a Roman Emperor whose philosophical leanings embraced Stoicism.

His reflections, written in Greek during his military campaigns, constitute the *Meditations*.

Book I

From my grandfather Verus I learned good morals and the government of my temper.

From the reputation and remembrance of my father, modesty and a manly character.

From my mother, piety and beneficence, and abstinence, not only from evil deeds, but even from evil thoughts; and further, simplicity in my way of living, far removed from the habits of the rich.

From my great-grandfather, not to have frequented public schools, and to have had good teachers at home, and to know that on such things a man should spend liberally.

From my governor, to be neither of the green nor of the blue party at the games in the Circus, nor a partizan either of the Parmularius or the Scutarius at the gladiators' fights; from him too I learned endurance of labour, and to want little, and to work with my own hands, and not to meddle with other people's affairs, and not to be ready to listen to slander.

From Diognetus, not to busy myself about trifling things, and not to give credit to what was said by miracle-workers and jugglers about incantations and the driving away of daemons and such things; and not to breed quails, nor to give myself up passionately to such things; and to endure freedom of speech; and to have become intimate with philosophy; and to have been a hearer, first of Bacchius, then of Tandasis and Marcianus; and to have written dialogues in my youth; and to have desired a plank bed and skin, and whatever else of the kind belongs to the Grecian discipline.

From Rusticus I received the impression that my character required improvement and discipline; and from him I learned not to be led astray to sophistic emulation, nor to writing on speculative matters, nor to delivering little hortatory orations, nor to showing myself off as a man who practises much discipline, or does benevolent acts in order to make a display; and to abstain from rhetoric, and poetry, and fine writing; and not to walk about in the house in my outdoor dress, nor to do other things of the kind; and to write my letters with simplicity, like the letter which Rusticus wrote from Sinuessa to my mother; and with respect to those who have offended me by words, or done me wrong, to be easily disposed to be pacified and reconciled, as soon as they have shown a readiness to be reconciled; and to read carefully, and not to be satisfied with a superficial understanding of a book; nor hastily to give my assent to those who talk overmuch; and I am indebted to him for being acquainted with the discourses of Epictetus, which he communicated to me out of his own collection.

From Apollonius I learned freedom of will and undeviating steadiness of purpose; and to look to nothing else, not even for a moment, except to reason; and to be always the same, in sharp pains, on the occasion of the loss of a child, and in long illness; and to see clearly in a living example that the same man can be both most resolute and yielding, and not peevish in giving his instruction; and to have had before my eyes a man who clearly considered his experience and his skill in expounding philosophical principles as the smallest of his merits; and from him I learned how to receive from friends what are esteemed favours, without being either humbled by them or letting them pass unnoticed.

From Sextus, a benevolent disposition, and the example of a family governed in a fatherly manner, and the idea of living conformably to nature; and gravity without affectation, and to look carefully after the interest of friends, and to tolerate ignorant persons, and those who form opinions without consideration: he had the power of readily accommodating himself to all, so that intercourse with him was more agreeable than any flattery; and at the same time he was most highly venerated by those who associated with him; and he had the faculty both of discovering and ordering, in an intelligent and methodical way, the principles necessary for life; and he never showed anger or any other passion, but was entirely free from passion, and also most affectionate; and he could express approbation without noisy display, and he possessed much knowledge without ostentation.

From Alexander the grammarian, to refrain from fault-finding, and not in a reproachful way to chide those who uttered any barbarous or solecistic or strange-sounding expression; but dexterously to introduce the very expression which ought to have been used, and in the way of answer or giving confirmation, or joining in an inquiry about the thing itself, not about the word, or by some other fit suggestion.

From Fronto I learned to observe what envy, and duplicity,

and hypocrisy are in a tyrant, and that generally those among us who are called Patricians are rather deficient in paternal affection.

From Alexander the Platonic, not frequently nor without necessity to say to any one, or to write in a letter, that I have no leisure; nor continually to excuse the neglect of duties required by our relation to those with whom we live, by alleging urgent occupations.

From Catulus, not to be indifferent when a friend finds fault, even if he should find fault without reason, but to try to restore him to his usual disposition; and to be ready to speak well of teachers, as it is reported of Domitius and Athenodotus; and to love my children truly.

From my brother Severus, to love my kin, and to love truth, and to love justice; and through him I learned to know Thrasea, Helvidius, Cato, Dion, Brutus; and from him I received the idea of a polity in which there is the same law for all, a polity administered with regard to equal rights and equal freedom of speech, and the idea of a kingly government which respects most of all the freedom of the governed; I learned from him also consistency and undeviating steadiness in my regard for philosophy; and a disposition to do good, and to give to others readily, and to cherish good hopes, and to believe that I am loved by my friends; and in him I observed no concealment of his opinions with respect to those whom he condemned, and that his friends had no need to conjecture what he wished or did not wish, but it was quite plain.

From Maximus I learned self-government, and not to be led aside by anything; and cheerfulness in all circumstances, as well as in illness; and a just admixture in the moral character of sweetness and dignity, and to do what was set before me without complaining. I observed that everybody believed that he thought as he spoke, and that in all that he did he never had any bad intention; and he never showed amazement and surprise, and was never in a hurry, and never put off doing a thing, nor was perplexed nor dejected, nor did he ever laugh to disguise his vexation, nor, on the other hand, was he ever passionate or suspicious. He was accustomed to do acts of beneficence, and was ready to forgive, and was free from all falsehood; and he presented the appearance of a man who could not be diverted from right rather than of a man who had been improved. I observed, too, that no man could ever think that he was despised by Maximus, or ever venture to think himself a better man. He had also the art of being humorous in an agreeable way.

In my father I observed mildness of temper, and unchangeable in the things which he had determined after due deliberation; and no vainglory in those things which men call honours; and a love of labour and perseverance; and a readiness to listen to those who had anything to propose for the common weal; and undeviating firmness in giving to every man according to his deserts; and a knowledge derived from experience of the occasions for vigorous action and for remission. And I observed that he had overcome all passion for boys; and he considered himself no more than any other citizen; and he released his friends from all obligation to sup with him or to attend him of necessity when he went abroad, and those who had failed to accompany him, by reason of any circumstances, always found him the same. I observed too his habit of careful inquiry in all matters of deliberation, and his persistency, and that he never stopped his investigation through being satisfied with appearances which first present themselves; and that his disposition was to keep his friends, and not to be soon tired of them, nor yet to be extravagant in his affection; and to be satisfied on all occasions, and cheerful; and to foresee things a long way off, and to provide for the smallest without display; and to check immediately popular applause and all flattery; and to be ever watchful over the things which were necessary for the administration of the empire, and to be a good manager of the expenditure, and patiently to endure the blame which he got for such conduct; and he was neither superstitious with respect to the gods, nor did he court men by gifts or by trying to please them, or by flattering the populace; but he showed sobriety in all things and firmness, and never any mean thoughts or action, nor love of novelty. And the things which conduce in any way to the commodity of life, and of which fortune gives an abundant supply, he used without arrogance and without excusing himself; so that when he had them, he enjoyed them without affectation, and when he had them not, he did not want them. No one could ever say of him that he was either a sophist of a flippant slave or a pedant; but every one acknowledged him to be a man ripe, perfect, above flattery, able to manage his own and other men's affairs. Besides this, he honoured those who were true philosophers, and he did not reproach those who pretended to be philosophers, nor yet was he easily led by them. He was also easy in conversation, and he made himself agreeable without any offensive affectation. He took a reasonable care of his body's health, not as one who is greatly attached to life, nor out of regard to personal appearance, nor yet in a careless way, but so that, through his own attention, he very seldom stood in need of the physician's art or of medicine or external applications. He was most ready to give way without envy to those who possessed any particular faculty, such as that of eloquence or knowledge of the law or of morals, or of anything else; and he gave them his help, that each might enjoy reputation according to his deserts; and he always acted conformably to the institutions of his country, without showing any affectation of doing so. Further, he was not fond of change nor unsteady, but he loved to stay in the same places, and to employ himself about the same things; and after his paroxysms of headache he came immediately fresh and vigorous to his usual occupations. His secrets were not many, but very few and very rare, and these only about public matters; and he showed prudence and economy in the exhibition of the public spectacles and the construction of public buildings, his donations to the people, and in such things, for he was a man who looked to what ought to be done, not to the reputation which is got by a man's acts. He did not take the bath at unseasonable hours; he was not fond of building houses, nor curious about what he ate, nor about the texture and color of his clothes, nor about the beauty of his slaves. His dress came from Lorium, his villa on the coast, and from Lanuvium generally. We know how he behaved to the toll-collector at Tusculum who asked his pardon; and such was all his behaviour. There was in him nothing harsh, nor implacable, nor violent, nor, as one may say, anything carried to the sweating point; but he examined all things severally, as if he had abundance of time and without confusion, in an orderly way, vigorously and consistently. And that might be applied to him which is recorded of Socrates, that he was able both to abstain from, and to enjoy, those things which many are too weak to abstain from, and cannot enjoy without excess. But to be strong enough both to bear the one and to be sober in the other is the mark of a man who has a perfect and invincible soul, such as he showed in the illness of Maximus.

To the gods I am indebted for having good grandfathers, good parents, a good sister, good teachers, good associates, good kinsmen and friends, nearly everything good. Further, I owe it to the gods that I was not hurried into any offence against any of them, though I had a disposition which, if opportunity had offered, might have led me to do something of this kind; but, through their favour, there never was such a concurrence of circumstances as put me to the trial. Further, I am thankful to the gods that I was not longer brought up with my grandfather's concubine, and that I preserved the flower of my youth, and that I did not make proof of my virility before the proper season, but even deferred the time; that I was subjected to a ruler and a father who was able to take away all pride from me, and to bring me to the knowledge that it is possible for a man to live in a palace without wanting either guards or embroidered dresses, or torches and statues, and such-like show; but that it is in such a man's power to bring himself very near to the fashion of a private person, without being for this reason either meaner in thought, or more remiss in action, with respect to the things which must be done for the public interest in a manner that befits a ruler. I thank the gods for giving me such a brother, who was able by his moral character to rouse me to vigilance over myself, and who, at the same time, pleased me by his respect and affection; that my children have not been stupid nor deformed in body; that I did not make more proficiency in rhetoric, poetry, and the other studies, in which I should perhaps have been completely engaged, if I had seen that I was making progress in them; that I made haste to place those who brought me up in the station of honour, which they seemed to desire, without putting them off with hope of my doing it some time after, because they were then still young; that I knew Apollonius, Rusticus, Maximus; that I received clear and frequent impressions about living according to nature, and what kind of a life that is, so that, so far as depended on the gods, and their gifts, and help, and inspirations, nothing hindered me from forthwith living according to nature, though I still fall short of it through my own fault, and through not observing the admonitions of the gods, and, I may almost say, their direct instructions; that my body has held out so long in such a kind of life; that I never touched either Benedicta or Theodotus, and that, after having fallen into amatory passions, I was cured; and, though I was often out of humour with Rusticus, I never did anything of which I had occasion to repent; that, though it was my mother's fate to die young, she spent the last years of her life with me; that, whenever I wished to help any man in his need, or on any other occasion, I was never told that I had not the means of doing it; and that to myself the same necessity never happened, to receive anything from another; that I have such a wife, so obedient, and so affectionate, and so simple; that I had abundance of good masters for my children; and that remedies have been shown to me by dreams, both others, and against bloodspitting and giddiness; and that, when I had an inclination to philosophy, I did not fall into the hands of any sophist, and that I did not waste my time on writers, or in the resolution of syllogisms, or occupy myself about the investigation of appearances in the heavens; for all these things require the help of the gods and fortune.

Among the Quadi at the Granua.

Book II

Begin the morning by saying to thyself, I shall meet with the busybody, the ungrateful, arrogant, deceitful, envious, unsocial. All these things happen to them by reason of their ignorance of what is good and evil. But I who have seen the nature of the good that it is beautiful, and of the bad that it is ugly, and the nature of him who does wrong, that it is akin to me, not of the same blood or seed, but that it participates in the same intelligence and the same portion of the divinity, I can neither be injured by any of them, for no one can fix on me what is ugly, nor can I be angry with my kinsman, nor

395

hate him. For we are made for co-operation, like hands, like eyelids, like the rows of the upper and lower teeth. To act against one another then is contrary to nature; and it is acting against one another to be vexed and to turn away.

Whatever this is that I am, it is a little flesh and breath, and the ruling part. Throw away thy books; no longer distract thyself: it is not allowed; but as if thou wast now dying, despise the flesh; it is blood and bones and a network, a contexture of nerves, veins, and arteries. See the breath also, what kind of a thing it is, air, and not always the same, but every moment sent out and again sucked in. The third then is the ruling part: consider thus: Thou art an old man; no longer let this be a slave, no longer be pulled by the strings like a puppet to unsocial movements, no longer be either dissatisfied with thy present lot, or shrink from the future.

All that is from the gods is full of providence. That which is from fortune is not separated from nature or without an interweaving and involution with the things which are ordered by providence. From thence all things flow; and there is besides necessity, and that which is for the advantage of the whole universe, of which thou art a part. But that is good for every part of nature which the nature of the whole brings, and what serves to maintain this nature. Now the universe is preserved, as by the changes of the elements so by the changes of things compounded of the elements. Let these principles be enough for thee, let them always be fixed opinions. But cast away the thirst after books, that thou mayest not die murmuring, but cheerfully, truly, and from thy heart thankful to the gods.

Remember how long thou hast been putting off these things, and how often thou hast received an opportunity from the gods, and yet dost not use it. Thou must now at last perceive of what universe thou art a part, and of what administrator of the universe thy existence is an efflux, and that a limit of time is fixed for thee, which if thou dost not use for clearing away the clouds from thy mind, it will go and thou wilt go, and it will never return.

Every moment think steadily as a Roman and a man to do what thou hast in hand with perfect and simple dignity, and feeling of affection, and freedom, and justice; and to give thyself relief from all other thoughts. And thou wilt give thyself relief, if thou doest every act of thy life as if it were the last, laying aside all carelessness and passionate aversion from the commands of reason, and all hypocrisy, and self-love, and discontent with the portion which has been given to thee. Thou seest how few the things are, the which, if a man lays hold of, he is able to live a life which flows in quiet, and is like the existence of the gods; for the gods on their part will require nothing more from him who observes these things.

Do wrong to thyself, do wrong to thyself, my soul; but thou wilt no longer have the opportunity of honouring thyself. Every man's life is sufficient. But thine is nearly finished, though thy soul reverences not itself, but places thy felicity in the souls of others.

Do the things external which fall upon thee distract thee? Give thyself time to learn something new and good, and cease to be whirled around. But then thou must also avoid being carried about the other way. For those too are triflers who have wearied themselves in life by their activity, and yet have no object to which to direct every movement, and, in a word, all their thoughts.

Through not observing what is in the mind of another a man has seldom been seen to be unhappy; but those who do not observe the movements of their own minds must of necessity be unhappy.

This thou must always bear in mind, what is the nature of the whole, and what is my nature, and how this is related to that, and what kind of a part it is of what kind of a whole, and that there is no one who hinders thee from always doing and saying the things which are according to the nature of which thou art a part.

Theophrastus, in his comparison of bad acts — such a comparison as one would make in accordance with the common notions of man-kind — says, like a true philosopher, that the offences which are committed through desire are more blamable than those which are committed through anger. For he who is excited by anger seems to turn away from reason with a certain pain and unconscious contraction; but he who offends through desire, being overpowered by pleasure, seems to be in a manner more intemperate and more womanish in his offences. Rightly then, and in a way worthy of philosophy, he said that the offence which is committed with pleasure is more blamable than that which is committed with pain; and on the whole the one is more like a person who has been first wronged and through pain is compelled to be angry; but the other is moved by his own impulse to do wrong, being carried towards doing something by desire.

Since it is possible that thou mayest depart from life this very moment, regulate every act and thought accordingly. But to go away from among men, if there are gods, is not a thing to be afraid of, for the gods will not involve thee in evil; but if indeed they do not exist, or if they have no concern about human affairs, what is it to me to live in a universe devoid of gods or devoid of providence? But in truth they do exist, and they do care for human beings, and they have put all the means in man's power to enable him not to fall into real evils. And as to the rest, if there was anything evil, they would have provided for this also, that it should be altogether in a man's power not to fall into it. Now that which does not make a man worse, how can it make

397

a man's life worse? But neither through ignorance, nor having the knowledge, but not the power to guard against or correct these things, is it possible that the nature of the universe has overlooked them; nor is it possible that it has made so great a mistake, either through want of skill, that good and evil should happen indiscriminately to the good and the bad. But death certainly, and life, honour and dishonour, pain and pleasure, all these things equally happen to good men and bad, being things which make us neither better nor worse. Therefore they are neither good nor evil.

How quickly all things disappear, in the universe the bodies themselves, but in time the remembrance of them; what is the nature of all sensible things, and particularly those which attract with the bait of pleasure or terrify by pain, or are noised abroad by vapoury fame; how worthless, and contemptible, and sordid, and perishable, and dead they are — all this it is the part of the intellectual faculty to observe. To observe too who these are whose opinions and voices give reputation; what death is, and the fact that, if a man looks at it in itself, and by the abstractive power of reflection resolves into their parts all the things which present themselves to the imagination in it, he will then consider it to be nothing else than an operation of nature; and if any one is afraid of an operation of nature, he is a child. This, however, is not only an operation of nature, but it is also a thing which conduces to the purposes of nature. To observe too how man comes near to the Deity, and by what part of him, and when this part of man is so disposed.

Nothing is more wretched than a man who traverses everything in a round and pries into the things beneath the earth, as the poet says, and seeks by conjecture what is in the minds of his neighbours, without perceiving that it is sufficient to attend to the daemon within him, and to reverence it sincerely. And reverence of the daemon consists in keeping it pure from passion and thoughtlessness, and dissatisfaction with what comes from gods and men. For the things from the gods merit veneration for their excellence; and the things from men should be dear to us by reason of kinship; and sometimes even, in a manner, they move our pity by reason of men's ignorance of good and bad; this defect being not less than that which deprives us of the power of distinguishing things that are white and black.

Though thou shouldest be going to live three thousand years, and as many times ten thousand years, still remember that no man loses any other life than this which he now lives, nor lives any other than this which he now loses. The longest and shortest are thus brought to the same. For the present is the same to all, though that which perishes is not the same; and so that which is lost appears to be a mere

398

moment. For a man cannot lose either the past or the future: for what a man has not, how can any one take this from him? These two things then thou must bear in mind; the one, that all things from eternity are of like forms and come round in a circle, and that it makes no difference whether a man shall see the same things during a hundred years or two hundred, or an infinite time; and the second, that the longest liver and he who will die soonest lose just the same. For the present is the only thing of which a man can be deprived, if it is true that this is the only thing which he has, and that a man cannot lose a thing if he has it not.

Remember that all is opinion. For what was said by the Cynic Monimus is manifest: and manifest too is the use of what was said, if a man receives what may be got out of it as far as it is true.

The soul of man does violence to itself, first of all, when it becomes an abscess and, as it were, a tumour on the universe, so far as it can. For to be vexed at anything which happens is a separation of ourselves from nature, in some part of which the natures of all other things are contained. In the next place, the soul does violence to itself when it turns away from any man, or even moves towards him with the intention of injuring, such as are the souls of those who are angry. In the third place, the soul does violence to itself when it is overpowered by pleasure or by pain. Fourthly, when it plays a part, and does or says anything insincerely and untruly. Fifthly, when it allows an act of its own and any movement to be without an aim, and does anything thoughtlessly and without considering what it is, it being right that even the smallest things be done with reference to an end; and the end of rational animals is to follow the reason and the law of the most ancient city and polity.

Of human life the time is a point, and the substance is in a flux, and the perception dull, and the composition of the whole body subject to putrefaction, and the soul a whirl, and fortune hard to divine, and fame a thing devoid of judgment. And, to say all in a word, everything which belongs to the body is a stream, and what belongs to the soul is a dream and vapour, and life is a warfare and a stranger's sojourn, and after-fame is oblivion. What then is that which is able to conduct a man? One thing and only one, philosophy. But this consists in keeping the daemon within a man free from violence and unharmed, superior to pains and pleasures, doing nothing without a purpose, nor yet falsely and with hypocrisy, not feeling the need of another man's doing or not doing anything; and besides, accepting all that happens, and all that is allotted, as coming from thence, wherever it is, from whence he himself came; and, finally, waiting for death with a cheerful mind, as being nothing else than a dissolution of the elements of which every living being is compounded. But if there is no harm to the elements themselves in each continually changing into another, why should a man have any apprehension about the change and dissolution of all the elements? For it is according to nature, and nothing is evil which is according to nature.

This in Carnuntum.

George Long

SENECA

For biographical note, see under Letters.

Clemency

Clemency defined. Mercy is the interest both of prince and people. Illustrations of imperial clemency.

The humanity and excellence of this virtue is confessed at all hands, as well by the men of pleasure, and those that think every man was made for himself, as by the Stoics, that make "man a sociable creature, and born for the common good of mankind": for it is of all dispositions the most peaceable and quiet. But before we enter any farther upon the discourse, it should be first known what clemency is, that we may distinguish it from pity; which is a weakness, though many times mistaken for a virtue: and the next thing will be, to bring the mind to the habit and exercise of it.

"Clemency is a favourable disposition of the mind, in the matter of inflicting punishment; or, a moderation that remits somewhat of the penalty incurred; as pardon is the total remission of a deserved punishment." We must be careful not to confound clemency with pity; for as religion worships God, and superstition profanes that worship; so should we distinguish betwixt clemency and pity; practising the one, and avoiding the other. For pity proceeds from a narrowness of mind, that respects rather the fortune than the cause. It is a kind of moral sickness, contracted from other people's misfortune: such another weakness as laughing or yawning for company, or as that of sick eyes that cannot look upon others that are bleared without dropping themselves. I will give a shipwrecked man a plank, a lodging to a stranger, or a piece of money to him that wants it: I will dry up the tears of my friend, yet I will not weep with him, but treat him with constancy and humanity, as one man ought to treat another.

It is objected by some, that clemency is an insignificant virtue; and that only the bad are the better for it, for the good have no need of it.

But in the first place, as physic is in use only among the sick, and yet in honour with the sound, so the innocent have a reverence for clemency, though criminals are properly the objects of it. And then again, a man may be innocent, and yet have occasion for it too; for by the accidents of fortune, or the condition of times, virtue itself may come to be in danger. Consider the most populous city or nation; what a solitude would it be if none should be left there but those that could stand the test of a severe justice? We should have neither judges nor accusers; none either to grant a pardon or to ask it. More or less, we are all sinners; and he that has best purged his conscience, was brought by errors to repentance. And it is farther profitable to mankind; for many delinquents come to be converted. There is a tenderness to be used even toward our slaves, and those that we have bought with our money: how much more then to free and to honest men, that are rather under our protection than dominion? Not that I would have it so general neither as not to distinguish betwixt the good and the bad; for that would introduce a confusion, and give a kind of encouragement to wickedness. It must therefore have a respect to the quality of the offender, and separate the curable from the desperate; for it is an equal cruelty to pardon all and to pardon none. Where the matter is in balance, let mercy turn the scale: if all wicked men should be punished, who should escape?

Though mercy and gentleness of nature keeps all in peace and tranquility, even in a cottage; yet it is much more beneficial and conspicuous in a palace. Private men in their condition are likewise private in their virtues and in their vices; but the words and the actions of princes are the subject of public rumour; and therefore they had need have a care, what occasion they give people for discourse, of whom people will be always a talking. There is the government of a prince over his people, a father over his children, a master over his scholars, an officer over his soldiers. He is an unnatural father, that for every trifle beats his children. Who is the better master, he that rages over his scholars for but missing a word in a lesson, or he that tries by admonition and fair words, to instruct and reform them? An outrageous officer makes his men run from their colours. A skilful rider brings his horse to obedience by mingling fair means with foul; whereas to be perpetually switching and spurring, makes him vicious and jadish: and shall we not have more care of men than of beasts? It breaks the hope of generous inclinations, when they are depressed by servility and terror. There is no creature so hard to be pleased with ill usage as man.

Clemency does well with all, but best with princes; for it makes their power comfortable and beneficial, which would otherwise be the pest of mankind. It establishes their greatness, when they make the good of the public their particular care, and employ their power for

402

the safety of the people. The prince, in effect, is but the soul of the community, as the community is only the body of the prince; so that being merciful to others, he is tender of himself: nor is any man so mean but his master feels the loss of him, as a part of his empire: and he takes care not only of the lives of his people, but also of their reputation. Now, giving for granted that all virtues are in themselves equal, it will not yet be denied, that they may be more beneficial to mankind in one person than in another. A beggar may be as magnanimous as a king: for what can be greater or braver than to baffle ill fortune? This does not hinder but that a man in authority and plenty has more matter for his generosity to work upon than a private person; and it is also more taken notice of upon the bench than upon the level. When a gracious prince shows himself to his people, they do not fly from him as from a tiger that rousess himself out of his den, but they worship him as a benevolent influence; they secure him against all conspiracies, and interpose their bodies betwixt him and danger. They guard him while he sleeps, and defend him in the field against his enemies. Nor is it without reason, this unanimous agreement in love and loyalty, and this heroical zeal of abandoning themselves for the safety of their prince, but it is as well the interest of the people. In the breath of a prince there is life and death; and his sentence stands good, right or wrong. If he be angry, nobody dares advise him; and if he does amiss, who shall call him to account? Now, for him that has so much mischief in his power, and yet applies that power to the common utility and comfort of his people, diffusing also clemency and goodness into their hearts too, what can be a greater blessing than such a prince? Any man may kill another against the law, but only a prince can save him so. Let him so deal with his own subjects as he desires God should deal with him. If heaven should be inexorable to sinners, and destroy all without mercy, what flesh could be safe? But as the faults of great men are not presently punished with thunder from above, let them have a like regard to their inferiors here upon earth. He that has revenge in his power, and does not use it, is the great man. Which is the more beautiful and agreeable state, that of a calm, a temperate, and a clear day; or that of lightning, thunder, and tempests? and this is the very difference betwixt a moderate and a turbulent government. It is for low and vulgar spirits to brawl, storm, and transport themselves: but it is not for the majesty of a prince to lash out into intemperance of words. Some will think it rather slavery than empire to be debarred liberty of speech: and what if it be, when government itself is but a more illustrious servitude? He that uses his power as he should, takes as much delight in making it comfortable to his people as glorious to himself. He is affable and easy of access; his very countenance makes him the joy of his people's eyes, and the delight of mankind. He is beloved, defended, and reverenced by all his subjects; and men speak as well of him in private as in public. He is safe without guards, and the sword is rather his ornament than his defence. In his duty, he is like that of a good father, that sometimes gently reproves a son, sometimes threatens him; nay, and perhaps corrects him; but no father in his right wits will disinherit a son for the first fault: there must be many and great offences, and only desperate consequences, that should bring him to that decretory resolution. He will make experiments to try if he can reclaim him first, and nothing but the utmost despair must put him upon extremities. It is not flattery that calls a prince the father of his country; the titles of *great* and *august* are matter of compliment and honour; but in calling him father, we mind him of that moderation and indulgence which he owes to his children. His subjects are his members; where, if there must be an amputation, let him come slowly to it; and when the part is cut off, let him wish it were on again: let him grieve in the doing of it. He that passes a sentence hastily, looks as if he did it willingly; and then there is an injustice in the excess.

It is a glorious contemplation for a prince, first to consider the vast multitudes of his people, whose seditious, divided, and impotent passions, would cast all in confusion, and destroy themselves, and public order too, if the band of government did not restrain them; and thence to pass to the examination of his conscience, saying thus to himself: "It is by the choice of Providence that I am here made God's deputy upon earth, the arbiter of life and death; and that upon my breath depends the fortune of my people. My lips are the oracles of their fate, and upon them hangs the destiny both of cities and of men. It is under my favour that people seek either for prosperity or protection; thousands of swords are drawn or sheathed at my pleasure. What towns shall be advanced or destroyed, who shall be slaves, or who free, depends upon my will; and yet, in this arbitrary power of acting without control, I was never transported to do any cruel thing, either by anger or hot blood in myself, or by the contumacy, rashness, or provocations of other men, though sufficient to turn mercy itself into fury. I was never moved by the odious vanity of making myself terrible by my power, (that accursed, though common humour of ostentation and glory that haunts imperious natures.) My sword has not only been buried in the scabbard, but in a manner bound to the peace and tender, even of the cheapest blood: and where I find no other motive to compassion, humanity itself is sufficient. I have been always slow to severity, and prone to forgive; and under as strict a guard to observe the laws as if I were accountable for the breaking of them. Some I pardoned for their youth, others for their age. I spare one man for his dignity, another for his humility; and when I find no other matter to work upon, I spare myself. So that if God should at this instant call me to an account, the whole world would agree to witness for me, that I have not by any force, either public or private, either by myself or by any other, defrauded the commonwealth; and the reputation that I have ever sought for has been that which few princes have obtained, the conscience of my proper innocence. And I have not lost my labour neither; for no man was ever so dear to another, as I have made myself to the whole body of my people." Under such a prince the subject has nothing to wish for beyond what he enjoys; their fears are quieted, and their prayers heard; and there is nothing can make their felicity greater, unless to make it perpetual; and there is no liberty denied to the people but that of destroying one another.

It is the interest of the people, by the consent of all nations, to run all hazards for the safety of their prince, and by a thousand deaths to redeem that one life, upon which so many millions depend. Does not the whole body serve the mind, though only the one is exposed to the eye and the other not, but thin and invisible, the very seat of it being uncertain? Yet the hands, feet, and eyes, observe the motions of it. We lie down, run about and ramble, as that commands us. If we be covetous, we fish the seas and ransack the earth for treasure: if ambitious, we burn our own flesh with Scaevola; we cast ourselves into the gulf with Curtius; so would that vast multitude of people, which is animated but with one soul, governed by one spirit, and moved by one reason, destroy itself with its own strength, if it were not supported by wisdom and government. Wherefore, it is for their own security that the people expose their lives for their prince, as the very bond that ties the republic together; the vital spirit of so many thousands, which would be nothing else but a burden and prey without a governor. When this union comes once to be dissolved, all falls to pieces; for empire and obedience must stand and fall together. It is no wonder then if a prince be dear to his people, when the community is wrapt up in him, and the good of both as inseparable as the body and the head; the one for strength, and the other for counsel; for what signifies the force of the body without the direction of the understanding? While the prince watches, his people sleep; his labour keeps them at ease, and his business keeps them quiet. The natural intent of monarchy appears even from the very discipline of bees; they assign to their master the fairest lodgings, the safest place; and his office is only to see that the rest perform their duties. When their king is lost, the whole swarm dissolve: more than one they will not admit; and then they contend who shall have the best. They are of all creatures the fiercest for their bigness; and leave their stings behind them in their quarrels; only the king himself has none, intimating that kings should neither be vindictive nor cruel. Is it not a shame, after such an example of moderation in these creatures, that men should be yet intemperate! It were well if they lost their stings too in their revenge, as well as the other, that they might hurt but once, and do no mischief by their proxies. It would tire them out, if either they were to execute all with their own hands, or to wound others at the peril of their own lives.

A prince should behave himself generously in the power which God has given him of life and death, especially toward those that have been at any time his equals; for the one has his revenge, and the other his punishment in it. He that stands indebted for his life has lost it; but he that receives his life at the foot of his enemy, lives to the honour of his preserver: he lives the lasting monument of his virtue; whereas, if he had been led in triumph, the spectacle would have been quickly over. Or what if he should restore him to his kingdom again? would it not be an ample accession to his honour to show that he found nothing about the conquered that was worthy of the conqueror? There is nothing more venerable than a prince that does not revenge an injury. He that is gracious is beloved and reverenced as a common father; but a tyrant stands in fear and in danger even of his own guards. No prince can be safe himself of whom all others are afraid; for to spare none is to enrage all. It is an error to imagine that any man can be secure that suffers nobody else to be so too. How can any man endure to lead an uneasy, suspicious, anxious life, when he may be safe if he please, and enjoy all the blessings of power, together with the prayers of his people? Clemency protects a prince without a guard; there is no need of troops, castles, or fortifications: security on the one side is the condition of security on the other; and the affections of the subject are the most invincible fortress. What can be fairer, than for a prince to live the object of his people's love; to have the vows of their heart as well as of their lips, and his health and sickness their common hopes and fears? There will be no danger of plots; nay, on the contrary, who would not frankly venture his blood to save him, under whose government, justice, peace, modesty, and dignity, flourish? under whose influence men grow rich and happy; and whom men look upon with such veneration, as they would do upon the immortal gods, if they were capable of seeing them? And, as the true representative of the Almighty they consider him, when he is gracious and bountiful, and employs his power to the advantage of his subjects.

When a prince proceeds to punishment, it must be either to vindicate himself or others. It is a hard matter to govern himself in his own case. If a man should advise him not to be credulous, but to examine matters, and indulge the innocent, this is rather a point of justice than of clemency: but in case that he be manifestly injured, I would have him

406

forgive, where he may safely do it: and be tender even where he cannot forgive; but far more exorable in his own case, however, than in another's. It is nothing to be free of another man's purse; and it is as little to be merciful in another man's cause. He is the great man that masters his passion where he is stung himself, and pardons when he might destroy. The end of punishment is either to comfort the party injured, or to secure him for the future. A prince's fortune is above the need of such a comfort, and his power is too eminent to seek an advance of reputation by doing a private man a mischief. This I speak in case of an affront from those that are below us: but he that of an equal has made any man his inferior, has his revenge in the bringing of him down. A prince has been killed by a servant, destroyed by a serpent; but whosoever preserves a man, must be greater than the person that he preserves. With citizens, strangers, and people of low condition, a prince is not to contend, for they are beneath him: he may spare some out of good-will, and others as he would do some little creatures that a man cannot touch without fouling his fingers: but for those that are to be pardoned, or exposed to public punishment, he may use mercy as he sees occasion; and a generous mind can never want inducements and motives to it; and whether it be age or sex, high or low, nothing comes amiss.

To pass now to the vindication of others, there must be had a regard either to the amendment of the person punished, or the making others better for fear of punishment, or the taking the offender out of the way for the security of others. An amendment may be procured by a small punishment: for he lives more carefully that has something yet to lose; it is a kind of impunity to be incapable of a farther punishment. The corruptions of a city are best cured by a few and sparing severities; for the multitude of offenders creates a custom of offending, and company authorises a crime, and there is more good to be done upon a dissolute age by patience than by rigour; provided that it pass not for an approbation of ill-manners, but only as an unwillingness to proceed to extremities. Under a merciful prince, a man will be ashamed to offend, because a punishment that is inflicted by a gentle governor seems to fall heavier, and with more reproach: and it is remarkable also, that "those sins are often committed which are very often punished." Caligula, in five years, condemned more people to the sack than ever were before him: and there were "fewer parricides before the law against them than after." For our ancestors did wisely presume, that the crime would never be committed, until by law for punishing it, they found that it might be done. Parricides began with the law against them, and the punishment instructed men in the crime. Where there are few punishments, innocency is indulged as a public good, and it is a dangerous thing to show a city how strong it is in delinquents. There is a certain contumacy in the nature of man, that makes him oppose difficulties. We are better to follow than to drive; as a generous horse rides best with an easy bit. People obey willingly where they are commanded kindly. When Burrhus the prefect was to sentence two malefactors, he brought the warrant to Nero to sign; who after a long reluctancy, came to it at last with this exclamation, "I would I could not write!" A speech that deserved the whole world for an auditory, but all princes especially; and that the hearts of all the subjects would conform to the likeness of their masters. As the head is well or ill, so is the mind dull or merry. What is the difference betwixt a king and a tyrant, but a diversity of will under one and the same power? The one destroys for his pleasure, the other upon necessity; a distinction rather in fact than in name.

A gracious prince is armed as well as a tyrant; but it is for the defence of his people, and not for the ruin of them. No king can ever have faithful servants that accustoms them to tortures and executions: the very guilty themselves do not lead so anxious a life as the persecutors: for they are not only afraid of justice, both divine and human, but it is dangerous for them to mend their manners; so that when they are once in, they must continue to be wicked upon necessity. An universal hatred unites in a popular rage. A temperate fear may be kept in order; but when it comes once to be continual and sharp, it provokes people to extremities, and transports them to desperate resolutions; as wild beasts, when they are pressed upon the toil, turn back, and assault the very pursuers. A turbulent government is a perpetual trouble both to prince and people; and he that is a terror to all others is not without terror also himself. Frequent punishments and revenges may suppress the hatred of a few, but then it stirs up the detestation of all. So that there is no destroying one enemy without making many. It is good to master the will of being cruel, even while there may be cause for it, and matter to work upon.

Augustus was a gracious prince when he had the power in his own hand; but in the triumviracy he made use of his sword, and had his friends ready armed to set upon Anthony during that dispute. But he behaved himself afterwards at another rate; for when he was betwixt forty and fifty years of age he was told that Cinna was in a plot to murder him, with the time, place, and manner of the design; and this from one of the confederates. Upon this he resolved upon a revenge, and sent for several of his friends to advise upon it. The thought of it kept him waking, to consider, that there was the life of a young nobleman in the case, the nephew of Pompey, and a person otherwise innocent. He was off and on several times whether he should put him to death or not. "What," says he, "shall I live in trouble and in danger myself, and the contriver of my death walk free and secure? Will nothing serve him but that life which Providence has preserved in so many civil wars; in so many battles both by sea and land; and now in the state of an universal peace too? and not a simple murder neither, but a sacrifice; for I am to be assaulted at the very altar; and shall the contriver of all this villainy escape unpunished?" Here Augustus made a little pause, and then recollecting himself: "No, no, Caesar," says he, "it is rather Caesar than Cinna that I am to be angry with: why do I myself live any longer after that my death is become the interest of so many people? And if I go on, what end will there be of blood, and of punishment? If it be against my life that the nobility arms itself, and levels their weapons, my single life is not worth the while, if so many must be destroyed that I may be preserved." His wife Livia gave him here an interruption, and desired him that he would for once hear a woman's counsel. "Do," says she, "like a physician, that when common remedies fail will try the contrary: you have got nothing hitherto by severity; after Salvidianus, there followed Lepidus; after him Muraena: Caepio followed him, and Egnatius followed Caepio; try now what mercy will do, forgive Cinna. He is discovered, and can do no hurt in your person; and it will yet advantage you in your reputation." Augustus was glad of the advice, and he gave thanks for it; and thereupon countermanded the meeting of his friends, and ordered Cinna to be brought to him alone; for whom he caused a chair to be set, and then discharged the rest of the company. "Cinna," says Augustus, "before I go any farther, you must promise not to give me the interruption of one syllable until I have told you all I have to say, and you shall have liberty afterwards to say what you please. You cannot forget, that when I found you in arms against me, and not only made my enemy, but born so, I gave you your life and fortune. Upon your petition for the priesthood, I granted it, with a repulse to the sons of those that had been my fellow-soldiers; and you are at this day so happy and so rich, that even the conquerors envy him that is overcome; and yet after all this, you are in a plot, Cinna, to murder me." At that word Cinna started, and interposed with exclamations, "that certainly he was far from being either so wicked or so mad." "This is breach of conditions, Cinna," says Augustus, "it is not your time to speak yet, I tell you again, that you are in a plot to murder me:" and so he told him the time, the place, the confederates, the order and manner of the design, and who it was that was to do the deed. Cinna, upon this, fixed his eye upon the ground without any reply: not for his word's sake, but as in a confusion of conscience: and so Augustus went on. "What," says he, "may your design be in all this? Is it that you would pretend to step into my place? The commonwealth were in an ill condition, if only Augustus were in the way betwixt you and the government. You were cast the other day in a cause by one of your own freemen, and do you expect to find a weaker adversary of Caesar? But what if I were removed? There is Aemilius Paulus, Fabius Maximus, and twenty other families of great blood and interest, that would never bear it." To cut off the story short; (for it was a discourse of above two hours; and Augustus lengthened the punishment in words, since he intended that should be all;) "Well, Cinna," says he, "the life that I gave you once as an enemy, I will now repeat it to a traitor and to a parricide; and this shall be the last reproach I will give you. For the time to come there shall be no other contention betwixt you and me, than which shall outdo the other in point of friendship." After this Augustus made Cinna consul, (an honour which he confessed he durst not so much as desire) and Cinna was ever affectionately faithful to him: he made Caesar his sole heir; and this was the last conspiracy that ever was formed against him.

This moderation of Augustus was the excellency of his mature age; for in his youth he was passionate and sudden; and he did many things which afterwards he looked back upon with trouble; after the battle of Actium, so many navies broken in Sicily, both Roman and strangers: the Perusian altars, (where 300 lives were sacrificed to the ghost of Julius); his frequent proscriptions, and other severities; his temperance at last seemed to be little more than a weary cruelty. If he had not forgiven those that he conquered, whom should he have governed? He chose his very life-guard from among his enemies, and the flower of the Romans owed their lives to his clemency. Nay, he only punished Lepidus himself with banishment, and permitted him to wear the ensigns of his dignity, without taking the pontificate to himself so long as Lepidus was living; for he would not possess it as a spoil, but as an honour. This clemency it was that secured him in his greatness, and ingratiated him to the people, though he laid his hand upon the government before they had thoroughly submitted to the yoke; and this clemency it was that made his name famous to posterity. This is it that makes us reckon him divine without the authority of an apotheosis. He was so tender and patient, that though many a bitter jest was broken upon him, (and contumelies upon princes are the most intolerable of all injuries) yet he never punished any man upon that subject. It is, then, generous to be merciful, when we have it in our power to take revenge.

A son of Titus Arius, being examined and found guilty of parricide, was banished Rome, and confined to Marseilles, where his father allowed him the same annuity that he had before; which made all people conclude him guilty, when they saw that his father had yet condemned the son that he could not hate. Augustus was pleased to sit upon the fact in the house of Arius, only as a single member of

410

the council that was to examine it: if it had been in Caesar's palace, the judgment must have been Caesar's and not the father's. Upon a full hearing of the matter, Caesar directed that every man should write his opinion whether guilty or not, and without declaring of his own, for fear of a partial vote. Before the opening of the books Caesar passed an oath, that he would not be Arius's heir; and to show that he had no interest in his sentence, as appeared afterward; for he was not condemned to the ordinary punishments of parricides, nor to a prison, but, by the mediation of Caesar, only banished Rome, and confined to the place which his father should name: Augustus insisting upon it, that the father should content himself with an easy punishment; and arguing that the young man was not moved to the attempt by malice, and that he was but half resolved upon the fact, for he wavered in it; and therefore, to remove him from the city, and from his father's sight, would be sufficient. This is a glorious mercy, and worthy of a prince, to make all things gentler wherever he comes. How miserable is that man in himself, who, when he has employed his power in rapines and cruelty upon others, is yet more unhappy in himself? He stands in fear both of his domestics and of strangers; the faith of his friends and the piety of his children, and flies to actual violence to secure him from the violence he fears. When he comes to look about him, and to consider what he has done, what he must, and what he is about to do; what with the wickedness, and with the torments of his conscience, many times he fears death, oftener he wishes for it; and lives more odious to himself than to his subjects; whereas on the contrary, he that takes a care of the public, though of one part more perhaps than of another, yet there is not any part of it but he looks upon as part of himself. His mind is tender and gentle; and even where punishment is necessary and profitable, he comes to it unwillingly, and without any rancour or enmity in his heart. Let the authority, in fine, be what it will, clemency becomes it; and the greater the power, the greater is the glory of it. "It is a truly royal virtue for a prince to deliver his people from other men's anger, and not to oppress them with his own."

Roger L'Estrange

ORATORY

Cicero

Tacitus

CICERO

MARCUS TULLIUS CICERO (C. 106-43 B.C.) was one of the most distinguished Romans, as statesman, orator, philosopher, and letter writer. Born at Arpinum, of an equestrian family, he rose to the highest office in the state, becoming consul in 63 B. C. In this capacity be crushed the conspiracy of Catiline.

Cicero determinedly fought against political corruption, and suffered the consequences. He was banished through the machinations of Clodius. In the Civil War he supported Pompey against Caesar. He was finally assassinated for his attacks against Antony.

Among his extant works are political and legal speeches, philosophical essays, and a large correspondence. His chief reputation rests on his Latinity, which in his hands became a pliant, sensitive instrument of expression and a model for later centuries.

THE FIRST ORATION AGAINST VERRES

THE ARGUMENT

After the last oration it was decided that Cicero was to conduct the prosecution against Verres: accordingly, a hundred and ten days were allowed him to prepare the evidence, with which object he went himself to Sicily to examine witnesses, and to collect facts in support of his charges, taking with him his cousin Lucius Cicero as an assistant, and in this journey, contrary to all precedent, he bore his own expenses, resolving to put the island to no charge on his account. At Syracuse the praetor, Metellus, endeavoured to obstruct him in his inquiries, but the magistrates received him with great respect, and declaring to him that all that they had previously done in favour of Verres (for they had erected a gilt statue of him, and had sent a testimonial of his good conduct and kind government of them to Rome) had been extorted from them by intrigue and terror, they delivered into his hands authentic accounts of many injuries their city had received from Verres, and they revoked by a formal decree the public praises which they had given him. Messana, however, continued firm in its engagements to Verres, and denied Cicero all the honours to which he was entitled. When he finished his investigations, apprehending that he might be waylaid by the contrivance of Verres, he returned by sea to Rome, where he found intrigues carrying on to protract the affair as much as possible, in order to delay the decision of it till the year following, when Hortensius and Metellus were to be the consuls, and the brother of Metellus was to be praetor, by whose united authority the prosecution might be stifled: and it was now so late in the year that there was not time to bring the trial to an end, if the ordinary course of proceeding was adhered to. But Cicero, determined to bring on the decision while Glabrio continued praetor, abandoned his idea of making a long speech, and of taking up time in dilating on and enforcing the different counts of the indictment, and resolved to do nothing more than produce his witnesses, and offer them to examination; and this novel method of conducting the case, together with the powerful evidence produced, which he could not invalidate, so confounded Hortensius, that he could find nothing to say in his client's defence, who in despair went of his own accord into banishment.

The object of Cicero in this oration is to show that it is out of sheer necessity that he does this, and that he is driven to such a proceeding by the intrigues of the opposite party. He therefore exhorts the judges not to be intimidated or cajoled into a dishonest decision, and threatens the opposite party with punishment for endeavouring to corrupt the judges.

I.   That which was above all things to be desired, O judges, and which above all things was calculated to have the greatest influence towards allaying the unpopularity of your order, and putting an end to the discredit into which your judicial decisions have fallen, appears to have been thrown in your way, and given to you not by any human contrivance, but almost by the interposition of the gods, at a most important crisis of the republic. For an opinion has now become established, pernicious to us, and pernicious to the republic, which has been the common talk of every one, not only at Rome, but among foreign nations also, — that in the courts of law as they exist at present, no wealthy man, however guilty he may be, can possibly be convicted. Now at this time of peril to your order and to your tribunals, when men are ready to attempt by harangues, and by the proposal of new laws, to increase the existing unpopularity of the senate, Caius Verres is brought to trial as a criminal, a man condemned in the opinion of every one by his life and actions, but acquitted by the enormousness of his wealth according to his own hope and boast. I, O judges, have undertaken this cause as prosecutor with the greatest good wishes and expectation on the part of the Roman people, not in order to increase the unpopularity of the senate, but to relieve it from the discredit which I share with it. For I have brought before you a man,

414

by acting justly in whose case you have an opportunity of retrieving the lost credit of your judicial proceedings, of regaining your credit with the Roman people, and of giving satisfaction to foreign nations; a man, the embezzler of the public funds, the petty tyrant of Asia and Pamphylia, the robber who deprived the city of its rights, the disgrace and ruin of the province of Sicily. And if you come to a decision about this man with severity and a due regard to your oaths, that authority which ought to remain in you will cling to you still; but if that man's vast riches shall break down the sanctity and honesty of the courts of justice, at least I shall achieve this, that it shall be plain that it was rather honest judgment that was wanting to the republic, than a criminal to the judges, or an accuser to the criminal.

II.   I, indeed, that I may confess to you the truth about myself, O judges, though many snares were laid for me by Caius Verres, both by land and sea, which I partly avoided by my own vigilance, and partly warded off by the zeal and kindness of my friends, yet I never seemed to be incurring so much danger, and I never was in such a state of great apprehension, as I am now in this very court of law. Nor does the expectation which people have formed of my conduct of this prosecution, nor this concourse of so vast a multitude as is here assembled, influence me (though indeed I am greatly agitated by these circumstances) so much as his nefarious plots which he is endeavouring to lay at one and the same time against me, against you, against Marcus Glabrio the praetor, and against the allies, against foreign nations, against the senate, and even against the very name of senator; whose favourite saying it is that they have got to fear who have stolen only as much as is enough for themselves, but that he has stolen so much that it may easily be plenty for many; that nothing is so holy that it cannot be corrupted, or so strongly fortified that it cannot be stormed by money. But if he were as secret in acting as he is audacious in attempting, perhaps in some particular he might some time or other have escaped our notice. But it happens very fortunately that to his incredible audacity there is joined a most unexampled folly. For as he was unconcealed in committing his robberies of money, so in his hope of corrupting the judges he has made his intentions and endeavours visible to every one. He says that once only in his life has he felt fear, at the time when he was first impeached as a criminal by me; because he was only lately arrived from his province, and was branded with unpopularity and infamy, not modern but ancient and of long standing; and, besides that, the time was unlucky, being very ill-suited for corrupting the judges. Therefore, when I had demanded a very short time to prosecute my inquiries in Sicily, he found a man to ask for two days less to make investigations in Achaia; not with any real intention of doing the same with his diligence and industry, that I have accomplished by my labour, and daily and nightly investigations. For the Achaean inquisitor never even arrived at Brundusium. I in fifty days so travelled over the whole of Sicily that I examined into the records and injuries of all the tribes and of all private individuals, so that it was easily visible to every one, that he had been seeking out a man not really for the purpose of bringing the defendant whom he accused to trial but merely to occupy the time which ought to belong to me.

III. Now that most audacious and most senseless man thinks this. He is aware that I am come into court so thoroughly prepared and armed, that I shall fix all his thefts and crimes not only in your ears, but in the very eyes of all men. He sees that many senators are witnesses of his audacity; he sees that many Roman knights are so too, and many citizens, and many of the allies besides to whom he has done unmistakeable injuries. He sees also that very numerous and very important deputations have come here at the same time from most friendly cities, armed with the public authority and evidence collected by their states. And though this is the case, still he thinks so ill of all virtuous men, to such an extent does he believe the decisions of the senators to be corrupt and profligate, that he makes a custom of openly boasting that it was not without reason that he was greedy of money, since he now finds that there is such protection in money, and that he has bought (what was the hardest thing of all) the very time of his trial, in order to be able to buy everything else more easily; so that, as he could not by any possibility shirk the force of the accusations altogether, he might avoid the most violent gusts of the storm. But if he had placed any hope at all, not only in his cause, but in any honourable defence, or in the eloquence or in the influence of any one, he would not be so eager in collecting and catching at all these things; he would not scorn and despise the senatorial body to such a degree, as to procure a man to be selected out of the senate at his will to be made a criminal of, who should plead his cause before him, while he in the meantime was preparing whatever he had need of. And what the circumstances are on which he founds his hopes, and what hopes he builds on them, and what he is fixing his mind on, I see clearly. But how he can have the confidence to think that he can effect anything with the present praetor, and the present bench of judges, I cannot conceive. This one thing I know, which the Roman people perceived too when he rejected the judges, that his hopes were of that nature that he placed all his expectations of safety in his money; and that if this protection were taken from him, he thought nothing would be any help to him.

416

IV. In truth, what genius is there so powerful, what faculty of speaking, what eloquence so mighty, as to be in any particular able to defend the life of that man, convicted as it is of so many vices and crimes, and long since condemned by the inclinations and private sentiments of every one. And, to say nothing of the stains and disgraces of his youth, what other remarkable event is there in his quaestorship, that first step to honour, except that Cnaeus Carbo was robbed by his quaestor of the public money? that the consul was plundered and betrayed? his army deserted? his province abandoned? the holy nature and obligations imposed on him by lot violated? — whose lieutenancy was the ruin of all Asia and Pamphylia, in which provinces he plundered many houses, very many cities, all the shrines and temples; when he renewed and repeated against Cnaeus Dolabella his ancient wicked tricks when he had been quaestor, and did not only his danger desert, but even attack and betray the man to whom he had been lieutenant, and proquaestor, and whom he had brought into odium by his crimes; — whose city praetorship was the destruction of the sacred temples and the public works, and, as to his legal decisions, was the adjudging and awarding of property contrary to all established rules and precedents. But now he has established great and numerous monuments and proofs of all his vices in the province of Sicily, which he for three years so harassed and ruined that it can by no possibility be restored to its former condition, and appears scarcely able to be at all recovered after a long series of years, and a long succession of virtuous praetors. While this man was praetor the Sicilians enjoyed neither their own laws, nor the decrees of our senate, nor the common rights of every nation. Every one in Sicily has only so much left as either escaped the notice or was disregarded by the satiety of that most avaricious and licentious man.

V. No legal decision for three years was given on any other ground but his will; no property was so secure to any man, even if it had descended to him from his father and grandfather, but he was deprived of it at his command; enormous sums of money were exacted from the property of the cultivators of the soil by a new and nefarious system. The most faithful of the allies were classed in the number of enemies. Roman citizens were tortured and put to death like slaves; the greatest criminals were acquitted in the courts of justice through bribery; the most upright and honourable men, being prosecuted while absent, were condemned and banished without being heard in their own defence; the most fortified harbours, the greatest and strongest cities, were laid open to pirates and robbers; the sailors and soldiers of the Sicilians, our own allies and friends, died of hunger; the best built fleets on the most important stations were lost and destroyed, to the great disgrace of the Roman people. This same man while praetor plundered and stripped those most ancient monuments, some erected by wealthy monarchs and intended by them as ornaments for their cities; some, too, the work of our own generals, which they either gave or restored as conquerors to the different states in Sicily. And he did this not only in the case of public statues and ornaments, but he also plundered all the temples consecrated in the deepest religious feelings of the people. He did not leave, in short, one god to the Sicilians which appeared to him to be made in a tolerably workmanlike manner, and with any of the skill of the ancients. I am prevented by actual shame from speaking of his nefarious licentiousness as shown in rapes and other such enormities; and I am unwilling also to increase the distress of those men who have been unable to preserve their children and their wives unpolluted by his wanton lust. But, you will say, these things were done by him in such a manner as not to be notorious to all men. I think there is no man who has heard his name who cannot also relate wicked actions of his; so that I ought rather to be afraid of being thought to omit many of his crimes, than to invent any charges against him. And indeed I do not think that this multitude which has collected to listen to me wishes so much to learn of me what the facts of the case are, as to go over it with me, refreshing its recollection of what it knows already.

VI. And as this is the case, that senseless and profligate man attempts to combat me in another manner. He does not seek to oppose the eloquence of any one else to me; he does not rely on the popularity, or influence, or authority of any one. He pretends that he trusts to these things; but I see what he is really aiming at; (and indeed he is not acting with any concealment.) He sets before me empty titles of nobility, that is to say the names of arrogant men, who do not hinder me so much by being noble, as assist me by being notorious; — he pretends to rely on their protection; when he has in reality been contriving something else this long time. What hope he now has, and what he is endeavoring to do, I will now briefly explain to you, O judges. But first of all, remark, I beg you, how the matter has been arranged by him from the beginning. When he first returned from the province, he endeavoured to get rid of this prosecution by corrupting the judges at a great expense; and this object he continued to keep in view till the conclusion of the appointment of the judges. After the judges were appointed, because in drawing lots for them the fortune of the Roman people had defeated his hopes, and in the rejecting some my diligence had defeated his impudence, the whole attempt at bribery was abandoned. The affair was going on admirably; lists of your names and of the whole tribunal were in every one's hands. It did not seem possible to mark the votes of these men with any distinguishing mark or colour or spot of dirt; and that fellow, from having been brisk and in high spirits, became on a sudden so downcast and humbled, that he seemed to be condemned not only by the Roman people but even by himself. But lo! all of a sudden, within these few days, since the consular comitia have taken place, he has gone back to his original plan with more money, and the same plots are now laid against your reputation and against the fortunes of every one, by the instrumentality of the same people; which fact at first, O judges, was pointed out to me by a very slight hint and indication; but afterwards, when my suspicions were once aroused, I arrived at the knowledge of all the most secret counsels of that party without any mistake.

VII. For as Hortensius the consul elect was being attended home again from the Campus by a great concourse and multitude of people, Caius Curio fell in with that multitude by chance, — a man whom I wish to name by way of honour rather than of disparagement. I will tell you what, if he had been unwilling to have it mentioned, he would not have spoken in so large an assembly so openly and undisguisedly; which, however, shall be mentioned by me deliberately and cautiously, that it may be seen that I pay due regard to our friendship and to his dignity. He sees Verres in the crowd by the arch of Fabius; he speaks to the man, and with a loud voice congratulates him on his victory. He does not say a word to Hortensius himself, who had been made consul, or to his friends and relations who were present attending on him; but he stops to speak to this man, embraces him, and bids him cast off all anxiety. "I give you notice," said he, "that you have been acquitted by this day's comitia." And as many most honourable men heard this, it is immediately reported to me; indeed, every one who saw me mentioned it to me the first thing. To some it appeared scandalous, to others ridiculous; ridiculous to those who thought that this cause depended on the credibility of the witnesses, on the importance of the charges, and on the power of the judges, and not on the consular comitia; scandalous to those who looked deeper, and who thought that this congratulation had reference to the corruption of the judges. In truth, they argued in this manner — the most honourable men spoke to one another and to me in this manner — that there were now manifestly and undeniably no courts of justice at all. The very criminal who the day before thought that he was already condemned, is acquitted now that his defender has been made consul. What are we to think then? Will it avail nothing that all Sicily, all the Sicilians, that all the merchants who have business in that country, that all public and private documents are now at Rome? Nothing, if the consul elect wills it otherwise. What! will not the judges be influenced by the accusation, by the evidence, by the universal opinion of the Roman people? No. Everything will be governed by the power and authority of one man.

VIII. I will speak the truth, O judges. This thing agitated me greatly; for every good man was speaking in this way "That fellow will be taken out of your hands; but we shall not preserve our judicial authority much longer; for who, when Verres is acquitted, will be able to make any objection to transferring it from us?" It was a grievous thing to every one, and the sudden elation of that profligate man did not weigh with them as much as that fresh congratulation of a very honourable one. I wished to dissemble my own vexation at it; I wished to conceal my own grief of mind under a cheerful countenance, and to bury it in silence. But lo! on the very day when the praetors elected were dividing their duties by lot, and when it fell to the share of Marcus Metellus to hold trials concerning extortion, information is given me that that fellow was receiving such congratulations, that he also sent men home to announce it to his wife. And this too in truth displeased me; and yet I was not quite aware what I had so much to fear from this allotment of the praetor's duties. But I ascertained this one thing from trustworthy men from whom I received all my intelligence; that many chests full of Sicilian money had been sent by some senator to a Roman knight, and that of these about ten chests had been left at that senator's house, with the statement that they were left to be used in the comitia when I expected to be elected aedile, and the men to distribute this money among all the tribes had been summoned to attend him by night. Of whom one, who thought himself under the greatest obligations to me, came to me that same night; reports to me the speech which that fellow had addressed to them; that he had reminded them how liberally he had treated them formerly when he was candidate for the praetorship, and at the last consular and praetorian comitia; and in the second place that he had promised them immediately whatever money they required, if they could procure my rejection from the aedileship. That on this some of them said that they did not dare attempt it; that others answered that they did not think it could be managed; but that one bold friend was found, a man of the same family as himself, Quintus Verres, of the Romilian tribe, of the most perfect school of bribers, the pupil and friend of Verres's father, who promised that, if five hundred thousand sesterces were provided, he would manage it; and that there were some others who said that they would cooperate with him. And as this was the case, he warned me beforehand with a friendly disposition, to take great care.

IX. I was disquieted about many most important matters at one and the same moment, and with very little time to deliberate. The comitia were at hand; and at them I was to be opposed at immense expenditure of money. This trial was at hand; the Sicilian treasurers menaced that matter also. I was afraid, from apprehension about the comitia, to conduct the matters relating to the trial with freedom; and because of the trial, I was unable to attend with all my heart to my canvass. Threatening the agents of bribery was out of the question, because I saw that they were aware that I was hampered and fettered by this trial. And at this same moment I hear that notice has been given to the Sicilians by Hortensius to come to speak to him at his house; that the Sicilians behaved in that matter with a proper sense of their own liberty, and, when they understood on what account they were sent for, they would not go. In the meantime my comitia began to be held; of which that fellow thought himself the master, as he had been of all the other comitia this year. He began to run about, that influential man, with his son, a youth of engaging and popular manners, among the tribes. The son began to address and to call on all the friends of his father, that is to say, all his agents for bribery; and when this was noticed and perceived, the Roman people took care with the most earnest good-will that I should not be deprived of my honour through the money of that man, whose riches had not been able to make me violate my good faith. After that I was released from that great anxiety about my canvass. I began, with a mind much more unoccupied and much more at ease, to think of nothing and to do nothing except what related to this trial. I find, O judges, these plans formed and begun to be put in execution by them, to protract the matter, whatever steps it might be necessary to take in order to do so, so that the cause might be pleaded before Marcus Metellus as praetor. That by doing so they would have these advantages; firstly, that Marcus Metellus was most friendly to them; secondly, that not only would Hortensius be consul, but Quintus Metellus also: and listen while I show you how great a friend he is to them. For he gave him a token of his good-will of such a sort, that he seemed to be giving it as return for the suffrages of the tribes which he had secured to him. Did you think that I would say nothing of such serious matters as these? and that, at a crisis of such danger to the republic and my own character, I would consult anything rather than my duty and my dignity? The other consul elect sent for the Sicilians; some came, because Lucius Metellus was praetor in Sicily. To them he speaks in this manner: that he is the consul; that one of his brothers has Sicily for his province; that the other is to be judge in all prosecutions for extortion; and that care had been taken in many ways that there should be no possibility of Verres being injured.

X. I ask you, Metellus, what is corrupting the course of justice, if this is not, — to seek to frighten witnesses, and especially Sicilians, timid and oppressed men, not only by your own private influence, but by their fear of the consul, and by the power of two praetors? What would you do for an innocent man or for a relation, when for the sake of a most guilty man, entirely unconnected with you, you depart from your duty and your dignity, and allow what he is constantly saying to appear true to any one who is not acquainted with you? For they said that Verres said, that you had not been made consul by destiny, as the rest of your family had been, but by his assistance. Two consuls, therefore, and the judge are to be such because of his will. We shall not only, says he, avoid having a man too scrupulous in investigating, too subservient to the opinion of the people, Marcus Glabrio, but we shall have this advantage also: — Marcus Caesonius is the judge, the colleague of our accuser, a man of tried and proved experience in the decision of actions. It will never do for us to have such a man as that on the bench, which we are endeavouring to corrupt by some means or other; for before, when he was one of the judges on the tribunal of which Junius was president, he was not only very indignant at that shameful transaction, but he even betrayed and denounced it. After the first of January we shall not have this man for our judge, — we shall not have Quintus Manlius and Quintus Cornificius, two most severe and upright judges, for judges, because they will then be tribunes of the people. Publius Sulpicius, a solemn and upright judge, must enter on his magistracy on the fifth of November. Marcus Crepereius, of that renowned equestrian family and of that incorruptible character; Lucius Cassius, of a family renowned for its severity in all things, and especially as judges; Cnaeus Tremellius, a man of the greatest scrupulousness and diligence; — these three men of ancient strictness of principle are all military tribunes elect. After the first of January they will not be able to act as judges. And besides this, we elect by lot a successor in the room of Marcus Metellus, since he is to preside over this very trial. And so after the first of January, the praetor, and almost the whole bench of judges being changed, we shall elude the terrible threats of the prosecutor, and the great expectations entertained of this trial, and manage it according to our own will and pleasure. Today is the fifth of August. You began to assemble at the ninth hour. This day they do not even count. There are ten days between this and the votive games which Cnaeus Pompey is going to celebrate. These games will take up fifteen days; then immediately the Roman games will follow. And so, when nearly forty days have intervened, then at length they think they shall have to answer what has been said by us; and they think that, what with speeches, and what with excuses, they will easily be able to protract the cause till the period of the games of Victory. With these the plebeian games are connected, after which there will be either no day at all, or very few for pleading in. And so, when the accusation has got stale and cold, the matter will come all fresh before Marcus Metellus as praetor. And if I had distrusted his good faith, I should not have retained him as a judge; but now I have such an opinion of him, that I would rather this matter was brought to a close while he is judge than while he is praetor; and I would rather entrust to him his own tablet while he is on his oath, than the tablets of others when he is restrained by no such obligation.

XI. Now, O judges, I consult you as to what you think I ought to do. For you will, in truth, without speaking, give me that advice which I understand that I must inevitably adopt. If I occupy the time which I legitimately might in speaking, I shall reap the fruit of my labour, industry, and diligence; and by this prosecution I shall make it manifest that no one in the memory of man appears ever to have come before a court of justice better prepared, more vigilant, or with his cause better got up. But while I am getting this credit for my industry, there is great danger lest the criminal may escape. What, then, is there which can be done? I think it is neither obscure nor hidden. I will reserve for another time that fruit of praise which may be derived from a long uninterrupted speech. At present I must support this accusation by documentary evidence, by witnesses, by letters of private individuals and of public bodies, and by various other kinds of proof. The whole of this contest is between you and me, O Hortensius. I will speak openly. If I thought that you were contending with me in the matter of speaking, and of getting rid of the charges I bring against your client in this cause, I, too, would devote much pains to making an elaborate accusation, and to dilating on my charges. Now, since you have determined to contend against me with artifice, not so much in obedience to the promptings of your own nature, as from consulting his occasions and his cause, it is necessary for me to oppose conduct of that sort with prudence. Your plan is, to begin to answer me after two sets of games have been celebrated; mine is to have the adjournment over before the first games. And the result will be that that plan of yours will be thought crafty, but this determination of mine necessary.

XII. But as for what I had begun to say,—namely, that the contest is between you and me, this is it,—I, when I had undertaken this cause at the request of the Sicilians, and had thought it a very honourable and glorious thing for me that they were willing to make experiment of my integrity and diligence, who already knew by experience my innocence and temperance: then, when I had undertaken this business, I proposed to myself some greater action also by which the Roman people should be able to see my good-will towards the republic. For that seemed to me to be by no means worthy of my industry and efforts, for that man to be brought to trial by me who had been already condemned by the judgment of all men, unless that intolerable influence of yours, and that grasping nature which you have displayed for some years in many trials, was interposed also in the case of that desperate man. But now, since all this dominion and sovereignty of yours over the courts of justice delights you so much, and since there are some men who are neither ashamed of their licentiousness and their infamy, nor weary of it, and who, as if on purpose, seem to wish to encounter hatred and unpopularity from the Roman people, I profess that I have undertaken this, — a great burden perhaps, and one dangerous to myself, but still worthy of my applying myself to it with all the vigour of my age, and all diligence. And since the whole order of the senate is weighed down by the discredit brought on it by the wickedness and audacity of a few, and is overwhelmed by the infamy of the tribunals, I profess myself an enemy to this race of men, an accuser worthy of their hatred, a persevering, a bitter adversary. I arrogate this to myself, I claim this for myself, and I will carry out this enmity in my magistracy, and from that post in which the Roman people has willed that from the next first of January I shall act in concert with it in matters concerning the republic, and concerning wicked men. I promise the Roman people that this shall be the most honourable and the fairest employment of my aedileship. I warn, I forewarn, I give notice beforehand to those men who are wont either to put money down, to undertake for others, to receive money, or to promise money, or to act as agents in bribery, or as go-betweens in corrupting the seat of judgment, and who have promised their influence or their impudence in aid of such a business, in this trial to keep their hands and inclination from this nefarious wickedness.

XIII.   Hortensius will then be consul with the chief command and authority, but I shall be aedile — that is, I shall be a little more than a private individual; and yet this business, which I promise that I am going to advocate, is of such a nature, so pleasing and agreeable to the Roman people, that the consul himself will appear in this cause, if that be possible, even less than a private individual in comparison of me. All those things shall not only be mentioned, but even, when certain matters have been explained, shall be fully discussed, which for the last ten years, ever since the office of the judge has been transferred to the senate, have been nefariously and wickedly done in the decision of judicial matters. The Roman people shall know from me why it is that when the equestrian body supplied the judges for nearly fifty years together, not even the slightest suspicion ever arose of bribes having been accepted for the purpose of influencing a decision; why it is, I say, when the judicial authority was transferred to the senatorial body, and the power of the Roman people over every one of us was taken away, Quintus Calidius, when he was condemned, said that a man of praetorian rank could not honestly be condemned at a less price than three hundred thousand sesterces; why it is that when Publius Septimius, a senator, was condemned for extortion, when Quintus Hortensius was praetor, damages were assessed against him, including money which he had received as judge to decide causes which came before him; why it is, that in the case of Caius Herennius, and in that of Caius Popillius, senators, both of whom were convicted of peculation — why it is, that in the case of Marcus Atilius, who was convicted of treason — this was made plain, — that they had all received money for the purpose of influencing their judicial decisions; why it is, that senators have been found who, when Caius Verres, as praetor of the city, gave out the lots, voted against the criminal whom they were condemning without having inquired into his case; why it is, that a senator was found who, when he was judge, took money in one and the same trial both from the defendant to distribute among the judges, and from the accuser to condemn the defendant. But how shall I adequately complain of that stain, that disgrace, that calamity of the whole senatorial order, — that this thing actually happened in the city while the senatorial order furnished the judges, that the votes of men on their oaths were marked by coloured tablets? I pledge myself that I will urge all these things with diligence and with strictness.

XIV. And what do you suppose will be my thoughts, if I find in this very trial any violation of the laws committed in any similar manner? especially when I can prove by many witnesses that Caius Verres often said in Sicily, in the hearing of many persons, "that he had a powerful friend, in confidence in whom he was plundering the province; and that he was not seeking money for himself alone, but that he had so distributed the three years of his Sicilian praetorship, that he should say he did exceedingly well, if he appropriated the gains of one year to the augmentation of his own property, those of the second year to his patrons and defenders, and reserved the whole of the third year, the most productive and gainful of all, for the judges." From which it came into my mind to say that which, when I had said lately before Marcus Glabrio at the time of striking the list of judges, I perceived the Roman people greatly moved by; that I thought that foreign nations would send ambassadors to the Roman people to procure the abrogation of the law, and of all trials, about extortion; for if there were no trials, they think that each man would only plunder them of as much as he would think sufficient for himself and his children; but now, because there are trials of that sort, every one carries off as much as it will take to satisfy himself, his patrons, his advocates, the praetor, and the judges; and that this is an enormous sum; that they may be able to satisfy the cupidity of one most avaricious man, but are quite unable to incur the expense of his most guilty victory over the laws. O trials worthy of being recorded! O splendid reputation of our order! when the allies of the Roman people are unwilling that trials for extortion should take place, which were instituted by our ancestors for the sake of the allies. Would that man ever have had a favourable hope of his own safety, if he had not conceived in his mind a bad opinion of you? on which account, he ought, if possible, to be still more hated by you than he is by the Roman people, because he considers you like himself in avarice and wickedness and perjury.

XV. And I beg you, in the name of the immortal gods, O judges, think of and guard against this; I warn you, I give notice to you, of what I am well assured, that this most seasonable opportunity has been given to you by the favour of the gods, for the purpose of delivering your whole order from hatred, from unpopularity, from infamy, and from disgrace. There is no severity believed to exist in the tribunals, nor any scruples with regard to religion; in short, there are not believed to be any tribunals at all. Therefore we are despised and scorned by the Roman people; we are branded with a heavy and now a long standing infamy. Nor, in fact, is there any other reason for which the Roman people has with so much earnestness sought the restoration of the tribunitian power: but when it was demanding that in words, it seemed to be asking for that, but in reality it was asking for tribunals which it could trust. And this did not escape the notice of Quintus Catulus, a most sagacious and honourable man, who, when Cnaeus Pompeius, a most gallant and illustrious man, made a motion about the tribunitian power, and when he was asked his opinion, began his speech in this manner, speaking with the greatest authority, "that the conscript fathers presided over the courts of justice badly and wickedly; but if in deciding judicial trials they had been willing to satisfy the expectations of the Roman people, men would not so greatly regret the tribunitian power." Lastly, when Cnaeus Pompeius himself, when first he delivered an address to the people as consul elect, mentioned (what seemed above all things to be watched for) that he would restore the power of the tribunes, a great shout was raised at his words, and a grateful murmur pervaded the assembly. And when he had said also in the same assembly "that the provinces were depopulated and tyrannised over, that the courts of justice were become base and wicked, and that he desired to provide for and to remedy that evil," the Roman people then signified their good will, not with a shout, but with a universal uproar.

XVI. But now men are on the watch towers; they observe how every one of you behaves himself in respecting religion and in preserving the laws. They see that, ever since the passing of the law for restoring the power of the tribunes, only one senator, and he too a very insignificant one, has been condemned. And though they do not blame this, yet they have nothing which they can very much commend. For there is no credit in being upright in a case where there is no one who is either able or who endeavours to corrupt one. This is a trial in which you will be deciding about the defendant, the Roman people about you; — by the example of what happens to this man it will be determined whether, when senators are the judges, a very guilty and a very rich man can be condemned. Moreover, he is a criminal of such, a sort that there is absolutely nothing whatever in him except the greatest crimes, and excessive riches; so that if he be acquitted, no other opinion can be formed of the matter except that which is the most discreditable possible. Such numerous and enormous vices as his will not be considered to have been cancelled by influence, by family connection, by some things which may have been done well, or even by the minor vices of flattery and subservience; in short, I will conduct the cause in this manner; I will bring forward things of such a sort, so well known, so proved by evidence, so important, and so undeniable, that no one shall venture to use his influence to obtain from you the acquittal of that man; for I have a sure path and method by which I can investigate and become acquainted with all their endeavours. The matter will be so managed by me that not only the ears but even the eyes of the Roman people shall seem to be present at all their counsels. You have in your power to remove and to eradicate the disgrace and infamy which has now for many years attached to your order. It is evident to all men, that since these tribunals have been established which we now have, there has never been a bench of judges of the same splendour and dignity as this. If anything is done wrongly in this case, all men will think not that other more capable judges should be appointed of the same order of men, which is not possible; but that another order must be sought for, from which to select the judges for the future.

XVII. On which account, in the first place, I beg this of the immortal gods, which I seem to myself to have hopes of too, that in this trial no one may be found to be wicked except one who has long since been found to be such; secondly, if there are many wicked men,

I promise this to you, O judges, I promise this to the Roman people, that my life shall fail rather than my vigour and perseverance in prosecuting their iniquity. But that iniquity, which, if it should be committed, I promise to prosecute severely, with however much trouble and danger to myself, and whatever enmities I may bring on myself so doing, you, O Marcus Glabrio, can guard against ever taking place by your wisdom, and authority, and diligence. Do you undertake the cause of the tribunals. Do you undertake the cause of impartiality, of integrity, of good faith and of religion. Do you undertake the cause of the senate; that, being proved worthy by its conduct in this trial, it may come into favour and popularity with the Roman people. Think who you are, and in what a situation you are placed; what you ought to give to the Roman people, what you ought to repay to your ancestors. Let the recollection of the Acilian law passed by your father occur to your mind, owing to which law the Roman people has had this advantage of most admirable decisions and very strict judges in cases of extortion. High authorities surround you which will not suffer you to forget your family credit; which will remind you day and night that your father was a most brave man, your grandfather a most wise one, and your father-in-law a most worthy man. Wherefore, if you have inherited the vigour and energy of your father Glabrio in resisting audacious men; if you have inherited the prudence of your grandfather Scaevola in forseeing intrigues which are prepared against your fame and that of your fellow-judges; if you have any share of the constancy of your father-in-law Scaurus, so that no one can move you from your genuine and deliberate opinion, the Roman people will understand that with an upright and honourable praetor, and a carefully selected bench of judges, abundance of wealth has more influence in bringing a criminal into suspicion, than in contributing to his safety.

XVIII. I am resolved not to permit the praetor or the judges to be changed in this cause. I will not permit the matter to be delayed till the lictors of the consuls can go and summon the Sicilians, whom the servants of the consuls elect did not influence before, when by an unprecedented course of proceeding they sent for them all; I will not permit those miserable men, formerly the allies and friends of the Roman people, now their slaves and suppliants, to lose not only their rights and fortunes by their tyranny, but to be deprived of even the power of bewailing their condition; I will not, I say, when the cause has been summed up by me, permit them after a delay of forty days has intervened, then at last to reply to me when my accusation has already fallen into oblivion through lapse of time; I will not permit the decision to be given when this crowd collected from all Italy has departed from Rome, which has assembled from all quarters at the same time on account of the comitia, of the games, and of the census. The reward of the credit gained by your decision, or the danger arising from the unpopularity which will accrue to you if you decide unjustly, I think ought to belong to you; the labour and anxiety to me; the knowledge of what is done and the recollection of what has been said by every one, to all. I will adopt this course, not an unprecedented one, but one that has been adopted before, by those who are now the chief men of our state, — the course, I mean, of at once producing the witnesses. What you will find novel, O judges, is this, that I will so marshal my witnesses as to unfold the whole of my accusation; that when I have established it by examining my witnesses, by arguments, and by my speech, then I shall show the agreement of the evidence with my accusation: so that there shall be no difference between the established mode of prosecuting, and this new one, except that, according to the established mode, when everything has been said which is to be said, then the witnesses are produced; here they shall be produced as each count is brought forward; so that the other side shall have the same opportunity of examining them, of arguing and making speeches on their evidence. If there be any one who prefers an uninterrupted speech and the old mode of conducting a prosecution without any break, he shall have it in some other trial. But for this time let him understand that what we do is done by us on compulsion, (for we only do it with the design of opposing the artifice of the opposite party by our prudence.) This will be the first part of the prosecution. We say that Caius Verres has not only done many licentious acts, many cruel ones, towards Roman citizens, and towards some of the allies, many wicked acts against both gods and men; but especially that he has taken away four hundred thousand sesterces out of Sicily contrary to the laws. We will make this so plain to you by witnesses, by private documents, and by public records, that you shall decide that, even if we had abundant space and leisure days for making a long speech without any inconvenience, still there was no need at all of a long speech in this matter.

C. D. Yonge

TACITUS

For biographical note, see under History.

A Dialogue Concerning Oratory

This is a discussion of the causes of the corruption of eloquence. The scene is laid in the sixth year of the reign of the Emperor Vespasian, 75 A.D.

You have often inquired of me, Justus Fabius, why it is, that while ancient times display a race of great and splendid orators, the present age, divested of all claim to the praise of oratory, has scarcely retained even the name. By the appellation of orator we now distinguish none but those who flourished in a former period; while the eminent speakers of the present day are styled pleaders, advocates, patrons, in short, every thing but orators.

The inquiry is in its nature delicate; tending, if we are not able to vie with antiquity, to impeach our genius, and if we are not willing, to arraign our judgment. An answer to so nice a question is more than I should venture to undertake, were I to rely altogether upon myself: but it happens, that I am able to state the sentiments of men distinguished by their eloquence, such as it is in modern times; having, in the early part of my life, been present at their conversation on the very subject now before us. What I have to offer, will not be the result of my own thinking: it is the work of memory only; a mere recital of what fell from the most celebrated orators of their time: men who thought with subtlety, and expressed themselves with energy and precision; each, in his turn, assigning different but probable causes, at times insisting on the same, and, in the course of the debate, maintaining his own proper character, and the peculiar cast of his mind. What they said upon the occasion, I shall relate, as nearly as may be, in the style and manner of the several speakers, observing always the regular course and order of the controversy. For a controversy it certainly was, where the speakers of the present age did not want an advocate, who supported their cause with zeal, and, after treating antiquity with severity, and even derision, assigned the palm of eloquence to modern times.

430

Curiatius Maternus gave a public reading of his tragedy of Cato. On the following day a report prevailed, that the piece had given umbrage to the men in power. The author, it was said, had labored only to enhance the character of his hero, regardless of himself. This soon became the topic of public conversation. Maternus received a visit from Marcus Aper and Julius Secundus, then the first ornaments of the forum. I was, at that time, a constant attendant on those eminent men; I heard them, not only in their courts of judicature, but feeling an inclination to the same studies, I followed them with youthful ardor, in public and in private, to hear their familiar talk, their discussions, and the most intimate expression of their sentiments. True it is that by many it was captiously objected to Secundus, that he had no command of words, no flow of language; and to Aper, that he was indebted for his fame, not to art or literature, but to the natural powers of a vigorous understanding. The truth is, the style of the former was remarkable for its purity; concise, yet sufficiently free and copious: and the latter was well versed in general erudition. It might be said of him, that he despised literature, not that he wanted it. He thought, perhaps, that, by scorning the aid of letters, and by drawing altogether from his own fund, his fame would stand on a more solid foundation.

We went together to pay our visit to Maternus. Upon entering his study, we found him with the tragedy, which he had read on the preceding day, lying before him. Secundus began: — Are you then so little affected by the censure of malignant critics, as to persist in cherishing this obnoxious tragedy of yours? Perhaps you are revising the piece, and, after retrenching certain passages, intend to send your Cato into the world, in, I will not say an improved, but certainly a safer form. — There lies the poem, said Maternus; you may peruse it, if you think proper; you will find it just the same as when you heard it read. If Cato has omitted any thing, Thyestes, at my next reading, shall supply the deficiency. I have formed the fable of a tragedy on that subject; the plan is warm in my imagination, and, that I may give my whole time to it, I now am eager to dispatch an edition of Cato. — Marcus Aper interposed: Are you, indeed, so enamored of your dramatic muse, as to renounce your oratorical character, and your forensic pursuits, in order to sacrifice all your time to — Medea, I think it was lately, and now to Thyestes? though, meanwhile, the causes of so many friends, and the interests of so many colonies and municipal cities, call you to the forum. Surely these would give you more than sufficient employment, though you had not imposed upon yourself this new task, laboring to add Domitius and Cato, that is to say, the incidents and characters of Roman story, to the fables of Greece.

431

The sharpness of that reproof, replied Maternus, would perhaps have disconcerted me, if, by frequent repetition, it had not lost its sting. To differ on this subject is grown familiar to us both. For you wage an incessant war against the poets; and I, who am charged with deserting my clients, have yet every day the cause of poetry to defend. I rejoice the more, therefore, that we have a person present, of ability to decide between us: a judge, who will either lay me under an injunction to write no more verses, or, as I rather hope, encourage me, by his authority, to renounce forever the dry enployment of forensic causes (in which I have had my share of drudgery), that I may, for the future, be at leisure to cultivate the more august and sacred eloquence of the tragic muse.

But I, said Secundus, before Aper refuses me as an umpire, will follow the example of all fair and upright judges, who, in particular cases, when they feel a partiality for one of the contending parties, desire to be excused from hearing the cause. The friendship and habitual intercourse which I have ever cultivated with Saleius Bassus, that excellent man, and no less excellent poet, are well known: and let me add, if poetry is to be arraigned, I know no client that can offer such handsome bribes.

My business, replied Aper, is not with Saleius Bassus: let him, and all of his description, who, without talents for the bar, devote their time to the Muses, pursue their favorite amusement without interruption. But, since we are now before a competent judge, Maternus must not think to escape in the crowd. I single him out from the rest. I call upon him to answer, how it happens, that a man of his talents, formed by nature to reach the heights of manly eloquence, whereby he might at once both acquire friendships and support them, and have the glory to see whole provinces and nations rank themselves under his patronage, does yet thus renounce a pursuit of all others the most advantageous, whether considered with respect to interest or to honors; a pursuit that affords the most illustrious means of propagating a reputation, not only within our own walls, but throughout the whole compass of the Roman empire, and indeed to the most distant nations of the globe?

If utility ought to be the governing motive of every action and every design of our lives; can we possibly be employed to better purpose, than in the exercise of an art which enables a man, upon all occasions, to support the interest of his friend, to protect the rights of the stranger, to defend the cause of the injured, to strike with terror and dismay his open and secret adversaries, himself secure the while, and guarded, as it were, by an imperishable potency?

In the calm seasons of life, the true use of oratory is discerned in the protection of others. Have we reason to be alarmed for ourselves? — the sword and breast-plate are not a better defense in the heat of battle. It is at once a buckler to cover yourself, and a weapon to brandish against your enemy. Armed with this, you may appear with courage before the tribunals of justice, in the senate, and even in the presence of the prince. What had Eprius Marcellus to oppose to the united resentment of the whole senate but his eloquence? Collected in himself, and looking terror to his enemies, he foiled Helvidius Priscus; a man, no doubt, of consummate wisdom, but unpracticed and inexpert in contests of that kind. Such is the advantage of oratory: to enlarge upon it were superfluous. My friend Maternus will not dispute the point.

I proceed to the pleasure arising from the exercise of eloquence; a pleasure which does not consist in the mere sensation of the moment, but is repeated every day, and almost every hour. For let me ask, to a man of an ingenuous and liberal mind, who knows the relish of elegant enjoyments, what can yield such true delight, as to see his house always thronged by a concourse of the most distinguished persons; and to know that the honor is not paid to his money, or to his heirless condition, or to his possession of a public office, but to his very self? The rich who have no issue, and the men in high rank and power, are his followers. Though he is still young, and probably destitute of fortune, all concur in paying their court to solicit his patronage for themselves, or to recommend their friends to his protection. In the most splendid fortune, in all the dignity and pride of power, is there any thing that can equal the satisfaction of seeing the most illustrious citizens, men respected for their years, and flourishing in the opinion of the public, yet courting your assistance, and, in the midst of wealth and grandeur, fairly owning, that they still want something superior to all their possessions?

Then think, too, of the honorable crowd of clients conducting the orator from his house, and attending him in his return; what a glorious appearance he makes in public! what distinguishing respect is paid to him in the courts of judicature! with what exultation of heart he rises up before a full audience, hushed in solemn silence, and fixed attention, pressing round the admired speaker, and receiving every passion he deems proper to raise! Yet these are but the ordinary joys of eloquence, and visible to every common observer. There are others, and those far superior, of a more concealed and delicate kind, and of which the orator himself can alone be sensible. Does he stand forth prepared with a studied harangue? As the composition, so the pleasure, in this instance, is more solid and equal. Does he, on the other hand, rise not without a certain fluttering of spirit, in a new and unexpected debate?

The very solicitude he has felt, enhances the pleasure of his success. Indeed the most exquisite satisfaction of this kind is, when he boldly hazards an unpremeditated speech, or it is in the productions of genius, as in the fruits of the earth; many things are shown and brought to maturity with toil and care, but those which spring up spontaneously are ever the most agreeable.

As to myself, if I may allude to my own feelings, the day on which I obtained the laticlave, and even the days when I, an obscure man, born in a city that did not favor my pretensions, entered upon the offices of quaestor, tribune, and praetor, were not so joyful to me as those on which it befalls me, with such little power of speech as I possess, to defend the accused; to argue successfully before the centumviri, or, in the presence of the prince, to plead for his free men, and the procurators appointed by himself. Upon those occasions I seem to rise above the dignities of tribune, praetor, and consul; and feel within myself a grandeur that springs from no external cause, that is not conferred by patent, nor obtained by favor.

Where is the art or science, the renown of which can vie with the celebrity of a great orator? His fame does not depend on the opinion of thinking men, who attend to business and watch the administration of affairs; he is applauded by the youth of Rome, at least by such of them as are of a laudable disposition, and hope to rise by honorable means. Whose example do parents more recommend to their sons? Whom do the ignorant common people oftener name, and point at as he passes by? The strangers, too, who arrive from all parts, are eager to behold the man of whom they have heard so much in their towns and colonies.

I will be bold to say that Eprius Marcellus, whom I have already mentioned, and Crispus Vibius, (I cite living examples, in preference to the names of a former day,) are not less known in the remotest parts of the empire, than they are at Capua, or Vercellae, where, we are told, they were born; nor does either of them owe this extensive fame to his three hundred thousand sesterces, (though their eloquence may be said to have built up their fortunes;) and, indeed, such is the divine power of eloquence, that in every age we have examples of men, who by their talents raised themselves to the summit of their ambition. But these, as I have already said, are recent instances; nor are we to glean an imperfect knowledge of them from tradition; they are every day before our eyes. The more abject the origin of these two men, and the more sordid the poverty in which they set out, the more brilliant illustration and proof do they afford of the advantages of oratory; since it is apparent, that, without birth or fortune, neither of them recommended by his moral character, and one of them deformed in his person, they have made themselves, for a series of years, the first men in the state. They were the first men in the forum as long as they chose to be so; now they are the first in Caesar's friendship; they direct and govern all things, and the favor with which the prince regards them is little short of veneration. In fact, Vespasian, that venerable old prince, always open to the voice of truth, clearly sees that the rest of his favorites derive all their lustre from the favors which his munificence has bestowed: but with Marcellus and Crispus the case is different; they carry with them, as their recommendations, what no prince can give, and no subject can receive. Compared with the advantages which those men possess, what are family pictures, statues, busts, and titles of honor? Not that these things are without their value; it is with them as with wealth and honors, advantages against which you will easily find men who declaim, but none who in their hearts despise them. Hence it is, that in the houses of all who have distinguished themselves in the career of eloquence, we see titles, statues, and splendid ornaments, the reward of talents, and, at all times, the decorations of the great and powerful orator.

But to come to the point from which we started; poetry, to which my friend Maternus wishes to dedicate all his time, has none of these advantages. It confers no dignity, nor does it serve any useful purpose. It is attended with some pleasure, but it is the pleasure of a moment springing from vain applause, and bringing with it no solid advantage. What I have said, and am going to add, may probably, my good friend Maternus, be unwelcome to your ear; and yet I must take the liberty to ask you, if Agamemnon or Jason speaks in your piece with dignity of language, what useful consequence follows from it? What client has been defended? Who returns to his own house with a grateful heart? Our friend Saleius Bassus is, beyond all questions, a poet of eminence, or, to use a warmer expression, he has the god within him: but who attends his levee? who seeks his patronage, or follows in his train? Should he himself, or his intimate friend, or his near relation, happen to be involved in a troublesome litigation, he would of course apply to his friend Secundus; or to you Maternus; not because you are a poet, nor yet to obtain a copy of verses from you; of those he has a sufficient stock at home, elegant, it must be owned, and exquisite in their kind. But after all his labor and waste of genius, what is his reward?

When in the course of a year, after toiling day and night, he has brought a single poem to perfection, he is obliged to solicit his friends, and exert his interest, in order to bring together an audience so obliging as to hear a recital of the piece. Nor can this be done without expense. A room must be hired, a stage or pulpit must be erected; benches must be arranged, and tickets distributed throughout the city. What if the reading succeeds to the height of his wishes? Pass but a day or two, and the whole harvest of praise and admiration fades away, like a flower that withers in its bloom, and never ripens into fruit. By the event, however flattering, he gains no friend, he obtains no patronage, nor does a single person go away impressed with the idea of an obligation conferred upon him. The poet has been heard with applause; he has been received with acclamations; and he has enjoyed a short-lived transport. We lately lauded it as an uncommon instance of generosity in Vespasian, that he made Saleius Bassus a present of fifty thousand sesterces. To deserve so distinguished a proof of the sovereign's esteem is, no doubt, highly honorable; but is it not still more honorable, if your circumstances require it, to serve yourself, to be your own benefactor, and to be the object of your own liberality? It must not be forgotten, that the poet who would produce any thing excellent, must bid farewell to the conversation of his friends; he must renounce, not only the pleasures of Rome, but also the duties of social life; he must retire, as the poets say, "to groves and grottoes," in other words, to solitude.

Fame even, which alone they worship, and which they confess to be the sole reward of all their toil, does not attend poets in the same degree as orators. The indifferent poet has no readers, the best but few. Let there be a reading of a poem by the ablest master of his art: will the fame of his performance reach all quarters, I will not say of the empire, but of Rome only? Among the strangers who arrive from Spain, from Asia, or from our Gaul, who inquires after Saleius Bassus? Should it happen that there is one, who thinks of him, his curiosity is soon satisfied; he passes on, content with a transient view, as if he had seen a picture or a statue.

In what I have advanced, let me not be misunderstood: I do not mean to deter such as are not blessed with the gift of oratory, from the practice of their favorite art, if it serves to amuse their leisure, and gain them a degree of reputation. I am an admirer of all eloquence; I hold it venerable, and even sacred, in all its departments; in solemn tragedy, of which you, Maternus, are so great a master; in the majesty of the epic, the gayety of the lyric muse, the wanton elegy, the keen iambic, and the pointed epigram; all have their charms; and Eloquence, whatever may be the subject which she chooses to adorn, is in my mind to be preferred to all other arts. But this, Maternus, is no apology for you, who, formed by nature to reach the summit of perfection, yet choose to wander into devious paths, and rest contented with a humble station in the vale beneath.

Were you a native of Greece, where to exhibit in the public games is an honorable employment; and if the gods had bestowed upon you the force and sinew of the athletic Nicostratus, do you imagine that I could tamely look on, and see that amazing vigor waste itself away in nothing better than the frivolous art of darting the javelin, or throwing the quoit? With the same feeling I summon you now from the theatre and public recitals to the business of the forum, to the tribunals of justice, to scenes of real contention, to a conflict worthy of your abilities; especially since you can not fall back upon the excuse alleged by many, that poetry is safer than oratory, less liable to give offense; for the ardor of your fine genius has already blazed forth, and you have given offense, not for the sake of a friend — that would be far less dangerous — but on behalf of Cato! Nor can you offer in excuse, either the duty of your profession, justice to your client, or the unguarded heat of debate. It is manifest that you fixed upon a great historical personage with deliberate design, and as a character that would give weight and authority to your sentiments. You will reply, I am aware, it was that very circumstance which gained you such universal applause, and rendered you the general topic of discourse. Talk no more then, I beseech you, of security and repose, while you thus industriously raise up to yourself so potent an adversary. For my own part, at least, I am contented with engaging in questions of a more modern and private nature; wherein, if in defense of a friend I am under a necessity of taking liberties, unacceptable, perhaps, to my superiors, the honest freedom of my zeal will, I trust, not only be excused, but applauded.

Aper having delivered this with his usual warmth and earnestness, Maternus replied in a milder tone, and with an air of pleasantry: Prepared as I was to prefer against the orators an indictment no less copious than my friend's panegyric in their behalf, (for I expected that he would proceed to decry the poets, and confound their art,) he has somewhat ingeniously softened my asperity by certain concessions he is pleased to make in their favor. He is willing to allow those whose genius does not point to oratory, to apply themselves to poetry; but I, who might do something, and obtain some distinction as a pleader, have chosen, nevertheless, to build my reputation on dramatic poetry. (The first attempt I made for this purpose, was by exposing the dangerous power of Vatinius: a power which even Nero himself disapproved, and which that infamous favorite abused to the profanation of the sacred Muses.) And I am persuaded, if I enjoy any share of fame, it is to poetry rather than to oratory that I am indebted for the acquisition. It is my fixed purpose, therefore, entirely to withdraw myself from the fatigue of the bar. The homage of visitors, the train of attendants, and the multitude of clients, which Aper has represented in such pompous colors, have no charms for me; no more have those sculptured honors which he mentioned; though they too have made their way into my house, notwithstanding my inclinations to the contrary. Hitherto I find my condition and my peace of mind better secured by innocence than by eloquence; and I am under no apprehension I shall ever have occasion to open my lips in the senate, unless, perhaps, in defense of a friend.

But woods, and groves, and solitude itself, the objects of Aper's invective, to me afford such delight, that I reckon it among the chief blessings of poetry that it is cultivated far from the noise and bustle of the world, without a client to besiege my doors, or a criminal to distress me with his tears and squalor. Free from those distractions, the poet retires to scenes of solitude, where peace and innocence reside, and there he treads on consecrated ground. It was there that Eloquence modern growth, the offspring of corrupt manners, and degenerate first grew up, and there she reared her temple. In such retreats she first adorned herself with those graces which have made mankind enamored of her charms; and there she inspired the hearts of the blameless and the good. Oracles first spoke in woods and sacred groves. As to the species of oratory which practices for lucre, or with views of ambition; that sanguinary eloquence now so much in vogue; it is of times; and as you, Aper, expressed it, it is adopted as a deadly weapon.

The early and more happy period of the world, or, as we poets call it, the golden age, free alike from orators and from crimes, abounded with inspired poets, who exerted their noble talents, not in defending the guilty, but in celebrating the good. Accordingly, no character was ever more eminently distinguished, or more augustly honored: first by the gods themselves, by whom the poets were supposed to be admitted to their feasts, and employed as messengers of their high behests; and afterward by that sacred offspring of the gods, the first venerable race of legislators. In that glorious list we read the names, not of orators indeed, but of Orpheus, and Linus, or, if we are inclined to trace the illustrious roll still higher, even of Apollo himself.

But these things, perhaps, will be treated by Aper as fables, and inventions of fancy. He can not, however, deny that Homer has received as signal honors from posterity as Demosthenes; or that the fame of Sophocles or Euripides is as extensive as that of Lysias or Hyperides; that Cicero's merit is less universally confessed than Virgil's; or that not one of the orations of Asinius or Messala is in so much request as the Medea of Ovid, or the Thyestes of Varius.

By no means do I shrink from comparing the fortune and the happy communion of poets, with the restless and anxious life of the orator; even though the hazardous contentions of the latter may possibly raise him to the consular dignity. Far more desirable, in my estimation,

438

was the calm retreat of Virgil: where yet he lived not unhonored by his prince, nor unregarded by the Roman people: witness the letters of Augustus; witness the conduct of the people itself, who, when some of Virgil's verses were repeated in the theatre, where he happened to be present, rose up to a man, and saluted him with the same respect that they would have paid to Augustus.

Even in our own times, will any man say that Secundus Pomponius, in point of dignity or extent of fame, is inferior to Domitius Afer? As for Crispus and Marcellus, who have been cited as bright examples, what is there in their elevation to be coveted? Is it that they are feared by numbers, and live in fear themselves? That they are daily courted for their favors, and the men who obtain their suit hate them? That they are bound to such a degree of adulation, as never to be thought by their masters sufficiently servile, nor by the people sufficiently free? And after all, what is the amount of this boasted power of theirs? The emperor's freedmen commonly enjoy as much. But as Virgil sings, "Me let the sweet Muses lead to their soft retreats, their living fountains, and melodious groves, where I may dwell remote from care, master of myself, and under no necessity of doing every day what my heart condemns. Let me no more be seen in the wrangling forum, a pale and anxious candidate for precarious fame; and let neither the tumult of visitors crowding to my levee, nor the eager haste of officious freedmen, disturb my morning rest. Let me live free from solicitude, a stranger to the art of promising legacies, in order to buy the friendship of the great; and when nature shall give the signal to retire, may I possess no more than I may bequeath to whom I will. At my funeral let no token of sorrow be seen, no pompous mockery of woe. Crown me with chaplets; strew ewers on my grave, and let my friends erect no vain memorial, to tell where my remains are lodged."

Maternus finished with an air of enthusiasm, that seemed to lift him above himself. In that moment, Vipstanus Messala entered the room. From the attention that appeared in every countenance, he concluded that some important business was the subject of debate. I am afraid, said he, that I break in upon you at an unseasonable time. You have some secret to discuss, or, perhaps, a consultation upon your hands. — Far from it, replied Secundus; I wish you had come sooner. You would have had the pleasure of hearing an eloquent discourse from our friend Aper, who has been endeavoring to persuade Maternus to dedicate the whole strength of his genius and his studies to the business of the forum; and an animated reply from Maternus, wherein, as became one who was defending his favorite art, he delivered himself

439

with a boldness and elevation of style more akin to the poetical than the oratorical character.

It would have afforded me infinite pleasure, replied Messala, to have been present at a debate of this kind. And I can not but express my satisfaction, in finding the most eminent orators of our times, not confining their genius to points relating to their profession, but canvassing in their conversation such other questions of taste and literature as give a very advantageous exercise to their faculties, at the same time that they furnish an entertainment of the most agreeable kind, not only to themselves, but to those who hear them. And believe me, Secundus, the world received with much approbation your history of J. Asiaticus, as an earnest that you intend to publish more pieces of the same nature. On the other side, it is observed with equal satisfaction, that Aper has not yet bid adieu to the questions of the schools, but employs his leisure rather after the example of the modern rhetoricians, than of the ancient orators.

I perceive, returned Aper, that you continue to treat the moderns with your usual derision and contempt; while the ancients alone are in full possession of your esteem. It is a maxim, indeed, I have frequently heard you advance, (and, allow me to say, with much injustice to yourself and to your brother,) that there is no such thing in the present age as an orator. This you are the less scrupulous to maintain, as you imagine it can not be imputed to a spirit of envy; since you deny yourself a distinction which every body concedes to you.

I have hitherto, replied Messala, found no reason to change my opinion; and I am persuaded, that neither Secundus, nor Maternus, nor yourself, Aper, (whatever you may sometimes affect to the contrary,) think differently from me. I should, indeed, be glad, if I could prevail on any of you to investigate and expound the causes of so remarkable a disparity, which I often seek to explore in my own thoughts. What to some appears a satisfactory solution of this phenomenon, to me, I confess, heightens the difficulty: for I find the very same difference prevails among the Grecian orators; and that the priest Nicetes, together with other of the Ephesian and Mitylenean schools, who content themselves with raising the acclamations of their tasteless auditors, deviate much farther from Aeschines or Demosthenes, than Afer and Africanus, or you, my friends, from Tully or Asinius.

The question you have started, said Secundus, is a very important one, and well worthy of consideration. But who so capable of doing justice to it as yourself? who, besides the advantages of a fine genius and great literature, have given, it seems, particular attention to this inquiry. — I am very willing, answered Messala, to lay before you my thoughts upon the subject, provided you will assist me with yours as

I go along. — I will engage for two of us, replied Maternus: Secundus and myself will speak to such points as you shall, I do not say omit, but think proper to leave to us. As for Aper, you just now informed us that it is usual with him to dissent from you in this matter: and, indeed, I see he is already preparing to oppose us, and will not tamely bear to see us thus leagued in support of the ancients.

Undoubtedly, returned Aper, I shall not suffer the moderns to be condemned, unheard and undefended, by this conspiracy of yours. But first let me ask, who it is you call ancients? What age of orators do you distinguish by that designation? The word always suggests to me a Nestor, or a Ulysses, men who lived about twelve hundred years since: whereas you seem to apply it to Demosthenes and Hyperides, who, it is agreed, flourished so late as the times of Philip and Alexander, and indeed, survived them. It appears from hence, that there is not much above four hundred years' distance between our age and that of Demosthenes: an interval which, considered with respect to human duration, appears, I acknowledge, extremely long; but if compared with that immense space of time which includes the several ages of the world, is exceedingly contracted, and seems almost but of yesterday. For if it be true, what Cicero observes in his treatise inscribed to Hortensius, that the great and genuine year is that period in which the heavenly bodies return to the same position, wherein they were placed when they first began their respective orbits; and this revolution contains 12,954 of our solar years; then Demosthenes, this ancient Demosthenes of yours, lived in the same year, or rather I might say, in the same month, with ourselves.

But to mention the Roman orators: I presume, it is not Menenius Agrippa (who may with some propriety, indeed, be called an ancient,) you prefer to the men of eloquence among the moderns; but Cicero, Caesar, Caelius, Calvus, Brutus, Asinius, and Messala, to whom you give this honorable precedency: though why these should be deemed ancients rather than moderns, I am at a loss to know. To instance in Cicero: he was killed, as his freedman Tiro informs us, on the 26th of December, in the consulship of Hirtius and Pansa, in which year Augustus and Pedius succeeded them in that dignity. Now, if we take fifty-six years for the reign of Augustus, and add twenty-three for that of Tiberius, about four for that of Caius, fourteen apiece for Claudius and Nero, one for Galba, Otho, and Vitellius, together with the six that our present excellent prince has enjoyed the empire, we shall have about one hundred and twenty years from the death of Cicero to these times: a period to which it is not impossible that a man's life may extend. I remember, when I was in Britain, to have met with an old soldier, who assured me, he had taken part in the battle in which his

441

countrymen opposed Caesar's descent upon that island. If we suppose this person, by being taken prisoner, or by any other means, to have been brought to Rome, he might have heard Caesar and Cicero, and likewise any of our contemporaries. At the last public donative, you yourselves saw several of the populace who acknowledged they had received the same bounty more than once from the hands of Augustus. It is evident, therefore, that these people might have been present at the pleadings both of Corvinus and Asinius: for Corvinus lived to the middle of the reign of Augustus, and Asinius nearly to its close. Surely, then, you will not split a century, and call one orator an ancient, and another a modern, when the very same person might be an auditor of both; and thus, as it were, render them contemporaries.

I have made these preliminary remarks to show that the glory, whatever it be, that accrued to the age in which those orators lived, is not confined to that particular period, but reaches down to the present time, and may more properly be said to belong to us, than to Servius Galba, or to Carbo, and others whom with good reason we call ancients. Of that whole race of orators I may freely say, that their manner can not now be relished. The language of these last is coarse, and their composition rough, uncouth, and harsh; and I could wish that your Calvus, your Caelius, and even Cicero himself, had not thought such models worthy of imitation. I mean to speak my mind with freedom; but I must premise that eloquence changes its form and style with the manners and the taste of the age. Thus we find, that Gracchus, compared with the elder Cato, is full and copious; but, in his turn, yields to Crassus, an orator more polished and ornate. Cicero rises superior to both; more pointed, more harmonious and sublime. Corvinus is considerably more smooth and harmonious in his periods, as well as more correct in his language, than Cicero. I am not considering which of them is most eloquent: all I endeavor to prove at present is, that oratory does not manifest itself in one uniform figure, but is exhibited by those whom you call ancients under a variety of aspects. However, it is by no means a just way of reasoning, to infer, that one thing must necessarily be worse than another, merely because it is not the same. Yet such is the unaccountable perversity of human nature, that whatever has antiquity to boast, is sure to be admired, and every thing novel is certainly disapproved.

Can we doubt that there have been critics who were better pleased with Appius Caecus than with Cato? Cicero had his censurers, who objected that his style was redundant, turgid, never compressed, immoderately self-complacent, and destitute of Attic elegance. We all have read the letters of Calvus and Brutus to your famous orator. In the course of that correspondence, we plainly see what was Cicero's opinion of those eminent men. The former appeared to him cold and languid; the later, disjointed, loose, and negligent. On the other hand, we know what they thought in return: Calvus did not hesitate to say, that Cicero was diffuse, luxuriant to a fault, and florid without vigor. Brutus, in express terms, says, he was lengthened out into weakness, and wanted sinew. If you ask my opinion, each of them had reason on his side. But I shall hereafter examine them separately. At present, I speak of them in general terms.

The admirers of antiquity are agreed, I think, in extending the area of the ancients as far as Cassius Severus, whom they assert to have been the first that struck out from the plain and simple manner, which till then prevailed. Now I affirm that he did so, not from any deficiency in point of genius or learning, but from his superior judgment and good sense. He saw it was necessary to accommodate oratory, as I observed before, to the different times and tastes of the audience. In early times, the people, rude and unpolished, might well be contented with the tedious length of unskillful speeches; and, indeed, to be able to harangue for a whole day together, was itself looked upon, at that illiterate period, as a talent worthy of admiration. The prolix exordium, the circumstantial detail, the ostentatious division of the argument under different heads, the endless degrees of logical deduction, with whatever else you may find laid down among the precepts of those driest of all writers, Hermagoras and Apollodorus, were then held in supreme honor. And, to complete all, if the orator had just dipped into philosophy, and could sprinkle his harangue with some of the trite maxims of that science, he was extolled to the skies. And no wonder; for these were new and uncommon topics to them; indeed very few of the orators themselves had any acquaintance with the writings either of the philosophers or the rhetoricians.

In the present age, the tenets of philosophy and the precepts of rhetoric are no longer a secret. The lowest of our popular assemblies are now, I will not say fully instructed, but certainly acquainted with the elements of literature. The orator, by consequence, finds himself obliged to seek new and more subtle avenues to the heart, that he may not offend fastidious ears, especially before a tribunal where the judge is no longer bound by precedent, but determines according to his will and pleasure not, as formerly, observing the measure of time allowed to the advocate, but taking upon himself to prescribe the limits. Nor is this all: the judge, at present, will not condescend to wait till the orator, in his own way, opens his case; but, of his own authority, reminds him of the point in question, and, if he wanders, calls him back from his digression, not without a hint that the court wishes to dispatch.

443

Who at this time would bear to hear an advocate introducing himself with a tedious preface about the infirmities of his constitution? Yet that is the usual exordium of Corvinus. We have five books against Verres. Who now could endure that vast redundance? Who could listen to those endless arguments upon points of form, and caviling exceptions, which we find in the orations of the same celebrated advocate for Marcus Tullius and Aulus Caecina? Our modern judges are able to anticipate the argument. Their quickness goes before the speaker. If not allured and biased by the vivacity of his manner, the elegance of his sentiments, and the glowing colors of his descriptions, they soon grow weary of the flat insipid discourse. Even the populace that come to hear have now a taste that requires the gay, the florid, and the brilliant. The dull uncouth style of antiquity would now succeed as ill at the bar, as the modern actor who should attempt to copy the deportment of Roscius, or Ambivius Turpio. Even the young men who are preparing for the career of eloquence, and for that purpose attend the forum and the tribunals of justice, expect not merely to hear, but to carry home some bright illustration, some splendid passage, that deserves to be remembered. What has struck their fancy, they communicate to each other: and in their letters, the glittering thought, given with sententious brevity, the poetical allusion that enlivened the discourse, and the dazzling imagery, are sure to be transmitted to their respective colonies and provinces. The ornaments of poetic diction are now required, not indeed copied from the rude obsolete style of Accius and Pacuvius, but embellished with the graces of Horace, Virgil, and Lucan. In compliance with the taste of the age, our orators grow every day more polished and adorned. Let it not be said that their speeches are less effective, because they fall pleasingly on the ears of the judges. Are the temples, raised by our modern architects, of a weaker structure, because they are not formed with shapeless stones, but with polished marble, and lustrous gilding?

Shall I fairly own to you the impression which I generally receive from the ancient orators? They make me laugh, or lull me to sleep. Nor is this the case only when I read the orations of Canutius, Arrius, Furnius, Torianus, and others of the same schools, or rather, the same infirmary; a lean and bloodless sickly race of orators, without sinew, color, or proportion. But what shall be said of your admired Calvus? He, I think, has left no less than one-and-twenty volumes: in the whole collection, there is not more than one or two short orations with which I am satisfied. Upon this point there is no difference of opinion. Who now reads his declamations against Asitius or Drusus? His speeches against Vatinius are in the hands of the curious, particularly the second: for the language is elegant; the sentiments are striking, and the ear is satisfied with the roundness of the periods. In this specimen we see that he had an idea of just composition, but his genius was not equal to his judgment. What of the orations of Caelius? Though upon the whole defective, they are not without their beauties. Some passages are highly finished. In those we acknowledge the nice touches of modern elegance. In general, however, the coarse expression, the halting period, and the vulgarity of the sentiments, have too much of the leaven of antiquity; nor do I think there is any one so enamored of the ancients as to admire him in that part of his character.

With regard to Julius Caesar, engaged as he was in vast designs and enterprises, we may forgive him the want of that perfection which might, otherwise, be expected from so sublime a genius. Brutus, in like manner, may be excused on account of his philosophical speculations. Both he and Caesar, in their oratorical attempts, fell short of themselves. Their warmest admirers acknowledge the fact, nor is there an instance to the contrary, unless there be here and there a reader of Caesar's speech for Decius the Samnite, and that of Brutus for king Deiotarus, and others of the same languid and lukewarm character; or some one to admire their verses; for verses they both made, and published too, I will not say, with more merit than Cicero, but certainly with better fortune, for fewer know of their existence.

Asinius too, though he lived nearer to our own times, gives me the idea of one who had studied among the Menenii and Appii; he certainly imitated Pacuvius and Accius, not only in his tragedies, but also in his orations, so cold and dry he is. But the beauty of an oration, like that of the human body, is then perfect, when the veins do not project, nor can the bones be counted; but a wholesome blood fills the limbs, rises up through the flesh, and mantles over the thews and sinews with the comely hue of health. I am not willing to disturb the memory of Corvinus Messala. If he did not reach the graces of modern composition, the defect does not seem to have sprung from choice. The vigor of his genius was not equal to his judgment.

I now come to Cicero, who had the same contest with those of his own times, as mine, my friends, with you. They, it seems, were favorers of the ancients; while he preferred the eloquence of his contemporaries: and, in truth, he excels the orators of his own age in nothing more remarkably than in the solidity of his judgment. He was the first who set a polish upon oratory; the first who cultivated delicacy of expression, and the art of composition. He introduced into his discourses passages of lively coloring, and phrases of pregnant brevity; particularly in his later performances, when much practice and experience had taught him a more improved manner. But his earlier compositions are not without the blemishes of antiquity. He is tedious in his exordiums, too circumstantial in his narrations, and careless in retrenching luxuriances. He seems not easily affected, and is but rarely fired; his periods are seldom either properly rounded, or happily pointed: he has nothing, in fine, you would wish to make your own. His speeches, like a rude edifice, have strength, indeed, and permanency; but are destitute of that elegance and splendor which are necessary to render them perfectly agreeable.

Now I would have the orator be like the man of wealth and station, for whom it is not enough that his house will keep out the wind and the rain; it must strike the eye, and present a pleasing object. Nor will it suffice that the furniture may answer all domestic purposes; it should have gold and gems so curiously wrought, that they will bear examination, often viewed, and always admired. The common utensils, which are either mean or sordid, should be carefully removed out of sight. In like manner, the true orator should avoid the trite and vulgar. Let him reject the antiquated phrase, and whatever is covered with the rust of time; let his sentiments be expressed with spirit, not in clumsy, ill-constructed periods, like those of a dull writer of annals; let him know how to vary the structure of his periods, so as not to end every sentence with the same unvaried cadence.

I will not expose the meanness of Cicero's conceits, such as his "wheel of Fortune," and his punning on the word "Verres," nor his affectation of concluding almost every other period with, "as it should seem." instead of pointing them with some luminous and sententious turn. I mention even these with reluctance, and pass over many others of the same injudicious cast. It is singly, however, in little affectations of this kind, that they who are pleased to style themselves ancient orators seem to admire and imitate him. I shall content myself with describing their characters, without mentioning their names: but you are aware there are certain pretenders to taste who prefer Lucilius to Horace, and Lucretius to Virgil; who hold the eloquence of your favorite Bassus or Nonianus in the utmost contempt, when compared with that of Sisenna or Varro; in a word, who despise the productions of our modern rhetoricians, yet are in raptures with those of Calvus. We see these men prosing in the courts of judicature after the manner of the ancients (as they call it), till they are deserted by the whole audience, and are scarce supportable even to their very clients; so dreary and squalid they are; so much is their boasted healthy sobriety an evidence of a sickly habit and valetudinary abstinence. No physician would call that a sound constitution, which requires constant care and anxiety of mind. To be only not indisposed, is but a small acquisition; it is spirits, vivacity, and vigor, that I require: he who can just say that he is well, and no more, is not far from being unwell.

Be it then (as with great ease it may, and in fact is) the glorious distinction of you, my illustrious friends, to ennoble our age with the most refined eloquence. It is with infinite satisfaction, Messala, I observe, that you single out the liveliest models among the ancients for your imitation. You too, Maternus, and you, Secundus, how happily unite strength of sentiment with beauty of expression; such a pregnancy of imagination, such a symmetry of ordonnance distinguish your speeches; so copious or so concise in your elocution, as different occasions require; such gracefulness of style and such lucid terseness adorn and dignify your compositions: in a word, so absolutely you command the passions of your audience, and so happily temper your own, that, however the envy and malignity of the present age may withhold that applause which is so justly your due, posterity will surely speak of you as you well deserve.

Anonymous
19th century

447

THE NOVEL

Petronius

Apuleius

PETRONIUS

GAIUS PETRONIUS belongs in the first century A. D. As *elegantiae arbiter* he was the fashion critic at the court of the Emperor Nero. He attained the consulship, but as the historian Tacitus remarks, his reputation was that of a licentious voluptuary. In 66 A.D. he committed suicide, at the instance of the Emperor.

Petronius is the author of a remarkably realistic novel, known as the *Satyricon,* that describes the largely disreputable, amatory, and exciting adventures of Encolpius, Ascyltus, and Giton in the towns and seaports of southern Italy. One of the most vivid scenes depicts the banquet given by Trimalchio, a lowly parvenu, to a strange assortment of guests. The narrator is Encolpius. Throughout the elaborate and fantastic meal the intimate, pseudo-learned and completely uninhibited talk is unique in expression and content.

The Banquet of Trimalchio

And now came the third day, that is the expectation of an entertainment at Trimalchio's, where every one might speak what he would: But having received some wounds, we thought flight might be of more use to us than sitting still: We got to our inn therefore, as fast as we could, and our wounds not being great, cured them as we lay in bed, with wine and oyl.

But the rogue whom Ascyltos had hewn down, lay in the street, and we were in fear of being discovered, while therefore we were pensively considering which way to avoid the impending storm, a servant of Agamemnon's interrupted our fears: "And do not ye know," said he, "with whom we eat today? Trimalchio, a trim finical humorist has a clock in his dining-room, and one on purpose to let him know how many minutes of his life he had lost." We therefore drest our selves carefully, and Gito willingly taking upon him the part of a servant, as he had hitherto done, we bade him put our things together, and follow us to the bath.

Being in the mean time got ready, we walk'd we knew not where, or, rather, having a mind to divert us, struck into a tennis-court, where we saw an old bald-pated fellow in a carnation-color'd coat, playing at ball with a company of boys, nor was it so much the boys, tho' it was worth our while, that engaged us to be lookers on as the master of the house himself in pumps, who altogether tossed the ball, and

449

never struck it after it once came to the ground, but had a servant by him, with a bag full of them, and enough for all that play'd.

We observed also some new things; for in the gallery stood two eunuchs, one of whom held a silver chamber-pot, the other counted the balls, not those they kept tossing, but such as fell to the ground. While we admir'd the humor, one Menelaus came up to us, and told us we were come where we must set up for the night, and that we had seen the beginning of our entertainment. As he was yet talking, Trimalchio snapp'd his fingers, at which sign the eunuch held the chamber-pot to him as he was playing; then calling for water, he dipped the tips of his fingers in it, and dry'd them on the boys head. 'Twould be too long to recount every thing: We went into the hot-house, and having sweated a little, into the cold bath; and while Trimalchio was anointed from head to foot with a liquid perfume, and rubb'd clean again, not with linnen but with finest flannen, his three chyrurgeons ply'd the muscadine, but brawling over their cups; Trimalchio said it was his turn to drink; then wrapt in a scarlet mantle, he was laid on a litter born by six servants, with four lacqueys in rich liveries running before him, and by his side a sedan, in which was carried his darling, a stale bleer-eyed catamite, more ill-favored than his master Trimalchio; who as they went on, kept close to his ear with a flagellet, as if he had whispered him, and made him musick all the way. Wondering, we followed, and, with Agamemnon, came to the gate, on which hung a tablet with this inscription:

WHAT EVER SERVANT GOES FORTH WITHOUT
HIS MASTER'S COMMAND, HE SHALL
RECEIVE AN HUNDRED STRIPES

In the porch stood the porter in a green livery, girt about with a cherry-colored girdle, garbling of pease in a silver charger; and over head hung a golden cage with a magpye in it, which gave us an All Hail as we entred: But while I was gaping at these things, I had like to have broken my neck backward, for on the left hand, not far from the porter's lodge, there was a great dog in a chain painted on the wall, and over him written in capital letters, BEWARE THE DOG. My companions could not forbear laughing; but I recollecting my spirits, pursued my design of going to the end of the wall; it was the draught of a market-place where slaves were bought and sold with bills over them: There was also Trimalchio with a white staff in his hand, and Minerva with a train after her entring Rome: Then having learnt how to cast accompt, he was made auditor; all exquisitely painted with their proper titles; and at the end of the gallery Mercury lifting him by the chin, and placing him on a judgment-seat. Fortune stood by him with a cornucopia, and the three fatal sisters winding a golden thread.

I observed also in the same place a troop of light-horsemen, with their commander exercising them, as also a large armory, in one of the angles of which stood a shrine with the gods of the house in silver, a marble statue of Venus, and a large golden box, in which it was said he kept the first shavings of his beard. Then asking the servant that had the charge of these things, what pictures those were in the middle? The Iliads and the Odysses, said he, and on the left-hand two spectacles of sword-playing. We could not bestow much time on it, for by this time we were coming to the dining-room, in the entry of which sate his steward, taking every one's account: But what I most admir'd, were those bundles of rods, with their axes, that were fastened to the sides of the door, and stood, as it were, on the brazen prow of a ship, on which was written:

TO CAIUS POMPEIUS TRIMALCHIO
OF PRAETORIAN DIGNITY;
CINNAMUS THE STEWARD

Under the same title also, hung a lamp of two lights from the roof of the room, and two tablets on either side of the door; of which one, if I well remember, had this inscription:

THE THIRD AND SECOND OF THE KALENDS OF
JANUARY, OUR PATRON CAIUS EATS ABROAD

On the other was represented the course of the moon, and the seven stars; and what days were lucky, what unlucky, with an emboss'd studd to distinguish the one from the other.

Full of this sensuality we were now entring the room, where one of his boys, set there for that purpose, call'd aloud to us, "ADVANCE ORDERLY." Nor is it to be doubted, but we were somewhat concern'd for fear of breaking the orders of the place. But while we were footing it accordingly, a servant stript off his livery, fell at our feet, and besought us to save him a whipping; for he said his fault was no great matter, but that some cloths of the stewards had been stolen from him in the bath, and all of them were not worth eighteen-pence.

We returned therefore in good order, and finding the steward in the counting-house telling some gold, besought him to remit the servant's punishment: When putting on a haughty face "It is not," said he, "the loss of the thing troubles me, but the negligence of a careless rascal. He has lost me the garments I sate at table in, and which a client of mine presented me on my birth-day: no man can deny them to be right purple, tho' not double dye; yet whatever it be, I grant your request."

Having receiv'd so great a favor, as we were entring the dining-room, the servant for whom we had been suitors, met us, and kissing us, who stood wondring what the humor meant, over and over gave us thanks for our civility; and in short, told us we should know by and by, who it was we had oblig'd: The wine which our master keeps for his own drinking, is the waiters kindness.

At length we sate down, when a bigger and sprucer sort of boys coming about us, some of them poured snow-water on our heads, and others par'd the nails of our feet, with a mighty dexterity, and that not silently, but singing as it were by the bye: I resolved to try if the whole family sang; and therefore called for drink, which one of the boys a readily brought me with an odd kind of tune; and the same did every one as you asked for any thing: You'd have taken it for a Morris dancers hall, not the table of a person of quality.

Then came a sumptuous antepast; for we were all seated, but only Trimalchio, for whom, after a new fashion, the chief place was re-serv'd. Besides that, as a part of the entertainment, there was set by us a large vessel of metheglin, with a pannier, in the one part of which were white olives, in the other black; two broad platters covered the vessel, on the brims of which were engraven Trimalchio's name, and the weight of the silver, with little bridges soldered together, and on them dormice strew'd over with honey and poppy: There were also piping-hot sausages on a silver gridiron, and under that large damsons, with the kernels of pomegranats.

In this condition were we when Trimalchio himself was waddled into the consort; and being close bolster'd with neck-cloaths and pil-lows to keep off the air, we could not forbear laughing unawares: For his bald pate peep'd out of a scarlet mantle, and over the load of cloaths he lay under, there hung an embroidered towel, with purple tassels and fringes dingle dangle about it: He had also on the little finger of his left hand, a large gilt ring, and on the outmost joint of the finger next it, one lesser, which I took for all gold; but at last it appeared to be jointed together with a kind of stars of steel. And that we might see these were not all his bravery, he stripp'd his right arm, on which he wore a golden bracelet, and an ivory circle, bound together with a glittering locket and a medal at the end of it: Then picking his teeth with a silver pin, "I had not, my friends," said he, "any inclination to have come among you so soon, but fearing my absence

452

might make you wait too long, I deny'd myself my own satisfaction; however suffer me to make an end of my game:" There followed him a boy with an inlaid table and christal dice; and I took notice of one thing more pleasant than the rest; for instead of black and white counters, his were all silver and gold pieces of money.

In the mean time while he was squandering his heap at play, and we were yet picking a relish here and there, a cupboard was brought in with a basket, in which was a hen carved in wood, her wings lying round and hollow, as sitting on brood; when presently the consort struck up, and two servants fell a searching the straw under her, and taking out some peahens eggs, distributed them among the company: At this Trimalchio changing countenance, "I commanded my friends," said he "the hen to be set with peahens eggs; and so help me Hercules, am afraid they may be half hatcht: however we'll try if they are yet suppable."

The thing we received was a kind of shell of at least six pounds weight, made of paste, and moulded into the figure of an egg, which we easily broke; and for my part, I was like to have thrown away my share; for it seemed to me to have a chick in it; till hearing an old guest of the tables saying, it was some good bit or other, I searched further into it, and found a delicate fat wheatear in the middle of a well-pepper'd yolk: On this Trimalchio stopped his play for a while, and requiring the like for himself, proclaim'd, if any of us would have any more metheglin, he was at liberty to take it; when of a sudden the music gave the sign, and the first course was scrabled away by a company of singers and dancers; but in the rustle it happening that a dish fell on the floor, a boy took it up, and Trimalchio taking notice of it, pluck'd him by the ears, and commanded him to throw it down again; on which the groom of the chamber came with a broom and swept away the silver dish, with whatsoever else had fallen from the table.

When presently came in two long-hair'd blacks, with small leather bottles, such as with which they strew sand on the stage, and gave us wine to wash our hands, but no one offered us water. We all admiring the finicalness of the entertainment, "Mars," said he, "is a lover of justice, and therefore let every one have a table to himself, for having more elbow-room, these nasty stinking boys will be less troublesome to us"; and thereupon large double-ear'd vessels of glass close plaistered over, were brought up with labels about their necks, upon which was this inscription:

OPIMIAN MUSCADINE OF AN HUNDRED YEARS OLD

While we were reading the titles, Trimalchio clapped his hands, and "Alas, alas," said he, "that wine should live longer than man!

Wine is life, and we'll try if it has held good ever since the consulship of Lucius Opimius, or not. 'Tis right Opimian, and therefore make ready; I brought not out so good yesterday, yet there were persons of better quality sup'd with me."

We drank and admired every thing, when in came a servant with a silver puppet, so jointed and put together that it turned every way; and being more than once thrown upon the table, cast it self into several figures; on which Trimalchio came out with his poetry:

> Unhappy mortals, on how fine a thread
> Our lives depend! How like this puppet man,
> Shall we, alas! be all when we are dead!
> Therefore let's live merrily while we can.

The applause we gave him, was followed with a service, but respecting the place not so considerable as might have been expected: However, the novelty of the thing drew every man's eye upon it; it was a large charger, with the twelve signs round it; upon every one of which the master cook had laid somewhat or other suitable to the sign. Upon Aries, chick-pease, (a pulse not unlike a ram's head); upon Taurus, a piece of beef; upon Gemini a pair of pendulums and kidneys; upon Cancer a coronet; upon Leo an African figg; upon Virgo a well-grown boy; upon Libra a pair of scales, in one of which was a tart, in the other a custard; upon Scorpio a pilchard; upon Sagittary a grey-hound; upon Capricorn a lobster; upon Aquarius a goose; upon Pisces two mullets; and in the middle a plat of herbs, cut out like a green turf, and over them a honey-comb. During this, a lesser black carry'd about bread in a silver oven, and with a hideous voice, forced a bawdy song from a buffon that stunk like assa foetida.

When Trimalchio perceiv'd we look'd somewhat awkwardly on such coarse fare, "Come, come," said he, "fall to and eat, this is the custom of the place."

Nor had he sooner said it, than the fourth consort struck up; at which the waiters fell a dancing, and took off the upper part of the charger, under which was a dish of cramm'd fowl, and the hinder paps of a sow that had farrowed but a day before, well powdered, and in the middle a hare, stuck in with finns of fish in his side, that he look'd like a flying horse; and on the sides of the fish four little images, that spouted a relishing sauce on some fish that lay near them, all of them brought from the river Euripus.

We also seconded the shout begun by the family, and fell merrily aboard this; and Trimalchio no less pleas'd than our selves, cryed "Cut"; at which the music sounding again, the carver humor'd it,

454

and cut up the meat with such antick postures, you'd have thought him a carman fighting to an organ.

Nevertheless Trimalchio in a lower note, cryed out again "Cut." I hearing the sound so often repeated, suspecting there might be some joke in it, was not ashamed to ask him that sate next above me, what it meant? And he that had often been present at the like, "You see," said he, "him that carves about, his name is cutter; and as often as he says 'Cut,' he both calls and commands."

The humour spoiled my stomach for eating; but turning to him that I might learn more, I made some pleasant discourse to him at a distance; and at last asked him what that woman was that so often scutled up and down the room. "It is," said he, "Trimalchio's wife, her name Fortunata, she measures money by the bushel; but what was she not long since? Pardon me sir, you would not have touch'd her with a pair of tongs, but now, no one knows how or wherefore, she's got into heaven; and is Trimalchio's all in all: In short, if she says it is mid-night at mid-day, he'll believe her. He's so very wealthy, he knows not what he has; but she has an eye everywhere; and when you least think to meet her: She's void of all good counsel, and withal of all ill tongue; a very pyre at his bolster; whom she loves, she loves; and whom she does not love, she does not love.

"Then for Trimalchio, he has more lands than a crow can fly over; monies upon monies: There lies more silver in his porters lodge, than any one man's whole estate. And for his family, hey-day, hey-day, there is not (so help me Hercules) one tenth of them that know their master. In brief, there is not one of those fools about him, but he can turn him into a cabbage-stalk. Nor is there any occasion to buy any thing, he has all at his own door; wooll, marte, pepper, nay hens milk; do but beat about and you'll find it. In a word, time was, his wooll was none of the best, and therefore he bought rams at Tarentum to mend this breed; and in like manner he did by his honey, by bringing his bees from Athens. It is not long since but he sent to the Indies for mushroom-seed: Nor has he so much as a mule that did not come of a wild ass. See you all these quilts? there is not one of them whose wadding is not the finest comb'd wooll of violet or scarlet colour, dy'd in grain. O happy man! but have a care how you put a slight on those freed men, they are rich rogues: See you him that sits at the lower-end of the table, he has now the Lord knows what; and 'tis not long since he was not worth a groat, and carried billets and faggots at his back; it is said, but I know nothing of it myself, but as I have heard, either he got in with an old hog-grubbler, or had to do with an incubus, and found a treasure: For my part, I envy no man, (if God gives anything

455

it is a bit of a blow, and wills no evil to himself) he lately set up this proclamation:

"C. POMPEIUS DIOGENES HAS SOME LODGINGS
TO LET, FOR HE HATH BOUGHT A HOUSE."

"But what think you of him who sits in the place of a late slave? how well was he once? I do not upbraid him: He was once worth a hundred thousand sestertias, but has not now a hair of his head that is not engaged; nor, so help me Hercules, is it his own fault: There is not a better humour'd man than himself; but those rascally freed-men have cheated him of all: For know, when the pot boyls, and a man's estate declines, farewell friends. And what trade do you think he drove? He had the setting forth of grave men's funerals; and with that eat like a prince: He had his wild boars served up covered; pastry-meats, fowl-cooks, bakers: More wine was thrown under his table, than most men have in their cellars; a meer phantasm: And when his estate was going, and he feared his creditors might fall upon him, he made an auction under this title:

"Julius Proculus Will Make an Auction
of Several Goods He Has No Use of."

The dish was by this time taken away, and the guests grown merry with wine, began to talk of what was done abroad, when Trimalchio broke the discourse; and leaning on his elbow, "This wine," said he, "is worth drinking, and fish must swim; but do you think I am satisfied with that part of your supper you saw in the charger? Is Ulysses no better known? what then; we ought to exercise our brains as well as our chaps; and shew, that we are not only lovers of learning, but understand it: Peace rest my old tutor's bones who made me a man amongst men: No man can tell me any thing that is new to me; for, like him, I am master of the practicks.

"This heaven, that's inhabited by twelve gods, turns it self into as many figures; and now 'tis Aries: He that's born under that sign has much cattle, much wooll, and to that a jolt-head, a brazen-face, and will be certainly a cuckold: There are many scholars, advocates, and horned beasts, come into the world under this sign. We praised our nativity-caster's pleasantness, and he went on again: The whole Heaven is Taurus, and wonder it e'er bore foot-ball-players, herds-men, and such as can shift for themselves. Under Gemini are foaled coach-horses, oxen calved, great baubles, and such as can claw both sides are born. I was born my self under Cancer, and therefore stand on many feet,

456

as having large possessions both by sea and land. For Cancer suits one as well as the other, and therefore I put nothing upon him, that I might not press my own geniture. Under Leo, spendthrifts and bullies: under Virgo, women, runagates, and such as wear iron garters: under Libra, butchers, slipslop-makers, and men of business: under Scorpio, empoisoners and cut-throats: under Sagittary, such as are goggle-eyed, herb-women, and bacon-stealers: under Capricorn, poor helpless rascals, to whom yet Nature intended horns to defend themselves: under Aquarius, cooks and paunch-bellies: under Pisces, caterers and orators: And so the world goes round like a mill, and is never without its mischief; that men be either born or perish. But for that tuft of herbs in the middle, and the honey-comb upon it, I do nothing without just reason for it: Our mother the earth is in the middle, made round like an egg, and has all good things in her self, like a honey-comb."

"Most learnedly," we all cry'd; and lifting our hands, swore, neither Hipparebus nor Aratus were to be compared to him, till at last other servants came in and spread coverlets on the beds, on which were painted nets, men in ambush with hunting-poles, and whatever apper-tained to hunting: Nor could we yet tell what to make of it: when we heard a great cry without, and a pack of beagles came and ran round the table, and after them a large tray, on which was a boar of the first magnitude, with a cap on his head, (such as slaves at their making free, had set on theirs in token of liberties) on his tusks hung two wicker baskets, the one full of dates, the other of almonds; and about him lay little pigs of marchpane, as if they were sucking: They signified a sow had farrowed, and hang there as presents for the guests to carry away with them.

To the cutting up this boar, here came not he that had carried about the fowl as before, but a swinging fellow with a two-handed beard, buskins on his leggs, and a short embroidered coat; who drawing his wood-knife, made a large hole in the boar's side, out of which flew a company of blackbirds: Then fowlers stood ready with their engines and caught them in a trice as they fluttered about the room: On which Trimalchio ordering to every man his bird, "See," said he, "what kind of acorns this wild boar fed on:" When presently the boys took off the baskets and distributed the dates and almonds among the guests.

In the mean time, I, who had private thoughts of my own, was much concerned, to know why the boar was brought in with a cap upon his head; and therefore having run out my tittle-tattle, I told my interpreter what troubled me: To which he answered, "Your boy can even tell ye what it means, for there's no riddle in it, but all as clear

457

as day. This boar stood the last of yester-nights supper, and dismiss'd by the guests, returns now as a free-man among us."

I curst my dulness, and asked him no more questions, that I might not be thought to have never eaten before with men of sense.

While we were yet talking, in came a handsome boy with a wreath of vine leaves and ivy about his head; declaring himself one while Bromius, another while Lyccus, and another Euphyus (several names of Bacchus) he carried about a server of grapes, and with a clear voice, repeated some of his master's poetry, at which Trimalchio turning to him, "Dionysius," said he, "be thou Liber," (i.e.) free, (two other names of Bacchus) whereupon the boy took the cap from off the boar's head, and putting it on his own, Trimalchio added, "You will not deny me but I have a father, Liber." We all praised the conceit, and soundly kissed the boy as he went round us.

From this up rose Trimalchio, and went to the close-stool; we also being at liberty, without a tyrant over us fell to some table-talk.

When presently one calling for a bumper, "The day," said he, "is nothing, 'tis night e're the scene turn, and therefore nothing is better than to go straight from bed to board. We have had a great deal of frost, the bagnio has scarce heated me; but a warm drinking is my wardrobe-keeper: For my part, I have spun this days thread; the wine is got into my noddle, and I am down-right —"

Selucus went on with the rest, "And I," said he, "do not bathe every day, for he where I use to bathe is a fuller: Cold water has teeth in it, and my head grows every day more washy than others, but when I have got my dose in my guts, I bid defiance to cold: Nor could I well do it to day, for I was at a funeral, a jolly companion, and a good man was he, Crysanthus has breathed his last: 'Tis not long since we were together, and methinks I talk with him now. Alas, alas! we are but blown bladders, less than flies, yet they have somewhat in them: But we are meer bubbles. You'll say he would not be rul'd; not a drop of water, or crumb of bread went down his throat in five days: And yet he's gone, or that he died of the doctor. But I am of opinion his time was come; for a physician is a great comfort. However, he was well carried out of his house upon a rich bed, and mightily lamented, he made some of his servants free; but his wife seem'd not much concerned for him. You'll say again he was not kind to her; but women are kind of kites; whatever good is done them, 'tis the same as if it were thrown in a well; and old love is as bad as a goal."

At this Philaos grew troublesome, and cryed out, "Let us remember the living: He had what was due to him; as he liv'd so he dy'd: and what has he now that any man moans the want of it? He came from nothing, and to his dying-day would have taken a farthing from

458

a dunghil with his teeth; therefore as he grew up, he grew like a honey-comb. He dy'd worth the Lord knows what, all ready money. But to the matter; I have eaten a dog's tongue and dare speak truth: He had a foul mouth, was all babble; a very make-bate, not a man. His brother was a brave fellow, a friend to his friends, of an open hand, and kept a full table: He did not order his affairs so well at first as he might have done; but the first vintage made him up again; for he sold what wine he would; and what kept up his chin was the expectation of a reversion; the credit of which brought him more than was left him; for his brother taking a pelt at him, devised the estate to I know not whose bastard: He flies far that flies his relations. Besides, this brother of his had whisperers about him, that were back-friends to the other: but he shall never do right that is quick of belief, especially in matter of business; and yet 'tis true, he'll be counted wise while he lives, to whom the thing whatever it be is given, nor he that ought to have had it. He was without doubt, one of fortune's sons; lead in his hand would turn to gold, and without trouble too, where there are not rubbs in the way. And how many years think ye he liv'd: Seventy-odd: but he was as hard as horn, bore his age well, and as black as a crow.

"I knew him some years ago an oilman, and to his last a good womans man; but withal such a miser, that (so help me Hercules) I think he left not a dogg in his house. He was also a great whore-master, and a jack of all trades; nor do I condemn him for't, for this was the only secret he kept to himself and carry'd with him."

Thus Phileros and Gammedes, as followeth: "Ye talk of what concerns neither Heaven nor Earth, when in the mean time no man regards what makes all victuals so scarce: I could not (so help me Hercules) get a mouthful of bread to day: and how? The drought continues: For my part, I have not fill'd my belly this twelve-month: A plague on these clerks of the market, the baker and they juggle together; take no notice of me, I'll take no notice of thee; which make the poorer sort labour for nothing, while those greater jaw-bones make festival every day. Oh that we had those lyons I now find here, when I first came out of Asia, that had been to live: The inner part of Sicily had the like of them, but they so handled the goblins, even Jupiter bore them no good-will. I remember Safinius, when I was a boy, he liv'd by the old arch; you'd have taken him for pepper-corn rather than a man; where-ever he went the earth parched under him; yet he was honest at bottom; one might depend on him; a friend to his friend, and whom you might boldly trust in the dark. But how did he behave himself on the bench? He toss'd every one like a ball; made no starch'd speeches, but downright, as he were, doing himself what he would persuade others: But in the market his noise was like a trumpet, without sweating or spueing. I fancy he had somewhat, I know not what, of the Asian humour: then so ready to return a salute, and call every one by his name, as if he had been one of us. In his time corn was as common as loam; you might have bought more bread for half a farthing, than any two could eat; but now the eye of an ox will cost you twice as much: Alas! Alas! we are every day worse and worse, and grow like a cows tail, downward: And why all this? We have a clerk of the market not worth three figgs, and values more the getting of a doit himself, than any of our lives: 'Tis this makes him laugh in his sleeve: for he gets more money in a day than many an honest man's whole estate: I know not how he got the estate he has; but if we had any thing of men about us, he would not hug himself as he does, but now the people are grown to this pass, that they are lyons at home, and foxes abroad: For my part, I have eaten up my cloaths already, and if corn holds at the rate it does, I shall be forc'd to sell house and all: For what will become of us, if neither gods nor men pity us? Let me never enjoy my friends more, than I believe all this comes from Heaven; for no one thinks there is any such thing; no one keeps a fast, or value Jupiter a hair, but shuts his eyes and reckons what he is worth. Time was, when matrons went bare-foot with dishevel'd hair, pure minds, and pray'd him to send rain, and forthwith it rained pitcher-fulls, or then or never, and every one was pleased: Now the gods are no better than mice; as they tread, their feet are wrap't in wooll; and because ye are not superstitious your lands yield nothing."

"More civilly, I beseech ye," said Echion the hundred-constable; "it is one while this way, and another while that, said the country-man when he lost his speckled hogg: What is not to day may be to morrow; and thus is life hurried about, so help me Hercules, a country is said not to be the better that it has many people in it, tho' ours at present labours under that difficulty, but it is no fault of hers: We must not be so nice, Heaven is equally distant every where; were you in another place you'd say hoggs walked here ready dress'd: And now I think on't, we shall have an excellent show these holy-days, a fencing-prize exhibited to the people; not of slaves bought for that purpose, but most of them free-men. Our patron Titus has a large soul, but a very devil in his drink, and cares not a straw which side gets the better; I think I should know him, for I belong to him; he's of a right breed both by father and mother, no mongril. They are well provided with weapons, and will fight it out to the last: the theatre will look like a butchers shambles, and he has where-withal to do it; his father left him a vast sum, and let him make ducks and drakes with it never so much, the Estate will bear it, and he always carries the reputation of it. He has his waggon horses, a woman-carter, and Glyco's steward,

460

who was taken a-bed with his mistress; what a busle's here between cuckolds and cuckold-makers! But this Glyco a money-broker, condemned his steward to fight with beasts; and what was that but to expose himself for another? where lay the servant's crime, who perhaps was oblig'd to do what he did: She rather deserv'd to be brain'd, than the bull that tossed her; but he that cannot come at the arse, thrashes at the pack-saddle: yet how could Glyco expect Hermogine's daughter should make a good end? She'd have pared the claws of a flying kite! a snake does not bring forth a halter: Glyco might do what he would with his own; but it will be a brand on him as long as he lives; nor can any thing but Hell blot it out; however, every man's faults are his own. I perceive now what entertainment Mammea is like to give us; he 'll be at twopence charges for me and my company; which if he does, he will pull Narbanus clean out of favour; for you must know, he'll live at the full height; yet in truth what good has he done us? He gave us a company of pittiful sword-players, but so old and decrepid, that had you blown of them, they'd have fallen of themselves: I have seen many a better at a funeral pile; he would not be at the charge of lamps for them; you'd have taken them for dunghil cocks fighting in the dark; one was a downright fool, and withal gouty; another crump-footed, and a third half dead, and ham-strung: There was one of them a Thracian, that made a figure, and kept up to the rule of fighting; but upon the whole matter, all of them were parted, and nothing came of this great block-headed rabble, but a downright running away: And yet, said he, I made ye a show, and I clap my hands for company; but cast up the account, I gave more than I received; one hand rubs another. You Agamemnon seem to tell me what would that trouble some fellow be at; because you that can speak, and do not, you are not of our form, and therefore ridicule what poor men say; tho', saving the repute of a scholar, we know you are but a meer fool. Where lies the matter then? let me persuade you to take a walk in the country, and see our cottage, you'll find somewhat to eat; a chicken, some eggs, or the like: The tempestuous season had like to have broke us all, yet we'll get enough to fill the belly. Your scholar, my boy Cicero, is mightily improved, and if he lives, you'll have a servant of him; he is pretty forward already, and whatever spare time he has, never off a book: He's a witty lad, well-featur'd, takes a thing without much study, tho' yet he be sickly: I killed three of his linnets the other day, and told him the weasels had eaten them; yet he found other things to play with, and has a pretty knack at painting: He has a perfect aversion to Greek, but seems better inclined to Latin; tho' the master he has now humours him in the other; nor can he be kept to one thing, but is still craving more, and will not take pains with any. There is also

461

another of this sort, not much troubled with learning, but very diligent, and teaches more than he knows himself: He comes to our house on holidays, and whatever you give him he's contented; I therefore bought the boy some ruled books, because I will have him get a smattering in accounts and the law; it will be his own another day. He has learning enough already, but if he takes back to it again, I design him for a trade, a barber, a parson, or a lawyer, which nothing but the devil can take from him: How oft have I told him, Thou art (Sirrah), my first begotten, and believe thy father, whatever thou learnest 'tis all thy own: See there Philero the lawyer, if he had not been a scholar he might have starved: but now see what trinkums he has about his neck, and dares nose Narbanus. Letters are a treasure, and a trade never dies."

Thus, or the like, we were bandying it about when Trimalchio return'd, and having wip'd the slops from his face, wash'd his hands, and in a very little time, "Pardon me, my friends," said he, "I have been costive for several days, and my physicians were to seek about it, when a suppository of pomegranate wine, with the liquor of a pine-tree and vinegar relieved me; and now I hope my belly may be ashamed if it keep no better order; for otherwise I have such a rumbling in my guts, you'd think an ox bellowed; and therefore if any of you has a mind, he need not blush for the matter; there's not one of us born without some defect or other, and I think no torment greater than wanting the benefit of going to stool, which is the only thing even Jupiter himself cannot prevent: And do you laugh, Fortunata, you that break me so often of my sleep by nights; I never denied any man do that in my room might pleasure himself, and physicians will not allow us to keep any thing in our bodies longer than we needs must; or if ye have any farther occasion, every thing is ready in the next room: Water, chamber-pots, close-stools, or whatever else ye may need; believe me, this being hard-bound, if it get into the head, disturbs the whole body; I have known many a man lost by it, when they have been so modest to themselves as not to tell what they ailed."

We thank'd him for his freeness, and the liberty he gave us, when yet to suppress our laughter, we set the glasses about again; nor did we yet know that in the midst of such dainties we were, as they say, to clamber another hill; for the cloth being again taken away, upon the next musick were brought in three fat hogs with collars and bells about their necks; and he that had the charge of them told us, the one was two years old, the other three, and the third full grown. I took it at first to have been a company of tumblers, and that the hogs, as the manner is, were to have shewn us some tricks in a ring, till Trimalchio breaking my expectation, "Which of them," said he, "will ye have for supper? for cocks, pheasants, and the like trifles are but country fare, but my cooks have coppers will boil a calf whole;" and therewith commanding a cook to be called for, he prevented our choice by ordering him to kill the largest, and with a loud voice, asked him, Of what rank of servants in that house he was? to which he answering, of the fortieth: "Were you bought," said the other, "or born in my house?" "Neither," said the cook, "but left you by Pansa's testament." "See then," said Trimalchio, "that you dress it as it should be, or I'll send you to the galleys." On which the cook, advertised of his power, went into the kitchin to mind his charge.

But Trimalchio turning to us with a pleasanter look, asked if the wine pleased us, "If not," said he, "I'll have it changed, and if it does, let me see it by your drinking: I thank the gods I do not buy it, but have everything that may get an appetite growing on my own grounds, without the city, which no man that I know but my self has; and yet it has been taken for Tarracino and Taranto. I have a project to joyn Sicily to my lands on the continent, that when I have a mind to go into Africa, I may sail by my own coasts. But prithee Agamemnon tell me what moot-point was it you argued to day; for tho' I plead no causes my self, yet I have had a share of letters in my time; and that you may not think me sick of them now, have three libraries, the one Greek, the other two Latin; therefore as you love me tell me what was the state of the question:" "The poor and the rich are enemies," said Agamemnon: "And what is poor?" answered Trimalchio "Spoke like a gentlemen," replied Agamemnon. But making nothing of the matter, "If it be so," said Trimalchio, "where lies the dispute? And if it be not so, 'tis nothing."

While we all humm'd this and the like stuff, "I beseech ye," said he, "my dear Agamemnon, do you remember the twelve labours of Hercules, or the story of Ulysses, how a Cyclop put his thumb out of joint with a mawkin? I read such things in Homer when I was a boy; nay, saw my self the Sybil of Curna hanging in a glass bottle: And when the boys asked her, 'Sybil, what wouldst thou?' She answered, 'I would die.'"

He had not yet run to the end of the rope, when an over-grown hog was brought to the table. We all wondered at the quickness of the thing, and swore a capon could not be dress'd in the time; and that the more, because the hog seemed larger than was a boar, we had a little before: When Trimalchio looking more intent upon him, "What, what," said he, "are not his guts taken out? No, (so help me Hercules) they are not! Bring hither, bring hither this rogue of a cook." And when he stood hanging his head before us, and said, he was so much in haste he forgot it. "How, forgot it," cry'd out Trimalchio! "Do ye think he has given it no seasoning of pepper and cummin? Strip him:" When in a trice 'twas done, and himself set between two tormentors: However, we all interceded for him, as a fault that might now and then happen, and therefore beg'd his pardon; but if he ever did the like, there was no one would speak for him; tho' for my part, I think he deserved what he got: And so turning to Agamemnon's ear, "This fellow," said I, "must be a naughty knave; could any one forget to bowel a hog? I would not (so help me Hercules) have forgiven him if he had served me so with a single fish." But Trimalchio it seems, had somewhat else in his head; for falling a laughing, "You," said he, "that have so short a memory, let's see if you can do it now." On which, the cook having gotten his coat again, took up a knife, and with a feigned trembling, ripp'd up the hog's belly long and thwart, when immediately its own weight tumbled out a heap of hogs-puddings and sausages.

After this, as it had been done of it self, the family gave a shout, and cry'd out, "Health and prosperity to Caius!" The cook also was presented with wine, a silver coronet, and a drinking goblet, on a broad Corinthian plate: which Agamemnon more narrowly viewing; "I am," said Trimalchio, "the only person that has the true Corinthian vessels."

I expected, that according to the rest of his haughtiness, he would have told us they had been brought him from Corinth: But he better: "And perhaps," said he, "you'll ask me why I am the only person that have them. And why, but that the copper-smith from whom I buy them, is called Corinthus? And what is Corinthian but what is made by Corinthus? But that ye may not take me for a man of no sence, I understand well enough whence the word first came. When Troy was taken, Hannibal, a cunning fellow, but withal mischievous, made a pile of all the brazen, gold and silver statues, and burnt them together, and thence came this mixt metal; which workmen afterwards carried off; and of this mass made platters, dishes, and several other things; so that these vessels are neither this nor that metal, but made of all of them. Pardon me what I say; however others may be of another mind, I had rather have glass ware; and if it were not so subject to breaking, I'd reckon it before gold: but now it is of no esteem.

"There was a copper-smith that made glass vessels of that pliant harness, that they were no more to be broken than gold and silver ones: It so happened, that having made a drinking-pot, with a wide mouth of that kind, but the finest glass, fit for no man, as he thought, less than Caesar himself; he went with his present to Caesar, and had admittance: The kind of the gift was praised, the hand of the workman commended, and the design of the giver accepted. He again, that he might turn the admiration of the beholders into astonishment, and work himself the more into the Emperor's favour, prayed the glass out of the Emperor's hand; and having received it, threw it with such a

464

force against the paved floor, that the most solid and firmest metal could not but have received some hurt thereby. Caesar also was no less amazed at it, than concerned for it; but the other took up the pot from the ground, not broken but bulg'd a little; as if the substance of metal had put on the likeness of a glass; and therewith taking a hammer out of his pocket, he hammer'd it as it had been a brass kettle, and beat out the bruise: And now the fellow thought himself in Heaven, in having, as he fansied, gotten the acquaintance of Caesar, and the admiration of all: But it fell out quite contrary: Caesar asking him if any one knew how to make this malleable glass but himself? And he answering, there was not, the Emperor commanded his head to be struck off: 'For,' said he, 'if this art were once known, gold and silver will be of no more esteem than dirt.'

"And for silver, I more than ordinarily affect it: I have several water-pots more or less, whereon is the story how Cassandra killed her son's, and the dead boys are so well embossed, you'd think them real. I have also a drinking cup left me by an advocate of mine, where Daedalus puts Niobe into the Trojan horse, as also that other of Hermerotes; that they may stand as a testimony, there's truth in cups, and all this massy; nor will I part with what I understand of them at any rate."

While he was thus talking, a cup dropt out of a boy's hand; on which, Trimalchio looking over his shoulder at him, bad him begone, and kill himself immediately; "for," said he, "thou art careless and mind'st not what thou art about." The boy hung his lip, and besought him; but he said, "What! dost thou beseech me, as if I required some difficult matter of thee? I only bid thee obtain this of thy self, that thou be not careless again." But at last he discharged him upon our entreaty. On this the boy ran round the table and cry'd, "Water without doors, and wine within." We all took the jest, but more especially Agamemnon, who knew on what account himself had been brought thither.

Trimalchio in the mean time hearing himself commended, drank all the merrier, and being within an ace of quite out, "Will none of you," said he, "invite my Fortunata to dance? Believe me, there's no one leads a country dance better:" And with that, tossing his hands round his head, fell to act a jack-pudding: the family all the while singing, 'youth it self, most exactly youth it self;' and he gotten into the middle of the room, but that Fortunata whispered him, and I believe told him, such gambols did not become his gravity. Nor was there any thing more uneven to it self: for one while he turned to his Fortunata, and another while to his natural inclination: But what disturbed the pleasure of her dancing was his notaries coming in; who, as they had been the acts of a common council, read aloud:

'VII of the Calends of August born in Trimalchio's manner of cumanum, thirty boys and forty girls, brought from the threshing-floor into the granary, five hundred thousand bushels of wheat. The same day broke out a fire in a pleasure-garden that was Pompey's, first began in one of his bayliffs houses.'

"How's this," said Trimalchio: "When were those gardens bought for me?" "The year before," answered his notary, "and therefore not yet brought to account."

At this Trimalchio fell into a fume; and "whatever lands," said he, "shall be bought me herafter, if I hear nothing of it in six months, let them never, I charge ye, be brought to any account of mine." Then also were read the orders of the clerks of the markets, and the testaments of his woodwards, rangers, and park-keepers, by which they disinherited their relations, and with ample praise of him, declare Trimalchio their heir. Next that, the names of his bayliffs; and how one of them that made his circuits in the country, turned off his wife for having taken her in bed with a barber; the door-keeper of his baths turn'd out of his place; the auditor found short in his accounts, and the dispute between the grooms of his chamber ended.

At last came in the dancers on the rope; and a gorbelly'd blockhead standing out with a ladder, commanded his boy to hopp every round singing, and dance a jigg on the top of it, and then tumble through burning hoops of iron, with a glass in his mouth. Trimalchio was the only person that admir'd it, but withal said, he did not like it; but there were two things he could willingly behold, and they were the flyers on the high rope, and quails; and that all other creatures and shows were meer gewgaws: "For," said he, "I bought once a sett of stroulers, and chose rather to make them merry-andrews than comedians; and commanded my bag-piper to sing in Latin to them."

While he was chattering all at this rate, a boy chanced to stumble upon him, on which the family gave a shriek, the same also did the guests; not for such a beast of a man, whose neck they could willingly have seen broken, but for fear the supper should break up ill, and they be forc'd to wail the death of the boy.

Whatever it were, Trimalchio gave a deep groan; and leaning upon his arm as if it had been hurt, the physicians ran thick about him, and with the first, Fortunata, her hair about her ears, a bottle of wine in her hand, still howling, miserable unfortunate woman that she was! Undone, undone. The boy on the other hand, ran under our feet, and beseeched us to procure him a discharge: But I was much concern'd, lest our interposition might make an ill end of the matter; for the cook that had forgotten to bowel the hog was still in my thoughts. I began therefore to look about the room, for fear somewhat or other

466

might drop through the ceiling; while the servant that had bound up his arm in white, not scarlet-colour flannen, was soundly beaten: Now was I much out, for instead of another course, came in an order of Trimalchio's by which he gave the boy his freedom; that it might not be said, so honourable a person had been hurt by his slave. We all commended the action, but chatted among our selves with what little consideration the things of this world were done. "You're in the right," said Trimalchio; "nor ought this accident to pass without booking;" and so calling for the journal, commanded it to be entered; and with, as little thought, tumbled out these verses:

> "What's least expected falls into our dish,
> And fortune's more indulgent than our wish:
> Therefore, boy, fill the generous wine about."

This epigram gave occasion to talk of the poets, and Marsus, the Trachian, carry'd the bays a long while: till Trimalchio (turning to some wit amongst them) "I bessech ye, master of mine," said he, "tell me what difference take ye between Cicero the orator, and Publius the poet? for my part I think one was more eloquent, the other the honester man; for what could be said better than this."

> "Now sinking Rome grows weak with luxury,
> To please her appetite cram'd peacocks die:
> Their gaudy plumes a modish dress supply.
>
> For her the guinea hen and capon's drest:
> The stork it self for Rome's luxurious taste,
> Must in a caldron build its humbl'd nest.
>
> That foreign, friendly, pious, long-leg'd thing,
> Grateful, that with shrill sounding notes dost sing
> All winter's gone; yet ushers in the spring.
> Why in one ring must three rich pearls be worn,
> But that your wives th'exhausted seas adorn,
> Abroad t'increase their lust, at home their scorn?
>
> Why is the costly emerald so desir'd,
> Or richer glittering carbuncle admir'd,
> Because they sparkle, is't with that you're fir'd?
> Well, honesty's a jewel. Now none knows
> A modest bride from a kept whore by 'er cloaths;
> For cobweb lawns both spouse and wench expose."

"But, now we talk after the rate of the learned, which," said he, "are the most difficult trades? I think a physician and a banker: a physician, because he know's a man's very heart, and when the fits of an ague will return; tho' by the way, I hate them mortally; for by their good will I should have nothing but slubber-slops: And a banker, because he'll find out a piece of brass money, tho' plated with silver.

"There are also brute beasts, sheep and oxen, laborious in their kind: Oxen, to whom we are beholding for the bread we eat; and sheep, for the wooll, that makes us so fine. But O horrid! we both eat the mutton, and make us warm with the fleece. I take the bees for divine creatures; they give us honey, tho' 'tis said they stole it from Jupiter, and that's the reason why they sting: For where-ever ye meet any thing that's sweet, you'll ever find a sting at the end of it."

He also excluded philosophers from business, while the memoirs of the family were carrying round the table, and a boy, set for that purpose, read aloud the names of the presents, appointed for the guests, to carry home with them. Wicked silver, what can it not? Then a gammon of bacon was set on the table, and above that several sharp sauces, a night-cap for himself, pudding-pies, and I know not what kind of birds: There was also brought in a rundlet of wine, boiled off a third part, and kept under ground to preserve its strength: There were also several other things I can give no account of; besides apples, scallions, peaches, a whip, a knife, and what had been sent him; as sparrows, a flye-flap, raisons, Attick honey, night-gowns, judges robes, dry'd paste, table-books, with a pipe and a foot-stool: After which came in an hare and a sole-fish: And there was further sent him a lamprey, a water-rat, with a frog at his tail, and a bundle of beets.

Long time we smiled at these, and five hundred the like, that have now slipt my memory: But now when Ascyltos, who could not moderate himself, held up his hands and laught at every thing; nay so downright, that he was ready to cry: A free-man of Trimalchio's that sate next above me, grew hot upon't; and "What," said he, "thou sheep, what dost thou laugh at? does not this sumptuousness of my master please you? you're richer (forsooth) and eat better every day; so may the guardian of this place favour me, as had I sate near him, I'd hit him a box on the ear ere this: A hopeful cullion, that mocks others; some pitiful night-walker, not worth the very urine he makes; and should I throw mine on him, knows not where to dry himself. I am not (so help me Hercules) quickly angry, yet worms are bred even in tender flesh. He laughs! what has he to laugh at? what wooll did his father give for the bantling? Is he a Roman knight? I am the son of a king. How came I then, you'll say, to serve another? I did it of my self, and had rather be a citizen of Rome, than a tributary king, and

468

now hope to live so, as to be no man's jeast. I walk like other men, with an open face, and can shew my head among the best, for I owe no man a groat; I never had an action brought against me, or said to me on the exchange, Pay me what thou owest me. I bought some acres in the country, and have everything suitable to it: I feed twenty mouths, besides dogs: I ransomed by bond-woman, lest another should wipe his hands on her smock; and between our selves, she cost me more than I'll tell ye at present. I was made a captain of horse gratis, and hope so to die, that I shall have no occasion to blush in my grave: But art thou so prying into others, that thou never considerest thy self? Canst thou spy a louse on another man's coat, and not see the tyck on thy own? Your master then is ancienter than your self, and 't please him; but yet thou, whose milk is not yet out of thy nose; that can'st not say boh to a goose; must you be making observations? Are you the wealthier man? If you are, dine twice, and sup twice; for my part, I value my credit more than treasures: Upon the whole matter, where's the man that ever dunn'd me twice? Thou pipkin of a man, more limber, but nothing better than a strap of wet leather, I have served forty years in this house, came into it with my hair full grown; this palace was not then built, yet I made it my business to please my master, a person of honour, the parings of whose nails are more worth than thy whole body. I met several rubs in my way, but by the help of my good angel, I broke through them all: This is truth; it is as easie to make a hunting-horn of a sow's tail, as to get into this company. What make ye in a dump now, like a goat at a heap of stones?"

On this Gito, who stood behind him, which the other taking notice of, fell upon the boy; and, "Do you," said he, "laugh too, you curl-pated chattering magpye? O the Saturnals! Why how now, sirrah! is it the month of December? When were you twenty, I pray? What would this collop dropt from the gibbet, this crows-meat, be at? I'll find some or other way for Jupiter to plague thee, and him that bred thee no better, or never let me eat a good meals-meat again: I could, sirrah, but for the companies sake, I spare thee; tho' either we understand not aright, or they are sots themselves that carry no better a hand over thee; for without doubt it is true, like master like man. I am hot by nature, and can scarce contain my self; give me but a mess of pease-porridge, and I care not two-pence for my mother. Very well, I shall meet thee abroad, thou mouse; nay, rather mole-hill. May I never thrive more, but I'll drive that master of thine into a blade of rue; nor shalt thou (so help me Hercules) 'scape me, tho' thou could'st call in Jupiter to thy aid: I shall off with those locks, and take thee when that trifling master of thine shall be out of the way; thou wilt certainly fall into my hands, and either I know not my self, or I'll make thee leave that buffoonry: Tho' thy beard were of gold, I'll have thee bruised in a mortar, and him that first taught thee; I never studied geometry, criticism, and meer words without sence, but I understand the fitting of stones for buildings; can run you over a hundred things, as to metal weight, coin, and that to a tittle; if you have a mind you and I will try it between us: I'll lay thee a wager, thou wizard, and tho' I am wholly ignorant of rhetorick, thou'lt presently see thou hast lost: Let no one run about the bush to me: I come up to him: Resolve me, I say, 'which of us runs, yet stirs not out of his place: which of us grows bigger, and yet is less.' Do you scamper? Can't you tell what to make of it, that you look so like a mouse in a trap? Therefore either hold thy tongue, or don't provoke a better man than thy self, who does not think thee fram'd of nature, unless thou fansiest me taken with those yellow curl'd locks, which thou hast already vowed to some whore or other. O lucky opportunity! Come, let's walk the exchange, and see which of us can take up money: You'll be satisfied then, this iron has credit upon't; a pretty thing, is it not! a drunken fox. So may I gain while I live, and die well; but the people will brain me if I follow not that coat on thy back, which is not for thy wearing, where-ever thou goest: He's a precious tool, too, whoever he were, that taught thee; a piece of green cheese, no master. I have learn'd as well as another man, and my master said it would be my own another day. Save your worship! get home as fast as you can, but look well about you, and have a care how you speak irreverently of your betters, or vie estates with them; he that does it, his purse shall feel it: For my self, that you see me as I am, I thank my stars for the art I have."

Ascyltos was making answer to his railing; when Trimalchio, pleased with that good grace of speaking, "Go to," said he, "no more of this wild talk, let us rather be pleasant: And you Hermeros, bear with the young-man, his blood boils; be thou the soberer man; he that is overcome in this matter, goes off conqueror: Even thy self, when thou wert such another capon, hadst nothing but coco, coco, and no heart at all. Let us therefore, which is the better of the two, be heartily merry, and expect some admirers of Homer, that will be here presently."

Nor were the words scarce out of his mouth, when in came a band of men, and made a rustling with their spears and targets. Trimalchio leaned on his elbow, the Homerists rattled out Greek verses, as, arrogantly enough, they were wont to do, and he read a Latin book, with a loud voice: whereupon silence being made, "Know ye," said he, "what fable they were upon?"

"Diomedes and Ganymede were two brothers, and Helen was their sister; Agamemnon stole him away, and shamm'd Diana with a hind in his room, as says Homer in this place; and how the Trojans, and the Parentines fought among themselves; but at last he got the better of it, and married his daughter Iphigenia to Achilles; on which Ajax ran mad. And there's an end of the tale."

On this the Homerists set up a shout, and a young boiled heifer with an helmet on her head, was handed in upon a mighty charger: Ajax followed, and with a drawn sword, as if he were mad, made at it, now in one place, then in another, still acting a Morris-dancer; till having cut it into joints, he took them upon the point of his sword, and distributed them. Nor had we much time to admire the conceit; for of a sudden the roof gave a crack, and the whole room shook: For my part, I got on my feet, but all in confusion, for fear some tumbler might drop on my head; the same also were the rest of the guests; still gaping and expecting what new thing should come from the clouds: when straight the main beams opened, and a vast circle was let down, all around which hung golden garlands, and alabaster pots of sweet ointments.

While we were required to take up these presents, I chanced to cast an eye upon the table, where there lay a fresh service of cheese-cakes and tarts, and in the midst of them a lusty rundlet, stuck round with all sorts of apples and grapes, as they commonly draw that figure.

We greedily reached our hands towards it, when of a sudden, a new diversion gave us fresh mirth; for all the cheese-cakes, apples and tarts, upon the least touch, threw out a delicious liquid perfume, which fell upon us.

We judging the mess to be sacred, that was so gorgeously set out, stood up and began a health to the august founder, the father of his country: After which reverence, failing to catch that catch could, we filled our napkins and I chiefly, who thought nothing too good for my boy Gito.

During this, in came three boys in white, their coats tuck'd about them; of whom, two set on the table three household gods with broaches about their necks, and the other bearing round us a goblet of wine, cry'd aloud, "Be the gods favourable!" "The name of this," said he, "is cobler, that other's good-luck, and the third's spend-all." And as the image of Trimalchio was carryed round, and every one kiss'd it, we thought it a shame not to do as the rest of the company.

After this, when all of us had wished him health and happiness, Trimalchio, turning to Niceros, "You were wont," said he, "to be a good companion, but what's the matter we get not a word from ye now? Let me entreat ye, as you would see me happy, do not break an old custom."

Niceros, pleased with the frankness of his friend: "Let me never thrive," said he, "if I am not ready to caper out of my skin, to see you in so good a humours; therefore what I say shall be all mirth; tho' I am afraid those grave fopps may laugh: but let them look to't, I'll go on nevertheless; for what am I the worse for any one swearing? I had rather they laugh at what I say, than at my self."

Thus when he spoke he began this tale: — "While I was yet a servant we liv'd in a narrow lane, now the house of Gavilla: There, as the gods would have it, I fell in love with Tarentius's wife; he kept an eating-house. Ye all knew Melissa Tarentina, a pretty little punching-block, and withal beautiful; but (so help me Hercules) I minded her not so much for the matter of the point of that, as that she was good-humour'd; if I asked her any thing, she never deny'd me; and what money I had, I trusted her with it; nor did she ever fail me when I'd occasion. It so happened, that a she-companion of hers had dy'd in the country, and she was gone thither; how to come at her I could not tell; but a friend is seen at a dead lift; it also happened my master was gone to Capua to dispatch somewhat or other: I laid hold of the opportunity, and persuaded mine host to take an evenings walk of four or five miles out of town, for he was a stout fellow, and as bold as a devil: The moon shone as bright as day, and about cock-crowing we fell in with a burying-place, and certain monuments of the dead: my man loitered behind me a-star-gazing, and I sitting expecting him, fell a singing and numbering them; when looking round me, what should I see but mine host stript stark-naked, and his cloaths lying by the high-wayside. The sight struck me every where, and I stood as if I had been dead; but all of a sudden he was turned to a wolf: Don't think I jest; I value no man's estate at the rate, as to tell a lye. But as I was saying, after he was turned to a wolf, he set up a howl, and fled to the woods. At first I knew not where I was, till going to take up his cloaths, I found them also turn'd to stone. Another man would have dy'd for fear, but I drew my sword, and slaying all the ghosts that came in my way, lighted at last on the place where my mistress was: I entered the first door; my eyes were sunk in my head, the sweat ran off me by more streams than one, and I was just breathing my last, without thought of recovery; when my Melissa coming up to me, began to wonder why I'd be walking so late; and 'if,' said she, 'you had come a little sooner, you might have done us a kindness; for a wolf came into the farm, and has made butchers work enough among the cattle; but tho' he got off, he has no reason to laugh, for a servant of ours ran him through the neck with a pitch-fork.' As soon as I heard her, I could not hold open my eyes any longer, and ran home by daylight, like a vintner whose house had been robb'd: But coming by the place where the cloaths were turned to stone, I saw nothing but a puddle of blood; and when I got home, found mine host lying a-bed like an oxe in his stall, and a chirurgeon dressing his neck. I understood afterwards he was a fellow that could change his skin; but from that day, forward, could never eat a bit of bread with him, no, if you'd have kill'd me. Let them that don't believe me, examine the truth of it; may your good angels plague me as I tell ye a lye."

The company were all wondering, when, "Saving what you have said," quoth Trimalchio, "if there be faith in man, my hair stands on end, because I know Niceros is no trifler; he's sure of what he says, and not given to talking: Nay, I'll tell ye as horrible a thing myself; but see there, what's that behind the hangings?

"When I was yet a long-hair'd boy, for even then I liv'd a pleasant life, I had a minion, and he dy'd: He was (so help me Hercules) a pearl, a paragon, nay perfection it self: But when the poor mother lamented him, and we also were doing the same, some witches got round the house on a sudden, you'd have taken them for hounds hunting a hare. We had then in the house a Cappadocian, a tall fellow, stout and hardy, that would not have stept an inch out of his way for Jupiter. He boldly drew his sword, and wrapping his coat about his left arm, leaped out of the house, and as it might be here, (no hurt to the thing I touch) ran a woman clean through. We heard a pitiful groan, but not to lye, saw none of them. Our champion came in and threw himself on a bed, but all black and blue, so he had been trosh'd with flails; for it seems some ill hand had touched him. We shut the door, and went on with our mourning; but the mother taking her son in her arms, and stroaking him, found nothing but a bolster of straw; it had neither heart, entrals, nor any thing, for the fairies belike had stollen him out of his cradle, and left that of straw instead of him. Give me credit, I beseech ye, women are craftier than we are, play their tricks by night, and turn every thing topsy-turvy. After this our tall fellow never came to his colour again, but in a few days died raving-mad."

We all wondred, as not doubting what he said, and kissing the table in reverence to him, pray'd the privilege of the night, and that our places might be kept till we returned.

And now we thought the lamps look'd double, and the whole room seem'd quite another thing, when Trimalchio again, "I speak to you Plorimus, won't you come in for a share? Will ye entertain us with nothing, thou usedst to be a pleasant companion, couldst sing a song and tell a tale with the best; but alas! alas! the sweetmeats are gone." "My horses," said the other, "ran away with my coach, I have been troubled with the gout ever since. When I was a young fellow, I sung so long I had well nigh brought my self into a consumption. What

473

do ye tell me of songs, tales, or barber shops? Who ever came near me but one, only Apelles;" and with setting his hand to his mouth, whistled out somewhat, I know not what, which afterwards he swore was Greek. Trimalchio also when he mimicked the trumpets, looked on his minion and called him Croesus: Yet the boy was blear-eye'd, and swathing up a little black bitch with nasty teeth, and over-grown with fat, in green swadling-clouts, he set half a loaf on the table, which she refusing, he cram'd her with it: on which Trimalchio commanded the guardian of his house and family, Scylax, to be brought; when presently was led in a beautiful mastiff in a chain, who having a hint given him by a knock of the porter's foot, lay down before the table: whreupon Trimalchio throwing him a manchet; "There's no one," said he, "in this house of mine, loves me better than this dog." The boy taking it in dudgeon that Scylax should be so commended, laid the bitch on the floor, and challenged the dog to have a rubber with him. On this Scylax, after the manner of dogs, set up such a hideous barking, that it fill'd the room; and snapping at him, almost rent off a brooch that hung on Croesus's breast; nor did the scuffle end here, for the great candle being overturn'd on the table, broke all the chrystal glasses, and threw the scalding oil on the guests.

Trimalchio, not to seem concerned at the loss, kissed the boy, and commanded him to get on his back; nor was it long e're he was a cock-horse, and slapping his masters shoulders, and laughing, cry'd out, "Fool, fool, and how many of them have we here?"

Trimalchio thus kept under for a while, commanded a bumper to be fill'd and given round to the waiters, with this further, that whosoever refused it should have it poured down his collar. Thus one while we were grave, and other while merry.

After this came junkets and made dishes, the very remembrance of which, if I may be believed, will not yet down with me; for there were several cram'd hens given about under the notion of thrushes, and goose eggs with caps upon them; while Trimalchio, nor without ostentation press'd us to eat; adding withal, that their bones were taken out.

Nor were the words scarce out of his mouth, when a beadle rapp'd at the door, and one in white, with a company of roisters following him, came in upon us: For my part I was not a little surprized; and by his lordliness taking him for the Mayor of a town, and our selves within his liberties, was getting upon my feet. Agamemnon laught to see me so concerned, and bade me sit still; "for," said he, "this Habinas is a captain of horse, a good mason, and has a special faculty in making monuments."

Recovered again with his words, I kept my seat, and wholly fix't my eye on Habinas: He came in drunk, and lolling on his wife's shoulders, with some garlands about him, his face all trickling down with ointment, he seated himself at the head of the table, and incontinently called for wine and hot water.

Trimalchio was pleased with the humour, and calling for a bigger glass, asked him what entertainment he had whence he came?

"Every thing," said the other, "but thy self; for my inclination was here; tho' (so help me Hercules) it was all well. Scissa kept a nine-days feast for his servant Miscellus, whom he infranchised after he was dead: It is said he had a round sum in the chequer, for they reckon he died worth 50,000 sesterces; yet this was all done in good order; tho' every one of us were obliged to pour half his drink on the grave." "But," said Trimalchio, "what had ye to eat?" "I'll tell ye," quoth Habinas, "as near as I can, for my memory is not so good, but that sometimes I forget my own name: However, for the first dish we had a goodly porker, with a garland upon him, and puddings, goose giblets, lamb-stones, sweetbreads, and gizzards round him; there were also beets and household-bread of his own baking, for himself, which I would rather have than white; it makes a man strong, and I never complain of what I like. The next was a cold tart, with excellent warm honey, and that Spanish, running upon it. I eat little of the tart, but more of the honey; I tasted also the red pulse, and lupines, by the advice of Calvus, and several apples, of which I took away two in my handkerchief: for if I bring home nothing to my little she slave, I shall have snubs enough: this dame of mine puts me often in mind of her. We had also on a side-table the haunch of a bear, which Scintilla tasting ere she was aware, had like to have thrown up her guts: I on the other hand eat a pound of it or better, for methought it tasted like boars flesh; and said I, if a bear eats a man, why may not a man much more eat a bear? To be short, we had cream cheese, wine boil'd off to a third part, fry'd snails, chitterlings, livers, eggs, turneps, mustard, and a bowl that held a gallon. Don't disturb me, Palamedes; there were also handled about a basket of sugar-cakes, of which we wantonly took some, and sent away the gammon of bacon. But tell me Caius, I beseech you, what's the matter that Fortunata sits not among us?" "How came you to know her?" quoth Trimalchio; "for till she has gotten her plate together, and distributed what we leave among the servants, not a sip of any thing goes into her mouth."

"But unless she sits down," replied Habinas, "I'll be gone;" and was getting up, but that the word being four times given about for her, she came at last in a greenish gown and a cherry-colour'd stomacher, beneath which might be seen her petticoat and embroidered

475

garters; then wiping her hands on her neckcloth, she sate on that bed whereon Scintilla the wife of Habinas was; and having given her a kiss, told her it was in compliment to her that she was there. At length it came to this, that she took off her weighty bracelets, and shewed them to Scintilla; which she admiring, she also unbuckled her garters and a net-work purse, which she said was of the finest gold.

Trimalchio observed it, and commanding all to be laid before him, "See," said he, "this womans finery, and what fools our wives make us; they should be six pound and a half; yet I've another of Mercury's making, that weighs ten": And that he might not be thought to tell a lye, called for his gold scales, and commanded them to be weighed: Nor had Scintilla more wit than t'other, for pulling a golden box out of her bosom, which she called good luck, she took out of it two large pearl pendants, giving them in like manner to Fortunata to view: "See," quoth she, "what 'tis to have a kind husband, I am sure no woman has better." "What," said Habinas, "has thou put the shame on me? thou toldst me thou couldst be contented with glass beads; and for this trick, if I had a daughter I'd cut off her ears; tho' were there no women what were the rest worth?"

Mean time the women perceiving they were toucht, twitter'd among themselves, and being got drunk, fell to kissing one another; one commended the mistress of the house, t'other the master: when during this chatter, Habinas stealing behind Fortunata, gave her such a toss on the bed, that her heels flew as high as her head, on which she gave a squeak or two, and finding her thighs bare, ran her head under Scintilla's smock.

This held a while, till Trimalchio calling for a second service to entertain his new guests, the servants took away the tables that were before us, and having brought others, strew'd the room with pin-dust, mixt vermilion and saffron; and what I never saw before, the dust of a looking-glass ground to powder.

When immediately, quoth Trimalchio, "I could have been contented with those first dishes; but since we have got other tables, we must also have another service; and if there be any thing worth our having, bring it."

On which, a spruce boy that serviced us with warm water, began to imitate a nightingale; till Trimalchio giving the word, a servant that waited on Habinas, set up another humour, and, as I believe, commanded by his master, nois'd out:

"Meantime Aeneas had put off to sea."

Nor was there ever a harsher sound yet pierced my ears; for besides his disordered country tone, his pitiful and starvling way of delivery,

476

he so stufft it with scraps of verses, that even Virgil then first disrelished me; till at last so tyr'd, that he could hold no longer; "D'ye think," said Habinas, "this boy has learn'd nothing? I bred him with juglers that follow the fair: Nor has he his fellow, whether he humours a muliteer or a jester. This never-be-good has abundance of wit; he's a taylor, a cook, a baker, a jack of all trades, and but for two faults, were exact to a hair: He's crack-brain'd, and snores in his sleep: For that cast of his eye I value it not, he looks like Venus, and therefore his tongue is ever running; and were that eye out he were worth the money I gave for him."

On which Scintilla interrupting him, told him he was a naughty man, for not telling all his servant's good qualities: "He's a pimp," said he, "if not worse, but I'll take care he be branded for that."

Trimalchio laught, and said he knew he was a Cappadocian that never beguiled himself of any thing, and "(so help me Hercules) I commend him for't: when will you find such another, but Scintilla, you must not be jealous! Believe me, and I know you too; may I so enjoy the health you wish me, as I play'd at leap-frog so long with our boy, that my master grew jealous, and sent me to dig in the country: But hold thy tongue and I'll give thee a loaf."

Hereupon the rascal, as if he had been praised all this while, took out an earthen candlestick, and for half an hour or better, counterfeited the hautboys, Habinas singing the base to him, and blabbering his under lip with his finger; that done, he went into the middle of the room, and clattering some canes together, one while imitated the bagpipes, and danced a jigg to it; and other while with a ragged frock and a whip, humour'd a fellow driving his mules; till Habinas having called him, first kiss'd him, and then drank to him, which the other pledged; and wishing him better and better, I give you, said he, a pair of buskins.

Nor had there ever been an end of this trumpery, had not that last service of blackbirds, baked in good pie-crust with raisins and chess-nuts, been brought up, and after them quince-peaches, so stuck with prickles, that they look'd like hedgehogs: Yet this might have been borne with, if the next dish had not been such, that we had rather have starved than touch'd it: For when it was set upon the table, and as we thought, a fat goose, with fishes and all kind of fowl around it, whatever you see here, said Trimalchio is all made of the same substance.

I, like a cunning cur, straight apprehended what it might be; and turning to Agamemnon, "I marvel," said I, "whether they be all mash'd together or made of loam; for in a Saturnal at Rome, my self saw the like imaginery shew of a supper."

Nor had I scarce said it, when — quoth Trimalchio, "Let me so grow in estate, not bulk, as my cook made all of this out of one hog; there is not an excellenter fellow than himself; he shall, if he please, make ye a poll of ling of a sows tripe; a wood-culver of fat bacon; a turtle of a spring of pork; and a hen of a collar of brawn; and therefore of my own fancy, I gave him a name proper to him, for he is called Daedalus: And because he understands his business, I had chopping-knives of the best steel brought him from Rome"; and with that, calling for them, he turn'd them over, and admiring them, offered us the liberty of trying their edge on his cheek.

On this came in two servants as quarrelling about their collars, at which each of them had a large earthen pot hanging; and when Trimalchio determined the matter between them, neither of them stood to his sentence, but fell to club-law, and broke each others pots.

This drunken presumption put us out of order; yet casting an eye on the combatants, we saw oisters and scallops running from the pots, and another boy receiving them in a charger, which he carried round the guests.

Nor was the cook's ingenuity short of the rest, for he brought us a dish of grill'd snails on a silver gridiron, and with a shrill unpleasant voice, sang as he went. I am asham'd of what folow'd; for, what was never heard of till then, the boys came in with a bason of liquid perfumes, and first binding our legs, ancles and feet, with garlands, anointed them with it, and put the rest into the wine vessel and the lamps.

And now Fortunata began to dance, and Scintilla's hands went faster than her tongue; when, quoth Trimalchio, "Sit down Philargyrus, I give ye leave, and you Carrio, because you are a green-ribbon-man, and you Minophilus bid your comrade do the like"; what shall I say more? The family so crowded upon us, that we were almost thrust off our beds; and who should be seated above me, but the cook who had made a goose of a hog, all stinking of pickle and kitchen-stuff; nor yet content that he sate amongst us, he fell immediately to personate Thespis the tragedian, and dare his master to a wager which of them two should win a prize next wrestling.

Trimalchio abash'd at the challenge; "My friends," said he, "even servants are men; and however oppress'd by ill luck, sucked the same milk our selves did; and for mine, it shall not be long e're I make them free without prejudice to my self: to be short, I enfranchise all of them by my last will and testament.

"I give Philargus a country farm, and his she-comrade; to Carrio an island, with a twentieth part of my moveables, a bed and its furniture; for I make Fortunata my heiress, whom I recommend to all my friends, and publish what I have done, to the end my family may so love me now, as if I were dead."

All thanked their master for his kindness; and he, as having forgotten trifles, called for a copy of his will, which he read from one end to the other, the family all the while sighing and sobbing; afterwards turning to Habinas, "Tell me, my best of friends," said he, "do you go on with my monument as I directed ye, I earnestly entreat ye, that at the feet of my statue you carve me my little bitch, as also garlands and ointments, and all the battles I have been in, that by your kindness I may live when I am dead: Be sure too that it have an hundred feet as it fronts the highway, and as it looks towards the fields two hundred: I will also, that there be all sorts of fruit and vines round my ashes, and that in great abundance: For it is a gross mistake to furnish houses for the living, and take no care of those we are to abide in for ever: And therefore in the first place, I will have it engraven —

'Let no heir of mine pretend to this Monument.'

"And that I may receive no injury after I am dead, I'll have a codicil annext to my will, whereby I'll appoint one of my freed-men the keeper of this monument, that the people make not a house-of-office of it. Make me also, I beseech you, on this my monument, ships under full sail, and my self in my robes sitting on the bench, with five gold rings on my fingers, and scattering moneys among the common people; for you know I have ordered ye a funeral feast, and two-pence a-piece in money. You shall also, if you think fit, shape me some of these beds we now sit on, and all the people making their court to me. On my right hand place my Fortunata's statue, with a dove in one hand, and leading a little dog in her girdle with the other: As also my Cicero, and large wine vessels close cork'd that the wine don't run out, and yet carve one of them as broken, and a boy weeping over it; as also a sun-dial in the middle, that whoever comes to see what's-a-clock, may read my name whether he will or no. And lastly, have a special consideration whether you think this epitaph sufficient enough:

'Here rests Caius Pompeius Trimalchio, patron of the learned. A troop of horse was decreed him, without suing for, and might have been a senator would he have accepted it. A pious man, honest, valiant, and true to his friend. He raised himself from little or nothing, but left behind him a prodigious estate, yet never heard a philosopher. Farewell to you also.'"

This said, Trimalchio wept plentifully, Fortunata wept, Habinas wept, and the whole family set up a cry as it had been his funeral; nay, I also whin'd for company: when, quoth Trimalchio, "Since you know we must die, why don't we live while we may? so let me live my self to see you happy; as, if we plunge our selves in the bath we shall not repent it: At my peril be it; I'll lead the way, for this room is grown as hot as an oven."

"Say you so," quoth Habinas, "nor am I afraid to make two days of one"; and therewith got up barefoot and follow'd Trimalchio.

I on the other hand turning to Ascyltos, asked him what he thought of it, for "if I but see the bath I shall swoon away."

"Let's lagg behind then," said he, "and whilst they are getting in, we'll slip off in the crowd."

The contrivance pleased us; and so Gito leading the way through the portico, we came to the last gate, where a chained dog bolted upon us so furiously, that Ascyltos fell into the fish-pond. I, who had been frighted at the painted dog, and now gotten as drunk as Ascyltos, while I endeavoured to get hold of him, fell in my self; at last the porter's coming in saved us, for he quieted the dog and drew us out; but Gito, like a sharp rascal, delivered himself, for whatever had been given him at supper to carry home with him, he threw it the dog, and that mollified him.

But, when shivering with cold, we desired the porter to let us out: "You're mistaken," said he, "if ye think to go out the same way ye came in, for no guest ere yet did; they came in at one gate and are let out by another."

In this sad pickle, what should we do? we found ourselves in a new kind of labyrinth, and for bathing, we'd enough of it already: However, necessity enforcing us, we pray'd him to show us the way to the bath: and Gito having hung out our cloaths a drying in the porch, we entred the bath, which was somewhat narrow, and sunk in the earth, not unlike a rainwater cistern; in this stood Trimalchio stark-naked: Nor could we avoid his filthy tricks; for he said, nothing was better than to bathe in a crowd; and that every place had in times past been a grinding-house. Being weary at length, he sate down, and provok'd by the noisiness of the bath, set up his drunken throat, and fell a murdering some songs of Menecrates, as they that understood him told us.

Other guests ran round the cistern with their arms across, and made a clamorous slap with their mouths; others either try'd to take up a ring from the pavement, with their hands bound behind them, or putting one knee to the ground, to kiss their great toes backward.

While they thus entertained one another, we went into the hothouse that had been heated for Trimalchio; and being now recovered of our drunkenness, were brought into another room, where Fortunata had set out a fresh entertainment. Above the lamps I observed some women's gewgaws. The tables were massy silver, the earthen ware double gilt, and a conduit running with wine; when, quoth Trimalchio, "This day, my friends, a servant of mine opened a barber-shop; he's well to pass, a thrifty fellow, and a favourite of mine: Come, let the floor have a drink as well as our selves; and for our part, we'll sit to it till day-light."

While he was yet speaking, a cock crow'd, at which Trimalchio grew disordered, and commanded the wine to be thrown under table, and sprinkle the lamps with it; then changing a ring to his right hand, "it is not for nothing," said he, "this trumpeter has given us notice; for either the house should be on fire, or one of the neighbourhood will kill himself: Far from us be it, and therefore, whoever brings me this discoverer, I'll give him a reward."

When immediately a cock was brought in, and Trimalchio, commanding to have him drest, he was torn in pieces by that exquisite cook, who a little before had made us fish and fowl of a hog, and put in a stew-pan, and while Daedalus was taking a lusty draught, Fortunata ground pepper.

After which Trimalchio taking some of the banquet, bid the waiters go to supper, and let others supply their places.

Whereupon came in another rank of servants, and as the former going cry'd out, "Farewell, Caius," those coming in cry'd out, "Sit thou merry, Caius."

And here our mirth first began to be disturb'd; for a beautiful boy coming in among those new servants, Trimalchio plucked the boy to him, and did nothing but kiss him over and over: Whereupon Fortunata to maintain her right, began to rail at Trimalchio, called him pitiful fellow, one that could not bridle his lust, shame and dishonour to an honest woman, and a very dog. Trimalchio on the other hand, all confounded and vex'd at her taunts, threw a goblet at her head: She fell a roaring as if she had lost an eye, and clapt both her hands before it.

Scintilla also stood amazed, and covered Fortunata all trembling as she was, in her bosom; the boy also put a cold pitcher to her cheek, on which she leaned and made a lamentable wailing and blubbing.

But Trimalchio quite contrary; "for," said he, "what am I the better for this graceless buttock? 'Tis well known I took her out of a bawdy-house, and made her an honest woman, but now blown up like a frog she bespatters herself; a very block, no woman: But this

481

poor boy born in a hovel, never dreams of palaces. May my good genius so befriend me, as I'll bring down this seeming saint, but in her actions a whore rampant: As inconsiderable as she makes me, I might have had a wife with two hundred and fifty pistols; you know I don't lye; but she was somewhat in years, and Agatho the sweet oil-man, persuaded me not to let my name run out, when instead of doing good to her, I have put a thorn in my own foot; but I'll have a care that she dig me not out of my grave with her nails: And that she may know what I'll do at present, I will not, Habinas, have you put her statue in my monument, that I have no words with her when I am dead: Nay, that she may know I am able to plague her, she shall not so much as kiss me when I die." After this ratling, Habinas entreated him to give over his anger; "There's none of us all," said he, "but some time or other does amiss; we are but men, not gods." Weeping Scintilla said the same, called him Caius, and by his own good nature, besought him to be pacified.

Trimalchio not able to hold tears any longer, "I beg of you, Habinas," said he, "and as you wish to enjoy what you have gotten, if I have done any thing without cause, spit in my face: I kiss'd the boy 'tis true, not for his beauty, but that he's a hopeful thrifty lad: He has several sentences by heart, can read a book at first sight; saves money out of his days provision; has a binn of his own to keep it, and two drinking cups; and does he not deserve to be in my eye? but Fortunata, forsooth, will not have it so; your bandy legs won't away with it. Be content with your own, thou she-kite, and don't disquiet me, thou harlotry, or otherwise thou'lt find what I am; thou knowest well enough, if I once set on't, 'tis immoveable. But we'll remember the living.

"Come, my friends, let's see how merry ye can be, for in my time I have been no better than your selves, but by my own industry I am what I am: 'Tis the heart makes a man, all the rest is but stuff. I buy cheap and sell dear; another man may sell ye other things, but I enjoy my self; and thou dunghillraker, are thou yet gruntling, I'll make ye hereafter do it for somewhat.

"But as I was saying my frugality brought the fortune I have: I came out of Asia no taller than this candlestick, and daily measured my self by it; and that I might get a beard the sooner, rubb'd my lips with the candle-grease; yet I kept Ganymede to my master fourteen years (nor is any thing dishonourable that the master commands) and the same time contented my mistress: Ye know what I mean, I'll say no more, for I am no boaster. By this means, as the gods would have it, the governing the house was committed to me, and nothing was done but by my guidance: What need many words? He made me joint-

heir with Caesar, and I had by it a Senator's estate; but no man thinks
he has enough, and I had a mighty desire to turn merchant. Not to
detain you longer; I built five ships, freighted them with wines, which
at that time were as dear as gold, and sent them to Rome; you'll think
I desir'd to have it so: All my ships founder'd at sea; 'tis a great truth,
no story; Neptune swallowed me in one day three hundred thousand
sesterties. Do ye think I broke upon't, (so help me Hercules) no; the
loss was but a flea-bite: For as if there had been no such thing, I built
others, larger, better, and more fortunate than the former; so that
every one called me a man of courage. As you know a great ship
carries a great deal of force, I loaded them again with wine, bacon,
beans, unguents, planes: And here Fortunata shewed her affection;
for she sold what she had; nay, her very cloaths, and put a round sum
in my pocket; tho' yet it was but a pig of my own sow. What the gods
will is quickly done; I got an hundred thousand sesterties by the voyage,
and forthwith redeemed the lands my patron had left me, built me a
house, bought cattle to sell them again, and whatever I went about
gathered like a snow-ball: But when I grew richer than all the country
besides, I took up, and from a merchant turn'd usurer, and bought
servants.

"Thus resolved to give over trading, a certain astrologer that
chanc'd to light on this village, would have persuaded me to the contrary. He was a Graecian, his name Soerapa, one that held correspondence with the gods. He told me a deal that I had forgotten, and laid
everything before me from top to bottom: He knew all I had within
me, and told me what I had the night before to supper: you'd have
thought he had liv'd with me all his life.

"I beseech you, Habinas, for I think you were there; he told
me the intrigue between my mistress and me; that I had but ill luck
at friends; that no one ever made me a return of my kindnesses: That
I had large possessions, but nourished a viper in my bosom: Why
should I not tell you all? I have by his account, thirty years, four months,
and two days yet to live; and in a short time shall have another estate
left me.

"Thus my fortune-teller. But if I can join my lands here to those
in Apulia, I shall do well enough: in the mean, and while Mercury is
my guardian, I have built this house; it was once you know, a pitiful
cabin, but now as magnificent as a temple: it has four dining rooms,
twenty bed-chambers, two marble porticoes, a gallery above stairs,
my own apartment, another for this viper; a very good porter's lodge,
and the house capable of receiving a thousand guests: To be short,
when ever Scaurus comes this way, he had rather lodge here than at
his own house, tho' it lie to the seaward: and many other conveniences

it has, which I'll shew you by and by. Believe me, he that has a penny in his purse, is worth a penny: Have and you shall be esteemed. And so your friend, once no better than a frog, is now a king.

"And now Stichus bring me the furniture in which I design to be carried to my funeral pile; bring also the unguent, and some of that pot, which I ordered for the cleansing my bones."

Stichus lingered not, but brought in a white coverlet, and robe of state, and pray'd us to try if they were not fine wooll, and well woven. "And see you Stichus," said Trimalchio smiling, "that neither mice nor moths come at them, for if they do I'll burn you alive. I will be brought out in pomp, that all the people may speak well of me."

With that opening a glass bottle of spicknard, he caused us all to be anointed; and "I hope," said he, "it will do as much good when I am dead, as it does while I am living": Then commanding the wine vessels to be filled again; "Fausie," said he, "you are invited to my funeral feast." We by this time nauseated were ready to vomit; Trimalchio also was gotten confoundedly drunk, when behold, a new interlude; he called for the coronets to come in; and, underset with pillows, and stretching himself at length on the bed, "suppose me," said he, "now dead, say somewhat, I beseech you, in praise of me."

Whereupon the coronets sounded as it had been at a funeral; but one above the rest, a servant of that freed-man of Trimalchio's, that was best condition'd of 'em all, made such a thundring, that it rais'd the neighbourhood: On which the watch thinking the house was on fire, broke open the gate, and making an uproar after their manner, ran in with water and hatchets: When finding so fair an opportunity, we gave Agamemnon the slip, and scamper'd off, as if it had been a real fire.

William Burnaby

APULEIUS

APULEIUS, LUCIUS: Born c. 123 A.D. at Madaura, in North Africa. Date of death uncertain.

Apuleius studied and traveled widely, was initiated into mystery cults, and gained marked recognition as a philosopher, orator, and poet. His marriage to Pudentilla, a wealthy widow, brought the charge of practicing magic, but Apuleius defended himself in his *Apologia* or *De Magia*. His philosophical works include the *Florida*, a miscellany of pieces from his declamations, and *De Deo Socratis*. His literary reputation, however, rests on his *Metamorphoses* or *The Golden Ass*, a fantastic novel packed with strange adventures, brigandage, mystic rites, and witchcraft. The hero, Lucius, is changed magically into an ass, but finally succeeds in regaining his human form.

How Apuleius by Roses and Prayer Returned to his Humane Shape

When midnight came that I had slept my first sleepe, I awaked with suddaine feare, and saw the Moone shining bright, as when shee is at the full, and seeming as though she leaped out of the sea. Then thought I with my selfe, that that was the most secret time, when the goddesse Ceres had most puissance and force, considering that all humane things be governed by her providence: and not onely all beasts private and tame, but also all wild and savage beasts be under her protection. And considering that all bodies in the heavens, the earth and the seas, be by her increasing motions increased, and by her diminishing motions diminished: as weary of all my cruell fortune and calamity, I found good hope and soveraigne remedy, though it were very late, to be delivered from all my misery, by invocation and prayer, to the excellent beauty of the Goddesse, whom I saw shining before mine eyes, wherefore shaking off mine Assie and drowsie sleepe, I arose with a joyfull face, and mooved by a great affection to purifie my selfe, I plunged my selfe seven times into the water of the Sea, which number of seven is conveniable and agreeable to holy and divine things, as the worthy and sage Philosopher Pythagoras hath declared. Then with a weeping countenance, I made this Orison to the puissant Goddesse, saying: O blessed Queene of heaven, whether thou be the Dame Ceres which art the originall and motherly nource of all fruitfull things

485

in earth, who after the finding of thy daughter Proserpina, through the great joy which thou diddest presently conceive, madest barraine and unfruitfull ground to be plowed and sowne, and now thou inhabitest in the land of Eleusie; or whether thou be the celestiall Venus, who in the beginning of the world diddest couple together all kind of things with an ingendered love, by an eternall propagation of humane kind, art now worshipped within the Temples of the Ile Paphos, thou which art the sister of the God Phoebus, who nourishest so many people by the generation of beasts, and art now adored at the sacred places of Ephesus, thou which art horrible Proserpina, by reason of the deadly howlings which thou yeeldest, that hast power to stoppe and put away the invasion of the hags and Ghoasts which appeare unto men, and to keepe them downe in the closures of the earth; thou which art worshipped in divers manners, and doest illuminate all the borders of the earth by thy feminine shape, thou which nourishest all the fruits of the world by thy vigor and force; with whatsoever name or fashion it is lawfull to call upon thee, I pray thee, to end my great travaile and misery, and deliver mee from the wretched fortune, which had so long time pursued me. Grant peace and rest if it please thee to my adversities, for I have endured too too much labour and perill. Remoove from me my shape of mine Asse, and render to me my pristine estate, and if I have offended in any point of divine Majesty, let me rather dye then live, for I am full weary of my life. When I had ended this orison, and discovered my plaints to the Goddesse, I fortuned to fall asleepe, and by and by appeared unto me a divine and venerable face, worshipped even of the Gods themselves. Then by little and little I seemed to see the whole figure of her body, mounting out of the sea and standing before mee, wherefore I purpose to describe her divine semblance, if the poverty of my humane speech will suffer me, or her divine power give me eloquence thereto. First, shee had a great abundance of haire, dispersed and scattered about her neck, on the crowne of her head she bare many garlands enterlaced with floures, in the middle of her forehead was a compasse in fashion of a glasse, or resembling the light of the Moone, in one of her hands she bare serpents, in the other, blades of corne, her vestiment was of fine silke yeelding divers colours, sometime yellow, sometime rosie, sometime flamy, and sometime (which troubled my spirit sore) darke and obscure, covered with a blacke robe in manner of a shield, and pleated in most subtill fashion at the skirts of her garments, the welts appeared comely, whereas here and there the starres glimpsed, and in the middle of them was placed the Moone, which shone like a flame of fire, round about the robe was a coronet or garland made with flowers and fruits. In her right hand shee had a timbrell of brasse, which gave a pleasant sound, in her left hand shee bare a cup of gold, out of the mouth whereof the serpent Aspis lifted up his head, with a swelling throat, her odoriferous feete were covered with shoes interlaced and wrought with victorious palme. Thus the divine shape breathing out the pleasant spice of fertill Arabia, disdained not with her divine voyce to utter these words unto me: Behold Lucius I am come, thy weeping and prayers hath mooved mee to succour thee. I am shee that is the naturall mother of all things, mistresse and governesse of all the Elements, the initiall progeny of worlds, chiefe of powers divine, Queene of heaven, the principall of the Gods celestiall, the light of the goddesses: at my will the planets of the ayre, the wholesome winds of the Seas, and the silences of hell be disposed: my name, my divinity is adored throughout all the world in divers manners, in variable customes and in many names, for the Phrygians call me the mother of the Gods: the Athenians, Minerva: the Cyprians, Venus: the Candians, Diana: the Sicilians, Proserpina: the Eleusians, Ceres: some Juno, other Bellona, other Hecate: and principally the Aethiopians which dwell in the Orient, and the Aegyptians which are excellent in all kind of ancient doctrine, and by their proper ceremonies accustome to worship mee, doe call mee Queene Isis. Behold I am come to take pitty of thy fortune and tribulation, behold I am present to favour and ayd thee, leave off thy weeping and lamentation, put away all thy sorrow, for behold the healthfull day which is ordained by my providence, therefore be ready to attend to my commandement. This day which shall come after this night, is dedicated to my service, by an eternall religion, my Priests and Ministers doe accustome after the tempest of the Sea be ceased, to offer in my name a new ship as a first fruit of my Navigation. I command thee not to prophane or despise the sacrifice in any wise, for the great Priest shall carry this day following in procession by my exhortation, a Garland of Roses, next the timbrell of his right hand: follow thou my procession amongst the people, and when thou commest to the Priest make as though thou wouldest kisse his hand, but snatch at the Roses, whereby I will put away the skin and shape of an Asse, which kind of beast I have long time abhorred and despised, but above all things beware thou doubt not nor feare any of those things, as hard and difficill to bee brought to passe, for in the same houre that I am come to thee, I have commanded the Priest by a vision what he shall doe, and all the people by my commandement shall be compelled to give thee place and say nothing! Moreover, think not that amongst so faire and joyfull Ceremonies, and in so good a company that any person shall abhorre thy ill-favoured and deformed figure, or that any man shall be so hardy, as to blame and reprove thy suddaine restoration to humane shape, whereby they should gather or conceive any sinister

487

opinion: and know thou this of certaine, that the residue of thy life untill the houre of death shall be bound and subject to me! And think it not an injury to be alwayes serviceable towards me, since as by my meane and benefit thou shalt become a man: thou shalt live blessed in this world, thou shalt live glorious by my guide and protection, and when thou descendest to Hell, where thou shalt see me shine in that subterene place, shining (as thou seest me now) in the darkness of Acheron, and raigning in the deepe profundity of Stix, thou shalt worship me, as one that hath bin favorable to thee, and if I perceive that thou arte obedient to my commandement, addict to my religion, and merite my divine grace, know thou, that I will prolong thy daies above the time that the fates have appointed, and the celestial Planets ordeined. When the divine Image had spoken these words, she vanished away! By and by when I awaked, I arose, haveing the members of my bodie mixed with feare, joy and sweate, and marvailed at the cleare presence of the puissant goddesse, and being sprinkled with the water of the sea, I recounted orderly her admonitions and divine commande-ments. Sonne after, the darknes chased away, and the cleare and golden sunne arose, whenas behold I saw the streets replenished with people going in a religious sort and in great triumph. All things seemed that day to be joyfull, as well all manner of beasts and houses, as also the very day it selfe seemed to rejoyce. For after the hore-frost, ensued the hot and temperat sun, whereby the little birds weening that the spring time had bin come, did chirp and sing in their steven melodiously: the mother of stars, the parent of times, and mistres of all the world: The fruitful trees rejoyced at their fertility: The barren and sterill were contented at their shadow, rendering sweete and pleasant shrills! The seas were quiet from winds and tempests: The heaven had chaced away the clouds, and appeared faire and cleare with his proper light. Behold then more and more appeared the pomps and processions, attired in regall manner and singing joyfully: One was girded about the middle like a man of armes: Another bare and spare, and had a cloke and high-shooes like a hunter! another was attired in a robe of silke, and socks of gold, having his haire laid out, and dressed in forme of a woman! There was another ware legge-harnesse, and bare a target, a sallet, and a speare like a martial souldier: after him marched one attired in purple with vergers before him like a magistrate! after him followed one with a maurell, a staffe a paire of pantofles, and with a gray beard, signifying a philosopher: after him went one with lime, betokening a fowler, another with hookes declaring a fisher: I saw there a meeke and tame beare, which in matron habite was carried on a stoole: An Ape with a bonet on his head, and covered with lawne, resembling a shepheard, and bearing a cup of gold in his hand: an

Asse which had wings glewed to his backe, and went after an old man, whereby you would judge the one to be Pegasus, and the other Bellerophon. Amongst the pleasures and popular delectations, which wandered hither and thither, you might see the pompe of the goddesse triumphantly march forward: The women attired in white vestiments, and rejoysing, in that they bare garlands and flowers upon their heads, bespread the waies with hearbes, which they bare in their aprons, where this regall and devout procession should passe: Other carried glasses on their backes, to testifie obeysance to the goddes which came after. Other bare combes of Ivory, and declared by their gesture and motions of their armes, that they were ordained and readie to dresse the goddesse: Others dropped in the wayes as they went Balme and other pretious ointments: Then came a great number, as well of men as women, with candels, torches, and other lights, doing honour to the celestiall goddesse: After that sounded the musicall harmony of instruments: then came a faire companie of youth, apparelled in white vestiments, singing both meeter and verse, with a comely grace which some studious Poet had made in honour of the Muses: In the meane season, arrived the blowers of trumpets, which were dedicated unto Serapis, and to the temple before them were officers and bedles, preparing roome for the goddes to passe. Then came the great company of men and women, which had taken divine orders, whose garments glistered all the streets over. The women had their haire annointed and their heads covered with linnen: but the men had their crownes shaven, which were the terrene stars of the goddesse, holding in their hands instruments of brasse, silver and gold, which rendered a pleasant sound. The principall Priests which were apparelled with white surplesses hanging downe to the ground, bare the relikes of the puissant goddesse. One carried in his hand a light, not unlike to those which we used in our houses, saving that in the middle thereof appeared a bole which rendred a more bright flame. The second attired like the other bare in his hand an Altar, which the goddesse her selfe named the succor of nations. The third held a tree of palme with leaves of gold, and the verge of Mercurie. The fourth shewed out a token of equitie by his left hand, which was deformed in every place, signifying thereby more equitie then by the right hand. The same Priest carried a round vessell of gold, in forme of a cap. The fift bare a van, wrought with springs of gold, and another carried a vessell for wine: By and by after the goddesse followed a foot as men do, and specially Mercurie, the messenger of the goddesse infernall and supernall, with his face sometime blacke, sometime faire, lifting up the head of the dogges Annubis, and bearing in his left, his verge, and in his right, the branches of a palme tree, after whom followed a cow with an upright gate, representing the figure of the great goddesse, and he that guided her, marched on with much gravity. Another carried after the secrets of their religion, closed in a coffer. There was one that bare on his stomacke a figure of his god, not formed like any beast, bird, savage thing or humane shape, but made by a new invention, whereby was signified that such a religion should not be discovered or revealed to any person. There was a vessell wrought with a round bottome, haveing on the one side, pictures figured like unto the manner of the Egyptians, and on the other side was an eare, whereupon stood the Serpent Aspis, holding out his scaly necke. Finally, came he which was appointed to my good fortun according to the promise of the goddesse. For the great Priest which bare the restoration of my human shape, by the commandement of the goddes, approached more and more, bearing in his left hand the timbrill, and in the other a garland of Roses to give me, to the end I might be delivered from cruel fortune, which was alwaies mine enemie, after the sufferance of so much calamitie and paine, and after the endurance of so manie perilles: Then I not returning hastilie, by reason of sodaine joye, lest I should disturbe the quiet procession with mine importunitie, but going softly through the prease of the people, which gave me place on every side, went after the Priest. The priest being admonished the night before, as I might well perceive stood still and holding out his hand, thrust out the garland of roses into my mouth, I (trembling) devoured with a great affection: And as soon as I had eaten them, I was not deceived of the promise made unto me. For my deforme and Assie face abated, and first the rugged haire of my body fell off, my thick skin waxed soft and tender, the hoves of my feet changed into toes, my hands returned againe, my neck grew short, my head and mouth began round, my long eares were made little, my great and stonie teeth waxed lesse like the teeth of men, and my tayle which combred me most, appeared no where: then the people began to marvaile, and the religious honoured the goddesse, for so evident a miracle, they wondred at the visions which they saw in the night, and the facilitie of my reformation, whereby they rendered testimonie of so great a benefit which I received of the goddessse. When I saw my selfe in such estate, I stood still a good space and said nothing, for I could not tell what to say, nor what word I shoulde first speake, nor what thanks I should render to the goddesse, but the great Priest understanding all my fortune and miserie, by divine advertisement, commanded that one should give me garments to cover me: Howbeit as soone as I was transformed from an asse to my humane shape, I hid the privitie of my body with my hands as shame and necessity compelled mee. Then one of the company put off his upper robe and put it on my backe: which done, the Priest looked upon me, with a sweete and benigne voice, gan say in this sort: O my friend Lucius, after the endurance of so many labours, and the escape of so many tempests of fortune, thou art at length come to the port and haven of rest and mercy: neither did thy noble linage, thy dignity, thy doctrine, or any thing prevaile, but that thou hast endured so many servil pleasures, by a little folly of thy youthfullness, whereby thou hast had a sinister reward for thy unprosperous curiositie, but howsoever the blindness of fortune tormented thee in divers dangers: so it is, that now unwares to her, thou art come to this present felicitie: let fortune go, and fume with fury in another place, let her finde some other matter to execute her cruelty, for fortune hath no puissance against them which serve and honour our goddesse. For what availed the theeves: the beasts savage: thy great servitude: the ill and dangerous waies: the long passages: the feare of death every day? Know thou, that now thou art sage, and under the protection of her, who by her cleare light doth lighten the other gods: wherefore rejoyce and take a convenable countenance to thy white habit, follow the pomp of this devout and honorable procession, to the end that such which be not devout to the Goddes, may see and acknowledge their errour. Behold Lucius, thou art delivered from so great miseries, by the providence of the goddesse Isis, rejoyce therefore and triumph of the victory of fortune; to the end thou maist live more safe and sure, make thy selfe one of this holy order, dedicate thy minde to the Obsequy of our Religion, and take upon thee a Voluntary yoake of ministrie: And when thou beginnest to serve and honour the goddes, then thou shalt feele the fruit of thy liberty: After that the great Priest had prophesied in this manner, with often breathings, he made a conclusion of his words: Then I went amongst the company of the rest and followed the procession: everie one of the people knew me, and pointing at me with their fingers, said in this sort: Behold him who is this day transformed into a man by the puissance of the soveraigne goddesse, verily he is blessed and most blessed that hath merited so great grace from heaven, as by the innocencie of his former life, and as it were by a new regeneration is reserved to the obsequie of the goddesse. In the mean season by little and little we approached nigh unto the sea cost, even to that place where I lay the night before being an Asse. There after the images and reliques were orderly disposed, the great Priest compassed about with divers pictures according to the fashion of the Aegyptians, did dedicate and consecrate with certaine prayers a fair ship made very cunningly, and purified the same with a torch, an egge, and sulphur; the saile was of white linnen cloath, whereon was written certaine letters, which testified the navigation to be prosperous, the mast was of a great length, made of a Pine tree, round and very excellent with a shining top, the cabin was covered over with coverings of gold, and all the shippe was made of Citron tree very faire; then all the people as well religious as prophane took a great number of Vannes, replenished with odours and pleasant smells and threw them into the sea mingled with milke, untill the ship was filled up with large gifts and prosperous devotions, when as with a pleasant wind it lanched out into the deep. But when they had lost the sight of the ship, every man caried againe that he brought, and went toward the temple in like pompe and order as they came to the sea side. When we were come to the temple the great priest and those which were deputed to carrie the divine figures, but especially those which had long time bin worshippers of the religion, went into the secret chamber of the goddesse, where they put and placed the images according to their ordor. This done, one of the company which was a scribe or interpreter of letters, who in forme of a preacher stood up in a chaire before the place of the holy college, and began to reade out of a booke, and to interpret to the great prince, the senate, and to all the noble order of chivalry, and generally to all the Romane people, and to all such as be under the jurisdiction of Rome, these words following — Laois Aphesus — which signified the end of their divin service and that it was lawfull for every man to depart, whereat all the people gave a great showt, and replenished with much joy, bare all kind of hearbs and garlands of flowers home to their houses, kissing and imbracing the steps where the goddesse passed: howbeit I could not doe as the rest, for my mind would not suffer me to depart one foot away, so attentiv was I to behold the beauty of the goddesse, with remembrance of the great miserie I had endured.

William Adlington

LETTERS

Cicero

Pliny the Younger

Seneca

CICERO

For biographical note, see under *Oratory*.

Cicero's letters have the unusual feature in that they were not a literary exercise intended primarily for publication. Hence their contents are all the more intimate and revealing.

To Atticus

Q. Caecilius Pomponianus was one of Cicero's closest friends. He was called Atticus on account of his long residence in Athens, the chief city of Attica.

When I praise any of your friends in a letter to you, I should like you to let him know that I did so. You know I recently wrote to you about Varro's relationship to myself, and you wrote back that you were very pleased about it. But I should like to inform him that I am satisfied with him, not really, but potentially. For he contrived strange delays: as you know, his thoughts are all crooked. But I remember the precept: it is expedient to endure the ignorance of the masters. But Hortalus, your other friend, praised me to the skies generously and frankly and elegantly, when he spoke of the praetorship of Flaccus and the episode of the Allobroges. Be assured, it could not have been expressed more affectionately or honorably or liberally.

I am very anxious to have you write him that I have sent you this message. But what about writing yourself? I suppose you are coming and already close by: for that's what we discussed in our previous letters. I am eagerly awaiting you, and miss you very much — no more than the situation itself and the critical times demand. About matters here, what shall I write, except the usual thing? Nothing is in a more desperate condition, nothing more an object of hate than the commonwealth: all due to those men. I, as I believe and hope and surmise, am under the strong protection of men of good will.

So fly here. You will either release me from all this trouble or share it. I shall be brief, therefore, because I hope it will shortly be possible to discuss in person what we choose. Take care of yourself.

H. E. W.

To Atticus

I received some letters from you, that gave me to understand how anxious and eager you are to hear the news. We are under restraint on all sides, and we no longer object to being slaves, but fear death and banishment as if they were greater terrors, though they are much lesser evils. This is the position: there is general lamentation: not a word from anyone to bring relief. The aim, I suspect, of those who hold the reins is to leave no one else an opportunity of giving. Young Curio alone speaks out and shows open opposition. Everyone applauds him most respectfully, and in addition loyal citizens shower on him indications of their goodwill. They pursue Fufius with shouts and insults and hisses. These facts do not bespeak hope, but greater grief, when you see that the people's wishes are free, while their courage is under restraint. And if you ask for details item by item, the entire situation is reduced to this that there is no prospect that private citizens, or even state officers, will be free. However, in this state of tyranny speech is freer in social gatherings at least and at parties than it was. Distress is beginning to transcend fear, without preventing widespread despondency. Also, the Campanian Law prescribes an oath taken publicly by candidates not to mention any other method of occupying land except in accordance with the Julian Laws. The others don't hesitate to take the oath. Laterensis is believed to have acted admirably in refusing to do so and giving up his candidacy for the tribunate. But it is not pleasant to write more about the commonwealth.

I am out of humor and I am writing in the deepest dejection. I act, considering the general oppression, without humiliation, and considering the present tumultuous situation, with feeble courage. I am very generously invited by Caesar to be his legate and a nominal legation, for the purpose of fulfilling a vow, is offered to me. But this legation is not sufficient protection in view of Clodius' honor, and removes me from the city at the moment of my brother's return. The legation is safer and does not prevent me from being here when I want. I hold on to this position, but I don't think I shall make use of it: nobody knows what will happen. It is not pleasant to flee; I am anxious to fight it out. There is a wave of zealous feeling for me. I make no definite assertion: you keep silent about this. I am worried about Statius' manumission and other matters, but I have now become hardened. I should like or rather desire very much your presence here. I would have your advice and sympathy. But be prepared to rush here, if I call upon you.

H. E. W.

495

To Atticus

Although, while I am on the march and actually on the road, the messengers of the tax-collectors are leaving and I am in a hurry, I still think I ought to steal a moment so that you don't think I have forgotten your injunction to write. And so I am making a halt on the way, to give you a brief summary of what really needs a longer letter. Know then that, with the utmost expectation, I arrived on the last day of July in this wretched and totally and eternally ruined province, after a delay of three days at Laodicea, three days at Apamea, and three at Synnas. I hear nothing but talk of the imposition of poll taxes, everyone's property being sold, wailing and lamentation in the communities, certain reports of monstrous acts, not human, but wildly bestial. What can I tell you? I'm just sick of it all. However, there is some relief for the miserable communities, because they don't incur any expense for me or my legates, quaestors, or any one of my staff. And not only do I not take hay or whatever is usually given according to the Julian Law, but not even wood, and none of my officers gets anything more than four cots and hut, in many places not even a hut, but usually stays in a tent. And so it is incredible how they flock from the fields and villages, from every house. On my mere arrival their spirits revive, on account of the justice, forbearance, and clemency of your own Cicero. Thus he exceeds all expectations. Appius, hearing of my coming, has retired to the most remote region of the province, as far as Tarsus, where he presides as a magistrate. About the Parthians, there is no news. However, those who come from Syria, report that our cavalry has been cut to pieces by the barbarians. Bibulus has not yet to date thought of entering his province. They say it is because he wants to withdraw in a less abrupt way. I am hastening to my camp, two days' distant.

H. E. W.

To P. Lentulus Spinther

A letter addressed by Cicero to one of his political friends. The subject is largely a debate in the Roman Senate.

On January 13 no business was settled in the Senate, because the time was largely spent in a dispute between the consul Lentulus and Caninius the tribune of the plebs. On that day I too spoke and seemed to impress the Senate deeply by my reference to your good feelings toward the Senate. And so next day it was resolved that three commissioners bring back King Ptolemy: then Hortensius' suggestion that you bring him back without armed force: thirdly, when Volcatius moved that Pompey bring him back, it was proposed that Bibulus' view be submitted to separate votes. In so far as he spoke of religious scruples, a point that could not be opposed, Bibulus' proposal was approved. In regard to three commissioners, they rejected the motion by a large majority. Hortensius' opinion came up next for discussion, when Lupus, the tribune of the plebs — since he himself opened a debate on Pompey — began to maintain that he ought to divide the house before the consuls did. There was general and violent opposition to his speech: for it was unfair and unprecedented. On the part of the consuls there was neither acquiescence nor strong rejection: they just wanted the day to be spent in debate. This was carried. For they perceived that many members would approve to a large extent Hortensius' motion, although they openly voted with Volcatius. Many were asked their opinion, and that too contrary to the consul's wishes: for they were eager for the acceptance of Bibulus' motion. This debate was prolonged into the evening; then the Senate rose.

That evening I happened to dine with Pompey, and seizing the opportunity, more favorable than any I ever had before — because after your departure for your province the day had been most auspicious for us in the Senate — talked with him and seemed to divert his thoughts from all other considerations except your own prestige. When I listen to him, I exonerate him completely from all suspicion of selfish ambition: but when I see his friends of all ranks, I notice — what is now generally evident — that the entire affair has been ruined long since by certain people, with the king's own consent and that of his advisers.

This letter I wrote before dawn, on January 17. There will be a senate meeting today. I shall maintain my dignity, I hope, as far as may be possible with such treacherous and unscrupulous people. As for the plan of a popular referendum, I think we succeeded in having no measure brought before the people without violation of the laws of the auspices nor without force of arms. On these points, a very weighty resolution of the Senate was passed yesterday. I think it was sent on to you.

In regard to other matters, whatever measures are taken, I shall write to you and see that they are as honorable as possible: trust my interest, my efforts, watchfulness, and my vigilance.

H. E. W.

To Cn. Pompey, Commander-in-Chief

If you and your army are doing well, it is good. From your despatches that you sent by state courier, I derive the greatest pleasure, as everyone does. For you imply as great a hope of peace as I predicted to all when I put my reliance on you exclusively. But you should know that your former enemies, now your new friends, are utterly confounded by your despatches and are perturbed and prostrated by the news of this great hope.

Now although the letter you sent me revealed only a slight expression of your goodwill toward me, still I want to inform you how pleasant it was: for I customarily enjoy nothing so much as the consciousness of services performed. If there is no proper response, I very readily let the balance of services rest on my side. I do not doubt, if my very great interest in your behalf has not brought us closer, that the common weal will unite us in friendly cooperation. And for your information as to what I expected from your letter, I shall speak frankly, as my nature and our friendship demand. I have performed acts for which, considering our association in public affairs, I expected some acknowledgment. I think you disregarded this matter, because you were afraid of offending anyone. But you should know that what I achieved for the welfare of our country is esteemed by universal testimony. When you arrive, you will realize that my achievements were accomplished with great perspicacity and nobility of purpose: and you will readily concede that I am not far below Laelius in the matter of friendship and concern for the state, just as you are much superior to Africanus.

H. E. W.

498

PLINY THE YOUNGER

PUBLIUS CAECILIUS SECUNDUS, who assumed the name of Plinius in accordance with his uncle's will, was one of the great letter writers, a kind of prototype of Addison, akin to Charles Lamb.

Born in 62 A. D., at Novum Comum, Pliny died in 114 A. D. He was wealthy and philanthropic, and pursued a legal and official career, ultimately reaching the consulship. His humanity induced him to offer his services frequently to the public welfare, especially in lawsuits. As governor of the province of Bithynia, Pliny represented the Emperor Trajan, with whom he corresponded on the subject of the Christians in his province.

Pliny's ten books of letters are all extant. The most famous letters describe the eruption of Mount Vesuvius.

To Romanus

I believe you were not present at a very droll circumstance which lately happened: I was not indeed a witness to it myself; however, I had an early account of what passed. Passienus Paulus, an eminent Roman knight, and particularly conspicuous for his literary abilities, has a genius for Elegiac Poetry; a talent which runs in the family, for Propertius was his relation as well as his countryman. He was lately reciting a poem which opened thus:

Priscus, at thy command —

Whereupon Priscus, who happened to be present as a particular friend of the poet's, cry'd out — *But he is mistaken, I did not command him.* Think what a roar of laughter this occasioned. The intellect of Priscus, you must know, is thought to be somewhat disordered; however, as he enters into the common offices of life, is called to consultations, and publicly acts as a lawyer, this behavior was the more remarkable and ridiculous: and in fact Paulus was a good deal disconcerted by his friend's absurdity. You see, it is necessary for those who are solicitous to receive their works in public, to take care that the audience, as well as the author, should be of sound intellects. Farewel.

To Tacitus

Your request that I would send you an account of my uncle's death, in order to transmit a more exact relation of it to posterity, merits my acknowledgments; for, if the glorious circumstances which occasioned this accident shall be celebrated by your pen, the manner of his exit will be rendered for ever illustrious. Notwithstanding he perished by a misfortune, which, as it involved at the same time a most beautiful country in ruins, and destroyed so many populous cities, seems to promise him an everlasting remembrance; notwithstanding he has himself composed many works which will descend to the latest times; yet I am persuaded, the mentioning of him in your immortal writings, will greatly contribute to eternize his name. Happy I deem those to be, whom the gods have distinguished with the abilities either of performing such actions as are worthy of being related, or of relating them in a manner worthy of being read; but doubly happy are they who are blessed with both these uncommon endowments: and in that number my uncle, as his own writings, and your history will prove, may justly be ranked. It is with extreme willingness, therefore, I execute your commands; and I should indeed have claimed the task if you had not enjoined it. He was at that time with the fleet under his command at Misenum. On the 24th of August, about one in the afternoon, my mother desired him to observe a cloud which appeared of a very unusual size and shape. He had just returned from enjoying the benefit of the sun, and after bathing in cold water, and taking a slight repast, was retired to his study: he immediately arose and went out upon an eminence, from whence he might more distinctly view this very singular phenomenon. It was not at that distance discernible from what mountain this cloud issued, but it was found afterwards to proceed from Vesuvius. I cannot give you a more exact description of its figure, than by re-sembling it to that of a pine-tree; for, it shot up a great height in the form of a tall trunk, which spread at the top into a sort of branches; occasioned, I suppose, either that the force of the internal vapour which impelled the cloud upwards, decreased in strength as it advanced, or that the cloud being pressed back by its own weight, expanded itself in the manner I have mentioned: it appeared sometimes bright, and sometimes dark and spotted, as it was either more or less impregnated with earth and cinders. This unccommon appearance excited my uncle's philosophical curiosity to take a nearer view of it. He accordingly ordered a light vessel to be prepared, and offered me the liberty, if I thought proper, to attend him. I rather chose to continue the employment in which I was engaged; for, it happened, that he had given me a certain writing to copy. As he was going out of the house with his tablets in his hand, he was met by the mariners belonging to the gallies stationed at Retina, from which they had fled in the utmost terrour; for, that port being situated at the foot of Vesuvius, they had no other way to escape than by sea. They conjured him therefore not to proceed and expose his life to imminent and inevitable danger. In compliance with their advice, he changed his original intention, and instead of gratifying his philosophical spirit, he resigned it to the more magnanimous principle of aiding the distressed. With this view, he ordered the fleet immediately to put to sea, and went himself on board with an intention of assisting not only Retina, but the several other towns which stood thick upon that beautiful coast. Hastening to the place therefore from whence others fled with the utmost terrour, he fleeted his direct course to the point of danger, and with so much calmness and presence of mind, as to be able to make and dictate his observations upon the appearance and progress of that dreadful scene. He was now so near the mountain, that the cinders, which grew thicker and hotter the more he advanced, fell into the ships, together with pumice-stones, and black pieces of burning rock: they were likewise in danger not only of being a-ground by the sudden retreat of the sea, but also from the vast fragments which rolled down from the mountains, and obstructed all the shore. Here he stopped to consider whether he should return back; to which the pilot advising him, *Fortune*, said he, *befriends the brave; steer to Pomponianus*. Pomponianus was then at Stabiae, separated by a gulf, which the sea, after several insensible windings, forms upon that shore. Pomponianus had already sent his baggage on board; for, tho' he was not at that time in actual danger, yet being within the view of it, and indeed extremely near, he was determined, if it should in the least increase, to put to sea as soon as the wind should change. It was favourable, however, for carrying my uncle to Pomponianus, whom he found in the greatest consternation: and embracing him with tenderness, he encouraged and exhorted him to keep up his spirits. The more to dissipate his fears, he ordered his servants, with an air of unconcern, to carry him to the baths; and after having bathed, he sat down to supper with great, or at least (what is equally heroic) with all the appearance of cheerfulness. In the mean while, the fire from Vesuvius flamed forth from several parts of the mountain with great violence; which the dark-ness of the night contributed to render still more visible and dreadful. But my uncle, in order to calm the apprehensions of his friend, assured him it was only the conflagration of the villages, which the country people had abandoned: after this, he retired to rest, and it is most certain, he was so little discomposed as to fall into a deep sleep; for, being corpulent, and breathing hard, the attendants in the antechamber actually heard him snore. The court which led to his apartment being

501

now almost filled with stones and ashes, it would have been impossible for him, if he had continued there any longer, to have made his way out; it was thought proper therefore to awaken him. He got up, and joined Pomponianus and the rest of the company, who had not been sufficiently unconcerned to think of going to bed. They consulted together whether it would be most prudent to trust to the houses, which now shook from side to side with frequent and violent concussions; or flee to the open fields, where the calcined stones and cinders, tho' levigated indeed, yet fell in large showers, and threatened them with instant destruction. In this distress they resolved for the fields, as the less dangerous situation of the two: a resolution which, while the rest of the company were hurried into by their fears, my uncle embraced upon cool and deliberate consideration. They went out then, having pillows tied upon their heads with napkins; and this was their whole defence against the storm of stones that fell around them. It was now day every where else, but *there* a deeper darkness prevailed than in the blackest night; which however was in some degree dissipated by torches and other lights of various kinds. They thought it expedient to go down farther upon the shore in order to observe if they might safely put out to sea; but they found the waves still run extremely high and boisterous. There my uncle, having drunk a draught or two of cold water, laid himself down upon a sail-cloth which was spread for him; when immediately the flames, preceded by a strong smell of sulphur, dispersed the rest of the company, and obliged him to rise. He raised himself up with the assistance of two of his servants, and instantly fell down dead; suffocated, I conjecture, by some gross and noxious vapour, as having always had weak lungs, and being frequently subject to a difficulty of breathing. As soon as it was light again, which was not till the third day after this melancholy accident, his body was found entire, and without any marks of violence, exactly in the same posture in which he fell, and looking more like a man asleep than dead. During all this time my mother and I who were at Misenum — But as this has no connection with your history, so your inquiry went no farther than concerning my uncle's death: with that therefore I will put an end to my letter. Suffer me only to add, that I have faithfully related to you what I was either an eye-witness of myself, or received immediately after the accident happened, and before there was time to vary the truth. You will choose out of this narrative such circumstances as shall be most suitable to your purpose: for, there is a great difference between writing a letter, and composing a history; between addressing a friend, and addressing the public. Farewel.

To Cornelius Tacitus

The letter which, in compliance with your request, I wrote to you concerning the death of my uncle, has raised, it seems, your curiosity to know what terrours and dangers attended me while I continued at Misenum; for there, I think, the account in my former letter broke off:

Tho' my shock'd soul recoils, my tongue shall tell.

My uncle having left us, I continued the employment which prevented my going with him, till it was time to bathe. After which I went to supper, and then fell into a short and unquiet sleep. There had been during many days before some shocks of an earthquake, which the less alarmed us as they are frequent in Campania; but they were so particularly violent that night, that they not only shook every thing about us, but seemed indeed to threaten total destruction. My mother flew to my chamber, where she found me rising in order to awaken her. We went out into a small court belonging to the house, which separated the sea from the building. As I was at that time but eighteen years of age, I know not whether I should call my behavior in this perilous conjuncture, courage or rashness; but I took up Livy, and amused myself with turning over that author, and even making extracts from him, as if I had been perfectly at my case. While we were in this situation, a friend of my uncle's, who was just come from Spain to pay him a visit, joined us, and observing me sitting by my mother with a book in my hand, reproved her patience, and my security: nevertheless I still went on with my author. It was now morning, but the light was exceedingly faint and languid; the building all around us tottered, and tho' we stood upon open ground, yet as the place was narrow and confined, there was no remaining without imminent danger: we therefore resolved to leave the town. The people followed us in the utmost consternation, and (as to a mind distracted with terror, every suggestion seems more prudent than its own) pressed in great crowds about us in our way out. Being advanced at a convenient distance from the houses, we stood still, in the midst of a most hazardous and tremendous scene. The chariots which we had ordered to be drawn out, were so agitated backwards and forwards, tho' upon the most level ground, that we could not keep them steady, even by supporting them with large stones. The sea seemed to roll back upon itself, and to be driven from its banks by the convulsive motion of the earth; it is certain at least the shore was considerably enlarged, and several sea-animals were left upon it. On the other side a black and dreadful cloud bursting with an igneous serpentine vapour, darted out a long train of fire, resembling slashes of lightning, but much larger. Upon this our Spanish friend, whom I mentioned above, addressing himself to my mother and me with great warmth and earnestness: *If your brother and your uncle, said he, is safe, he certainly wishes you may be so too; but if he perished, it was his desire, no doubt, that you might both survive him: Why therefore do you delay your escape a moment?* We could never think of our own safety, we replied, while we were uncertain of his: upon which our friend left us, and withdrew from the danger with the utmost precipitation. Soon afterwards, the cloud seemed to descend, and cover the whole ocean; as indeed, it entirely hid the island of Caprea, and the promontory of Misenum. My mother conjured me to make my escape at any rate, which as I was young I might easily effect; as for herself, she said, her age and corpulency rendered all attempts of that sort impossible; however she would willingly meet death, if she could have the satisfaction of feeling that she was not the occasion of mine. But I absolutely refused to leave her, and taking her by the hand I led her on: she complied with great reluctance, and not without many reproaches to herself for being the occasion of retarding my flight. The ashes now began to fall upon us, tho' in no great quantity. I turned my head, and observed behind us a thick smoke, which came rolling after us like a torrent. I proposed, while we had yet any light, to turn out of the high road, lest she should be pressed to death in the dark, by the crowd that followed us. We had scarcely stepped out of the path, when darkness over-spread us, not like that of a cloudy night, or when there is no moon, but of a room when it is shut up, and all the lights extinct. Nothing then was to be heard but the shrieks of women, the screams of children, and the cries of men; some calling for their children, others for their parents, others for their husbands, and only distinguishing each other by their voices; one lamenting his own fate, another that of his family; some wishing to die, from the very fear of dying; some lifting their hands to the gods; but the greater part imagining that the last and eternal night was come, which was to destroy both the gods and the world together. Among these there were some who augmented the real terrors by imaginary ones, and made the frighted multitude falsly believe that Misenum was actually in flames. At length a glimmering light appeared, which we imagined to be rather the forerunner of an approaching burst of flames, (as in fact it was) than the return of day; however, the fire fell at a distance from us: then again we were immersed in thick darkness, and a heavy shower of ashes rained upon us, which we were obliged every now and then to shake off, otherwise we should have been overwhelmed and buried in the heap. I might boast, that during all this scene of horrour, not a sigh, or expression of fear, escaped from me, had not my support been founded on that miserable, though strong consolation, that all mankind were involved in the same calamity, and that I imagined I was perishing

504

with the world itself. At last this terrible darkness was dissipated by degrees, like a cloud or smoke; the real day returned, and even the sun appeared, tho' very faintly, and as when an eclipse is coming on. Every object that presented itself to our eyes (which were extremely weakened) seemed changed, being covered with white ashes, as with a deep snow. We returned to Misenum, where we refreshed ourselves as well as we could, and passed an anxious night between hope and fear; tho' indeed, with a much larger share of the latter: for, the earth still continued to shake, while several enthusiastic persons ran wildly among the people, throwing out terrifying predictions, and making a kind of frantic sport of their own and their friends' wretched situation. However, my mother and I, notwithstanding the danger we had passed, and that which still threatened us, had no intention of leaving Misenum, till we should receive some account of my uncle. ——

And now, you will read this narrative without any view of inserting it in your history, of which it is by no means worthy; and indeed you must impute it to your own request, if it should appear not to deserve even the trouble of a letter. Farewel.

To Caninius

Tho' I am an admirer of the ancients, yet I am far from despising, as some affect, the genius of the moderns; nor can I suppose, that nature in these latter ages is so worn out, as to be incapable of any valuable production. On the contrary, I have lately had the pleasure of hearing Verginius Romanus read to a few select friends, a Comedy so happily formed in the spirit of the ancients, that it may hereafter be considered as a model. I know not whether the author is in the number of your acquaintance; I am sure at least he ought to be, as he is greatly distinguished by the probity of his manners, the elegance of his genius, and the variety of his compositions. He has written some very agreeable pieces of the burlesque kind in Iambics, with much delicacy, wit, and humour, and I will add too, even eloquence; for every species of composition, which is perfect in its kind, may with propriety be termed eloquent. He has also published some Comedies after the manner of Menander and other approved authors of that age, which deserve to be ranked with those of Plautus and Terence. He has now, for the first time, attempted the ancient Comedy, but in such a manner, as to shew he is a perfect master in this way. Strength and majesty, delicacy and softness, elegance and wit, are the distingushing graces of this performance. He places virtuous characters in the most amiable point of view, and exposes vicious ones with the warmest indignation: whenever he makes use of feigned names, it is with great propriety, as he employs real ones with equal justness. In respect only to myself, I should say he has erred thro' an excess of friendship, if I did not know that fiction is the privilege of poets. In a word, I will insist upon his letting me have the copy, that I may send it to you for your perusal, or rather that you may get it by heart; for I am well persuaded, when you have once taken it up, you will not easily lay it down. Farewel.

To Sparsus

You tell me, that of all my works, the last I sent you is your greatest favourite. The same judgement has likewise been passed upon it by another of my very knowing and ingenious friends: and I am the more inclined to believe that neither of you is mistaken, not only as it is improbable you both should, but because I am much disposed to flatter myself. I always endeavour indeed, that my last performance may appear the most finished; and for that reason I prefer the speech I lately published, to that which you mention: I will send it you as soon as I can meet with a safe conveyance. And now I have raised your expectations of this piece, I doubt you will be disappointed when it comes to your hands. In the mean while, however, you may indulge the agreeable persuasion (and perhaps too without, being disappointed) that it is a composition you will read with pleasure. Farewel.

To Calvisius

I have spent these several last days in my study with the most pleasing tranquillity. You will ask how that can be possible in the midst of Rome? It happened to be the season of celebrating the Circensian games; an entertainment for which I have not the least taste. They have no noveltry, no variety to recommend them; nothing, in short, one would wish to be present at twice. It is the more surprizing therefore, that so many thousand people should be possessed with the childish passion of desiring often to see a parcel of horses gallop, and men standing erect in their chariots. If indeed, it were the swiftness of the horses, or the skill of the charioteers that attracted them, there might be some little pretence of reason on their side. But it is the *dress* they favour; it is the dress that captivates them. And if in the midst of the course the different contenders were to change habits, their different partizans would change sides, and instantly desert the very same men and horses, whom they just before were eagerly following with their eyes as far as they could see, and shouting their names with all the warmth of vociferous exclamations. Such mighty charms, such wondrous power is there in the colour of a paltry tunic! and this in the sentiments, not only of the vulgar (more contemptible than the uniform they espouse) but even in the opinion of some grave personages. When I observe such men thus insatiably fond of so silly, so low, so uninteresting, so common an entertainment, I congratulate myself that I am insensible to these pleasures; and am glad to employ the leisure of this season upon my studies, which others throw away upon the most idle occupations. Farewel.

To Hispulla

When I consider that you love your niece even more fondly than if she were your own daughter, I ought in the first place to inform you of her recovery, before I tell you she has been ill; that the sentiments of joy at the one, may leave you no leisure to be afflicted at the other. Tho' I fear indeed, after your first transports of gratulation are over, you will feel some concern; and in the midst of your joy for the danger she has escaped, will tremble at the thought of that which she has undergone. She is now, however, in good spirits, and again restored to herself and to me; and is recovering her strength and health, as fast as she lost them. To say the truth, (and I may now safely tell it you) her life was in the utmost danger; not indeed from any fault of her own, but a little from the inexperience of her youth. To this must be imputed the cause of her miscarriage, and the sad experience she has had of the consequence of not knowing she was breeding. But tho' this misfortune has deprived you at present of a nephew, or a niece, to console you for the loss of your brother; you should reflect that it is a blessing which seems rather to be deserved than denied, since *her* life is preserved from whom that happiness is to be expected. I intreat you then to represent this accident to your father in the most favourable light; as your sex are the best advocates in cases of this kind. Farewel.

To Minutianus

I beg you to excuse me this one day: Titinus Capito is to recite a performance of his, and I know not whether it is most my inclination, or my duty to attend him. He is a man of a most amiable disposition, and justly to be numbered among the brightest ornaments of the present age. He diligently cultivates the polite arts himself, and generously admires and encourages them in others; to many of whom he is the protector, the refuge, and the liberal patron; as he is to all of them a bright and exemplary model. In a word, he is the restorer and reformer of literature, now alas! well nigh sinking into total neglect and decay. His house is open to every man of genius who has any works to rehearse; and it is not *there* alone that he attends these assemblies with the most obliging good-nature. I am sure at least he never once excused himself from mine, if he happened to be at Rome. I should therefore with a more than ordinary ill grace refuse to return him the same favour, especially upon so honourable an occasion. Should not I think myself obliged to a man, who, if I were engaged in any law-suit, generously attended the cause in which I was interested? And am I less indebted, now that my whole care and business is of the literary kind, for his assiduity in my concerns of this sort; which, if not the only, is however the principal instance wherein I can be obliged? But tho' I owed him no return of this nature; tho' I were not engaged to him by the reciprocal tie of the same good offices he has done me; yet not only the powers of his extensive genius, as elegantly polished as it is severely correct, but the dignity of his subject, would strongly incite me to be of his audience. He has written an account of the deaths of several illustrious persons, some of whom were my particular friends. It is a pious office then, it should seem, as I could not be present at their obsequies, to attend at least, this (as I may call it) their funeral oration; which tho' a late, is however for that very reason, a more unsuspected tribute to their memories. Farewel.

To Genialis

I much approve of your having read my orations with your father. It is highly for your advantage to learn from a man of his eloquence, what to admire in compositions of this kind, and what to condemn; as you will at the same time be trained up in an habitual custom of speaking your real sentiments. You see whose steps it is you ought to follow; and happy are you in having a living example before you, which is at once the nearest and the noblest model you can pursue! In a word, that he whom nature designed you should most resemble, is, of all others, the person whom you should most endeavour to imitate. Farewel.

This letter was written by Pliny not more than forty years after the death of St. Paul. It was preserved by the early Christians and the writers of the Church as evidence of Christian doctrine in refutation against pagan calumnies.

To the Emperor Trajan

It is a rule, Sir, which I inviolably observe, to refer myself to you in all my doubts; for, who is more capable of removing my scruples, or informing my ignorance? Having never been present at any trials concerning those persons who are Christians, I am unacquainted not only with the nature of their crimes, or the measure of their punishment, but how far it is proper to enter into an examination concerning them. Whether therefore any difference is usually made with respect to the ages of the guilty, or no distinction is to be observed between the young and the adult; whether repentance intitles them to a pardon; or if a man has been once a Christian, it avails nothing to desist from his error; whether the very profession of Christianity, unattended with any criminal act, or only the crimes themselves inherent in the profession are punishable; in all these points I am greatly doubtful. In the mean while the method I have observed towards those who have been brought before me as Christians, is this: I interrogated them whether they were Christians: if they confessed, I repeated the question twice, adding threats at the same time; and if they still persevered, I ordered them to be immediately punished. For, I was persuaded, whatever the nature of their opinions might be, a contumacious and inflexible obstinacy certainly deserved correction. There were others also brought before me possessed with the same infatuation, but being citizens of Rome, I directed that they should be conveyed thither. But this crime spreading (as is usually the case) while it was actually under prosecution, several instances of the same nature occurred. An information was presented to me without any name subscribed, containing a charge against several persons: these, upon examination, denied they were, or ever had been, Christians. They repeated after me an invocation to the gods, and offered religious rites with wine and frankincense before your statue; (which for that purpose I had ordered to be brought together with those of the Gods) and even reviled the name of Christ; whereas there is no forcing, it is said, those who are really Christians, into any of these compliances. I thought it proper therefore, to discharge them. Some among those who were accused by a witness in person, at first confessed themselves Christians, but immediately after denied it; the rest own'd indeed they had been of that number formerly, but had now (some above three, others more, and a few above twenty years ago) renounced that errour. They all worshipped your statue and the images of the Gods, uttering imprecations at the same time against the name of Christ. They affirmed the whole of their guilt, or their errour, was, that they met on a certain stated day before it was light, and addressed themselves in a form of prayer to Christ, as to some God, binding themselves by a solemn oath, not for the purposes of any wicked design, but never to commit any fraud, theft, or adultery, never to falsify their word, nor deny a trust when they should be called upon to deliver it up: after which, it was their custom to separate, and then re-assemble, to eat in common a harmless meal. From this custom, however, they desisted after the publication of my edict, by which, according to your commands, I forbade the meeting of any assemblies. In consequence of this their declaration, I judged it the more necessary to endeavour to extort the real truth, by putting two female slaves to the torture, who were said to officiate in their religious functions; but all I could discover was, that these people were actuated by an absurd and excessive superstition. I deemed it expedient, therefore, to adjourn all farther proceedings, in order to consult you. For, it appears to be a matter highly deserving your consideration; more especially as great numbers must be involved in the danger of these prosecutions, which have already extended, and are still likely to extend, to persons of all ranks and ages, and even of both sexes. In fact, this contagious superstition is not confined to the cities only, but has spread its infection among the neighbouring villages and country. Nevertheless, it still seems possible to restrain its progress. The temples, at least, which were once almost deserted, begin now to be frequented; and the sacred solemnities, after a long intermission are revived; to which I must add, there is again also a general demand for the victims, which for some time past had met with but few purchasers. From the circumstances I have mentioned, it is easy to conjecture what numbers might be reclaimed, if a general pardon were granted to those who shall repent of their error.

Trajan to Pliny

The method you have pursued, my dear Pliny, in the proceedings against those Christians which were brought before you, is extremely proper; as it is not possible to lay down any fixed rule by which to act in all cases of this nature. But I would not have you *officiously* enter into any inquiries concerning them. If indeed they should be brought before you, and the crime should be proved, they must be punished; with this restriction however; that where the party denies he is a Christian, and shall make it evident that he is not by invoking our Gods; let him (notwithstanding any former suspicion) be pardoned upon his repentance. Informations without the accuser's name subscribed, ought not to be received in prosecutions of any sort; as it is introducing a very dangerous precedent, and by no means agreeable to the equity of my government.

Wm. Melmoth

SENECA

LUCIUS ANNAEUS SENECA (c. 5 b. c. - 65 a. d.) was a Stoic philosopher, who for some time was tutor to the Emperor Nero. He was banished to Corsica but was recalled. Involved in the conspiracy of Piso against the Emperor, he committed suicide.

Seneca's works include philosophical essays, a large body of letters, a series of scientific discussions, and nine tragedies. These dramas served as models during the Middle Ages and far into Restoration times.

Letters

Ostensibly, Seneca's letters were addressed to his friend Lucilius: virtually, they are brief essays on morals, literature, leisure, indulgence, moderation, and similar topics that impinge on everyday life: to which Seneca added a good number of literary or philosophical allusions and illustrative anecdotes.

Epistle I

Speech as an Index of the Mind

You say well, that in speaking, the very ordering of the voice (to say nothing of the actions, countenances, and other circumstances that accompany it) is a consideration worthy of a wise man. There are that prescribe certain modes of rising and falling; nay, if you will be governed by them, you shall not speak a word, move a step, or eat a bit, but by a rule; and these perhaps are too critical. Do not understand me yet as if I made no difference betwixt entering upon a discourse, loud or soft; for the affections do naturally rise by degrees, and in all disputes or pleadings, whether public or private, a man should properly begin with modesty and temper; and so advance by little and little, if need be, into clamour and vociferation. And as the voice rises by degrees, let it fall so too; not snapping off upon a sudden, but abating as upon moderation: the other is unmannerly and rude. He that has a precipitate speech is commonly violent in his manners; beside, that there is in it much of vanity and emptiness; and no man takes satisfaction in a flux of words without choice, where the noise is more than the value. Fabius was a man eminent both for his life and learning, and no less for his eloquence; his speech was rather easy and sliding than quick; which he accounted to be not only liable to many errors, but to a suspicion of immodesty. Nay, let a man have words never so much at will, he will no more speak fast than he will run, for fear his tongue should go before his wit. The speech of a philosopher should be, like his life, composed, without pressing or stumbling; which is fitter for a mountebank than a man of sobriety and business. And then, to drop one word after another is as bad on the other side: the interruption is tedious, and tires out the auditor with expectation. Truth and morality should be delivered in words plain, and without affectation; for, like remedies, unless they stay with us, we are never the better for them. He that would work upon his hearers, must no more expect to do it upon the post, than a physician to cure his patients only in passing by them. Not but that I would have a wise man, in some cases, to raise himself, and mend his pace, but still with a regard to the dignity of his manners: though there may be a great force also in moderation. I would have his discourse smooth and flowing, like a river; not impetuous, like a torrent. There is a rapid, lawless, and irrevocable velocity of speech, which I would scarce allow even to an orator; for if he be transported with passion or ostentation, a man's attention can hardly keep him company. It is not the quantity, but the pertinence, that does the business. Let the words of an ancient man flow soft and gentle; let those of an orator come off round and powerful; but not run on without fear or wit, as if a whole declamation were to be but one period. Cicero wrote with care, and that which will for ever stand the test. All public languages are according to the humour of the age. A wantonness and effeminacy of speech denotes luxury; for the wit follows the mind: if the latter be sound, composed, temperate, and grave, the wit is dry and sober too; but if the one be corrupted, the other is likewise unsound. Do we not see when a man's mind is heavy, how he creeps and draws his legs after him? A finical temper is read in the very gestures and clothes; if a man be choleric and violent, it is also discovered in his motions. An angry man speaks short and quick; the speech of an effeminate man is loose and melting. A quaint and solicitous way of speaking is the sign of a weak mind; but a great man speaks with ease and freedom; and with more assurance; though less care. Speech is the index of the mind: when you see a man dress, and set his clothes in print, you shall be sure to find his words so too, and nothing in them that is firm and weighty:

it does not become a man to be delicate. As it is in drink, the tongue never trips till the mind be overborne, so it is with speech; so long as the mind is whole and sound, the speech is masculine and strong, but if one fails, the other follows.

Roger L'Estrange

Epistle IV

Correspondence Among Friends.
Precept and Wisdom

Your last letter was very short; and the whole letter itself was little more than an excuse for the shortness of it. One while you are so full of business that you cannot write at all; and another while you have so little news that you do not know what to write. Now, assure yourself, that whosoever has a mind to write may find leisure for it: and for your other pretence, it looks as if we ourselves were the least part of our own business. Put the case, that the whole world were becalmed, and that there were neither wars, amours, factions, designs, disappointments, competitors, or law-suits; no prodigals, usurers, or fornicators, in nature, there would be a large field yet left for the offices of friendship, and for the exercise of philosophy and virtue. Let us rather consider what we ourselves ought to do than hearken after the doings of other people. What signifies the story of our neighbour's errors to the reforming of our own? Is it not a more glorious and profitable employment to write the history of *Providence*, than to record the usurpation of *ambitious princes*? and rather to celebrate the bounties of the Almighty than the robberies of Alexander? Nor is business any excuse for the neglect either of our studies or of our friends. First, we continue our own business, and then we increase it: and instead of lending, we do wholly give ourselves up to it, and haunt for coloured pretences of misspending our time. But I say, that wherever we are, or with whomsoever or howsoever employed, we have our thoughts at liberty.

You have here drawn a long letter from me; and if you find it tedious, you may thank yourself for calling upon me to be as good as my word. Not but that I write by inclination too. For if we love the pictures of our friends, by what hand soever they be drawn, how much more then shall we joy in a friend's letters, which are undoubtedly

513

the most lively pictures of one another? It is a shame, you will say, to stand in need of any remembrancers of an absent friend; and yet sometimes the place, a servant, a relation, a house, a garment, may honestly excite the memory; and it renders every thing as fresh to us as if we were still joined in our embraces, and drinking up one another's tears. It is by the benefit of letters that absent friends are in a manner brought together; beside that, epistolary discourses are much more profitable than public and premeditated declamations; for they insinuate themselves into the affections with more freedom and effect, though with less pomp and pretence. You do expect, perhaps, that I should tell you how gentle and short a winter we have had; how cold and unseasonable a spring, or some other fooleries to as little purpose. But what are you or I the better of such discourses? We should rather be laying the foundations of a good mind; and learning to distinguish betwixt the blessings of virtue and the amusements of imagination. There came in some friends to me yesterday, that made the chimney smoke a little more than ordinary, but not at a rate to make the neighbourhood cry out *fire*. We had a variety of discourse; and passing from one thing to another, we came at last to read something of Quintus Sextius; (a great man, upon my credit, deny it that will). Good God! the force and vigour of that man's writings! And how much are they above the common level of other philosophers! I cannot read them, methinks, without challenging of fortune, and defying all the powers of ambition and violence. The more I consider him the more I admire him; for I find in him (as in the world itself,) every day to be a new spectacle, and to afford fresh matter still for more veneration. And yet the wisdom of our forefathers has left work enough for their posterity; even if there were no more in it than the application of what they have transmitted to us of their own invention. As suppose they had left us remedies for such and such diseases, so certain that we should not need to look for any other medicines, there would be some skill yet required in the applying of them in the proper case, proportion, and season. I have an honour for the memorials of our worthy progenitors. If I meet a consul or a praetor upon the road, I will alight from my horse, uncover my head, and give him the way; and shall I have no veneration now for the names of the governors of mankind? No man is so wise as to know all things; or if he did, one wise man may yet be helpful to another in finding out a nearer way to the finishing of his work: for let a man make never so much haste, it is some sort of assistance, the bare encouraging of him to continue his course; beside the comfort and benefits of communication in loving, and being loved, and in the mutual approbation of each other.

514

The last point, you know, that you and I had in debate was, "Whether or not wisdom may be perfected by precept." There are some that account only that part of philosophy to be profitable to mankind which delivers itself in particular precepts to particular persons, without forming the whole man: teaching the husband (for the purpose) how to behave himself to his wife, the father how to train up and discipline his children, and the master how to govern his servants; as if any man could be sufficiently instructed in the parts of life without comprehending the whole sum and scope of it. Others (as Aristo the Stoic) are rather for the general degrees of philosophers; which, whosoever knows in the main, that person understands in every particular how to tutor himself. As he that learns to cast a dart, when he has by practice and exercise gotten a true aim, he will not only strike this or that mark, but whatever he has a mind to: so he that is well informed in the whole will need no direction in the parts, but under the principles of a good life learn how to behave himself in all the circumstances of it. Cleanthes allows the paroenetic or preceptive philosophy to be in some sort profitable; but yet very short and defective, unless as it flows from the universal understanding of the heads and degrees of philosophy. Now, the question is, Whether this alone can make a good man? and whether it be superfluous itself, or so sufficient as to make all other knowledge appear so? They that will have it superfluous, argue thus: If the eyes be covered, there is no seeing without removing the impediment; and in that condition, it is to no purpose to bid a man go to such and such a place, or to reach this or that with his hand: and so it fares with the mind; so long as that continues clouded with ignorance and error, it is idle to give particular precepts; as if you should teach a poor man to act the part of a rich, or one that is hungry how to behave himself with a full stomach; while the one is necessitous, and the other half-starved, they are neither of them the better for it. And then, shall we give precepts in manifest cases or in doubtful? The former need none, and in the latter we shall not be believed. Nor is it enough simply to advise, unless we also give reasons for it. There are two errors which we are liable to in this case; either the wickedness of perverse opinions, which have taken possession of us; or at least a disposition to entertain error under any resemblance of truth. So that our work must be, either to cure a sick mind that is already tainted, or to prepossess an evil inclination before it comes to an ill habitant. Now, the degrees of philosophy enable us in both these cases: nor is it possible, by particulars, to obviate all particular occasions. One man marries a widow, another a maid: she may be rich, or poor, barren or fruitful, young or ancient; superior, inferior, or equal. One man follows public business, another flies it; so that the same advice that is profitable to the one may be mischievous

515

to the other. Every one's is a particular case, and must be suited with a particular counsel. The laws of philosophy are brief, and extend to all; but the variety of the other is incomprehensible, and can never make that good to all which it promises to a few. The precepts of wisdom lie open, but the degrees of it are hidden in the dark.

Now, in answer, it does not hold with the mind as with the eye: if there be a diffusion, it is to be helped by remedy and not by precept. The eye is not to be taught to distinguish colours; but the mind must be informed what to do in life. And yet the physician will prescribe order also to the patient, as well as physic; and tell him, "You must bring your eye to endure the light by degrees; have a care of studying upon a full stomach," etc. We are told, that precepts do neither distinguish nor abate false opinions in us of good or evil; and it shall be granted, that of themselves they are not able to subdue vicious inclinations; but this does not hinder them from being very useful to us in conjunction with other helps. First, as they refresh the memory; and, secondly, as they bring us to a more distinct view of the parts, which we saw but confusedly in the whole. At the same rate, consolatories and exhortations will be found superfluous as well as precepts; which yet upon daily experience we know to be otherwise. Nay, we are the better, not only for the precepts, but for the converse of philosophers; for we still carry away somewhat of the tincture of virtue whether we will or not; but the deepest impression they make is upon children. It is urged, that precepts are insufficient without proof; but I say, that the very authority of the adviser goes a great way in the credit of the advice; as we depend upon the opinion of the lawyer without demanding his reason for it. And again, whereas the variety of precepts is said to be infinite, I cannot allow it. For the greatest and most necessary affairs are not many; and for the application to time, places, and persons, the differences are so small that a few general rules will serve the turn. Nay, let a man be never so right in his opinion, he may yet be more confirmed in it by admonition. There are many things that may assist a cure, though they do not perfect it; even mad men themselves may be kept in awe by menaces and correction. But it is a hard matter, I must confess, to give counsel at a distance; for advice depends much upon opportunity; and that, perhaps, which was proper when it was desired, may come to be pernicious before it is received. Some indeed, may be prescribed, as some remedies, at any distance, and transmitted to posterity; but for others, a man must be upon the place and deliberate upon circumstances, and be not only present, but watchful, to strike in with the very nick of the occasion.

Roger L'Estrange

Epistle V

Seneca's Studies. Reflections on Human Life

Your letters were old before they came to my hand: so that
I made no inquiry of the messenger what you were a-doing; besides
that, wherever you are, I take it for granted that I know your business,
and that you are still upon the great work of perfecting yourself: a
thing not to be done by chance but by industry and labour. We
are all of us wicked before we come to be good. We are prepos-
sessed, so that we must unlearn iniquity, and study virtue. The great
difficulty is to begin the enterprise; for a weak mind is afraid of new
experiments. I have now given over troubling myself for fear of you;
because I have that security for your well-being that never failed any
man. The love of truth and of goodness is become habitual to you. It
may so fall out that Fortune perhaps may do you an injury; but there
is no fear of your doing yourself one. Go on as you have begun,
and compose your resolutions; not to an effeminate ease, but to a
frame of virtuous quiet. It is a double kindness that you call me to so
strict an account of my time, that nothing less than a diary of my life
will satisfy you; for I take it as a mark both of your good opinion
and of your friendship; the former, in believing that I do nothing
which I care to conceal; and the other, in assuring yourself that I
will hereafter set a watch upon myself, and do as you would have me;
and acquaint you not only with the course and method, but with the
very business, of my life.

This day I have had entire to myself, without any knocking at
my door, or lifting up of the hanging; but I have divided it betwixt
my book and my bed, and been left at liberty to do my own business:
for all the impertinents were either at the theatre, at bowls, or at the
horse-match. My body does not require much exercise, and I am
beholden to my age for it: a little makes me weary; and that is the
end also of that which is most robust. My dinner is a piece of dry
bread, without a table, and without fouling my fingers. My sleeps are
short, and in truth a little doubtful betwixt slumbering and waking.
One while I am reflecting upon the errors of antiquity; and then I
apply myself to the correcting of my own. In my reading, with reverence
to the ancients, some things I take, others I alter; and some again, I
reject, others I invent; without enthralling myself so to another's
judgment as not to preserve the freedom of my own. Sometimes, of
a sudden, in the middle of my meditations, my ears are struck with
the shout of a thousand people together, from some spectacle or other;

517

the noise does not at all discompose my thought; it is no more to me than the dashing of waves, or the wind in a wood; but possibly sometimes it may divert them. "Good Lord," think I, "if men would but exercise their brains as they do their bodies; and take as much pains for virtue as they do for pleasure!" For difficulties strengthen the mind as well as labour does the body.

You tell me that you want my books more than my counsels; which I take just as kindly as if you should have asked me for my picture. For I have the very same opinion of my wit that I have of my beauty. You shall have both the one and the other, with my very self into the bargain.

In the examination of my own heart, I find some vices that lie open; others more obscure and out of sight; and some that take me only by fits. Which last I look upon as the most dangerous and troublesome; for they lie upon the catch, and keep a man upon a perpetual guard: being neither provided against them, as in a state of war; nor secure, as in any assurance of peace. To say the truth, we are all of us as cruel, as ambitious, and as luxurious, as our fellows; but we want the fortune, or the occasion, perchance, to show it. When the snake is frozen, it is safe; but the poison is still in it though it be numbed, We hate upstarts, that use their power with insolence; when yet, if we had the same means, it is odds that we should do the same thing ourselves. Only our corruptions are private for want of opportunity to employ them. Some things we look upon as superfluous, and others, as not worth the while; but we never consider that we pay dearest for that which we pretend to receive gratis; as anxiety, loss of credit, liberty, and time. So cheap is every man in effect that pretends to be most dear to himself. Some are dipt in their lusts as in a river; there must be a hand to help them out: others are strangely careless of good counsel, and yet well enough disposed to follow example. Some again must be forced to their duties, because there is no good to be done upon them by persuasion; but out of the whole race of mankind, how few are there that are able to help themselves! Being thus conscious of our own frailty, we should do well to keep ourselves quiet, and not to trust weak minds with wine, beauty, or pleasure. We have much ado, you see, to keep our feet upon dry ground; what will become of us then if we venture ourselves where it is slippery? It is not to say, "This is a hard lesson, and we cannot go through with it!" for we can, if we would endeavour it; but we cannot, because we give it for granted that we cannot, without trying whether we can or not. And what is the meaning of all this but that we are pleased with our vices, and willing to be mastered by them? so that we had rather excuse than cast them off. The true reason is, we will not, but the pretence is, that we cannot: and we are not only under a necessity of error, but the very love of it.

To give you now a brief of my own character: I am none of those that take delight in tumults, and in struggling with difficulties. I had rather be quiet than in arms; for I account it my duty to bear up against ill fortune; but still without choosing it. I am no friend to contention, especially to that of the bar; but I am very much a servant to all honest business that may be done in a corner. And there is no retreat so unhappy as not to yield entertainment for a great mind; by which a man may make himself profitable both to his country and to his friends, by his wisdom, by his interest, and by his counsel. It is the part of a good patriot to prefer men of worth; to defend the innocent; to provide good laws; and to advise in war, and in peace. But is not he as good a patriot that instructs youth in virtue; that furnishes the world with precepts of morality, and keeps human nature within the bounds of right reason? Who is the greater man, he that pronounces a sentence upon the bench, or he that in his study reads us a lecture of justice, piety, patience, fortitude, the knowledge of Heaven, the contempt of death, and the blessing of a good conscience? The soldier that guards the ammunition and the baggage is as necessary as he that fights the battle. Was not Cato a greater example than either Ulysses or Hercules? They had the fame, you know, of being indefatigable; despisers of pleasure; and great conquerors, both of their enemies and of their appetites. But Cato, I must confess, had no encounters with monsters; nor did he fall into those times of credulity, when people believed that the weight of the heavens rested upon one man's shoulders; but he grappled with ambition, and the unlimited desire of power; which the whole world, divided under a triumvirate, was not able to satisfy. He opposed himself to the vices of a degenerate city, even when it was now sinking under its own weight. He stood single, and supported the falling commonwealth, until at last, as inseparable friends, they were crushed together; for neither would Cato survive the public liberty, nor did that liberty outlive Cato. To give you now a farther account of myself: I am naturally a friend to all the rules and methods of sobriety and moderation. I like the old-fashioned plate that was left me by my country-father: it is plain and heavy; and yet, for all this, there is a kind of dazzling, methinks, in ostentations of splendour and luxury. But it strikes the eye more than the mind; and though it may shake a wise man, it cannot alter him. Yet it sends me home many times more sad, perhaps, than I went out; but yet I hope not worse; though not without some secret dissatisfaction at my own condition. Upon these thoughts I betake myself to my philosophy; and then, methinks, I am not well unless I put myself into

519

some public employment: not for the honour or the profit of it, but only to place myself in a station where I may be serviceable to my country and to my friends. But when I come, on the other side, to consider the uneasiness, the abuses, and the loss of time, that attends public affairs, I get me home again as fast as I can, and take up a resolution of spending the remainder of my days within the privacy of my own walls. How great a madness is it to set our heart upon trifles; especially to the neglect of the most serious offices of our lives, and the most important end of our being? How miserable, as well as short, is their life, that compass with great labour what they possess with greater; and hold with anxiety what they acquire with trouble! But we are governed in all things by opinion, and every thing is to us as we believe it. What is poverty but a privation; and not intended of what a man has, but of that which he has not? The great subject of human calamities is money. Take all the rest together, as death, sickness, fear, desire, pain, labour; and those which proceed from money exceed them all. It is a wonderful folly, that of tumblers, rope-dancers, divers; what pains they take, and what hazards they run, for an inconsiderable gain! And yet we have not patience for the thousandth part of that trouble, though it would put us into the possession of an everlasting quiet. Epicurus for experiment sake, confined himself to a narrower allowance than that of the severest prisons to the most capital offenders; and found himself at ease too in a stricter diet than a man in the worst condition needs to fear. This was to prevent Fortune, and to frustrate the worst which she can do. We should never know any thing to be superfluous but by the want of it. How many things do we provide only because others have them, and for fashion-sake? Caligula offered Demetrius 500 crowns; who rejected them with a smile, as who should say, "It was so little it did him no honour the refusing of it. Nothing less," says he, "than the offer of his whole empire would have been a temptation to have tried the firmness of my virtue." By this contempt of riches is intended only the fearless possession of them; and the way to attain that is to persuade ourselves that we may live happily without them. How many of those things, which reason formerly told us were superfluous and mimical, do we now find to be so by experience? But we are misled by the counterfeit of good on the one hand, and the suspicion of evil on the other. Not that riches are an efficient cause of mischief; but they are a precedent cause, by way of irritation and attraction: for they have so near a resemblance of good, that most people take them to be good. Nay, virtue itself is also a precedent cause of evil; as many are envied for their wisdom, or for their justice; which does not arise from the thing itself, but from the irreproveable power of virtue, that forces all men to admire and to love it. That is not good that is more advantageous to us, but that which is only so.

Roger L'Estrange

Epistle XIX

An Exposition of True Courage

"Fortitude is" properly "the contempt of all hazards, according to reason;" though it be commonly and promiscuously used also, "for a contempt of all hazards, even without or against reason": which is rather a daring and a brutal fierceness than an honourable courage. A brave man fears nothing more than the weakness of being affected with popular glory. His eyes are not dazzled either with gold or steel; he tramples upon all the terrors and glories of Fortune; he looks upon himself as a citizen and soldier of the world; and, in despite of all accidents and oppositions, he maintains his station. He does not only suffer, but court, the most perilous occasions of virtue, and those adventures which are most terrible to others: for he values himself upon experiment, and is more ambitious of being reputed good than happy. Mucius lost his hand with more honour than he could have preserved it: he was a greater conqueror without it than he could have been with it; for with the very stump of it he overcame two kings, Tarquin and Porsenna. Rutilia followed Cotta into banishment; she staid, and she returned with him too; and soon after she lost him without so much as shedding a tear: a great instance of her courage in his banishment, and of her prudence in his death. This (says Epicurus) is the last and the blessedest day of my life, when he was ready to expire in an extreme torment of the stone. It is never said of the 300 Fabii that they were overcome, but that they were slain; nor of Regulus, that he was vanquished by the Carthaginians, but that he was taken. The Spartans prohibited all exercises where the victory was declared by the voice and submission of him that was worsted. When Phaeton begged of Phoebus the government of the chariot of the sun for one day, the poets make him so far from being discouraged by his father's telling him of the danger of the undertaking, and how he himself had much ado to keep his seat for fear, when he looked down from the meridian, that it proved a spur to his importunity.

"That is the thing," say Phaeton, "that I would be at; to stand firm in that difficulty where Phoebus himself trembles." Security is the caution of narrow minds; but as fire tries gold, so does difficulty and hazards try virtuous men. Not but that he may be as valiant that watches upon the tower as he that fights upon his knees; only the one has had the good fortune of an occasion for the proof of his resolution. As some creatures are cruel, others crafty, and some timorous; so man is endued with a glorious and an excellent spirit, that prompts him not so much to regard a safe life as an honest. Providence has made him the master of this lower world, and he reckons it his duty to sacrifice his own particular to the advantage of the whole. And yet there is a vast difference even in the same action done by a brave person and by a stupid; as the death of Cato was honourable, but that of Brutus was shameful. Nor is it death itself that we recommend for glorious; but it is a glorious thing to die as we ought. Neither is it poverty, banishment, or pain, that we commend; but the man that behaves himself bravely under those afflictions. How were the gladiators contemned that called for quarter, and those on the other side favoured that despised it? Many a man saves his life by not fearing to lose it; and many a man loses his life by being over-solicitous to save it. We are many times afraid of dying by one thing, and we come to die by another. As for example, we are threatened by an enemy, and we die by a pleurisy. The fear of death enlarges all other things that we fear. To bear it with constancy, we should compute, that whether our lives be long or short, it comes all to a point; some hours we lose; what if they were days, months, years? what matters it, if I never arrive at that which I must certainly part with when I have it? Life is but one point of flying time, and that which is to come is no more mine than that which is past. And we have this for our comfort too, that whosoever now fears death, will some time or other come to wish it. If death be troublesome or terrible, the fault is in us, and not in death itself. It is as great madness for a man to fear that which he is not to feel, as that which he is not to suffer; the difference lies in the manner of dying, and not in the issue of death itself. It is a more inglorious death to be smothered with perfume than to be torn to pieces with pincers. Provided my mind be not sick, I shall not much heed my body. I am prepared for my last hour without tormenting myself when it will come. It is betwixt the Stoics and other philosophers, as betwixt men and women; they are both equally necessary for society; only the one is born for government, and the other for subjection. Other sects deal with their disciples as plausible physicians do with their patients, they flatter and humour them; whereas the Stoics go a bolder way to work, and consider rather their profit than their pleasure.

Roger L'Estrange

522

Epistle XX

Learning. Private and Public Life

Let no man presume to advise others, that has not first given good counsel to himself, and he may then pretend to help his neighbour. It is, in short, as hard a matter to give good counsel as to take it; let it, however, be agreed betwixt the two parties, that the one designs to confer a benefit, and the other to receive it. Some people scorn to be taught; others are ashamed of it, as they would be of going to school when they are old; but it is never too late to learn what it is always necessary to know; and it is no shame to learn so long as we are ignorant, that is to say, so long as we live. When any thing is amiss in our bodies or estates, we have recourse presently to the physician or the lawyer for help; and why not to the philosopher in the disorders of our mind? No man lives but he that applies himself to wisdom; for he takes into his own life the supplement of all past ages. It is a fair step toward happiness and virtue, to delight in the conversation of good and of wise men; and where that cannot be had, the next point is, to keep no company at all. Solitude affords business enough, and the entertainment is comfortable and easy; whereas public offices are vexatious and restless. There is a great difference betwixt a life of leisure and of laziness. When people will express their envy of a man in a happy condition, they will say, "He lives at his ease;" when in truth the man is dead alive. There is a long life, and there is a long death; the former when we enjoy the benefits of a right mind, and the other when the senses are extinguished, and the body dead beforehand. He that makes me the master of my own time, and places me in a state of freedom, lays a great obligation upon me. As a merchant that has a considerable fortune abroad, is more sensible of the blessing of a fair wind and safe passage, than he that has only ballast, or some coarse commodity in the vessel; so that man that employs his privacy upon thoughts divine and precious, is more sensible of the comfort of that freedom than he that bends his meditations an ill way. For he considers all the benefits of his exemption from common duties, he enjoys himself with infinite delight, and makes his gratitude answerable to his obligations. He is the best of subjects, and the happiest of men; and he lives to Nature and to himself. Most men are to themselves the worst company they can keep. If they be good, quiet, and temperate, they are as good alone as in company: but if otherwise, let them converse with others, and avoid themselves; but he that has made himself good company, can never be too much alone. Many a ship is lost in the harbour, but more in the ocean; as many an honest man is condemned, but more guilty. This, however, is certain, he that cannot secure himself in privacy, shall be much more exposed itself, and exposed to the greediness of others. Prosperity, like a fair gale upon a strong current, carries a man in a trice out of the very sight of peace and quiet; and if it be not tempered and regulated, it is so far from easing us, that it proves an oppression to us. A busy and a fortunate man in the world, calls many men his friends, that are at most but his guests. And if people flock to him, it is but as they do to a fountain, which they both exhaust and trouble.

What greater slavery can there be than that of princes in this very respect, that they are chained to their post, and cannot make themselves less? All their words and actions are descanted upon, and made public discourse; and there are many things allowable to a private man that are not fit for a governor. I can walk alone, where I please without a sword, without fear, and without company; whereas a prince must be armed in peace, and cannot with dignity quit his guards. Fortune has him in custody: a train besets him wherever he goes, and there is no making of any escape. He is little better than nailed to his place, and it is the perfection of his misery that he cannot go less. He can no more conceal himself than the sun in the firmament: whereas his subjects may go and come, change habits and humour, without being taken notice of. Servitude is the fate of palaces, the splendour of a crown draws all men's eyes upon it. When Caesar speaks, the whole world hears his voice, and trembles at his displeasure; and where it falls, it shakes whatsoever is near it. His lips are the oracles of the people, and government is the cement that binds them together; but still he that is master of many is the servant yet of more. The power, it is true, of all things belongs to the prince, but the property to particular persons; and the same thing may be both yours and mine in several respects. We cannot say that a son or a servant has nothing, because a master or a father, may take it away if he will; or that he cannot give willingly, because they may hinder it, whether he will or not. "This is power and true dominion; and not to rule and command, when we may do it when we please." The strength of a prince is in the love of his people; for there is nothing so great but it must itself perish, when it is become the common safety that it should be so. Tyrants are hated because they are feared: and because they are hated, they will be feared. They are rendered odious to posterity, and they had better never been born, than to stand upon record for the plagues of mankind. Miserable is that people where their very keepers are their executioners. And it is not an armed tyranny neither, but the unarmed vices of avarice and envy that we ought to be most afraid of. Some will not endure to have their vices touched, but will shrink and struggle under the operation as if they were under the hand of a surgeon. But this shall not hinder me from lancing and probing, because of the cries and groans of the patient. Every man should have a monitor at his elbow to keep him from avarice, by showing him how rich a man may be with a little: from ambition, by representing the disquiets and hazards that accompany greatness; which makes him as great a burden to others as he is to himself. When it comes to that once, fear, anxiety, and weariness, make us philosophers. A sickly fortune produces wholesome counsels; and we reap this fruit from our adversity, that it brings us at last to wisdom.

Now, though clemency in a prince be so necessary and so profitable a virtue: and cruelty so dangerous an excess; it is yet the office of a governor, as of the master of an hospital, to keep sick and madmen in order, and in cases of extremity, the very member is to be cut off with the ulcer. All punishment is either for amendment or for example, or that others may live more secure. What is the end of destroying those poisonous and dangerous creatures, which are never to be reclaimed but to prevent mischief? And yet there may be as much hazard in doing too much as too little. A particular mutineer may be punished, but when the whole army is in a revolt, there must be a general pardon. The multitude of offenders, is their security and protection; for there is no quarreling with a public vice, where the custom of offending takes away the shame of it; and it is not prudent neither, by many punishments, to show a city that the wicked are so much the major part: beside, that it is as great a dishonour for a prince to have many executions, as for a physician to have many funerals. Shall a father disinherit a son for the first offence? Let him first admonish, then threaten, and afterward punish him. So long as there is hope, we should apply gentle remedies; but some nations are intractable, and neither willing to serve, nor fit to command; and some persons are incorrigible too.

Roger L'Estrange

Epistle XXI

A Sound Body and a Quiet Mind

Epicurus makes the two blessings of life to be a sound body and a quiet mind; which is only a compendious reduction of human felicity to a state of health and of virtue. The way to be happy is to make vice not only odious, but ridiculous, and every man to mind his own business; for he that torments himself for other people's misfortunes shall never be at rest. A virtuous life must be all of a piece, and not advanced by starts and intervals, and then to go on where it left; for, this is of losing ground. We are to press and persevere; for the main difficulties are yet to come. If I discontinue my course, when shall I come to pronounce these words? *I am a conqueror.* Not a conqueror of barbarous enemies and savage nations; but I have subdued avarice, ambition, and those lusts that have subjected even the greatest of conquerors. Who was a greater than Alexander, that extended his empire from Thracia to the utmost bounds of the East? but yet he burnt Persepolis at the request of a prostitute, to gratify his lust. He overcame Darius, and slew many thousands of the Persians; but yet he murdered Calisthenes, and that single blot has tarnished the glory of all his victories. All the wishes of mortals, and all the benefits which we can either give or receive, are of very little conducement to a happy life. Those things which the common people gape after, are transitory and vain; whereas happiness is permanent: nor is it to be estimated by number, measure, or parts; for it is full and perfect. I do not speak as if I myself were arrived at that blessed state of repose; but it is something yet to be on the mending hand. It is with me as with a man that is creeping out of a disease; he feels yet some grudgings of it, he is every foot examining of his pulse, and suspects every touch of heat to be a relique of his fever. Just at that rate I am jealous of myself. The best remedy that I know in this case is to go on with confidence, and not to be misled by the errors of other people. It is with our manners as with our healths; it is a degree of virtue, the abatement of vice, as it is a degree of health, the abatement of a fit.

Some place their happiness in wealth, some in the liberty of the body, and others in the pleasures of the sense and palate. But what are metals, tastes, sounds, or colours, to the mind of a reasonable creature? He that sets his heart upon riches, the very fear of poverty will be grievous to him; he that is ambitious, shall be galled with envy at any man that gets before him: for, in that case, he that is not first is last. I do not speak against riches neither; for if they hurt a man, it is his own folly. They may be indeed the cause of mischief, as they are a temptation to those that do it. Instead of courage, they may inspire us with arrogance; and instead of greatness of mind, with insolence; which is in truth but the counterfeit of magnanimity. What is it to be a prisoner, and in chains? It is no more than that condition to which many princes have been reduced, and out of which many men have been advanced to the authority of princes. It is not to say, "I have no master:" in time you may have one. Might not Hecuba, Croesus, and the mother of Darius, have said as much? And where is the happiness of luxury either, when a man divides his life betwixt the kitchen and the stews; betwixt an anxious conscience and nauseous stomach? Caligula, who was born to show the world what mischief might be done by concurrence of great wickedness and a great fortune, spent near 10,000 pounds Sterling upon a supper. The works and inventions of it are prodigious, not only in the counterfeiting of nature, but even in surpassing it. The Romans had their brooks even in their parlours; and their dinners under their tables. The mullet was reckoned stale unless it died in the hand of the guest: and they had their glasses to put them into, that they might the better observe all the changes and motions of them in the last agony betwixt life and death. So that they fed their eyes before their bodies. "Look how it reddens," says one; "there is no vermilion like it. Take notice of these veins; and that same gray brightness upon the head of it. And now he is at his last gasp: see how pale he turns, and all of a colour." These people would not have given themselves half the trouble with a dying friend; nay, they would leave a father or a brother at his last hour to entertain themselves with the barbarous spectacle of an expiring fish. And that which enhances the esteem of every thing, is the price of it: insomuch that water itself, which ought to be gratuitous, is exposed to sale in their conservatories of ice and snow. Nay, we are troubled that we cannot buy breath, light, and that we have the air itself gratis, as if our conditions were evil because Nature has left something to us in common. But luxury contrives ways to set a price upon the most necessary and communicable benefits in nature: even those benefits which are free to birds and beasts, as well as to men, and serve indifferently for the use of the most sluggish creatures. But how comes it that fountain-water is not cold enough to serve us, unless it be bound up in ice? So long as the stomach is sound, Nature discharges her functions without trouble; but when the blood comes to be inflamed with excess of wine or meats, simple water is not cold enough to allay that heat; and we are forced to make use of remedies; which remedies themselves are vices. We heap suppers upon dinners, and dinners upon suppers, without intermission. Good God! How easy is it to quench a sound and an honest thirst? But when the palate is grown callous, we taste nothing; and that which we take for thirst, is only the rage of a fever. Hippocratus delivered it as an aphorism, that "women were never bald nor gouty, but in one singular case." Women have not altered their nature since, but they have changed the course of their lives; for, by taking the liberties of men, they partake as well of their diseases as of their wickedness. They sit up as much, drink as much; nay, in their very appetites they are masculine too; they have lost the advantages of their sex by their vices.

Our ancestors, when they were free, lived either in caves or in arbours; but slavery came in with gildings and with marble. I would have him that comes into my house take more notice of the master than of the furniture. The golden age was before architecture: art came in with luxury, and we do not hear of any philosopher that was either a locksmith or a painter. Who was the wiser man, think you, he that invented a saw, or the other who, upon seeing a boy drink water out of the hollow of his hand, brake his pitcher, with this check to himself; "What a fool am I to trouble myself with superfluities?" Carving is one man's trade, cooking is another's; only he is more miserable that teaches it for pleasure than he that learns it for necessity. It was luxury, not philosophy, that invented fish-pools as well as palaces; where, in case of foul weather at sea, they might have fishes to supply their gluttony in harbour. We do not only pamper our lusts, but provoke them; as if we were to learn the very art of voluptuousness. What was it but avarice that originally brake the union of society, and proved the cause of poverty, even to those that were the most wealthy? Every man possessed all, until the world came to appropriate possessions to themselves. In the first age Nature was both a law and a guide, and the best governed; which was but according to Nature too. The largest and the strongest bull leads the herd; the goodliest elephant; and among men too, in the blessed times of innocence, the best was uppermost. They chose governors for their manners, who neither acted any violence nor suffered any. They protected the weak against the mighty; and persuaded or dissuaded as they saw occasion. Their prudence provided for their people; their courage kept them safe from angers; their bounty both supplied and adorned their subjects. It was a duty then to command, not a government. No man in those days had either a mind to do an injury or a cause for it. He that commanded well was well obeyed; and the worst menace the governors could then make to the disobedient, was to forsake them. But with the corruption of times, tyranny crept in, and the world began to have need of laws; and those laws were made by wise men too, as Solon and Lycurgus, who learned their trade in the school of Pythagoras.

Roger L'Estrange

Epistle XXV

Protections Against Fate

The book you promised me is now come to my hand; and I opened it with an intent to read it over at leisure. But when I was once in, I could not lay it down again until I had gone through with it. At present I shall only tell you that I am exceedingly pleased with the choice of the subject; but I am transported with the spirit and gentleness of it. You shall hear farther from me upon a second reading; and you need not fear the hearing of the truth, for your goodness leaves a man no place for flattery. I find you still to be one and the same man, which is a great matter, and only proper to a wise man; for fools are various: one while thrifty and grave, another while profuse and vain. Happy is the man that sets himself right at first, and continues so to the end. All fools, we say, are mad men, though they are not all of them in Bedlam. We find some at the bar, some upon the bench, and not a few even in the senate itself. One man's folly is sad; another's wanton; and a third is busy and impertinent. A wise man carries all his treasures within himself: what Fortune gives she may take; but he leaves nothing at her mercy. He stands firm, and keeps his ground against all misfortunes, without so much as changing countenance. He is free, inviolable, unshaken; proof against all accidents, and not only invincible, but inflexible. So long as he cannot lose any thing of his own, he never troubles himself for what is another's. He is a friend to Providence, and will not murmur at any thing that comes to pass by God's appointment. He is not only resolute, but generous and good-natured, and ready to lay down his life in a good cause; and for the public safety to sacrifice his own. He does not so much consider the pleasure of his life as the need that the world has of him; and he is not so nice neither as to be weary of his life while he may either serve his wife or his friends. Nor is it all that his life is profitable to them, but it is likewise delightful to himself, and carries its own reward; for what can be more comfortable than to be so dear to another, as for that very reason to become dearer to himself? If he lose a child, he is pensive; he is compassionate to the sick, and only troubled when he sees men wallowing in infamy and vice; whereas, on the other side, you shall see nothing but restlessness; one man hankering after his neighbour's wife; another in pain about his own; a third in grief for a repulse; another as much out of humour for his success. If he lose an estate, he parts with it as a thing that was only adventitious: or if it was of his own acquiring, he computes the possession and loss; and thus says to himself, I shall live as well afterwards as I did before.

Our houses (says he) may be burnt or robbed, our lands taken from us; and we can call nothing our own that is under the dominion of Fortune. It is a foolish avarice that restrains all things to a propriety, and believes nothing to be a man's own that is public: whereas a wise man judges nothing so much his own as that wherein mankind is allowed a share. It is not with the blessings of Providence as it is with a dole; where every man receives so much ahead; but every man there has all. That which we eat, and either give or receive with the hand, may be broken into parts; but peace and freedom of mind, are not to be divided. He that has first cast off the empire of Fortune, needs not fear that of great men; for they are but Fortune's hands; nor was any man ever broken by adversity that was not first betrayed by prosperity. "But what signifies philosophy," you will say, "if there be a fate; if we be governed by Fortune, or some over-ruling power? For certainties are unchangeable, and there is no providing against uncertainties. If what I shall do and resolve, be already determined, what use of philosophy?" Yes, great use; for granted, philosophy instructs and advises us to obey God, and to follow him willingly; to oppose Fortune resolutely, and to bear all accidents.

Fate is an irrevocable, and invincible, and an unchangeable decree; a necessity of all things and actions according to eternal appointment. Like the course of a river, it moves forward, without contradiction or delay, in an irresistible flux, where one wave pushes on another. He knows little of God that imagines it may be controlled. There is no changing of the purpose even of a wise man; for he sees beforehand what will be best for the future. How much more unchangeable then is the Almighty, to whom all futurity is always present? "To what end then is it, if Fate is inexorable, to offer up prayers, and sacrifices, any farther than to relieve the scruples and the weakness of sickly minds?" My answer is, first, That the gods take no delight in the sacrifices of beasts, or in the images of gold and silver, but in a pious and obedient will. And, secondly, That by prayers and sacrifices, dangers and afflictions may be sometimes removed; sometimes lessened; other whiles deferred: and all this without any offence to the power or necessity of Fate. There are some things which Providence has left so far in suspense, that they seem to be (in a manner) conditional; in such sort, that even appearing evils may, upon our prayers and supplications, be turned into goods, which is so far from being against Fate, that it is even a part of Fate itself. You will say, "That either this shall come to pass or not. If the former, it will be the same thing if we do not pray: and if the other, it will be the same thing if we do." To this I must reply, that the proposition is false, for want of the middle exception betwixt the one and the other. This will be, (say I) that is, if there shall any prayers interpose in the case. But then do they object, on the other side, that this very thing also is necessary: for it is likewise determined by Fate either that we shall pray or not? What if I should now grant you that there is a fate also even in our very prayers; a determination that we shall pray, and that therefore we shall pray? It is decreed that a man shall be eloquent; but upon condition that he apply himself to letters; by the same fate it is decreed that he shall so apply himself, and that therefore he shall learn. Such a man shall be rich if he betake himself to navigation: but the same fate that promises him a great estate appoints also that he shall sail, and therefore he puts to sea. It is the same case in expiations; a man shall avoid dangers, if he can by his prayers avoid the threatenings of divine vengeance: but this is part of his fate also that he shall so do, and therefore he does it. These arguments are made use of to prove, that there is nothing left to our will, but that we are all over-ruled by fatalities. When we come to handle that matter, we shall show the consistency of free-will with fate, having already made it appear that, notwithstanding the certain order of Fate, judgments may be averted by prayers and supplications, and without any repugnancy to Fate; for they are part even of the law of Fate itself. You will say, perhaps, "What am I the better for the priest or the prophet; for whether he bids me sacrifice or not, I lie under the necessity of doing it?" Yes, in this I am the better for it, as he is a minister of Fate. We may as well say that it is matter of Fate that we are in health: and yet we are indebted for it to the physician; because the benefit of that fate is conveyed to us by his hand.

Roger L'Estrange

SATIRE

Horace

Persius

Juvenal

HORACE

For biographical note, see under *Poetry*.

Book I — Satire I

It is folly to wish instead of to enjoy. Consider the case of the
hoarder of wealth.

How does it happen, Maecenas, that no one lives content with
the lot that either choice has assigned to him or chance has thrust upon
him: and that everyone commends those who pursue another path?
'How fortunate traders are!' declares the veteran soldier, whose
frame is worn out with hard toil. The trader, on the other hand,
whose ship is buffeted by the south winds, asserts: 'Soldiering is
preferable. Why! There is the shock of battle: in the brief space of
one hour death comes swiftly and the joy of victory.'
The lawyer, trained in the processes of law and justice, envies the
countryman, when at cock-crow a client knocks at the door. The poor
defendant, after naming sureties, has been dragged from the country
into town, and exclaims that only those who live in town are happy.
Other similar instances are so numerous, they would tire loquacious
Fabius. To make it short, listen to the sum of the entire matter. If
some god should say: 'See, here I am. I shall do as you wish: you,
recently a soldier, shall be a trader. You, a while ago a barrister, shall
be a countryman. Off with you, go and change your parts! Quick!
What are you waiting for?' they would not want to change. And yet
they could be happy. What reason is there really why Jupiter, in his
anger at them, does not puff out his cheeks and say he will not henceforth be so indulgent as to lend an ear to their wishes?
Now, let me not make a jest of this and lightly pass it over as
badinage: and yet what is to prevent me from telling the truth with a
smile? Like teachers, who sometimes coaxingly give children pastries,
to make them learn their alphabet. However, let us dismiss all drollery

533

and consider serious problems. The poor wretch who turns the heavy ground with his tough plough, the cheating inn-keeper, the soldier and the sailor who daringly sail all the seas, say they endure their work so that in old age they can rest tranquilly, since they now have collected enough for their subsistence. Like the example of the tiny ant, that laboriously with its mouth gathers up whatever it can and adds it to the store that it builds up, aware and careful of the future. But as soon as Aquarius saddens the upturned year, the ant does not creep about anywhere and wisely uses the supplies previously collected: while neither the raging heat drives you from gain, nor does winter, fire, the sea or the sword stop you, as long as there is a second person richer than yourself.

What pleasure is there in fearfully storing secretly in the earth a vast amount of gold and silver?

'But if you diminish it, it would dwindle to a paltry as.' But if you don't diminish it, what is the joy in a huge heap of wealth?

If your threshing-floor ground a hundred thousand bushels of grain, your stomach will not on that account hold more than mine. If you happen to carry on your loaded shoulder a net bag and bread in your train of slaves, you would not get more than the man who carries nothing.

Or, tell me, what does it matter to the man who lives within the bounds of Nature whether he has a hundred or a thousand acres to plough?

'But it is pleasant to draw from a large store.' Provided you let us draw from the store the same amount, why do you praise your granaries more than our corn bins? As though you did not need more than a pitcher of water or a cup, and said: 'I should prefer to draw from a large river rather than this little spring, though the amount might be the same.' So it comes to pass that if a man likes an excessive amount, the violent torrent Aufidus drags him along with its banks. But the man who needs only the little amount necessary, neither swallows the muddied water nor loses his life in the waves. But the majority of men, caught by a mistaken passion, say: 'Nothing is enough. For you are esteemed according to your possessions.' What can one say to such? You bid him be miserly gladly, in so far as he is a miser. It is told of a certain rich and miserly Athenian that he used to spurn popular opinion in these words: 'The people hiss me. But I applaud myself whenever I contemplate my money boxes at home.'

Tantalus in his thirst catches at the streams of water receding from his lips. Why do you laugh? Change the name and the fable applies to yourself. You sleep on your heaps of money bags, alert, and are forced to refrain from them as if they were sacred or to enjoy them as if they were painted pictures. Don't you know the value of money, or its use?

Bread may be bought, and vegetables, and a pint of wine. To deprive yourself of these things would be a disservice to human nature. Or is this your idea of pleasure: to stay awake dying from fright, and dreading wicked thieves night and day, and fires, and escaped slaves who may rob you? I should invariably want to be free from these fine things.

'But if the body is attacked by cold and the pain spreads all over, or some other condition has nailed you to your bed, you have someone to sit by your side and prepare fomentations, and to ask the doctor to revive you and restore you to your sons and dear kinsmen.'

Your wife does not wish you well, nor your son: all your neighbors hate you, young and old. Do you wonder, since you place money before everything, if no one shows you the love you don't earn? Or, if you want to hold and keep the love of the kin that nature gives you without any effort on your part, would you, unhappy wretch, be wasting your pains, like the man teaching an ass to obey the bit and run in the Campus? In short, let there be an end to hoarding. And, since having more you fear poverty less, start finishing your task, for you have acquired what you wanted. Or you may end up like a certain Ummidius. The tale is brief. He was so rich that he weighed out his money. He was so mean that he never dressed better than a slave. To his dying day he was afraid that penury would overtake him. But his freedwoman, the bravest of the children of Tyndarus, split his head with an axe.

'What then do you advise? To live like Naevius or like Nomentanus?'

You proceed to reconcile things that, face to face, are in mutual opposition. When I tell you not to be a miser I don't ask you to be a rake and a scamp. There is a difference between Tanais and Visellius' father-in-law. There is moderation in things: there are, finally, certain limits, and what is proper cannot exist beyond these limits and short of them. I return to my original theme how no one is satisfied with himself, like the miser, and rather envies those who pursue a different course, and dies with jealousy because a neighbor's goat has larger udders, and does not compare himself with the vast majority of poorer fellows, but labors to outdo one after the other. The richer man is always in the way of the frantic hoarder. When the horses pull away the chariots dashing from the starting-point, the driver closes in on the horses that outstrip his own, and sneers at the rival he passes for being among the hindmost.

Hence it is that we can rarely find a man who admits that he has had a happy life, and withdraws from it when the time comes, like a satisfied guest. Enough. You might think that I have robbed the book shelves of purblind Crispinus: so I shall not say another word.

H. E. W.

Book I — Satire IX

The Bore

It chanced that I, the other day,
Was sauntering up the Sacred Way,
And musing, as my habit is,
Some trivial random fantasies,
That for the time absorbed me quite, —
When there comes running up a wight,
Whom only by his name I knew:
"Ha, my dear fellow, how d'ye do?"
Grasping my hand, he shouted. "Why,
As times go, pretty well," said I:
"And you, I trust, can say the same."
But after me as still he came,
"Sir, is there anything." I cried,
"You want of me?" "Oh," he replied,
"I'm just the man you ought to know:
A scholar, author!" — "Is it so?
For this I'll like you all the more!"
Then, writhing to evade the bore,
I quicken now my pace, now stop,
And in my servant's ear let drop
Some words, and all the while I feel
Bathed in cold sweat from head to heel.
    "Oh for a touch," I moaned in pain,
"Bolanus, of thy slap-dash vein,
To put this incubus to rout!"
As he went chattering on about
Whatever he descries or meets,
The crowds, the beauty of the streets,
The city's growth, its splendor, size,

"You're dying to be off," he cries —
For all the while I'd been struck dumb:
"I've noticed it some time. But come,
Let's clearly understand each other:
It's no use making all this pother.
My mind's made up to stick by you;
So where you go, there I go too."
    "Don't put yourself," I answered, "pray,
So very far out of your way.
I'm on the road to see a friend,
Whom you don't know, that's near his end,
Away beyond the Tiber far,
Close by where Caesar's gardens are."
    "I've nothing in the world to do,
And what's a paltry mile or two?
I like it, so I'll follow you!"
Now we were close on Vesta's fane;
'Twas hard on ten, and he, my bane,
Was bound to answer to his bail,
Or lose his cause if he should fail.
    "Do, if you love me, step aside
One moment with me here," he cried.
    "Upon my life, indeed I can't:
Of law I'm wholly ignorant,
And you know where I'm hurrying to."
    "I'm fairly puzzled what to do:
Give you up, or my cause." — "Oh, me,
Me, by all means!" — "I won't," quoth he,
And stalks on, holding by me tight.
As with your conqueror to fight
Is hard, I follow. "How," anon
He rambles off — "How get you on,
You and Maecenas? To so few
He keeps himself. So clever, too!
No man more dexterous to seize
And use his opportunities.
Just introduce me, and you'll see
We'll pull together famously;
And hang me then, if with my backing
You don't send all your rivals packing!"
    "Things in that quarter, sir, proceed
In very different style indeed.
No house more free from all that's base,

In none cabals more out of place.
It hurts me not if there I spy
Men richer, better read than I.
Each has his place!" — "Amazing tact!
Scarce credible!" — "But 'tis the fact." —
"You quicken my desire to get
An introduction to his set." . . .

                    We ran
At the next turn against the man
Who had the lawsuit with my bore.
"Ha, knave," he cried with loud uproar,
"Where are you off to? Will you here
Stand witness?" I present my ear.
To court he hustles him along;
High words are bandied, high and strong;
A mob collects, the fray to see:
So did Apollo rescue me.

Theodore Martin

538

P E R S I U S

AULUS PERSIUS FLACCUS (34-62 A.D.) was a wealthy, ivory-tower poet, intimate with the Stoics of his day.

Persius, the first Stoic Roman satirist in verse, produced six brief satires. They deal with the corruption of literature, prayer, right living, self-knowledge, vice, and the use of wealth.

Satire I

ARGUMENT

This Satire opens in form of a dialogue between Persius and a friend. — We may suppose Persius to be just seated in his study, and beginning to vent his indignation in satire. An acquaintance comes in, and, on hearing the first line, dissuades the poet from an undertaking so dangerous; advising him, if he must write, to accommodate his wit to the taste of the times, and to write like other people.

Persius acknowledges, that this would be the means of gaining applause; but adds, that the approbation of such patrons as this compliance would recommend him to was a thing not to be desired.

After this, he exposes the wretched taste which then prevailed in Rome, both in verse and prose, and shews what sad stuff the nobles wrote themselves, and encouraged in others. He laments that he dares not speak out, as Lucilius and Horace did — but it is no very difficult matter to perceive that he frequently aims at the emperor Nero.

He concludes, with a contempt of all blockheads, and says, that the only readers, whose applause he courts, must be men of virtue and sense.

Persius — Monitor

PERSIUS: O the cares of men! O how much vanity is there in things!
MONITOR: Who will read these?
PERSIUS: Do you say that to me?
MONITOR: Nobody, truly.
PERSIUS: Nobody?

MONITOR: Perhaps two, perhaps nobody; it is a shameful and lamentable thing.

PERSIUS: Wherefore?

    Lest Polydamas and the Troiads should prefer Labeo
    To me? — trifles! — do not, if turbid Rome should disparage
    Any thing, agree with it, nor correct a false balance
    By that scale: seek not thyself out of thyself.
    For at Rome who does not—? Ah, if I might say! — But I may
    Then, when I have beheld greyness, and that our grave way of life,
    And whatever we do after our playthings are left;
    When we have the relish of uncles — then, then forgive.

MONITOR: I will not.

PERSIUS: What shall I do? for I am a great laugher with a petulant spleen.

MONITOR: We write shut up. One numbers, another prose,
    Sometimes grand. —

PERSIUS: Which lungs, large of air, may breathe.

    Doubtless these to the people, comb'd, and with a new gown,
    White, and lastly with a birth-day sardonyx,
    You will read, in a high seat, when with a liquid gargle you have
        wash'd
    Your moveable throat, and effeminate with a lascivious eye:
    Here, neither in a modest manner, nor with a serene voice,
    You may see the great Titi tremble, when the verses enter the loins,
    And when the inwards are scratch'd with the tremulous verse.

        Dost thou, O old man, collect food for the ears of others?
    For ears, to which even thou, in skin destroy'd, may'st say —
        "Enough."
        "For what purpose to have learnt, unless this ferment", and
        what once
    "Is within innate, the wild fig-tree, should come forth from "the
        bursten liver?"
    Lo, paleness and old-age! O manners! is your knowing, then
    Altogether nothing, unless another should know that you know it?
        "But it is pleasant to be shewn with the finger, and to be
        said — This is he."
    "For thee to have the exercises of an hundred curl-pates,
    "Dost thou esteem as nothing?" Lo, among their cups, the satiated
    Romans inquire, what divine poems may relate.
    Here, some one, who has round his shoulders a hyacinthine cloak,
    (Having spoken something rankish from a snuffling nostril)
    If he hath gently sung Phyllises, Hypsipyle, and some lamentable
        matter

Of the poets, and supplants words with a tender palate,
The men have assented: now are not the ashes of that poet
Happy? now does not a lighter hillock mark his bones?
The guests praise: now will there not from those manes,
Now will there not from the tomb, and the fortunate ember,
Violets spring up? — You laugh, says he, and too much indulge
Your hooked nostrils. Will there be, who can refuse to be willing
To have deserved the countenance of the people? and, having
    spoken things worthy of cedar,
To leave verses fearing neither little fishes, nor frankincense?
    Whoever thou art, O thou, whom I just now made to speak
        on the adverse part,
I, when I write, if haply something more apt comes forth,
(Since this is a rare bird,) yet if something more apt comes forth,
Would not fear to be praised; nor indeed are my inwards so horny.
But to be the end extreme of right. I deny
Your "Well done!" and your "O fine!" for examine this whole
        "O fine,"
What has it not within? Is not the Iliad of Accius here,
Drunk with hellebore? Is there not, if crude nobles have dictated
Any little elegies? Is there not, lastly, whatever is written
In citron beds? — You know how to place a hot sow's-udder;
You know to present a shabby client with a worn garment;
And "I love truth (say you); tell me the truth concerning me."
    How is it possible? — Would you have me say it? you trifle,
        when, O bald head,
Your fat paunch stands forth with a hanging-down foot and
    an half.
    O Janus! whom no stork pecks behind your back,
Nor has the moveable hand imitated white ears,
Nor so much of the tongue, as an Apulian bitch when athirst.
Ye, O patrician blood, whose condition it is to live with
The hinder part of the head blind, prevent flouts behind your backs!
    What is the speech of the people? — What forsooth, unless
        that the verses
Now at last flow with soft measure, so that, across the polish, the
    joining
May pour forth severe nails. He knows how to extend a verse,
Not otherwise than if he should direct the rubric with one eye;
Whether the work is on manners, on luxury, or the dinners of kings,
The Muse gives our poet to say great things.
    Behold now we see those bring heroic thoughts,
Who used to trifle in Greek, nor to describe a grove

Skilful; nor to praise a fertile country, where are baskets,
And a fire-hearth, and swine, and the feasts of Pales smoky
  with hay:
From whence Remus, and thou, O Quintius, wearing coulters in a
  furrow,
Whom thy trembling wife clothed dictator before the oxen,
And thy ploughs the lictor carried home. Well done, O poet!
    There is now, whom the veiny book of Brisaen Accius;
There are those whom both Pacuvius, and rugged Antiope
Might detain, having propp'd her mournful heart with sorrows.
    When you see blear-eyed fathers pour these admonitions into
Their children, do you seek whence this bombast manner of
  speaking
Came on their tongues? Whence that disgrace, in which
The smooth Trossulus exults to thee thro' the benches?
Does it nothing shame you, not to be able to drive away
  dangers from
Your grey head, but you must wish to hear this lukewarm —
  Decently?
    Thou art a thief (says one to Pedius) — What Pedius? his
  crimes
He weighs in polished antitheses: to have laid down learned figures
He is praised: this is fine! — this is fine? O Romulus, do you wag
  the tail?
For if a shipwreck'd mariner sings, could he move me, and a penny
Should I bring forth? do you sing, when yourself painted on a
  broken plank
You carry from your shoulder? A true (misfortune), not prepared
  by night,
He shall deplore, who would bend me by his complaint.
MONITOR: But there is beauty and composition added to crude numbers.
PERSIUS: Thus hath he learnt to conclude a verse: "Berecynthian Attys,
    "And the dolphin which divided caerulean Nereus —
    "Thus we removed a rib from the long Apennine."
MONITOR: "Arms and the man" — is not this frothy, and with a fat bark?
PERSIUS: As an old bough dried with a very large bark.
MONITOR: What then is tender, and to be read with a loose neck?
PERSIUS: "They fill'd their fierce horns with Mimallonean blasts,
    "And Bassaris, about to take away the head snatched from the
      proud
    "Calf, and Maenas, about to guide a lynx with ivy,
    "Redoubles Evion: the reparable echo sounds to it."
    Would these be made, if any vein of our paternal manliness

542

Lived in us? This feeble stuff, on the topmost spittle,
Swims in the lips, and in the wet is Maenas and Attys.
Nor does he beat his desk, nor taste his gnawn nails.

MONITOR: But where's the need to grate tender ears with biting truth?
See to it, lest haply the thresholds of the great
Should grow cold to you: here from the nostrils sounds the
    canine letter —

PERSIUS: For my part, truly, let every thing be henceforward white.
I hinder not. O brave! all things, ye shall all be very wonderful.
This pleases. — Here, say you, I forbid that any should make
    a pissing place:
Paint two snakes: boys, the place is sacred: without
Make water — I depart. — Lucilius cut the city,
Thee, Lupus, thee, Mutius; and he brake his jaw-tooth upon them.
Sly Horace touches every vice, his friend laughing:
And admitted round the heart, plays,
Cunning to hang up the people with an unwrinkled nose.
Is it unlawful for me to mutter? neither secretly, nor with a ditch?

MONITOR: Nowhere.

PERSIUS: Nevertheless I will dig here. "I have seen, I myself have seen,
    O little book: —
"Who has not the ears of an ass?" I this hidden thing,
This laugh of mine, such a nothing, I sell to thee for no
Iliad. O thou whosoever art inspired by cold Cratinus,
Art pale over angry Eupolis, with the very great old man,
These too behold: if haply any thing more refined you hear,
Let the reader glow towards me with an ear evaporated from
    thence.
Not he, who delights to sport on the slippers of the Grecians,
Sordid, and who can say to the blinkard, thou blinkard:
Thinking himself somebody; because, lifted up with Italian honour,
An aedile he may have broken false measures at Aretium.
Nor who, arch, knows to laugh at the numbers of an accountable,
And bounds in divided dust; prepared to rejoice much,
If petulant Nonaria should pluck a Cynic's beard.
I give to these, in the morning, an edict; after dinner, Callirhoë.

M. Madan

JUVENAL

The life of Decimus Junius Juvenalis (c. 50 A.D. - 140 A.D.) is obscure. He spent many years in Rome itself and had made a visit to Egypt. His extant work consists of sixteen satires, that fulminate against the social, political, and moral conditions that prevailed in contemporary Roman society.

Book I — Satire III

Expose of the Corruption of Rome

Grieved though I am to see the man depart,
Who long has shared, and still must share, my heart
Yet (when I call by better judgment home)
I praise his purpose; to retire from Rome,
And give, on Cumae's solitary coast,
The Sibyl — one inhabitant to boast!
    Full on the road to Baiae, Cumae lies,
And many a sweet retreat her shore supplies —
Though I prefer ev'n Prochyta's bare strand
To the Suburra: — for, what desert land,
What wild, uncultured spot, can more affright,
Than fires, wide blazing through the gloom of night,
Houses, with ceaseless ruin, thundering down,
And all the horrors of this hateful town?
Where poets, while the dog-star glows, rehearse,
To gasping multitudes, their barbarous verse!
Now had my friend, impatient to depart,
Consigned his little all to one poor cart:
For this, without the town, he chose to wait;
But stopped a moment at the Conduit-gate. —
Here Numa erst his nightly visits paid,
And held high converse with the Egerian maid:
Now the once-hallowed fountain, grove, and fane,
Are let to Jews, a wretched, wandering train,
Whose furniture's basket filled with hay, —

For every tree is forced a tax to pay;
And while the heaven-born Nine in exile rove,
The beggar rents their consecrated grove!
    Thence slowly winding down the vale, we view
The Egerian grots — ah, how unlike the true!
Nymph of the Spring; more honoured hadst thou been,
If, free from art, an edge of living green,
The bubbling fount had circumscribed alone
And marble ne'er profaned the native stone.
    Umbritius here his sullen silence broke,
And turned on Rome, indignant, as he spoke.
Since virtue droops, he cried, without regard,
And honest toil scarce hopes a poor reward;
Since every morrow sees my means decay,
And still makes less the little of today;
I go, where Daedalus, as poets sing,
First checked his flight, and closed his weary wing:
While something yet of health and strength remains,
And yet no staff my faltering step sustains;
While few grey hairs upon my head are seen,
And my old age is vigorous still, and green.
Here, then, I bid my much-loved home farewell —
Ah, mine no more! — there let Arturius dwell,
And Catulus; knaves, who, in truth's despite,
Can white to black transform, and black to white,
Build temples, furnish funerals, auctions hold,
Farm rivers, ports, and scour the drains for gold.
    Once they were trumpeters, and always found,
With strolling fencers, in their annual round,
While their puffed cheeks, which every village knew,
Called to "high feats of arms" the rustic crew:
Now they give shows themselves; and, at the will
Of the base rabble, raise the sign — to kill,
Ambitious of their voice: then turn, once more,
To their vile gains, and farm the common shore!
And why not every thing? — since Fortune throws
Her more peculiar smiles on such as those,
Whene'er, to wanton merriment inclined,
She lifts to thrones the dregs of human kind!
    But why, my friend, should I at Rome remain?
I cannot teach my stubborn lips to feign;
Nor, when I hear a great man's verses, smile,
And beg a copy, if I think them vile.

A sublunary wight, I have no skill
To read the stars; I neither can, nor will,
Presage a father's death; I never pried,
In toads, for poison, nor — in aught beside.
Others may aid the adulterer's vile design,
And bear the insidious gift, and melting line,
Seduction's agents. I such deeds detest;
And, honest, let no thief partake by breast.
For this, without a friend, the world I quit;
A palsied limb, for every use unfit.

     Who now is loved, but he whose conscious breast
Swells with dark deeds still, still to be supprest?
He pays, he owes, thee nothing, (strictly just,)
Who gives an honest secret to thy trust;
But, a dishonest! — there he feels thy power,
And buys thy friendship high from hour to hour.
But let not all the wealth which Tagus pours
In Ocean's lap, not all his glittering stores,
Be deemed a bribe, sufficient to requite
The loss of peace by day, of sleep by night: —
O take not, take not, what they soul rejects,
Nor sell the faith, which he, who buys, suspects!

     The nation, by the great, admired, caresst,
And hated, shunned by me, above the rest,
No longer, now, restrained by wounded pride,
I haste to show, (nor thou my warmth deride,)
I cannot rule my spleen, and calmly see,
A Grecian capital, in Italy!
Grecian? O, no! with this vast sewer compared,
The dregs of Greece are scarcely worth regard:
Long since, the stream that wanton Syria laves
Has disembogued its filth in Tiber's waves,
Its language, arts; o'erwhelmed us with the scum
Of Antioch's streets, its minstrel, harp, and drum.
Hie to the Circus! ye who pant to prove
A barbarous mistress, an outlandish love;
Hoe to the Circus! there, in crowds they stand,
Tires on their head, and timbrels in their hand.
     Thy rustic, Mars, the trechedipna wears,
And on his breast, smeared with ceroma, bears
A paltry prize, well-pleased; while every land,
Sicyon, and Amydos, and Alaband,
Tralles, and Samos, and a thousand more,

Thrive on his indolence, and daily pour
Their starving myriads forth; hither they come,
And batten on the genial soil of Rome;
Minions, then lords, of every princely dome!
A flattering, cringing, treacherous, artful race,
Of torrent tongue, and never-blushing face;
A Protean tribe, one knows not what to call,
Which shifts to every form, and shines in all:
Grammarian, painter, augur, rhetorician,
Rope-dancer, conjurer, fiddler, and physician,
All trades his own, your hungry Greekling counts;
And bid him mount the sky — the sky he mounts!
You smile — was't a barbarian, then, that flew?
No, 'twas a Greek; 'twas an Athenian, too!
— Bear with their state who will: for I disdain
To feed their upstart pride, or swell their train:
Slaves, that in Syrian lighters stowed, so late,
With figs and prunes, (an inauspicious freight,)
Already see their faith preferred to mine,
And sit above me! and before me sign! —
That on the Aventine I first drew air,
And, from the womb, was nursed on Sabine fare,
Avails me not! our birthright now is lost,
And all our privilege, an empty boast!

    For lo! where versed in every soothing art,
The wily Greek assails his patron's heart,
Finds in each dull harangue an air, a grace,
And all Adonis in a Gorgon face;
Admires the voice that grates upon the ear,
Like the shrill scream of amorous chanticleer;
And equals the crane neck, and narrow chest,
To Hercules, when, straining to his breast
The giant son of Earth, his every vein
Swells with the toil, and more than mortal pain.

    We too can cringe as low, and praise as warm,
But flattery from the Greeks alone can charm.
See! they step forth, and figure to the life,
The naked nymph, the mistress, or the wife,
So just, you view the very woman there,
And fancy all beneath the girdle bare!
No longer now, the favourites of the stage
Boast their exclusive power to charm the age;
The happy art with them a nation shares,

Greece is a theatre, where all are players.
For lo! their patron smiles, — they burst with mirth;
He weeps, — they droop, the saddest souls on earth;
He calls for fire, — they court the mantle's heat;
'Tis warm, he cries, — and they dissolve in sweat.
Ill-matched! — secure of victory they start,
Who, taught from youth to play a borrowed part,
Can, with a glance, the rising passion trace,
And mould their own, to suit their patron's face;
At deeds of shame their hands admiring raise,
And mad debauchery's worst excesses praise.
     Besides, no mound their raging lust restrains,
All ties it breaks, all sanctity profanes;
Wife, virgin-daughter, son unstained before, —
And, where they fail, they tempt the grandam hoar:
They notice every word, haunt every ear,
Your secrets learn, and fix you theirs from fear.
     Turn to their schools: — yon grey professor see,
Smeared with the sanguine stains of perfidy!
That tutor most accursed his pupil sold!
That Stoic sacrificed his friend to gold!
A true-born Grecian! littered on the coast,
Where the Gorgonian hack a pinion lost.
     Hence, Romans, hence! no place for you remains,
Where Diphilus, where Erimanthus reigns;
Miscreants, who, faithful to their native art,
Admit no rival in a patron's heart: —
For let them fasten on his easy ear,
And drop one hint, one secret slander there,
Sucked from their country's venom, or their own,
That instant they possess the man alone;
While we are spurned, contemptuous, from the door,
Our long, long slavery thought upon no more.
'Tis but a client lost! — and that, we find,
Sits wondrous lightly on a patron's mind:
And (not to flatter our poor pride, my friend)
What merit with the great can we pretend,
Though, in our duty, we prevent the day,
And, darkling, run our humble court to pay;
When the brisk praetor, long before, is gone,
And hastening, with stern voice, his lictors on,
Lest his colleagues o'erpass him in the street,
And first the rich and childless matrons greet,

548

Alba and Modia, who impatient wait,
And think the morning homage comes too late!
　　Here freeborn youths wait the rich servant's call,
And, if they walk beside him, yield the wall;
And wherefore? this, forsooth, can fling away,
On one voluptuous night, a legion's pay.
While those, when some Calvina, sweeping by,
Inflames the fancy, check their roving eye,
And frugal of their scanty means, forbear,
To tempt the wanton from her splendid chair.
　　Produce, at Rome, your witness: let him boast,
The sanctity of Berecynthia's host,
Of Numa, or of him, whose zeal divine
Snatched pale Minerva from her blazing shrine:
To search his rent-roll, first the bench prepares,
His honesty employs their latest cares:
What table does he keep, what slaves maintain,
And what, they ask, and where, is his domain?
These weighty matters known, his faith they rate,
And square his probity to his estate.
The poor may swear by all the immortal Powers,
By the Great Gods of Samothrace, and ours,
His oaths are false, they cry; he scoffs at heaven,
And all its thunders; scoffs, — and is forgiven!
Add, that the wretch is still the theme of scorn,
If the soiled cloak be patched, the gown o'erworn;
If, through the bursting shoe, the foot be seen,
Or the coarse seam tell where the rent has been.
O Poverty, thy thousand ills combined
Sink not so deep into the generous mind,
As the contempt and laughter of mankind!
　　"Up! up! these cushioned benches," Lectius cries,
"Befit not your estates: for shame! arise."
For "shame!" — but you say well: the pander's heir,
The spawn of bulks and stews, is seated there;
The cryer's spruce son, fresh from the fencer's school,
And prompt the taste to settle and to rule. —
So Otho fixed it, whose preposterous pride
First dared to chase us from their Honours' side.
　　In these cursed walls, devote alone to gain,
When do the poor a wealthy wife obtain?
When are they named in Wills? when called to share
The Aedile's council, and assist the chair? —

Long since should they have risen, thus slighted, spurned,
And left their home, but — not to have returned!
    Depressed by indigence, the good and wise,
In every clime, by painful efforts rise;
Here, by more painful still, where scanty cheer,
Poor lodging, mean attendance, — all is dear.
In earthen ware he scorns, at Rome, to eat,
Who, called abruptly to the Marsian's seat,
From such, well pleased, would take his simple food,
Nor blush to wear the cheap Venetian hood.
    There's many a part of Italy, 'tis said,
Where none assume the toga but the dead:
There, when the toil foregone and annual play,
Mark, from the rest, some high and solemn day,
To theatres of turf the rustics throng,
Charmed with the farce that charmed their sires so long;
While the pale infant, of the mask in dread,
Hides, in his mother's breast, his little head.
No modes of dress high birth distinguish there;
All ranks, all orders, the same habit wear,
And the dread Aedile's dignity is known,
O sacred badge! by his white vest alone.
But here, beyond our power arrayed we go,
In all the gay varieties of show;
And when our purse supplies the charge no more,
Borrow, unblushing, from our neighbour's store:
Such is the reigning vice; and so we flaunt,
Proud in distress, and prodigal in want!
Briefly, my friend, here all are slaves to gold,
And words, and smiles, and every thing is sold.
What will you give for Cossus' nod? how high
The silent notice of Veiento buy?
— One favourite youth is shaved, another shorn;
And, while to Jove the precious spoil is borne,
Clients are taxed for offerings, and, (yet more
To gall their patience,) from their little store,
Constrained to swell the minion's ample hoard,
And bribe the page, for leave to bribe his lord.
    Who fears the crash of houses in retreat?
At simple Gabii, bleak Praeneste's seat,
Volsinium's craggy heights, embowered in wood,
Or Tibur, beetling o'er prone Anio's flood?
While half the city here by shores is staid,

550

And feeble cramps, that lend a treacherous aid:
For thus the stewards patch the riven wall,
Thus prop the mansion, tottering to its fall;
Then bid the tenant court secure repose,
While the pile nods to every blast that blows.

O! may I live where no such fears molest,
No midnight fires burst on my hour of rest!
For here 'tis terror all; midst the loud cry
Of "water! water!" the scared neighbours fly,
With all their haste can seize — the flames aspire,
And the third floor is wrapt in smoke and fire,
While you, unconscious, doze: Up, ho! and know,
The impetuous blaze which spreads dismay below,
By swift degrees will reach the aerial cell,
Where, crouching, underneath the tiles you dwell,
Where your tame doves their golden couplets rear,
"And you could no mischance, but drowning, fear!"
"Codrus had but one bed, and that too short
For his short wife;" his goods, of every sort,
Were else but few: — six little pipkins graced
His cupboard head, a little can was placed
On a snug shelf beneath, and near it lay
A Chiron, of the same cheap marble, — clay.
And was this all? O no: he yet possest
A few Greek books, shrined in an ancient chest,
Where barbarous mice through many an inlet crept,
And fed on heavenly numbers, while he slept. —
"Codrus, in short, had nothing." You say true;
And yet poor Codrus lost that nothing too!
One curse alone was wanting to complete
His woes: that, cold and hungry, through the street,
The wretch should beg, and, in the hour of need,
Find none to lodge, to clothe him, or to feed!

But should the raging flames on grandeur prey,
And low in dust Asturius' place lay,
The squalid matron sighs, the senate mourns,
The pleaders cease, the judge the court adjourns;
All join to wail the city's hapless fate,
And rail at fire with more than common hate.
Lo! while it burns, the obsequious courtiers haste,
With rich materials, to repair the waste:
This, brings him marble, that, a finished piece,

551

The far-famed boast of Polyclete and Greece;
This, ornaments, which graced of old the fane
Of Asia's gods; that, figured plate and plain;
This, cases, books, and busts the shelves to grace,
And piles of coin his specie to replace. —
So much the childless Persian swells his store,
(Though deemed the richest of the rich before,)
That all ascribe the flames to thirst of pelf,
And swear, Asturius fires his house himself.

O, had you, from the Circus, power to fly,
In many a halcyon village might you buy
Some elegant retreat, for what will, here,
Scarce hire a gloomy dungeon through the year!
There wells, by nature formed, which need no rope,
No labouring arm, to crane their waters up,
Around your lawn their facile streams shall shower,
And cheer the springing plant and opening flower.
There live, delighted with the rustic's lot,
And till, with your own hands, the little spot;
The little spot shall yield you large amends,
And glad, with many a feast, your Samian friends.
And, sure, — in any corner we can get,
To call one lizard ours, is something yet!

Flushed with a mass of indigested food,
Which clogs the stomach and inflames the blood,
What crowds, with watching wearied and o'erprest,
Curse the slow hours, and die for want of rest!
For who can hope his languid lids to close,
Where brawling taverns banish all repose?
Sleep, to the rich alone, "his visits pays:"
And hence the seeds of many a dire disease.
The carts loud rumbling through the narrow way,
The drivers' clamours at each casual stay,
From drowsy Drusus would his slumber take,
And keep the calves of Proteus broad awake!

If business call, obsequious crowds divide,
While o'er their heads the rich securely ride,
By tall Illyrians borne, and read, or write,
Or, (should the early hour to rest invite,)
Close the soft litter, and enjoy the night.
Yet reach they first the goal; while, by the throng
Elbowed and jostled, scarce we creep along;
Sharp strokes from poles, tubs, rafters, doomed to feel;

And plastered o'er with mud, from head to heel:
While the rude soldier gores us as he goes,
Or marks, in blood, his progress on our toes!
    See, from the Dole, a vast tumultuous throng,
Each followed by his kitchen, pours along!
Huge pans, which Corbulo could scarce uprear,
With steady neck a puny slave must bear,
And, lest amid the way the flames expire,
Glide nimbly on, and gliding, fan the fire;
Through the close press with sinuous efforts wind,
And, piece by piece, leave his botched rags behind.
    Hark! groaning on, the unwieldy waggon spreads
Its cumbrous load, tremendous! o'er our heads,
Projecting elm or pine, that nods on high,
And threatens death to every passer by.
Heavens! should the axle crack, which bears a weight
Of huge Ligurian stone, and pour the freight
On the pale crowd beneath, what would remain
What joint, what bone, what atom of the slain?
The body, with the soul, would vanish quite,
Invisible as air, to mortal sight! —
Meanwhile, unconscious of their fellow's fate,
At home, they heat the water, scour the plate,
Arrange the strigils, fill the cruse with oil,
And ply their several tasks with fruitless toil:
For he who bore the dole, poor mangled ghost,
Sits pale and trembling on the Stygian coast,
Scared at the horrors of the novel scene,
At Charon's threatening voice, and scowling mien;
Nor hopes a passage, thus abruptly hurled,
Without his farthing, to the nether world.
    Pass we these fearful dangers, and survey
What other evils threat our nightly way.
And first, behold the mansion's towering size,
Where floors on floors on the tenth story rise;
Whence heedless garretteers their potsherds throw,
And crush the unwary wretch that walks below!
Clattering the storm descends from heights unknown,
Ploughs up the street, and wounds the flinty stone!
'Tis madness, dire improvidence of ill,
To sup abroad, before you sign your Will;
Since fate in ambush lies, and marks his prey,
From every wakeful window in the way:

Pray, then,—and count your humble prayer well sped,
If pots be only—emptied on your head.

    The drunken bully, ere his man be slain,
Frets through the night, and courts repose in vain;
And while the thirst of blood his bosom burns,
From side to side, in restless anguish, turns,
Like Peleus' son, when, quelled by Hector's hand,
His loved Patroclus prest the Phrygian strand.

    There are, who murder as an opiate take,
And only when no brawls await them wake:
Yet even these heroes, flushed with youth and wine,
All contest with the purple robe decline;
Securely give the lengthened train to pass,
The sun-bright flambeaux, and the lamps of brass.—
Me, whom the moon, or candle's paler gleam,
Whose wick I husband to the last extreme,
Guides through the gloom, he braves, devoid of fear:
The prelude to our doughty quarrel hear,
If that be deemed a quarrel, where, heaven knows,
He only gives, and I receive, the blows!
Across my path he strides, and bids me stand.
I bow, obsequious to the dread command;
What else remains, where madness, rage combine
With youth, and strength superior far to mine?
"Whence come you, rogue?" he cries; "whose beans to-night
Have stuffed you thus? what cobbler clubbed his mite,
For leeks and sheep's-head porridge? Dumb! quite dumb!
Speak, or be kicked.—Yet, once again! your home?
Where shall I find you? At what beggar's stand
(Temple or bridge) whimp'ring with out-stretched hand?"

    Whether I strive some humble plea to frame,
Or steal in silence by, 'tis just the same;
I'm beaten first, then dragged in rage away;
Bound to the peace, or punished for the fray!

    Mark here the boasted freedom of the poor!
Beaten and bruised, that goodness to adore,
Which, at their humble prayer, suspends its ire,
And sends them home, with yet a bone entire!

    Nor this the worst; for when deep midnight reigns,
And bolts secure our doors, and massy chains,
When noisy inns a transient silence keep,
And harassed nature woos the balm of sleep,

Then, thieves and murderers ply their dreadful trade;
With stealthy steps our secret couch invade: —
Roused from the treacherous calm, aghast we start,
And the fleshed sword — is buried in our heart!
     Hither from bogs, from rocks, and caves pursued,
(The Pontine march, and Gallinarian wood,)
The dark assassins flock, as to their home,
And fill with dire alarms the streets of Rome.
Such countless multitudes our peace annoy,
That bolts and shackles every forge employ,
And cause so wide a waste, the country fears
A want of ore for mattocks, rakes, and shares.
     O! happy were our sires, estranged from crimes;
And happy, happy, were the good old times,
Which saw, beneath their kings', their tribunes' reign,
One cell the nation's criminals contain!
     Much could I add, more reasons could I cite,
If time were ours, to justify my flight;
But see! the impatient team is moving on,
The sun declining; and I must be gone:
Long since, the driver murmured at my stay,
And jerked his whip, to beckon me away.
Farewell, my friend! with this embrace we part:
Cherish my memory ever in your heart;
And when, from crowds and business, you repair,
To breathe at your Aquinum freer air,
Fail not to draw me from my loved retreat,
To Elvine Ceres, and Diana's seat: —
For your bleak hills my Cumae I'll resign,
And (if you blush not at such aid as mine)
Come well equipped, to wage, in angry rhymes,
Fierce war, with you, on follies and on crimes.

William Gifford

555

SELECTIVE BIBLIOGRAPHY

Bailey, Cyril. The Legacy of Rome. Oxford: Clarendon Press, 1924.

Fowler, W. W. The City-state of the Greeks and the Romans. 2nd. ed. New York: The Macmillan Co., 1907.

Greene, Wm. C. The Achievement of Rome. Cambridge: Harvard University Press, 1933.

Highet, Gilbert. The Classical Tradition. New York: Oxford University Press, 1949.

Rose, H. J. A Handbook of Latin Literature. New York: E. P. Dutton and Co., 1936.

Rostovtzeff, M. A History of the Ancient World. 2 volumes. 2nd. ed. Oxford: Clarendon Press, 1930.

Showerman, Grant. Monuments and Men of Ancient Rome. New York: D. Appleton-Century Co., 1935.